Personality and Behavior

Jesse E. Gordon, Ph.D.

DEPARTMENT OF PSYCHOLOGY
THE UNIVERSITY OF MICHIGAN

The Macmillan Company, New York
Collier-Macmillan Limited, London

To Sophie and Harry Gordon

First Printing

Library of Congress catalog card number: 62-11920

The Macmillan Company, New York
Collier-Macmillan Canada, Ltd., Toronto, Ontario
Divisions of The Crowell-Collier Publishing Company

Printed in the United States of America

Design by R. A. Kaseler

Preface

This work was undertaken in order to provide the writer with a book that would meet his requirements for a text for introductory courses in personality and human adjustment. The book is designed to deal with personality as a substantive matter, rather than to make an exhortation to the student to accept a psychological viewpoint. It is intended primarily for courses *in* psychology, rather than for courses that *use* psychology as a vehicle for the improvement of student adjustment. The emphasis is on conveying a summary of the products of a field of scholarly investigation. The relevance of personality psychology to the immediate concerns of students is a two-edged sword. It provides the teacher with a ready source of motivation in his students, and one on which a text can capitalize. But this intrinsic relevance also tends to obscure psychology's validity as an area of intellectual endeavor providing its own rewards quite beyond its immediate utility. Thus I have tried to use examples which appeal to student interest, but the content of the text is not restricted to the psychology of late adolescence and early adulthood.

The psychology of personality covers a broad area, and it is not possible adequately and coherently to cover its entire range in one volume. My preference is to leave out material that cannot be covered in sufficient depth. It has often seemed to me that the brief presentation of complex material in an effort to present a complete survey defeats its own purpose. For example, a two page summary of something as complicated as a theory of personality or the principles of psychotherapy must necessarily so elide, simplify, and condense the material that the theory or principles appear simplistic, banal, irrelevant, or nonsensical to the student. A richer flavor of what personality is about can be better obtained from a detailed reading of some high points and representative topics than it can from a comprehensive but brief survey. A detailed reading can provide the student with the tools and concepts, and practice in their use, for generalizing to topics not specifically covered, while the presentation of the details also warns him of the complexities hidden in what may appear superficially to be simple matters.

Having decided to limit the range of topics covered, I have relied on several principles to guide decisions about what should be included and what the style of presentation should be. The most important of these principles is a stress on the relatedness of the various branches of psychology. I view personality as a "derived" phenomenon. That is, it is the study of the application of fundamental laws of behavior to the form and content of human social functioning. This kind of approach bridges several areas of psychology, each with its own vocabulary and concepts. I have therefore found it necessary to select one vocabulary and set of concepts as a base, and to interpret the phenomena dealt with in the several branches of psychology in terms of that base. I have no particular preference for one or another of the languages available, and the increasing production of points of contact among the branches (between physiological psychology and learning through studies of brain functions, between psychoanalytic ego psychology and general-experimental research on concept formation, and so forth) reduces the hegemony of any one language. My selection of the language of learning psychology therefore does not imply a rejection of the meaning and import of other branches, or an alliance with the specific point of view of learning psychology. Rather, I selected this language, and translated back and forth to other languages, because it has the most unambiguous denotative structure and seems to me to be the most flexible for application to a wide range of phenomena. Finally, it best communicates the relevance of the various branches of psychological knowledge to personality.

The use of a language identified with one part of psychology has its dangers. It readily leads to interpretations of personality of the "nothing but" variety — interpretations that run the risk of throwing the baby out with the bath water. It is one thing to say that a symptom is "nothing but" a product of the dynamics of conditioning; it is quite another to explore the particular mechanisms and circumstances in which this specific symptom was acquired, an exploration that discovers in the symptom a psychological meaning that goes beyond accidental conditioning of a random operant as a result of fortuitous reinforcement. Such exploration resolves the apparent inconsistency between the learning interpretation of a symptom as the product of past reinforcements and the psychoanalytic emphasis on the symbolic meaningfulness of the symptom for the individual's drive gratifications. I have drawn heavily on dynamic psychology for the phenomena and meanings with which the text deals, and have tried to interpret them in the language of general-experimental psychology without losing either the phenomena or the meanings — that is, without stripping behavior of the very features that make it of more than passing interest.

A second guideline for the design of the book is its utility as a teaching text rather than as a reference work. Therefore I have been more con-

cerned with citing illustrative research findings and methodologies than
with an exegesis of the research literature. I want students to understand the relationship between data and the hypotheses on which they
bear, and to see the relevance of specific substantive findings to more
general issues. This, too, has its dangers. While it is not necessary for
the student to learn specific data, he should come away from his studies
with more than empty generalizations that cover ignorance of their
bases. Interpretations of data change with time and new information,
but the relationships to which the interpretations are directed do not.
I think that it is important for students to know the phenomena, and, by
learning how contemporary theories have been derived, to understand
something of the way in which theories are adduced from the phenomena. This procedure leaves the student free to appreciate principles which may emerge from new data in the future, rather than
restricting him to temporary formulations.

Another implication of the emphasis on a teaching text is that the
book must avoid too-heavy dependence on the student's memory for
material he might have learned in an earlier psychology course. Thus
the first part of the book contains a fairly extensive review of the
relevant material on which the remainder of the text builds. This makes
the book particularly appropriate for students who have not already
studied general psychology. But even students who have taken an
introductory course often do not retain the concepts with sufficient
clarity to use them in understanding more complex material; for them,
the first part serves as a necessary review. This early section has another
function. It sets the stage for the detailed presentation that follows, and
develops in the reader a "set" for the close analysis of behavior in terms
of the basic vocabulary used throughout the text.

Students' tendencies to impose value judgments on behavior often
interfere with their ability to explore and understand the behavior. Once
they have decided that a particular action is inconsistent with their own
political and social belief systems, they find it difficult to see anything but
"maladjustment" and "mental illness" in the action. Beginning students
are more likely to ask if such and such is the "right" way to bring up
children (the propogation of their belief systems being implicitly
accepted as the goal in terms of which behaviors are right or wrong) than
they are to ask about the various ways in which they might react and the
several possible consequences to themselves and others of each alternative. I have tried to deal with this problem by emphasizing a nonjudgmental approach to behavior and avoiding built-in evaluations

based on cultural biases. I hope to communicate to the student that traits, motives, and other behavioral determinants can have both desirable and undesirable consequences. Independence of judgment, for example, is a characteristic of both the creative writer and the sociopath, and submissive conformity includes the kind of sensitivity to other people that also participates in making one a perceptive host. The student must be aware of these possibilities before he decides that he is in favor of whatever makes people have independence of judgment or social graciousness. A corollary of a nonjudgmental approach is the avoidance of concepts such as "adjustment" and "mental illness" which have built-in evaluations of the worth or utility of the behaviors so labelled. The variables determining the occurrence of a particular act may be described, as far as they are known or guessed, and the probable consequences of the act considered, without making moral or medical prejudgments of the consequences on the basis of judgments about the act itself.

The organization of the text is a product of these principles. Following the review of basic materials, the content rises to the first level of complexity in which these materials interact to produce some simple integrated behavioral structures. When these are explored another level of complexity is introduced, through the combination of interaction of the simple behavioral structures, and so on until the main outlines of complete functioning personalities can be presented without too many gross oversimplifications. Through this graduated introduction of complexity I hope to lead the reader from the relevance of molecular concepts to a feeling for the worlds of meaning inherent in even superficially simple actions, without also overwhelming him.

This kind of organization requires frequent returns, at new levels of complexity, to material presented earlier. At some of the points of return the text summarizes the material presented earlier, as a review for the student and as a stimulus for his redintegration of the earlier material. At others I have tried to encourage the needed redintegration by using illustrative material similar to that used in the earlier and simpler presentation, but emphasizing in the illustration a new dimension of complexity. Similarly, many of the illustrative case descriptions deal with the same symptoms, to add substance to the student's realization of the many meanings which the same behavior can have in different contexts. The last chapter points out some conclusions and comments on the picture of personality that emerges as the reader works through the text. I hope that these leitmotifs will also add a sense of the unity of the material, a unity that is easily destroyed by the necessity to divide behavior up into teachable chunks.

In some sections the organization has necessitated a new treatment of the material. But where suitable formulations have been made by other writers, I have felt free to use them. Thus the text relies heavily on the contributions of Freud, Dollard and Miller, McClelland, Cameron, Sears, and many other researchers, theorists, and practitioners. I hope that by so doing I have been able to draw a faithful portrait of personality psychology for the student.

JESSE E. GORDON

Table of Contents

1. Introduction

This section introduces the field of study of this book. It includes a discussion of the domain of personality and the definition of the term as it has guided the structure and presentation of the material in the text. In effect, the text proper represents an extended exploration of the meaning of the points made in the introduction; while the introduction attempts to prepare the reader for the text proper, it is therefore also true that the full meaning of the introduction lies in the body of this work.

1. The Study of Personality and Behavior

Sometimes people study personality as an area of knowledge, the pursuit of which provides its own satisfactions in increasing their fund of knowledge and the boundaries of their thought. Sometimes they study personality because they seek information about themselves. They may seek reasons for their behavior or advice that will reduce unhappinesses about themselves. Still others have the same interests in a more generalized form, as an expression of their concern about the human condition and its nature.

A text may be written for each kind of student slanted toward the appropriate concerns. But often the student is motivated by several of these factors in combination. Thus a text slanted in one direction would be inappropriate to some part of his curiosity. This book is written to provide a summary of what is known about personality and behavior, with the hope that the student will be able to draw from it some of the applications of the knowledge he seeks. There is little evidence that courses in personality actually produce a direct improvement in the ways in which students deal with themselves, but there is an intrinsic validity to the acquisition of knowledge about a legitimate (and highly fascinating) field of study and research. Let the reader use his own resources to manipulate and extend the knowledge he gains of personality, to develop generalizations and applications that are pertinent to his concerns. It is, however, first necessary that he be familiar with the basis of such generalizations in valid data about behavior.

The study of personality covers a varied and complex domain. It seeks to discover the reasons for a wide range of human behaviors, to account for their occurrence, and to assess their role in the total person. Some aspects of behavior with which the study of personality attempts to deal are described in this chapter. Following this discussion of these phenomena, a meaning for the term *personality* is outlined and the plan of this book is introduced.

Some Qualities of Human Behavior

Each of the several different aspects of behavior cited by psychologists as important components of personality has at one time or another been included in a definition of personality. A comprehensive view of human behavior, however, requires that each aspect be included in a total picture of personality.

Enduring Characteristics. Personality includes the *enduring characteristics* of the drives and traits which modulate the individual's behavior throughout his life. Fads, fancies, and temporary fashions in behavior are peripheral. The particular fashion in dress or behavior an individual follows at a particular time is not important. It is important that he tends to be fashionable throughout his life, following each new style as it presents itself. Similarly, temporary disturbances in behavior occasioned by unique circumstances or situations—for example, the temporary changes in behavior which occur while in military service, or following the death of a loved one—are significant because they shed light on those enduring personality processes which account for the individual's susceptibility to such situations. Life may be likened to a long river; the major currents of the river are its most salient characteristics, although in studying these the role of the minor eddies becomes significant.

Unique Characteristics. Another phenomenon of particular interest in the study of personality is the existence of *unique characteristics*. No two people seem to be exactly alike. The rules of science pose problems for the exploration of uniqueness. The truly unique event must necessarily be excluded from scientific study, because of the nature of the rules of induction.

Before one can draw a conclusion from a relationship between an event and the conditions that control it, or which were necessary for the event to occur, one must demonstrate that the relationship is reliable, that it occurs consistently in the same way. A scientific law that can be applied to other cases cannot be discovered from a single case, and of course a truly unique event is a single case. At best such a case may illustrate a law, but it cannot validate the law. Other scientists have to be able to reproduce the event, so that they can check the accuracy of the observations from which the law was derived. And, of course, a unique event is one that is not reproduced. A law derived from several observations of a single case applies to that case alone, but such a law would be of little use in general, and would not represent much of a contribution to knowledge. For all other events but that one, the law would be valueless. We seek laws that will apply to many situations, and to obtain such laws, we must study events which are reproducible, or which are similar to other events, i.e., not unique.

The discussion of this point has a long and impassioned history in psychology, and is known as the *idiographic* (single case)—*nomothetic* (many similar cases) controversy. There are laws that refer only to the single case. Within the behavior of a single individual one may very well discover consistencies which are not found in other people, and one may adduce the law which these consistencies obey. Obviously, the laws would be different from one person to another. But one can also find general laws that apply to all individuals. These laws are much more useful, since they can be used to predict behavior in many people, instead of one person alone. They, therefore, include the single case within them.

The acceptance of the nomothetic approach does not necessarily imply a denial of individual uniqueness. Many unique events are composed of subparts which are represented in several different "wholes." Thus each personality may be entirely unique as a whole, but this uniqueness rests in the combination of elements which are themselves not unique, and which, therefore, permit scientific study. Once reliable general laws of behavior have been established, then individual variations in behavior may be accounted for by reference to the general laws. For example, if there is a general law that B is some function of an antecedent A, such that the more A there is, the more B will occur, then we are able to draw a conclusion about an individual who differs from others in the amount of B in his behavior. We would conclude that the difference between this person and others came about because of differences between himself and others in A. Thus a general law, applicable to all, is of use in accounting for the individuality of the particular case, without any implication that individual differences are subordinated to group norms, or exist only as errors in measurement.

Of course, most psychological relationships are not as simple as the $A = fB$ example. More typically, we have relationships of the form: A is a function of B under conditions X and Y, but not under conditions R and S, in which case it is a function of variables K and L, and so on, to more and more complicated interrelationships. Thus while it is seldom true in psychology that one event necessarily implies another particular event, there is still lawfulness of behavior of a higher order of complexity. For many people, it is this complexity which constitutes the fascination and challenge of psychology, and which reflects the complexity of the human being.

Life Style. *Life style* refers to the manner in which an individual does what he does. We are interested in how people go about doing things, as well as what they do. We wish to know more than that a person eats three meals a day. We wish to know whether he dresses formally for dinner and uses one or three forks during a meal. The life style aspect of personality requires us to pay particular attention to those traits that describe an individual's customary ways of doing things, as well as to the things he is likely to do and to avoid doing.

Behavioral Organization. *Normative Measurement.* Most people in a society have about the same motives and traits, but they tend to differ considerably in the relative strengths of the motives and traits they share. It is for this reason that psychologists are interested in the *organization* of behaviors within a person. The organizational aspect of personality is most clearly indicated by psychographs. A psychograph is a visual technique used to present an individual's test scores in such a way that the relationships among the various tests—the organization of the measured attributes—become apparent. Figure 1 presents the psychographs of two people; it reveals the pattern of their scores on the scales of the Edwards Personal Preference Schedule.[1] The test assumes that all people have all of the traits, but that personality includes the *extent* to which the various traits are represented in the individual. Inasmuch as both subjects in Figure 1 have the same traits, they are alike, but they differ in personality because they do not have these traits to the same extent.

Scores on trait tests such as the Edwards are normative, or relative, not absolute—that is, an individual's score is obtained by comparing his test responses with those made by others similar to him. His score is relative to the comparison group used in the establishment of the test standards. For example, if a subject's responses are scored in terms of how they compare with the responses of American college freshmen,

Figure 1. Scores of Two Subjects
on the Edwards Personal Preference Schedule

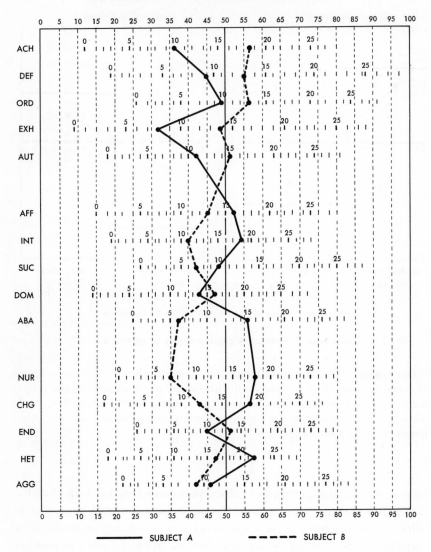

On the psychograph* are plotted the test scores of Subject *A* and Subject *B*.

*Reprinted by permission of the publishers from A. Edwards EDWARDS PERSONAL PREFERENCE SCHEDULE. New York: The Psychological Corporation, Copyright, 1954, by The Psychological Corporation.

Figure 2. Does the Subject Have a
Stronger Achievement or Affiliation Drive?

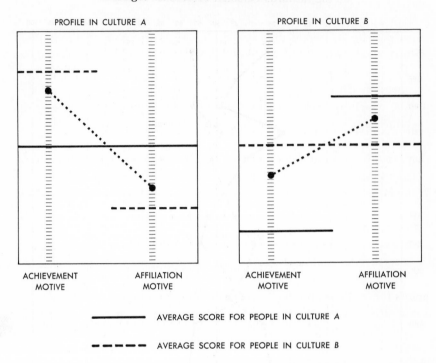

PROFILE IN CULTURE *A*   PROFILE IN CULTURE *B*

ACHIEVEMENT   AFFILIATION   ACHIEVEMENT   AFFILIATION
MOTIVE   MOTIVE   MOTIVE   MOTIVE

——————— AVERAGE SCORE FOR PEOPLE IN CULTURE *A*

— — — — AVERAGE SCORE FOR PEOPLE IN CULTURE *B*

One subject's scores on two trait tests are plotted with reference to the norms of two different cultures. Compared with the people in Culture *A*, the subject might be described as more ambitious than friendly, but in Culture *B* he would seem to be more friendly than ambitious, even though his answers to the test questions remain unchanged.

he may have a stronger trait of achievement and a weaker trait of affiliation than the comparison group. His personality is said to be that of an achievement-oriented person who tends not to engage in cooperative social activities. But let us suppose that the subject moves to another country or to another society or culture within his native country and continues to behave in the same manner. If he were to take the same test, and his performance were compared with the responses of people in the new culture, he might obtain a score low on achievement and high on affiliation. Compared to one group, his achievement needs are high and his affiliation needs low, but if he changes to a fiercely competitive society and is compared with their standards of behavior, there may be a reversal in his trait pattern.

This approach seems to make personality a rather slippery concept. According to it, personality would change as the subject moves from culture to culture, even though there is no change in his actual behavior. It is, therefore, important to distinguish between traits as they are presumed to exist, and traits as they are measured. The measurements, which are relative, refer to behavioral tendencies that exist in absolute although unknown quantities. Without knowledge of these quantities, it is not possible to compare traits within an individual for their relative strengths and thus be able to observe the organization of his personality. As in the example above, the strengths of the traits relative to each other vary with the norms of the group against which the person is compared. Thus in one culture a person may seem more achievement-oriented than he is cooperative and affiliative, while in another he may seem more affiliative than competitive. It is important to keep this cultural relativism in mind when examining test scores, but it is also important to remember that beneath these normative measurements there are absolute strengths for the traits being considered. The study of personality must account for these absolute strengths and their organization. The point is that knowledge of the organization of behavior requires knowledge of the absolute extent to which various behaviors are present in the individual's repertoire. Relativistic scores do not permit organizational inferences about an individual that would be valid for that person regardless of the society in which he lived.

The Holistic Approach. Behavioral organization also may refer to the manner in which the various different and discrete behavioral sequences or acts—the behavioral building blocks—are ultimately related (usually by means of common motives) into a coherent, sensible, interrelated structure. According to this approach, the individual behaves not simply as dictated by a collection of conditioned responses produced in his past, with each such response unrelated to the others. The discrete unitary responses are articulated or organized by their participation in a unifying emotional or motivational scheme, with each response contributing to the satisfaction of the motives that "organize" all responses. Thus the individual is seen as a whole, with all parts of his behavior interrelated and interdependent. He is more than a collection of learned and random responses. Rather, these elements are combined (usually uniquely for each individual) in such a way as to give coherence to the whole and meaning to the parts which make up the whole.

This interpretation of personality is derived from the Gestalt theory in psychology, and to a great extent represents an analogy based on perceptual phenomena. Figure 3 presents a typical "gestalt" (complex or patterned whole). The circle is composed of dashes. Each dash by itself is only a dash, and has nothing in it related to circularity. But the dashes are organized into a pattern we call a circle. The circle cannot be said to be composed simply of a group of dashes; it is composed of dashes in a special combination, or having particular relationships among themselves. Figure 3 is seen not as a collection of dashes. It is perceived immediately as a circle. And the whole circle is seen as different from the sum of its related parts. Similarly, personality is different from the sum of the individual behaviors that comprise it. The relationships among the behaviors organize them into a personality.

Figure 3. A Simple Gestalt

The figure is recognized as a circle, although it is composed of dashes that do not contain any features of circularity within them. Thus the Gestalters emphasized the *relationships* among parts of a whole.

Emphasizing the relationships among behavioral events and sequences appears to be an important contribution. A personality description based in part on information regarding these relationships would be much more complete than one that was not. Thus our study of personality must include a consideration of how such interrelationships of traits and behavioral elements are accomplished and the nature of the configurations found in people.

Adjustment and Homeostasis. When psychologists approach the study of personality, they often pay particular attention to the ways in which people respond to the stresses and demands of their environments. The word *adjustment* has been used to describe the individual's efforts to achieve some kind of stable and satisfying relationship with his environment. Adjustment also refers to the interrelationships within the individual of his various behavioral tendencies; the extent to which his habits conflict with or are consistent with his motives is one aspect of this internal adjustment.[2]

The concept of adjustment is related to the principle stated by Cannon, a leading physiologist of the recent past, that the organism strives to maintain "homeostasis,"[3] a kind of steady state, in which all forces operating within or on it are in optimal balance — it is neither hungry nor too full, neither too cold nor too warm, etc. An organism that has achieved complete homeostasis would be in a state not unlike Nirvana.

Homeostasis is basically a physiological concept, designed to call attention to the tendency of the several systems of the body to respond in an interrelated manner, and in such a way that the total disruptive effect of stimulation is minimized. The status of homeostasis as an *explanatory* principle in physiological behavior is questionable. The achievement of homeostasis does not necessarily mean that such was the "purpose" of the organism, any more than a broken leg which results from a skiing trip can be interpreted as the purpose of the trip. Further, some physiologists have even rejected the homeostatic interpretation of physiological events. They point out that socalled homeostatic mechanisms do not necessarily result in minimum disruption. A rise in body temperature, interpreted by Cannon as an illustration of a body system compensating for the disruptive effect of disease, sometimes is a cause of death in itself, through the destruction of brain tissue by excessive heat. This compensatory behavior, then, certainly does not seem to lead to homeostasis; if anything, it may make matters worse.

Some argue that personality functions are sufficiently analogous to purely physiological functions to justify applying the concept of homeostasis to human behavior. They maintain that humans behave in such a manner as to achieve some kind of balance or adjustment between themselves and their environments. Frustration, anxiety, or threat arising from environmental sources or from hidden desires in the individual create an "imbalance" that the individual tries to correct through a variety of techniques which ultimately result in either a reduction of the threat or an avoidance of it. In other words, the organism strives for homeostasis within his environment.

The validity of the concept of homeostasis as an explanatory principle in personality is questionable (see discussion above). Recent research indicates that the tendency to return to a state of minimal arousal or disruption is not nearly the simple thing Cannon and his followers believed. The discovery of drives involving curiosity, sensory stimulation, and activity, drives whose physiological status was unsuspected in

Cannon's day, indicates that organisms also tend toward increased stimulation. The operation of these tendencies and their implications for personality will be discussed in later chapters. They are mentioned here to indicate that homeostasis is not the straightforward and all encompassing principle it once was thought to be.

The concept of adjustment has been challenged for much the same reasons homeostasis is questioned. Obviously, people respond to their environments and change their behavior with changes in the stresses and demands of their lives. However, such behavior does not mean that people have some kind of intention or determining tendency to adjust. This interpretation would mean that a drive toward conformity is a basic and prepotent human characteristic. At best this interpretation represents a gross oversimplification. If people conform, and if they adjust, it is for reasons that go beyond a need to be adjusted or conforming.

Adjustment almost immediately leads to qualitative considerations, such as those involved in the labels "good adjustment," "well adjusted," or "maladjusted." Ultimately, such qualitative judgments turn out to be made on the basis of the value system of the person making the judgments. Maladjusted behavior does not exist as any particular kind of behavior; what may be maladjustive in one setting may not be in another, and what may constitute good adjustment for some judges may not for others. For example, observers in our society would probably say that the person who sees visions is hallucinating, and hallucinations are profoundly maladjustive. But then, what would be said of the man who hallucinates in a society in which visions are interpreted as marks of special mystical or religious favor? Would we be willing to agree that Bernadette of Lourdes was maladjusted? Would we be willing to consider maladjusted the American Indians who must have visions of their totem animal spirits in order to be considered mature braves by their tribes? Let us take another example: a person who has strong needs to be orderly and precise may find himself in an occupation, such as bookkeeping, in which these traits lead to success. But if he should be promoted to an executive position calling for the ability to make rapid decisions based on minimal information, his traits of orderliness and precision might handicap him. If personality is defined in terms of how well the person is adjusted to internal and external demands, it would imply that the bookkeeper's personality changed when he was promoted because the quality of his adjustment changed.

It might be argued that the truly adjusted man would be able to adapt to both jobs. Within limits, most personalities are adaptable. Nevertheless, it is impossible for a person to reach adulthood without acquiring leanings toward some activities that would make him less suitable for other activities. It might not even be desirable for personalities to be so adaptable that they include no such leanings and specializations: such "good" adjustment would create more difficulties for society than those produced by the man who loved every woman he knew.

Finally, the ideal of good adjustment does not contain any specific limitations on its range of application. If it is good adjustment for a man to adapt to his occupation, is it also good adjustment for him to adapt to his imprisonment for a crime? How about adjustment to unjust imprisonment, or to subjugation to the rule of a victorious political enemy? In each of these situations, the individual responds to the conditions he meets. His responses are jointly determined by the nature of the conditions and by the internal psychological processes he brings to the situation. Sometimes his responses will be adaptive to the environment, but sometimes they will not conform to others' judgments about what would be best for the situation. The determinants of the individual's responses may be studied and his personality described in terms of his responses and their determinants, without any necessary implication that the responses were designed to "fit in" with the environment, and without evaluating the adequacy of the individual's personality in terms of whether such a fit was achieved.

In summary, we can study the reactions that occur between the individual and his environment, but we must avoid the implication that a state of minimal disruption is the purpose or goal of the individual. And we must avoid thinking that when minimal disruption takes place, the behavior leading to it was necessarily good, healthy, or adequate, just as we must avoid assuming that the behavior that leads to a great deal of discomfort or disruption is necessarily bad or unhealthy; it might be that the inadequacy is in the environment which does not "fit" the individual's behavior.

It is for reasons such as these that the concept of adjustment will not be used in this book. We will examine the individual's responses to the demands of his own drives or motives and to demands having their source in the environment. We will seek the determinants of these responses and their consequences for the individual, without evaluating the responses in terms of adequacy, effectiveness, acceptability, and other such criteria of adjustment, and without assuming that the end state of the organism brought about by its response was a purposed, intended state to which the organism was striving. Our study then, will be the study of the determinants and consequences of responses to internal and external stimulating conditions.

Meaning of Personality

Personality characteristics and processes are enduring over time. People differ from each other; they vary not only in what they do but also in how they do it. Their behavioral processes and responses are interrelated, including responses to internal and external stimuli. Each of these aspects of human behavior has played a central role in one or another definition of personality. A comprehensive meaning for the term must account for all of them.

We have just suggested that the study of personality may be approached through a study of the determinants and consequences of responses to stimulating conditions. There are many psychologists who mean by this *all* human behavior. Personality often is defined as the "sum total" of an individual's behavior.[4] Definitions such as this arise because it is difficult to draw consistent lines between behaviors that are to be excluded from personality and those which are to be included. For example, by and large, personality psychologists are uninterested in stomach contractions and other components of the hunger drive. But they are interested in the person who overeats in response to frustration (or another who loses his appetite), and the study of this behavior necessarily involves an understanding of the operation and characteristics of the hunger drive. It therefore becomes almost impossible to exclude any particular behavior from consideration in the study of personality.

However, personality psychologists do study different things than say, learning psychologists or sensory psychologists; or they study the same things in different ways. Our definition of personality must make explicit the distinctions made in practice. The "sum total" definition is incomplete for our purposes because it does not adequately indicate the nature of the distinctions. If one should study the reports published in those professional journals concerned primarily with the area of personality, he would find very few if any studies of the variables that affect the learning process, of the physiological correlates of drive states, emotions, and the like, or of the mechanics and behavior of the sense receptors—the eyes, ears, touch receptors. Research reported in the personality journals deals with such topics as how particular attitudes are acquired, the situations that lead to agressiveness, how success and failure experiences influence aspirations, how certain kinds of experiences influence perceptual behavior, how certain perceptions are influenced by variations in the environmental stimuli, the relationship between achievement motivation and performance under stress or performance following failure, physiological responses to particular situations (stress, threat, success, failure, acceptance, rejection, etc.), the relationships between various kinds of behavioral tendencies and performance on various kinds of tasks, occupational selection, occupational success, reactions to failure, acceptance of social influence, etc.

Specificity. What are the differences between the studies encountered in and those excluded from the personality journals? While both groups involve learning, motivation, sensation and perception, and physiology, there are two important differences. The first is *specificity*.

A learning psychologist is more interested in the variables affecting learning than he is in what is learned. He is not primarily concerned with the particular response whose acquisition is being studied; that response has been selected for study because of its representativeness of a class of responses.

The personality psychologist, on the other hand, is interested in the circumstances under which particular responses—aggressive behavior, achievement needs, avoidance of anxiety, tendency to deny one's own feelings, and the like—are learned. His interest, then, is not in the general factors that influence all learning, such as frequency of reward or time interval between response and reward. He focuses on the specific factors that determine specific responses, such as parental domination as a determining factor in feelings of inadequacy or food deprivation in infancy as a determiner of later hoarding behavior. He and the learning psychologist may study the same responses; he is not necessarily interested in different kinds of behavior. Hence it is difficult to draw a line between behaviors included in personality and those which are not. But in studying these responses, the personality psychologist looks for the factors that determine that a subject will learn one rather than another response. Frequently this interest will mean that he will have to study characteristics of the subject's environment and past experience in order to discover these factors.

The last paragraph may be rephrased: The personality psychologist is concerned not with the mechanics by means of which learning takes place, but with what people learn and what events determine their particular learning experiences. Similarly he is concerned with why and how particular motives are acquired, not how motivation in general is acquired and how motives in general operate. Again, the personality psychologist does not ask how the eye operates, but rather why people perceive things in the particular ways they do.

It is obvious that this specificity in the study of personality is *derived*. That is, it is based on more fundamental laws, such as those of learning, motivation, physiology, and sensation. Before one can ask how and why a particular behavior is acquired, one must understand the general laws governing the acquisition of responses and then apply them to the individual and his environment. Such a background in the basic laws aids the personality investigator by suggesting what he should look for and by preventing his searching for things that cannot exist. For example, an investigator familiar with the structure and physiology of the elbow joint will not hypothesize that a person's bending his arm forward, not backward, results from his experiences and environment. He will not draw gratuitous conclusions such as: the human being must have an instinct to bend his arms forward, because no one can be found who bends his arms the other way, and there do not appear to be any particular experiences in the past of all people, or in their environments, which can account for the universality of this arm-bending propensity. To cite a more realistic example, it appears evident from the study of the development of the sensory processes that newborn infants do not have the capacity to sense and record events in their environments sufficiently well that these sensations may be recalled at later ages. Had Otto Rank known this, he would not have postulated that all anxiety which occurs during the individual's life is a reflection of the anxiety experienced at birth — the "birth trauma" — which recurs because something in the individual's present situation reminds him of his birth experience, particularly the fear of separation from a loved one.[5]

Consequences. Studies in personality differ from those in other areas in a second major respect. They are concerned, either directly or indirectly, with the *consequences* of particular learnings or particular motives or perceptions, with the influence of such events on subsequent experiences, learnings, motives, and perceptions. Examples of this emphasis include studies of the effect of achievement motivation on intellectual task performance, the relationship between some learned response tendencies and successful performance in particular occupations, the biasing effect of certain response tendencies on the perception of the characteristics of other people, and the way in which certain acquired response dispositions influence political and social attitudes. The learning psychologist studies the acquisition of response tendencies; the personality psychologist is interested in the consequences of these learnings for the learning of other responses, for perceptual behavior, for performance in various tasks, and for the development of interests and attitudes.

Personality Defined. These two distinctions, specificity and consequences, provide what is needed for a definition of our area of study. *Personality consists of the specific contents and consequences of behavior and the processes responsible for these contents and consequences.*[6] This definition emphasizes a particular kind of approach to the study of behavior more than it does any particular aspect of the behaving organism. After all, there is no "thing" within people that is their personality. The word is an abstraction referring to the contents of behaviors, the experiences and processes that determine these contents, and the consequences of all these for further behavior. In this sense, we would say that a scientist is studying personality when he (1) studies what motivates people, what they learn, what they sense, what their internal organs respond to, and why these particular events occur in particular people, rather than the general laws that govern the development and behavior of these phenomena; and (2) studies the consequences of particular phenomena for further learnings and other motives, perceptions, and performances of the individual. That is, he studies how what has gone on between the individual and his environment influences what happens to him in the future.

The Plan of Study

Part II presents the "terms of the organism," which include the physiological status of humans and the general laws of behavior which will, through interaction with the environment, produce the contents and consequences of personality. The section is thus largely concerned with the basic processes involved and attempts to summarize the pertinent information derived from general experimental psychology. It was mentioned earlier that the study of personality is largely derived from more basic studies. Part II presents these basics as the groundwork on which personality is built. Students who have already studied some psychology may be familiar with many of the concepts but their review will facilitate the integration of this material into a description of human personality. This material includes the physiological backgrounds of behavior, learning, the development of motives, and the nature of the cognitive processes of thinking, perceiving, and consciousness.

Part III is concerned with the organism-environment interactions which produce the specific contents of personality. The treatment is largely developmental. That is, we will begin with the infant's earliest socialization experiences and discuss the socialization of the physiological drives in the order in which these socialization processes occur in our society. This chapter will parallel the chapter in Part II dealing with physiological backgrounds. Then we will deal with the socialization of acquired drives, paralleling the chapters on learning and drive acquisition. Finally, Part III will discuss the socialization of cognitions, as a parallel to the earlier chapter on the nature of thought, perception, and consciousness.

Part IV takes us into the consequences of behavior, first through the study of conflict and the behaviors that conflict engenders, then through a presentation of patterns which are most clearly delineated in the exaggerated states of psychosis and neurosis and their associated character structures. It is in this section that we will deal with the unity of personality. The last chapter, "Human Nature and Value," is a summary of the major points of the book presented through a discussion of the value-consequences of personality.

The emphasis throughout will be on the determinants of behavior that operate in the functioning individual. This will require detailed analysis of a variety of behavioral acts; the guiding questions in psychology are "Why does this behavior occur when it occurs?" and "Why does this rather than any other behavior occur?" These questions will be asked of the most flamboyant and bizarre behaviors as well as of those aspects of behavior which are so mundane that one would hardly think it possible to question their nature. But the study of personality includes all behaviors, and all are candidates for being the subjects of why and how questions. It is part of the delight of studying human behavior in this close fashion that the answers to the questions often turn out to be quite other than one might expect. Both the ordinary and the bizarre may have highly complex and involved determinants, the discovery of which increases our fascination with people and constitutes an ultimate compliment to human nature.

Our focus on the functioning individual means that we will be concerned with the operation of physiological, learning, social, and cultural forces at the level of their participation in ongoing behavior of the individual. Such a study does not replace or exclude analysis of these forces as they are presented in courses in physiology, learning, sociology, and anthropology. Rather, the study of personality is supplementary to these areas. We will draw on them for information in the course of this book, but our use of the information will be to explicate the behavior of the individual, and only as these forces participate directly in determining the behavior of the individual within a society will they become pertinent. For example, large-scale social movements of the kind that sociologists study, and which have large-scale effects on many families, become important in the study of individual personality only as they involve particular behaviors in the parents whose relationships to their children are important determiners of conduct in their children.

REPRISE. The main points of this introduction are:

1. The study of personality attempts to account for enduring characteristics of people, their uniquenesses, the style as well as the what of their behavior, the organization of behavior, and the relationships among events within and without the individual.

2. Personality consists of the specific contents and consequences of behavior and the processes involved in producing these contents and consequences.

3. The plan of study takes us from the general determinants of behavior to the specifics involved in personality, and then to consequences.

4. Our study of personality involves the close analysis of behaviors at the level of the intact individual.

II. The Basic Processes

This section reviews those aspects of general psychology which define the processes through which personality develops and by means of which it operates. These general laws of behavior thus set the limits as well as potentialities for human behavior. The concepts and theories discussed in this section will be invoked repeatedly in later sections to account for the determinants of particular behavioral contents. Familiarity with them is necessary for an understanding of what will be said about personality.

2. Physiological Backgrounds

Man is a biological organism. He is an animal intimately connected with other animals morphologically and physiologically. He is different from other animals in his capacities for behavior (but is not always superior; cockroaches learn the path through some mazes more readily than do many people), but this is largely a difference of degree, rather than in kind. Ultimately all the behavior man displays, indeed, all behavior of which he is capable, is coordinate with internal biochemical and electrical events. This statement has some important implications. It implies that man is capable of no behavior which runs counter to the laws of biology. Thus no account of behavior can be considered adequate if it is not consistent with the laws of biology. It further implies that associated with all behavior are biological events by means of which the behavior takes place. And of course it means that the individual's biological functioning has a profound determining and limiting effect on his behavior. These are compelling reasons for including the study of man's physiological functioning in any study of behavior. Our aim in this chapter is to summarize what is known (which is very much, and yet not enough) about those aspects of human physiology most relevant to the study of personality.

It is at birth (and before) that the biological determinants of human behavior are most readily apparent. Except for the effects of the intra-uterine environment on the development of the organism, the individual's behavior has been but little modified by experience with the social and impersonal environment. What characteristics, propensities, and equipment come into the world with the birth of an infant?

23

Birth Equipment

The infant is born with a developing skeletal structure, a set of internal organs, a musculature, and, perhaps most important for its behavior, a nervous system including a set of sense organs — light, sound, touch, temperature, and olfactory receptors, and taste, pain, and kinesthetic (movement and position in space) sensers. While modifications may result from environmental factors in the maternal womb, most of the characteristics of these systems are largely determined by inheritance. The pattern of development of these organs, their potentialities for growth and maturation, also are fully established by the genetic material that comes together at conception. Of course, whether these potentialities are realized depends on the infant's subsequent activities — his nourishment and experiences.

Noninheritance of Acquired Characteristics. Notice that in this list of birth equipment there is no mention of ideas, thoughts, interests, attitudes, or any other mental contents. The organism is born with the necessary equipment for acquiring such things, but so far has experienced no interaction with an environment that would lead to the acquisition of thoughts or interests. Such behaviors are not inherited or innate. The ideas, values, morals, and all other mental activities of the parents are not biologically transmitted to their children. This is an expression of the principle that characteristics acquired during one's life cannot be passed on via genetic means to the offspring. Recent developments in genetics suggest that the genes, the carriers of the genetic material that determines the characteristics of the offspring, are in effect complex protein molecules which act as patterns for the conversion of nutrient materials into the protein chains which form the chemical building materials of the body;[1] the genes an individual inherits, which, in combination with those of this mate, will determine the characteristics of his offspring, are completely unaffected by his own experiences. Their characteristics were completely determined when he was born, except for possible modifications which may have been introduced, for example, by illness, disease, or radiation. Since a father's genes were established when he was conceived, and are so unaffected by his experiences, his acquired characteristics are not passed on biologically to his children.

The human individual is born with potentialities as part of his birth equipment, and vast ones. At birth he is simply an animal, not very different from most mammalian animals, although considerably less mature than many, and much more fragile. But he has the capacity to develop into a sophisticated, knowledgeable, civilized human being. This capacity, far beyond that possessed by other animals, is realized, turned into actuality, through the process of maturation and learning.

Individual Differences. It is obvious that people differ in an almost infinite variety of ways. Some of these differences are present at birth, as are the structural backgrounds out of which many other differences develop. One experiment showed that by selective breeding it was possible to develop one strain of white rats that was highly emotional and "nervous," and another strain, started by a member of the same litter that gave rise to the emotional strain, that was much less volatile, more phlegmatic and calm.[2] It is the same with people. Some, born with nervous systems which are more reactive than those of others, may be more active. As infants they may display faster and more intense reactions to sound, light, touch, and other stimuli. These babies might be particularly alert or responsive infants, and, as a result of their hyperactive nervous systems, their experiences may be markedly different from those of passive, unresponsive infants. And it is as a result of these differences in experiences that each child learns different traits and develops a different personality. One series of studies showed that almost from the moment of birth, individuals demonstrate reliable and enduring distinctive styles of reacting to events. Newborns who reacted rapidly to a loud sound continued to react rapidly as older children. While the *contents* of their reactions and the nature of the things that started the reactions varied among different "fast reactors," they did have this fast "style" in common.[3,4,5]

In addition to the biological systems already mentioned, their individual differences, and their genetically determined potentialities for future growth and development, the infant is born with some ready-formed capacities for behavior. These exist in the nature of the infant's nervous and sensory systems, which deserve a closer examination.

General Characteristics of the Nervous System

The nervous system may be thought of as a communications network, not unlike a telephone system. "Messages" are transmitted from receiver organs, which sense or respond to physical environmental stimuli such as light, sound, odors, and pressure, to other parts of the body, often through a central switchboard (the brain), and eventually to muscles, which are effector organs capable of producing movement and action.

The nerves that carry the messages from the sense organs are called *afferent* nerves. They carry the nervous impulses to the control or integration center where they may be combined with impulses coming in from other nerves. This control or integration center is called the *central nervous system,* and consists of the brain and spinal cord. The spinal cord has some integrating functions, but it is also of great importance as the main trunk line for carrying impulses to and from the brain. In fact, the brain is really a highly complicated elaboration of the spinal cord, and develops out from it. Many lower animals have almost no brain at all; the spinal cord and the limited kinds of behavior of which such a simple nervous system is capable are sufficient for such animals' growth and reproduction. In human embryos, the spinal cord is established first, and the brain differentiates out of it.

The nerves which transmit impulses from the central nervous system to the muscles of the body organs, which react and produce action and behavior when stimulated, are called *efferent* nerves. The muscular systems that respond to their impulses are called *effectors.* Taken together, the afferent and efferent nerves, most of which branch off from the spinal cord (although many go directly to the brain), are called the *peripheral nervous system,* to differentiate them from the central nervous system.

The Neurons. The building blocks of the nervous system, the wires over which impulses are carried, are elongated cells called *neurons.* Some neurons are relatively short, such as those that connect and interconnect various areas of the brain; some are quite long, such as those that carry impulses from the touch receptors at the tips of the toes to the spinal cord. What we refer to as *nerves* are really many such neurons collected together in bundles, much as a cable consists of many wires grouped together.

The impulses conducted along the neurons are really electrical phenomena, as shown in Figure 4. An impulse consists of a change in the electrical potential of the neuron; that is, it is a change in the relationship between the charge on the surface of the cell membrane and the charge within the cell. This change travels along the neuron by producing a breakdown in the permeability of the cell membrane in the area right next to the impulse. When this breakdown occurs, the charges at that point change in their relationship, so that that point then gets the impulse, and the area which previously had the impulse begins to restore itself. This change in electrical potential is associated with an exchange of potassium and sodium ions between the cell interior and exterior.[6] Thus a nerve impulse travels along the neuron, either to or away from the central nervous system, depending on whether the neuron is afferent or efferent.

The All-or-None Principle. The speed with which an impulse travels and the amplitude or "size" of the impulse vary from one neuron to another, but within a neuron they are relatively invariant. That is, a particular neuron, assuming it is healthy and rested, always conducts impulses at the same rate and amplitude, regardless of how powerful the stimulus, the light, sound, odor, or pressure which started the impulse. This characteristic is referred to as the "all-or-none" principle.

Figure 4. Neural Impulse Propagation

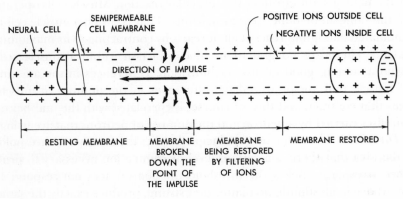

The impulse travels along the axon of a neuron; it consists of an interchange of ions through the semipermeable cell membrane, thus neutralizing the difference in potential between cell interior and exterior.

The impulse's speed of transmission and its amplitude are determined by differences in charge on the cell membranes and the nature of the ion interchange through the membrane. These factors exist within the neuron and its environment and have nothing to do with the size of the stimulus. Thus the all-or-none principle means that the energy for neural impulses resides within the neuron, rather than in the stimulus. A neuron is like a fuse made of gunpowder. Such a fuse burns at the same rate and with the same amount of heat regardless of whether the fuse is lit by a match or a blowtorch. The neuron is similar to the fuse in that the rate and amplitude of the impulse depend entirely on the state of the conductor—whether it is healthy, well nourished, and not depleted of essential biochemical substances.

How then are differences in the strength of stimuli transmitted? We do perceive differences between a bright light and a dim one, and it is apparent that our nerves can "instruct" our muscles to respond quickly and powerfully or slowly and with little force. The answer is that such differences are reflected, in part, by the number of impulses conducted by a neuron in a given time or by the distance between impulses (a strong stimulus produces a series of impulses one after another; a weak stimulus might produce fewer impulses with greater time intervals between them), and, in part, by the number of neurons fired. The more intense the stimulus, the greater the number of neurons which transmit impulses.

In the efferent system, the more muscle cells stimulated to contract by the neurons, the stronger the muscular reaction. Muscle cells operate on the same all-or-none basis as neurons. That is, when a muscle cell is stimulated enough to react at all, it reacts by contracting to its maximum extent. There are no gradations of contraction within a muscle cell, again assuming good health and nutrition. Differences in the amount of muscle pull are produced by differences in the number of muscle cells that contract, and this, of course, is correlated with the number of impulses carried by a neuron and the number of neurons that are firing.

Threshold. The all-or-none principle implies the concept of threshold — the idea that there is a certain level of stimulation necessary to produce a response. Below the threshold the neuron does not respond at all. Above it, all stimuli, no matter how strong, produce exactly the same effect on the neuron, in terms of the rate of transmission and the amplitude of the impulse (although thresholds may be altered by repeated stimulation, and weak stimuli may summate to the point where they are above the threshold). Thus a neuron either fires at the maximum strength permitted by its chemical structure, or it does not fire at all. Individual neurons differ widely in their thresholds.

The Sense Organs. The sense organs are highly specialized structures that convert physical energies into neural impulses. The eye is a complex machine that reacts to light in such a way as to produce neural impulses. It also responds to pressure. The ear is specialized to react to sound pressure waves and thus produce impulses in the neurons going from the ear to the central nervous system. So it is with the temperature, pressure, and chemical (smell and taste) sense organs. There are also kinesthetic organs which lie in the muscles. They transmit impulses when the muscles move or are enervated. Thus we are aware of changes in the positions of our body members even when our eyes are closed.

There is also a sense organ, part of the vestibular system located near the ears, which is sensitive to deviations of the head from an upright position. It is partially by means of impulses from this organ that we are enabled to keep our balance.

The History of a Response

When a sense organ is stimulated by the physical energy to which it is sensitive, such as the eye by light, a neural impulse is produced and travels along the neuron to its end. Let us suppose that a temperature receptor in the finger has been stimulated by the heat of a hot cup of coffee touching the fingers. The afferent impulse thus produced travels along the neuron to its end in the spinal cord. There, within the cord, the impulse meets several other neurons. One of these new neurons is a short one, extending from one side of the spinal cord to the other, where it meets an efferent neuron, which goes out of the cord to the finger and/or arm muscles. This short neuron, called an *association fiber*, is stimulated by the impulse from the afferent neuron and so conducts its own impulse to the efferent neuron. In its turn, the afferent neuron is stimulated, producing an impulse that travels to the muscles along the backs of the fingers. These muscles react to the impulse by contracting; the fingers spring open; and the hot cup drops. All this would happen, provided that the threshold for the firing of the association neuron was low enough and the impulse from the afferent neuron strong enough to stimulate it. The same is true of the threshold of the efferent nerve. It is possible that the thresholds of these second-order neurons will be so high that afferent impulses coming to them fail to produce a response in them. In this case, there would be no response to the sensory stimulus. If the cup were only mildly warm, so that relatively few impulses were stimulated in the heat-sensitive receptors, the total amount of stimulation might be too little to fire the association neuron, or the efferent neuron, so the cup would not be dropped.

The Reflex. This complete sequence of behavior is the *reflex*, the most basic response system. In the case of the hot coffeecup, a complete reaction to an environmental stimulus was produced, centered around the behavior of a sense receptor, three neurons, and effector muscles. The reaction was rapid and nonvolitional. That is, it occurred without being planned, and as usually happens, the cup was dropped even before the holder grew completely aware of the burning in his fingers. His cry of "ouch!" usually is not made until the cup is already on its way to the floor. This "cup dropping" reflex, integrated in the spinal cord, does not even require a brain for its occurrence. In fact, similar reflexes have been observed in frog legs detached from the frog bodies. This behavior is also unlearned, although learning may modify or alter such reflexes.

But only in an individual whose brain had been removed, an impossible situation for death would occur in humans at once, would a reflex involve so little. The afferent impulses coming from the burning fingers meet not only an association fiber, but also other neurons which go up to the brain and some which go to other points along the spinal cord. If their thresholds are low enough, the neurons going to the brain may also be stimulated, and so conduct impulses to that "master switchboard." In the brain these impulses might stimulate other association fibers and become integrated with other impulses coming in, such as those from the eye which produce the visual perception of the steaming cup. Eventually impulses travelling through the brain might stimulate efferent nerves which go to many different muscle structures. Thus impulses might travel to the legs, so the burned person jumps up; some impulses might go from the brain to the voice box so that an unpleasant word is uttered; some to the heart, which may suddenly beat faster, and so on. These secondary reactions may also include an awareness of what happened, if the threshold relationships among the various neurons involved are such that the necessary associations among fibers in the brain are activated by neural impulses. Because these secondary reactions involve a somewhat longer route for the neural impulses, they tend to occur some time after the simple spinal reflex which resulted in the cup being dropped.

Synapse. The meeting site of neurons, such as the juncture of an afferent with an association neuron, is called a *synapse*. Little is known about what goes on at a synaptic connection. We do not know, for instance, how one neuron stimulates the other to respond. The neural impulse does not jump the gap like a spark. It ends when it reaches the furthest extremity of the neuron along which it is traveling. It has been established that biochemical substances are secreted at the synapse, and that these secretions are affected by the impulse. Some physiologists are investigating what seems to be a kind of biochemical wet cell battery at the synapse, which stimulates the second neuron

Innate Reflex Structures. Let us return to the newborn baby now, to add another item to the list of original equipment: the great variety of innate reflex structures which enable the infant to make a wide range of responses. One of the most important is the sucking and swallowing reflex. Stimulation of the back of the mouth will automatically produce sucking and swallowing. The baby has no innate knowledge of milk, breasts, and nipples, but when an object such as a distended nipple touches the back roof of the mouth, a reflex is stimulated which produces sucking and swallowing muscle movements (as well as waving of the arms and legs). The baby did not have to learn how to swallow. Similarly, the responses of the internal organs, the digestive and excretory systems, are reflex mediated, and are, thus, innate response capacities, requiring only an effective stimulus to set them off.

Although the infant has a full set of reflexes, he has very little, if any, control over his actions. He cannot walk, talk, turn over—indeed, there is little he can do but wave his arms and legs in a random fashion, turn his head, open and close his eyes and mouth, and, of course, cry. This lack of control is a feature of the infant's physiological immaturity. Earlier, in the description of the phenomena found in reflexes, the synaptic connections between afferent neurons and the association neurons going up to the brain were mentioned. It is by means of connections within the cerebral cortex, the gray outermost layer of the brain, comprised of millions upon millions of nerve cell bodies, that the cortex can exert a controlling influence on the muscles involved in the reflex act. In fact, in the normal adult a steady stream of impulses flows from the cortex and other brain centers to the muscles of the body. This flow results in the muscles maintaining a state of mild contraction, or muscle "tone." It is in the cortex that efferent impulses, which are necessary for "voluntary" or "conscious" movement, originate. The cortex also functions to regulate muscle action by inhibiting it. Spinally mediated reflexes result in extreme muscular responses. When the cortex functions, it inhibits these responses to an extent, by sending impulses to the opposed muscle groups to counteract the responses of the reflexively acting muscles. Thus a person who suffers from an interruption in the neural paths going to the brain from the spinal cord kicks quite wildly when the patellar just below the knee is stimulated by a blow when a physician tests the "kneejerk" reflex, while the normal adult kicks much less violently.

The infant lacks conscious control over most of his muscles; his cortex has not yet begun to exercise its inhibitory and excitatory functions. As he develops, he gradually acquires such control. When it is the result of the elaboration and development of physiological structures and functions, this development of control is called *maturation.*

Maturation. There seem to be some fairly definite sequences in maturation which are common to all animals possessing spinal cords. One is the *cephalo-caudal* direction of maturation: the acquisition of control over muscular movements occurs first at the head and neck, next the shoulders, and so on, spreading downward in a head-to-tail direction. Thus an infant is first able to lift his head, and later his shoulders off the bed. The next step is sitting up; the last is standing and walking. This sequence has also been demonstrated in tadpoles, which swim by producing alternating 2- and S-shaped bends in their bodies. Leonard Charmichael found that in very recently hatched tadpoles, only the head could be bent. After a while, the trunk was also bent, and last the tail. He also found that tadpoles begin swimming at the same age, whether or not they have been allowed to practice, thus indicating that the observed cephalo-caudal development is maturational, rather than learned.[7] Confirmatory evidence has come from a study of human infants. In some societies, such as the Hopi Indian, it was the practice to bind infants to boards for the first several months of their lives (except for a short time each day when the baby was untied and permitted to play). Thus Hopi infants had very little opportunity to practice the responses they would need to make in walking. Despite this, Dennis and Dennis report that infants so bound learn to walk no later than infants not bound to boards, further illustrating that walking behavior is largely a product of the maturation of neural control, rather than learning.[8]

Another maturational sequence observed in many species is the *proximo-distal* direction of development: the acquisition of control over muscle groups beginning first at the midline of the body and proceeding outward. Thus the upper arm is controlled before the lower arm, the wrist before the hand, and last the fingers.

These two directions of development, when combined, indicate that the most highly developed control the very young infant has is centered around the mouth area. Oral activities, particularly eating, will consequently be of very great importance in the early life of the baby, and will be a focus of learning that has farreaching effects.

Many nerve cells in the mature body are covered by a layer of fatty tissue called the *myelin sheath*. Neurons that eventually become myelinated will not transmit impulses until the myelin sheath is complete and intact. Poliomyelitis is a dramatic instance of this characteristic. The myelin sheath is attacked by the virus, and paralysis of the muscles served by the affected neurons results. The myelinization of the nerve fibers is not complete by the time birth occurs. The building up of the myelin sheath continues for some time after birth in the general cephalo-caudal and proximo-distal directions. There is, thus, some reason for thinking that maturation and the acquisition of cortical control over body muscles is a result of the myelinization of nerve fibers.

We now have a fairly complete baby, including a nervous system and readymade reflexes, which, however, are not yet subject to cortical control. As we observe the baby, we note that many reflexes are being displayed in overt behavior, which includes crying, possibly because of hunger. Such behavior suggests that one more group of items must be added to the list of birth equipment: the array of *needs* that must be satisfied if the baby is to grow and develop.

Needs

A person's most significant experiences occur in relation to the satisfaction of his need. And it is through need-satisfaction that the learnings occur which, together with the products of maturation, form the constellation called "personality." In fact, without needs, there might be no behavior at all.

A comprehensive list of the infant's biological needs would be very long, and many of the items which should appear on it are unknown as yet. For example, to be truly comprehensive, it would be necessary not simply to list food, but to break this item down into the food nutrients, the vitamins, minerals, and roughage, necessary for optimal growth. However, it is not necessary to be so atomistic for our purposes, so the principle needs will be briefly noted in general terms.

Food. We are most aware of our need for food, principally because of hunger "pangs." Cannon has shown that our experiencing or sensing hunger pangs is directly associated with the contractions of the stomach that occur reflexively when the stomach is empty. He demonstrated this by having subjects swallow a deflated balloon tied to a tube. When the balloon came to rest in the stomach, air was pumped into it through the attached tube. The tube was then connected to a device that was sensitive to changes in the air pressure in the tube and that recorded these changes by means of a line on a moving strip of paper. When the stomach contracted, it put pressure on the balloon, thus increasing the air pressure in the tube. The subjects were asked to report to the experimenter each time they felt a hunger pang. Cannon found that the subject's reports regularly followed stomach contractions as these were recorded on the apparatus.[9]

On the basis of Cannon's studies, it was concluded that food need was expressed through stomach contractions that stimulated organisms to seek food and eat.[10] However, more recent evidence suggests that although stomach contractions may play a role in the subjective feelings of hunger, they are not the most important regulators of food intake. For example, if the nerves that carry impulses from the stomach to the brain are severed, the animal cannot experience or sense its own stomach contractions. It will nevertheless continue to eat and to regulate its food intake so that it will eat neither more nor less than an animal which has not been so surgically prepared.[11] Further, it has been found that organisms whose stomachs have been totally removed, so that there can be no contractions, still eat essentially normal amounts of food.[12,13,14] Thus it appears that mechanisms other than stomach contractions regulate the satisfaction of food needs. Currently, investigators are looking for such mechanisms, or regulatory centers, in the midbrain and the base of the brain.

The effects of a need for food on human behavior may be seen clearly in a study in which children's temper outbursts were observed throughout the day. It was found that the frequency and intensity of angry outbursts increased just before the children's customary feeding times, suggesting that hunger was affecting their emotional behavior.[15] This conclusion was corroborated by studies on semi-starvation for which conscientious objectors volunteered during World War II. After several weeks on a minimal diet, the men were found to be very irritable and uncooperative.[16]

There are specific hungers for particular food components. A young boy was taken to a physician because of an almost insatiable demand for salt. The mother reported that as a young baby he was very fussy and irritable, but that one day he accidentally knocked over a salt shaker and ate the spilled contents, and this quieted him so much that since that time she had freely indulged his desire for salt. The mother was advised to reduce the child's salt intake, and shortly after that the boy died. An autopsy revealed a defect in the physiological mechanisms by means of which salt is stored in the body and made available for use; this condition made it necessary that the child continuously take in salt.[17] This case suggests that some quite specific needs can markedly influence behavior. It is not known whether some specific mechanism is activated or stimulated as the result of salt deprivation, or whether the diffuse bodily effects of the salt deprivation simply made the boy feel bad in general, a feeling that was reduced when he accidentally discovered and ate salt.

Water. Cannon believed thirst to be a purely local matter, as in hunger, but centering in the mouth and throat. He concluded that when body tissues became dry, as a result of loss of body water through perspiration, urination, or evaporation in the lungs, the mouth and throat tissues also become dry and stimulate a flow of nervous impulses that result in drinking responses. However, we know now that this is not the whole story. Although a dry mouth may stimulate a person to drink, recent evidence indicates that other mechanisms control the amount of water intake. Dogs whose salivary glands are tied off so that their mouths become dry tend to drink more often than animals not so prepared, but they drink less each time, so that in the long run their total water intake is no different from what it was before the operation.[18]

Other studies have pointed to hypothalamic centers in the brain that in some as yet unknown way are sensitive to the water content of the body cells.[19,20] When the body cells become dehydrated, drinking occurs, regardless of how dry or wet the mouth is, although it is true that the dryness of the mouth is usually correlated with the water content of the body cells in normal organisms.

The essential point about water is that there is an optimal level of hydration. Dropping below that level represents a need for water, while exceeding that level is likely to result in some processes by which the excess water is shed, usually through urination.

Air. We are certainly aware of our own needs for food and drink, but we seldom think much about our physiological need for oxygen. No doubt this is because we seldom if ever experience deprivation of oxygen, which is so readily available that deprivation rarely occurs. This abundance is fortunate, because the need for oxygen is very likely the body's most imperative need. If their oxygen supply is cut off brain cells begin to perish in a matter of minutes, and in humans there is no regeneration of nerve cells. Hence the great importance of getting a newborn infant to breath as soon as possible after he has been separated from his source of oxygen, his mother's blood supply.

When there is a deficiency of oxygen in the cells, relative to the amount of carbon dioxide, chemical changes occur in the blood and in the cells. These changes result in a greater absorption of the oxygen content of the blood by the cells and in a richer oxygen mixture in the blood. But perhaps most significantly for personality, such a relative deficiency also results in an increased breathing rate and a faster heart beat. Sometimes people confuse these effects with similar symptoms caused by anxiety and other psychological states. This confusion will be more fully explored in a later section.

Temperature. The body produces heat as a product of oxidation. There is an optimal amount of heat necessary for the efficient operation of the body. Too much heat will cook body cells—the destruction of brain cells by cooking is the prime danger of high and prolonged fever. Too little heat will slow down bodily processes, particularly blood circulation, and thus produce a shortage of oxygen in the body cells. There is a very complicated relationship between the capillary blood vessels and nerve endings in the skin that operates so that disparities between the body's heat and the heat of the environment results in the initiation of neural impulses. These neural impulses become integrated in the brain's hypothalamic region—the same general area involved in the regulation of food and water intake—from which flow impulses that activate a variety of mechanisms. In the main, these mechanisms result in some modification of the organism which operates so that the body temperature remains relatively constant despite changes in the external environment. For example, if the external temperature is such that the nerve endings in the skin that are sensitive to cold become stimulated, neural impulses that go to the hypothalamic region are produced. There, through many synaptic connections, efferent impulses travel to the capillaries which become constricted, thus lessening the amount of heat at the skin which might be lost through radiation to the colder environment. Impulses go to the sweat glands which close, so that again heat loss is diminished. Functioning of the thyroid gland is accelerated, and greater production of heat through increased metabolic rate results. Shivering occurs, which further increases body heat by producing movement. In addition, the organism may do some things, such as increase its activities (you stamp your feet and swing your arms when you are cold) which increases heat production, or roll up in a ball to reduce heat loss by reducing surface area through which heat is lost to the environment by radiation.

Body temperature has some quite direct relationships to people's emotional behavior. For example, it has been reported that the body temperature of people who are particularly irritable and grumpy when they awaken in the morning is somewhat lower than that of people who wake up readily and feel fit and happy upon arising. The mechanism of this relationship is not known; it may be that the lowering of body temperature results in the stimulation of the temperature center of the hypothalamus, and in turn of the internal organs which respond in a manner experienced as unpleasant by the person, making him "jumpy" and irritable. The impulses from the hypothalamus may also produce heightened muscular tension, increased heart rate, and the rest of the general pattern of emotional arousal.

The main point is that mammals are sensitive to heat and cold and make many physiological responses which result in the maintenance of a constant body temperature. Deviations from the conditions that favor this constant body temperature are thus occasions for a great deal of physiological activity, and for behavior.

Elimination. Defecation and urination result from innate reflexes activated by events in the intestine and bladder. When these organs fill with waste material beyond a certain point, the reflex actions involved in urination and defecation are set in motion. Although originally on a reflex basis, these behaviors may be brought under the control of the cerebral cortex so that reflex elimination may be inhibited or facilitated depending not only on the state of the bowels and the bladder, but also on factors in the external environment. Both maturation and learning are involved in this acquisition of control over elimination.[21]

Sex. Sexual needs are probably our least understood biological needs. What is known suggests that sexual behavior is initiated by the action of hormones on brain centers, and the neural impulses thus produced are integrated in the hypothalamus from which impulses flow to the various internal organs and skeletal muscles involved in sexual behavior.

It is difficult to say when sexual needs develop. While very young infant boys have relatively frequent erections, the responses involved in ejaculation do not mature until adolescence. To complicate matters further, it is noted that sexually immature animals appear to engage in sexual activities as part of their play. Young dogs will mount each other even though complete sexual acts are not committed. And there is some evidence that sexual needs do not require orgasm for their relief; rats will learn to solve problems if they are simply permitted to mount a female when they have solved a problem correctly, even when they are not permitted to copulate to orgasm.[22] Sexual needs are somewhat different from the other needs discussed in that the organism can survive and be quite healthy even when it never has an opportunity to engage in sexual intercourse.[23] In contrast to sexual needs, food, water, and temperature needs must be gratified if the organism is to survive and remain in good health.

One of the problems in studying human sexuality is that it is so markedly different from sexual behavior in lower species. As one goes up the phylogenetic scale from the simplest animals to man, behavior becomes less and less stereotyped and automatic. Another way of stating this is: much behavior comes under the control of the cerebral cortex and thus can vary within wide limits to meet particular environmental situations, knowledge of which depends primarily on the cortex. As noted earlier, the cortex can exercise an inhibiting or arousing effect on behaviors integrated at lower centers. Thus, man's sexual behavior, though integrated at the hypothalamus, can be so extensively modified by the cortex that the direct expression of sexual needs and the variables that arouse it cannot be seen in him. Another factor related to this is that human societies establish quite rigid codes of conduct governing sexual behavior. These codes, made possible by man's capacity for cortical control of sexual behavior, and made imperative by the drastic effects on social groups of uncontrolled sexuality, result in such great modification of sexual behavior that what is seen in man may be only very distantly related to the innate patterns of sexual need and arousal. Every society includes more or less effective prohibitions on sexual relations with mother or father and brother or sister. Other restrictions vary from one society to another.

What we do know suggests that in the sexually untrained organism, sexual behavior may be initiated by the action of hormones on hypothalamic centers, and as the action continues physiological responses of a sexual nature are initiated and become stronger the longer the hormonal action continues. This action may be neutralized or ended by the physiological consequences of orgasm. Usually a partner is needed for orgasm to occur. Thus the sexual need is essentially a need for a partner in relation to whom sexual responses leading to orgasm may be carried out.

Absence of Pain. We shall classify tentatively the absence of pain as a human need which appears to be innate. As with the needs discussed above, there are special receptors or mechanisms that, when stimulated by the energies to which they are sensitive, produce a variety of physiological effects which generally continue until the stimulation of the receptors ceases. With pain as with temperature needs, the stimulus that starts the flow of afferent impulses to the central nervous system frequently comes from the environment, (e.g., a pin prick), but may also come from within the organism (e.g., muscular aches produced by overexercise). In the latter case, the need for the absence of pain is similar to sexual, food, and water needs in that stimulation is produced by events within the body. In other words, the pain receptors are located both deep in the body interior and on the body exterior, in the skin.

Much of the research on pain indicates that it is the result of stimulation of special receptors in the skin, the internal organs, and particularly in the walls of the blood vessels. The receptors in the skin, which seem to be free nerve endings having no special receptor mechanism or organs, are connected to two different kinds of neurons, one of which gives rise to the sensation of sharp, tingling pain, and the other, a slower neuron, which gives the sensation of dull and aching pain. Only the latter type seems to be present in the internal organs.

Pain receptors, when stimulated, produce a variety of internal responses. Some, such as spasms in the walls of blood vessels at the site of stimulation, may be strictly reflexive, mediated in the spinal cord. Other internal responses are more generalized. Quickening of the heart, a rise in blood pressure produced by constriction of the blood vessels, "catching" the breath, interruption of digestion, and localizing and identifying the painful area, are the results of neural activity in higher brain centers. Specifically, pain pathways carry impulses through the spinal cord to the brain's thalamic area. From there they travel to the cortex and the hypothalamus. The cortex becomes involved in the localization of the pain and the integration of afferent impulses to the skeletal muscles so that body members may be used in removing or avoiding the painful stimulus. The hypothalamus integrates impulses to the internal organs which produce the more general responses to pain stimulation. Although the cortex receives the sensory impulses of pain and is involved in awareness or consciousness of a painful stimulus, it is more likely the hypothalamically mediated responses of the internal organs that give pain its aspect of intensity and suffering. While the role of the cortex in consciousness and its relationship to the hypothalamus and other lower centers will be discussed more fully below, it is necessary to indicate here that pain responses can occur in the absence of the cortex and without the conscious experience of pain being present. The important thing about pain and physiological needs is that when pain endings are stimulated, internal organs respond through the integrating action of the hypothalamus, and these responses usually do not cease until the pain receptors no longer transmit their impulses.

Needs for Stimulation, Activity, and Change. Curiosity and Sensory Stimulation. Until recently, the list of physiological needs might have ended with the absence of pain. However, several new lines of research show the presence of another need. Several years ago Harlow and Butler of the University of Wisconsin discovered that if a monkey were kept in a completely enclosed box with a latched door on it, the monkey would learn to open the latch provided he was allowed to look out of the door at something interesting, such as a set of model trains on the floor outside of the box.[24,25,26] Harlow reasoned that the animal would not learn how to open the door if there were not some need operating, or if there were not some factor that made the sight of the toy trains more rewarding than not seeing anything. He hypothesized that the animal was being motivated by a curiosity drive; there did not seem to be any other reason for the animal to learn to open the door. He was not being rewarded by having his needs for food, water, oxygen, sex, comfortable temperatures, and absence of pain reduced by his opening the door. Harlow suggested that this "curiosity" drive could account for the exploratory behavior of animals who seem to look around whenever they find themselves in a new environment.

There is another line of research which may be related to Harlow's. In a very interesting series of experiments at McGill University, Heron has found that students placed in almost complete isolation from changes in their environment begin to demonstrate quite bizarre behavior. They found their experience so intolerable that they quit the experiment despite the high payment they received.[27] In the experiment each subject was placed in a room into which "white noise" was piped. "White noise" is a constant noisy sound, something like a hiss, which covers all frequencies and has no pattern and which serves to mask or block out other, incidental noises. The subject wore translucent goggles so that all he could see was an unvarying diffuse white light. Thus stimulation from variations in sound and light was reduced nearly to zero. The room was evenly heated to a constant temperature. The subject lay on a bed. Around his arms and legs were large cardboard cuffs, similar to cardboard mailing tubes. The subject was arranged in such a way that there was minimal contact between his body and other objects, including the bed clothes. Under these conditions subjects soon began to grow fidgety and anxious, to report "strange" feelings and hallucinations (they heard and saw things that were not there). The subjects' performances on intellectual tasks markedly deteriorated, and many reported that they were "unable to think." After two or three days under these conditions, most subjects quit, apparently unable to stand the deprivation of sensory stimulation, and feeling quite shaken from the experience.[28] These results are interpreted to indicate that humans have a need for sensory stimulation; when such stimulation is absent for any long period of time, diffuse psychological and physiological changes occur.[29]

Although Harlow's monkeys were not as completely isolated from sensory stimulation as Heron's college students, visual and auditory stimulation were drastically reduced when the monkeys were in their "curiosity drive" boxes. There is thus some reason to think that the monkeys' behavior was really an escape from mild sensory deprivation, rather than a result of a "curiosity drive."

Reactive Inhibition. There is one more line of work that relates to this problem. Clark L. Hull and his followers have discovered and explored a process in animals that is exactly opposed to learning. It was discovered that the more often an animal repeats a response, the less likely it is that he will repeat the response again.[30] In effect, animals seemingly get bored repeating the same response and are inclined to do something else. That this is not fatigue is indicated by the fact that the animal may use the very same muscles involved in the response to produce a different one when this "inhibition" builds up. This phenomenon is called *reactive inhibition.* It may be illustrated by soldiers who have been on a march. As the march progresses, they complain more and more and are less inclined to continue marching. If their disinclination is the result of muscle fatigue, they would not want to do anything that would involve the fatigued muscles. But if the disinclination is reactive inhibition, they would be willing to engage in other activities involving the same muscles as those used on the march, as long as the new activity is different from marching. The physically fatigued soldier would not want to go to a dance after the march; the soldier whose feeling of tiredness is really reactive inhibition would be willing to use his leg muscles in dancing, although he would feel too "tired" to use them in further marching.

Reactive inhibition is really part of the subject of learning because it is a reaction to an experience. Any animal that shows reactive inhibition is obviously showing the effect on his behavior of past experience. Thus the presence of reactive inhibition is evidence for learning. It has been used to show that even such simple animals as the one-celled paramecium learn: if a paramecium makes a right turn at a place where it can go either right or left (a choice point) then it is more likely to make a left turn than a right one at the next choice point. If what happened at the first turning had no effect on the second turning, then the direction of turn at the second choice point would be strictly a chance affair: the animal would have a 50/50 chance of turning one way or the other. But the experiment showed that the animal is more likely to turn in a direction opposite to the way it turned at the last choice point.

Reactive inhibition may be related to Harlow's curiosity drive and to Heron's need for sensory stimulation. It is possible that the monkeys' latch-opening behavior and the students' emotional upset at being isolated were really the results of reactive inhibition—the build-up of a need to do something other than what they had been doing, which in both experiments was the doing of close to nothing.

At any rate, no matter how the behavior may be explained, there is sufficient evidence to indicate that organisms do have some internal responses to the lack of stimulation (although the sense organs that initiate afferent impulses in response to the lack of stimulation and the neural paths those impulses follow, are still unknown), and that these responses result in some kind of behavior. Thus we list sensory stimulation as a "need," although this may not turn out to be an appropriate name for it.

Marasmus. With human infants, a very severe behavior disorder may result if this need becomes too great as a result of too prolonged deprivation. Margaret Ribble has studied in great detail a disorder known as *marasmus,* which is said to have accounted for an estimated one-half of the infant deaths below the age of one year up to the 1920s. Probably because of the marked changes in child rearing practices since that time, one no longer hears of marasmus.

Marasmus is a disorder in which the infant seems just to waste away. The intake of food and water is reduced, the child appears to be very unresponsive and unspontaneous, and there is no development of interest in the environment. Even though there seems to be nothing organically wrong that might produce such an impairment of behavior, the reduction of functioning may continue until death occurs.

Ribble found that this disease tended to occur in infants who for one reason or another either were deprived of their mothers or had reduced contact with their mothers. Since their physiological needs for food and water were being met, Ribble suggests that these infants were suffering from a lack of the handling, fondling, cuddling, holding and playing that usually occurs as an aspect of contact with an affectionate mother.[31] In a sense, then, marasmus may well have been a disorder resulting from a lack of sensory stimulation. As indicated above, little is known about the physiological operations involved in reactions to sensory deprivation, and the same is true for marasmus. We cannot be sure that the two are related until these questions have been answered.

Activity. It is not at all certain that there is a specific need for activity for its own sake. There is considerable evidence that activity level increases as other needs become stronger. A moderately thirsty or hungry animal, for example, is much more active than a satiated one (although if hunger or thirst increases beyond a certain point, activity begins to decline as a result of the reduction of cell metabolic functioning). Activity is highly correlated with sexual needs. A female rat in an activity cage (a drum that revolves when the rat inside it runs) will run the equivalent of four miles on an average day. But when she is in heat — when sexual hormones are being poured into the blood stream — she runs up to and exceeding 10 miles a day.[32] Male rats do not have such sexual cycles and so do not show such variation in activity. However, it has been suggested that the exuberance of human adolescents, male and female, may be a result of the building up of sex needs.

Although it may appear that activity results from other needs, the considerations mentioned with reference to the need for sensory stimulation may apply with equal weight to activity. The behavior of Harlow's and Heron's subjects may have resulted from a need for activity, rather than from a need for sensory stimulation. In fact, it would be hard to separate the two, because activity does produce sensory stimulation. Nerve endings in the muscles transmit impulses to the central nervous system when the muscles move. When such afferent impulses arrive in the central nervous system, efferent impulses are sent to other muscles which produce complicated reactions to the movement, the net result of which is to keep the body coordinated and balanced, and which enable the body movements to be consistent with the positions and attitudes of the body members. Although coordination and balance may be learned, the neural mechanisms for sensing and responding to body movements are innately present. Where there is consciousness, as in the waking and alert human, these mechanisms permit an awareness of the position of the body members. One need not look at one's arm in order to locate its position in space.

As a result of the firing of these sensory mechanisms in the muscles, activity produces stimulation. Thus it is difficult to know whether some behaviors are responses to lack of stimulation or to lack of activity. Although an animal satiated for all its other physiological needs tends to sleep, it remains awake if its need for sleep is also satisfied. Though activity may be minimal, there is still some present. Because some needs, such as those for food, water, elimination, and sex, are reduced only periodically rather than continuously, one might argue that the waking of the animal and its minimal activity are the results of the building of such needs, low as the need level may be, rather than the result of an activity drive per se. The definitive experiments on this question have not yet been performed. A need for activity, then, though present in this list of needs, must be considered a tentative formulation for the time being.[33]

Sleep. The physiological mechanisms that mediate and control sleep and wakefulness are but little understood. There is a small area in the hypothalamus which, if injured, results in chronic somnolence. This area, then, being responsible for wakefulness, has been called the *waking center.* There is another area in the hypothalamus which, if damaged, produces chronic wakefulness. This area is called the *sleep center.* There is evidence that the two interact, and that the cortex interacts with both centers. One theory suggests that the cortex gradually acquires control over these hypothalamic centers, and that this is how an infant progresses from many naps a day to the adult pattern in which sleep is postponed until one long stretch daily.

The sleep and waking centers may be involved in the need for sensory stimulation. It has been suggested that impulses from the sense organs go to an area allied with these two centers, which in response sends neural impulses to the cortex which keep the cortex "alert" or responsive. This "arousal system" requires variation in sensory stimuli in order to maintain alertness; it readily adapts to "steady" or "even" stimulation, and so soon ceases to send impulses to the cortex. It is *change* in stimulation that results in the sending of bursts of "arousing" impulses to the cortex.

It is sufficient to recognize that particular arrangements are usually necessary for sleep to occur. There must be an absence of intrusive stimulation (a steady voice even if loud does not disturb sleep so much as do occasional noises which produce contrast in the stimulus situation). There must also be provision for lying down. Whatever mechanism it is that produces sleep, its operation is facilitated by the presence of these two conditions, and the individual usually learns to arrange these conditions when the need for sleep arises. If these conditions are not present, it may not be possible to satisfy the need for sleep. As the need increases, the individual becomes tense, irritable and emotionally aroused — that is, until exhaustion begins to set in, with its associated reduction in behavior, hallucinations, and "blank spells."[34]

Several recent experiments on sleep deprivation show that the prolonged absence of sleep can produce severe behavioral disorganization, including delusions and hallucinations. These studies also indicate that physiological correlates of sleeping continue to occur at the subject's usual time for sleeping, even if he does not sleep, and that the patterns typical of the waking state begin to appear at the time the subject would usually awaken, even if he had not been asleep. Thus, he seems more awake during the day after a sleepless night than he was during the sleepless night. This suggests that the centers that control sleep and wakefulness are at least to some extent independent of the person's activities. These studies also point up how important sleep is for continued well-being. Some people who had voluntarily deprived themselves of sleep for long periods had to be hospitalized under psychiatric care as a result of the psychological changes produced by the sleep deprivation.

We do not know the mechanisms by which emotional arousal occurs as a response to sleep deprivation. It is known that the hypothalamus plays a major role in both sleep and emotional arousal.[35] We do not know what particular stimuli set off the actions of the sleep and waking centers. Some theories suggest that a chemical messenger acts on the sleep and waking centers. Other theories suggest that some kind of rhythmic pulsing center "times" the day and stimulates the sleep and waking centers at intervals.

The Importance of Needs

For our purposes, the significant thing about all these needs is that they are composed of complex physiological activities. The physiological arousal that occurs can be reduced or ended by a change in the relationship between the individual and his environment. In other words, when physiological arousal occurs, and the organism then behaves in such a way as to reduce the need (which usually means that he alters the environment or his relationship to it), then the physiological arousal state through which the need has become manifest is reduced or ended. In this way, needs lead to action.

In a sense, a need represents some state of deprivation of the organism or some departure from those conditions that are optimal for the organism's functioning. The extent of departure may be expressed in terms of length of deprivation—that is, how long since the need was last satisfied, or through the magnitude of the departure. The colder the environment the greater the need for heat. Time since last satisfaction and magnitude of departure thus serve as indices of strength of need.

Before birth, very few needs exist because of the nature of the developing infant's relationship to its mother. The mechanics of the relationship are such that the developing infant receives all the necessary materials on a continual basis, so that deprivation does not usually occur to any considerable extent. As long as it is served by the mother's blood supply, the infant receives ample food, water, and oxygen constantly. Its waste products are continually carried off, and the mother's body maintains a constant temperature for the infant's environment. Further, there is protection from pain stimulation by the cushioning of the amniotic fluids in the womb.

However, the fact of birth changes all this. From this time on, the infant is supplied with food and water on a periodic rather than a continual basis. Evacuation occurs at intervals rather than continually. In other words, from birth on the infant is subject to the building up and growth of needs, because he receives essential materials from the environment only on occasion. Psychologically speaking, this change is the major significance of birth.

It is probably fair to say that the organism is always in some state of need; all needs are probably never completely satisfied at the same moment in time. It takes time to satisfy a need; while one need is being reduced another is growing. And certain needs are quite incompatible and by their nature cannot be met concurrently. For example, the need for rest obviously cannot be satisfied when the need for activity or sensory stimulation is being met. This means that from birth on, the human is always in a state of need, and therefore always tending toward some action.

Motives. We have seen that there are mechanisms in which a state of deprivation or deviation from optimal conditions produces afferent neural impulses in the various organs that are sensitive to the deprivation. These impulses generally flow to integration centers in the brain's hypothalamic region. From the hypothalamus they proceed to the various effector organs—the blood vessels, the muscles of the internal organs, and the skin, the glands—which respond to the state of need. These physiological responses are what psychologists call *drive states* or *motives*. That is, the organism makes some internal responses to the need; these responses include the conversion of stored potential energy into the kinetic energy dissipated in behavior in the form of heat and motion. The conversion of energy usually results in some overt behavior in which the organism acts on or in his environment, and this action tends to continue until some change is effected in the environment or in the organism's relationship to it which reduces the need state and thus the drive to behave. The organism in a state of need appears to be trying to do something to reduce its need. In short, needs produce internal responses which result in behavior. The behavior is then said to be motivated (i.e., aroused and directed) by a state of need (deprivation or deviation from an optimal state which initiates the flow of nervous impulses). Motives are named in terms either of the needs which produced them, corresponding to the objects in the environment that will end the needs and thus the motivated behavior, or of the internal states that describe the deprivation (hunger, thirst, pain). These internal states are the products of neural integration of the need-produced impulses in the hypothalamic area, which then activates the internal organs by sending impulses through a special division of the nervous system called the *autonomic nervous system.*

Robert Malmo of McGill University has shown that the activity of the autonomic nervous system is associated with higher performance on the tasks assigned to his subjects; in other words, the level of autonomic activity was associated with the amount of motivation his subjects had.[36] It was also found that, when instructions to the subjects were varied, so that some instructions did not motivate the subjects very highly, and others provided very strong incentives for the subjects to perform well, there was a direct relationship between the amount of autonomic activity and how motivating the instructions were.

We have been discussing what are generally called *primary* motives—the motives implicit in the human organism by virtue of its biological structure. They may be considered part of the infant's birth equipment. As will be seen throughout this book, there are other motives, usually called *secondary, learned,* or *social* motives, which may be acquired after birth; these will be discussed in a later chapter. From the preceding discussion it is apparent that a motive exists when the autonomic nervous system is aroused or involved. The *goal-object* or *goal-activity* of the motivated organism is that which will reduce the autonomic arousal, usually by reducing the organism's state of need, and thereby removing the source of the neural impulses that produced the motive state.

Some theorists have accounted for motivation by pointing out that states of physiological need are all more or less painful, and that in general all motivated behavior may be thought of as an effort to reduce pain, or a response to pain. However, in the interests of exactness this interpretation may best be avoided. While intense hunger, for example, may be experienced as unpleasant and in that sense painful, pain has a more exact and different meaning, neurophysically speaking. In its exact meaning, pain refers to the experience produced by stimulation of particular nerve endings, the pain receptors. Obviously the mechanics of the two motives vary, as do the goal activities and objects that will reduce the motive and the need. To avoid confusion, it is probably better not to assume that the pain drive is the prototype for all the others.

John Dollard and Neal Miller, two men noted for their outstanding contributions to the science of personality, have suggested that any strong stimulus operates as a drive. They point out that the presence of any strong stimulus will impel an organism to behave—too bright a light, too loud a sound, or strong internal stimuli.[37] The autonomic nervous system's responses to needs involve reactions in the muscles of the internal organs. These muscles have sensory neurons attached to them, so that the muscles' responses can serve as strong stimuli for neural impulses in the sensory fibers. As Dollard and Miller define "drive," it could be said that the greater the autonomic arousal the stronger the drive. Since it has been shown that strong stimuli existing outside of the organism, such as bright lights and sounds, do produce autonomic arousal, their view of drive implicates autonomic arousal as the basis for motivation. Although the data concerning the effects of absence of stimulation produce some difficulties for Dollard and Miller's conception, it is obvious that the autonomic arousal produced by sensory deprivation does impel the individual to act, and so does give rise to motivated behavior.

Man, Active and Reactive. Curiosity, manipulation, activity, sensory stimulation—these various needs have a common element which is of profound significance for psychology, and which has made these needs a focus of important research. The common element is that these all involve a "reaching out" to the environment by the organism, in which the reaching out provides its own rewards. Speaking metaphorically, the appetitive needs, such as hunger, thirst, or sex, *push* until some incentive—food, water, a sexual partner—has been achieved. But there is no object *per se* appropriate to the reaching out drives, no incentive to be achieved. In a sense, the appetitive drives may be reduced by objects; the reaching out drives are reduced by *activities*. This means that some behaviors may be engaged in simply for the sake of behaving, even if no goal object is attained. The existence of such drives could account for play behavior, for thinking and imagination which are not problem solving in nature, and for such processes as needs to work, to be entertained, to be relieved of boredom.[38, 39] These drives may be closely involved in determining the kinds of behaviors most central to the development of culture, knowledge, and art. Man not only reacts to appetitive needs; he is also active. One implication of the reaching out drives is that human behavior includes more than a selfish search for needed objects — it includes also behaviors which are intrinsically satisfying.

It is for reasons such as these that psychologists have become very interested in exploring the active drives. Recent research focuses on how these drives operate, and on the variables that determine their occurrence and strength. Of primary importance in validating these drives is the elucidation of the physiological processes on which the active reaching out drives are based. Current thinking points to the reticular formation, an area of the brain allied to the hypothalamus. It is called the *reticular arousal system* (RAS) because stimulation of this area produces a flow of neurons to the cortex of the brain, which makes the organism act as if it were interested, curious, expectant, or alert. The organism seems aroused.[40]

The Role of the RAS. The RAS receives impulses from the hypothalamus. When appetitive needs are present and the hypothalamus is activated, it sends impulses to the RAS as well as to the internal organs. The impulses to the organs produce activity through the conversion of stored energy into movement; the impulses to the RAS produce a flow of impulses from the RAS to the cortex of the brain which is thereby alerted or aroused. The result of this cortical alerting is that stimuli in the environment that might reduce the drive can be more readily perceived and, thus, acquired. When the RAS arouses the cortex, the organism is in a heightened state of readiness to react to the environment. When the RAS is stimulated by the hypothalamus as part of the organism's motivational state, it thus functions to make the organism better able to satisfy its motives.

It has also been suggested that in the absence of need-produced stimuli from the hypothalamus, or supplementing them, environmental stimuli can produce impulses that activate the RAS on their way to the visual and auditory areas of the cortex, so that the animal acts alert and interested in the source of these stimuli. Harry F. Harlow, who very early proposed the possibility of such externally aroused drives as an explanation for curiosity, drew the illustration in Figure 5 to show what might be involved.[41]

This theory, including the research on the RAS and its neural pathways, thus suggests that organisms are motivated not only by pushes from within, but also by pulls from the environment, and that cortical

Figure 5. Motivational Arousal by Internal (Interoceptor) and External (Exteroceptor) Stimulation

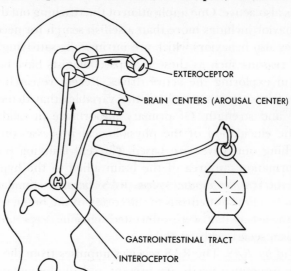

EXTEROCEPTOR

BRAIN CENTERS (AROUSAL CENTER)

GASTROINTESTINAL TRACT

INTEROCEPTOR

Harry F. Harlow drew this figure to show how motivational centers in the brain can be stimulated by both internal and external events.*

activity such as thinking or being alert to stimuli may be physiologically determined behavior whose occurrence is motivated even when appetitive needs are satisfied. Thus, we must recognize the possibility that organisms may be motivated by environmental events operating on the arousal system. However, even in such cases, the motivational state still involves hypothalamically mediated activation of the autonomic nervous system, by means of which internal organ responses and a preparation to act and behave are produced.

In short, any situation which produces autonomic activity arouses motivation. In the inexperienced and naive organism, such as the infant shortly after birth, stimulation of organs sensitive to states of bodily need and intense stimulation of any sense modality are the conditions which produce such autonomic activity. It is necessary for some change to be made in the organism's environment for the need to be reduced

*Reprinted by permission of Harry F. Harlow and the publishers from M. Jones (ed.) CURRENT THEORY AND RESEARCH IN MOTIVATION. Lincoln, Neb.: University of Nebraska Press, Copyright, 1953, by The University of Nebraska Press.

and the motive satisfied. In practice, this usually means that the organism has to do something about his needs.

Functions of Motives. The operation of motives will be explored in greater detail in succeeding chapters; it will suffice to mention here that motives serve to initiate activity, direct behavior toward a goal object or activity; they produce a readiness to respond to the goal, and in general arouse the organism or sensitize it to its environment and particularly to those portions of the environment that might reduce the autonomic arousal. In these senses, motivation provides the energy for behavior and is the central factor that makes it possible to transform the savage infant into a sophisticated adult. Put simply, the world may be arranged so that certain behaviors, produced by particular motives, may be encouraged and others discouraged. How this is done is the main topic of the next chapter and falls under the heading of learning.

These functions of motives are inherent in the nature of the autonomic nervous system. Because of the importance of motives in the development of personality, and in particular because of its role in fear and anxiety (avoidance motivation) which are such important variables in personality, it is important that we take a close look at this system.

The Autonomic Nervous System. Earlier, the nervous system was divided into a central nervous system and a peripheral system. The nervous system may also be divided another way: into the *somatic* and the *autonomic* components. The somatic nervous system consists of those nerves that carry afferent impulses from the sense organs and efferent impulses to the skeletal muscles, which control the movements of our bodies and the body members. These muscles are largely under the control of the cerebral cortex, so that the individual has the feeling of consciously controlling their action. The muscles so controlled are the *striate* muscles, named so because of their striped appearance.

But a great portion of the body's activities are concerned with internal affairs—the actions of the visceral organs, the glands, the digestive organs, the heart and lungs, the muscles in the walls of the blood vessels. The muscles of these organs and structures, being unstriped, are called *smooth* muscles (except for the heart muscle which is a special type of striped muscle). The branch of the nervous system that controls these muscles is called the *autonomic nervous system*.

The name is a curious one. The system was so named because many autonomic neurons go to nodules (*ganglia*)—clumps of nerve cells bodies and synapses—which lie in chains on each side of the spinal column. It was thought that these two chains of ganglia were independent of the rest of the nervous system—that the functioning of the nerves that connected with the ganglia was autonomous of the spinally-mediated nervous system. Thus the system was considered "autonomic," and the name has persisted despite the discovery that the ganglia send and receive many neurons directly from the spine and thus are not independent of it at all.

Sympathetic and Parasympathetic Systems. There are two complementary subdivisions of the autonomic system: the *sympathetic* and the *parasympathetic*. By and large the two systems serve the same internal organs and structures. But they do differ greatly in their effects on the organs they serve. In the case of any particular organ, the two subsystems are antagonistic in that impulses received from one result in an increase in the activity of the organ and impulses from the other produce a decrease. Thus sympathetic activity produces an increase in heart rate, while parasympathetic activity produces a reduction in heart rate. However, neither system functions exclusively to excite all the organs it serves or to inhibit them. Each system excites some and inhibits others.

The sympathetic and parasympathetic systems maintain a balance of power over each organ they serve. The smooth behavior of the organ depends upon the checks and balances between the two systems, so that the organ's behavior is a kind of compromise between the antagonistic actions of the two systems.

Need states, as indicated earlier, tend to operate through the integrating functions of the hypothalamus.[42] The hypothalamic center becomes stimulated when a need arises, either through sensory neurons from sense organs, or through hormonal stimulation, as is the case with sexual needs. It may even respond to changes in the temperature of the blood supply which serves it (this may be one of the ways in which temperature needs operate). The hypothalamus is the major central nervous system area for the control of the autonomic nervous system. When stimulated as a result of a need state, it sends efferent impulses to the internal organs through the autonomic system. It has been pointed out that the internal responses to hypothalamic stimulation constitute our physiological motives. These responses come about through changes in the reciprocal relations between the sympathetic and parasympathetic enervations of the internal organs. Thus in food deprivation the stomach contracts; sensory fibers going from the stomach to the cortex carry impulses produced by the stomach contractions, resulting in our awareness of our need for food. The hypothalamus also sends impulses directly to the cortex, which, therefore, also participates in motivation.

The sympathetic system is the part of the autonomic system usually involved most directly in motivational arousal, such as fear or pain. When it is so aroused, the balance of control shifts so that this system tends to exercise the major control over the organs it serves. The result is that digestion slows down, because the stomach and intestines are inhibited by the sympathetic system. The blood vessels in the viscera and the skin contract, driving blood to the muscles of the extremities (and incidentally producing the paleness characteristic of a frightened or a pained person), because the sympathetic system tends to contract the muscles in the walls of the vessels. The heart beat accelerates under sympathetic arousal; the adrenal gland is stimulated to release adrenalin into the blood, which adds a chemical reinforcement of the effect of the sympathetic system on the internal organs; the body and skeletal muscles react by tensing; the lungs take in larger quantities of air; the hairs of the body are pulled erect by the tiny muscles attached to them which are enervated by the sympathetic system; the action of the parasympathetic system in contracting the pupils of the eyes is dominated by the opposed action of the sympathetic system, which results in dilation of the pupils; the sweat glands are stimulated to secrete perspiration. You will recognize these internal changes as being the things that give fear or pain their emotional force. When one is frightened, he feels his hands perspire and his heart pound; he is tense; he may describe himself as feeling that his stomach is tied up in knots. These responses result in a mobilization of the body resources for the expenditure of energy, in the kinds of behavior that generally occur in a frightened or pained organism running or fighting. Greatly excited (i.e., highly motivated) people are capable of feats of strength and resistance to fatigue; one of the reasons for this is that adrenalin, being poured into the blood stream as the result of activation of the gland by hypothalamic impulses, drastically lowers the muscle cell thresholds of response to stimulation, thus counteracting the effects of fatigue, which tends to raise muscle cell thresholds. Adrenalin also makes it possible for a greater number of muscle cells (those with normally high thresholds) to respond to neural stimulation. The result is stronger muscular responses to neural impulses when adrenalin is present and a resistance to the rise in threshold usually produced by fatigue (i.e., excessive "firing" of the muscle cells).

Because the sympathetic system tends to be involved when intense needs arise, it is often referred to as the *emergency* system. However, it would be erroneous to conclude that the sympathetic system only functions on such occasions. During periods of rest and inactivity it is less active but is still a check on the parasympathetic system, which would otherwise produce too drastic a slowdown of activity.

If the sympathetic system is greatly involved in emergency reactions, it may be said that, by and large, the parasympathetic functions are those of a "housekeeping" nature. When it is dominant, the organs it serves behave in such a manner as to carry on life building processes. Digestion takes place, the heart is relaxed, blood pressure is lowered. In general then, sympathetic dominance results in physiological arousal and the expenditure of body resources, whereas parasympathetic dominance usually results in a rebuilding of the body and in physiological relaxation.

It was mentioned earlier that there are two chains of autonomic ganglia lying alongside the spinal cord. These ganglia are way stations for sympathetic neurons, and in the ganglia each neuron has synaptic connections with many other neurons, including fibers which travel to the other ganglia in the chains. Because of this anatomical arrangement, sympathetic arousal tends to be quite generalized. Each sympathetic neuron connects with so many others that impulses are sent to almost all the internal organs. For this reason, the states of the internal organs produced by sympathetic arousal tend to be indistinguishable from each other, despite the differences in the need states which produced the sympathetic activity, be they pain, fear, or sex.

Some experiments indicate that there are consistent individual differences in the pattern of internal organ activation as a result of autonomic activity. For some subjects, the heart is more reactive or sensitive than the stomach; for the others, the sweat glands or the vascular system may respond more strongly.[43, 44] These individual differences in what is the most reactive organ system are probably consistent regardless of the need-state that produced the autonomic arousal.

Discriminability. The parasympathetic neurons have their synaptic connections in ganglia lying close to the body organs. Thus they tend not to connect with the parasympathetic neurons that serve other organs. As a result, the action of the parasympathetic system is much more specific and focalized on particular organs than is the action of the sympathetic system. Thus it is possible, through the general effects of sympathetic activity and the more selective counterbalancing effects of the parasympathetic, that a variety of differing internal responses to differing need states may be produced.[45] The organism can thus discriminate between various need states, so that specific motives are aroused. This discrimination is based on the differing patterns of autonomic arousal; however, it is noted that when very intense needs are present so that there is massive sympathetic arousal, discriminability is reduced. Hospitalized mental patients, for example, who have extremely strong motivations, find it difficult to discriminate well enough between various states of their feelings so that they can label their motive states.

It is important to note that the patterns of autonomic arousal produced by various need states differ in their discriminability. For example, one can identify a hunger motive because the contractions of the stomach, even though not the essential part of a food need, nevertheless are present when the need for food arises. These stomach contractions are cues the individual can easily identify and thus readily learn what he can do to reduce the hunger motive. But sexual needs do not produce such easily discriminated cues as a result of the autonomic responses to the need. A hypothalamically mediated increase in activity is a fairly subtle response to sexual need, as are the other internal responses, such as muscular tension or dilation of the blood vessels in particular body areas. These same effects may be produced by a number of other need states and by the learned motives discussed in the next chapter. As a result, the individual cannot readily label the motive expressed through these vague and diffuse internal responses. Being unable to discriminate cues, he finds it difficult to label his feelings and to learn appropriate behaviors which will reduce the need. This is one of the reasons that sexual needs are so often unsatisfied and are so often found to be part of the basis for neurotic and psychotic behavior, which may be thought of as extreme reactions to unsatisfied needs and motives. Norman Cameron tellingly notes that the same stomach shares both hunger and hate, and the same heart that sighs for air sighs for love.[46] Because the same organs participate in a variety of need states, it may sometimes be difficult to discriminate adequately between states, and so respond appropriately. Thus some people feel hungry and eat when they are really frightened or angry. The tremendous significance of this fact for personality will be explored in later sections of this book.

Motivation and Emotion

It has been customary in psychology to make a distinction between motives and emotions. However, the two are intimately related: motives are accompanied by the experience of emotional feelings and emotions themselves serve to motivate behavior. The angry man is motivated to strike someone, the weeping to find someone who will provide solace and comfort. Because of these interrelationships, psychologists are coming to view emotion as a part of motivation. The term "emotion" by and large is applied to the individual's visceral, facial, and skeletal responses which give him the "feelings" that he experiences. They are responses of the same organs that respond to need states and are largely carried out through the operation of the autonomic nervous system. The term "motive," on the other hand, includes these same responses in connection with the stimuli that produced them — either a state of need or some external situation which elicits the emotion — and refers in particular to the instigation to action these internal responses produce. Thus emotion usually refers to subjective feelings associated with visceral activities, while motivation refers to the instigation to action associated with these responses. Motivation and emotion thus refer to two somewhat different viewpoints from which to regard the same behavior.

The Role of the Cerebral Cortex. Although it has been pointed out that as a biological organism, man is very similar to other, lower, animals, it is also true that as a behaving animal, he is much more complex than other animals. His behavior is more variable and modifiable. Whereas a lower animal may eat only when hungry, humans may eat when the need for food is quite low. Man may kill without being angry and love without passion. He is much less dependent upon external cues for his behavior (the adult male does not begin to make sexual responses upon first sight of a female), and his behavior is less completely determined by internal events (he does not eat at the first sign of hunger, nor does he build a "nest" only in certain seasons). Thus his behavior may be more variable and also, therefore, more readily modified. It is generally agreed that man's greater capacity for such modification and adaptability is made possible by his more highly developed *cerebral cortex.* The cortex is the covering, or outer layer of the brain, composed of millions of nerve cell bodies. There is more surface area to the human cortex relative to the volume of the brain than in any other animal. If you should study the brains of animals, you would note that as you go up the phylogenetic scale, the cerebral cortex shows a regular progression from being almost nonexistent in the lower animals to being the major portion of the brain of man.

The cortex in itself is not the source or neural center for any behavior. All behavior is mediated by centers below the cortex. Even one's visual experiences, which are generally thought to be located in the so-called "visual cortex" at the back end of the brain, have lower representations, so that decorticate animals — those whose cortexes have been surgically removed — can make some visual discriminations. What then is the role of the cortex?

Although there are specialized areas of the cortex which participate in particular kinds of behavior, by and large one may think of the cortex as an association device — the neural complex in which connections among various neurally mediated behavioral elements are made. In man, most if not all of the lower centers send neural fibers to the cortex, and receive fibers from the cortex in return. Because of the cortex's relatively large area, there is plenty of room for neural events mediated at lower centers to have representations in the cortex and for there to be billions of possible connections among cortical centers.

These billions of possible interconnections make it possible for a human to learn so much. They also make it possible for the sensory reports coming to the brain from several different sense receptors, and from several different parts of the body, together with all the associations among these sensory reports and the responses connected with them, to become integrated with the behavior of lower centers. This massive integration goes on and on as the individual constantly experiences and acts. The marked development of symbolic processes — producing and understanding words, numbers, and other such symbols, visual and auditory images, thinking and imagining — appears to be the result of the great potentiality of the human cortex for forming associations between afferent and efferent neural events.

Inhibition and Excitation. The cortex may operate either to inhibit or excite lower centers. This capacity of the cortex is probably based upon its associative activity. The associations mediated in the cortex produce impulses going to lower centers, which either inhibit or stimulate these centers or the muscles they activate. For example, in dogs in which the cortex has been removed, one may observe what has been called "sham rage." As a response to almost any even mildly noxious stimulus, the dog will give an extremely intense rage response, which is identical to rage in normal dogs in every respect except that it is so easily aroused and is not appropriately directed. This latter is probably because of the absence of cortical tissue in which associations between the neural traces of the stimulus events in the environment and the animal's own reactions can be made. That is, the absence of the cortex deprives the dog of the part of the brain in which his reactions can be coordinated with the sensations that bring him information about his environment. Thus he cannot direct his rage appropriately to the environment. The main significance of this experiment is that the rage reaction is completely integrated and organized in lower centers (the hypothalamus) so that, even without a cortex, the full pattern of rage is elicited. But the extremeness of the rage response indicates that the cortex normally inhibits rage in intact dogs. This kind of inhibition is constantly going on. In fact, studies of the electrical activity of the brain using the electroencephalogram (EEG), which is essentially a device for picking up and amplifying many times the neuroelectrical currents in the brain, indicate that at no time is the cortex at rest; there is always a pattern of activity, even during sleep. This constant discharge from the cortex, it is theorized, serves to inhibit lower centers and the body activities, inhibiting muscular reactions by maintaining enervation of opposing muscle groups. Even when the arm is not being used, the reciprocal enervation of the opposing muscles (those that would produce a bending of the arm *vs.* those that would straighten the arm out) keeps the arm in a state of minimal tension so that, for example, it does not swing quite as freely as a pendulum as one walks.

The inhibitory functions of the cortex are seen quite clearly in the patellar (knee jerk) reflex. If you will recall the example of the hot cup of coffee, you will remember that in a simple reflex there is an afferent impulse which goes to the spine where it synapses with an association neuron which in turn stimulates an impulse in an efferent neuron. In the case of a sharp blow just below the knee cap, the response produced is a kick. But the kick is a controlled kick. It has been noted that in cases in which neural connections between the spine and the cortex are interrupted, the kick is an uncontrolled, wild one — and quite dangerous to the physician who administers the stimulus, unless he has learned to stand to one side. What normally happens in the patellar reflex, as in other reflexes, is that the afferent neuron synapses not only with an association neuron which stimulates the efferent neuron, but also with neurons that carry impulses to the cortex. There, probably as a result of associations with other neural events, such as those which represent the position of the body in space or those which are stimulated by light in the environment producing vision, an impulse is shunted back down the spinal cord to the muscle of the leg which opposes the kick, thus inhibiting the magnitude of the response. Physicians make use of this fact to locate approximately neural lesions by testing the patellar reflex and noting whether the kick is wild or cortically inhibited.

That the cortex can also excite or facilitate behavior is shown by experiments in which subjects, instructed to think about having a blow to the knee, give amplified or less inhibited reflexes. Thinking is largely a cortically mediated activity. Certainly it is true that cortically mediated visual and auditory experiences may stimulate and arouse motive states — the smell, sight, and sound of frying chicken is quite likely to stimulate (or perhaps more accurately, amplify) food motivation. Thus the cortex may both facilitate and inhibit hypothalamically integrated responses on different occasions.

Behavioral Variability. Lower animals, not having such highly developed cerebral cortexes, do not show such cortically produced inhibition and excitation to the extent revealed in man. Their behavior, being more completely controlled by lower centers, is therefore more stereotyped. This is best illustrated by the studies of sexual behavior in various animals by Clelland Ford and Frank Beach of Yale University.[47] They note that as one goes down the phylogenetic scale from man, patterns of sexual responses become more and more stereotyped. In man, sexual behavior may take a tremendous variety of forms depending upon the particular situation. Lower primates such as monkeys show some variability in their sexual behavior, but not as much as man, and when one gets down as far as the birds, the pattern of courtship and mating is almost invariable from one occasion to the next, with very little modification related to differences in environmental situations. The greater corticalization of behavior in man is not an unmixed blessing — it also means that damage to his cortex results in a much greater alteration in his behavior than it does in lower animals. Man is more dependent upon his cortex.

Thought. Although thought and consciousness will be treated in greater detail in a later chapter, it is necessary to mention here that thought is very largely a cerebral activity. The association functions make it possible for people to "know" — that is, have conscious experience. The mechanics of this phenomenon are not well understood at all. The problems of studying thought are the most formidable in all of psychology. But the role of thought in behavior has been explored to some extent. It is obvious that thought has a marked effect on many kinds of overt behavior but it is also true that behavior is possible without thought at all. An experiment illustrates this point very well. Subjects were instructed to reply to numbers between zero and ten spoken by the experimenter. Whenever the subject replied with a number two higher than the number spoken by the experimenter, the subject was told he was correct. It was noted in this experiment that subjects gradually gave the "correct" answers more and more frequently, indicating that their behavior was being modified by the experimenter's telling them they were correct at certain times, and that this happened even when the subjects reported that *they hadn't the slightest idea of why their answers were right or wrong.* That is, there was no idea or thought that identified the principle "What he said plus two" gives the correct response. Thus behavior is not necessarily dependent upon "knowing."[48]

Animals will eat, drink, and satisfy other physiological needs even when their cortexes are removed. Certainly infants, in whom it is presumed that thought and knowing are almost totally absent because of the immaturity of the cortex and the lack of experience necessary to form associations, are motivated to meet their biological needs. Thus needs may arise, motives develop through hypothalamic activity, and behavior leading to need reduction (sucking, for example, in the infant) may occur without thought, without knowing or labeling one's motives.

The Cortex, Lower Brain Centers, and the Effectors. We have reached the jackpot questions in psychology today. How does the cortex operate to allow man the flexibility of behavior he shows? How does the cortex acquire and operate the control over the body reflexes that grows with the maturation of the infant? How does the cortex inhibit and facilitate responses? How does it participate in motivation and emotion? In the answers to these questions we shall gain some understanding of how man has come to succeed so well as an animal and on what basis the "humanity" of man rests.

We have already noted that the explanation for the great capacity of the human cortex to control the body and its behavior lies in its tremendous potentiality for forming associations between sensory and motor impulses and for integrating (i.e., connecting and interconnecting) these associational networks.

Let us return to the example of the hot coffee cup. Suppose that simultaneously with or even preceding the arrival at the cortex of the neural impulses produced in the afferent nerves by the heat stimulus, impulses are received from the eyes which "report" to the person a representation of what it is on which he is standing. These visual impulses stimulate networks of association fibers in the cortex through whose activation the person "interprets" the visual stimulus to be a costly Persian rug. The association network which represents this perception sends impulses to the muscles of the fingers which contract, resulting in a tighter grasp on the cup. The connections between the visual stimulus (the Persian rug) and the motor response of tightly grasping are learned, probably through having been punished for holding liquid containers too loosely when standing on or near expensive things.

While the fingers grip the cup tightly in response to the sight of the rug, several other things are happening. Impulses stimulated by the heat of the cup go toward the cortex. In addition, the spinal reflex that leads to dropping the cup is activated. These reflexes may already be in progress, because the spinal reflex involves a shorter circuit than the circuits that go up to the cortex. When the spinal reflex is activated, neural impulses go from the muscles of the fingers to the brain "reporting" the contraction of the muscles that would make the fingers loosen their hold on the cup. Thus while the Persian rug-grasp tightly circuits are operating, two sources are sending impulses to the cortex; those that sense the heat of the cup and those that sense the tendency of the finger muscles to open reflexively. When the impulses from these two sources reach the cortex, they reinforce the impulses from the sight of the rug to reinforce the grasp tightly circuit, thus producing increased contraction of the grasping muscles to counteract the tendency to drop the cup. As a result, the person hangs onto the cup, enduring the heat until he can set the cup down gently without spilling it. Thus the cortex has operated, through the integration of sensory impulses from hand and eye and their associated efferent impulses, to control a spinally mediated reflex. Here we see how the cortex's capacity for interconnections can result in the inhibition of responses mediated at lower centers. Of course, whether the cup is dropped depends on the relative strengths of the stimulus-response connections—how hot the cup is compared with how strong is the learned response of grasping.

We have just described one possible explanation for the operation of cortical control over spinal reflexes; it is one which has been the most commonly accepted in psychology until recently. However, several interesting studies suggest that there may be an alternative explanation, or perhaps a supplementary mechanism. These studies show that peripheral neurons fail to transmit impulses under certain conditions in which the direction of the subject's attention is controlled.[49] These studies suggest that there is some kind of "gating" or selective blocking process in the brain which cuts off or closes out neural pathways—raises their thresholds for firing to a great extent—so that they will not transmit impulses under ordinary conditions of stimulation. In effect, "gating" may mean that the reason the person does not drop the cup is as follows: activation of the cortical "sight of expensive rug—grasp tightly" circuits somehow raises the threshold for response of the neurons that serve those hand muscles that, when contracted, make the fingers fly open. The person fails to drop the cup because, as a result of his awareness of the nature of the rug, there is increased resistance to firing of motor neurons to the hand muscles, and thus a reduction in the stimulation of the muscles that must contract for the cup to be dropped. "Gating" has been demonstrated with sensory neurons. In cats, the nerves that transmit to the brain impulses produced by auditory stimulation of the ear become resistant to firing (i.e., their thresholds are raised) when the cat's attention is diverted from the auditory stimulus by the sight of a mouse.[50, 51] It is possible that a similar "gating" occurs on motor neurons, as in the suggested explanation for how the cortex controls the spinally mediated, cup-dropping reflex. However, so far the mechanics by means of which such "gating" takes place are unknown.

The acquisition of control—referred to as "voluntary control" in the discussion of maturation in the infant—thus includes the use of the cortex in integrating learned stimulus-response associations with reflexive events to inhibit (either through enervation of opposing muscle groups or through "gating" of motor neurons) the reflexes. But the flexibility of behavior in man, his freedom from rigid hormonal control over sexual behavior, his ability to eat when not hungry and kill without anger, includes not only the ability of the cortex to inhibit responses, but also the ability of the cortex to participate in the arousal, activation, or facilitation of behavior. This subject, however, because it very directly involves the acquisition and development of motives and the learned arousal of motives, is in itself vast and controversial. It deserves an extended discussion, which is reserved for Chapter 4.

The Cortex in Emotion and Motivation. The mechanics of the cortex's participation in emotion and motivation are inadequately known. Two major theories have dominated psychological work in this area. The older theory, known as the James-Lange theory, named after the two men who independently announced it, states that neural impulses go from the internal organs which are engaged in an emotional or motivational response to the cortex. These "feedback" impulses result in a cortical representation of the internal organ responses. It is supposedly in the cortex that thinking and awareness occur; through the associations established there between the afferent neurons that report the behaviors of internal organs and the neural representations of learning, the person "knows" or becomes aware of his motive or emotional state. Thus one knows he is hungry when he feels his stomach contract. Hence, according to the James-Lange theory, motivated behavior occurs *before* the cortex is implicated. The patterns of eating responses, for example, are thought to be integrated at the hypothalamic level. It has been shown in surgically decorticated lower animals that eating behavior still occurs. The cortex was not necessary for this motivated behavior to take place. It has already been indicated that the cortex is not necessary for rage emotions to occur in dogs. However, the motivated and emotional behaviors displayed by the decorticate animals are stereotyped and unvarying, and frequently are ineffective in that they are not directed toward the appropriate objects in the environment. The enraged decorticate dog may completely misdirect his attack so that he lashes out at an irrelevant object rather than the experimenter who is "annoying" him. It seems apparent, then, that something occurs in the cortex to inhibit and direct motivated (emotional) responses, and thus produce greater flexibility in behavior. In terms of the James-Lange theory, it is likely that the feedback impulses from the body organs stimulate cortical association neurons which integrate these impulses with those coming from other sense modalities "reporting" the nature of the environment and their associated efferent patterns, so that the efferent discharge to the body muscles producing overt behavior is a modified product of the integration of the association fibers. These interactive associations are thought to be a product of learning.

Thus the James-Lange theory suggests that impulses to the hypothalamus set off internal organ reactions and also some fairly "primitive" or simple response patterns, and that feedback to the cortex from the internal organs and the simple response patterns become integrated in the cortex with other neural events producing efferent discharge to muscles which modify and alter and elaborate on and/or perhaps even inhibit the simple response patterns. It is not known whether, in terms of this theory, the hypothalamus itself directly integrates the primitive, simple pattern, or whether this is cued off or stimulated by feedback from the internal organs to other lower brain centers. And it is also not known whether the cortex modifies the simple pattern by sending efferent impulses directly to the body muscles, or by impulses that inhibit the hypothalamic area itself from sending its impulses to the internal organs, or both.

Although the James-Lange theory seems reasonable, some studies indicate that people can report feelings even when they have no sensory impulses coming from their internal organs. And in some neurological disease states, patients' facial expressions of their feelings are completely at variance with their internal physiological states. An experiment by Bard was crucial in showing that the expression of feelings was not dependent on the arousal of internal organ states. He sympathectomized cats — severed the sympathetic system from the spinal cord so that there could be no internal arousal, and thus no cortical representation of an arousal state—and found that, when presented with noxious stimuli, the cats nevertheless growled, spat, and engaged in behavior that did not appear to differ at all from the behavior of normal cats in the same situations. In other words, Bard's cats responded with fear and anger even though they could not possibly "feel" internal fear responses. Thus Cannon and Bard concluded that the James-Lange theory had been disproven, and they offered an alternative.[52, 53] The Cannon-Bard theory suggested that impulses from the sense organs produced by some threatening or noxious stimulus (or from need-sensitive centers) entered the hypothalamus, which then sent impulses to the cortex. The cortex in turn integrated these impulses with others through association fibers connected to the neurons coming from the hypothalamus (either innately or as a result of learning) and to efferent neurons going to the internal organs and body muscles. Thus an efferent discharge from the cortex is sent to the internal organs and the body muscles which produce action, resulting in an emotional (in this case, fear) state in the body. The main difference between the James-Lange and the Cannon-Bard theories is that in the former, emotional states are produced directly by the hypothalamus and these in turn affect the cortex, while in the latter the cortex directly produces the emotional state in the body organs.

As is often the case with opposing theories, each with its own mass of research data to support its position, the truth probably lies somewhere in between. It has been demonstrated that decorticate animals can give rage responses. Thus a cortex is not necessary for the basic emotional and motivational response pattern to occur. It has also been demonstrated that people without stomachs continue to eat and that drinking does not depend on a dry mouth. In a sense then, internal organ responses are not necessary for motivated behavior to occur, and Bard's study with sympathectomized cats showed that they are not necessary for emotions. These data suggest that the hypothalamus is the focus for emotional and motivated behavior,[54, 55] and may be all that is strictly necessary for simple response patterns to occur. It may be that the hypothalamus simultaneously sends impulses to the cortex and to the effector muscles. The impulses arriving at the cortex result in awareness of the motivational or emotional situation, and by stimulating association neurons with connections (innate or learned) to efferent neurons, may also produce modifications in the motivated behavior pattern. The impulses going to the internal organs and the body muscles result in the primitive, simple response patterns and in the involvement of the internal organs. Feedback from these organs to the cortex may there produce the feelings of emotion. The peculiar "drive" or "force" of motivational (emotional) states may depend on this feedback in which the cortex's cold "knowledge" of the situation is supplemented by impulses from the internal organs which "report" the physiological uproar in the body organs and which provide the "feeling" as opposed to pure knowledge of the motivation (emotional) state. In short, stimulation of the hypothalamus may directly integrate primitive bodily motivational (emotional) responses, efferent discharge to the muscles may produce the "passion" usually associated with motives and emotions, and discharge to the cortex may produce awareness and control over the "passion" and the overt responses. At any rate, the precise relationships among the cortex, the hypothalamus, and the body organs are still a matter for debate and further research, so far as their involvement in motivation and emotion is concerned.

Individual Differences in Autonomic Arousal. The extent or intensity of sympathetic arousal can be measured in a number of ways. It is known that sympathetic arousal increases breathing rate, so that the pneumograph, an apparatus strapped around the chest which measures breathing rate, may be used as a measure of arousal. Because the sympathetic system activates the adrenal gland to pour adrenalin into the blood, which produces muscular tension, measures of the electrical activities in the skeletal muscles may also be used.

By far the most popular measure of sympathetic arousal is the galvanic skin response (GSR). The sympathetic system, it will be recalled, sends neural impulses to the sweat glands of the skin which respond by releasing sweat through the body pores. This fact is responsible for the clammy hands which one feels when his sympathetic system is involved in a strong emotional state. Parasympathetic activity dilates the small blood vessels in the skin. Thus, autonomic activity affects the skin in two ways. The autonomic outflow of impulses, through both the sympathetic and parasympathetic divisions, also produces a decrease in the resistance of the skin to the passage of electrical currents by making the skin membranes more permeable. If one places electrodes on the skin at two different points, one can measure the resistance of the skin to the passage of electrical current. Changes in resistance are called GSRs.

All of these measures—heart rate, muscle tension, breathing, GSR— tend to give about the same results, but some evidence suggests that the physiological makeups of people differ such that whereas one person's autonomic arousal most markedly affects his breathing, in another it most markedly affects his GSR.

Studies using these measures of autonomic arousal suggest that there are consistent individual differences in the extent to which their autonomic nervous systems respond to standard, mild, noxious stimulation. It is found that some people react more intensely and have stronger autonomic responses to a particular stimulus, than do others. Further, there are also differences among people in how long it takes for the autonomic arousal to die down to normal after a noxious stimulus has been withdrawn.[56] You can readily see how these individual differences in autonomic reactivity imply differences in the strengths of motives. These studies suggest that a good part of the individual differences in intensity and duration of arousal are innate and genetically determined. Thus infants differ among themselves in how violently they react to need states. This characteristic has tremendous significance for their behavior, and particularly for the kinds of things these infants will learn in order to satisfy their motives. Thus one infant may be relatively placid and unexcitable, while another will become easily and strongly aroused by relatively minor need states. Obviously parents also differ in their responses to infants. If a highly anxious, insecure parent happens to have an easily aroused baby, it is quite likely that the interaction will lead to learnings and experiences in the infant which might not occur if either the parents' responses or the infant's arousal tendencies had been different.[57] Although these factors will be explored in greater detail in ensuing chapters, it is apparent that genetically determined individual differences in birth equipment (autonomic arousal in particular) may have a profound influence on the later learnings, and thus the personality of the infant.

REPRISE. Thus our catalog of the equipment and potentialities of the human infant as they relate to the emergence and development of behavior is complete. We have on our hands a newborn baby with a complete set of needs, the physiological equipment through which these needs operate, a nervous system which makes behavior possible, internal motivational states produced by need, and a stamp of uniqueness in all these. There is also the potentiality for maturation, for the acquisition of new behaviors, and for the development of thought and other symbolic processes. The baby is ready to begin its social existence, to interact with its environment, and to learn, so that it may progress from its biological animal status to that of a socialized and civilized human adult. How this progress occurs, and in particular, the role and operation of learning in the transformation, are the subjects of the next chapters.

These are the significant points of this chapter:

1. Infants are born as biological structures, with no mental contents, but with reflexive response systems.

2. The importance of birth is that for the first time in the individual's life, conditions deviating from optimal occur, constituting states of need.

3. A drive consists of various internal organ reactions to neural impulses initiated by receptors which are sensitive to need states (deviations from the organism's optimal state); these reactions are integrated in the hypothalamus and are transmitted by the autonomic nervous system.

4. Drive or motivation states vary in their discriminability.

5. The cortex can both inhibit and facilitate motivational behavior, but motivational states can occur without the cortex.

6. Such cortical control is not present at birth, but the structures making it possible mature in cephalo-caudal and proximo-distal sequences.

7. Emotions are based on the visceral components of drive states.

8. There are individual differences in extent of response to need, in ease of autonomic arousal and duration, and in the pattern of reactivity of the visceral organs.

3. Learning: How Behavior Is Acquired

The infant enters the world with builtin response systems—reflexes—which allow for some limited kinds of behavior, such as sucking, breathing, and kicking. But this is a very small repertoire of behavior. The infant will have to acquire a great deal more if he is to show the great variety of behavior characteristic of humans. He has all that is needed for the acquisition of new behaviors and a need to behave, that is, motives are present. The infant is ready to *learn*.

In the last chapter we saw how motives arise in states of need, and how the hypothalamic area, the internal organs, and the cortex participate in the expression of motivated behavior. It is the task of this chapter to discover *what* behaviors become expressed and how they are selected or acquired. Thus we will study the factors that influence the acquisition and performance of responses, or in other words, the laws of learning.

One caution: we often think the word "learning" refers to a school activity involving the memorization of material and the acquisition of school-subject skills. School life may appear to be, after all, a fairly insignificant portion of our total living experiences, and many students wonder why psychologists spend so much time on such a seemingly limited subject. The answer to this is that learning refers to more than absorbing course material. Psychologists use the term to refer to any modification in a living organism's behavior as a result of experience, whether or not the organism is even aware that he is learning. Our interest in the changes from the infant's limited behavioral repertoire to the adult's vast behavioral stockpile is an interest in learning and how it occurs, whether or not someone specifically designated as "teacher" is present, and whether or not the behaving organism, be it the single-celled paramecium or the multicelled human, considers itself to be a student.

In examining learning, we will look at the main variables involved: the role of *motivation, responses* and their nature, the effects of *reward,* and the functions of *stimuli* in learning. Then we shall present some special learning phenomena—*stimulus generalization* and *discrimination learning,* and the *extinction* of learned responses. Finally, after reviewing the effects of learning experiences, we will take another look at events in the brain in order to see what happens there that makes learning operate the way it does.

Motivation

Motivation makes learning possible. If the organism had no motive-arousing needs, there would be no "urge to behave." There would be no reason to act. As a result of birth, needs no longer are satisfied automatically, so that motives develop. Human structure is such that at no time after birth are all motives likely to be satisfied. If you rest in order to satisfy a fatigue or sleep need, then a need for activity builds up. While one is eating, the need for water increases. The temporal nature of behavior is such that at no instant are all needs likely to be fully satiated. Thus people are almost constantly motivated to behave, to act upon their environments in order to satisfy their needs, and so to learn.

Selective Effects of Motives. Motivation does more than simply create the conditions in which behavior is likely to occur, thus making it possible for responses to be learned. Motivation also operates selectively. When a particular motive is present, the range of behaviors which might be learned becomes limited. For example, it is quite unlikely that an animal suffering mild food deprivation will learn to sleep. First of all, a hungry animal is active, and so is unlikely even to try sleeping as a way of "feeling better" or reducing his motive. And if a behavior does not occur, it cannot be learned. Secondly, since sleeping would not end the animal's food deprivation, it would not reduce the motive, or satisfy it. So the animal would keep right on behaving, usually until by hit or miss he emitted the kind of behavior that reduces the need.

Thus motivation serves two functions: it accounts for why behavior occurs at all, and it sustains behavior until the motive is satisfied.

How Motives Affect Learning. The necessity of motivation (or "drive") for learning to occur is open to question. Some theorists regard it as essential. In Hull's theory, the first requirement that must be fulfilled if a response is to be learned is that the response must occur. That is, the organism must "try out" a response before it can learn to make that response habitually. One does not learn to swim without practicing with arms and legs. And a response will not be "tried out" unless motivation, or a drive to behave, is present.

The Energy for Behavior Comes from Motives. Behavior involves the expenditures of energy, the conversion of stored food resources in the body into forms of energy dissipated in action. In order for kinetic energy (the energy consumed in action) to be created, there must be a conversion of potential energy (food resources, fuel). It is largely the autonomic nervous system under the command of the hypothalamus that carries the impulses to the organs and systems of the body that produce this conversion of energy into action.[1] And as we have seen, the hypothalamus does this when stimulated by a need state. Thus there must be motivation, involving the creation of kinetic energy, for behavior to occur at all. An unmotivated animal, (one that is not converting fuel into energy forms) cannot behave; he cannot produce kinetic energy. In this sense, motivation is the energizing function of the body. An illustration of this function is found in a study by Bertram Cohen, who measured the amount of ATP produced in his subjects.[2] ATP is a biochemical substance involved in metabolism; it enables body cells to burn food and thus convert stored energy into movement. Cohen found that the more ATP released in a subject, the more work the subject was able to accomplish in a simple task assigned to him.

Motives Are Necessary for Performance of Learned Responses. The second point at which motivation enters Hull's theory is in the principle that only those responses that lead to a reduction in the animal's drive will be learned. Other theorists, and Hull's later formulation, make a distinction between learning and performance. They suggest that learning occurs merely by the close association of two events — a stimulus and a response — which establishes some kind of connection between the two events such that the stimulus tends to evoke the response. In this way a learned potential to respond in a particular way to a stimulus is built up. However, the conversion of this potentiality into actuality — performance of a learned response — occurs only when motivation or drive is present which can be reduced by the performance. The energy of motivation is necessary, if not for learning, then for overt performance.

In other words, although there may be an increase in the potential strength of a response as a result of experience, this response will not be given overt expression, and will not result in behavior, until there is some incentive to behave. And of course, an incentive implies an unsatisfied need, and thus a motive.

Most current theorists accept the principle that a response must be performed if it is to be learned. Without going into the details of the controversy over whether motivation affects learning directly, or only the performance of learned responses, we can conclude that some motivational state is necessary for overt behavior to occur, without which responses cannot be learned.

Motives Are Necessary for Drive Reduction to Occur. In addition to the necessity for motives if responses are to be practiced, most psychologists accept the idea that when motives are satisfied (when drive reduction occurs) there is a reduction in the tendency to behave, so that other responses which might have been made fail to occur. In this way, the reduction of drive results in only some responses being practiced, rather than all of which the organism might be capable. And finally, all theorists agree that when there is a drive present which may be reduced, and if incentive (something that will reduce the drive) is available, the acquisition of responses is at its most efficient.

Drive Reduction "Selects" the Correct Response. Practically speaking, then, the stimulation of sensitive neural centers by some physiological state of need produces afferent neural impulses to the autonomic and visceral muscle systems which produce behavior. This behavior will continue until, in some way or another, the motivational state of the organism is ended. In this way, the motivational state guides and sustains behavior. The behaviors that occur closest to the point at which the motivational state is ended (when an incentive or goal is achieved and drive reduction occurs) will tend to occur again the next time the same drive is present. That is, these responses have been learned. Thus motivation operates in a manner to select the responses that will be acquired. Those responses will be learned which so fit the nature of the environment that an incentive or goal is achieved and drive reduction occurs. Crying in response to a food need is very likely to result in the placing of a nipple and milk into the infant's mouth, so that a goal or incentive has been achieved; no further responses are necessary, do not occur, and are not learned. The crying response, having occurred most closely to the reduction of the hunger drive, will tend to occur again the next time stimulation from food deprivation occurs. The crying response thus is practiced and learned. The next time hunger is present, the infant will cry sooner and perhaps louder, indicating that this response has increased in its strength as a result of the infant's previous experience of the connection between crying and being fed. The reduction of hunger in response to crying thus operated to "select" crying as the "correct" response.

We are talking here only about physiological drives, often referred to as *primary drives,* because we wish to observe the learning process in its basic elements, which means in a completely naive organism that has not already learned so much that the pattern of learning is obscured. In such an organism, the only motives present are the primary drives. Social motives (*secondary drives*) are acquired or learned through experience. The acquisition of such drives will be discussed when we have outlined the basic mechanisms of the processes by means of which all learning occurs.

A Distinction Between Drive Reduction and Need Reduction. There is a very important distinction between need and drive, or motive. Many needs, or deprivational states, never result in motivation. There are no sense receptors sensitive to these deprivational states; thus there can be no arousal of the hypothalamic centers and no efferent impulses producing internal responses. For example, no receptors are sensitive to carbon monoxide; hence the presence of carbon monoxide cannot lead to a motive to avoid the gas.

Another reason for the distinction between need and drive, or motive, involves the concept of drive reduction. Humans have the very important capacity to reduce their motives without necessarily reducing their need states or changing the conditions that initiate the motive states. Although drive reduction through need satisfaction is probably the most efficient way of behaving, it is often difficult or impossible. For example, premarital sexual responses are punished in our society. Most adolescents are not permitted to reduce their sex needs directly. But they can reduce their sex drives by imagining themselves to be the hero of a love story in the movies, and they can resort to physical activity to reduce the physiological tensions which are part of the motive state. Substitute responses can reduce drive states and so be learned, without reducing needs. The importance of this fact for personality is incalculable; it helps account for the acquisition of the inappropriate behaviors usually labeled neurotic, and also for the development of so many of the cultural forms which are the great achievements of civilization. But the exploration of this vast topic is reserved for later.

Alternatives to Drive Reduction Theory. The account of the role of motivation in learning given here is basically hedonistic; it suggests that animals behave and learn primarily because of body needs. It is possible to develop a theory which includes altruistic behavior from this hedonic base. However, recently many psychologists have questioned this interpretation. They suggest that drives and motives need not be invoked to explain the "energizing" of behavior; it is sufficient to point out that it is in the nature of living systems to behave. Given this innate tendency to behave, it is the function of the brain simply to "know" the environment—that is, to make connections between stimuli and responses, whether or not drive is present, and whether or not a drive is reduced or the response rewarded.

William Estes of Indiana University explains the increased learning which occurs when an animal is under high drive, compared to when it is poorly motivated, by pointing out that the higher the drive, the more stimuli are produced by the drive for responses to be associated with.[3] In Estes' theory, responses are controlled by the number of stimuli or cues present, rather than by drive. He regards the assumption of hedonism as unnecessary. There is a whole family of new theories which interpret learning as the formation of associations in the nervous system; drive, and therefore reward, are considered unnecessary. These theories, in general, stress a view of man as a cognitive animal who functions in such a way as to "know" his environment. If you will recall the distinction made between learning and performance, with motivation and drive reduction playing its role in controlling performance, then these theories may be seen to be concerned primarily with the acquisition of learnings (cognitions), rather than response performance. These theories differ from drive reduction theories by suggesting that performance is based on the cognitive associations established in learning, rather than being controlled by motivation. This point of view focuses attention on the dynamics and nature of performance—upon the study of responses.

Response

A response is a reaction of a muscle or muscle group to chemical and neural stimulation. It may vary in its complexity from a slight muscle twitch so small in magnitude that it can only be detected by amplification of the tiny electrical potential of the muscle, to a smoothly coordinated interplay of most of the skeletal muscles, patterned so as to produce such overt and easily recognized behavior as going to a movie or painting a picture. Thus responses may be overt or covert.

The Response Hierarchy. It was said before that a response must occur, or be practiced, if it is to be learned. If this is the case, then how does the organism come to make the response for the first time? Is it completely new?

In a sense, no response is completely new. That is, responses involving the interaction of many different muscle groups, or even the simple response of reaching and grasping, involve muscles all of which have responded before to neural impulses, if only in the hungry infant's wild reflex activity. What is new is the *combination* of muscle reactions; the particular arrangement and sequence of responses may never have appeared before. But even in the naive organism, some muscle groups have had more practice than others, and some, because of immaturity of neural and cortical functioning, are incapable of being fitted into a coordinated response sequence. Thus there exists an innate response hierarchy, or order of response "preference," even in the most inexperienced animal.

The word "response" is confusing in its meaning; it refers not only to the behavior of individual muscle cells, but also to a total sequence of behavior having a fairly well defined beginning and end. Thus psychologists talk about a pecking response in chicks or a key-pressing response in humans. But logically it is impossible adequately to define these molar sequential responses. When does the key-pressing response begin? When the finger approaches the telegraph key? When the finger touches the key? When pressure is exerted on the key by the finger? Or when the key is pressed sufficiently so that an electrical circuit is closed? Similarly it would be difficult to define the end of a response. In order to avoid this logical dilemma, it would be convenient to define as a response all muscular actions occurring in an organism at a particular moment in time. Many of these muscle actions may be irrelevant to the organism's situation, but any or all of them can be learned (conditioned) so that they can occur again in the same or similar situations.

If we accept this meaning of the term, it is apparent that responses occur in an order. This order, which exists in the most naive organism, is the response hierarchy. It was suggested above that one factor that might determine the placement of responses in the order is the amount of practice various muscle groups have already had; those muscle actions that have occurred most often in the past would tend to occur high in the response hierarchy. It was also suggested that maturational state may influence position of a response in the response hierarchy. This area has been explored so incompletely that there is little information about other possible determining factors. Very likely the ease of a response, the degree to which it does not arouse or create further need states such as fatigue-produced pain, contributes to its place in the hierarchy. There may also be a compatibility factor. Under strong arousal, a response involving relaxation of muscle groups would be very difficult to make, and probably would be very low in the response hierarchy.

When an organism is motivated, it will "emit" responses in the order in which they exist in the response hierarchy. Theoretically, every possible human behavior lies somewhere in the response hierarchy of humans. The combinations of muscle group reactions, which are continually varied as the organism reels off various behaviors, may appear to be quite random, and this random responding could continue, theoretically, until all possible human behaviors—those already "invented" and those not yet known—are displayed. In practice, of course, this is impossible. Fatigue sets in, lowering the tendency to respond, and the fatigue may become so great that the motivated tendency to stop responding is stronger than the motivational state initiating the responses. Further, the nature of the drive the individual is under tends to eliminate the completely inappropriate responses, so that fairly early in the sequence of unreeling the response hierarchy an appropriate response, which would lead to drive reduction and to the cessation of responding, might occur. In this way, the completely unusual responses the individual *could* make tend not to be elicited because a more satisfactory response occurs first and brings the reeling off of responses to a halt. Thus most people do not write letters in rhyme, because prose is higher in their response hierarchies, and prose sufficiently satisfies their wish to communicate that they do not seek other ways of writing that might be lower in their hierarchies.

Invention and Innovation. If all possible human responses are available somewhere in the response hierarchy, then how is invention and innovation still possible for man? The answer may be that invention does not involve the production of totally new responses, but rather involves the ability to make new use of responses that have already occurred and whose value has escaped notice through lack of reinforcement. The inventor or innovator may be a person who is able to see potentialities for reinforcement of responses others have ignored.

Learning Is a Change in the Response Hierarchy. Learning, then, does not really refer to the acquisition of a new response (although the particular pattern of muscular activities may never have occurred before in the organism). Rather, learning is better conceived as the establishment of some functional connection between the neural events produced by a drive state and a response, such that there is an increase in the probability that under the same or similar drives, the response will occur again. The existence of the response at some point in the hierarchy means that its probability of occurrence is always greater than zero. Learning produces a shift in the position of the response in the hierarchy so that the response is given more readily, thus increasing the probability that the response will occur in behavior.

The Role of Instructions. Verbal instructions and "set" (the production of a readiness to respond in a particular way, such as in the preparation to be critical of another person produced by hearing unpleasant things about him) operate to limit the response hierarchy, so that irrelevant responses are not tried out, and the individual is limited to trying only those classes of responses which are pertinent to the situation. One tells a subject to answer questions by saying either "yes" or "no," so that other possible responses to the questions, answers in which the questioner is not interested, are not made. In this way the response hierarchy can be limited to as few as two alternatives.

Reinforcement

When a response occurs that results in a reduction in motive strength or intensity, there is an increase in the tendency to repeat the response on later occasions. The response is said to have been reinforced.

An event is reinforcing if it reduces the strength of a drive. This usually means that food will be a reinforcer for behavior initiated by a food need, but it is possible for responses other than finding food and eating to be reinforced when the organism is motivated by hunger; smoking a cigarette, for example, may reduce some of the motive "state of arousal" in an individual, without reducing his need for food. In this case, the responses of reaching for and lighting a cigarette will be reinforced, and this behavior will be increased in strength.

In our discussion of the role of motivation, we mentioned that several new theories of behavior stress the cognitive functions of organisms and do without the concepts of drive, or motive, as an energizer of behavior.[4] Naturally, such theories must also take a different view of reinforcement. If it is not necessary for drive to be present for learning to occur, then drive reduction is also not necessary. These theorists suggest that the important function served by reinforcers is not that they reduce drives, but rather that they serve as cues or stimuli, the apprehension of which tells the organism something more about his environment. The classic experiment on this subject is one in which an animal received food reward in one arm of a simple T-maze randomly only about 75 per cent of the time that he went to that arm of the maze.[5] If the importance of the food was that by reducing a hunger drive the animal acquired stronger learning to go to that arm of the maze, then it would be expected that when hungry he would run only to that side of the maze, since he seldom received food on the other side. But if the presence of the food served only as another stimulus element in the situation and the function of the animal is to know his environment, then it would be expected that even when hungry, his experience should tell him that he can find food in that arm of the maze only 75 per cent of the time. Therefore he would run to that side of the maze only 75 per cent of the time, instead of running there on every trial. This is in fact what happened in the experiment. This experiment provides evidence that the presence of a reinforcer serves primarily to provide information about the environment, and that animals behave in terms of the information (the cognitive associations) they have established. On the other hand, other research indicates that simply revealing to subjects the consequences of their responses is not sufficient, and that reinforcement is necessary for learning.[6] Another study has shown that where the amount of reinforcement is equal for two goals, the number of cues available at each (i.e., information) determined the animals' performances.[7] Thus there is conflicting evidence on the part played in learning by reinforcers. Further alternative explanations of these experiments, and of others like them, are possible.

However, for all practical purposes something happens when a drive is reduced which results in the strengthening of a functional connection between the drive and the responses which preceded the reinforcer. Pending further advances in theory and research, we will have to think of reinforcement as an event in which drive reduction strengthens learning. Whether other events, such as the presentation of information, also serve as reinforcers is still open to question.

Reinforcement Determines Which Responses Will Be Correct. In laboratory experiments on learning, the experimenter "selects" the response which he will reinforce. Having produced a drive in his experimental animals, he specifies beforehand that he will reduce the drive only when the organism behaves in a certain way, that is, makes the "correct" response. Initially the experimental animal behaves in a seemingly random fashion as he reels off responses from his response hierarchy until he "hits" the correct response and receives a reward in the form of whatever is needed to reduce his drive state. Thus the organism comes to effect some change in his relationship to his environment which reduces his motivational arousal, and on later occasions he tends more and more to make the "correct" response. The "correct" response may be quite arbitrary; such varied responses as scratching the ear, pressing a bar, striking an object, or saying plural words can be reinforced if the situation is established by the experimenter in such a way that these behaviors are followed by reward. One investigator was able, for example, to condition a smiling response in young infants. By picking up and soothing the infant whenever he smiled, the experimenter was able to produce an increase in the frequency of smiling, and a corresponding decrease in the frequency of crying, which was not rewarded.[8] Another was able to produce increases in such nervous habits as playing with a pencil, scratching an ear, or twisting a lock of hair, by saying "good" to subjects whenever they made these responses during the course of an interview with the subjects.[9]

Socio-cultural Factors in Reinforcement. But in real life, the responses which get reinforced do not vary quite so widely. An infant is much more likely to have crying reinforced than smiling. His parents hear him crying, so that they can respond; a smiling infant in a crib in the nursery does not create the kind of energy that can stimulate the parents in the next room. The "correctness" of a response, whether or not it will receive a reward, is determined outside the laboratory not by the whim or intent of an experimenter, but by the nature of the environment, particularly the social environment. The cultural norms, the society's folkways and mores, expressed through the reactions of people to each other's behavior, determine which behaviors will be reinforced and which will not. It is in this manner that common elements in the personalities of people within a culture become established, and it is this factor which creates the differences in behavior among people from different cultures.

Universal Learning Experiences. There are some interactions among people which are almost invariant among cultures, particularly those interactions which have a biological basis. For example, all infants almost regardless of culture are likely to be rewarded by women for crying, because it is only women who can nurse and thus reduce the hunger drive. The emotional feeling of affection towards mother figures fairly common in most cultures can therefore be traced to common experiences in all cultures, despite the great differences among them in other respects. Similarly, the fact that women bear the children makes it highly probable in all cultures that domestic activities and those economic activities which can be performed close to home will receive much greater reinforcement when they occur in women than when they occur in men. The point to be made here is that the almost universal affection of young children for their mothers, and the almost universal domesticity of women should not be considered to be innate and instinctive simply because these responses are displayed in widely divergent cultures.[10] It should be kept in mind that some experiences which have biological bases occur wherever people are, regardless of the state of their civilization, although technological advance produces more and more freedom from the biological base in technological societies.

If one wishes to ask what kinds of behaviors, what kinds of personalities, are likely to be acquired by particular individuals, it is necessary to examine the cultures which surround them, so that one may know what kinds of behaviors are likely to be reinforced. Similarly, if one wishes to analyze some component of personality, it is necessary to understand the condition which produced it, including the factors in the culture which operated to reinforce that component.[11] We shall have to take a long look at our culture to understand the origins of such behaviors as competitiveness, achievement striving, sexual guilt, gregariousness, and other traits which are common among Americans.

The Gradient of Reinforcement. The effect of a reinforcer on behavior is not specific, but general. Reinforcement results in an increase in the probability that the reinforced response will occur again, and it also increases (to a lesser extent) the probability that the other responses preceding the reinforced one also will occur again. The effect of reward is strongest on the response which occurs closest to the reinforcement. It has a lesser effect on those that occurred earlier. The effect decreases with time, so that those responses which occurred a long time before the reinforcement show very little increase in strength as a result of the reinforcement. This is referred to as the *gradient of reinforcement.*[12] When a motivated animal is placed in a new situation and begins to unreel responses from its response hierarchy, and finally emits one which is followed almost immediately by reward, that response is strengthened the most. If all the responses were strengthened equally, then the animals would never learn the particular correct response. That is, the correct response would not move up in the animals' response hierarchies, and the animals would continue to give the wrong as well as the right ones. But the gradient of reinforcement makes it possible for a correct response to grow stronger than those responses which may initially have been higher in the response hierarchy, so that the correct response will be given sooner and sooner, as practice increases. Further, the fact that responses occurring before the correct one get some reinforcement, although less than the correct one, allows an organism to learn to give sequences of responses which may be necessary before the correct one can be given. A rat in a maze must learn to make the next-to-last turn correctly before he can make the last response correctly, and thus be rewarded. The fact that the next-to-last turn also receives some effect of the reinforcer when the rat enters the goal box and eats makes the learning of that turn possible without it being necessary specifically to reinforce that turn. Thus sequences of behavior producing progress toward a goal (a reinforcer) may be learned fairly efficiently, although the responses occurring latest (closest to the goal) tend to be learned first, and those occurring earlier in the sequence, because they are further from the goal, are learned more slowly.

The backward spread of reinforcement makes it possible for irrelevant responses to be eliminated. When the correct response gains dominance over other responses because it has received the most reinforcement, the other responses will tend to drop out. In this way unnecessary responses may be eliminated. If one of the responses that drop out is necessary for the final goal-achieving response to be made, no reinforcement will occur on that trial. There will be a reshuffling of the response hierarchy because of the nonreinforcement and the necessary response may appear again in the sequence; if it does, reinforcement will occur again. Over a number of trials, then, reinforcement will occur only when the necessary responses are all present, and will occur regardless of whether the unnecessary responses are present. Learned behaviors, after enough of this kind of practice, therefore become fairly efficient and economical of effort. An infant gradually learns to cry without also waving his arms and legs, and comes to the point where he can cry while lying quite still. The irrelevant responses of gross body activity are not reinforced as strongly and as often as the crying which, through learning, occurs more and more rapidly as a response to a drive. In general, then, reinforcement results in efficiency in behavior. For example, given several paths (or alternative responses) leading to the same reinforcement, an organism will tend to learn that path or that response which allows him to reach the reinforcing goal soonest. This is so because that is the path which gets the greatest effect of the reinforcer.

Another factor which favors efficiency of behavior is the ease of making a response. Given two possible responses to achieve the same goal, both requiring the same amount of time but one involving much less effort than the other, the organism will more readily learn the easier response. This is because the more effortful response produces more fatigue (punishment). The drive to avoid punishment will operate such that the *total* reinforcement obtained by the organism giving a very fatiguing response will be less than that obtained by the organism giving a less fatiguing response. Therefore the easier response gets more net reinforcement and is learned more readily. Thus various factors combine in producing the principle of economy of learned behavior.

As in the discussion of the role of motivation, this presentation of reinforcement refers primarily to the reduction of biological drives. Reinforcements can be learned, just as new motivations can be learned. The example, used earlier, of infants who were held and soothed in order to reinforce smiling responses, concerned a learned reinforcement. The holding and soothing reduces no primary drive, and is not therefore a primary reinforcer. In the section in which the acquisition of secondary drives is presented, secondary reinforcement will also be discussed: how nonprimary drive reducing situations and events come to be reinforcing.

The Management of Reinforcement. It is apparent that reinforcement is a powerful tool in the control of learning. When one examines a situation with reference to when reinforcement occurs, and what responses are reinforced, one often discovers quite unexpected things. For example, one discovers that as much as parents deplore crying in their infants, they usually act so as to reinforce the crying. As Dollard and Miller point out, reinforcement of crying also reinforces the infant's doing *something* in response to a drive.[13] Thus the parent who responds to crying is teaching the infant that by behaving, by doing something or taking action, discomfort and pain can be reduced. In other words, the infant is learning to react, rather than passively endure discomfort. To take another example, a nagging wife may fail to reinforce any response in her husband if every time she attempts to reward a new behavior by praising it, she inadvertently also punishes it by accusing her husband of not having made the "correct" response in the past. The control of learning by the management of reinforcers can be seen when a teacher makes an effort to end the class hour in an enjoyable rather than punishing activity, in order to avoid having the response of leaving class at the end of the hour reinforced by a reduction of discomfort. The students, then, do not learn "leaving class" responses so well that at the first sound of the bell, they bolt from their seats. Rather, they act more as if they do not care to make such a response, because they get little or no reinforcement for doing so.

Avoidance of Pain Is Also Reinforcing. The reduction of a drive does not necessarily occur only when the organism achieves some positive goal, such as food for the hungry and water for the thirsty. It is only necessary that a response result in the reduction of a drive, and for some drives this might more readily be accomplished by an avoidance response than by a specific goal-oriented response. For example, responses given under a pain drive can be reinforced by avoiding or getting away from a painful stimulus. This is an important consideration to keep in mind; it plays a key role in fear and anxiety drives, the motives which are frequently involved in the learning of avoidance responses.[14]

Stimuli and Cues

It was said that the reinforcement of a correct response increases the probability that the same response will occur again in the same or similar situations. The phrase "same or similar situations" requires closer examination. A situation is a physical event or phenomenon possessing energies to which sense organs in an organism are sensitive. A situation refers to all the stimuli impinging on an organism at a particular moment, including those coming from his internal organs and muscles, and those coming from outside in the form of light, heat, sound, and pressure. Ordinarily, the term "stimulus" is used to refer only to those physical energies to which the organism responds. That is, when studying a stimulus situation, one does not need to study the nature of all physical forces; this is the subject matter of physics and chemistry. The psychologist is interested in only those physical events with which the living organism can interact. The gravity of stars constitutes a physical energy which would not be considered a stimulus for organisms on the Earth. In other words, the psychologist is not interested in the total reality as it may exist, but rather only those parts of it which are included in the psychological "field" or environment; these are defined as those to which organisms respond. We label as stimuli only those energies which are capable of modifying the behavior of an organism.

Usually a small group out of the total physical energy field becomes particularly salient as an effective stimulus. One learns to step on the brake when a traffic light within the visual field turns red, regardless of variations in the rest of the energy or stimulus field. One stops whether the day is sunny or overcast, whether in a coupe or a truck, day and night. The red light is the *effective* stimulus, so far as this response is concerned.

We can now restate learning as the establishment of a functional connection between a response and an effective stimulus. The effective stimulus or stimuli include those coming from the individual's state of motivational arousal, and those coming from sources external to the organism.

The Role of Stimuli in Learning. Effective stimuli act as cues for the organism instructing him as to when, where, and how to respond. A response becomes conditioned or attached to the effective stimulus and so comes to be elicited only when the effective stimulus is present. One does not make eating responses whenever a hunger drive is present; eating responses are associated not only with the stimulation of food deprivation, but also with the sight and smell of food. Thus the cues arising from food elicit the eating response, or determine in conjunction with drive, when and where the response is to be made.

Discriminability of Stimuli. Motives or drives vary in their cue value. The physiological responses to needs vary in the extent to which they produce internal cues or stimuli. The physiological reactions to sexual deprivations are diffuse. The neurons which are stimulated by the internal activities involved in this drive are involved in so many other responses that the cues arising from sexual motivation are indiscriminable from the cues produced by many other physiological situations. This means that it is difficult to attach a unique response to sexual motivation, or to learn a response which will be particularly effective in reducing sexual needs. It is no wonder then that many people, feeling diffusely upset, fail to realize that they are suffering from a strong sexual drive. Without discriminating or distinctive cues, they cannot make the appropriate, sexual response. It is in this sense that cues "instruct" the organism how to respond.

There is another very important example of this. Fear drives involve the activation of the same internal organ systems as do many other need states. In general, most of the internal organs produce relatively few and quite poorly defined cues when they react. Thus discriminations between fear and other internal states such as stomach upset or diseased heart functioning are difficult to make. Many people who are really frightened believe that instead they have upset stomaches or "bad" hearts. This relative indiscriminability of cues therefore plays a major role in the development of some neuroses, and is also a factor in making treatment of such neurotic behaviors very difficult. It is not easy to get a hypochondriac to accept psychotherapy that would help him make the discrimination between fear and illness, when he thinks that all his difficulties are organic and should be treated by a specialist in internal medicine.

Some theorists suggest that in fact people do not learn to discriminate between their emotional-motivational states on the basis of cues coming from their internal organs. It is possible that the discriminations made are entirely on the basis of the person's awareness of the situation that produced the feelings. In terms of this theory, one knows he is hungry rather than frightened because he sees nothing in his environment which would produce fear and he knows that he has not eaten anything for several hours.

In some cases the mechanism by which a need produces internal drive responses has little to do with the cues produced by the drive state, and in others the mechanism has a great deal to do with cue production. Pain has very discriminable cues, particularly pain resulting from stimulation of the pain receptors in the skin. Pain cues are so distinctive that one can respond differently to pain in different body areas. That is, one can localize the pain. The neurons whose stimulation produces pain are the same ones that produce the cues allowing localization (or discriminating responses) to occur. But in hunger, cues produced by a spasmodically contracting stomach help the individual to recognize the nature of his drive quite readily, even though stomach contractions do not play a necessary role in producing hunger drive. Similarly, a dry mouth makes it easier to identify one's discomfort as thirst, even though one does not necessarily have to experience a dry mouth for a thirst drive to develop. In other words, the cues associated with pain arise from the same sense organs as those which arouse the motive, whereas in hunger and thirst the cues arise from organs which are not involved in producing the motives.

Cue-Producing Responses. Internal cues are not limited to those associated with motives. The responses of skeletal muscles when the individual is doing something produce kinesthetic stimuli, so that one can locate his body parts in space. These kinesthetic stimuli function as cues, in that responses may become attached to them. The response of moving the shift lever in a car becomes attached to a large number of stimuli, including those arising from the left leg as a result of having depressed the clutch with that leg. The depression of the clutch is a *cue-producing response* to which the response of shifting gears is attached through learning. Cue-producing responses contribute to learning of sequential coordinated behaviors. They also make possible the many self-reactions and self-evaluations which figure so largely in personality. The production of verbal responses is a particularly important example of cue-producing responses. One may start by making the verbal responses called a sentence. These responses produce cues to which other responses (actions or another sentence) may be made. Thus one may produce a chain of reasoning, or an imagined story, and actions may be stimulated by thoughts, with the conclusion (the action, or the end of the reasoning or imagined story) coming as the end of a chain of cue-producing responses.

Stimulus Generalization

The association between a stimulus situation and a response usually does not occur full blown after only one trial. It takes some amount of practice for a response to be well learned. There are conflicting theories about why this is so. Some theorists suggest that the *connection* between a stimulus and a response grows stronger with practice.[15] Others suggest that a response is learned in one trial only, but that on each trial a different part of the whole response pattern is learned.[16] Thus on one trial one small *part* of the organism's response is "fixed" (learned); on the next, another part is learned, and so on. In this theory, the role of practice is to provide an opportunity for all the components of the response to be learned and thus be repeatable. For example, in the former theories, practice results in an increase in the speed of responding by gradually adding new strength to the stimulus-response connection with each trial. In the latter theory practice results in increased speed of responding by gradually adding new but essential components to the total learned pattern with each trial. The existence of response thresholds, below which a neuron or a muscle does not fire and above which it fires to its maximum extent tends to support the latter position.

This issue is yet to be resolved. But even without a resolution one would conclude from either theory that practice does increase efficiency in emitting a response. By practice is meant reiterated presentations of the stimulus situation, (including drive components), and repetition of the response.

But there is an odd thing about repetitions of the stimulus-response-reinforcement sequence. It is in fact impossible ever to reproduce *exactly* the stimulus situation present at any particular moment. As a result of being reinforced (let us say the drive is hunger and the reinforcement is food) the animal has a somewhat smaller drive, be the reinforcement ever so little. Time passes between practice trials, and things change in time – the learning apparatus used in the experiment is not as strange on later trials as it is on earlier ones; the learning animal is a little more fatigued (and perhaps a little thirstier); the light may change as day wanes; the apparatus acquires the odor from the organism's body. Even if all of these factors are carefully controlled in a very "cleanly" run experiment, some variability enters the situation. On the first trial the animal may look at the stimulus situation primarily with his right eye. On the next trial his head may tilt just a little differently from the way it did on the first, and so the animal gets a slightly different view of things. The stimulation he receives from the various physical energies of light, sound, heat, and pressure is therefore necessarily and inevitably different from trial to trial. In a laboratory experiment these differences may be minimal but in natural, real learning situations, the differences from one trial to another may be much greater. The first time an infant responds to hunger and the other stimuli present by crying, it may be daytime and he might be lying on his stomach; the next time might be at night with the infant on his back. The first time his diapers may have been wet, the second time dry, and so forth. Obviously, the stimuli present when a response occurs tend to be at least somewhat different the next time it occurs. If this is so, then what does practice do to the stimulus-response association?

The first answer is that it broadens it. Repeated practice in which the stimuli vary results in connections among the response and a *range* of stimulus conditions. This seems to be what happens: on trial 1 the organism sooner or later gives a response which is rewarded. An associative connection between the stimulus situation present and the response is established, (or between part of the stimulus situation and one element of the response). On trial 2, although the stimulus situation is inevitably slightly different, the animal does not get reinforcement until it gives the same response as on trial 1. When this occurs, an association is established between the response and the stimuli present in trial 2. The same process occurs throughout the practice trials. Thus the animal learns an association between a response and a *family* of stimuli which vary within perhaps fairly narrow limits. In addition, however, the animal has learned to generalize. He has learned, in effect, that it is "correct" to give the same response to different although similar stimuli. The result is the development of a *gradient of stimulus generalization.* Stimulus generalization means that responses acquired in association with a set of stimulus conditions tend to be made to stimuli which vary from that set of conditions, and that the strength of the response decreases as the differences among the stimulus situations increase.

**Figure 6. Generalization of a Response
to a Tone Stimulus**

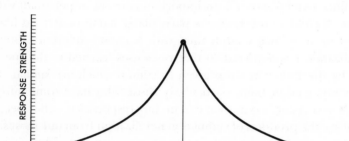

The tone to which the response was conditioned receives the strongest response; higher and lower tones also receive responses, but at reduced strength as shown by the gradient.

An illustration of this principle is seen in Figure 6 which describes what happened to a response that was originally learned to a tone of 1,000 cycles. This was the particular stimulus which, when presented, provided the cue for the organism to respond. Upon the presentation of other tones the subjects did respond, but not as quickly as to the 1,000-cycle tone. There is a falling off of response strength as the presented tones differ more and more from the original one.[17]

It is this stimulus generalization which makes it possible for an organism to respond in many different situations without having to learn specifically a correct response for each one. Earlier an example was used of the driver who learns to stop his car at red traffic lights, regardless of variations in many aspects of the stimulus conditions. The red traffic light was singled out as the particular effective or salient stimulus to which the driver responds. That example is a practical illustration of stimulus generalization. The event which is most common to all the various situations present on the driver's many practice trials is the red traffic light. His car may be different, his destination, the time of day, and so forth. But the traffic light is less variant from one situation to another and makes the various situations similar. Its presence places all the various stimulus situations in the different trials on the same continuum.

Stimulus generalization is an important concept in personality development. A child whose father is particularly harsh or strict is likely to respond to all or many adult men with fear and deference. Stimulus generalization has occurred so that responses learned to the cues produced by the father are also given to stimuli which are similar to the father—other adult men, particularly those who have some authority over the youngster. To a great extent, our responses to other people in general are the products of stimulus generalization from our most significant and early interpersonal situations—our parents. Thus it is that there is a connection between our attitudes toward our parents and our attitudes toward other people in general. In one study subjects who had more positive feelings toward their mothers rated photographs of women's faces higher than did subjects who did not feel as positively toward their mothers.[18] The fact that most children have experience with two parents makes it possible for them to develop more varied reactions to other people than would be the case where stimulus generalization proceeds from only one parent.

Responding to a stimulus at any point on the stimulus generalization continuum always presupposes the presence of motivation, without which there would be no responding at all. As motivation changes in intensity, there is a corresponding change in the tendency to make the response learned in relation to that motive. As hunger increases, there is an increased tendency to eat when food is presented. There are also corresponding changes in the strength of response at other points on the stimulus generalization gradient. As the strength of the response to the originally learned stimulus increases, so does the strength of the responses to variants of that stimulus. In effect, then, with an increase in drive, the height of the entire stimulus generalization gradient is increased. As the *shape* of the gradient remains the same, this means that more distant variants of the stimulus situation become included under the gradient. That is, the width of the gradient at the base line increases, thus including a greater range of stimulus conditions, when drive increases. For example, as hunger increases one is more strongly tempted to eat certain foods which, when drive is not so great are completely excluded from consideration.

Discrimination Learning

The other side of the stimulus generalization coin is discrimination learning. Obviously the driver mentioned in the earlier example learns to make a discrimination—make different responses—to red and green traffic lights, and to discriminate between red traffic lights and red neon signs. On the basis of stimulus generalization alone, one would expect that a stopping response learned to a red light would also tend to be elicited, though at reduced strength, by a light of a different shade, such as a green light. This in fact does happen, but discrimination learning also occurs to correct the situation.

In a laboratory experiment, the experimenter may arrange conditions such that a response of entering a dark grey door is correct (rewarded by giving food to a hungry animal). An animal so trained will also tend to enter a door painted a lighter shade of grey. If the experimenter wishes the animal to learn to discriminate between the two doors, he will arrange the situation so that when the animal makes the generalized response of going into the "wrong" door, he gets no food. In fact, if he is also given an electric shock when he makes such an error, producing a pain drive to avoid the wrong door, the animal will even more readily learn to avoid the incorrect door. In this way a discrimination between a dark and a light grey door is learned. A boy who is fearful of all authority figures as a result of stimulus generalization from a punishing father must learn to discriminate between other authority figures and father if his behavior is not to be inappropriately fearful. Often this discrimination is learned naturally. In the normal course of experience the boy may be rewarded for approaching some authority figure, thus producing an increase in the tendency to approach this person. The learned approach may become stronger than the fear and avoidance resulting from stimulus generalization from the father. The boy therefore learns a discrimination. If such a discrimination is not learned "accidentally," it may be necessary for the fearful boy to seek counseling, the function of which would be to aid him in learning the necessary discrimination.

Discrimination Learning and Conflict. The learning of a discrimination is pictured in Figure 7. The left-hand gradient represents the generalization of an approach response; the right-hand gradient represents

Figure 7. The Learning of a Discrimination

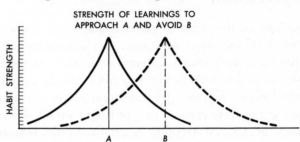

STRENGTH OF LEARNINGS TO
APPROACH A AND AVOID B

HABIT STRENGTH

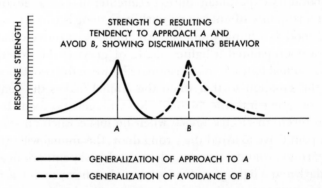

STRENGTH OF RESULTING
TENDENCY TO APPROACH A AND
AVOID B, SHOWING DISCRIMINATING BEHAVIOR

RESPONSE STRENGTH

———— GENERALIZATION OF APPROACH TO A
– – – – GENERALIZATION OF AVOIDANCE OF B

As a result of the learning of an avoidance response to
B, the generalized response to A becomes restricted to a
narrower range of stimuli.

the generalization of an avoidance response to a similar, yet different, stimulus. The nonoverlapping areas beneath the curves are the areas in which discriminations are made. There is an overlapping area where the stimuli are ambiguous in the sense that they are similar to both A and B, and thus tend to elicit both an approach and avoidance response. This is an area of conflict, or "ambivalence." The two curves interact so that one subtracts from the other. A large approach tendency together with a small avoidance tendency will produce a moderate approach. Where the two tendencies are exactly equal, the individual is faced with a difficult conflict to resolve. How he responds to such conflicts plays a major role in personality; the exploration of conflict will receive a great deal of attention in Chapter 9.

Some discriminations are difficult to learn, and some are just impossible. The red-green color blind person cannot learn a discrimination between a red and green signal lamp. The learning of discriminations is limited by the sensitivity of sense receptors to physical stimuli, and as the limits of such sensitivity are approached, discriminations become more and more difficult. This fact has been used in the experimental study of conflict; by requiring an animal to make successively finer and finer discriminations to the point where his sense organs can no longer respond differently to the stimuli, experimenters have produced conflict in animals. These conflicts are in some respects similar to those which produce neuroses and other abnormal behaviors in people. By producing conflicts in animals, experimenters hope to discover more about the nature and effects of conflict. The most famous experiment of this type was one done by Norman Maier of the University of Michigan who trained rats to jump across a gap to one of two doors in a goal box.[19] If the rats jumped to the wrong door, which was distinguished by being painted a different color, they bumped their noses against it and fell into a net. The rats therefore learned the discrimination. But then the experimenter modified the colors of the doors so that gradually the right and wrong doors became indistinguishable to the animals. The result was neurotic-like behavior; some rats showed very inappropriate stereotyped responses, such as always jumping to the left-hand door, even when the experimenter later removed the right-hand door so that the animals could see that there was food inside the right-hand compartment. Maier likened this behavior to the inappropriate stereotyped behavior of neurotic people, thus suggesting that human neuroses may be caused by the inability to make the proper discriminations.

Extinction

The opposite of acquiring a response is referred to as extinguishing it. A response is extinguished when it is no longer elicited by the stimuli which used to elicit it, even though drive is present. A hungry rat that has learned to press on a bar in order to get pellets of food will stop responding — pressing the bar — if food is no longer presented when the response is performed. When the rat completely ceases to press the bar, the response is said to have been extinguished. The trials in which the bar-pressing was not rewarded by food are called extinction trials.

We have already met extinction in the discussion of discrimination learning. In order for a response to be learned to a green traffic light which is different from the response learned to a red light, the generalization of the stopping response to a green light has to be extinguished. After it is extinguished, a different response such as stepping on the gas can be acquired.

This example suggests an important principle in producing extinction. It is most efficiently produced by teaching the animal an incompatible response. The more incompatible the new response is, the easier will the old response extinguish. A well known example of this is the experiment performed by John B. Watson on a little boy named Albert.[20] Watson taught Albert to make a fear response to a rabbit by suddenly clashing a pair of cymbals behind Albert's head whenever the rabbit was presented. The cymbal clash became associated with the cues of the rabbit. Albert very readily became frightened of the rabbit, and cried whenever it was presented. The next step in the experiment was to extinguish the fear response. This was done by bringing the rabbit into the room with Albert while Albert was eating dinner in his highchair. At first the rabbit was kept far from Albert, at the opposite side of the room. Eating responses are quite incompatible with fear since eating involves predominately parasympathetic activity, and fear involves largely sympathetic arousal. The rabbit, being kept far away, aroused only very mild fear which was too weak to compete with the eating response. Albert was hungry, and the hunger drive was much stronger than the fear drive when the rabbit was so far away. In this way Albert was prevented from making a fear response to the rabbit, and the rabbit became part of the stimulus situation to which eating and hunger drive-reduction was associated. Gradually the rabbit was moved closer and closer to Albert; the end result was the extinction of fearful responses and Albert was even able to eat while petting the rabbit.

Theories of Extinction. What happens when extinction occurs? The answer depends on one's theoretical position. Those who state that reinforcement plays a role only in the performance of a response, but not in the learning itself, assert that extinction trials decrease the probability that the response will occur again, but that the basic learning of the response has been unaffected. That is, as soon as a reinforcement is again present, the response should appear at high strength. This in fact does occur. According to this theory, then, once a response has been acquired, the organism can never be the same as it was before the response was acquired. The learning can never be completely undone. Perhaps this accounts for the great difficulty in producing successful psychotherapy, much of which is directed at extinguishing inappropriate responses. This may also account for the fact that sometimes people whose psychotherapy has appeared to be successful eventually slip back into their former neurotic behaviors; some reinforcement may accidentally have occurred, reinstating the "extinguished" responses at high strength.

On the other hand there are theorists who, arguing that reinforcement plays a direct role in the learning of responses, state that the lack of reinforcement during extinction trials actually results in a lessening of the strength of the learning. If an extinguished response should suddenly reappear later in life as a result of an accidental reinforcement, these theorists would say that extinction simply had not been complete enough.

There is a third theory of extinction which states that extinction is not really the opposite of learning but is in fact a learning situation in itself. During extinction trials an organism learns to not respond; the reinforcement for not responding is the avoidance of effort. In essence, the response of not responding—sitting still, lying down, etc.—becomes learned in relation to the stimuli which previously elicited a different kind of response. When the "not responding" response acquires more strength than the response which had been given in the situation previously, then it will be given more frequently, and so it will appear as if the earlier response had been extinguished. At first glance it may seem difficult to think of "not responding" as a learned response, but on closer analysis it is obvious that, for example, one may learn to stop a car when a light turns red, and to not start the car until the light turns green. This is a practical example of learning to "not respond."

The theoretical picture is therefore still cloudy. It is not yet known definitely whether the learning of an incompatible response really reduces the strength of the previously learned behavior or only replaces the previous response with a stronger one, leaving the original learning intact and still capable of expression in behavior.

Partial Reinforcement and Resistance to Extinction. Responses vary in their resistance to extinction, depending on the conditions under which they were learned. A response learned in a situation in which it is reinforced on only some of the trials will be more resistant to extinction than one which is reinforced 100 per cent of the time, although it will take more trials for the former response to become as habitual as the latter.[21] Under *partial reinforcement* it is really a complex response which is learned. Suppose that an animal is reinforced in a random fashion for making a bar-pressing response, but arranged so that three out of every five correct responses are rewarded. In this situation, the animal learns not only to press the bar once, but to press the bar several times in order to be rewarded. When extinction trials have begun, the animal has had practice at continuing to respond when no food is present, and so continues to do so. The partially reinforced animal cannot discriminate as readily between learning and extinction trials as can an animal that had received 100 per cent reinforcement, because in his past experience several nonreinforced responses have been followed by reward. The fact that no food follows a bar-pressing response during extinction trials does not make the extinction series any different from the learning trials for the partially reinforced animal. Therefore he continues to respond during extinction at a greater rate than does the 100 per cent reinforced animal.[22]

Effects of Partial Reinforcement. Partial reinforcement helps account for the difficulty encountered in extinguishing human responses which have been acquired in other than experimental laboratory conditions. In natural life, reinforcement usually does not occur every time the correct response is made. Therefore the responses people learn are often highly resistant to extinction. This is particularly true in infancy and childhood. When an adult performs a response correctly, he may still be reinforced even though no one sees him perform the response, because the adult has sufficient verbal skills to reinforce himself by telling himself that he has done well, and, at a later time, to tell others who will then reinforce him by giving approval. Thus an adult can be reinforced close to 100 per cent of the time. An infant or child does not have the verbal skills to reinforce himself or to tell others that he has performed "correctly," if the correct response was made when there were no observers to give immediate reinforcement. Therefore an infant or child is likely to perform correctly many times without being reinforced. Thus it is that responses acquired in infancy and childhood are likely to be much more resistant to extinction than responses acquired in adulthood, because they tend to be more partially reinforced than adult responses.

One might define "hope" as behaving as if a reinforcement will eventually occur. People seem to have more hope, the more irregular or partial their reinforcements have been in the past.

It is because of the effects of partial reinforcement that psychologists have stressed the undesirable effects of inconsistency in parental behavior to children. Parental rejection of a child, if it is consistent, will produce learnings in the child which can be more readily extinguished than the same learnings which might be produced by only intermittent rejection and punishment. In this sense, the consistently rejected child may show less resistance to modifying his behavior than the partially rejected one. In addition, inconsistency in parental behavior also leads to the development of conflict in the child, as will be discussed in Chapter 9.

The Effects of Learning

The learning of a response is reflected in a number of different ways, some of which provide useful measurements for the extent of learning.

The better a response is learned, or the stronger the response tendency, the more frequently the response will appear in behavior. *Number or per cent of correct responses* is a frequently used measure of learning. The converse of this is that the better learned a response, the fewer "errors" are made. In some situations, *number of errors* is a more convenient measure of learning.

The stronger the habit, the more enduring it is through extinction trials. *Resistance to extinction* is therefore another good measure of the strength of learning.

The better learned a response, the more quickly it will occur when the appropriate cues are presented. The student who has learned well a response does not hesitate when the appropriate question is asked, while the student whose learning has not been as strong may have to "search around" in his response hierarchy for the correct answer. The time interval between a cue and the beginning of the correct response is called the response *latency*. As learning progresses, latency is reduced. Response latency is therefore used as a measure of learning.

As a response is practiced, it becomes more and more efficient. Irrelevant responses are eliminated. This is true of the response as a global unit, such as pressing a bar, and it is also true of the individual response elements. Irrelevant muscle actions are eliminated, and latencies among the response elements are reduced. The overall effect is to produce a reduction in the time a global response takes to be performed, once it has begun. Thus *response time* is a measure of learning.

These various measurements assume that strength of motivation at the time of measurement is the same for all subjects, or for the same subject throughout all the measurements. Obviously, if motivation at the time of testing is extraordinarily high, even a poorly learned response may be quite resistant to extinction, and have short latency and response times. The better learned a response, the lower need be the motivation necessary to elicit it. It may require a good deal of hunger to train a dog to perform a particular trick for a food reward. But as training progresses, the response may be elicited under less and less food deprivation. Eventually the point may be reached when the dog will perform the trick (such as sitting up and begging for food) shortly after being fed, when he could hardly be considered to be very hungry. Thus lower and lower levels of drive are needed for a response to be elicited, as learning progresses. This is an important fact in personality. Behaviors learned under a pain drive, and reinforced by pain reduction, will be elicited by ever lower levels of pain as learning progresses. Eventually the pain-reducing response may be elicited by even the slightest discomfort. As long as the response continues to be reinforced, learning becomes stronger and stronger. The response is elicited so often, and is reinforced so often, that the response becomes characteristic of the person. A vicious cycle is set up in which the response occurs more and more frequently, and by virtue of being reinforced, increases still further the probability that it will occur again. The response may begin to seem inappropriate, because it is elicited by such low levels of drive that outside observers would not even suspect that any drive is present. Often such responses, having developed to such an extent, are called *overlearned.* Their tremendous resistance to extinction is apparent, partly because they have had so many reinforcements, and partly because so little drive reduction is necessary for them to be reinforced that it is difficult to arrange an extinction situation which would have no reinforcement for the response at all.

The same development occurs in relation to cues. As a response becomes better learned, the strength of cues necessary to elicit the response is reduced. At first it may be necessary to repeat loudly and firmly to the dog, "Sit and beg!" But as training progresses, it will not be so necessary to repeat the entire phrase. The same phrase, or even only part of it, given in a normal tone of voice, will be adequate to elicit the response. After a while, simply raising the arm slightly as if one had a morsel of food in it may be sufficient to elicit the response in the dog. A child learns not to touch certain objects around the house to the cues of a firm "No!" by his mother. As training progresses, the child will make withdrawal responses to merely a cross look on his mother's face, and perhaps even to only a warning glance in his direction.

Because the strength of cues necessary to elicit a response is reduced through learning, the response will tend to occur more frequently, thus contributing to overlearning.

The better learned a response, the greater will be the stimulus generalization of the response. More and more different stimuli will elicit the response. The child who has learned to respond with fear to his father also will tend to give the same response to other adult men. As learning progresses, the same response will be given to even more generalized stimuli—to slightly older boys, to older women, to mannikins, to projected images of people on a movie screen, to voices from a radio. Thus the same response will tend to be evoked more and more frequently as new stimuli become capable of eliciting it, further contributing to overlearning, unless discrimination learning keeps pace with this development.

Thus a well-learned response will be made to very low levels of drive, to quite subtle cues, and to more and different stimuli. The result is increased practice of the response, increased resistance to extinction, apparent inappropriateness in making the response, very short latencies, and very rapid responding. And of course, the further this is developed, the more potentialities are created for the still further development of the response. The response may come to the point where it is stereotyped, seems rigidly unvarying, and is so automatic that the responding individual does not even have to think about it before making the response. It occurs without planning or thought; it is unconscious. This is illustrated by the front seat passenger who gives a stepping-on-the-brake response when a dangerous situation develops. This response can become so overlearned that it is elicited by relatively minor cues, and it generalizes to a cue situation which does not even include the presence of a steering wheel in the responder's hands. The response is so automatic that the individual fails to think about it; if he did, he would realize how inappropriate it is to step on an imaginary brake, and he would try to inhibit the response. Even this inappropriate response tends to be reinforced. The driver usually avoids the possible accident, so that drive reduction occurs almost immediately after the brake-stepping response, and overlearning progresses. Further, by making the response without thinking or planning, the passenger feels that he has lost control over this bit of behavior, that it occurs unconsciously without his ability to inhibit it. Embarrassed, he may try to inhibit himself by making incompatible responses such as drawing his leg up under him and sitting on his foot. However, even then he may find his leg tensing the next time the cues are presented for a stepping-on-the-brake response.

The development of such a high level of skill in responding is a salutory thing in some situations. It allows a worker to perform skilled operations with maximum efficiency. It permits extremely rapid responses such as those which may be necessary to prevent injury or death when driving a car or flying a plane. By freeing the individual from the necessity for thinking about what he is doing, the routine worker can occupy his thought with imagination, with plans, and with ideas about himself and others, thus making his routine task more tolerable to him. It allows one to continue a conversation while looking for, extracting from the pack, and lighting a cigarette, the cigarette smoking routine having been learned to a high degree of skill. This, incidentally, may be why it is so difficult to give up smoking. The responses involved have become so automatic and are cued off by so many stimulus situations, that the tendency to make the response (what is experienced as wanting and desire) is ever present although one may not be aware of the desire *per se* until the response is interrupted or frustrated by the lack of the necessary materials.

But the capacity for the attainment of such high levels of skill and efficiency also creates the possibility of neurosis. Neurotic behaviors consist of just such overlearned responses, as the following example illustrates.

A two year old boy, Lester, was just beginning to develop adequate speech. He was the first child and his parents were quite anxious to bring him up right. They were insecure people, given to worrying a great deal over relatively minor events. Both parents were sure that they did not want their son to have as unpleasant a childhood as they felt theirs had been. They encouraged their son to talk and were very proud when he began using words but were also greatly worried that they may have "pushed" him too much. At about this time a sister was born. Although Lester's mother did all she could to avoid Lester's becoming jealous of his sister, he nevertheless received less attention from his parents than he used to. One day, when Lester was particularly excited at finding a picture of a monkey in a new book his parents had given him, he brought the book to his mother, pointed to the illustration, and tried to say "monkey." His excitement was so great that his as yet poorly learned speech responses were interrupted. In effect, Lester stuttered when he spoke the word. The interference with learned behaviors by nervousness and excitement is a normal phenomenon; it is most apparent in the mutism and stuttering of stage fright. Ordinarily the response is not permanently affected. When the excitement passes the individual is again able to produce responses correctly and without interference. But Lester's parents became so alarmed over his stuttering, feeling guilty that they might have been neglecting him too much for the baby sister, and still concerned that they might have pushed him too hard into speech, that they overreacted to his accidental stuttering. They immediately thought that it meant that Lester was going to be a stutterer. They became so upset at this thought that Lester's mother immediately took him into her arms, tried to calm him down from his excited state, and comforted him. Thus a stuttering response was reinforced.

Lester's parents began to pay very close attention to his speech. Whenever he produced the slightest blocking on a sound, (which happened often because Lester had so little experience in speaking), new alarm was raised in them, they gave him increased attention and so continued to reward stuttering. Lester therefore regained almost completely the attention that he had before the baby was born. His stuttering increased. His parents took him to their family physician, again making Lester the center of attention. At the physician's office, parents and doctor made great efforts to make Lester talk. Fright combined with the already established stuttering tendency produced increased stuttering. The reaction as before was an immediate show of affection and concern and thus further reinforcement.

Thereafter, each time Lester stuttered on a word his parents made renewed attempts to get him to repeat the word without blocking. Thus reinforcement continued. The pattern of learning was initiated which led to repeated stuttering, repeated reinforcement, lower levels of drive (loneliness, excitement, anxiety) necessary to elicit the response, more and more stimuli capable of eliciting it, and a reduction in the strength of the cues necessary to elicit the response. Lester became a confirmed stutterer and was quite unable to control it. At first he was quite unconcerned about it and did not think of stuttering as being wrong or unusual. But as he grew older, entered school and had contacts with other children and adults who mimicked his stuttering, made fun of it, and avoided him because it was so difficult to wait until Lester was able to speak a whole sentence (considering all the repeated syllables), he began to feel rejected by others, disliked, and inferior. The anxiety and worry thus produced naturally increased his stuttering, making matters worse. The vicious cycle of neurosis was established on the basis of more and more overlearning. As an adult, Lester was destined to be shy, afraid of others, rejected from social participation, unable to achieve satisfactory sexual relationships because of rejection and lack of practice, chronically worrying, less able to find satisfactory employment, and of course, chronically stuttering.

There are some important points to consider in this case. It was not the initial stuttering as a two year old that was the cause of it all. Rather, it was the parents' reinforcement occurring as a result of their own fears and worries which, repeated time and time again, created the problem. It was not the original experience of excitement over recognizing a monkey; it was what was learned as a result of this experience that produced the habitual stuttering. Further, the fact of stuttering, in interaction with other people — schoolmates, teachers — resulted in new problems to which Lester brought the response he had learned best, and the behavior which had worked most effectively in winning him his parents' attention and affection — stuttering. Finally, even though stuttering was "maladjustive," in that it began to create for Lester more problems than it solved, it was the best learned response he had acquired to the cues of worry, and so was the response he made most frequently even though he certainly did not want to stutter. The response had become automatic. (It should not be understood that this is representative of the origin and development of stuttering in all cases. The causes of stuttering are many and complex, and it is quite likely that they may vary from case to case.)

One last point about Lester's case: the dynamic factors which led into his neurotic developments were exactly the same as those responsible for the acquisition of all learned behaviors — motive, response, cues, and reinforcement. Since these factors operate in all people, and are capable of producing neurotic overlearning, then why are not all people neurotic? The answer is in the nature of the particular drives, the particular learned response, the nature of the environment which may or may not reinforce the response, and how adequate discrimination learning is. Lester's unsatisfied needs for affection and attention are particularly potent drives because they can be present at all times, and can almost always be reduced to a greater extent than they are at any particular moment. One may eat a hearty meal and eat so well that the hunger drive is completely reduced to zero. But it is always possible to have affection and attention from more people than are giving it and to have more and more convincing demonstrations of affection. Lester's drive was one which can be insatiable. The response of stuttering which Lester emitted quite naturally unfortunately was one which his cultural environment (his mother and father) was quite likely to reinforce. Other responses might not have received such immediate and powerful reinforcement and stuttering might not have been reinforced to such an extent by other parents, and so would not have been so overlearned. Lester's particular social environment was such that this particular response was likely to be encouraged. Finally, the larger society in which Lester moved when a schoolboy and an adult was such that stuttering produced reactions in people that led to the further frustration of Lester's drives.

If Lester had learned a discrimination so that stuttering would only occur to the cues produced by his parents, he might not have stuttered so often and in so many different situations, and his stuttering would not have had such a bad effect on his social relationships. But because he was so young and had no other cues presented to him until much later when he went to school, he did not learn a discrimination to counteract stimulus generalization. Had discrimination learning occurred, the frustration of other motives, such as his sexual drive, his need for academic achievement, for regard and status among people his own age, might not have occurred, there would have been reduced motive strength, and thus reduced stuttering.

The learnings which produce a neurosis, as you can see, are quite complex, and tend to produce the vicious circle seen in Lester's case, wherein increased drives produce increased neurotic behavior which results in still further increases in drive level and in the tendency to make the neurotic response.

This description of the acquisition of a neurotic personality does not do justice to the richness and complexity of a human life. The depths of Lester's feelings, his hopes and aspirations, the warmth of his humanity, are not included or commented upon. Our description is a bleak reflection of him. But it is not the function of this description to convey to the reader such impressions, or to give an intimate knowledge of Lester as a person. Perhaps these are functions best served by literature or poetry. The purpose here is to account for certain aspects of Lester's behavior. If the account seems far removed from a human life, it is probably no more so than the account of atomic activities is removed from our experience of what a chair is like. A scientific statement need not conjure up an image of the phenomenon described. It need only be predictive of behavior to be valid, and the more economical the statement is without sacrificing predictive accuracy, the better it is. This presentation is an oversimplification of Lester's personality in many respects, but many more concepts must be presented before more realistically complicated descriptions can be given.

Where Learning Takes Place

We have surveyed the main events involved in learning. But we have not yet indicated exactly the nature of the association between a response and the stimuli which elicit it. What is this association like? Where does it take place? What modifications in the physiological functioning of the organism take place, through which learning operates? The inquisitive mind cannot help asking these questions but at present there can be very little by way of an answer.

Some things are known. Learning can occur when the muscle whose response is being "conditioned" (associated with a new stimulus) is inoperative because of drugs during the learning trials. When the drugs wear off, it is found that the muscle responds upon presentation of the new stimulus. Learning has taken place in some spot other than the reacting muscle.[23, 24]

It is also known that a response can become associated with visual stimulation when the stimulus, instead of being an object presented before the eye, is an electrical stimulus applied to the visual cortex — the part of the brain which receives the neural impulses from the eyes.[25] Therefore it is not necessary to stimulate a sense organ directly for learning to occur.

Leaning therefore seems to occur in the body somewhere between the sense receptors and the effector muscles. Most of the research on the problem has centered around the brain, the cortex in particular. There have been many experiments involving the general pattern of teaching a response to an animal, removing part of the brain, and then testing for retention or ability to relearn the response. This is done in an effort to locate the brain areas which mediate the learned response. The results of these experiments are extremely ambiguous. The brain area involved in a response seems to depend both upon the kind of response and the nature of the stimulus to which the response is attached. Making complex visual discriminations, where the differential responses to stimulus 1 and stimulus 2 are fairly simple seems to require an intact visual cortex (an area at the back of the brain). But simple discriminations between levels of brightness of a stimulus can be made even when this brain area is completely destroyed. Apparently learning involving relatively simple cue-dimensions occurs or can occur at lower levels of the brain.

Cortical Localization. Which areas of the cortex are involved depends to some extent on the particular cues to be associated. Auditory stimuli excite one area, visual cues another, olfactory, kinesthetic, and other cues excite other areas. Thus learning a response to a cue cannot occur if the area or areas which receive the impulses produced by the cue are not functioning.

Similarly, learning cannot occur (or rather, it cannot yet be known if learning occurs) when the areas involved in making motor responses are destroyed. There are areas in the cortex which, when stimulated, produce muscular reactions in body parts. The body members are localized, so that each member has a section of the cortex for itself. If these motor areas are destroyed, spinal reflexes remain intact, but the body members do not respond to stimuli which excite the cortex. In those learning situations in which a muscular response becomes associated with some cortically mediated cue situation (such as complex visual cues, or a complex auditory cue involving pattern, pitch, and loudness variables, or a cue situation made up of the cortical representations of other motor responses coming from other parts of the body) no response of the body members can be made, and therefore it cannot be known whether an association (learning) has occurred.

There are thus motor and sensory localized areas in the cortex, but we have also seen that lower centers in the brain can mediate simple motor and sensory neural activities. The afferent and efferent neural pathways go through the lower areas before they reach the cortex, and have many opportunities to form synaptic connections with each other even before they reach the cortex. However, in the cortex the connections among the neurons are probably much more numerous than at lower levels. Perhaps this is why learning responses to complex afferent patterns, and learning involving complex efferent activities, seems to require the presence of intact cortical areas. This may also account for the greater range of complexity in the learnings of which humans are capable; they have much more developed and elaborated cortexes.

Mass Action. Despite such localization of sensory and motor functions (and perhaps because many such functions are also mediated at lower levels of the brain) the principle of *mass action* seems to hold in the case of complex learning involving trial-and-error problem solving, which probably constitutes the majority of the learning involved in personality. Mass action means that the ability to learn in such complex problems seems to depend, not upon any particular area of the cortex, but rather on the amount of the cortex present and functional, regardless of its location. The most famous study in this area, by Karl S. Lashley, indicates that the more complex a learning task, the more it can be interfered with by destruction of the cortex, and the more cortex destroyed, regardless of location, the more interference there is with the learning.[26] The principle of mass action suggests that there may be no such thing as a location or site for complex learning. Although this may be difficult to understand, the evidence has been confirmed over and over again that despite certain particular losses which may occur as a result of local cortical destruction, such as loss of attention to stimuli resulting from destruction of the prefrontal cortex, or loss of awareness of the visual cues resulting from destruction of the parietal cortex—despite such particular losses, ability to perform sucessfully in complex trial-and-error learning tasks shows no variability associated with the location of the damage, but only variability associated with the amount of tissue destroyed.

Some physiological psychologists have suggested possible explanations for this. It has been pointed out that there are usually alternative ways of performing successfully in a given problem-solving task. An animal may concentrate on kinesthetic cues in learning a path through a maze, or he may use visual cues primarily. He may make a correct turn in a maze because turning his head at the corner is associated with a particular pattern of light cues, or because auditory cues produced by echoes in the maze stimulate one ear before the other, become associated with cocking that ear and thus turning the head; or the animal literally might be following its nose as it places its nose closer and closer to olfactory cues. In the intact animal, very likely several such alternative ways of solving a problem are utilized simultaneously. That is, the correct response is associated with several or all of these various cues. It has been shown by Krechevsky that intact animals, in a situation in which only one method can be used at a time, tend to alternate methods on alternate trials.[27] This suggests that intact animals can use all the methods available to them. But animals which have lost some cortical tissue are more limited in the methods for reaching a goal which they have available to them. Some classes of cues can no longer stimulate them; perhaps some response patterns can no longer be integrated. In

Krechevsky's study, these cortically-impaired animals did not vary in their methods for reaching the goal from one trial to the next, when alternatives were possible. It then was found that the particular method the operated animals selected and stuck to depended on the location of the cortical damage. If three methods for solving a problem are possible, and the cortical centers mediating two such methods are destroyed, then the animal must make do with the one method yet remaining to him. Perhaps in very simple situations, if all three centers are destroyed, the animal may still learn if the situation is such that it can be solved by simple integrations and neural activities at levels below the cortex. This is more possible for lower animals than for man; in humans the cortex carries a much greater responsibility for behavior than in lower species. But as the problems increase in complexity, requiring the utilization of more than one sense modality and response pattern, the more such localized areas that are destroyed, the fewer methods the animal has available for solving the problem, and the poorer his performance will be. Therefore, in simple problems there may be relatively little interference in performance by widespread cortical destruction, as long as at least one method for solving the problem is available to the animal, and as long as the problem is simple enough to be solved by the use of only one method. But as the problem becomes more complicated, the animal must use more than one method, and perhaps the more methods it uses, the more efficient his performance. In such problems, the more cortex destroyed, (the more localized areas necessary for each method are eliminated), the greater the reduction in the animal's ability to solve the problem. It is suggested therefore that the reason for the correlation between amount of tissue destroyed and ability to solve problems, regardless of the location of the destruction, is that problem-solving allows for a number of alternative methods, and the greater the *number* of localized alternatives eliminated, the more difficult it is to solve the problem.

Some methods used in solving a problem may be more effective or efficient than others. Krechevsky found that rats using visual cues rather than position cues were "brighter" (learned the problem more readily) than those using other cues. This suggests that the nature of the problem Krechevsky used was one in which the visual was the more effective method. Other problems might more easily be solved by other methods. One can untie a knot by "feel" alone, or by reference to visual cues alone, but the use of visual cues is more efficient than the use of touch cues. Other problems might be such that other sense modalities might convey the most effective or discriminable cues. Sound and also touch are more useful at night, and touch is more effective than sound for getting around a furnished room without accident, although auditory cues also may help. Thus the specific areas damaged, and the specific functions lost play a part in the effectiveness with which different problems are solved, depending upon the abilities most effective for solving the particular problem, and the discriminability of the cues to which the animal may respond.

Intelligence. Intelligence may refer to the ability to utilize various alternative methods to solve problems. Experiments by Goldstein and his coworkers indicate that in brain injury, there is a correlation between the extent of the injury and the ability of subjects to group things into categories.[28] One test frequently used for detection of brain injury is the Vigotsky.[29] In this test the subject is presented with a number of blocks of various colors, sizes, thicknesses, and shapes. The blocks can be grouped together on the basis of similarities on any of those dimensions: color, size, thickness, or shape. In brain injury the ability to shift concepts—that is, the ability to group the blocks in various alternative ways is lost. This supports the idea that cortical injury reduces the number of possible methods available to an organism in solving a problem. People of below average intelligence have difficulty in shifting—in grouping the blocks in various different ways—further suggesting that intelligence may involve the ability to select or use various methods for solving problems, depending on the appropriateness of each available method to the problem.

One further point about the location of learning: no investigator has yet found any anatomical or functional changes in neurons or synapses mediating a learned response, as a function of the learning. If learning does change the characteristics of neural functioning, such as producing a lowering of the threshold of a neuron to stimulation from other particular neurons, such a change has not been detected, despite a great deal of intensive effort.

How Reinforcement Affects the Organism. In the most original and exciting series of experiments to be performed recently in psychology, James Olds of the University of Michigan has found evidence for the existence of a "reward system" in the brain.[30]

Olds was attempting to study the effect of electrical stimulation of lower brain centers in unanesthetized rats by permanently implanting small silver electrodes in their brains. By means of a stereotaxic instrument, it is possible to drill a tiny hole in the skull of an anesthetized rat and insert in the hole very fine electrodes with a fair degree of precision, so that the electrodes enter into the areas of the brain in which the experimenter is interested. The electrodes have a plastic base which is then screwed to the skull by means of tiny jewelers' screws to hold the electrodes firmly in place. Upon recovering from anesthesia, the rats do not seem to mind the electrodes at all, although the observer may be somewhat startled to see animals reminiscent of science fiction stories with what look like antennae coming out of their heads.

With the animals prepared this way, Olds allowed them to walk around in a large box, the corners of which he labeled A, B, C, D. Through wires attached to the electrodes, he administered small electric currents to the rats' brains. He found that if he did this when a rat was in corner B, the rat seemed to find that corner very interesting and acted as if he preferred it. Olds then tried to "transfer" the effect to corner A by administering the electric current whenever the rat made any moves in the direction of A. It was not long before the rat found himself in corner A and now seemed to prefer this corner. Thus by the administration of electric currents to the structures deep within the brain Olds was able to control the rat's movements.

In a modification of this procedure, Olds put his rats in boxes with a lever on one wall (Skinner boxes). The lever was hooked up to the wire through which current was administered to the rat's brain, so that if the rat pressed the lever he received the stimulation. In this setup, the rats learned to press the lever very readily and performed at very high levels, going up to 5,000 responses per hour. Olds found that the animals would rather receive electrical stimulation than eat, even when strong hunger drive was induced, and some animals would continue pressing the lever until they were exhausted!

Olds accounts for these remarkable results (which are obtained only in certain areas of the limbic system, which is closely related to hypothalamic structures and the reticular arousal system) by labeling this as a reward or reinforcement center of the brain. It is not known whether it is the direct effect of stimulation on this area which constitutes a reward, or whether stimulation of this area produces a reduction in the animal's motivational state through discharge over the parasympathetic system, counteracting the effects of sympathetically mediated drive and emotional states in the internal organs. The very rapid responding of Olds' animals makes this latter explanation seem reasonable. Animals not so implanted never respond at such high rates. This may be because each time a normal animal is rewarded by being given a pellet of food when he presses the bar in a Skinner box, there is some semi-permanent decrease of the hunger motive, at least until the food need has had time to redevelop. The animal therefore is not motivated to press the bar on a second trial as strongly as he was to press it on the first, and so the intervals between responses are longer. Also reinforcement by ingestion of food takes longer to occur than reinforcement by direct electrical stimulation because it takes longer for the food to result in a decrease of the firing of the food need sensitive receptors. Thus in the usual learning situation, reinforcement does not follow the response as directly and rapidly as it does in Olds' experiments, if one assumes that the electrical stimulation directly affects the motivational state. Therefore the bar-pressing response is not as well learned in traditional experiments and so is not made as rapidly. Finally, if the electrical stimulation temporarily reduces the motivational state, for the length of time in which the current is actually on, then this would explain why the animals respond again as soon as the current is turned off. As soon as the electrical "motivation reducing" stimulus is turned off, motivation returns to its full strength because the animal has done nothing to reduce his needs. The continual stimulation of the food need-sensitive receptors reestablishes the motivational state as soon as the electrical stimulation ceases.

Olds has elaborated his findings into a larger theory of drive and reinforcement. He points to some evidence which indicates that a moderate stimulation of the reward center produces an increase in the animal's activity such as one would observe in a hungry animal that has just smelled food. On the other hand, strong stimulation of the same center is said to produce a quieting of behavior, such as occurs when an animal has been reinforced and so ceases to emit further responses. Olds is here suggesting that what we have described as a cue to which responses are attached operates as a stimulus which produces a moderate arousal of the reward system.

The reward center discovered by Olds includes two important sub-systems, one of which seems to be sensitive to cues from the external environment, and the other (the hypothalamus) to internal drive states. Olds suggests that the former system may be activated by cortical events, such as thinking about an object associated with reward. If this system alone is activated, there is a moderate overall stimulation of the reward system which results in increased activity. In this way a cortical event of thinking about a stimulus (an anticipation of a goal) results in an increase in behavior (searching and seeking for the goal). But if both subsystems are activated, such as when the goal object stimulates the cortex at the same time as there is a reduction in a motivational state (as when the goal is achieved) the total excitation of both subsystems produces an overall high level of stimulation of the reward system. This high level of stimulation—the same as that which Olds found to be reinforcing in his brain-implanted rats—produces a cessation of behavior. The animal no longer searches and seeks but instead seems simply to "enjoy" the goal state. In effect then, anticipation arouses behavior and goal attainment (reinforcement) results in a decrease in activity; which occurs is determined by the level of arousal of the reward system deep in the brain.[31]

Olds' theory and research have excited a great deal of interest among psychologists. It has given us a lead as to how reinforcement may work, and also provides some interesting answers to how cues operate to elicit behavior. Certainly it is true that even a hungry animal may engage in relatively little activity in a Skinner box until the light goes on indicating to the animal that if he presses the bar, a pellet of food will be delivered. As soon as the light appears (the cue) there is an increase in activity until, as a result of the bar-pressing and the delivery of food, the animal is reinforced and thus quieted. Olds' theory suggests how the light cue is able to result in activation; a thought about the goal object, experienced as an anticipation, might serve as the very same kind of "arousing" cue.

This completes our review of the main facts of learning. Because the study of learning is of the greatest importance for understanding the behavior of living organisms, it is the most active field for research and speculation, and is in a continual state of ferment. We barely have suggested some of the problems being investigated and the nature of some of the solutions for which investigators are searching. But whatever may be the final answers, it seems likely that they will deal with the major concepts we have here discussed: control of responses by drives or motives, control by cues, and control by reinforcers.[32]

REPRISE. In this chapter we have seen that the infant acquires behavior as a result of the interaction among motivation, cues and the response systems already present. This characterizes the learning process in which responses become associated with drive and environmental cues through the operation of reinforcement, so that there is an increase in the probability that the same response will occur under similar conditions in the future. The roles of motivation in stimulating behavior and of reinforcement in reducing drive, providing information about the environment, or ending the sequence of responding, was discussed in terms of current theories. Some of the main issues of learning concerned with whether motivation and drive reduction are necessary for learning or for performance of responses were presented. Similar issues with respect to extinction, and whether it affects learned associations, or only performance were offered.

Practice as an essential condition for learning was discussed in terms of its role in producing stimulus generalization and discrimination learning. Two alternative explanations of the effects of practice were described.

Finally, the operation of learning in the development of a limited portion of one person's personality was described through the case of Lester, in which it was stressed that the responses which comprise personality are frequently overlearned as a result of continued practice arising from the individual's unique life situation and experiences.

The main points of this chapter are:

1. When motives arise, trial and error responding ensues, out of the organism's response hierarchy.

2. When a reinforcer occurs, a functional connection between the response occurring close to the reinforcement and the stimuli present, including those coming from the drive state, is established.

3. Repeated reinforced practice results in increased efficiency in giving the "correct" response.

4. Practice also results in the development of stimulus generalization.

5. The backward spread of reinforcement (goal gradient) operates to eliminate nonessential responses, and to permit the learning of response sequences leading to a goal.

6. Cues operate to "trigger" a response when motivation is present. When cues are ambiguous or indistinct, as in some drive states, it is difficult to associate responses to them reliably.

7. Responses produce cues to which other responses may be associated, contributing to sequences of responses.

8. Thoughts, such as anticipations, may serve as cues for the performance of a response.

9. Drives may be reduced at least temporarily without ending the conditions which arouse the drive, such as states of deprivation.

10. Increases in drive produce increases in the height of the stimulus generalization gradient but its shape remains the same, so that increase in drive results in the inclusion under the gradient of cues which were outside its area when drive was low.

11. Discrimination learning counteracts the effects of stimulus generalization.

12. Extinction through nonreinforcement may be conceived of as a weakening of the learned association, as learning to not respond, or as affecting only performance and not the learned association.

13. Extinction is most economically produced by reinforcing a response incompatible with the to-be-extinguished response.

14. Learned responses become efficient and economical in terms of time and effort, resistant to extinction, and elicitable by decreasingly strong cues and drive, going in the direction of becoming automatic and "overlearned" in a spiralling way.

15. Resistance to extinction is also influenced by the schedule of reinforcement during learning.

16. Some responses are more likely to be reinforced and learned than others, depending on the nature of the biological, physical, and social environment. As a result, some behaviors are relatively similar across culture, across sexes, and within cultures. Examination of the reinforcing tendencies of a particular social environment increases understanding of what behaviors are likely to be learned in that environment.

17. Personality characteristics are the result of extended practice resulting from particular situations and experiences, rather than from a single upsetting or "traumatic" event.

4. Motives and How They Are Acquired

Man becomes more than the eating, sleeping, defecating, and reproducing animal he is at birth. The newborn infant behaves exclusively on a biological level and is motivated exclusively by organic needs; the human adult is a socially oriented creature who might refuse food when hungry in order to be polite, suffer pain in order to achieve honor, and renounce sex to serve an ideal. In the course of development from infancy to adulthood, the human somehow acquires new motives which often are stronger than the biological drives with which he is born.

It is in the development of learned motives—for example, desires for status, prestige, money, appreciation, achievement, or honor and motives of covetousness, hatred, and of course, love—and in the appreciation of the social rewards that satisfy these motives, that man becomes so different from other animals. The development of civilizations and the elaboration of cultural forms in community living require man's greater capacity for developing social motives and striving for social rewards.

Inhibition and Facilitation

In Chapter 2 we explored some of the ways in which the nervous system, particularly the cortex, may inhibit the behavior mediated by lower centers. This capacity for *inhibition* is one of the reasons for the flexibility in man's behavior, compared with the stereotyped behavior patterns of lower animals. However, inhibition is only one agent of this

flexibility. Social motives and the laws of their acquisition and operation are such that *facilitation* of behavior also can occur. Man can develop new drives and display old ones without waiting to be goaded into
action by a state of need, as well as inhibit the expression of his drives.
Flexibility involves a freedom from absolute control over behavior by
biological needs; man can refrain from behaving when needs are present (inhibition), and he can engage in behavior even when needs appear
to be satisfied (facilitation). The study of acquired drives, or learned
motives, is the study of how facilitation is accomplished.

Requirements for a Theory of Acquired Motivation. We have not
studied the acquisition of motives as intensively as we have the acquisition of responses and the operation of motives once they have been
acquired. The analysis and study of motives is a late-comer to experimental psychology. The word "motive" is used in different ways, and
means different things to different researchers whose data, therefore,
are not always comparable. Hence, it will be necessary to deal with the
problem by examining different conceptualizations and theories.

The reader should keep in mind the functions served by motives, and
which therefore, a theory of motivation must encompass:

1. Expenditure of energy in behavior.
2. Elicitation, or "releasing" of behavior by cues in particular situations (searching, seeking, maze-running, bar-pressing), when the
   conditions creating energy expenditure are presumed to have
   existed over some period of time before the behavior is elicited.
3. Cessation or reduction in behavior following goal-attainment,
   together with the increased probability that the behavior will occur
   again as a result of the goal-attainment.

We have seen how biological drives operate to meet these requirements. Below, the same requirements are restated with particular reference to social or acquired drives. A theory of acquired drives must
account for the:

1. Expenditure of energy in behavior when presumably the need-
   sensitive receptors are not being fired by states of need.
2. Ability of certain stimulus situations (such as a "loving cup" as an
   award of merit) to elicit motivated behavior and striving.
3. Capacity of certain stimuli (such as the possession of the "loving
   cup") to produce a cessation, or reduction in such striving, when
   presumably such stimuli cannot alter the organism's need state or
   the motivational states produced by needs, and to "reinforce" the

behavior (i.e., increase the probability that it will occur again) which preceded the presentation of these stimuli.

These are the requirements for a theory of learned drive. The explanations offered in this chapter should be evaluated in terms of how they satisfy the requirements.

Secondary Reinforcement

One explanation for the acquisition of new goals, and for the ability of previously ineffective stimuli such as money to reinforce responses, invokes the concept of *secondary reinforcement.*

In a Skinner box experiment in which animals learned to depress a bar which resulted in a pellet of food being delivered into a dish in the cage with the hungry rat, it was found that the bar-pressing response did not extinguish very readily even when food no longer was being delivered. The experimenter discovered that if he modified the Skinner box to eliminate the "click" that occurred in the mechanism when the bar was pressed, then the bar-pressing response extinguished more rapidly.[1] Apparently the click, which had been associated closely with food reward during the training trials, operated in some way to. perpetuate the bar-pressing response. This finding was interpreted to mean that the click had acquired the ability to serve as a reinforcement. Thus extinction occurred more slowly in the clicking apparatus because the click had acquired some small capacity to reinforce the bar-pressing. With the clicks present, the bar-pressing was more resistant to extinction. This phenomenon is called *secondary reinforcement.*

Briefly stated, secondary reinforcers are stimuli which, by virtue of their close association with primary reinforcement, acquire the capacity to act as reinforcers themselves. Thus the rats continued to press the bar if bar-pressing was followed by presentation of the click which had occurred so closely to food reinforcers. If secondary reinforcers, like the clicks in the apparatus, are presented, an animal might even learn new responses. Thus, new responses might be learned even though no food, water, relief from pain, etc., is presented.

Obviously secondary reinforcement is an important topic; it may account for much human learning, most of which is never reinforced directly by biological drive reduction. We learn to do things for prestige, for love, for friendship, for a pat on the head – the list of potential secondary reinforcers is almost inexhaustible.

An Important Secondary Reinforcer. A hungry infant cries, and his mother responds by feeding him. The crying ceases. After several repetitions of this sequence, the mother may discover that the baby stops crying when she approaches, rather than waiting for the nipple to be placed in the mouth. After still more trials, the hungry infant's crying ceases when he hears his mother's voice or even just her footsteps. Because the mother constitutes a stimulus which has occurred in close proximity to a primary reinforcement, her presence, her voice, even the sound of her shoes on the floor acquire secondary reinforcing properties, so that there is a cessation of activity when these stimuli are presented, exactly similar to the cessation of activity which follows the primary reinforcement of the milk. In this manner the child learns to "value" the mother's presence, because of her close association with so many different occasions on which primary reinforcement has occurred. Such experiences, common to almost all cultures because of the biologically determined nature of mother-child relationships, could well be the basis for the very human trait of gregariousness, through stimulus generalization from the mother to other people. Thus people tend to live in colonies or groups. The secondary reinforcing capacity usually acquired by mothers also has been identified as forming the basis for the love children have for their mothers. However, it is important to note that if the mother should cease feeding the child when he cries and relies on her presence alone to quiet the hungry baby, then the association between her presence and primary reinforcement will be weakened. She may lose her secondary reinforcing capacities; the child may soon fail to cease crying when she comes, and will continue to cry until he is fed. Such experiences could well lead to a "sour" attitude toward people, an expectation that sooner or later they will fail you or prove to be frustrating, and thus weaken the usually acquired drive to be near others, and to have social relationships. Of course, such a pervasive social attitude would not be learned as a result of only one trial in which disappointment occurs. However, it probably is true that a mother who habitually fails to satisfy her infant's needs when she is present, would continue this kind of behavior throughout his childhood and so provide a great many occasions to further the development of such an attitude.

Partial Reinforcement and Ambivalence. If the association between mother and primary reinforcement is intermittent and random—such that sometimes the mother feeds the baby when he gets hungry and at other times remains in the baby's presence but fails to feed him—the infant is very likely to acquire *ambivalent* or conflicting attitudes toward her and toward people in general. The reward associated with the mother's presence may occur often enough so that the desire for her presence becomes established, but the frustration and failure to satisfy the hunger drive when she is present also may occur often enough so that her presence also is associated with the continuing tensions of unsatisfied drives, which the child may experience as a general uneasiness and discomfort in her presence. This kind of experience, repeated often enough and in many different situations, could produce a learning to be extremely dependent on having company, coupled with fear, discomfort, or extreme shyness when in company.[2] And as we have seen, the effect of such partial reinforcement by the mother is to make the responses learned much more highly resistant to extinction than had there been 100 per cent reinforcement. Such resistance to extinction makes therapy difficult.

The effects of a complete failure to present infants with secondary reinforcing stimuli are seen in institutionalized orphan children. Such children often have several different nurses, each one of whom spends only a little time with the baby when she satisfies his primary needs. Thus stimuli coming from a particular person, such as a mother or mother-substitute, fail to occur frequently enough in close conjunction with primary reinforcement for them to acquire secondary reinforcing properties. As a result, these institutionalized children often fail to develop close interpersonal ties even in adulthood. They marry less frequently than those raised by families and tend not to develop close ties with any particular location or town. They prefer living in public dwellings such as hotels, YMCA's, and the like. In other words, they have not learned to "value" people.[3]

Token Rewards. Secondary reinforcement has been studied extensively in experiments on token rewards. Chimpanzees, for example, were trained to work for no reward other than a poker chip which later could be exchanged for a grape or a banana.[4, 5]

The animals were taught to insert a chip in a machine—the Chip-O-Mat; when the chip was put in the slot a grape was delivered to the hungry animal. Because the chip thus was placed in close temporal proximity to a primary reinforcer, the chip itself became a "valued" object, or a secondary reinforcer. The animals then could be taught various responses with a chip as a token reward for giving correct responses. The "value" of the chip was maintained by periodically allowing the animals to exhange their chips for grapes in the Chip-O-Mat.

It is important to maintain such value. Promises too, are secondary reinforcers. Children will behave "correctly" in order to receive a promise of candy, but their acceptance of such a promise as a reward is based on the promises being kept eventually. Children who have had long experience with unkept promises cease to behave "correctly" in order to obtain a promise.

Dollard and Miller point out that unreliability of secondary reinforcers may play an important role in the lack of desire to learn academic subjects often found in children of low socioeconomic class.[6] Their teachers give rewards for academic success in the form of grades, which are associated with more primary drive reduction (approval and its associated reduction in punishment and pain at home, affection, perhaps more liberal servings of favorite foods, increased allowance for ice-cream, and the like) for middle-class children. But they are not so closely associated with such powerful rewards for lower-class children, whose parents do not value good grades, and therefore do not reward good grades by their children with primary reinforcements. Thus, lower-class children do not respond to good grades as secondary reinforcers, because they are, in fact, not reinforcers: they are not associated with primary drive reduction. Teachers also emphasize that good grades are associated with financial and social success, which, in turn, are associated with drive reduction. The child is told that he must get good grades in order to receive a good income, which he is going to need if he is to reduce his drives readily. For middle-class children who often have contact with "successful" people, the ultimate goal, or reinforcer, is known to exist, and the child will work toward it. But the lower-class child does not have such intimate contact with "success." He may even have learned from others that success in the middle-class sense is denied to people "from the wrong side of the tracks." He "knows" that the ultimate goal is not there for him, that good grades are not redeemable for more primary drive reduction, and so does not make responses — do acceptable academic work — which will move him toward such a goal. If, by chance, he does study hard, the grade "A" fails to reinforce it, hence such study will tend to extinguish. In such a manner culture guides the acquisition and extinction of responses.

Reinforcement Value. Secondary reinforcers thus may vary in value to different people; the *reinforcement value* of such stimuli is emphasized by Rotter as an explanation of why some people do not bypass immediate primary rewards in order to achieve other, perhaps greater, rewards in the future.[7] Secondary reinforcers mediate long-range goals; that is, they make the intermediate steps of value in the progression toward some far-off goal. The individual continues to progress, and the intermediate steps in his progress are rewarded by secondary reinforcers, If an intermediate step, such as graduation from elementary school, has no secondary reinforcing value (because it is not closely enough associated with primary reinforcement) it does not reinforce progress toward an eventual goal of a college education and a professional career. In this case the individual is likely to behave so as to receive immediate gratification (reward) — quitting school as soon as possible and getting a job — rather than give an alternative response which might lead to what are secondary rewards to others — getting a high school diploma — but not to him.

Some people are unable to defer gratification for a while in order to receive some greater, but more distant, reward — for example, those of whom it is said that "money burns holes in their pockets." They cannot save in order to insure financial security or pay off a mortgage, if it means passing up a more immediate reward such as an expensive dinner, a newer car, or the latest style clothes. Saving, or having a large bank account or a paid-up mortgage has low reinforcement value for such people. In some cases this failure to respond to potential secondary reinforcers is chronic or habitual. Such people frequently come into conflict with the law over failure to honor their long-term commitments or to consider the consequences of their immediate gratifications.

Learning Sets. How does such failure of stimuli to be secondarily reinforcing become chronic? The answer is suggested by a series of experiments on learning in monkeys done by Harry Harlow and his associates, at the University of Wisconsin. A monkey was presented with a simple discrimination problem in which he was shown two objects under one of which was a reward of a raisin. If the monkey selected the proper object, he got the reward. After a number of trials, the monkey would reach for the correct object on every trial, regardless of whether the correct object was to the right or left of the incorrect one. When the monkey had learned this discrimination, Harlow changed the two objects. Instead of using a square and circular block of wood, he used a triangle and a diamond. The animal also learned to make this discrimination, and in a shorter period of time than it had taken him to learn the first one. When this problem was learned, the objects were changed again and the animal was required to learn a new discrimination. Harlow discovered that as a whole series of such simple discrimination problems were presented, the animals took less and less time and fewer and fewer trials to learn each one and finally got to the point where they could solve each problem perfectly after only one trial.[8] It should be noted that even though each problem involved a discrimination different from those that preceded it, the animals still learned it faster. Harlow interpreted this to mean that on each problem the animals were learning not only how to solve that particular problem but also how to solve discrimination problems in general. They thus were learning how to learn. This phenomenon is referred to as *learning set.*

Chronic inability to respond to stimuli as secondary reinforcers may be the result of the operation of a learning set. That is, by continually repeated experiences in which secondary reinforcers are not redeemed — unkept promises, savings consumed by sudden inflation, honest work met by cheated rewards, deserved honors going to others with "pull" — an individual may develop a set to disvalue any secondary reinforcers of this nature. When one such reinforcer loses value because of unfortunate experience, others do by virtue of generalization. This kind of development is expressed in attitudes of "what's the use?" or of cynicism, or in the principle of "live today for tomorrow we may die," a principle characteristically found during periods of social upheaval when the dependability with which secondary reinforcers are redeemed is greatly reduced. The earlier in the individual's life that such disappointments occur, the greater is the generalization and the more pervasive and chronic is the inability to defer immediate gratification.

Secondary Reinforcement and the Gradient of Reinforcement. In the chapter on learning, the concept of a gradient of reinforcement was introduced to describe the backward spread of reinforcing effects. The gradient of reinforcement is deducible from the principle of secondary reinforcement.[9] The reason that responses closest to the reinforcement are learned more readily than responses that occur earlier in the sequence is that these responses are rewarded by stronger secondary reinforcers. The stimuli closest to the goal acquire secondary reinforcing power more readily than do those further away. The rat in the maze learns the last turn first because he is rewarded by the sight of the goal box which has been so closely associated with eating and the resultant hunger drive reduction. The first turn of the maze gets very little reward, because the stimuli presented to the rat when he makes this turn (the sight of the second leg of the maze) are associated but distantly with the drive reduction which takes place in the goal box at the far end of the maze. They therefore do not acquire strong secondary reinforcing properties and so do not operate to reward very strongly the correct turning response at the choice point.

Stimuli that occur in close proximity to an already established secondary reinforcer also may acquire secondary reinforcing capacities. Marks of status are secondary reinforcers, probably not because they themselves are associated with primary reinforcement, but because they are associated with affection and attention from parents, which are associated in turn with primary reinforcement. Thus, chains of secondary reinforcers are possible. This process is referred to as *higher order conditioning.*

Criticisms of Secondary Reinforcement As an Explanation for Acquired Motives. It would appear that secondary reinforcement can account for the learning and performance of responses reinforced by stimuli that in themselves are not directly need-satisfiers. However, there are problems connected with secondary reinforcement which have made psychologists question whether the concept really does account for learned drives and rewards.

The most important of these problems is the instability of secondary reinforcement in most learning experiments. The ability of goal-related stimuli to reinforce responses deteriorates very readily after relatively few trials. That is, while secondary reinforcers operate for a while, very shortly the animal ceases to perform if the secondary reinforcers are not followed by a primary reinforcer. If the reinforcing effects of such stimuli are weak and temporary, how then can an individual's life-long search for prestige, status, or even love be accounted for? If these are secondary reinforcers, it is argued, they should extinguish quite rapidly, as do secondary reinforcers in laboratory experiments, in which case they hardly could account for the enduring strivings found in people. It is pointed out, for example, that in no experiment has it been possible to make a secondary reinforcer more powerful than the primary reinforcer with which it had been associated. Then how can it be that in human behavior status, honor, love, and even money, often appear to be stronger or more powerful rewards than such primary reinforcers as food, sex, and even pain-relief?

Another very important criticism of the concept of secondary reinforcement as an explanation for acquired goals and rewards is that secondary reinforcers only operate on behavior initiated by an internal, primary physiological drive such as hunger, thirst, or sex. Chimpanzees will work for poker chips redeemable for bananas when they are under food deprivation. They also will perform for poker chips when under water or sex deprivation—but to a lesser extent if the chips have been associated only with bananas, demonstrating that there is an interaction of drives. But if the animals are completely satiated for most primary drives, they will not work at all for poker chips. How is it then that a man will get up from a dinner table, at which he has fairly completely satiated his drives for food and water, and assuming that his sexual drive has been recently satisfied, will nevertheless go to work, or engage in a hobby, or go to a movie? Presuming that these activities result in the acquisition of a secondary reinforcer, what drive is operating to produce the behavior in the first place? People do not work for money only when hungry or in some other physiological need state.

In fact, if secondary reinforcement operates only when the animal is under some primary, need-produced drive, then it is easy to understand why secondary reinforcing properties of stimuli are lost so readily when need reduction no longer follows regularly and closely. Because the secondary reinforcer alone fails to satisfy or reduce the animal's need state, the animal will tend to continue to behave. And in the trial and error emission of responses while motivated, the position of the previously rewarded, but now only secondarily rewarded response may so change in the response hierarchy that another response becomes more dominant. If the correct response fails to be followed by reduction of the animal's needs, the animal may eventually cease giving the correct response altogether. If primary reinforcement does not follow the secondary reinforcer often enough, the secondary reinforcing powers of stimuli deteriorate precisely because they do not reduce the animal's need-produced drives.

To summarize the criticisms of secondary reinforcement as a complete account of learned motives, it can be said that they operate only when the animal is already motivated, and further, that they produce no enduring drive reduction because they reduce no needs. Human social rewards, on the other hand, seem to be very enduring and resistant to extinction, and humans respond to such rewards when seemingly they are not in particularly strong states of need; in fact, people often respond to social goals in preference to goals which would produce primary drive reduction.

It is not known, however, whether the apparent instability of secondary reinforcers is a real problem. It has been shown that stimuli associated with a *partial* primary reinforcement acquire secondary reinforcing capacities more resistant to extinction than those which occur in association with continuous, or 100 per cent, reinforcement. If these "partially reinforced" secondary reinforcers are in turn used as rewards on a partial rather than a 100 per cent basis (so that the secondary reinforcers are presented less often than they would be under 100 per cent presentation, and thus are given less chance to extinguish), then the secondary reinforcers are quite a bit more stable in their ability to reinforce learned responses.[10]

In human daily life, reinforcement tends to be partial. We are not rewarded every time we make a correct response. Thus the secondary reinforcers established in real life are likely to be stronger and more stable than those established in experiments with 100 per cent reinforcement. Furthermore, human secondary reinforcements are largely higher order reinforcers based on their association with affection and love from parents, which are extremely powerful reinforcers in themselves, having been established and strengthened throughout all the years of infancy and childhood, when the person is most vulnerable and so most powerfully affected by rewards.

Finally, there is some evidence that the capacity of stimuli to acquire strong reinforcing properties increases as one goes up the phylogenetic scale. It is extremely difficult to teach rats new responses on the basis of secondary reinforcement (although resistance to extinction of an already learned response in the presence of secondary reinforcers has been demonstrated). But chimpanzees can learn new responses when the only reward is a poker chip. It is likely that humans can be even more powerfully affected by secondary reinforcement. Thus it is still a moot point whether the principle of secondary reinforcement is adequate to account for human social behavior. However, the criticism still remains that secondary reinforcement fails to account for the conversion of potential energy into the kinetic energy spent in behavior, when need states are not present; the motivational state of the organism is still to be accounted for.

Learned Drives

If people strive for social goals even when their needs for food and other primary reinforcers appear to be at a low level, perhaps they have acquired other kinds of drives which impel them to behave. The acquisition of drives has been explored extensively by Neal Miller. Indeed, the classic experiment in this area is his pain-avoidance, or fear, study.[11]

The apparatus for this study consisted of two compartments, one of which had a metal floor which could be electrified to deliver a shock to the rat's feet. There was a door between the two compartments, one of which was painted black and the other white. Shock was administered to the animal in one compartment. With shock-induced pain as the drive, the animal learned to press a bar in order to open the door so he could run to the other compartment, in which the floor was not electrified. Since the animal learned this response, it is obvious that the escape, or pain-reduction, served to reinforce the bar-pressing response.

When running to the white compartment was a well learned response, Miller turned off the electricity in the black compartment. Nevertheless, the animals continued to run to the white compartment. Under what drive was the animal now operating? Miller reasoned that by association with shock, the cues of the black compartment had acquired the capacity to elicit a fear response as well as running, and that this fear produced stimuli which operated as a drive. Thus fear became a learned drive, through association with cues which previously had been ineffective in producing fear. The fear response was reinforced by the drive reduction which occurred when the animal escaped from the black compartment.

To demonstrate further that such fear is really a drive, the reduction of which can reinforce new learning, Miller then changed the switch which operated the door between the compartments so that the frightened rats had to learn to press a button (and later turn a wheel) in order to open the door between the compartments. No shock was given, but even so, the animals learned the various new switching devices — the button, the wheel — provided that the correct response was followed by the door opening and allowing the animal to run to the nonshock-associated (white) compartment. The drive under which the animals were operating, which made the new learning possible, was fear; the responses of pressing the button and turning the wheel were reinforced by a reduction in fear which occurred when the animal was no longer in the presence of the fear-arousing cues of the black compartment.

The Learning and Reinforcement of Fear. Let us take a close look at this experiment and examine in generalized terms what has transpired. The administration of shock in the black compartment operates as a strong stimulus which affects the pain receptors. The animal responds to this stimulation in at least two ways: by a set of internal autonomic responses which Miller calls fear, and by a running response. When the animal has run to the white compartment, reinforcement occurs, in that the pain is reduced. Thus both the running and fear responses are learned in response to the shock and to the other stimuli present (the black compartment) and reinforced by the reduction in pain. When the animal is placed again in the black compartment, both responses occur, even though no shock is present on this trial. The animal learns to operate a latch that opens the door between compartments. Since learning occurs, it is presumed that drive reduction (reinforcement) takes place when the animal arrives in the white compartment. Because shock is no longer present, it is obviously not a pain drive which is reduced. Miller states that the fear response, which includes strong stimulation through autonomic arousal (stimulation from a rapidly beating heart, "nervousness," "tightness" in the stomach — all the feelings usually associated with autonomic arousal), operates as a drive, and it is this drive which is reduced when the animal arrives in the white compartment. It is reduced because the stimuli which elicited the response, the cues from the black compartment, are no longer present. On the basis of this and many similar experiments Miller suggests that fear is a *learned* drive because it can be elicited by previously ineffective cues (before the experiment was begun the black compartment did not elicit fear).

Some Characteristics of Fear. Fear appears to behave like other learned responses: (a) it is subject to stimulus generalization (when a boy was taught to fear a white rabbit he also showed fear of other furry objects — a dog, cat, teddy bear, a fur coat); (b) there are responses with which it is incompatible (it was not possible to teach the boy to fear the rabbit when he was sucking his thumb); (c) the gradient of reinforcement applies to fear as well as other responses; and (d) the strength of fear increases with the number of training trials and with increases in the amount of pain drive under which the fear was learned.[12]

It is a very strong response, often reaching the limit of response strength in only a few trials, and it is a powerful drive. A rat operating under a fear drive pulls four times as hard as a rat running under 48 hours of food deprivation.[13] Finally, fear is very resistant to extinction. It takes many, many trials before avoidance under a fear drive ceases, even when no pain is present, and it often appears as if it never ceases altogether. Further, even after many extinction trials, just one reinforced trial (one occasion on which pain is again produced) will often return the fear response to full strength. Finally, fear learned during partial reinforcement is much more resistant to extinction than that learned under 100 per cent reinforcement. Subjects in an experiment who get shocked randomly are afraid of the apparatus for a longer period of time than those who are shocked whenever the stimulus is presented and only then.

Fear is particularly resistant to extinction in daily life because the response which most readily reduces fear and is thus learned is an avoidance response.[14] As a result of the avoidance, the fearful person never permits himself to engage in extinction trials in which he remains in contact with the stimuli which, through past association with pain, had produced the fear. A young man who is afraid of girls as a result of stimulus generalization from a rejecting and punishing mother stays away from girls. The staying away is reinforced by the reduction in fear which occurs when he is away from the stimuli (girls) which are associated with pain. Because he avoids them, he cannot learn that most girls would not pain him or reject him, and so he gives himself no opportunity to lose his fear. He would have to remain in the presence of a non-pain-producing girl for the fear response to extinguish, and this he does not do because he has learned to avoid girls (or at least to avoid them in social situations similar to those which originally resulted in pain, punishment, and rejection).[15, 16, 17, 18]

People often are motivated by fear even when they cannot put their fingers on just what it is of which they are afraid. They cannot identify the source of their fear because they avoid not only the fear-arousing stimuli but also thoughts about these stimuli. Such thoughts, like the external "dangerous" stimuli themselves, would also produce fear, because they too were present when the pain was administered. Thus the person avoids not only the external stimuli which arouse fear, but also the internal stimuli, thoughts, which symbolize the feared situation. Through such avoidance, the person fails to think about what it is of which he is afraid and therefore cannot identify the source of his fear. This kind of nameless fear is often referred to as *anxiety*. From what has been said before of fear, it can be seen that anxiety is a particularly important and powerful human motive; it is perhaps even more of a problem because the suffering person cannot understand what it is from which he is suffering.

It has been mentioned already that humans can reduce drives without necessarily satisfying the needs which aroused them, and it is this capacity which makes neurosis possible. This capacity is particularly important with regard to anxiety. When the source of fear is unknown the individual finds it difficult to avoid the painful stimulus; instead, he concentrates on reducing anxiety, not on eliminating the source of his difficulty. The behaviors he may learn to reduce such anxiety without affecting the ability of the fear response to be elicited by environmental stimulation and thoughts are what can turn into the symptoms of neurosis. Much of the remainder of this book will be devoted to the exploration and elaboration of this state of affairs.

Let us summarize the steps in the acquisition of the fear drive. (1) Pain, leading to an avoidance response, is produced in the presence of distinctive stimuli. (2) Through repetition of the pairing of pain and the distinctive stimuli, these stimuli acquire the capacity to elicit motivated avoidance behavior in the absence of pain. (3) When such eliciting stimuli are presented to an animal, he will learn new responses, if these responses are followed by reduction or removal of the eliciting stimuli, and thus a reduction or removal of the drive which they elicited.

It should be emphasized that the learning involved is not really the learning of a new drive, but rather is the learning of new stimuli which acquire the capacity to elicit an innate physiological drive. Thus Miller's animals learned to respond with a pain drive to previously ineffective stimuli (the black compartment). Common usage names this drive as "fear," but it is in fact no different from the innate motivational response to stimulation of the pain receptors.

The Learning of Other Drives. This kind of learning has been demonstrated only for the aversive, or avoidance-type, drives. As a result, psychologists have tried to explain most acquired human drives as stemming from fear or its variant, anxiety. For example, the motive to hurry to class is supposedly basically a fear response to the discrepancy between the thoughts, "Class begins at 9:10; it is now 9:05." It thus would appear as if man were generally a fearful and anxious creature in most situations. That some people are, cannot be gainsaid, but probably most people are not so anxious so much of the time.

However, it is not necessary to restrict learned drives only to a basis in pain. This was demonstrated by an experiment in which hungry rats were required to learn a path through a maze. Correct performance was reinforced by a food reward (Maze A). The same animals were then satiated for food and put in Maze B. Although there was a food reward at the end of Maze B, the animals were not hungry and tended not to eat when they arrived in the goal compartment. But still they learned Maze B. Another group of animals was put in Maze B, but this group did not have the previous experience with food deprivation and learning of Maze A. This second group did not learn Maze B. The first group had learned Maze B because, through their experience in Maze A, an association was established between their hunger drive state and the stimuli of the maze. Maze B, which was in many respects similar to Maze A, had the capacity to elicit a hunger drive.[19] Thus stimuli which had been characteristically associated with hunger acquired the capacity to elicit a hunger drive,[20] just as the stimuli which had been associated with pain in Miller's experiment acquired the capacity to elicit pain (fear) motivation. The same principle may be applied to the other innate, need-produced drives. Many people, for example, have noted that the sound of chimes at noon is capable of making them react with a hunger drive response. The stimuli of the bells have thus acquired the capacity to elicit a hunger drive. This happens even if one has had a hearty late breakfast.

Thus new stimuli can elicit primary drive states, *even though the needs which are innately capable of producing the drive states are absent or at low levels.* These primary drives thus elicited are responsible for the energy conversion which makes behavior possible when the learned eliciting stimuli are present. Once such a drive is elicited by previously ineffective stimuli, the organism will behave, and if that behavior includes some response which removes the eliciting stimuli or reduces the drive state, that response is reinforced.

Individual Differences in Learned Arousal. It was mentioned in Chapter 2 that there seem to be consistent individual differences in the responsiveness of different organs to motivational arousal, so that for some people the heart is a more sensitive indicator of emotion than it is in others or for others the stomach may be the most sensitive organ.[21] Individual differences in organ responsiveness suggests that there may also be individual differences in the ease with which different organ responses may become associated with and elicited by new stimuli. And in general, some organ systems may be conditioned to new stimuli more readily than others. This forms the basis for what are called *psychosomatic disorders,* which are real disorders of body organs produced as a result of their chronic participation in reactions to stress. Thus heart conditions may be induced in some people as a result of chronic emotional arousal elicited by environmental stimuli, and ulcers may occur in others.

The Energy Sources of Learned Drives. Generally, learned drives (or really, learned eliciting stimuli) are named in terms of the situations which elicit them. A hunger drive in an infant may be elicited by the cues of being alone in his crib, as a result of frequent association between such cues and the presence of strong hunger. If the infant then cries, even though his need for food may have been satiated fairly recently, and this crying brings the mother, her presence removes the cues of aloneness, so that the hunger drive no longer is elicited. The hunger drive is reduced, thus reinforcing the crying response. In this case the drive usually is identified in terms of the goal state achieved, and so might be called "gregariousness." However, it must be kept in mind that physiologically, this gregariousness drive is no different from the hunger drive in relation to which it was learned. Thus acquired drives— covetousness, prestige, status, love, achievement—involve the same energy sources as those involved in the primary drives. What is new is that these primary drives can be elicited in the absence of states of need and thus can be reduced by stimuli which are not primary reinforcers. That is, they can be elicited by stimuli other than those internal ones which are innately capable of producing a drive state.

Appetitive motives which become conditioned to new stimuli in this manner do not appear to be as strong as the avoidance drives based on pain. This may be because the pain receptors are directly stimulable, so that a pain-avoidance drive can be produced promptly and suddenly by noxious stimuli. But the receptors reporting states of tissue need (hunger or thirst) are internal and hence immune from direct stimulation from the environment. Since they respond only to states of deprivation, which usually build up slowly over periods of time, the motive states produced are not characterized by the sudden intensity typical of pain-avoidance drives, and so are difficult to associate strongly with external stimuli.

Unconscious Motivation. Although new motives may give rise to or be related to ideas, wishes, intentions, desires, and other such mental states, they are not the essence of motives, and motives may arise without them. When a motivational state is elicited by cues which do not also elicit thoughts, so that in effect the motive state is unidentified by the person, he is said to be *unconsciously* motivated. That is, he is not aware of the nature of his drive state, what cues elicited it, and what responses are therefore likely to reduce the drive. A case history will illustrate unconscious motivation.

Mr. M. was a college student. He came to the clinic because he was failing several courses in his major field. The results of an intelligence test indicated that he was of superior ability and could be expected to do creditable work in his courses, but his responses to the test items varied greatly from extensive elaboration of some answers to responses on some items which were given so reluctantly and with so little trying that often they were inadequate. He reported that when he was in class he felt "just tense all over, and on edge" and that he "couldn't think straight" because of feeling so upset. He stated that his professors were research people but not good classroom teachers, and that everyone in class was confused. He also said that one of his professors spoke very indistinctly, that another had distracting mannerisms, that their tests were ambiguous, and further, they used "objective" exams in which he had no opportunity to show his understanding of the course material, and that the tests concentrated on "irrelevant fact-memorizing." As the student talked during the interview with the counselor, he became more and more critical of his professors, of the head resident of the dormitory in which he lived, and of the college administration. It became apparent to the counselor that the student's tension in class was due to his experience of a strong drive, apparently one to which he responded with aggressive behavior when he could, judging from his hypercriticalness of almost all the people in authority about whom he spoke. He was given a series of personality tests in order to discover why he was responding as he was. On one test, the Michigan Picture Test[22], he was asked to tell stories about what was happening in pictures shown to him. It was noted that every time he was shown a picture containing a young boy and an older man, he told a story in which the man was described as the boy's father and was lecturing the boy or punishing him for some misbehavior which the boy didn't really commit. It thus was concluded that the student's difficulties were the result of a strong fear drive which had come to be elicited by stimuli generalized from his father, who was apparently frequently associated with pain during the student's youth. He responded to such a drive by becoming hostile and aggressive but could not behave in such a fashion directly to his father, or other authority figures, because he would suffer further punishment if he did. He did not think of himself as a hostile or aggressive person and was not aware that he was responding to authority figures with a fear (or pain) drive. His motivation therefore was described as unconscious. The student wasn't even aware that he was behaving in a somewhat hostile and sarcastic manner to the interviewer, indicating that the stimulus of the psychologist was also eliciting motivated aggression.

It also was hypothesized that to some extent, at least, the student's class failure was unconsciously motivated as an expression of aggression, associated with the conditioned fear drive, against his father and the teachers — an effort to try to assert his independence from his father's demands and expectations for him, and by stimulus generalization, to resist his professors' demands and expectations. Of course, he was not aware that his behavior was consistently such as to increase the probability of failing: inadequate time devoted to study, oversleeping and missing class, using his extracurricular activities as an excuse for cutting class, "forgetting" to turn in assignments. He explained that he always had felt that there was time enough left before the end of the term for him to "knuckle down and get to work." But he worried a great deal about his classes and was under the impression that he was devoting to course work all the possible time any student could, except "when unavoidable circumstances come up." Thus his motivated failure was also unconscious, despite the fact that the drive resulted in the learning of several different "class avoidance" responses which were reinforced to some extent by his parents' dismay at his poor school work.

Primary drives which, through learning, have come to be elicited by new stimuli may be reduced either by removal of the eliciting stimuli, or by the acquisition of the primary reinforcer appropriate to the drive. Another case will illustrate this:

Mr. N., a businessman, was becoming obese. He ate almost constantly, particularly sweet foods. Thorough medical examination revealed no glandular imbalance, and the case history taken by the social worker revealed no history of chronic overeating in Mr. N's family to suggest the possibility of some inherited dysfunction of the food regulatory mechanisms. During the course of diagnostic interviews, Mr. N. indicated that there was an almost perpetual state of war between himself and his wife, who was apparently a very critical, easily dissatisfied woman. In addition to this stress at home, Mr. N's business partners also were constantly squabbling, and there was a great deal of petty jealousy of each other. His partners often were trying to involve Mr. N. in their arguments, each one trying to get him on his side.

Mr. N. then reported that whenever a conflict, either between himself and his wife (which was not much of a conflict, since Mr. N. generally bowed to her wishes), or among his partners "started brewing" (note the food reference), he would become tense and upset, would begin to feel hungry, and would eat as soon as he could.

In discussing these arguments, Mr. N. began to recount similar arguments which occurred between his parents. His father, who was a small shopkeeper, was in the store most of the day and evening, but took dinner with the family. Frequently this was the only time of the day when the father had any interaction with the wife, and so it was the only time available for engaging in the acrimonious debate which characterized their relationship. During the course of these arguments over the dinner table, both parents tried to get young N on their side, and each tried to outdo the other in shows of consideration for the boy, largely expressed through urgings to eat, and blaming each other for ruining the boy's appetite by starting an argument. In order to reduce this aspect of the parental conflict, N tried to eat as much as possible, so that he would not appear to have a spoiled appetite.

Thus the stimuli arising from interpersonal conflict occurred, in Mr. N's childhood, characteristically when his hunger drive was at its height, at the beginning of dinner. Mr. N's obesity was the result of early training in hunger, and an unfortunate set of circumstances in maturity which were similar to those present in his childhood, and to which he responded in the same way as he did as a child.

As a child, Mr. N. was frightened by his parents' arguments, but with his hunger drive also present, and the reason supplied him by his parents to eat, he responded by eating, a response which is incompatible with the sympathetic arousal present in fear. Thus eating reduced fear as well as hunger. When these drives were elicited by the stimuli of interpersonal conflict in Mr. N's marriage and business, he responded in the way he had learned in childhood. It might be said that this behavior was inappropriate or ineffectual, because it resulted in no change in the eliciting stimuli, the occurrence of the arguments, so that eating could produce no fairly permanent reduction in his drive state. In fact, his growing obesity tended to make Mrs. N. even more critical of her husband than before, so that conflict at home actually increased rather than decreased as a result of Mr. N's way of responding.

As it is with hunger, so is it true of other primary drives that have been conditioned to new stimuli: they may be reduced either by a change in the stimulus situation or by the appropriate drive-reducing behavior. Sexual drives that have come to be elicited by stimuli and thoughts suggestive of inferiority may be reduced by events which produce evidence of personal adequacy, or by satisfying the sexual drive by achieving orgasm. It was discovered in World War II studies that the incidence of venereal disease was greatest in the units with lowest morale.[23] The low-morale soldiers, constantly feeling as if they are not achieving and constantly faced with officers who occupied and emphasized their superior positions, making the soldiers feel inferior, responded with increased sex drives, increasing their frequency of sexual behavior, and so also increased the frequency with which they contracted venereal disease. The sexual behavior probably was satisfying, not only because it produced a reduction in sexual motivation, but also because it helped reduce the feelings of inadequacy which elicited the sex drive; sexual conquest is usually accepted as evidence of masculine prowess, and therefore contradicts inferiority. Furthermore, sexual promiscuity, because it is frowned upon in our society, and because the soldiers' officers were representatives of society, also served as a means for expressing opposition to the officers.

Alcoholism also may be related to the conditioning of drives – in this case, probably the thirst drive. Stimuli which have acquired the capacity to elicit thirst may be responded to by drinking. If the drinking is of alcoholic beverages, the reinforcement will be great, because the state of intoxication itself has important nervous system effects in reducing tension. However, the drunkeness is likely to lead to further problems, and the stimulation from worry which occurs as a result of these new problems is also likely to be responded to by drinking to intoxication. This drinking is further reinforced by reducing the upset of worry. Thus more and more stimuli acquire the capacity to elicit thirst, and the drinking of high alcohol content beverages continues to be reinforced, leading to chronic alcoholism in which drinking becomes an habitual response to a large variety of stimuli.

Similarly, sex drive may be elicited by a wide variety of stimuli. In man, the relative lack of hormonal control over sexual behavior makes it possible for him to behave sexually whether or not physiological needs are present. Females of lower species are entirely unreceptive to sexual advances by males except during the period of ovulation when they are described as being "in heat." Human females, while they display some vestiges of this hormonal control (they tend to be more receptive and more active during ovulation) nevertheless can be sexually aroused at any point in their menstrual cycle. Sex drive may be elicited by romantic thoughts, the sight of a handsome male, the sight of "sexy" clothes, music, looking at erotic pictures, and the like. In fetishism, a neurotic disorder, sex drive may be elicited even by the sight of a woman's clothes, including shoes, stockings, and purses.

In sum, then, people are almost constantly in a state of motivation or drive, either as a result of the repetitive building up of need states, or as a result of the acquired capacity of a large variety of stimuli to elicit drives. When the drives are elicited by new stimuli, they are referred to as learned or social motives, and may be reduced by non-primary reinforcers as well as primary reinforcers. To be precise, we should not talk about achievement motives, status motives, and prestige motives, but about hunger, sex, and other such drive states which can be elicited, through learning, by stimuli associated with competition, increases in power, or status symbols, and which can be reduced by the attainment of achievements, marks of honor, and so on.

Neural Mechanisms in Learned Drive. One may speculate on the neural mechanisms which mediate associations between need-produced drives and those other stimuli present with which the drives become connected. When a need state results in motivational arousal, there is stimulation occurring not only from the need-sensitive receptors, but also from the nerve cells in the eyes, ears, muscles, and other receptor organs. That is, stimulation occurs *exteroceptively* as well as *interoceptively*. The motivational state follows the over-all pattern of stimulation. The autonomic arousal state which is the energizer for behavior requires only the presence of need stimulation; but if exteroceptive stimulation is also consistently present when the need-sensitive neurons create a motive state, then the motive state becomes associated with these exteroceptive events, too. This association probably occurs in the cortex, which has such a great capacity for integrating sensory impulses arriving from many different sense receptors. The fact that the conditionability of drives is correlated with increasing size of the cortex as one goes up the phylogenetic scale also suggests this location.

The sympathetic division of the autonomic nervous system can be activated more readily by the cortex than can the parasympathetic division. Thus the sympathetic division, which is usually dominant in states of fear or anger, is activated more readily by the cortical representations of external events. The parasympathetic division, usually dominant in appetitive drives such as hunger and thirst, is less responsive to such external stimuli and is more responsive to internal ones. Thus fear and anger can be more readily associated with external events than can the appetitive drives.

A study using rats illustrates the connection between external cues and drives. In this study, thirsty rats showed increases in drive (as measured by their activity) when the lights were turned off, as a function of the number of trials in which the "lights out" period was followed by allowing the thirsty animals to drink. Thus the external stimuli (the "lights out" period) acquired the capacity to elicit high motivation, as expressed in activity.[24]

A location in the cortex for the connections between external events and drives is suggested by a number of facts. It has already been noted that the cortex has a great capacity for integrating sensory impulses arriving from many different receptors. Further, the conditionability of drives is correlated with increasing size of the cortex; the higher in the phylogenetic scale, the larger is the cortex and the more readily are drives conditioned.

A motive state occurs less frequently and less strongly in response to exteroceptive stimuli than it does to stimulation of the interoceptive need-sensitive receptors. The motive state is an innate response to need stimulation, and so occurs every time need is present, while the same pattern of environmentally produced stimulation does not occur every time needs arouse a motive state. Thus the connection between the environmental stimuli and the motivational response is relatively weaker. Perhaps that is why people are so seldom aware of the physiological components of their social motives; these components, though strong enough to produce responses and guide learning, are probably too weak to be adequately discriminated.

Learned Drives and Anticipatory Behavior. In Chapter 3, Olds' theory of the functioning of the brain's reward system was presented. His theory suggests that arousal of the reward system by cortical events, such as thoughts, could result in an increase in activity such as is involved in searching and seeking behavior when a hungry animal "noses around" seemingly in search of food. Applied to learned drives, the theory suggests that if a particular thought is consistently present when a need-produced drive state occurs, it should acquire the capacity to elicit the drive state, just as do exteroceptively mediated stimuli. Further, it is apparent that thoughts *about* external stimuli which have acquired the capacity to elicit drives are also capable of eliciting them. Such thoughts are frequently experienced as "anticipations" or "expectations," which usually prove to be highly motivating.

Anticipatory behavior was demonstrated in studies of food deprivation in infancy. Very young rats were put on minimal diets so that they were almost constantly in a state of hunger drive. After a period of time they were then put on a regular, more adequate diet. Later, in adulthood, food supplies were restricted again. It was discovered that during this period of restricted food, the rats who had been deprived in infancy began to hoard food when it became plentiful. Animals that had not been deprived in infancy did not respond to deprivation in adulthood by hoarding.[25] Animals deprived of food early in life had learned an anticipation of hunger in response to the sight of empty food cups, and the like, and this anticipation, because of its association with a hunger drive, had acquired the capacity to elicit hunger drive in adulthood, when the learned anticipation was stimulated by the absence of food on the floor of the cage during the second period of deprivation. The animals responded to the hunger drive by collecting and hoarding food. The collection of food in the cage reduced the elicited hunger drive by changing the situation from one of a cage empty of food, which elicited the anticipation and the drive, to one of a cage with food in it, which no longer elicited the anticipation, and thus the drive. This change in the stimulus situation produced by the hoarding reinforced the collecting and hoarding response.

Secondary reinforcers, because of their close association with primary reinforcers, may operate as the stimuli for such anticipations. That is, because they have been followed by primary reinforcement, they serve as signals to the organism that a primary reinforcement is available. In this manner, the presence of secondary reinforcers function to inhibit extinction by inducing anticipations of primary reward and thus eliciting higher drive states.

Thus, in a sense, man is a self-stimulating animal whose thoughts and cortical activities can induce motivational arousal. This is one of the mechanisms which produces the flexibility of human behavior. Man can be motivated in the absence of physiological needs and can, in fact, arouse his own motives through thinking.

In the discussion of learning and reinforcement in the previous chapter it was indicated that a knowledge of the social structure of an individual's society is important if one is to predict the kinds of behaviors likely to be reinforced and learned by the individuals in that society. The same consideration applies to the learning of drives: a knowledge of the individual's society can shed a great deal of light on the kinds of stimulation likely to occur frequently in the presence of need states and thus become cues capable of eliciting motivational states. Such a knowledge of social factors also would play a role in understanding the kinds of behaviors the individual will learn when so motivated, and the kinds of situations which would be reinforcing.

Are Motives Necessary?

In Chapter 3, a theory by Estes was described. The essence of his theory is that the concept of motives as energizers of behavior is unnecessary. Estes suggests that behavior is controlled exclusively by stimuli, and the only function of drive states such as hunger is to add more cues with which responses can be associated. In this theory, there is no need to seek for learned motives to account for human social behavior. That people behave and act and expend energy may be thought of as simply the nature of the animal. The only thing one must account for is why people act in the particular ways they do, and it is not necessary to invoke motives to explain this; the association between stimuli and responses may be sufficient.

Gordon Allport long ago introduced a concept similar to this; he called it *functional autonomy.*[26] According to Allport, habitual ways of behaving which may have become established as the result of motives, become autonomous in that they continue even when the motives are no longer operating. Although one may develop a strong achievement drive because of the rewards achievement brings, one may continue to compete even when rewards are not likely and when the originally rewarding figures—for instance, parents—are absent. In effect, one continues doing things for their own sake, and the learning of drives is not needed to account for the long term habit structures of adults.

Allport's theory is not specified in as much detail as Estes', and so has led to very little research. As a result, it has not been accepted widely. It affirms the *absence* of something, which is always difficult to demonstrate and which leads to a reduction in scientific searching. Few psychologists, therefore, have become involved directly in this theory, because it calls for no research. Thus functional autonomy has not been given much weight, particularly because there is no evidence directly supporting it.

Estes' theory, which is a more advanced statement of the expendability of learned motives, has stimulated more research. While his theory does not include drive as an energizer of behavior, it does take into account the internal cues produced by need states, to which responses may be associated. In terms of Estes' theory it would be said that environmental stimuli come to elicit hypothalamically mediated internal states or cue patterns, which we have called "drive states," and these in turn elicit the responses learned in association to them. Thus Estes' theory includes learned drives, although he refers to drives as internal stimulus states.

REPRISE. While everyone agrees that people behave in ways which do not always reduce their biological needs, that stimuli other than those of need come to elicit striving, and that stimuli other than those that reduce such needs serve as goals and reinforcers, there is little agreement on the principles and mechanisms by which these events occur. Those who invoke the concept of drive as an energizer of behavior have suggested explanations in terms of secondary reinforcement and

learned drives; those who have been investigating the control of responses by stimuli without drive energizers do not think in terms of
such acquired motives.

While secondary reinforcement and learned drives have been demonstrated in some limited laboratory situations, there is considerable
doubt about whether they can account for all the behavior ascribed to
them, such as enduring social motivations (and the lack of such motives
in some people), the ability of some primary reinforcers to substitute
for social goals such as the ability of eating, drinking, and sexual behavior to reduce drives elicited by social stimuli, and the development
of psychosomatic disorders. In particular, the conditioning of positive
or appetitive drives has not been adequately demonstrated experimentally, although the learning of aversive motivation (fear) has been well
established.[27] Thus the hypothesis of conditioned drives exists with little
direct support, though the hypothesis is demanded by and fits well
within a theory that has much support from other sources for its other
parts. This hypothesis is the one which is most generally accepted in
psychology today (although it is often stated in different terms).

In this chapter the following points have been included:

1. The acquisition of motives can account for the lack of exclusive
dependence upon biological need in human behavior in that it involves
the facilitation of behavior in the absence of need.

2. Secondary reinforcement and higher-order conditioning have
been used to explain the reward value of nonneed-relevant stimuli such
as money, marks of prestige, signs of affection, etc., although secondary
reinforcement presupposes an already aroused motive state and greater
stability of its effects than are obtained using laboratory animals.
Humans reinforced on a partial basis may show more adequately stable secondary reinforcing effects.

3. Reinforcement value of stimuli was introduced to explain differences among people in their responsiveness to culturally defined symbols and stimuli.

4. Learning sets applied to secondary reinforcement were introduced
to account for the generality or chronicity of responses to potential
secondary reinforcers.

5. The conditioning of responses to pain stimuli, resulting in the
learning of a fear drive, was described and was used as a model for the
way in which drive responses to need-produced stimuli can be conditioned to new stimuli and so be invoked when need stimuli are absent.
In this theory socially evoked motives involve the same physiological

drive states as those which are innately produced by the need-stimuli in relation to which they were acquired.

6. Such learned drives can be reduced either by those stimuli which reduce the need which is innately capable of producing the drive state, or by removing the environmental cues which, through learning, have acquired the capacity to elicit the drive. Thus reinforcement of the behavior impelled by learned drives occurs.

7. The particular physiological drive responses which are readily elicited in learned drives can play a part in the production of psychosomatic disorders.

8. Fear drive is particularly strong and resistant to extinction. When fear is present without any thoughts about the situation which elicits it, such fear is often labelled anxiety. When the motivated person is unable to discriminate his drive state, he is said to be unconsciously motivated.

9. Learned drives, such as fear, may be reduced by behaviors such as avoiding the eliciting stimuli. This keeps the drive at a low level without altering the existence of the conditions which allow the drive to be evoked by those stimuli; this fact makes neurotic behavior possible.

10. Learned drives may be evoked not only by external stimuli, but also by thoughts or anticipations, so that man is in this sense self-stimulating or self-arousing.

11. Functional autonomy was described as an alternative to the hypothesis of learned drives.

5. Thinking, Perception, and Consciousness

Each of the chapters in this section deals with concepts more complicated than those considered in the preceding chapters. And as the complexity of the material increases, our sound, scientifically valid knowledge decreases. And further, as information decreases, there appears to be an increase in the number of theories. Theory abounds where fact is scarce — nowhere more than in the related areas of thought, perception, and consciousness.

Of the basic phenomena with which psychology deals, none are as difficult to study scientifically, and none have as many fatal pitfalls awaiting the unwary trespasser, as the subjects of this chapter. And added to the inherent difficulties in studying these phenomena and further inhibiting the development of knowledge, there has been a prejudice against the concepts of thought, perception, and consciousness in the minds of many of psychology's most able investigators.

The main difficulty is that thinking, perceiving, and being aware still are private events and so cannot be directly observed by an impartial investigator. The investigator has only the word of the subject that he is thinking, and there are many reasons for that word not being the most reliable and valid report: possible intentional concealment and unintentional distortion; for many if not all subjects, it is impossible for them always to know their own thought processes. The reader, for example, may have discovered that it is possible to hold a conversation with a half-asleep room mate, who, upon awakening in the morning, vehemently denies all knowledge of the conversation.

Psychologists can, of course, study subjects' verbal reports about their thoughts and can discover variables which produce changes in the verbal reports. But studying verbal reports may not be the same thing as studying thoughts.

The prejudice against studying these phenomena probably is related to the ease with which vitalistic conceptions "creep in" to theorizing about thought and consciousness. Most experimental psychologists wish to avoid any such notions which ascribe independent existence and "power" to such non-material concepts as thought. As soon as one speaks about thoughts "arising," one has implied some independent existence and reality to a "thing," thought, which has never been seen, touched, weighed or measured. And of course, when thoughts are presumed to "do" things — drive out other thoughts or influence perception, motives, physiological functioning — one has implied that these immaterial and nonobjective objects, if there can be such things, have power or force; the door is opened to mysticism. Thus many investigators choose to avoid the problem altogether.

The Place of Thought in Psychological Systems

The attitude of the early behaviorists about thought was that, because thought is private and apparently immaterial, one has no scientifically valid evidence that it even exists. Certainly I may claim that I think, but I can never know whether you or any other creature is thinking. Am I conscious? Is a dog conscious? Does he think? How about a white rat? Or a cockroach? Or paramecium? It seems that we shall never know. And it is a principle in science that nothing can be presumed to exist without evidence. This principle is a part of scientific scepticism. Therefore, the early behaviorists denied the existence of thought and consciousness. They reasoned further that if one could make predictions of behavior adequately without involving the concepts of thought and consciousness, then these concepts are totally unnecessary and can explain nothing. For example, they would say that if one can predict the level of performance in a particular task solely on the basis of the amount of previous practice, motivation, and reinforcement, then nothing is gained by supposing that these variables affect thinking which in turn affects performance. More simply, if C (performance) is a direct function of B (thought), and B is a direct function of A (practice, motive, and reinforcement), it may be said that C is a function of A and B is an unnecessary concept.

So it was that for many years many psychologists quite successfully could ignore thought and consciousness and even deny their existence. At the opposite pole were Freud and his students who theorized extensively about impulses and thoughts conflicting with each other, arising, transforming, disguising themselves, hiding, and influencing behavior. And withal, there was no effort made to develop lawful relationships between experiences and thoughts, or between thoughts and overt behavior. Little wonder that experimental psychologists rejected Freud's ideas: his theory's ability to predict adequately could seldom be tested experimentally, because most of the theory concerned thoughts which, by their nature, are not open to direct observation.

More recently there has been a change in attitude about thought. Although many still try to develop laws of behavior which can dispense with thinking and ideas, there are few who claim that thinking does not occur. The main questions nevertheless remain: What is the nature of thought? Where do thoughts come from? What are the effects of thoughts? These same questions may be applied to consciousness and to perception, which may be considered a special form of thought — that which is stimulated more or less directly by events in the sensory organs.

The Gestalt Emphasis on Insight. This change probably is connected with the Gestalt movement in psychology. The Gestalters pointed out that most of the research on learning used apparatus and learning demonstrations, such as animals in mazes, which encouraged trial and error performance, but seldom were conditions arranged in such a way that the experimental subjects could solve the problem by thought or insight. A rat in a maze could not learn the maze by insight, because at no time could he see the entire plan of the maze. He could only see the small section he was in at any moment, and so could not discover mentally the relationships among the various maze sections. To correct this situation, the Getstalters worked with experimental situations in which the subject could solve the problem by an insightful mental event in which the solution depended upon the subject's perceiving a relationship among stimulus elements. For example, a hungry ape would be placed in a cage from the roof of which hung a banana out of the ape's reach. A wooden box was placed in the cage. When the ape perceived a relationship between the box, the banana, and himself, and then stood on the box to reach the banana, insight was said to occur, producing a solution to the problem. It appeared, at least from the animal's overt behavior, that no trial and error was involved.[1] The Gestalters did a great deal of work along these lines, forcing upon the attention of other psychologists that mental events were occurring and had an obvious bearing on problem solution and overt behavior. It thus has become a task of psychology to discover the nature of such "mental" events, their operation, and their effects.

Incidentally, the new methods introduced by Gestalt psychology illustrate how methods influence the nature of theory. It is a truism that theory determines the research method, but the reverse is also true: one's method of investigation exerts a subtle but powerful influence on the kind of theory which will emerge from the data.

Thought

Thought is an internal process or event. It may be said that thought *represents* or in some way stands for, or substitutes for, external events or conditions. To illustrate: an animal may be trained to go to one of three goals marked by turning on a light directly over the proper goal. When the response to the light has been acquired, the animal may be restrained and required to delay his reaction for various periods of time after the light indicating the proper goal has been turned off. If the animal, upon release, goes to the proper goal, it must be assumed that some internal event within the animal represents or symbolizes the turned on light, since the external light itself already has been turned off.[2] In this sense, thought is an internal substitution for external events which may or may not be immediately present and stimulating to the organism's senses.

This general description of thought as a *symbolic* or representational process includes many varieties of thought: simple recall, daydreaming, planning, undirected "woolgathering," reasoning, logic, analysis, synthesis, and creative problem-solving. All share the common element of involving internal substitutions for external events.

It has been assumed generally that thought occurs in the brain. The brain has been compared to a gland, in saying that it "secretes" thought as the gall bladder secretes bile. Because the brain is largely a neural organ, it would appear that thought is a neural process — some arrangement of differences in neuron sensitivities or synaptic transmissions which always work together, or which, when they do work together, constitute a "trace" or correlate of a previously sensed external event.[3] Nothing definite is known at all about such traces. Presumably each trace is associated or connected with many other traces, so that when one trace is activated by a stimulus it can stimulate neural activity in other traces, thus producing chains of association, or extended thinking. Also presumably, these traces are established by past experience; the neural firings which occurred when a stimulus was presented somehow produce or leave a trace. There are no thoughts about things or events which have not been experienced directly.

New Ideas. An event is a state of stimulation existing at a moment in time; the various momentary states may, in thought, be recombined into new or novel sequences making possible creative thought and imagination. For example, one has seen pictures of ballistic missiles, and one has seen enlarged photographs of distant planets. Therefore one can imagine himself in a rocket on a flight to Venus, by combining previously experienced stimulus situations.

Recent studies of creativity suggest that there are consistent individual differences in the tendency to combine traces in such ways as to produce novel outcomes.[4] A unique event occurs when one neural trace stimulates other traces which in most people are not associated with the initial stimulating trace. If the complete unique chain of thoughts is effective in solving a problem or results in a highly socially valued response, then it is likely to be called creative. It appears that the ability to associate traces in unique ways can be learned, in that reinforcement for unique associations produces an increase in their frequency of occurrence. Such reinforcement therefore also should increase the occurrence of creative acts; if a certain proportion of unique thoughts are creative, then an increase in the frequency of unique associations should include an increase in the number of creative thoughts.

Neural Traces and Thoughts. It is important to keep in mind that the activation of a trace *is* a thought; it does not produce a thought, which would then have to be described as a factor having existence beyond the neural trace itself. The inactive neural trace, whatever its nature, may be a latent thought, but it must be fired by an effective stimulus for the thought actually to occur. Generally it is assumed that such neural traces are composed of synaptic relations among neural cell groups, or assemblies, in which thresholds for transmission of impulses are raised and lowered differentially to produce patterned firing in the cell assemblies; each pattern is associated, again by means of differentially lowered and raised thresholds, with other patterns to produce thought chains.

This description is almost entirely in the nature of an hypothesis which seems reasonable and logical on the basis of what is known about neural firing and what may be inferred from behavior such as in the delayed reaction experiments. There are three main sources of evidence on this central (meaning central nervous system) theory of thought. One is the finding that unanesthetized patients during brain surgery report that they experience ideas or thoughts when the surgeon stimulates points on the cortex.[5] Another line of evidence comes from electro-encephalographic studies, in which the very tiny electrical activities in the brain are magnified greatly and recorded. These studies indicate that when a subject is actively thinking rather than completely relaxing, there is an interruption in the usual pattern of electrical activity, and often irregular "bursts" of activity. These are presumed to be produced by the subject's thoughts. A third line of evidence, coming from the problem solving performances of brain injured humans and animals, indicates an apparent reduction in thinking ability as a result of injury.[6] For example, some patients find it impossible to say the sentence, "The sun is shining" when it is night time. The production of the words themselves is a symbolic activity intimately connected with thinking, in that sounds are symbols for words; words themselves are symbols for things. These brain injured patients can produce sounds as symbols for words, but they cannot accomplish the next step in symbolization — using words as symbols for events not immediately present to the senses.[7]

Peripheralist Theory of Thought. However, these lines of evidence, although they implicate the brain in thinking, are not definitive. They tell us nothing about what actually goes on within the brain, and they fail to exclude other possible interpretations of thought, particularly the peripheralist theory. There have been two main theories in this area. The *central* theory is the one we have just discussed, in which thought is said to occur in the central nervous system. Opposed to this view is the *peripheral* theory. We have already met the central-peripheral controversy in a different form — in the discussion of the Cannon-Bard theory of emotion versus the James-Lange theory. The Cannon-Bard theory is essentially a central theory, placing the nexus of emotions in the brain, whereas the James-Lange theory, emphasizing the bodily components of emotion and motivation is a peripheralist theory. The peripheralist position on thought is that covert and tiny muscular reactions in the muscles characteristically involved in responses to stimuli constitute thoughts. That is, the muscle action itself is the thought; when the stimulus is not present, so that the response is not given overtly, the response may occur covertly, so greatly reduced in amplitude that it is not apparent to the external observer. Nevertheless, this tiny amplitude of response is enough to constitute a thought of the response, or to give rise to the thought through sensory neurons in the muscles being stimulated by the tiny muscle reaction and sending "reporting" impulses to the brain. Thus, in the peripheral theory thoughts are stimulated by or arise from the muscles, rather than from the central nervous system itself. A thought is an incipient muscular response.

An interesting demonstration of this theory is one in which memory is aided and stimulated. A college student who, when asked, could not remember the name of his first-grade teacher or those of any first-grade classmates, was asked to produce at least one memory of first grade. He remembered that he sat somewhere near the back of the room. The experimenter then placed the subject in a chair near the back of the experimental room. The subject was then asked to recall where the windows were situated. He vaguely felt that they were to his right. The experimenter then took the subject to a room in which, when he was placed at the rear, the windows were to the right. The subject was next asked to gaze through the windows and try to recall the view he had when in first grade. By so doing, the experimenter was gradually able to reconstruct the visual and kinesthetic cues present when the subject was in the first grade, and when a large enough number of such cues were present, so that the subject was responding in ways very similar to those in which he behaved in elementary school, he gradually began to recall the names and appearances of his teacher and classmates. This demonstration suggests, then, that muscular responses and positions produce cues which in turn elicit thoughts (memories). But where are the thoughts themselves located?

Thoughts As Incipient Motor Responses. Other experiments suggest an answer. If the tiny electrical activities produced by muscle action of the arm are amplified and recorded, an experimenter can obtain a visual record of even very small muscle actions which would not be visible to an observer, and of which the subject himself might be unaware. With the subject so prepared, the experimenter asks him to think of dealing two body blows to the world heavyweight champion. Immediately on the recording device appears a burst of activity from the arm muscle, and then another.[8]

Similarly, if the activity of the eye muscles is recorded, and the subject is asked to think of the tallest building in the world, a burst of activity in the muscles appears, as if the subject's eyes were looking up.

Other experiments have shown that thinking of words produces activity in the voice box, thinking of running produces implicit leg responses, and so forth. Thus, there is a great deal of evidence to show that thoughts do involve some activities in those muscles usually involved in the thought about response. Thought is, to some extent at least, a partial or incipient motor response, which can stand for or symbolize an overt response. In the delayed reaction studies described earlier, for example, it was found that the experimental animals would assume a pointing position when the light turned on to indicate the correct goal box; they would point to the correct goal by orienting their heads and bodies to that goal. When the light had been turned off, and the delay period expired so that the animals could run to the goal, they ran to the one to which they were pointing. They literally followed their noses. When animals were not permitted to point to the correct goal, their ability to "remember" which was the correct one after the signal light was extinguished was sharply curtailed.[9] In other words, the animals' "thought" consisted largely of preparatory or incipient responses of those muscles involved in the overt behavior of which the animal was presumably thinking.

The peripheral muscular involvement in thought may be demonstrated readily by any person. When you are lying down in a relaxed manner, begin thinking about playing football; when you have been thinking in a detailed and intensive manner about playing an exciting game, you may suddenly find yourself kicking the ball with your leg — the force of the response may, in fact, so startle you as to interrupt your reverie. Similarly, many people have found that while dreaming they have produced muscular responses associated with the activities occurring in their dreams; these overt responses may occur with such force that the dreamer is awakened by them.

Thoughts and Learning. These considerations suggest the intimate connection between thought and learning. The muscular responses involved in thought are those previously acquired through learning. The effect of learning on thought becomes particularly apparent with responses that have become so well learned as to be almost automatic. Often one finds it difficult to put such responses into words and think about them in order to explain them to someone else. If, however, one performs the response in pantomime, he then is able to think and talk about it. For example, if you were asked to tell whether the hot water faucet is on the right or left in your home sink, you probably would find that you could better describe it if first you give the overt response of reaching for the faucet in pantomime. Here again is a demonstration of the motor-response aspect of thought.

Finally, it has been noted often that body position sometimes stimulates memories of past occasions involving the same body position. This was dramatically illustrated in a movie version of Hemingway's *Old Man and the Sea*,[10] in which the old man, bracing his arm against the side of his boat in order to hang onto the line on which he has caught a large fish, is reminded of an occasion in his youth in which his arm was similarly braced for a "hand wrestling" competition. The similarity between the two situations, which was mediated by the kinesthetic cues of the arm, involved arm position and a competitive struggle of controlled strength against a silent and primitive adversary. When memories suddenly pop into consciousness, it is sometimes because of such cue-similarities between the present occasion and the remembered one, with the memory mediated by body position and internal cues of the emotional state present at the time.

Thought Involves Central and Peripheral Components. How does the evidence for the peripheral (motor response) nature of thought fit in with the central theory, which places thought in the brain? The central-peripheral controversy in psychology is an old one, and as with most such controversies, the truth probably lies somewhere between the two positions. It is unlikely that neural events occurring within the brain have no effect on the musculature. We have seen already that learning does not occur unless the response is performed and practiced; if such learning results in a neural trace, the activation of which is a thought of the response, then it is likely that there are several connections between the cells involved in the trace and the muscles involved in the response which produced the trace. If this is so, then activation of the trace very likely would include the transmission of impulses to the associated muscles. Similarly, it seems reasonable that activation of the muscles involved in a response, such as in an implicit or covert response, would result in activation of the neural trace associated with that response by means of feedback from the muscles to the central nervous system. It is probable, then, that thinking involves both central and peripheral (motor) activity.

Although both central and peripheral events are usually present in thought, the centralist-peripheralist controversy centers on which set of events is necessary and sufficient for thought to occur. The question, then, is of the nature of the relationship between central and peripheral factors. The evidence suggests that central events are necessary and sufficient for thought to occur, but that thinking may be more specific or extensive when implicit muscular responses are also present. In the delayed reaction experiments, when animals were not permitted to point to the correct goal, their performance was greatly reduced, but they still were able to go to the correct goal, although this ability disappeared after fairly short delays. When permitted to point or establish a position set, they could go to the correct goal after much longer periods of delay.

In another kind of experiment on thinking, animals are required to make alternate responses. That is, a rat may be required to run around a "block" to the right once and then to the left once, in order to receive a reward.[11] The sequence may be altered and extended indefinitely — RL, RRLL, RLRL, RRLLRR, and so forth. In the double alternation sequence, RRLL, which many rats can learn to master, it is apparent that some internal symbolic cues are operating; after the first R the rat makes a second R, but after the second R he makes an L. In other words, the rat can discriminate between a first and a second response when the two are identical so far as muscular movements are concerned. In a variant of this experimental procedure, some animals could perform an RRRRLLLL alternation. In other words, the animal was able to "count" to 4, or at least discriminate among 1, 2, 3, and 4 right turns, in order to make the first left turn after the correct right one.[12] Since the muscular responses in making the fourth turn were identical with those in making the third turn, it does not seem possible that the "thinking" or "counting" occurred in the muscles. The symbolization of the turns already made must occur elsewhere in the animal, and the central nervous system appears to be the likely place. Thus these experiments further suggest that the brain is the location for the symbolic activities of thought.

Finally, it is noted that patients suffering from paralysis and anesthesias of their limbs, such as hemiplegics and paraplegics, and those who have lost their limbs can think about activities — throwing a ball or walking — which ordinarily involve their disabled members. Thus it would appear from the delayed reaction studies, the alternation problems, and from studies of the disabled that thinking or symbolizing can occur in other than the body muscles.

However, paraplegics and other disabled patients also report that their thinking about activities involving their lost or paralyzed limbs tends to be vague and poorly defined. They can think about walking, but find it difficult vividly to imagine themselves actually walking. This, together with the evidence from delayed reaction experiments, in which the permissible period of delay was extended greatly when animals were permitted to make pointing muscular sets, suggests that the participation of implicit muscular responses aids thinking, probably by making it more specific and definite, and apparently also by extending the period in which symbolic activities can substitute effectively for real events. This participation by muscles may be why the performance of responses in pantomime aids recall; it may be that the association of implicit muscular responses with the activation of a neural trace and the feedback to the brain from such implicit responses bring the symbolic activity into a closer or more realistic relationship with the thing being symbolized, or provide more cues to which a thought response is attached. In general, then, it can be said at least that symbolic processes ordinarily involve both central and peripheral components, that it is possible for thought (perhaps only vague thought) to occur without peripheral components, and that, on the other hand, peripheral implicit responses can produce thoughts or aid in the production of thoughts, through feedback from the muscles to the central nervous system. Certainly it is true that there is no thought at all without activity in the brain; even during sleep, when the cortex is least active, dreams are marked by an increase in cortical electrical activity as measured by the electroencephalograph, and this increase approximates the kind of activity characteristic of the waking state.

Verbal Thought. Although there is some evidence that thinking often may be in terms of traces of visual images, and less often of auditory, olfactory, gustatory and tactile images, such modes of thoughts are fairly restricted to simple recall or memory related imaginations. This is probably true in general of thoughts which consist of implicit responses of the effector organs (body muscles, eye muscles, and so forth) and their associated neural traces.

But the most important mode of thought is verbal. In our discussion of the central-peripheral controversy, we dealt largely with thinking about concrete objects, events, and responses, which when present can directly stimulate the senses. But the kind of thinking usually involved in intellectual pursuits, logical analysis and synthesis, problem-solving, and creative thinking is of abstract concepts. That is, these thoughts often are concerned with concepts symbolized typically by words. When one thinks about a tall building this thought may include the implicit responses of the eye muscles involved in looking up. But what are the implicit responses — what part of the body moves or is involved in thoughts about such abstractions as truth, average, morality, squareness? Response systems (eye muscles or leg muscles) are not associated with such concepts as they are with seeing certain objects or playing football.

Implicit Speech. The answer is that such thoughts involve the muscles which are employed in the production of words, numbers, or other named symbols — those of the voice box, tongue, and larynx. Thinking about such abstractions is then a symbolic activity concerned with other (verbal) symbols. In other words, much abstract thinking involves implicit speech, just as more simple thoughts involve implicit body muscle responses. Implicit speech is evident in studies in which electrical activities in the voice box and tongue are recorded when a subject is thinking. An interesting confirmation of this comes from experiments on deaf subjects who use their hands for symbolic communication in place of words. Electrodes attached to the hands were connected with an amplifier which amplified and recorded the electrical activity of the hand muscles while the subjects slept. When there were bursts of activity in the hand muscles, the subjects were awakened and asked if they had been dreaming. Most of them reported "Yes." Subjects awakened when there was no activity in the hand muscles generally responded "no."[13]

Another very interesting experiment on the subject was William Scott's on opinion change.[14] Assuming that opinions, like other thoughts, are largely verbal, Scott reasoned that if people were rewarded for giving speeches contrary to their opinions, then their opinions should shift in the direction of the opinions expressed in the rewarded verbal speech-making. In order to test this hypothesis, he measured the opinions of college students on some issues and then required his subjects to debate the issues before their classmates, but with each debater taking the side opposite to his own opinion. Thus each subject was given practice at making certain verbal statements. After the debates, Scott told half of the subjects that they had won the debate, and the other half that they had lost. In this way he rewarded the verbal practice of half of his subjects. Then their opinions on the issues were measured again. Scott found that debaters who had been rewarded for arguing against their own opinions actually changed their opinions in the direction of the side they took in the debate. Debaters who were told they lost — who were not rewarded — did not shift their opinions. This experiment indicates that thoughts may be changed by selectively rewarding verbal behavior and therefore provides additional confirmation of the verbal nature of thought.

Words As Substitutes for Other Stimuli. Words are substitutes for real objects,[15] and people respond to words in much the same manner as they would to that for which the word substitutes.[16] There are many notable examples of changes produced in the English vocabulary because people do respond to words as if they were the things for which they stand. Aversion to and fear of death itself is attached to the words associated with death, so that where we used to have funeral parlors and undertakers, we now have mortuaries and morticians, and more recently, "chapels" and "bereavement consultants," as we search for new words to which we will not respond with aversion and fear. Similarly we are moving from "cemetery" to "memorial gardens."

People react to their thoughts as they do to the situations symbolized by the thoughts. An illustration of this was provided by a subject instructed simply to think quietly while a GSR device recorded changes in his emotional state. Whenever there was a sharp drop in skin resistance, the experimenter said "Good," thereby reinforcing whatever thought had produced the emotional state. The reinforcement seemed to increase the frequency of occurrence of such emotion arousing thoughts; that, at least, was the experimenter's interpretation of why the subject suddenly ripped the GSR electrodes off his hand, exclaiming in a perturbed manner "You're reading my mind!" as he stalked out of the experimental room.

One may frighten himself by thinking about objects and events which frighten him, and one can delight himself by covertly producing words about things and events which yield him pleasure. In this sense, man is self-stimulating, although there may be an ultimate external stimulus to the chain of thoughts. One of the ways in which man differs from lower animals is in the great extent to which, through symbolic activity, he is self-stimulating. It is of interest that as one ascends the phylogenetic scale, the amount of delay possible between the turning off of the cue and the performance of the correct response in a delayed reaction experiment (the period in which the animal is self-stimulating, following the initial external cue), becomes greater and greater. In rats it is seconds, in children many minutes, and in adult humans probably infinite.[17]

Words symbolize or identify concepts in which many different concrete events which have something in common are brought under the same rubric.[18] The common element is an abstraction from the collection of real objects for which the word stands. Thus words provide great economy in thinking; by thinking the word "chair" one accomplishes what it would otherwise be necessary to do by successive images of many different real chairs. In this way words are mediators of stimulus generalization; by applying the same word to several different objects, the response learned to one of the objects can be evoked by any of the objects so labeled. A child who avoids the radiator after having been burned by it and associates the word "hot" with the burn, will generalize his avoidance response to all other objects which are also labeled "hot" by his mother.

Words therefore are useful for effecting transfer of responses to new stimuli whose similarity to a previously learned stimulus is mediated by using the same verbal label for both. The opposite is also true: making discriminations among stimuli which appear similar may be encouraged by associating different words to the stimuli. A boy discriminates between two girls, who may be highly similar as stimuli, if one is labeled "married" and the other "a coed."

The operation of such verbally mediated discriminations may be observed readily in a common failure to make the proper discrimination. Frequently young schoolchildren respond to their teachers with such affection and dependency, stimulated by the teachers' motherliness and authority, that their responses to their teachers become similar to their responses to their mothers. Such a child is very likely to address his teacher inadvertently as "Mother." Because the responses to mother and teacher are similar, the child but poorly learns to discriminate between them and apply different labels to the two women. He therefore applies the same name to both, expressing the stimulus generalization which has occurred and his failure to make the discrimination.

By applying different labels to similar physical stimuli it is possible to encourage the making of differential responses to the stimuli. A child who has learned the appropriate responses to the words "hot" and "cool" is able, with minimal or no trial and error, to respond differentially to two almost identical radiators, one of which his mother has called "hot" and the other "cool."

In the last example, labeling reduced or eliminated trial and error behavior. By mediating generalization and discriminations, words are able to evoke the appropriate response to a stimulus; when a verbal stimulus is presented, a person gives the response learned to that stimulus. If an entirely new stimulus configuration is presented, and is labeled with a word to which the individual has already learned a response, the word serves to evoke the learned response, so that the trial-

and-error unreeling of behaviors from the response hierarchy is unnecessary in order for the individual to make a response to the new stimulus configuration. When presented with a totally new gadget, much trial and error is saved if the presentation is made with the statement: "This is a cigarette lighter." The receiver, having learned a set of responses to the label "cigarette lighter," limits his responses to those evoked by the label and thus also makes a discrimination between this gadget and others — pill boxes, compacts, paperweights, mechanical objects and parts — perhaps similar in color, shape, "feel," and/or weight, which are not cigarette lighters. In this sense there is a narrowing down of the field of possible and probable responses to the gadget, producing a great deal of efficiency in behavior.

Narrowing the possible range of responses is the purpose of verbal instructions. They are designed to mediate responses to a stimulus so that only the class of responses desired may be evoked. The research psychologist, for example, may distribute questionnaire booklets to a class with instructions which explain "this is not a test." The intention is to induce a discrimination between this stimulus and other similar questionnaires, so that fearful and anxious responses are not made to this stimulus. In other parts of the instructions the researcher will use other words, responses to which the members of the class have already learned, so that the class of responses evoked by the stimulus will be limited to those in which the researcher is interested, such as circling T for True and F for False.

Language, Thought, and Culture. There is a close and intimate relationship between language (and therefore thought) and culture.[19] Eskimos have a large number of words to name different kinds of snow; it is therefore possible for Eskimos to make discriminations among different snowfalls, and to think (make implicit verbal responses which can serve as stimuli for other responses) about various kinds of snow. We can do little more than discriminate between dry and wet snow, because our language contains few other verbal concepts related to kinds of snow. Similarly, where we can only make discriminations between ripe and unripe coconuts, and therefore can only think about the ripeness of coconuts in this highly restricted two valued manner, there are societies in the Southern Pacific in which the language contains a dozen different words describing various degrees of ripeness of coconuts. Societies which have very complex kinship customs and systems have names for various kinship relationships unnamed in our society, such as the mother of a wife's cousin's husband.

A study by Brown and Lenneberg clearly shows the interrelationships among culture, vocabulary, and ability to make discriminations.[20] They found that colors on which there was greatest agreement about the color names were also the colors most readily recognized. However, when the subjects were Zuni Indians, whose language contains only one word for both the colors we call orange and yellow, there was a confusion between these two colors. When shown yellow and then asked to recognize the same color from a group of color-cards, the Zuni often picked orange, and vice versa when asked to recognize orange. American students never made this mistake. Interestingly enough, those Zuni who spoke English made more mistakes than the white Americans, but fewer than their non-English-speaking tribemates.

It is apparent from these examples that the verbal concepts contained in a language are closely related to economic and social characteristics of the culture using the language, which therefore also play an important part in determining the things thought and thought about in a culture.

Word Order and Thinking. In a similar manner word order is related to culture and to thinking. Because of our great familiarity with English, we are prone to imagine that the word-order characteristic of English (subject as first element in a sentence, verb second, and object next) is "natural," and other orders unnecessarily and artificially complex. Our study of foreign languages, however, should convince us that it is entirely possible to communicate just as effectively with other word orders, such as that characteristic of German, in which the verb is at the end of the sentence. Young children just learning to speak use many different word orders in their attempts to communicate and yet do not appear to be confused about what they are trying to communicate.

The molding effect of language on thought is readily seen in the effects of word order in English. Because words of action tend to follow noun-subjects directly in a sentence, it is not surprising that one tends to think of the phenomena labeled by the noun-subject as acting. This usage often leads to illogical thinking when the noun-subject refers to a fairly high-level abstraction rather than to a physical object which is capable of acting. For example, if a speaker begins a sentence with the complex noun-subject "The unconscious mind," it is customary to continue with a verb — "The unconscious mind influences dreams" — so that the speaker is put in the position of ascribing a capacity for action to something which has no real physical properties or existence. Word order is thus another way in which thinking is influenced by the language conventions evoked by the culture.

Language may be considered a set of spoken and/or written symbols used according to a set of rules; both the symbols and the rules are related to characteristics of the culture in which they developed. Thinking is largely the implicit production of such symbols (or the covert process which symbolizes verbal symbols); it therefore is influenced inevitably by the nature of the verbal symbols available and the rules for their use which the individual has learned.

Problem-solving. Verbal thinking is particularly involved in planning, introspective analysis, creative efforts — that is, in those kinds of thinking in which the solution of a problem is a goal. One can manipulate words without manipulating the objects and events for which they stand. In this way one can avoid the effort of overt trial and the possible pain of error. One says words to himself, responds to these words with more words, and so entertains a series of thoughts. The initial stimulus for the first thought of the series is some problem — that is, some motivational state for which the individual is seeking a response that will reduce the drive. When he produces chains of thinking according to the rules of language and logic he has learned, he may produce a thought which symbolizes a goal state or drive-reducing activity. The thinker has solved his problem and acts out the responses which the conclusion of his thought sequence has symbolized. If the acted out response does in fact reduce his drives, he is reinforced not only for the acted out responses, but also for the chain of thought which led up to or preceded the reinforced response. This process is what most people describe as "insight."

The acting out of the solution, or the making of the overt response, allows the thinker to check his thinking for accuracy or logicality; if the overt response does indeed lead to reinforcement, the logic involved in the thinking is more likely to be correct and is itself reinforced. Thus realistic and accurate thinking tends to be reinforced. This process is analogous to conscious scientific investigation, in which the scientist checks the conclusions of his deductions by making a prediction of events based on his logic, and then checks the accuracy of his prediction. If his predictions are accurate, then the logic he has used also has been reinforced. In this sense, the thinking man is behaving in the same way as the scientist.

Thinking of this kind can vary along the dimension of contact with reality. That is, it may be more or less realistic. When it is habitually unrealistic, the individual is said to have poor reality contact.

Fantasy. Thinking which usually is not considered to be directly problem-solving — such as day-dreaming, fantasizing, night dreams, and "wool-gathering"—may differ from concentrated effort only in the extent to which the thinker's thought sequences are directed by the rules of logic he has acquired. These thoughts also are motivated by some drive state. Even in the most relaxed circumstances they are influenced by any residual unsatisfied drive state. In fact, many creative thinkers have stated that insights, meaning problem-solutions, have occurred to them while they were engaged in such informal thinking.[21] Ordinarily, however, the fantasizer suspends his logic, or proceeds from assumptions he knows to be incorrect (although they might be possible if he were someone or somewhere else), in order to create thoughts which please him even though he cannot act out the conclusions of these thoughts. Some people even engage in the more restricted problem-solving thinking described in the preceding paragraph when they have no intention of acting out their problem solutions. They simply enjoy thinking, and may engage in hobbies and games which will present problems for analysis. The enjoyment of thinking is part of the enjoyment chess players receive from the game. However, an important question about such thinking, in which no effort is made to act out a problem solution overtly, and in which thoughts are produced simply because they are pleasing, is the source and nature of the reinforcement implied by the word "pleasing."

Gratification Through Fantasy. What is satisfying to the hungry man when he dreams about food, to the sexually frustrated man when he imagines a beautiful nude girl, or to the poor and unattractive girl when she daydreams about being a lovely princess? Several sources of reinforcement may be hypothesized. Because the sight and thought of food has occurred frequently in close proximity to the actual ingestion of food when one is hungry, these cues and their associated images may have acquired secondary reinforcing properties. Thus, even when food is not available, the image and thought of food provides some reinforcement to the hungry man, thus producing some feelings of satisfaction and also increasing the frequency of the reinforced fantasizing. Because such sights and thoughts usually precede the actual eating, they also serve as cues for the eating responses associated with them. In the hungry man who has no food available, his secondarily reinforcing fantasy also will act, therefore, as cues for the eating responses he cannot make. Thus he may experience an increased desire or appetite for eating, or an increased readiness to eat, which, added to the already present hunger drive, may be experienced as very frustrating. Perhaps that is why fantasies about unavailable goal objects or activities tend to be both pleasing and upsetting. Because the upset (punishment) follows the pleasure (reward), there is usually a tendency for the deprived person to be alternately attracted and intrigued by thoughts of food, and then repelled by them; the fantasy then ceases temporarily. However, because the cues of the hunger drive usually have been followed by the responses of eating and viewing and thinking of food, these cues will tend to elicit the viewing (in imagination) and the thinking again, even though eating is impossible. Thus the sequence of fantasizing and then stopping the fantasy tends to be repeated.

The situation with drives not produced by need states appears to be somewhat more complicated. If cues arising from a competitive achievement situation are presented to a person in whose past experience such cues have been associated with a drive state, he will tend to respond to the presented cues in a motivated manner. If this response is one of fantasizing in which the high-achievement oriented person produces thoughts about meeting the challenge and winning success, and if he produces such thoughts strongly enough, he will be producing cues or stimuli which compete with those external ones which elicited the fantasy and the drive. These competing fantasy cues may so occupy his thoughts that he responds to them more strongly than to the external arousing cues. In this fantasy, he removes the cues which elicited the drive state—he meets the challenge, or achieves successfully—thus reducing the drive state. This reduction in the drive state may be experienced as satisfying, and the reduction will reinforce the fantasizing of successful achievement.

Fear-Reduction in Fantasy. Fantasy often is reinforced by a reduction in anxiety or fear. Fear elicited by some event in the person's environment may be reduced by creating thoughts which compete with the environmental stimuli for his attention. By thinking such competing thoughts, the individual produces cues which elicit responses incompatible with the fear. If he produces enough such internal cues, the fear response will be dominated by the competing responses and thus will be diminished. In this way the production of cues in fantasy reduces a fear drive, and the fantasy as a response to fear cues is reinforced. Teachers often observe this process. A child called on in class to answer a question may experience fear when he cannot give an adequate answer. If the teacher tells him to sit down in a rejecting tone, thus adding to the fear, the child is likely to begin to daydream, appearing lost in thought for a while. When the daydream reduces the fear sufficiently, and the fear-evoking cues in the environment have disappeared (the teacher leaves the room or engages in some activity which is not threatening to the student), he may "snap out of it." But meanwhile, the daydreaming has been reinforced, and while engaged in it the student has missed even more of what the teacher has been teaching, further increasing the probability that when called on again, he will not know the answer, fear will be aroused, and daydreaming again occurs. This is another example of the spiraling effect of overlearning discussed in Chapter 3. Many teachers are aware of this kind of process and are on guard against behaving in any way which will evoke fear or discomfort in their students.

If we compare fantasy with problem-solving we find that in fantasy the images produced reduce drives directly, while in problem-solving they lead to acting out a solution, which in turn can reduce the individual's drive. Acting out provides the possibility of reality-testing, a possibility not available in fantasizing.

Fantasy As Wish-Fulfillment. It is important to note that in order for such fantasy to be anxiety drive-reducing, it must involve cues which elicit responses that are incompatible with fear. Hence such fantasies tend to be pleasant and opposite in character to the situation which stimulates them. The plain looking girl must produce fantasies which will compete with her anxiety responses to thoughts of her homeliness. Thus she daydreams about being a princess or a movie star. The failing student daydreams of some great success, in or out of school. Such compensatory fantasies therefore tend to imply their opposites as eliciting conditions. When you encounter a fantasy concerning great wealth, you can guess that the fantasizer is upset by fear elicited by cues of not having enough money. It is in this sense that such fantasy involves a wish-fulfillment.

A variety of such compensatory fantasy is known as *restitutive.* In restitutive fantasy, the person imagines some goal object which is not present in the environment; the fantasy thus serves as a replacement for the absent real object.[22] The lonely child imagines his parents when they are away from him. Of course, such fantasy requires that the person already has had some experience in which the hallucinated or imagined object has functioned to reduce his drive state.

Drive-Reduction Through Fantasy. These uses of thought are examples of an important point made earlier in this text: drives may be reduced without needs necessarily being satisfied. Imagining food when hungry produces a temporary reduction in drive, and is thus reinforcing, even though no food is ingested. Similarly, imagining that one has had some remarkable achievement is reinforcing, even though the thoughts or feelings of failure which cued off the fantasy may persist when the fantasy ends, and the cues that stimulated the achievement drive remain in the environment. That fantasy reduces drives was illustrated by a study in which some subjects were asked to fantasize (make up imaginative stories) after the experimenter aroused their aggression.[23] Other subjects were given some task to do which made it difficult for them to spend much time in fantasizing after the aggression-arousing experience. Then all the subjects were given tests designed to measure how aggressive the subjects were as a result of the aggression-provocation the experimenter had produced. It was found that subjects who had been permitted and encouraged to engage in fantasy, much of which was concerned with aggression, were less aggressive afterward than those subjects who had not engaged in fantasy. Thus it appears that the fantasy served to reduce agressive drives.

The Effects of Fantasizing. Occasionally such fantasizing may result in the production of thoughts which, if acted out, would produce effective solutions to the motivating problems, as noted earlier.[24] Further, such thinking enables one to brook necessary delays in reaching goals and allows one to find some satisfaction even when frustration of a drive is inevitable, necessary, or impossible to remove. On the other hand, such fantasy often does not lead to realistic problem solutions, and because it is reinforced readily by the intrinsic reinforcement involved and because of certain social factors (the child who sits quietly in his seat in school, engaging in extensive daydreaming but not bothering the teacher or other students tends to be thought of by teachers as a "good" child and therefore rewarded), it can become habitual and overlearned. When such overlearning occurs, the individual may devote time to compensatory or restitutive fantasy in response to problems which he *could* solve, if he spent more time in problem-solving thinking and acting. Because of his extensive fantasizing, he does not solve them, and may even create more problems, further increasing the probability of engaging in fantasy. In this sense, fantasy may be an ineffective response to problems and may result in such extensive frustration and consequent imagining that the individual requires outside help in solving his problems and in responding to the external stimuli of reality.

Such fantasy tends not to result in problem solutions because the thinker may not be aware that a problem exists, or being aware of the problem, feels that it is unsolvable at the moment and engages in fantasy simply because of the intrinsic reinforcements involved. He does not intend to search for a solution which can be acted out. If he is not going to act out a solution, there is no need for him to follow logical rules in his thinking, or to base his fantasy on his knowledge of reality. He can begin by assuming that he is someone other than himself, or in a different place, or even in a different kind of world in which the usual relationships among people and events no longer obtain. This kind of fantasy does not need to be realistic, and so often is not (except in those cases of fantasizing for its intrinsic rewards in which the thinker adheres to a set of rules, as in playing chess and other such games of strategy. Here the thinker obtains enjoyment through finding solutions to the problems presented in the course of the game, but he must test his thinking against reality by acting upon the products of his thoughts. If his action results in a victory, then his thinking has been realistic and logical, even though the "reality" of it was the make-believe reality of a game. "Pleasure" thinking such as this may be motivated by competitive drive or by needs for sensory stimulation or by a gregariousness drive to be with another person).

Another reason that compensatory and restitutive fantasy often is unrealistic is that it is carried on largely through nonverbal, or imagistic thinking. Verbal reasoning and thinking tend to be logical, partly because of the structure and functions of language, and partly because the learning of language is usually accompanied by training to be logical. But imagistic fantasy can and does occur even before a child has learned to speak or use verbal symbols. Thus the imagistic thoughts available for use in fantasy are often infantile, because it was in infancy and childhood that such fantasies occurred most frequently and became established. Such infantile imaginings are illogical and unrealistic simply because the young child has had too little experience with the environment to make his fantasy logical and realistic.[25]

The illogicality of non-problem-solving fantasy is probably one of the reasons that people frequently are resistant to revealing their fantasies to others. It should be mentioned here that when such fantasizing becomes overlearned, the fantasizer may get more practice at it and reward for illogical and unrealistic thinking than he does for problem-solving thinking. As a result of this kind of development, illogical thinking may become habitual and the thinker no longer able to respond adequately to reality. Much more will be said about this later, in our discussion of delusional thinking and psychotic personality patterns.

Even though such thinking may be unrealistic, it is, nevertheless, motivated, and the content of the fantasy often may reveal something of the nature of the motivation which produced it. This is true whether or not the individual is aware of the nature of his drives. As far as he is concerned, he may simply be "wool-gathering" to fill up some idle moments, but even this "sensory stimulation" fantasy will include thoughts and images associated with or elicited by residual unsatisfied drives. Thus motives influence the content of even apparently "purposeless" fantasizing.

Fantasy and Problem-Solving Related. We have been dealing with problem-solving thinking and fantasizing as if they were different kinds of things. In fact, however, in each kind there is some of the other. We have already noted that fantasizing can produce problem-solutions. It is also true that motives in the problem-solving thinker that are not related directly to the problem can influence the kind of solution found or preferred. For example, a literary critic may be trying to solve a problem in the interpretation of a particular work, but if he has strong competitive or hostile drives, he may prefer an interpretation directly opposite to the one offered by some authority in the field. His own drives thus influence the course of a problem-solving effort, even though those drives might have no intrinsic connection with the literary problem.

Regression in the Service of the Ego. Fantasy and problem-solving thinking are related in another way, through their participation in creative thinking. It already has been noted that many creative problem solutions occur during fantasy. This is because creativity requires untraditional thinking. It was indicated earlier that invention and novelty come about through the making of connections between responses and ideas that are not usually associated.[26] Imaginative thinking or fantasy relaxes the constricting forces of traditional logical thinking, making it possible for new and distant associations to be made freely. Because fantasy is imagistic, deriving from a mode of thought developed earlier in life than logical thinking, a regression to this earlier mode encourages the finding of creative solutions.[27] The ability to allow oneself to regress in thinking, to relax the hold of logical, realistic, and conventional thinking, therefore, has been proposed as an important element in creativity. This process is referred to as *regression in the service of the ego,* meaning that the thinker allows himself to regress in order to eventually come up with a uniquely effective solution to a problem.[28] Of course, a creative solution depends on more than regression; it requires the presence of the latent ideas whose associations produce the solution and the ability to recognize a good solution (the ability to recognize problem solutions in the fantasy contents and to think logically about possible solutions so that the reinforcement potentials of various ideas can be evaluated).

How Motives Are Inferred from Fantasy. The determining nature of motives in fantasy is responsible for the development of dream analysis and personality tests (the "projective" techniques) which require subjects to fantasize, or create imaginative productions, in order to reveal their needs or motives as these influence their imaginative thought. It has been shown, for example, that subjects under a hunger drive increase the number of references to food in imaginative stories which they create as the hunger drive increases.[29,30] Similarly, as the desire for achievement increases, there is an increase in the frequency of achievement imagery or themes in the stories subjects tell.[31] The same is true of thirst, sex, aggression, affiliation, and other drives or motives. This fact is also the basis for a great deal of the activity of literary critics, who infer from an author's work many of the author's motives. Just as the thinking man is behaving very much like a scientist, so the fantasizing man is behaving much like the author or playwright. And just as people tend not to be aware of the ways in which their drives are influencing their fantasies, so writers are frequently unaware of the motives implicit in their work. That is why it is often of little value to compare an expert's interpretation of a literary work with the author's own statement or interpretations. The author, being unaware of his own motives, may frequently be in error when the expert is not.

How such interpretation of motives is permitted by fantasy productions is illustrated by the following stories told in response to a Thematic Apperception Test picture of a boy sitting before a table on which a violin rests.[32] He has his head resting on his hand, and is gazing at the violin.

1. "This boy was given a violin by his parents. He takes lessons on the violin every day, but hates it. Right now he is sitting there thinking about the other kids outside playing baseball, and wishing that he could be out playing also. He is trying to think of a way out of having to practice. Pretty soon he works out a plan. He breaks one of the strings, and tells his mother that he can't practice because of the broken string. So she lets him go out and play baseball with the other kids."

2. "This boy is dreaming of someday becoming a famous violinist. He has been practicing on the violin for the past hour and got a little tired and so is resting. While he rests, he is imagining himself some day in the future as a famous violinist who can create all kinds of wonderful music with his instrument. He's dreaming of giving a concert in Carnegie Hall, and of the great ovation he receives at the end of it."

Figure 8. Thematic Apperception Test Picture

This is Card 12F from Henry A. Murray's *Thematic Apperception Test.**

*Reprinted by permission of the publishers from Henry A. Murray THEMATIC APPERCEPTION TEST. Cambridge, Mass.: Harvard University Press, Copyright, 1943, by The President and Fellows of Harvard College.

There are obvious differences between the two boys who told these stories. Which one has the higher achievement drive? Which one is more likely to be resistant to further testing (a task he will perceive as imposed on him by the authoritarian psychologist)? Which author is more likely to work hard to achieve his goals? Which one is more likely to be resistant to his parents and to others in authority? Which one is more likely to doubt his personal power or skill?

One can see readily from these two examples that motives can be inferred from fantasy productions, and also dominant response patterns or the response tendencies (habits) learned in relation to those motives.[33]

Dreams. Another problem arises in considering non-problem-solving fantasy. In night dreams, or in other such fantasies which occur when the thinker is in some state which reduces the level of cortical functioning — as in sleep, general anesthesia, or intoxication — the thinker does not or cannot impose control over his associations in order to make them logical and coherent. His thoughts may be composed largely of images (perhaps because of a temporary suspension or disruption of activity in those parts of the cortex through which verbal behavior is mediated) which have not been subjected to the kind of learning of logical coherence which characterizes verbal behavior. Dream images therefore are quite illogical. There is no grammar or syntax of visual images. In such a situation, the dream images may reflect quite directly the dreamer's motivations and desires. The complication is that if such motivations or dreamed activities are unacceptable to the dreamer, in the sense that they may be stimuli for anxiety or fear, a process may take place in which the dream occurs in a symbolized rather than more direct manner. That is, the dreamer may have images, not of the feared objects themselves, but of other objects associated in some ways with the feared objects, and which for the dreamer are substitutes (symbols) for the feared object or activity. Such symbolization or substitution probably obeys the laws of stimulus generalization presented earlier. In this way the dreamer may dream of subjects intimately concerned with his most important and powerful fears, anxieties, and hidden desires, but in such a way that he does not respond with the anxiety he ordinarily would. If this anxiety occurred, the dreamer would awaken, because anxiety has an arousing effect which is incompatible with sleep, and awakening is a way of stopping the unpleasant and anxiety-arousing thoughts. Freud proposed that the function of dreaming was therefore to preserve sleep, in this way helping to satisfy a need of the body. Studies on dreaming provide some support for this interpretation. It has been found that when subjects are dreaming, as shown by an electroencephalographic recording of brain activity, it takes a louder sound to awaken them than when they are not dreaming.[34]

Dreaming preserves sleep in other ways, also. The presence of a dream may operate to focus the sleeper's attention on internal events — the dream elements — so that he does not attend to environmental events — sounds, lights, and other disturbances — which might otherwise awaken him. Often these potential disturbers become woven into the fabric of the dream and are reinterpreted in the dream so that the sleeper does not have to awaken. The ringing of the alarm clock may become part of a dream about fire engines, and someone knocking on the door may become part of a dream about hammering nails into wood. Several studies have shown that when stimulation is applied to sleeping subjects, the subjects have dreams containing similar stimuli. When the beds in which the subjects slept were rocked, the subjects reported dreams of sailboating, horseback riding, and the like.[35]

Of course, the dreamer does not realize that he is dreaming of important matters in disguised or symbolic form; if he did translate the symbols into the objects and events for which they stand, he would necessarily be thinking of such objects and events, and would respond to such thoughts with the anxiety and fear associated with them. Anxiety and fear can only be avoided by not making the translation from symbol to referent. This process is even more complicated by the fact that when reporting dreams, people must do it verbally, and usually when they are conscious — that is, when their production of words and other symbols is greatly influenced by the learned rules of logic and coherence. What may come out, then, is a more logical and realistic version or description of the dream, further disguising what is already a highly symbolized event.

Symbolizing occurs not only in night dreams, but also in daydreams and other waking fantasy, and works in essentially the same manner. An experiment on sexual arousal showed that when an unacceptable drive is aroused, ideas associated with the drive are expressed symbolically rather than directly.[36] In the experiment sexual drives were aroused by showing pin-up pictures to a group of college men, and fantasy was elicited by asking the subjects to make up stories about other pictures shown to them. When the sexual drive was aroused, there was a reduction in overt sexual references in the stories told, and an increase in symbolic sexual references. In another part of the experiment the same procedures were repeated at a party with subjects who consumed alcohol. Since alcohol lowers inhibitions such as those produced by anxiety and fear, it would be expected that in the inebriated condition there would be a reduction in symbolism and an increase in direct sexual references. This is just what was found. This study confirms the idea that symbolizing is a response to the inhibitions by anxiety which occur when drives that have been punished in the past are aroused.

Manifest and Latent Content. We are indebted to Freud for discovering the symbolic meaningfulness of dreams (although even Aristotle recognized that people dream of things which, when conscious, would involve totally unacceptable thoughts). Freud described dreams as consisting of a *manifest* content and a *latent* content.[37] The manifest content includes the objects and events actually thought about. It is what one would tell about if he were willing to relate his dreams to another person (although, as pointed out above, his retelling would probably involve some distortion of the manifest content, as he strives to tell it logically and coherently).

The manifest content of dreams is usually made up of symbols (verbal thoughts and images) representing recent events, experiences, and thoughts. They also may be the dreamer's reactions to stimuli impinging on his senses as he sleeps (as in the experiment in which there were reports of dreams about horse-back riding, sailing, or automobile driving when the beds in which the dreamers lay were given an undulating motion).

But of all the thoughts and experiences one has during the day, why does one dream about a particular event? One answer is that a person dreams about only those events which are in some way important to him. They may be important because they are cues related to an unsolved problem, or which elicit some response the person has been unable to perform overtly — as when he dreams about what he would have liked to say to his boss when he was bawled out for making an error, or as he does when he is looking forward to going to a party and can hardly wait for the big evening to arrive. In such cases, one is likely to dream directly about the events which stimulated the dream. In these dreams, the manifest content is close to the latent content of the dream.

Sometimes, however, the things one dreams about are important or significant because they remind him of or are cues for thoughts or responses which are highly motivated, but which have been punished in the past and so elicit fear responses when they occur. The fear is reduced by not symbolizing the thought which would elicit it — that is, by not thinking it. But the memory of the event with which the feared thought was associated remains. In this case, the feared thought is said to be unconscious. The individual does not remark upon the significance or meaning of the event or experience which has taken place, because to do so would cue off his fear and anxiety. But when he goes to sleep, he dreams about these events. The drive which lies behind the feared thought is still present, resulting in the feared responses being made in the dream. These responses may be made in a direct manner, or, as indicated earlier, they may be symbolized. Thus the dreamer produces fantasies about what appear to be passing and insignificant incidents which have occurred in the waking state, but these dreams are really the result of unconscious, anxiety-arousing thoughts and responses elicited by such incidents. In this sense, the dreamer could be said to be really dreaming about his unconscious responses. These responses are what Freud called the latent content of the dream — the meaning expressed through the things the person dreams about (the manifest content). The manifest content could be thought of as symbolic of the latent content, and it is because of the latent content that the particular events and experiences which occupy the dream are selected for dreaming about from the many events which occur to the individual during his lifetime. Thus highly symbolized or seemingly unimportant dreams often imply anxiety or fear, and the interpretation of such dreams frequently is in terms of sexual and/or aggressive themes. These are the drives which are, in our society, most likely to have been punished, and so elicit fear, and thus be reserved for dreaming in symbolic form. It is in this sense that dreaming protects or preserves sleep, as Freud suggested. If the dreams were not symbolized, and the dreamer responded with anxiety, the anxiety might become so great that the dreamer would awaken.

There may be another reason for the symbolic content of dreams. Many motives are so poorly discriminated that the person cannot directly react to them. However, external events may occur which "match" the person's feeling or symbolize it so well that these events or the visual image of them come to stand for the person's feelings in much the same way as words might. This is particularly likely to happen in connection with feelings or drives developed in childhood, before verbal skills in labeling experiences were developed. The child then symbolizes his experiences through visual images of the events which stimulated his feelings. Later dreams in adulthood may be composed of childhood images which have these meanings, although images also may be derived in this way in adulthood. Adult dream contents may then be very much like the visual symbols of complex or ambiguous ideas used by artists when descriptive language is inadequate to symbolize fully the feelings involved.

It is important to note that symbolization does not necessarily occur in all dreams. As noted above, many dreams are the result of strong anticipations or frustrations (blocking) of responses, not because they arouse anxiety, but because circumstances did not permit their occurrence. While these dreams are wish-fulfilling like compensatory fantasy, they are not symbolic — their latent meaning is the same as their manifest content. In fact, highly symbolic dreams seem to be relatively rare. Experimenters have tried to explore dream symbolism by hypnotizing subjects and telling them, under hypnosis, to dream about certain experiences which the experimenter thinks should elicit fear in the subjects.[38] Although some experimenters report symbolic dreams in response to this procedure, others report that most often their subjects dream directly and in an undisguised fashion about the feared experience. This suggests that the fear associated with such experiences simply may not be as strong a motivating force as once was thought. Many people do not symbolize their dream expressions of sexual drives, for example, simply because the expression of such drives is not fear-arousing enough to them to inhibit their direct expression.

People frequently remember their dreams for only a short period of time after awakening. Just why this is so is not known. It may be that as a result of sleep, there is a reduction of cortical functioning to such an extent that the dream events do not produce or leave enduring traces. Another possibility, which may interact with this, is that if the dream events are even mildly anxiety-arousing, the person fails to think about them during the waking state in order to avoid the anxiety; he does not rehearse or practice the verbal responses by means of which he thinks about the dream, and so is not able to recall the dream (make verbal responses describing it).

It thus appears that a large portion of a person's thinking is motivated, and its content is related to the kind of motives present in the person. This is true even for "irrelevant" thoughts, sudden ideas that seem to pop up from nowhere and seem to have no relationship to anything else that is going on, and "errors" in thought, such as "unintended" word substitutions, slips of the tongue, and the like. Freud analyzed many examples of these phenomena and showed convincingly that when a man "accidentally" refers to his wife as his "louse" rather than "spouse," it is because this word substitution is motivated by hostility toward the wife.[39] Such interruptions in speech or thought are often the result of sudden increases in drive, perhaps stimulated by cues in the environment and from the body, as in the example cited earlier of the thoughts which occurred to the old man in *The Old Man and the Sea*. The person who is not aware of the drive that was aroused thinks of the thought or idea that popped up as irrelevant and without any connection with himself, and without any real meaning. It is said to be *ego-dystonic* (not a part of the person's usual way of thinking about himself and others). Despite this feeling that the slip or interruption is just accident or chance, motivational determination of the thought is still present.

   Thinking for Its Own Sake. So far we have been talking about thinking as a motivated activity. However, we have also made reference to thinking for its own sake, as in people who enjoy playing a game of chess (even with themselves), where the only gratification involved seems to be the enjoyment the person gets from the act of thinking. Until very recently it was theorized that there is no such thing as thinking for its own sake. The general idea was that all thinking is motivated by some drive in the person which accounts for the existence of the thoughts and their contents. These drives might be primary, such as hunger or sex, or learned, such as achievement, fear, or dependency. However, the recent work on the reticular arousal system and the "reaching out" drives of curiosity, sensory stimulation, and activity, has called the earlier theory into question. Many theorists now accept the idea that there is a need for cortical activity — for thinking *per se* — even when appetitive drives all have been reduced. It has been suggested the the reticular arousal system activates the cortex, producing thoughts and actions, and that this arousal system can operate whether or not other need states are present. When the arousal system operates the individual looks around for objects and events in the environment about which to think or to act upon. If no such objects are present the cortex may show random firing, producing random thoughts, memories, and ideas. In one study subjects' visual fields were reduced to an even white light without features, similar to the "white-outs" experienced by pilots when flying through clouds. In a "white-out" the pilot loses his sense of bodily position and orientation and becomes quite confused. In the experiment in which these white-outs were produced artificially, it was found that some subjects began to report hallucinations, loss of orientation of their bodies in space, and general confusion. It was discovered that when this happened, there was an increase in the electrical activity in the part of the cortex which is the center for visual reception.[40] We already have described similar experiences of subjects in sensory deprivation experiments, which indicate that even when the environment does not provide stimulation for the cortex, the cortex will still be active.

Finally, recent work on dream deprivation indicates that there is some kind of strong need to dream. If subjects are awakened when their brain wave patterns indicate the start of a dream, they tend to begin dreaming again shortly after they are allowed to go back to sleep. If the experimenter continues to awaken them before they dream, he finds that the subjects begin dreaming sooner and sooner after falling back asleep, to the point where the experimenter can hardly awaken the subjects fast enough to prevent dreaming. This research thus suggests a need to dream.[41] Very likely this is just one aspect of a general need for cortical activity, a need mediated by the reticular arousal system.

All of this work suggests that thinking can occur as its own gratification, or that the existence of thinking is a product of the physiological operation of the brain. A problem, or some unsatisfied appetitive drive does not seem to be necessary for thinking to occur. In short, one may think and dream simply for the sake of thinking, regardless of problem solutions, and without the thinking having to produce problem solutions or symbolic drive reductions. The stimulation for such thinking, coming from the arousal system, has been called "neutralized energy," in psychoanalytic theory, because it does not come from appetitive drives or problems.[42] In psychoanalytic theory, which refers to the apparatus of thought as the "ego," such thinking is said to involve ego energies, rather than energy produced by appetitive drives (which are called "libidinal energies"). Although libidinal energies may not be necessary for thought, which can provide its own satisfaction, this does not mean that thinking is unmotivated. It is a product of man's biological structure, and is produced by neural events in the brain. There is a physiological base for thought just as there is for hunger and thirst. Man is built in such a way that he must think, just as he must also eat and drink.

It should also be kept in mind that the appetitive drives can stimulate the arousal system and lead to thoughts and fantasies, and further, that the *content* of the thoughts and fantasies stimulated by the arousal system is determined by past learnings in connection with whatever drives or problems face the person. Given an innate need to think, even when the need is not a result of a state of hunger or thirst, one still must account for the nature of what the person thinks about. This content aspect of thought is still believed to be determined by the cortical traces of experiences associated with drives or problems that are operating in the person. The more that thought or fantasy is stimulated by libidinal drives, the more its content will be drive-related. This leaves the possibility that some thought, or some part of thought, is free of libidinal drives, conflicts, or internal problems in the person. Current psychoanalytic writers refer to this as the "conflict-free sphere of the ego."[43] But even here the use made of the conflict-free sphere — the way in which non-libidinally motivated thinking is done — whether it is through a chess game, solving crossword puzzles, doing abstract mathematical problems, or creating formal designs — depends on past experiences which taught one how to satisfy his needs for sensory stimulation and activity, and is therefore significant for personality.

Perception

When physical energies strike the sense organs, series and patterns of neural impulses are produced. When the sense organs respond, it is spoken of as a *sensation*. However, such sensations are not meaningful to the person who experiences them; the process or event which results in the interpretation or ascription of meaning to sensations is called *perception*. Perception refers to the interaction of a sensation with the residuals (traces) of past experience such that from his experience one is able to label or identify the sensations. Somehow or other, the neural impulses stimulated in the sense organs activate traces of past experience in the brain; the associations elicited by the sensations define its meaning (or the perception which occurs). The more associations stimulated by a sensory input, the greater the meaningfulness of the sensation.

Clyde Noble has used this principle in developing a measure of the meaningfulness of words.[44] He asks subjects to list all the words they think of when a stimulus word is presented. The more words subjects associate with the stimulus, the greater is the meaningfulness of the stimulus. In this sense, perception consists of responding to sensory neural impulses; one can know that a perception has occurred when the perceiver makes a response to the physical energy impinging on his sense organs.

We already have met the concept of threshold — the point above which a single neuron fires and below which it does not. There are also thresholds associated with more global responses, so that for example, the threshold of stimulation necessary to produce overt verbal responses is different from (and higher than) that necessary to produce an implicit one. One may mutter to oneself when he knocks his finger against an object accidentally, but he does not cry out, because the stimulus was not strong enough — was not above the threshold — for a crying-out response. It would require a stronger blow for the individual to shout with pain. Similarly, the threshold for autonomic responses to visual stimuli appear to be lower than the thresholds for verbal responses. In one study it was found that subjects showed a GSR reaction to visual stimuli (nonsense syllables which previously had been paired with electric shocks so that galvanic skin responses were conditioned to the visual stimuli) when the visual stimuli were presented at levels of illumination too low and exposure speeds too fast for the subjects to give correct verbal responses.[45, 46] Their autonomic nervous system responses occurred when the stimuli were below their thresholds for making verbal responses. These subjects, then, reacted emotionally to stimuli they could not correctly identify. This phenomenon has been called "subliminal perception," but that is a misnomer. The response which indicated that perception had occurred was the GSR, and obviously the stimuli were above the limen (threshold) for that response, although they were below the threshold for conscious recognition.

The term *perception,* therefore, is not reserved for use only with conscious recognition; it refers to any response which indicates that the organism has discriminated the stimulus from other possible stimuli. There are several possible reasons for the difference in thresholds between galvanic skin responses and verbal responses. It could be that verbal responses are not learned as well as autonomic ones, so are not as strong as GSRs, and therefore are not so readily elicited by stimuli. It also may be that the neural firings necessary for a verbal response may involve neurons and/or synaptic connections which natively have higher thresholds than those required for GSRs. The autonomic response is integrated below the cortex, while verbal responses depend on the cortex, and cortical functions generally have higher thresholds than those functions integrated at lower levels. Finally, it is possible that there may be some inhibition of verbal responses which is not present for GSRs. For example, in one study subjects were shown words on a screen at very rapid exposure speeds. Some of the words were socially unacceptable. It was found that subjects did not correctly report the obscene words as well as they did the nonobscene words which were also shown. The obscene words had to be shown at slower speeds than the others in order to be reported correctly by the subjects.[47] At first these results was interpreted to mean that the obscene words were "unconsciously" perceived by the subjects, and that because the words were socially unacceptable, the subjects responded to them with anxiety and "refused" to perceive them consciously in order to avoid the anxiety. This process was referred to as "perceptual defense." However, subsequent studies have shown that subjects who know in advance that there may be obscene words shown them are as readily able to report them as they are the neutral words.[48] It thus has been reasoned that in the original study the subjects seemed to have higher perceptual thresholds for the dirty words, not because they didn't "see" them, but because they inhibited their verbal responses to them, feeling that they must have been in error, that their college professor experimenter simply *couldn't* have used the word they thought they saw, and they'd make fools of themselves if they said such a word aloud. Thus they waited until the exposure time on such words was lengthened to the point where they were dead certain of the word, before making such an error. This interpretation suggests, then, that the differences in thresholds for reporting "threat" and "neutral" words was not a result of perceptual defense (not seeing in order to avoid anxiety) but rather was a result of the suppression or inhibition of certain verbal responses. An accurate verbal report might not be given because it serves as a cue for fear which can be avoided by not verbalizing. Of course, in such studies there also is the problem that there may be differences in how well learned the threat and neutral words are, and therefore in how readily they will be given in response to stimuli.[49] As we have seen, the better learned a response, the lower the level of stimulation necessary to elicit it. It has been reasoned that words of equal frequency of usage should, on the average, be equally well learned, and so experimenters refer to the Thorndike-Lorge word list for lists of words of comparable frequency of usage in English.[50] However, even this is not satisfactory for use in obscene-word studies, because the Thorndike-Lorge list is based on frequency of use in written documents, and it seems likely that obscene words tend to be used orally to a much greater extent than they are in writing.

However, regardless of one's interpretation of these kinds of data, one may conclude that people can react emotionally to stimuli whose presence they are unable to report verbally — to stimuli of which they are not consciously aware, and that these differences in perception may be the result of differences in thresholds of the different response systems, and/or differences in the strength of the perceptual responses involved, and/or differences in inhibition of responses. A very clear example of this may be seen in a study in which subjects were shown pictures projected on a screen and asked to make up stories about the pictures. While the pictures were being shown, another projector flashed a word on the screen with the picture, but at an exposure speed too fast for the subjects even to know that a word was there. However, the stories made up by the subjects were influenced by the words. Subjects wrote stories with positive emotional tones when words like "happy" were flashed, but they wrote stories with unpleasant themes when words like "failure" and "cry" were used.[51]

Perception As Labeling. The process of conscious perceiving — of classifying, categorizing, or associating to a stimulus — is largely one of giving verbal responses to the neural impulses propagated by a stimulus, or of applying verbal labels to the stimuli. One can see here the close connection between thinking and perceiving: both are largely verbal. In effect, when a sensation occurs, the individual searches around in his past experiences for the verbal label he has affixed success-fully to similar patterns of stimulation. Like other responses, such verbal labels exist in a hierarchy. And as before, the order of responses in the hierarchy is determined by past learning, so that what one has expe-rienced or perceived (i.e., labeled) most frequently in the past will provide the most ready label for a new stimulation.

In this sense the process of perceiving is like the operation of an electronic computer. Coded impulses are sent into the machine (like neural impulses). In order to "perceive" these impulses, the machine must have a program, or a built-in template, with which the impulse patterns may be compared; when they match one of the built-in tem-plates, one may say that the input pattern has then been identified or "perceived," and the machine then responds through the electrical con-nections activated by the "perceiving" template. One could think of these templates as being analogous to the verbal response hierarchy in people. Thus perceiving may be thought of as a process in which sensory impulses are "matched" with the traces of learned verbal labels, to each of which verbal labels a different set of behavioral re-sponses have been attached through learning.[52]

Both machines and people scan the inputs in order to match them with their templates. People do this because a good match leads to rewards when the person finds the objects he needs to reduce his drive.

If he did not seek for a good match, he would be trying to use objects inappropriately, and so would not find drive reduction. A wax fruit may be misperceived to be real, but it cannot satisfy hunger.

In the machine, the templates and their connecting "action systems" are built in through arrangement of electronic components; in humans they are acquired through learning what objects are associated with what drives. In machines, the order in which the templates are compared with the input impulse pattern is predetermined and established. However, in people the order of responses in the response hierarchy is constantly changing as drives change. When the match between a pattern of neural impulses and the trace of a past experience (the template) is perfect, the stimulus is perceived correctly. If the pattern of impulses is somewhat different from all the templates, which template is activated by it will depend on which templates are first presented for comparison, and how similar to the impulse patterns the templates are. This is true for certain computers and may also describe the operation of that natural computer, the brain. The perceptual response made to a totally new stimulus will be the one of those high in the response hierarchy whose neural trace is most like the new stimulus pattern.

Set in Perception. As we have seen before, instructions (both explicit and implied) operate to limit the hierarchy of responses available to the perceiver. In this way situations (with their implied instructions) produce a "set" or readiness to perceive.[53] How this operated in "threat" words has already been described. When the subjects were told in advance that they could expect obscene words, the effect was to rearrange their response hierarchies so that words which ordinarily would be quite low in the hierarchies, considering the nature of the experimental situation, were made more available to the subjects, thus lowering the thresholds for their recognition. It should be mentioned that in the experiment in which subjects were instructed in advance about the nature of the words they could expect, the threshold for the "threat" words actually dropped below that for "neutral" words. They were more readily able to perceive or verbally recognize the "threat" words than the "neutral" words. This also shows the influence of availability of responses in the response hierarchy; knowing that they were going to see obscene words, the subjects were ready to interpret each stimulus as one of a relatively small class of words —those they think of as obscene. Thus the stimulus may be one of only fifteen or twenty possible words in the subject's response hierarchy. But each "neutral" word, being one of several thousand possible "neutral" words, has a much larger response hierarchy that must be searched for the stimulus to be identified, and so such words require longer exposure times for recognition than do the "threat" words, when the subjects have warning about the kind of words being used.

Drives in Perception. Just as instructions produce such a set or readiness to respond, so do drives. When an individual is hungry, the responses associated with eating tend to be high in the response hierarchy, because some of the cues to which these responses are attached — those arising from the drive state itself — are already present and tend to elicit the drive-related responses. The presence of a drive has a similar effect on perceptual readiness; one is more likely to perceive or respond to stimuli having reference to the drive which is present than to others which are not related to the drive, all things being equal (that is, the strength of the drive-related and the non-drive-related stimuli are equal).

The relationship between drive and perception is well illustrated in a famous study.[54] The experimenter measured the values or interests (the kinds of things which motivated them, or were associated with their motives) of subjects by means of the Allport-Vernon Study of Values, a test in which the subjects are asked to select activities they would like to engage in.[55] From the pattern of answers each subject makes, one can get scores showing the relative importance (or value) to the subject of several different kinds of activities: religion, science, business, social work, among others. A subject with a high score on theoretical and a low score on religious is one who is presumably more highly motivated to theorize than he is to attend church.

Next, a set of pictures of people engaging in various activities was gathered. The selected pictures related to each of the value areas measured by the Allport-Vernon test. A picture of a man looking at a test-tube, for example, was appropriate for scientific values. The subjects then were asked to look at the pictures as they were flashed on a screen at very rapid exposure speeds, and to tell the experimenter which ones they saw more clearly. It was found with this procedure that subjects with high values and motives in scientific activities reported seeing the scientific pictures clearly more frequently than did subjects whose values for science were low. The same was true for subjects with high values for other areas; in general, the subjects perceived most clearly pictures related to their chief values, and more infrequently those related to activities for which their values were low. In other words, they more readily perceived the stimuli related to their motives than those which were unrelated.

Perceptual Selectivity. In general, then, it may be said that selectivity in perception occurs, so that we do not perceive every stimulus which is presented to our senses. And it appears that the individual's drives are an important factor in determining the nature of his perceptual selectivity at any particular moment. How such selectivity operates physiologically has been suggested by a number of investigators who have been guided by the work of Donald O. Hebb. They point out that the reticular formation, a bundle of nerve cells deep within the brain, seems to operate as an arousal center. Sensory stimuli produce impulses which go to this center, which in turn sends impulses to the cortex. These impulses going to the cortex serve to alert or arouse the cortex; when the reticular formation is being stimulated, the brain waves in the cortex change from those characteristic of sleep to those usually present when the organism is awake and alert.

You may remember from Chapter 2 that this is how the effects of sensory deprivation are explained. When there are no sensory stimuli, the reticular formation does not send "alerting" impulses to the cortex. These theorists suggest that the presence of drives also arouses the reticular formation, which in turn alerts the cortex, or lowers response thresholds in the cortex so that in effect, a highly motivated organism, having lower perceptual response thresholds, perceives more rapidly than one which is not motivated. That may be why it is so difficult for one to fall asleep when he is worried, hungry, or suffering some other strong drive. In line with this theory, it was noted in the experiments on sensory deprivation that subjects frequently reported an inability to think, thus suggesting that without sensory stimulation, their cortexes were not operating at their usual level.

The cortical activity produced by drive-induced arousal alerts the organism to scan the environment for objects which will match the aroused neural circuits or templates. In this way one searches the environment for the thought-about goal objects of the drives which produced the arousal. The over-all effect is that one has an idea and searches the environment for objects that correspond to that idea, and which reduce the individual's drive states.

Sensory Gating. Although cortical arousal explains perceptual sensitivity under conditions of high drive, it does not account for the selective nature of such sensitivity; one is sensitive to the particular stimuli which have relevance to his drives. The concept of "sensory gating" (mentioned in Chapter 2) has been proposed to account for selectivity.

In computers, when the machine is busy reacting to some input signals, an electronic "gate" closes so that new input signals are held up in order to keep them from interfering with those still activating the machine. Similarly, it has been proposed, when a person is busy responding to a stimulus, some gating process occurs such that the individual does not perceive stimuli irrelevant to his drives. It also has been suggested that gating makes neurons resistant to firing.[56]

The process of perceiving, according to the gating theory, is as follows: (1) A strong drive lowers thresholds for giving learned responses to stimuli. This is the alert phase. (2) A stimulus related to his drives is presented to the alert organism, to which he gives a labeling response quite readily. He also will make other learned responses to the label which he has applied to the stimuli. (3) While he is doing this, the threshold for stimulation of neurons not being stimulated by the drive-relevant stimuli are raised, or "gated out." At this point, the organism is resistant to distraction. It is difficult to draw his attention away from the drive-relevant stimuli. When the gating mechanisms are closed, so that neural stimulation is difficult to produce, the individual's perceptions are narrowed or limited. Such narrowing is most apparent during sleep, in which the gating mechanisms are presumed to be maximally closed. Thus the sleeper is highly resistant to stimulation.

The nature of the gating mechanism also has been suggested. Bruner, who proposed the concept of gating, has pointed to research which may indicate that some very small neurons, whose functions have not yet been firmly established, are activated by the cortex and carry impulses to synapses. He has hypothesized that these neurons are the "gates" which we have been discussing. When they are firing as a result of stimulation in the cortex, they tend to raise the threshold of the synapse, so that neural impulses do not get passed along from one neuron to the next.[57] In a sense, the impulses coming into the synapse along the main neurons "die on the vine" as a result of the firing of the very small and heretofore mysterious neurons activated by the cortex. Thus the impulses are "gated out" and cannot produce a perception. This appears to be a reasonable hypothesis, in terms of what is now known, but the evidence for it is still quite scanty and so it is entertained only very tentatively.

It is also possible that selectivity occurs, because when drives are strong they produce many cues to which perceptual responses are attached. The person with strong drive may then need only very low level cues from the environment to have enough total cues present for the response to be elicited. Thus, the person with high drive is very sensitive to environmental cues that work in the same direction (elicit the same response) as the internal cues produced by his drives.

Drive, Set, and Practice Can Produce Misperceptions. An individual's drive state can be so strong that he may tend to misidentify stimuli in terms related to the nature of his drive. Generally speaking, the stronger the drive and the more ambiguous the stimulus, the greater the likelihood that the stimulus will elicit a response at the top of the hierarchy (the drive-relevant response), which will very often be an erroneous one. That is why errors and distortions in perception often reveal an individual's drives. An effect of drive on perception was demonstrated in an experiment in which two pictures of equal illumination, one of food and the other a landscape, were shown to hungry subjects. These subjects reported seeing the food picture more clearly and as being brighter than the other.[58] What they meant was that their responses to this picture were stronger than their responses to the other, because they were in a drive state which already tended to elicit the food-labeling or recognizing responses.

There is also some new evidence to indicate that when a person looks at an object related to his drives, there is an increase in the size of his pupils, which therefore admit more light to the retina. The effect is to make the drive-relevant object seem brighter than other, irrelevant objects.

Selectivity can also be observed in a study which found that psychotherapists who had certain kinds of personality problems tended either not to recognize (perceive) the same problems when they existed in their patients, or to perceive their patients as having the same problems even when the patients in fact did not have them.[59] Those therapists whose thinking about their problems produced fear and anxiety avoided such thoughts so as to reduce their anxiety drive. Therefore, their verbal labels for such problems were low in their response hierarchies, and were not ready for use or application to patients who presented stimuli which should have been so labeled. These therapists failed to perceive something that was there. The other therapists were those who did not react to their problems with such fear and anxiety, and so instead tended to think a great deal about them. For these therapists, the verbal labels with which to identify their difficulties were therefore high in their response hierarchies, having been well practiced, and so tended readily to be applied to the ambiguous stimuli produced by their patients, even when in error. It is because of the danger of this kind of perceptual error that it is important for psychotherapists to undergo therapy themselves, in order to solve their own personality problems.

Not only drives and "set," but also past practice has an effect on the order of responses in the response hierarchy, and therefore on perception. The effect of practice was demonstrated very neatly in an experiment in which two pictures were shown to subjects, one picture of a person in an aggressive act, and the other of a person in a nonaggressive act. The pictures were shown at the same time, one to the right eye only, and the other to the left eye, by means of a stereopticon. Binocular "rivalry" was produced by this arrangement, and the subjects were asked simply to describe what they saw. It was found in this study that detectives and criminal prisoners described the aggressive picture much more frequently than did college student subjects. The prisoners had the highest frequency of perceiving the aggressive act; presumably both aggressive drives and experience with aggression are high in this group. The detectives were next in frequency of seeing the aggressive picture; this group presumably does not have the aggressive drives of the criminals, but their experience with aggressive acts is probably greater. The college students, having neither high drive nor great experience, saw aggression least often.[60]

In practice, drive and experience usually work together. Recall the perception study that showed that people more readily perceive pictures related to their own interests or values. It might be argued that the people with strong interest in a particular occupational area have probably had more experience with that occupation, and so see more clearly those pictures which were about things with which they were familiar. It is obviously difficult to separate motives from set and from past practice. A person with strong dependency drive has probably had more experience or practice at behaving in a dependent fashion than one whose drive is low. The same is true for aggression and many other social drives. When selective perception occurs, it is therefore usually safe to infer the existence of both high drive and frequent past experience.

In sum, one can conclude that amount of past practice, the nature of one's current motives (particularly fear), and situational instructions (explicit or implied) interact among themselves and with the stimulus in determining a perception, the correctness of which depends on the relationship among the strengths of these various factors.

Perceptual Reality Testing. How then does one know if his perception is correct? Checking one's conclusions against those of others is at best a hazardous solution. Despite the old saying, forty million Frenchmen *can* be wrong. Bruner suggests that the answer is the same as that discussed in connection with thought: A perception involves a prediction; if this thing is what I think it is, then it should behave in thus and so a way, because that is the way such things have behaved in my experience in the past. If it does not so behave, then my perception or identification of the sensation may be in error. Just as one insures the accuracy of one's thinking by checking its results against reality, so one insures the accuracy of his perception by comparing its results with reality. This process is commonly known as "reality testing."

Accuracy of perception is thus not determined by simple agreement with everyone else (although many people use such a criterion, and so misperceive on occasion). Rather, one's apprehension of reality is correct because objects and events behave lawfully in relation to the individual's perceptions of them. Perceptual accuracy is, therefore, an individual matter, in which the person must rely on his own predictive processes to achieve accuracy, without regard to how others may be perceiving. Certainly, the extent of disagreement with others can often serve as a clue that one's perceptions may be in error, because most people's predictive processes are very much alike and yield the same results. But group consensus is not a final criterion.

Where motives are particularly strong because they have been frustrated for long periods of time, thus inclining one to inaccurate perceptions, and where reality testing has produced anxiety because it exposes the individual to cues which may stimulate fear responses (as is likely to be the case in a person who has been frustrated extensively), there may be a weakening of the habit of reality testing, which is reinforced by the avoidance of anxiety. Thus the person may come habitually to make erroneous perceptions and fail to discover his errors; more will be said of this later, in our discussion of delusions and hallucinations and other psychotic behaviors.

Some failures to perceive correctly may be ascribed to a failure to learn the appropriate verbal labels. A child tends to call all his mother's friends "Aunt" because he has not learned to discriminate between them and his parents' sisters. He does not learn to discriminate readily, because our language has no handy label to attach to one's mother's friends. One may therefore fail to perceive events or stimuli simply because one does not have a response to associate with the stimuli. This is particularly true for fears which are established in early childhood, before the child has learned sufficient words to label his experiences. As an adult he may experience nameless fears—that is, fears elicited by stimuli of which he is not aware, because the fear was learned in relation to stimuli for which he never learned a verbal label.

It is also possible for misperception to occur not as a result of a failure to learn the appropriate label, but rather as a result of inhibition of the labeling. If verbal labels are anxiety-arousing, they are not given in response to stimuli. We have seen one example of this in the study of therapists with personality problems. It is also frequently seen in patients in therapy, who seem to be unable to perceive relationships between their past experiences and their present problems (develop insight) which are quite obvious and transparent to the observer. The patient avoids identifying the relationship because the words involved would elicit anxiety, the reduction of which is possible only if the verbal responses are not made. Not producing the words is reinforced by anxiety-reduction, and so the words fail to be practiced, are low in the response hierarchy, and their production by the patient does not occur. He therefore fails to perceive a connection, to develop an insight, which others readily perceive. He sometimes uses alternative labels whose meanings are sufficiently different so that they do not evoke anxiety. One may describe his behavior as being "politely complimentary" rather than "lying" or "apple-polishing." Because the alternative words do not arouse anxiety, they are practiced more, and are thus higher in the response hierarchy. In these examples, it may be seen that anxiety drive influences perception in two ways: (1) by influencing practice, and therefore the position of the response in the response hierarchy, and (2) by punishing the response if it is made.[61]

Interpersonal Perception. The consequences of misperceiving are probably most important in interpersonal perception. When the stimuli are those arising from people, the chances of misperceiving are very great, and it is especially difficult to "check" such perceptions in order to correct them. Interpersonal stimuli tend to be misperceived for two reasons. First, they are quite ambiguous. An honest man doesn't behave too very differently from a dishonest one; a shy person behaves in ways similar to a guilty person, and a frightened person may act very much like an angry one. In other words, the cues are so similar that it is often difficult to discriminate among several human characteristics. The other reason is that most of our strongest motives relate to people, rather than objects. We have seen how motives influence perceptual responses;

the influence is likely to be greatest when the stimuli are those coming from people, because it is people who are most involved in satisfying our drives. An individual with a strong dependency drive is more likely to misperceive another person as a source of satisfaction of his drive than he is to misperceive inanimate objects in such a direction.

Such misperceptions are also very difficult to check, again because the stimuli of people are so ambiguous, and also because they present so many stimuli. If you perceive another person as vain, you can almost always find evidence to support your perception, by perceiving other aspects of his behavior in the same way. Where you decide that someone seems dishonest, you are very likely to perceive the rest of his behavior in the same terms. He is seen as crafty rather than reticent; his eyes are shifty rather than alert. And of course, if one labels another as dishonest, he will respond to the other in the ways he has learned to respond to dishonest people. This behavior is likely to affect the perceived person who may feel insulted and so act in an aggressive fashion, further confirming the perception of him as a bad person.

We have indicated earlier that correct perceiving is reinforcing, and now we have also said that incorrect perceiving may also be drive-reducing. But there is a difference between the two. Correct perceiving is drive-reducing because it brings the individual's drives into a relationship with reality such that the drive is reduced. Psychoanalytic theory labels such perceiving as "secondary process," which means that it is realistic. Incorrect perceiving is reinforcing because it avoids the unpleasantness of fear or anxiety in the course of which reality is violated. This kind of perceiving is similar to the psychoanalytic concept of "primary process," which means that thinking and perceiving is uninfluenced by external reality.[62]

Studying Personality Through Perception. As has been pointed out, perceptual habits are a product of learning; this is another way of saying that one's perceptions are related to his personality. A person's characteristic ways of perceiving other people are related to his own personality — to the drives and responses he has acquired. Put another way, what has been said in this chapter implies that an individual's personality is one of the important determinants of how he perceives and misperceives other people. In one study it was found that people with similar personality characteristics tend to perceive other people in similar ways, and that those with one set of characteristics perceive people differently from subjects with a different set. This was tested by categorizing a group of subjects on the basis of their answers to a personality test, and then having the subjects predict test responses of others, as a measure of the way they perceived the others.[63]

This same research also illustrates a principle mentioned above that it is difficult to correct one's interpersonal misperceptions. The subjects of the research were first asked to predict the test responses of another person whom they did not know; then they were introduced to another person and instructed to work with him at a puzzle task for an hour. After the hour, in which the subjects had an opportunity to get to know their partner, they were then asked to predict the partner's test responses. It was found that the predictions the subjects made this time were biased in the same way as they were before they met the people whom they were predicting. In fact, after meeting and working with their partners, the subject's predictions were even *more* biased, as if their contact with the partners further confirmed the pre-existing impressions, regardless of how much the partner was actually like the way the subjects perceived them.[64] This study therefore suggests that people have perceptual response tendencies about other people. They tend to perceive people in certain ways before they have actually met them. These ways are related to their own personalities, and people tend to confirm or become more sure of their interpersonal perceptions no matter how accurate they are, when they have an opportunity to check their perceptions against reality.

The influence of these variables of drive, practice, and readiness to respond on perception is used to advantage in some psychological tests in which ambiguous stimuli are presented to the subject, and his perceptions analyzed in order to discover his dominant motives and his customary habits in interpreting stimuli. From this information, the psychologist can frequently infer the kinds of experiences which the subject may have had to produce such motives and habits. The most famous test of this type is the Rorschach Test, which is made up of ambiguously shaped ink-blots.[65] Here are two responses given by two different people to the same ink-blot:

"This looks like a leering face — the face of a frightening ugly man."

"This looks like a happy cat — or maybe more like a kid's Halloween pumpkin at a party."

In which of these two people is a fear response higher in the response hierarchy? Which one is readier to interpret situations as dangerous? Which one has more likely experienced fear often in the past? Which is more playful? Which one has had more pleasant experiences with children? Which one is more likely to have had unpleasant experiences

Figure 9. A Card of the Rorschach Ink Blot Test

The text gives two responses to this blot.*

with his father? Which one is more likely to want the protection and comfort of other people?

Of course, none of these questions can be answered definitely on the basis of only one perception from each subject. That is why the questions were phrased as which is *more likely*. However, if, in a large number of perceptions, the same patterns appear, one can be more confident in his answers. Likelihood increases, the more consistent evidence one has.

Consciousness

When a person is attending to some particular stimulus (that is, responding to it) he may be unconscious of other stimuli present; that is, he makes no responses to other stimuli which are impinging on his sense organs. When reading an interesting book, one may ignore all the extraneous and irrelevant stimuli which are present — the pressure of the chair, the sounds of the street, of passing airplanes, of birds outside the window. One may become so engrossed that he may not even

*Reprinted by permission of the publishers from Hermann Rorschach PSYCHO-DIAGNOSTIK. Berne, Switzerland: Hans Huber Publishers, Copyright, 1942, by Hans Huber Publishers.

be aware of the contractions of his stomach resulting from hunger. It is only when he puts the book down that these stimuli may claim his attention. This capacity to ignore stimuli is an extremely important one for human behavior — it contributes to such varied behaviors as yogi, hysterical blindness, anesthesia, perseverence during stress and distraction, and is capitalized on in a number of ways. A physician may slap a child on the buttock just before giving him an injection, knowing that the pain of the slap will draw the child's attention away from the hypodermic needle, so that the injection may take place painlessly. Recently a technique for judging the interest-arousing capacity of motion pictures was developed in which recordings are made of the movements of the audience members in their seats as they watch the movie, by means of sensitive meters attached to the seats. This device is based on the idea that the more interesting the movie, the less the audience will respond to discomfitures of their seats, to muscle cramps, and to other extraneous stimuli, and so the less shifting of position in the seats will there be.

It would seem, therefore, that consciousness consists in making responses to stimuli. But what of responses of which the individual making them is unaware? One may put down an object while attending to something else, and not be "conscious" that he has done it. A college student may be awakened during the night by his roommate's return from a date, may hold a conversation for a few moments with the roommate, then fall back to sleep, and in the morning remember nothing at all about the conversation. Similarly, people have been known to respond to a ringing alarm clock by arising from bed, walking to the dresser on which the alarm clock sits, turning off the alarm, walking back to bed, climbing in again, adjusting the covers, and going back to sleep. The whole sequence of complicated events, involving quite effective goal-oriented behavior, may be completely unconscious by the time the sleeper awakens and wonders why the alarm clock did not go off and awaken him.

Unconsciousness. We have referred repeatedly to behavior which occurs without the behaving individual being aware of it. We have seen that galvanic skin responses can occur to stimuli which are at levels of illumination too low for correct verbal report, and have described this as unconscious perception. We have noted that many responses — particularly overlearned ones — can occur in the absence of thought and planning, and these responses are called unconscious. It has also been indicated that people may avoid attaching verbal labels to fairly obvious stimuli in avoiding anxiety, and so may be said to be unconscious of the stimuli.

Unconsciousness has been speculated about by philosophers for centuries, but it was Freud who really tackled the problem, in a sense spending his entire scientific career in exploring its content and functions. Freud was aware of the existence of unconsciousness; such a state was obvious in hypnosis, in which subjects could be brought to recall events which they seemed to have forgotten in the waking state, and hypnotized people awakened from their trance behaved in ways which indicated that they were completely unconscious of things that happened during the trance, even though their behavior was obviously influenced by the trance events. But Freud's great discovery was that there were forces operating in this unconscious which, when recognized, accounted reasonably well for behavior which otherwise seemed illogical and strange. For example, a small boy's unreasonable fear of horses appeared quite strange on the surface, but when Freud discovered that unconsciously the boy associated horses with his father (who was a sportsman), and also was unconsciously afraid of his father (the boy feared that his father would punish him), the fear of horses became reasonable. The boy did not act overtly fearful in his father's presence, and was not aware that he was seeing a connection between his father and horses — these events were unconscious.[66]

Freud elaborated on such discoveries as these in order to discover the mode of operation — the dynamics — of the unconscious. Much of what Freud wrote has been carried over into common culture, so that people speak of the unconscious mind, and think of it as something which distorts, symbolizes, and motivates people in ways more powerful and more subtle than the conscious mind. This kind of thinking tends to ascribe a personality and independent existence to a thing which in fact does not exist as an entity. There is no location or organ in the body which operates as or contains an unconscious mind.

Then what does one mean by the term unconscious? It might be defined as awareness, but then, what is awareness? Sometimes a person is aware of what is going on around him, in the sense that he responds to the stimuli present (particularly if his responses are overlearned), but he may be unable to describe his responses or the stimuli which elicited them. Examine again the kinds of behavior which we have described as unconscious. It may be seen that behavior is described as unconscious if the behaving individual fails to think or to symbolize his responses. Similarly, one is unconscious of stimuli when he does not identify (label) them. Consciousness, then, would consist of thinking of or symbolizing one's experiences. As such, it is an aspect of responding to stimuli. Descartes said, "I think, therefore I exist." He might better have said, "I think, therefore I am conscious." If thinking is largely verbal, then consciousness largely consists of "talking to one's self" about one's experiences.

However, there is a problem in connection with this definition. It is possible for people to talk without really being conscious of what they are doing. Hypnotized subjects, for example, can talk and yet appear not to be aware of it. What about the roommate who talks in his sleep, but is not aware that he is doing so? It seems that simply producing words or thoughts is not sufficient as a criterion of consciousness. There is some evidence on this. In one experiment, subjects were instructed, while hypnotized, not to think about a particular anxiety-arousing experience during part of an interview. GSRs were then recorded during the interview, and even in that part of it in which the subjects were not supposed to be thinking about the anxiety-arousing experience, there was a consistent and steady increase in anxiety as measured by the GSR.[67] Presumably the subjects were not consciously thinking about the upsetting experience, but then something must have been going on, of a thought-like nature, unconsciously to stimulate the anxiety. But in terms of the definition proposed above, if thought is present, the subjects have to be considered conscious.

This contradiction may be resolved if one more point is added to the conceptualization of consciousness: we would say that an individual is conscious when he responds in thought to his own behavior. One is conscious of his perceptions if he symbolizes the fact that he has responded to a sensory stimulus; he is conscious of his own muscular reactions when he symbolizes what he has done. Consciousness is a response to a response, and is self-related in character. When one talks to himself about what he is doing and perceiving, one is conscious of what he is doing and to what he is responding. This process becomes clear when it takes place in slow-motion. A person may have a feeling of being vaguely annoyed, but not know what it is that is producing the annoyance. The presence of the annoyance indicates that he is responding to stimulation, and by thinking about or symbolizing the fact of feeling annoyed, he is conscious that he is bothered (although this realization or consciousness may be belated, not appearing until the person has snapped at his wife and children and kicked the dog). Then he asks himself why he is annoyed, and may begin to examine various events which have taken place in order to identify the stimulus for his upset.

So far, though he perceives the stimulus in the sense that he responds to it with annoyance, he is *pre-conscious* of the stimulus or of his perception of it, because he cannot yet label or symbolize the perception he has made to which he is responding with annoyance. After some thinking, he may identify the stimulus. At this point, he is conscious of it.

It is in this sense that consciousness of external stimuli consists of symbolizing or thinking about them, and consciousness of internal events —one's own drives, responses, and in particular, thoughts and perceptions —consists of making self-related responses to such stimuli. Thus one may be conscious of an external stimulus (respond to it) but be unconscious of his perception and his response to it. This is what happens in a person who responds inappropriately to women of his own age as if they were his mother. Such a person is obviously conscious of women, and of his responses to them; however, he is not conscious that he perceives women as being like his mother, and he would have to engage in extensive introspection (that is, make many self-related responses) in order to achieve this insight.

Self-Concept. This analysis of consciousness focuses particular attention on one's self-related responses. If one were to summarize the general character of an individual's self-related responses, he would have a description of what psychologists refer to as the individual's self-concept. The self-concept consists of the things about one's self of which he is aware, the characteristic words he applies to himself; in short, how he perceives and acts toward himself as an object in the world. It is composed of things about one's self of which he is conscious. (However, it is not necessarily so that an individual is conscious of his self-concept. He may not respond to his own self-evaluational thoughts, and so may not be explicitly aware that he has a self-concept, or of the nature of that concept).

Words, as you remember, are cues to which other responses may be attached. Some words are cues for fear, either because they symbolize some real event to which one has learned to respond with fear, or because one has been punished for using the word itself, as when a parent punishes a child or disapproves the child for saying "nasty" words. Similarly, there are many words which are reassuring and reduce anxiety. If one is fearfully expecting punishment (a bad grade in a course, for example), the words which the teacher may use which are opposite to those expected (telling the student that he has done very well on the exam) are reassuring and serve as cues for fear reduction. Thus the word "good" serves as a reinforcer, not only because it has been associated with more primary rewards in the past, but also because it dispels the anxiety which is generated by one's thought of the possibility that he might be bad. The reinforcement value of an evaluation term like "good" was demonstrated in an experiment in which subjects were asked simply to say words aloud. Whenever a subject gave a plural word the examiner nodded approval and said "uh-huh." It was found that subjects increased the frequency of saying plural words, showing that the experimenter's behavior was reinforcing, even though later interviews indicated that the subjects were quite unaware of what the experimenter was doing, or of the fact that their verbal responses were being influenced.[68]

The point is that words are associated with rewards and punishments, which therefore influence the extent to which an individual uses the words. Words which elicit strong fear are not as likely to be given in response to cues arising from one's self as other words which do not elicit fear. If, for a particular person, certain words elicit strong fear, then that person will tend not to use such words in thinking about himself; they will be excluded from his self-concept. In other words, one's perceptions of himself, like his perceptions of others, are powerfully influenced by his motives. To the extent that excluded words are accurate descriptions of his behavior, to that extent will a person's self-concept be at variance with his behavior. A boy tells a lie to someone whom he is trying to avoid; he may be aware of his lying (that is, he may tell himself that he has lied) if, for this boy, saying such a thing does not elicit fear because he has not been punished extensively for lying in the past. "I sometimes tell lies" is therefore part of his self-concept. In psychoanalytic terms, lying is "ego-syntonic" to this person; that is, it is consistent with the rest of his perceptions. On the other hand, if past punishment for lying has been severe or extensive, the boy would not be able to label his action as lying; he might tell himself that he was being polite, considerate of other's feelings, and "socially correct." In this case, his self-concept would be "I am polite and well mannered. I am honest, and never lie to people"; and in such a case, the self-concept would be a less accurate description of his own behavior. Lying is "ego-dystonic" to this person. To the extent this is so, this person would be unconscious of his own behavior, and might be described as lacking insight.

Usually the words which one uses in labeling are controlled by the labeled events themselves. The individual learns to associate particular words with particular events as a result of repeated reinforcements for correct word usage. As a result, strong habits of labeling accurately (in terms shared by the individual's society) are established. Thus there is a certain level of insight or consciousness which we come to expect of people. However, as has been pointed out above, punishment and/or reward associated with particular words can, by influencing their positions in the response hierarchy, make it more or less likely that such words will be used by the individual in responding to himself. It was indicated earlier that as stimulus ambiguity increases, the individual becomes more and more likely to perceive in terms of the most dominant responses in his response hierarchy. The same may be said of the self-concept; the more ambiguous are the stimuli of the individual's own behavior, the more likely that the order of responses in his response hierarchy will determine the nature of his self-concept. If the order of responses in the verbal response hierarchy is determined not only by frequency of use in the past, but also by rewards and punishments which have been associated with particular concepts, then it is possible for the resulting order of responses to produce a "slanted" or "biased" self-concept, particularly when the stimuli are ambiguous. Thus, the self-concepts of people are not necessarily accurate reflections of their own behavior. Sometimes their self-concepts may be overly "good," in that they exclude the individual's faults or failings; sometimes self-concepts are overly bad, in that the individual perceives himself as inferior or inadequate even when others do not perceive him that way. How these kinds of self-concepts come about will be discussed later; the main point to be made here is that the rewards and punishments associated with self-evaluative words can result in distorted self-concepts, in the sense that the individual may use words in responding to his own behavior, not so much because they are accurate and appropriate labels for his behavior, but because he has learned that it is good to use such words. Similarly, an individual may exclude certain self-responses, not because they are inappropriate or inaccurate, but rather because it makes the individual "feel bad" to make such responses.

The origin of self-evaluative and descriptive responses lies in the process of introjection in indentification, in which parental responses are imitated by the child and become a part of his own response hierarchy. The self-concept is derived from parental responses to him as a person, which the child has imitated and taken over as his own. How introjection and identification operate will be explored in the next chapters.

Self-concepts tend to become self-perpetuating. If a person thinks of himself as honest, he will not perceive those behaviors in himself which ought to be labeled as dishonest. Over a period of time, he becomes more and more convinced of his honesty because he is aware of no evidence to the contrary. Self-concepts therefore become more stable and consistent as the individual ages, or as the time increases in which he confirms and reconfirms his thoughts about himself.[69] And of course, the more confirmed he is in his thinking (that is, the more often his self-related responses have been reinforced) the more likely that he will think the same way in the future and the stronger must be the stimulation from inconsistent or contradictory behaviors for the self-concept to be modified. It is more difficult to change an old person's self-concept than it is to change that of a young person.

One of the most important consequences of the self-concept is that, when it is inaccurate as a reflection of the individual's behavior, the person finds it difficult to understand the situations in which he finds himself and the reactions other people have toward him. Because he is not labeling his own behavior correctly, he cannot understand how his behavior gets him into difficulties, or why people respond to him in a way different from the way he expects, on the basis of his erroneous self-image. He may then come to feel that he has little control over himself and his environment, or that he never knows what to expect of himself and others. These feelings are likely to be quite upsetting, because most of us have learned to want to understand ourselves accurately and to be adequately able to predict our own behavior. Slanted or distorted self-concepts can therefore provide a basis for much worry and unhappiness.

Further, words and other symbols serve as cues for other responses. A person's self-concept is part of the cue situation which elicits other responses. If these responses are to be appropriate, then the self-concept must be fairly accurate. A girl whose self-concept is that of a dull student, is likely to avoid school and select a nonacademic or nonintellectual vocation, even though she might actually be quite bright. Perceiving herself as dull, she might also fail to study in school, thereby creating the conditions which would affirm her self-concept.

Ego Functions

The concepts discussed in this chapter — thought, fantasy, perception, consciousness, and self-concept — are all involved in what psychologists often refer to as contact with reality. That is, thinking, perceiving, and the self-concept may be more or less accurate, more or less correct representations of reality. All of these functions have a reciprocal relationship with drives and past practice. We have noted that drives operate on perception in such a way as to increase the speed with which the individual will perceive objects and events related to his drives. The thirsty person becomes readily aware of the Coke signs, although when not thirsty he may not perceive them. In this way perception is intimately involved in drive-satisfaction. We have also noted how thinking is motivated, and also plays a role in reducing drives, most clearly seen when thought yields a solution to a problem. It is in this sense that the functions presented in this chapter have been described by many psychologists (particularly those adhering to Freud's theories) as in the service of the individual's drives. They refer to these functions as *ego-functions*, the ego being a term used to describe the aspect of the individual which is concerned with reality contact.

Use of the term "ego" has been avoided so far for two reasons. First, it is a poor term because the expression "functions of *the ego*" sounds as if there is a thing or organ which is "the ego" and which behaves in certain ways or does certain things. Our analysis of thought, perception, and consciousness indicates that there is no such single organ; the use of the expression "the ego" could therefore be misleading and could readily contribute to incorrect thinking, considering the important part verbal behavior plays in thought. The second reason for not referring to "ego functions" as such is that, by breaking these behaviors down into their components, we are able to give a more complete and detailed analysis of them and their determinants than we would get if we discussed them in a lump as a discussion of the "ego." No one has seen an "ego," but we can see the tiny changes in muscle activity in the voice box. This exclusion of the term "ego" is part of the scientific principle of economy: If the "ego" is a product of past experience, rewards and punishments, and particularly practice in the use of words, and if reality contact (thinking, perceiving, knowing) is a function of the "ego," then it may be said that reality contact is a function of past experience, rewards, and punishments, and verbal skills, without any reference to an "ego."

Ego Strength. In general it may be said of the higher mental processes discussed in this chapter that there is a complicated relationship between them and drives. If habits of correct thinking, perceiving, and knowing have been established, then it is more difficult for strong drives to lead to inaccuracies. We have seen that very strong drives can lead to misperceptions (that is, making a labeling response which is incorrect) by producing a strong readiness to respond in terms related to the drive. But in people who have developed strong habits of accurate labeling and "reality testing," misperceptions are readily corrected. In those who have not developed such strong habits, the misperception may go uncorrected. To the extent that they are uncorrected, the individual may be said to be out of contact with reality. Similarly, to the extent that thinking is influenced so strongly by motives that the individual produces ideas which are inaccurate or which lead to conclusions which are false to fact, to that extent the individual's thinking may be said to be out of contact with reality. When such reality testing is weak, and when habits of correct labeling and logical thinking are poorly established, the individual is said to have a "weak ego" which is "dominated" by his drives. On the other hand, a "strong ego" is said to exist in a person whose habits of accurate thinking and perceiving and of checking his thoughts and perceptions are strong enough so that his drives, no matter how high they may get, do not result in inaccuracies. In such a person, it might be said that his "ego" dominates his drives, at the same time as it "serves the drives." Accurate thought and perception result in putting the person in a reality situation in which he can emit his learned responses and reduce his drives. It is in this sense that the ego "serves the drives." Whether an ego is weak or strong depends, according to the analysis in this chapter, on the strength of habits of correct labeling and logical thinking. The administration of rewards for correct thinking and labeling, particularly in childhood (that is, giving the child experience with successful problem-solving), is an important factor in reality contact. If a child is left to solve too many problems, or problems too complex for his level of symbolic ability, such that he does not achieve success for thinking logically, then his ability to think well as an adult — his reality contact — will be poor. A realistic self-concept and realistic perception depend on the extent to which the symbolizing involved in these perceptions does not serve as a cue for anxiety or fear which is stronger than the habits of correct or accurate perceiving. We will return to a closer examination of the factors which determine accurate thinking in later chapters.

Intelligence and Reality Contact. The role of intelligence in reality contact should be mentioned. The ability to think logically, to perceive accurately and rapidly, are aspects of intelligence, and obviously play a part in establishing and maintaining reality contact. It seems logical that children of low intelligence should have greater difficulty in obtaining rewards for logical thinking, and so develop weaker habits of thought, than children of higher intellectual ability. It is perhaps significant that when reality contact is weak in highly intelligent people, their thinking inaccuracies tend to be subtle, and it is often difficult to tell whether they are, in fact, delusional because their thinking seems to be so logical. This is best seen in *paranoia,* a psychosis which will be discussed more fully in later sections.

It has been emphasized in this chapter that much thought and perception depends on verbal skills. A relationship between intelligence and reality contact therefore is suggested further by the finding that the best single indicator of intelligence is vocabulary and verbal reasoning. Although many psychologists have suggested that intelligence plays an important role in the "ego functions," research and analysis of the precise nature of this role are still in their infancies.

Next Steps. This chapter completes the presentation of the general determinants of behavior. The main variables which control behavior, and the characteristics of their operation, have been discussed. It now remains for us to present the specific determinants of behavior. In the following sections discussions will be presented, not of reinforcements in general, but of particular kinds of reinforcers, administered by particular people, and their effects on particular responses. In other words, we have presented the skeleton or framework of personality; now we must fill in the outlines.

Our task in the succeeding chapters will be to examine human drives and responses as they exist in people, to ask how and why these particular drives and responses are acquired, what are the kinds of family situations which determine their occurrence in childhood, what are the characteristic situations which people meet in adolescence and adulthood which encourage their development, and what are the common agents of reinforcement and types of rewards and punishments. What are the characteristics of these agents, what happens when certain kinds of drives conflict with each other, what are the kinds of things that people learn to do when they are in conflict or are frustrated, and why do they learn those things rather than others and finally, what happens to people who develop certain common drives and responses?

REPRISE. In this chapter we have focussed on what are commonly called "the higher mental processes." Thought, perception, and consciousness were interpreted as symbolic responses to stimuli. The symbols used are usually verbal ones, probably because language provides a most flexible and extensive set of symbols. Considering this relationship between language and thinking, it is no accident that tests of verbal ability (vocabulary, in particular) are often the best measures of intelligence. It is also no accident that the thought disturbances and loss of contact with reality found in severely distorted personalities, such as psychotics, are associated with inaccurate and bizarre usages of words.

Because of the great importance of symbols in logical thinking, accurate perceptions, and realistic self-perceptions, we have examined some of the factors which determine what words shall be used and how. These factors include the nature of the individual's drives, extent of past practice, and the rewards and punishments associated with the ideas — in short, the same factors which determine the availability for use of any response, verbal or otherwise. Cultural and economic factors were also cited as influencing the kinds of words in the language which are available to the individual for use.

Three particular aspects of the higher mental processes were singled out for discussion: fantasy, perception of ambiguous stimuli, and the self-concept. Psychologists are interested in these phenomena because of their diagnostic significance, and for the important ways in which these phenomena influence the individual's future behavior. The nature of people's fantasy, of their perceptions, and of their self-concepts will be referred to frequently in subsequent sections of this book in order to explain personality developments and patterns frequently found.

III. Contents of Personality

In this section, the major emphasis will be on applying the general laws presented in Section II to the study of personality. We have seen that behavior includes components of several types or levels — any behavioral sequence involves physiological activities (largely motivational-emotional), learned responses (the behaving social self), and intellectual (thinking, perceiving, and knowing) events. For a complete picture of a behaving organism, it is necessary to view him in all three dimensions.

Our task during the remainder of the book will be to observe people in the round, to apply the general laws of behavior to people as they are known to us in daily life. We shall examine the kinds of motives that people characteristically develop in our society, the kinds of responses which they frequently acquire, and common thought patterns. We will be interested in the circumstances under which such behaviors are acquired, and the consequences to the individual of his acquiring them. In order to carry out this analysis, we will first present an over-all picture of typical personality development from infancy through adulthood; then we will examine in some detail a few common motives and thought patterns. Finally, we will consider the consequences of this developmental process in terms of conflict, typical responses to conflict, and the resulting personality patterns as they may be observed in normal people, in those labeled neurotic, and in those who are considered to be psychotic.

6. The Socialization of Primary Drives

The primary drives with which the infant is born were discussed in Chapter 2. We have seen that it is in relation to the satisfaction of these drives that the infant acquires response tendencies, or habits, and also new or secondary drives and reinforcements. The drives and responses an individual displays and their consequences, are the subject matter of the study of personality. It is the task of this chapter to discover the kinds of behaviors and drives people in our culture characteristically develop; in order to do this, then, we must examine the learnings which occur in relation to the drives the baby brings into the world with him. The character of these learnings and how they are managed are largely functions of the baby's parents and of the culture which is expressed through their behavior. The parents are the ones who determine how and under what circumstances the infant's drives will be reduced, thus directly determining what behaviors will be reinforced.

The acquisition of habits and drives through the action of the parents on the child is referred to as the *socialization* of the child. In this chapter we will discuss various kinds of procedures and the variables which influence the course of socialization, with reference to each of the drives which become socialized. For each of the primary drives, then, we will discuss several common kinds of socialization experiences in terms of the learnings each produces. Our approach is developmental; that is, the drives are presented in the order in which they are usually socialized. However, we must recognize that training is continuous and that socialization of one drive usually overlaps training of others.

Hunger and Thirst Drives

These two drives will be treated together because through much of the child's early socialization they are confounded; they are reduced by the same response and the same goal-object — sucking and milk.

Most of what is important in personality development during early infancy centers about the mouth and the hunger drive. You will recall that one of the most significant aspects of birth is that for the first time in the infant's experience, its needs are met periodically rather than continuously. For the first time, needs accumulate over time and motives develop which increase in strength as a function of time since the needs were last satisfied. Thus birth produces the infant's first occasions to be motivated. The motive most likely to be strongest is the hunger drive. Given a normal infant and a normal delivery, infants have very little difficulty in satisfying their other needs — oxygen, sleep, defecation, and urination. All these are satisfied automatically by innate reflexes or mechanisms. Further, most infants are kept adequately warm (too warm, since infants require less heat than do adults, contrary to popular opinion, because they have less surface area through which body heat may be lost relative to body mass)[1] and free from pain stimulation. But in order for their food needs to be satisfied, another person must take special action periodically. It is in this dependency for satisfaction of food needs that the possibilities for the development of very strong drive are present. It is difficult for an adult to know when an infant is hungry (some will not even nurse when hungry during the first few days of life, probably because they have not yet learned to do so in response to hunger drive), and it is seldom possible to feed the infant at intervals exactly appropriate to his needs so that hunger drive doesn't become very strong. Hence most of the young infant's learnings will be in relation to the hunger drive.

Motor Control of the Mouth. This fact combines with another to suggest the importance of feeding as a focus of the infant's first learnings. In the discussion of maturation in Chapter 2 we noted that cortical control over body muscles spreads in a cephalocaudal and a proximodistal direction. These sequences of development mean that at birth the only structure over which the infant's cortex has any control is that at the midline of the head — the mouth — and it is this structure which remains throughout life the best controlled set of muscles in the body, with the lips and tongue capable of extremely precise movements and coordinations. The area of the cortex given over to the control of the muscles of the mouth and tongue is larger than the areas controlling any other body muscles.[2] The mouth is thus the first, and for the first several very important weeks, the only group of muscles whose responses can be integrated within the brain with stimuli coming from the sense receptors, such that the responses of the mouth can be firmly associated with external and internal cues.

The infant's most significant learning experiences then center around the mouth. Indeed, this period of life was called the "oral stage" by Freud, who was the first to recognize the importance of early feeding experiences for personality development. Freud suggested that many of our attitudes about food, eating, and oral activities in general, such as smoking, chewing gum, and the like are based on infantile experiences centered around the satisfaction of our hunger drive.[3] We will examine this general hypothesis in more detail, in terms of the kinds of things infants might learn as a result of various types of feeding situation.

Importance of Oral Learnings. The learnings which occur in connection with infantile feeding may continue throughout the person's life, and also affect the direction which later learning takes. That is, the responses the infant acquires first are those most likely to be made in other, later, learning situations, so that the potentialities for later learning — the range of responses which might be learned later — is limited by the learnings which have occurred in this earlier period. In this way the infant's feeding experiences — as the center of the infant's first strong drives, learnable responses, and powerful reinforcements — set the tone for his later learnings. Another process which also operates to increase the permanence of the effects of infantile feeding experiences results from the parents' personalities; studies in the consistency of personality indicate that people do not change their general ways of behaving very readily.[4] Thus parents who act in certain ways when feeding their infants are likely to act in very similar ways in all of their responses to their children's needs — not only in infancy, but throughout babyhood, childhood, and adolescence. Consequently they are likely to teach their children similar things in a wide variety of situations over many years. The net effect is that the child in his parental home is reinforced for about the same kind of behavior countless times throughout his life and so acquires quite stable and enduring drives and responses, starting with oral training immediately after birth.

It is not asserted here that infancy and infantile experiences are the sole, or even primary, determinants of all later adult behavior. Infantile experiences are *one* strong source of influence on the direction which responses will take later in childhood which therefore will influence later responses and learnings in adolescence, which in turn will influence still later responses and learnings in adulthood. In other words, infantile learnings start a chain reaction, or trend, which still may be modified within wide limits at all later occasions. But as pointed out above, the consistency in parents' personalities which further encourages the consistency in childhood learning experiences operates to restrict the range within which the patterns established in infancy may be modified by later learnings during the child's period of dependency on his parents.

Major Variables of Oral Training. There are several ways in which infantile feeding experiences may vary and the effects of these experiences fall into several general areas. Infants may be breast or bottlefed; they may be fed on a schedule or upon demand; the feeding may be accompanied by various degrees of pleasant or unpleasant contact with the mother; weaning (the child's first major step toward independence and mature behavior) may be begun early or late; the child may be given few or many opportunities to suck; weaning may be harsh and unpleasant, or gradual and easy.

Each one of these variables influences the learnings associated with feeding, and it is likely that the many different possible combinations of these variables each produces an effect. Thus early weaning combined with pleasant stimulation is likely to have effects different from those of late weaning and pleasant stimulation, and both effects are likely to be different from those of unpleasant stimulation combined with either harsh or easy weaning.

These variables affect the learning of responses and drives in several different but related areas. It is obvious that they will affect the reinforcement value of food and the tendency to make oral responses, particularly sucking. Thus later attitudes toward food, nourishment, and ingestion and later habits involving mouth responses — such as thumb-sucking, lip-biting, smoking, chewing, enjoying drinking through a straw and sucking candies, lollipops, and the like — may have their groundworks established in infancy.[5]

These variables also appear to influence the learning of responses related to other people — affection and dependency in particular. This is so because of the particular nature of infantile feeding: it is (at first at least) always a social activity, in that another person is always present when the infant's hunger drive is reduced by nursing. This other person (in our culture, usually the mother) is thus a stimulus which occurs in close proximity to the reduction of a very powerful drive on many different occasions, every day of the week for several months at least. Therefore the mother and stimuli associated with her begin during early infancy to acquire very strong secondary reinforcing capacities and so become the goal objects of a great deal of motivated behavior, depending on the adequacy or strength of the primary reinforcement — the actual feeding — with which they are associated, and the consistency of the association. As a result, degree of affection toward the mother (and feelings toward others in general on the basis of stimulus generalization) is established during infantile feeding. The extent of the tendency to approach others, to rely upon their presence for the satisfaction of one's needs and the reduction of discomfort — all that is implied by the term *dependency drive* — is acquired similarly as a product of the social interaction which accompanies feeding, and would be expected to vary in strength with the variables involved in feeding. Thus hunger-socialization determines many responses and also what are called "object relations"— the relationships between drives and the human and nonhuman objects in the environment.[6]

Feeding Schedules. Infants usually are fed on a schedule which varies from rigid time intervals between feedings (usually four hours) to a complete "self-demand" schedule in which the infant is fed whenever he appears to be hungry. Dollard and Miller point out that the schedule itself may be an important determinant of infantile learnings. A baby fed on demand would be expected to learn to cry quite readily, because crying is quickly, promptly, and uniformly reinforced by a reduction in the hunger drive. Such a child might readily acquire the characteristics of a "demanding" child; however, it is probably also true that, because the reinforcement approaches a 100 per cent schedule (the child is fed every time he cries with hunger), the crying should extinguish more readily than would be the case with an interval-scheduled baby, when it comes time for the child to learn more mature ways of responding to his drives. In terms of what is known about learning, it would seem likely that the demand-fed baby would also be developing a "learning set"; that is, he would be learning not simply to cry, but also to take action in general when he is motivated. Thus Dollard and Miller suggest that the demand-fed infant is more likely to become an active child and adult—active in the sense that when emotionally aroused he does things actively to obtain relief.[7]

Because hunger in the demand-fed baby usually does not reach the height which it might in an interval-scheduled baby, it also seems likely that the learnings which occur in relation to feeding might not be as strong as those which occur in relation to scheduled feeding. Thus the demand-fed baby might be expected on this basis also to be able to extinguish habits more readily and replace them with new habits. In general then, one might expect a demand-fed baby to show less persistence in a habit and to be more readily modified in his behavior by changed situations.

It should be noted here that it appears to be quite rare for a child to be placed exclusively on a demand schedule although demand feeding is gaining in popularity. Parents who elect a demand schedule usually modify it by specifying some minimal time interval between feedings, such as two hours, with the feeding on demand any time after that minimum.

Although mothers seem to be changing in this regard, in accordance with popular fashion the most typical feeding schedule is that of four hour-intervals which are modified to varying extents by different parents in the direction of appropriateness relative to the baby's hunger. One mother may feed her child about every four hours, but be quite willing to feed him after three and a half hours if the baby seems to be very hungry before the full four hours have gone by. Another mother may, on the other hand, be quite inflexible, not deviating from her schedule to feed her baby a minute sooner than the clock requires. A child on a rigid schedule might on some occasions be awakened from a nap to be fed; on others he might be fed after he has been crying with hunger for a while. There would probably be many times when the infant would become very hungry, but would not be fed because the proper interval had not elapsed since the last feeding. Such an infant then, frequently might be fed even when not hungry, and conversely, often not fed even though he was very hungry (although infants do tend to adapt to the parents' feeding schedule on the whole).[8] In this kind of situation it appears likely that the feeding would tend not to reinforce any particular behaviors because the feeding is not dependent on such behaviors, as it is dependent on crying in the demand-feeding schedule. Thus it is unlikely that the rigidly interval-scheduled child would acquire any particular responses which reliably bring relief from discomfort. Dollard and Miller suggest that such a child may well learn in effect that there is little he can do to produce drive reduction and satisfaction of his desires; he not only fails to learn any particular response, but also fails to learn to respond in general when he requires help. In this sense, rigid interval-scheduling could produce a tendency toward passive acceptance or endurance of discomfort in a person who would fail actively to seek solutions to his problems and discomforts. If this pattern of unresponsiveness to the baby's needs in infancy should continue in connection with other drives that develop as the baby grows into and through childhood, the child might feel that he has not the capacity to take effective action when his drives or wants are high; he has learned that no matter what he does it does not bring satisfaction, so that doing things in general has failed to be reinforced. Enough experiences of this kind may teach a child to endure frustration, to take relatively little action to satisfy his needs, and to give up trying sooner than might be the case with children whose parents are consistently responsive to their needs.

However, such a child also should learn strong needs for his mother's presence. If the child's mother tends not to interact with the child except at the regularly scheduled feeding occasions, her presence will be closely and consistently associated with drive reduction, so that she too will acquire strong secondary reinforcing properties. And in fact, since the child of such a parent is likely to suffer very intense drives because his needs are allowed to accumulate until the schedule calls for parental intervention, the drive reduction which does occur when the mother feeds the child will be even greater than that which occurs in a child on a self-demand schedule; thus the mother is likely to acquire even stronger secondary reinforcing capacities than is the less rigid mother. Such a child would be expected to rely on parents even more heavily than the self-demand child and to be more dependent on others in general, but with this difference: compared to the self-demand child, who may learn that he can do things which will induce others to help him, the rigidly scheduled child, while developing equally strong if not stronger drives to be with other people, also learns to feel that there is little he can do to make others help him when he needs their help. As an infant and child who knows nothing of clocks and schedules, his parents' satisfaction of his needs appears capricious and unpredictable; at least there is nothing he can do which works reliably in getting them to satisfy his needs. Thus he may learn that though he looks toward others for help and comfort, he must wait until they offer it of themselves. He cannot make it happen himself.

That schedule which is adopted seems to be related to the mother's personality. A nervous, insecure mother is more likely to follow her pediatrician's advice closely, or to be greatly influenced by current fashion. When the trend in medical thinking favored interval scheduling, as it did very strongly in the 1940's, the more anxious mother tended to use rigid schedules to a greater extent than the relatively self-confident mothers did.[9]

Inconsistent Scheduling. In the discussion so far, it was assumed that the parents behaved consistently in their schedule. Now let us examine the likely consequences of irregular behavior, which can neither be classified as demand nor as interval-scheduled feeding. With such irregular parental behavior, it is quite difficult for the child to adapt to the parents' feeding schedule. The child quite frequently may show signs of hunger at times when his mother does not feed him; he may fail to be hungry on other occasions when she is prepared to feed him. It has been suggested that such a child therefore may experience extraordinarily high drive on some feeding occasions and very little drive on others. When hunger is intense, the infant sucks violently and is physically tense while nursing. As a result, he swallows large quantities of air along with the milk, which produces painful stomach upset that must be relieved by "burping." However, because of the strong hunger, the infant continues nursing instead of stopping to be "burped." At the same time, because of his physical tension he is uncomfortable while he nurses. These factors mean that although the infant's hunger drive is reduced, the reduction is itself accompanied by pain. On other occasions, when the mother tries to feed the child when he is not hungry, the feeding situation will again be unpleasant and he may fail to suck. It may happen that after she experiences this frustration, the mother becomes less inclined to feed the baby soon again, so that when he does become hungry enough to suck, feeding is delayed for a time, which allows the hunger drive to build up again to painful strength and makes a painful feeding situation likely to recur. In this kind of interaction, it is likely that the mother will acquire secondary reinforcing capacities, because she is still associated quite often with the reduction of a drive; however, she is also likely to acquire the capacity to elicit a pain or fear drive because she is present when painful nursing occurs. Thus the infant will tend to learn *ambivalent* feelings toward his mother, toward food, and toward oral activities in general. He will get hungry enough so that he literally is forced to eat, but the eating will not be a pleasurable activity and he will tend to cease eating as soon as possible. Such a child is likely to become known as a "fussy eater," a result that may disturb his parents so much that they may make mealtimes occasions for arguing, demanding, or forcing the child to eat, for punishing and rejecting him for not eating — thus further increasing the child's ambivalence toward food and toward his parents. A child so reared is likely to be one who is lonely and upset when he is without company — when stimuli from other people are absent — but who also is nervous, fearful, or "shy" when he is with others. In short, he is almost always in conflict over his social relationships.

Breast Vs. Bottle Feeding. Much impassioned prose, and even some poetry, has been written in the controversy as to whether it is better to feed an infant by breast or by bottle. In the recent past it was very unfashionable to breast-feed. Many women felt that there was something demeaning or low about using their bodies in such a primitive biological function. More recently there has been a marked upsurge in the popularity of breast feeding. As far as convenience is concerned, each method has its advantages; breast feeding obviates the need for mixing formula and sterilizing bottles, but in our society it usually is done in private, which means that a mother may not feed when she has company or is in a public place, and so has to make special arrangements to avoid doing so.

So far, no study has demonstrated satisfactorily that the choice of breast or bottle feeding of itself produces differences in babies. No particular psychological consequences of either method of feeding have been established, and one would not, on theoretical grounds, expect such consequences. Provided that the formula fed from a bottle reduces drives as readily as breast milk does, and provided that the nipple used approximates the natural nipple, it seems unlikely that the structural differences between bottle and breast are great enough for the infant to attach distinctive responses to them.

However, the choice of whether to feed by bottle or breast is related to factors in the mother which may be general enough that they also will influence the mother's behavior toward the infant in many ways. For example, one study found evidence that rejection of breast feeding is highest among women who are rated as being more anxious about sex.[10] A sexually inhibited or anxious mother would, according to this study, be more likely to bottle feed her baby. In all likelihood such a mother also avoids dealing openly with other sexual matters arising in the child's life. She would be very modest when washing her baby's genitals and when teaching the child about sex. Such a mother would be expected to develop prudish or anxious attitudes toward sex in her children — and these attitudes then would be found to correlate with lack of breast feeding. The point is that the correlation is due to some factor other than decision to breast or bottle feed.

There has not been any reliable evidence that the decision to bottle feed rather than breast feed is related to attitudes of rejection toward the baby, contrary to the belief of many people. However, an anxious or worried mother might think that there is a relationship between bottle feeding and rejection and so force herself to breast feed in order to avoid the psychological consequences of rejection though she would prefer to bottle feed. In such a situation the mother thereby may produce the very result which she is trying to avoid. Feeling anxious and upset about breast feeding, she tends to hold the baby uncomfortably and to cut short the feeding before the baby is fully satiated; she is too tense to fondle and play with the baby while she nurses him. The baby thus will become less strongly attached to her than if she had bottle fed him, and the feeding situation itself may become very similar to that described in the discussion of inconsistent scheduling with similar effects on the child. In one study it was demonstrated that mothers who decided against breast feeding actually secreted less milk the day after birth than mothers who decided in favor of breast feeding.[11] The mother who feels guilty about not wanting to breast feed but forces herself to use this method, might therefore feed her baby less adequately than if she used the bottle method. This would produce all the consequences of inadequate drive reduction which already have been described.

There is one consequence which is more likely to occur with breast feeding than with bottle feeding. Breast feeding requires intimate physical contact between the mother and the child. With bottle feeding after a baby is two or three months old, it becomes possible simply to prop the bottle and leave the baby alone to drink. Thus it is more likely with breast feeding that the stimuli of the mother will acquire secondary reinforcing capacities. Thus it also is more possible with bottle feeding for the feeding situation to become a private, lonely affair, with the consequences which one might expect as far as developing attitudes of love and of a desire to be near the mother, and through stimulus generalization, a weak attachment to other people as well.

Ambivalence. This discussion points up the role of the quality of the interpersonal contact between the infant and his mother. As has been noted, the less pain producing this contact, the greater the number of stimuli which the mother presents to her child (as in fondling the baby, talking to him, touching the baby over much of his body, and the like) the more likely that a wide variety of interpersonal stimuli will acquire secondary reinforcing capacities. In other words, the more pleasant and stimulating the interpersonal situation, the more likely that the child will develop feelings of love for the mother and a desire to be near her and people in general, provided of course that hunger drive reduction also has occurred satisfactorily while these stimuli were present.[12] As might be expected from the discussion of acquired drives, it would also be predicted that if the hunger drive were not reduced when these stimuli are characteristically present — if in fact such stimuli became associated with a high level of hunger drive, these stimuli would acquire the capacity to elicit increased hunger drive which could be most readily reduced by avoiding the stimuli; in such a situation, the child would learn a motivated avoidance of close interpersonal contact, love relationships and of environmental realities in general. Of course, it is not possible for a mother consistently to fail to satisfy her infant's hunger drive. Thus in the case of all infants reared by their mothers the mother always is associated to some degree with drive reduction, although many also may become associated with pain and intense hunger from time to time. Therefore, seldom is there an unqualified motivated avoidance of other people; such avoidance, when present, is almost always mixed with at least some motivated tendency to approach others — that is, ambivalence. The implications of such a conflict will be presented in more detail in a later chapter. At that time, it will become apparent that it is this kind of ambivalence, rather than outright avoidance of interpersonal contact, which is capable of producing neurotic and psychotic reactions.

Is There an Innate Sucking Drive? There is one further consideration associated with the decision to breast or bottle feed a baby, involving the question of the importance to the infant of sucking experience. When bottle feeding, a mother can adjust the nipple flow appropriately to the child's sucking drive, if such a drive exists, whereas the breast feeding mother must hope that her nipple is just right for her baby. However, the presence of an innate drive to suck is open to question. It has been hypothesized in the past that infants do in fact possess such an innate drive, which is most obviously manifested in thumbsucking. Thumbsucking has been explained as the child's effort to satisfy a need which may not be met completely during feeding because of a too fast nipple flow or too short feeding session. That many children are motivated to suck cannot be denied; one need only witness the many techniques a child will learn in order to suck his thumb, and the many ways in which children try to get around their parents' prohibitions against thumbsucking. What has been questioned is whether or not this drive is innate.

One of the earliest studies of this problem was by David Levy,[13] who divided litters of puppies into two groups, one of which he fed through a nipple with very small holes, so that the puppies had to suck for a long time in order to empty the bottle; the other fed the same amount of milk but through a nipple with a large hole so that they gained relatively little sucking experience. Levy then tested both groups for their tendency to engage in nonnutritive sucking, analogous to thumbsucking, and found that the puppies fed very rapidly tended to do more nonnutritive sucking than did the other group. This study therefore suggested that puppies at least have a need to suck which, if unsatisfied through feeding, can be satisfied outside of the feeding situation. However, a more recent study by Sears may be more definitive. Sears found that in general the earlier a child is weaned from a nipple (breast or bottle) the more likely he is to suck his thumb, apparently supporting Levy's findings.[14, 15] However, Sears also found that infants that never had had an opportunity to suck at all, having been fed from a cup from birth (something which had heretofore been thought impossible), tended not to engage in nonnutritive sucking at all. He explains this in terms of secondary reinforcement; children that have had any experience at all in sucking develop a strong desire to suck because this action has been so closely associated with hunger drive reduction. Once this drive has been established, and it seems to be established quite easily with relatively few trials, such a child will continue to suck, and if he does not do enough of it during his feeding because of a too rapid flow of milk, then he will suck his thumb. However, infants that never had sucked do not acquire a drive to do so, and so do not engage in thumbsucking at all. Thus it appears that while sucking is a drive quite readily acquired through association with hunger drive reduction, and is one usually acquired because of the way in which most babies are fed — as Freud originally suggested — it is not innate. However, once established, it is still true that the size of the hole in the nipple or the rapidity of the flow of milk then will be an important determiner of how completely the drive is reduced, and thus of how much nonnutritive sucking the child does.

Age and Severity of Weaning. In America children tend to be weaned earlier than in fifty-one preliterate societies with which America was compared by Whiting and Child.[16] Two-thirds of American babies had weaning started before they were eleven months old. This probably is a reflection of the great emphasis in our society on encouraging independence early in life. However, it should be noted that within American culture, there are large variations among subcultures; for example, Negro mothers tend to wean their children much later than do white parents.[17]

Weaning, in combination with the parents' efforts to modify the baby's schedule to approximate the eating schedule of adults, is one of the first experiences where the child is pushed toward independence of his parents and toward the acceptance of the modes of eating behavior characteristic of the society into which he was born. It is thus one of the baby's earliest socialization experiences. As such, the learnings which may become established during this training will be important in determining the nature of the child's responses to later steps toward independence and adult standards of behavior, thereby influencing the child's general responses to independence and to his society's folkways — the characteristic ways of doing things.

Associated with the belief that infants have an innate sucking drive was the logical conclusion that babies should be permitted to satisfy this drive, so that early weaning from the nipple was thought to be frustrating — indeed, the baby's first major frustration in which his natural propensities had to be denied in order for him to learn the more "artificial" ways of people in his culture. However, as we have seen, the innateness of the sucking drive is no longer a valid concept. The evidence seems to indicate that, as one would expect on the basis of the laws of learning, sucking is a learned drive. The laws of learning also would indicate, then, that the longer an infant is allowed to suck, the stronger would be his drive to suck, and the stronger would be the habits which he had acquired in connection with this drive. Thus the psychoanalytic idea that early weaning is especially frustrating conflicts with a hypothesis derived from the principles of learning that the later the weaning, the more resistant to weaning the infant should be.

Robert Sears and his co-workers have explored these hypotheses in several studies in which mothers were interviewed intensively with respect to their child-training practices, and their children either observed and rated by trained raters or rated by their mothers.[18] Sears found that the later weaning is started, the more emotional upset at weaning is produced in the children, according to the mothers' reports. In other words, the more firmly established the habit, the more difficult it is to extinguish.

However, these results must be compared with the data gathered by other investigators. Whiting and Child studied the child-rearing practices of a large number of preliterate societies and rated each society on a number of scales concerned with characteristics of their treatment of children.[19] They found that early weaning and relatively little indulgence of the infant's oral drives were associated with severe or harsh training in more mature ways of satisfying hunger drives. They suggest that perhaps two factors are at work; on the one hand, long-established sucking habits are more difficult to extinguish, but on the other hand, older children are more intelligent and so "catch on" to what is required of them in weaning, so that older children should wean more readily. This observation is supported by the fact that the older a child is when weaning is begun, the more quickly the weaning is completed.

Another factor which plays a part in weaning is the duration of the process. Weaning can be done suddenly and be completed in one day, as when a mother takes the baby's bottle away and refuses to give it back, or it may be done gradually by giving the child fruit juices to drink out of a cup, then encouraging the child to drink milk out of a cup for one meal a day, gradually increasing the number of times a cup is offered instead of a bottle. Similarly a mother simply may offer a child a cup and punish him when he asks for a bottle, or may give a great deal of reward for drinking out of a cup and remain noncommittal when the child asks for the bottle. It has been found that the more gradually a mother eases her child into solid foods and drinking from a cup, the less emotional upset the child shows.[20] However, the character of this gradualness seems to be important. If the weaning is long and drawn out, because the mother is inconsistent in her practices — at one time rewarding the child for drinking from a cup and at another preferring to give a bottle because she can't tolerate the mess produced by the child's inept handling of the cup — in such circumstances, as one would expect from partial reinforcement, the child's resistance to the extinction of sucking drive and responses will be greater, as will his disturbance. On the other hand, if a long duration weaning occurs because the mother is gradual and consistent in her introduction of new procedures, then weaning seems not to produce such upset.

Some Effects of Oral Trauma. An important question is the significance of the upset which the child may display during weaning. Is the upset an indication of some enduring insecurity, and are later personality traits correlated with the presence of such upset? There is some inferential evidence on this question.

Sears obtained information about child-rearing practices from mothers and studied the relationship between the practices used and ratings of aggressiveness and dependency in the children.[21] The ratings were made by the children's nursery school teachers and by trained observers who closely watched the children's play for fifteen minutes at a time on several different occasions. Sears found that total dependency was related to the children's frustration in nursing and weaning, such that the most frustrated children were those who showed the most dependent behavior. Just as the sucking drive gets stronger, the longer it is gratified, so does the acquired drive to be near the mother. The child learns on many occasions that loneliness is associated with high drive and the mother associated with drive reduction, so that loneliness acquires the capacity to elicit motivated behavior such as seeking his mother or crying, and these responses are reinforced by the mother's presence (which removes the cues of loneliness). Thus it is that a late-weaned child is likely to be more dependent than an early-weaned child.

Other evidence comes from a series of studies by Goldfarb who intensively studied the personalities of children who had been reared in institutions, where the close association between the presence of a single person and the satisfaction of hunger tends not to occur.[22] In institutions, children are fed by attendants, often by several different attendants who are usually too busy to provide the kind of close contact and stimulation that makes feeding a pleasant experience and that is necessary if the parent-substitutes are to acquire secondary reinforcing capacities. Children raised in such a setting and later adopted showed very strong dependency drive and sought attention constantly. They tended not to develop strong affectionate relationships with their adoptive parents, even after several years. As we interpret this result, there was no stimulus generalization of affectionate responses from a rewarding mother to other people in general. The interpersonal relationships of these children tended to be superficial. These characteristics were more pronounced in those placed in the institutions earliest (about six months of age), and in those who stayed longest before being adopted. Goldfarb's study thus shows that the variables which play a role in the feeding process are extremely powerful in determining relatively enduring personality characteristics.

Oral Training and Object-Relations. Freud and his followers have suggested that the groundwork for schizophrenia (a pattern of personality traits which are generally bizarre and exaggerated, such that the individual is not able to manage his affairs successfully, and is therefore hospitalized) is laid during infantile feeding. They have hypothesized that severe disturbance ("trauma") associated with the reduction of the hunger drive increases the probability that the individual will become schizophrenic later on in life. Schizophrenia is most frequently marked by a lack of reality contact and withdrawal from object relations; the schizophrenic engages extensively in inaccurate thinking and bizarre fantasy, and is prone to massive misperceptions. In explaining such behavior, psychoanalysts have proposed that if trauma occurs at this early stage, the infant does not get satisfactory gratification of his oral (sucking) drive, so that he either fails to progress beyond this point in life, or has a fixation at this point in life such that later difficulties are responded to by a return to ways of behaving characteristic of the young infant. Thus the thinking, fantasizing, and perception of the schizophrenic are thought to be essentially those of the person when he was an infant.

As we have seen, present evidence is not consistent with the hypothesis of an innate oral drive. In fact, there is little objective evidence that schizophrenia is related to trauma during the age when feeding training is so important. But it has been found that lack of pleasant affectional stimulation during infantile feeding experiences appears to be related to the development of traits similar to those found in schizophrenics — traits of emotional coldness and distance from people, apathy, and extreme dependence. It also has been found that a child's mental development tends to be much slower and to remain lower if he is brought up in the impersonal atmosphere of an institution than if he is brought up in an environment in which he could have maternal love. Further, many psychiatrists who have worked intensively with schizophrenics and have acquired a great deal of experience with the problem, are firmly convinced that the first few months of life are crucial in determining the occurrence of this personality pattern.

There are various possible events which may account for the presumed relationship between schizophrenia and infantile feeding. One possibility is that if the feeding experience is very unpleasant either because of too strong drive or rough handling by the mother, the child may learn that the most drive-reducing response is to turn away from the breast or bottle after minimal sucking. He thus learns an avoidance response which may be generalized to the mother and to other people, and perhaps to all external stimuli. Should this occur, such that the child does little reality testing in which he checks his thinking and perceptions for accuracy by attending to stimuli in the environment, he will not acquire habits of logical and correct thinking and perceiving; instead he will tend to engage in private fantasy to a great extent, developing the type of thought characteristic of schizophrenia. It has been found that the language development of children reared in institutions tends to be slower even years after their adoption than is that of noninstitutionally reared children;[23, 24] we already have explored the intimate connection between language and thought. Avoidance of reality is more likely to be learned at a very early age, before the child has developed sufficient maturation and intellectual power to try out and perhaps acquire other, less drastic responses to frustration and pain.

Another possible explanation is that too strong a drive at an age when the nervous system is still quite immature and is developing rapidly — that is, the first few months of life before the central and peripheral nervous systems have developed their full complement of cells and neural centers — may produce such drastic or violent neural firing that permanent injury to the young neurons or to their synapses may be produced. Such injury would most likely occur in the hypothalamic area, in which the need-sensitive receptors appear to lie, and which integrates the drive-emotion responses of the autonomic nervous system. A permanent impairment of this center might leave the individual subject to more frequent or more intense autonomic arousal, and thus more intense motives which are therefore more likely to be frustrated. Or impairment in the hypothalamus may reduce the individual's ability to learn responses to his drive states, so that he is continually frustrated. Such frustration or punishment occurring in relation to the individual's drives might then in turn make it more likely that he learn avoidance responses to environmental stimulation, thus weakening reality contact and inclining him to the thought pattern characteristic of schizophrenia. There has been a great deal of evidence that the autonomic functioning of schizophrenics is very different from that of non-schizophrenics.[25] However, this evidence is not conclusive for the theory as it is possible that the anomolies of autonomic functioning may have been produced by factors other than injury to the hypothalamus, such as intense drive.

Thus, though there is little direct support for any particular theory of schizophrenia, the available evidence and the weight of theorizing does seem to converge on that age in which infantile feeding experiences are the sources of learning, of drive satisfaction, and of the kind of frustration which is presumed to be the important determinant of later schizophrenia. Responsiveness to the environment, both social and physical, and habits of thinking based on such responsiveness, therefore are thought to be related to what goes on in connection with hunger drive reduction in early infancy.

Finally, schizophrenic behavior has been described as a lack of object-relations. We already have indicated that as a consequence of the feeding situation the individual's first object-relationships are established with the mother. Thus it is reasoned that schizophrenia is a result of the

failure to establish those interpersonal relations in connection with infantile feeding which serve as a basis for later object-relations or attitudes toward the people and objects of the environment.

Combinations of the Major Variables. It is probably true that a mother's
decision on any one of the variables we have discussed — schedule *vs.*
demand feeding, breast *vs.* bottle, intimate *vs.* distant contact with the
baby, early *vs.* late, and severe *vs.* gradual weaning, is related to her
decision on some of the other variables, though not necessarily. A
highly rejecting mother may tend to avoid breast feeding, wean her child
early and severely, and provide very little warmth in association with
the feeding process. In one study, mothers were asked if they would
prefer to have their babies "rooming in" with them in the hospital after
they were born — a relatively new innovation in which the baby is allowed to stay in the mother's room, rather than remain in the nursery
to be cared for by nurses most of the time. It was found that of those who
chose rooming in, most also decided to breast feed their child, while
the majority of those who decided against rooming in chose bottle feeding.[26] Thus these variables are not completely independent of each
other. However, it is probably also true that the pattern — a mother's
place on each of these variables — varies from one mother to another;
this is very likely one of the beginning points of the learned individual
difference in personality. This heterogeneity of patterns also makes it
impossible to make predictions at this time about what a particular child
will learn as a result of his infant feeding experiences. As yet, we know
too little of the complex effects of the interactions of these several
variables.

Because of this lack of knowledge of the specific effects of each variable and of each possible combination of variables, and also because of
the apparent tendency for decision on one variable to be correlated
somewhat with decision on other variables, investigators have tended to
deal with global or overall evaluations of feeding practices, rather than
restrict themselves to the particular variables involved. Thus many
psychologists have studied variables such as "rejection by the mother."
One mother might be rated as rejecting because she chose to bottle feed,
another because she did not provide the baby with pleasant stimulation
during feeding, and another because she was not responsive to the
child's state of need. More typically, rejection is measured by rating
the mother's attitudes toward her baby, with the assumption that in one
way or another, on one variable or another, a rejecting mother will
behave in a negative fashion to the child, or in a way such that she has

little contact with the child. To an extent, this approach may be in error. It is likely that rejection manifested through scheduled feeding will have very different effects than rejection expressed through early weaning. In other words, "rejection" is not a unitary trait, always having the same effects wherever it is found.

Oral Symbols. In summary, there is an association among attitudes toward food and oral activities in general, attitudes of affection toward or rejection of people, and responsiveness to external stimulation. This association is established because of the social nature of infantile feeding experiences, so that factors which affect the nature of the feeding experience and the closeness of the interpersonal relations between the mother and the child will affect the child's acquired habits and drives in these areas.[27] It is because of this strong association between satisfaction of hunger drive and interpersonal feeling, or a correspondence between them, that food may be thought of as symbolic of attitudes of love. That is, attitudes toward food or toward oral activities vary with attitudes toward people, so that it is frequently possible to infer one from the other. Thus a person with an insatiable appetite who eats far more than is required to satisfy his physiological state of need may really be responding to a dependency drive, manifested through the physiological state of hunger in association with which the individual acquired the drive to be near others who will take care of and help him. His eating, in this sense, is symbolic of his desire for love and protection. It is not uncommon for obese people whose obesity is not a result of glandular disturbance to be very dependent people.

The association between food and love is strengthened throughout childhood by circumstances that surround most of the child's feeding experiences. In American society where the father usually works outside of the home, eating time is one of the few times — often the only time of the day — when the whole family sits together and does something together as a unit. It is quite common for mealtime thus to become the time when important family affairs are discussed, and it is usually the only time that children are made privy to such affairs. These stimuli of family solidarity therefore acquire secondary reinforcing capacities through association with hunger drive reduction. It is not surprising then that when people wish to honor a person, or to show support and solidarity with him, they hold a banquet — they eat with him. Because of the central role of dining in family life, the quality of family relations is usually associated with eating. If the mother and father are in conflict, they argue at dinner so that eating becomes a symbol of discord and fear for their children. As in the case of infantile feeding, those variables which affect the nature of eating experiences will affect not only attitudes toward food and hunger, but also interpersonal feelings of love, affection, and "belongingness."

Air and Temperature

These two needs appear to be of little consequence so far as learning is concerned. The need for oxygen is so imperious that satisfaction of the drive must occur without delay. Thus it is not possible to teach children particular responses in which the learning is reinforced by allowing the child to obtain oxygen. In addition, it may be that the reflexive breathing response to the presence of carbon dioxide in the blood is quite a satisfactory one which does not create problems for group living, so that societies do not have any need to impose socialization procedures on this drive with a view to altering the reflexive response.

Socialization practices are carried on with reference to temperature needs, in that parents teach their children to reduce temperature drive in particular ways, that is, by wearing the clothing approved in the particular culture. However, there does not appear to be any direct manipulation of the drive itself, such as is the case with hunger, in which the height or intensity of the drive itself is dependent upon the parents' behavior. Temperature needs are met on a continual basis, rather than only now and again, so that people do not differ very much in the extent to which their drive is reduced or the frequency. Thus drive level and frequency of reinforcement do not seem to participate in producing particular kinds of learnings, except perhaps in the relatively rare case in American society in which poverty or parental neglect reduce the adequacy of the drive reduction.

However, clothes in our society and in many others are associated with social status, so that the clothes a child is permitted to wear and the age at which he is permitted to wear different garments may have some bearing on the child's acquisition of attitudes toward himself and on the development of status drives. In one study children were presented with dolls and costumes in which the dolls might be dressed. One of the costumes was a work costume (a maid's apron); nursery school children placed this costume on the Negro doll more often then they did on the non-Negro dolls, thus demonstrating that even at this age, there is a discrimination of stereotyped social roles as expressed through clothing.[28]

Clothing and Identification. An important aspect of the socialization process with respect to clothing is the extent to which the child is permitted to wear clothes similar to those of the like-sexed parent. Once the child is able to discriminate between his type of clothing and the type of clothing worn by his parents, his clothing becomes associated with his status within the family. The child may then give the same response to clothing as he gives to his social status or role within the family. Parents often try to capitalize on this in toilet training; they tell their children that if they cease wetting their pants, they may wear more grownup clothes, like father and mother wear. A child who has had discomfort associated with his role and status, or who has learned that increases in status are associated with more satisfactory drive reduction than is available to him, thus will be motivated to wear more adult clothing. Conversely dependency drive in a child who finds that a more mature role deprives him to some extent of the affection he has come to value may express this drive through a desire to continue wearing child-like clothing, or to return to wearing clothing which was associated with more direct drive reduction than he is experiencing currently.

The wearing of clothing similar to the parents' creates a situation in which responses associated with the cues produced by the parents now may come to be elicited by the child's own clothing. That is, by being like the parents the child tends to respond to himself in ways similar to the ways in which he responded to parents. This contributes to the process of *identification* with the parents and to growth of the tendency within the child to respond to and control his own behavior in ways similar to those which the parents had used. Thus the child *introjects* his parents' rules; he begins to punish himself when he initiates a response which the parents had previously punished and so inhibits his behavior by himself. The source of control shifts from the parent to himself. It is clear that identification and introjection have reference to the development of what is commonly referred to as conscience — the superego, in psychoanalytic terms.

Clothing and the Self-Concept. The wearing of clothing also has reference to the child's self-concept. The responses he gives to his parents will come to be elicited by his own dress, if that dress is similar to his parents. Thus the boy who perceives his father as big and strong will tend to feel more adequate himself when he wears fatherlike clothing. This seems to be why people often feel that getting "dressed up" gives them an emotional boost. The clothing they wear alters their self-concepts in the direction of feeling more like those people in relation to whom the same clothing serves as part of the cue-situation. A woman feels more sophisticated in an evening gown, for example. In such a situation, she may begin to make responses consistent with the social role she is playing. Because of the clothes she is wearing, others respond to her as sophisticated so that she may begin to acquire responses to the cues of others' behavior, thus actually becoming more graceful in her own behavior as a result of the practice she receives. However, it also may happen that disillusionment may occur. The little boy who feels strong like Daddy because he is wearing a tie like Daddy may attempt to imitate Daddy's behavior beyond the limits of his skill; the resulting failure and punishment may then teach him that regardless of clothing, he is inferior to his father. Anxiety or fear then becomes associated with any cue situation which requires mature or "Daddy-like" behavior, and with adult clothing in general. Such a person also may learn to discriminate between himself and his clothing, and experience anxiety over the discrepancy between his childlike self-concept and his more adult style of dress. He will feel that he simply is "putting up a front" and that he is very different from what he seems.

Through learning-sets and stimulus generalization, the child may also acquire a drive to wear whatever type of clothing is worn by people he admires in the same way as he admires his parents. This is more likely to occur if the child has learned to imitate, as a result of having being reinforced for giving responses like the responses made by his parents. Dollard and Miller have shown that nursery school children can learn to imitate other children in a situation in which they were given a jelly bean every time they moved a lever in the same direction as did the "leading" child.[29] These investigators also showed that the more reinforced practice the child received in imitating, the more skilled he became. It was possible to teach the child to imitate so well that he would respond in the same way as the imitated child on even the very first trial of a new task. Thus through a general set to imitate and stimulus generalization people may come to want to wear the same clothing as people similar to their parents; this is more likely to occur if the wearing of clothes like the parents' has been rewarded either by parental approval or by a reduction in anxiety which may occur when the person avoids the cues of his immature social status and role by wearing more mature clothing. This may be one of the reasons for the strong tendency of many people to follow fashions and to wear whatever prestige-marked people are wearing. This kind of behavior therefore implies that the "slave of fashion" may be a person who is highly motivated to wear prestige-associated clothing in order to feel that he or she is an adequate, mature, or affection-deserving person, and that the cue for following fashion is a feeling of inferiority in one's social role, or immaturity, or a drive for affection.

Elimination

It is in connection with the socialization of the elimination drive that many significant learnings may occur. There has been found no culture in the world, however primitive, which permits the innate reflex response to the elimination drive to go unmodified; every society has rules regarding when and where defecation and urination may occur. Toilet training is therefore a universal experience in relation to which the child learns the patterns of his culture through the training efforts of its parents or of whoever else has responsibility for this aspect of socialization.

The circumstances surrounding toilet training have been examined fairly closely by psychologists. This is for a number of reasons. (1) Because it is universal, different societies which teach their children different responses to the elimination drive may be compared with each other in terms of the effects on the learning of various factors such as severity of training, training methods, age of training, and others. If two societies differ in the approved eliminative responses but are similar in the age at which training is begun, then similarities in the learnings produced in the two societies may be ascribed to the influence of age of training, rather than to the content of the training. In this way it is possible to separate the variables involved in toilet training and see the unique effects of each. While one could analyze the other drives as well, it seems particularly important to study toilet training (and sex training) in which societies differ so markedly in the behavior they approve and disapprove. (2) Toilet training provides a focused situation in which the parents' general methods of training their children are readily apparent, so that different parents within a culture may be compared for their procedures in this "standard" training exercise. It is assumed by many investigators that the way each parent behaves in this situation is very similar to the ways in which the parent behaves in other child-training situations which are like toilet training in some respects. With this assumption, the effects of the parents' training methods may be studied by examining their behavior in this one situation which all parents face. However, it should be noted that this assumption is open to some question. John Whiting and Irvin Child rated many primitive cultures on

which dossiers were available in Yale's cross-cultural files wherein all information cultural anthropologists have obtained about the many societies they have studied is collected and indexed. Whiting and Child had ratings made, based on the material in the files, of such variables as age of socialization of hunger, sex, aggression, and elimination drives, and severity of socialization of these drives. They found that in general there are no correlations between the age at which toilet training is begun and the age at which other drives are socialized. That is, a society which tends to start toilet training relatively early is not necessarily one which begins sex training or aggression training early.[30]

However, it still is not known whether parents' training procedures in regard to the socialization of the eliminative drive are associated with their procedures in socializing *similar* behaviors. Many psychologists assume that a parent who is harsh in enforcing prohibitions against toilet "accidents" also may tend to be harsh in enforcing other prohibitions of society.

This last assumption indicates the third reason for the interest in toilet training. (3) It is similar in many respects to other experiences the child will have throughout his lifetime so that learnings which occur in this situation tend to generalize to a wide variety of similar stimuli, thus leading to strong and pervasive habits which account for a large proportion of the responses which an individual makes. To the extent that this is so these learnings constitute a large part of the person's personality.

In American culture the child is taught to defecate and urinate only in special places. Usually he is taught that the response is a private one and should not be observed by others, except perhaps by the parents. American children also are taught to avoid public discussion or reference to toilet functions and excreta. This taboo is apparent in the poverty of socially acceptable words which refer to toilet processes (or to the associated body parts) in the English language and in the proliferation of euphemistic words ("potty," "throne," "number one" and "number two," etc.). At the same time children are taught to respond with avoidance to the excreted material and to the body parts which participate in excretion. Thus American children learn responses on the dimensions of cleanliness-uncleanliness and modesty-immodesty. The learnings which occur are of such a nature that the child acquires a particular feeling about violations of the prohibitions — the feeling called guilt. Toilet training is very often the situation which contributes most to the learning of guilt in response to disobedience, immodesty, and dirtiness and in response to transgressions against the society's moral, ethical, and legal codes in general. Rules regarding elimination which indicate what the child may or may not do and under what circumstances essentially are rules of conduct existing within the culture in the same way as other moral, ethical, and legal codes are rules of conduct for the culture. Like these other rules, one seldom receives rewards for conforming but one is considered blameworthy or punishable for their violation. Thus responses learned in relation to the cues presented by the parents which represent elimination rules they are trying to teach readily generalize through stimulus generalization to other rules which may be represented through cues produced by other authority figures, and people in general (so-called social pressures). Because the individual constantly is faced with such pressures and with the moral, ethical, and legal rules of his society throughout his life, the responses he acquires to such cues in toilet training will tend to be made very often and comprise his habitual mode of responding to demands, rules, and authority. While it is unlikely that responses to toilet training alone are so strong and resistant to extinction that they can account for all of an individual's habitual responses to social controls, the responses parents teach their children to toilet rules probably are very similar to the responses they teach their children to make to other rules which they impose in the course of socialization, thus contributing to the generality of the learning. This generalization was demonstrated in a study in which parental practices in socializing eliminative behavior were correlated with their socialization practices regarding obedience, cleanliness, manners, aggression, sex and modesty, and school behavior.[31]

There is still another reason for the importance of the study of toilet training. This socialization experience is the most extensive one (in terms of number of trials and amount of time devoted to its learning) in which the child's earlier, reflexive responses must be changed and in which the parents have no way of controlling directly the occurrence or non-occurrence of the response. Toilet training is unlike eating training in this respect. In oral training the infant cannot satisfy his hunger drive except under those circumstances which the parents impose, because the parents' aid is necessary for the child to reduce his hunger drive. But in toilet training the child may reduce his drive in other than the approved ways, and at times ways which may be contrary to the parents' wishes. Further, the parents cannot control the drive (as they can the hunger drive by deciding the length of the interval between feedings) so that the drive will be high at the appropriate times (when the parents put the child on the toilet). Thus one of the main problems parents face in toilet training is arranging conditions so that the child performs correctly for the first time so that he can be rewarded for it. Time and time again the mother may put her child on the toilet only to find that he does not defecate, while he will continue to defecate in his diapers at other times throughout the day. The infant learning how to satisfy his hunger drive is in the position of the dog in Pavlov's experiment who must wait until the experimenter blows the meat powder in his mouth. But the child in toilet training is more like the rat in a Skinner box; one never knows when he will come to give the correct response out of all the possible responses in his hierarchy, and the experimenter must wait until the response is forthcoming, doing whatever he can to increase the probability that the correct response will occur but being unable to determine it precisely.

Toilet training places the child in a position unique in terms of his past experience. He has been reducing his elimination drive quite automatically several times a day, daily since he was born. More or less suddenly he is prohibited from doing so by his parents. Apart from his shifting from nursing to drinking from a cup, this may be the child's first experience with an attempt to extinguish a response which previously had been reinforced, and previously had been acceptable to the parents. In other words, the child is faced with a prohibition against a behavior which had acquired great habit strength in the past. The prohibitions are strong, and sooner or later must be effective. Toilet training therefore may be the child's first experience with efforts to make him comply with inflexible rules or laws which are inconsistent with his previous behavior, his strong habits, and his drive. In addition, the child is expected to acquire control over muscles which he doesn't know he has and which have been controlled on a strictly reflexive basis up to this time. This may be the child's first extensive experience in acquiring cortical control over reflexive behavior. The stimuli of the toilet must acquire greater capacity to elicit defecation than the innate stimuli produced in the bladder and bowel.

It also should be pointed out that toilet training is usually a learning experience in which the rewards for successful performance may be quite small. Most children do not find wet diapers to be uncomfortable, so that there is little intrinsic reward for being toilet trained. Unlike learning to climb, for example, in which success allows the child to gratify drives which otherwise are less readily gratified, such as by being able to reach the cookie jar without having to wait for mother to serve him, defecating and urinating in a toilet results in drive reduction that is no more efficient than eliminating in diapers —in fact, it is *less* drive reducing because it involves delay between the reinforcement and the responses which the child must make in order to defecate in a toilet. He must stop what he is doing, go to the bathroom, take down his pants, and climb on the seat. Thus toilet training is a situation in which the parents must supply some external motivation to the child, reinforcement of which is so powerful that it overrides the effects of the increased elimination drive level which the child must experience and tolerate as he learns the proper toilet behaviors. The motivations parents supply to accomplish this usually are either affection drive or pain drive, or some combination of the two. The parents manipulate these drives so that incorrect elimination produces an increase in drive state, despite the reduction of the elimination drive, and correct responding results in reinforcement sufficient to overcome the increased elimination drive which is involved in correct responding. For many children the toilet training situation is the first occasion on which their drive for love and freedom from pain is more or less systematically manipulated by their parents in a manner which is unpredictable to the child, who has not developed sufficient mental capacity and verbal ability to understand the need for toilet procedures, to perceive readily the relationship between his elimination and the love and/or punishment, and to learn the correct responses rapidly.

Major Variables in Toilet Training. With these considerations in mind, let us examine the effects of the main variables involved in toilet training on the kinds of learnings which may occur. These variables include the age at which training is begun, the severity or ease of the training, and the way in which rewards (usually praise and love) and punishments are used by the training agents. To a large extent, their use of reinforcers will be related to their own attitudes toward toilet training, eliminative activities, and excrement. Thus it also will be worthwhile to look at common parental attitudes in order to understand their use of reinforcers.

These variables will be examined for their effects on the kinds of learnings which occur: reactions to rules which may vary from resistance to compliance, reactions to the body parts involved in elimination which may vary on dimensions of shame and modesty, attitudes toward fecal and similar material which may vary on dimensions of disgust and cleanliness, reactions to complying with authoritative requests or demands which may vary from withholding to extreme generosity, and, finally, reactions involving elimination which may vary from constipation to diarrhea.

Age. Age at which toilet training is initiated appears to be an important variable, because successful toilet training requires that the child's neuromuscular system be mature enough for him to acquire the cortical control which is necessary.[32] It is not known precisely when this is and, of course, infants vary in rate of maturation. It is very likely that cephalocaudal maturation should have progressed at least to the point where the child is able to control his upper legs.[33] Thus a child who can crawl probably is sufficiently mature for toilet training to be effective, so far as muscle control is concerned. Development of ability to make intellectual connections between elimination drive and sitting on the toilet may come even later than this. Pediatricians suggest that in no case should toilet training be begun before the child is nine months old and some recommend waiting until the child is a year and a half for bowel training.[34]

Toilet training tends to be begun early in middle class families. The average age for starting, according to a recent survey, is eleven months, with bowel training taking an average of seven months to be completed. The length of time it takes to bowel train a baby grows shorter the older the baby is when training is initiated; while it takes about nine and a half months to train completely a child whose training is begun at five months of age, it takes less than half that much time (4.7 months) to train a child when the start of training has been delayed until the child is twenty months old.[35] The age at which a mother decides to begin toilet training her child has been found to depend to some extent on personality characteristics of the mother. Sears, Maccoby, and Levin found that mothers who started toilet training early tended to be rated as being more anxious in relation to sex matters than mothers who started later. They suggest that a child's lack of training stimulates further anxiety in the sexually anxious mothers who react by trying to get the job over with as soon as possible. It also has been suggested that middle class parents may tend to start toilet training early because in general they receive approval and rewards from their peers if their children have achieved this level of socialization at an early age. To be trained early is a testimony to both the child's and the parents' achievements. American society in general appears to begin toilet training quite early compared to other cultures; the median age at which toilet training is begun in the twenty-five primitive societies whose toilet training practices were studies by Whiting and Child was two years.[36]

Mothers who began toilet training their children when they were between fifteen and nineteen months old report more emotional upset in their children than mothers who started at other ages.[37] It seems reasonable that in this age range, the child already has had such extensive practice in defecating reflexively that it is a difficult habit to change; however, children of this age are not quite old enough to make the kind of discriminations which would facilitate toilet training (discriminations between parental rejection of wrong behavior and rejection of the child himself, and discrimination between the right and wrong places), and have not yet developed the kinds of motives (to be like Mommy or Daddy or to be grown up) which would be reduced by proper defecation. Thus the age range of fifteen to nineteen months seems to be one in which toilet training involves relatively more emotional upset than do earlier ages when the habit of eliminating reflexively is not so strong, and than do later ages, when the increased strength of the reflex habit is more than offset by the child's stronger social drives and greater learning ability.

Severity of Training. Although there has been a great deal of discussion about the age at which toilet training is begun, most of the available evidence suggests that age alone is not the important variable. Lower class mothers start training later than do middle class mothers, but are rated as being more severe in their training practices.[38] However, Whiting and Child found that there was a relationship between age of training and severity. Training begun early is generally more severe than training begun late. A very young child tends not to sit still long enough to give himself an opportunity to defecate on a toilet and so has great difficulty in learning the correct response. And of course, his discrimination and learning ability are less than optimal.

Training may be rated on the dimension of severity-leniency on the basis of such practices as punishing the child for accidents, requiring the child to sit on the toilet for long periods until he defecates, suddenly using a toilet which is unfamiliar to the child, and the like. The more severe such training is, the more emotional upset is reported by mothers. However, it has been found that severe training produces more emotional upset than lenient training only in children whose mothers are rated as emotionally "cold." There was no difference between the effects of severe and lenient training by mothers rated as emotionally "warm."[39] When a child is toilet trained, he loses the attention and stimulation he used to get from his mother when he was having his diapers changed; a warm mother is more likely to continue giving such attention and stimulation to the toilet trained child, even though the training is severe, which may be why such a child does not react with great emotional upset at being trained. However, this is less likely to be the case with a "cold" mother. Another factor which may play a role in this relationship is the extent to which the child is able to discriminate between his mother's rejection of his excreta and her rejection of him. An emotionally warm mother is more likely to behave in an accepting fashion to the child on many different occasions throughout the day, so that the child learns that punishment for toilet accidents does not mean that he himself is bad. He therefore does not reveal strong emotional upset even though toilet training is severe. On the other hand, the "cold" mother who avoids emotional affectionate interchanges with her child is less likely to compensate the child for the punishment she gives during toilet training by giving him love and affection at other times during the day. Her child therefore experiences a great loss of love to which he responds with emotional upset.

Although severe training thus appears to be an important variable in creating emotional reactions in the child, it is of interest that more severe training does not seem to speed the toilet training process at all. A severely trained child learns no faster than one who is trained in a gentler fashion. However, a severely trained child is more likely to continue wetting his bed longer than a gently trained child. Conversely, maternal warmth and gentle training are related to early night dryness. It is for this reason that nocturnal enuresis (habitual night bed wetting) is often taken as a sign of emotional upset, as the same factors which produce upset are responsible for the enuresis.

It also has been found that children who had feeding problems (food refusal, "hunger strikes," rejection of new foods) had more severe toilet training. Sears, Maccoby, and Levin found that feeding problems seem to be an alternative to enuresis as a response to severe toilet training; those children who were severely trained who also had feeding problems tended not to be enuretic, while those who had no feeding problems were late bed wetters. Thus feeding problems also are commonly interpreted as evidence of emotional upset.

Which of these two reactions —feeding problems or eneuresis —a child will have to severe training may depend on a number of factors. On the one hand, the fear produced in severe training involves activity of the autonomic nervous system which is incompatible with digestion, thus inclining children toward feeding problems. The autonomic responses also result in a loss of inhibition of reflexes, thus inclining the child to enuresis. That is why there was a great increase in bladder lapses in the frightened British children evacuated from the cities in World War II.[40] The response which prevails may depend upon that which receives the greater reinforcement. A child who as a result of feeding problems receives the kind of attention which reduces fear, will be reinforced for appetite loss and being "difficult" or "finicky" about food, whereas a child whose feeding problems are followed by increased punishment would probably extinguish this response. Further, in one family a wet bed is felt by the mother to be more bothersome than food refusal, while the situation may be reversed in another. It is possible that the severely trained child may give one or the other response out of hostility to the mother, the one he gives depending on which is more punishing to the mother. (The dynamics of aggression will be explored in more detail in the next chapter.) Still another factor related to which response the child gives is the kind of learning which has occurred during feeding training. A child who has acquired positive attitudes toward food as a result of effective drive reduction during oral training is less likely to make a food refusal response, and therefore is not likely to find such a response rewarding as far as reducing fear and emotional upset is concerned. It is of interest to note that maternal sex anxiety is associated both with a decision against breast feeding (and thus with a higher probability of less rewarding feeding situations) and with early toilet training (and thus with a higher probability of severe training and emotional upset).[41]

If toilet training is severe, the pain produced by the training person becomes associated with that person, and also with the other stimuli which are characteristically present when the pain is produced (such as the sight and touch of the toilet, when the child is punished for not sitting on it, or for not defecating on it). Such fear may be reduced by an avoidance of the pain-associated stimuli; therefore a severely trained child may tend to avoid his parents (thus prolonging the training by avoiding the very people who will teach him to perform correctly), and also to avoid the toilet, even though he may need to eliminate. Thus the parental training places the child in conflict; on the one hand, he will avoid punishment and win approval if he goes to the toilet, but on the other hand, his parents have taught him to fear the toilet and to stay away from it. The child may respond to this conflict by trying to inhibit defecation completely until, of course, he loses control because of too strong a drive. The loss of control will be followed by very great drive reduction since the elimination drive had become quite strong. Thus the child may develop a strong habit of general inhibition punctuated on occasion by sudden losses of control. Should the same kind of training occur in other situations as well (such as in aggression training), it is likely that the child may learn a general pattern of suppression and inhibition, but with a proneness to sudden and violent outbursts, as in temper tantrums.

Parental Training Practices. It was indicated earlier that one of the significant features of toilet training was that the child is required to learn a new set of responses which, though they do not result in more rapid or certain drive reduction than those which they replace, must be made if the child is to avoid pain and/or receive love. It is in this sense that the child learns that what his parents require of him is good, and those behaviors which earn pain (or the loss of love) are bad. Evaluations of behavior in terms of good and bad, and the facilitation of behavior labeled as good and the inhibition of behavior labeled as bad, thus are learned long before the child is capable of making such evaluations in terms of intellectual or logical considerations. It is for this reason that one's reactions to moral choices are often in terms of strong emotional feelings (that is, acquired drives) which seemingly defy logical analysis and are all but impossible to verbalize: the difference between good and bad is that one has been punished for being what his parents called "bad" and loved for being "good," and these rewards and punishments were the only meaning and the only criteria for what is good and what is bad. For the child, they are the only reasons for trying to be good and avoiding being bad. It is because of this feature of toilet training as the first important occasion for such learnings, that psychologists have stressed the consequences of toilet training for the child's moral attitudes and for the nature of his reactions to moral and ethical evaluations of the good-bad kind.[42] Does the child learn to be good in order to win love, or does he strive to be good in order to avoid the constant threat of punishment? Does he learn that he is generally a "good" or loveworthy person, or does he learn that he is generally bad or blameworthy? If he learns that he is bad, what does he learn to do to reduce the fear drive evoked by the label "bad?" What is the range of behaviors which become evaluated as good or bad? To what extent are these evaluative responses attached only to the act of elimination, and to what extent are they generalized to the child himself, to his body parts, to his sex organs, to his excreta, and to similar materials which are also labeled as dirty? To a large extent, the answers to these questions reside in the particular training procedures and behavior of each child's parents. In this section we will examine some of the procedures commonly used in terms of the answers which such procedures produce.

Because toilet training results in no increase in the satisfaction of the elimination drive, the parents must develop a drive in the child which is stronger than the elimination drive and which, unlike the elimination drive, can be reduced only by the correct behavior and not by the incorrect. If the child already has acquired such a drive, his toilet training can proceed more readily than if the parents must first set the stage for the acquisition of a usable drive. It is for this reason that the mother who already has established a close affectionate relationship with the child will have an easier time training him; her approval already has become an important reward usually acquired during the feeding training. For children who have acquired a drive for love and approval, successful or correct toilet performance readily can become the condition for satisfying the drive. The child learns that he can do things to earn love when it is withdrawn. However, where the feeding situation was such that this kind of drive was not developed so that the child rather feels more frightened than comforted by the mother's presence and is suspicious of her approval, maternal displays of affection are not likely to be drive reducing and hence will be ineffective in increasing the probability that the child will make the desired eliminative responses. In such a situation, the parent is likely instead to teach the child a fear drive or, since the child already has acquired a fear drive, she will merely make the fear drive evokable by the stimuli of elimination in the wrong or disapproved places. If the mother proceeds in this fashion, it means that the child must eliminate incorrectly sufficiently often and be punished for such behavior sufficiently for him to learn to react to his own eliminative response tendencies with fear, and so inhibit such responses in order to reduce the fear. In addition, he must perform correctly sufficiently often to make it possible for him to learn a discrimination so that he does not inhibit eliminative response when they occur in the approved places. As we know from out study of learning, the fear attached to elimination will generalize to elimination in all cue situations, including the toilet, so that discrimination learning must occur in order for the child to disinhibit when appropriate. It is necessary only that the training in eliminating in the proper place be sufficiently strong to acquire slightly more response strength than the inhibition which reduces the learned fear. This means that the punished child will learn to eliminate in the toilet but also will experience fear and a generalized tendency to inhibit while so doing which is only a little weaker than his tendency to eliminate. In this way, every occasion when he visits the toilet is one where he feels fear and tension even though he is performing correctly. Such a child may tend to inhibit eliminative responses as much as possible; as one of the consequences of his toilet training experiences, he will probably react to fear or to evaluations of himself as bad by sphincter inhibition producing a chronic tendency to constipation. Because of the extensiveness and frequency of punishment necessary to motivate learning in which the child must be punished for eliminating incorrectly in each situation, in each room of the house, in each outfit of clothes, if he is to learn a general fear and inhibition of elimination, the child is likely to be punished the major part of each day. He therefore will have many occasions when the term "bad" is applied to so many of his behaviors that he will learn to respond to himself as being in general a bad, punishable person. Thus as an adult, he frequently will make the kind of evaluative response to himself to which sphincter inhibition has become conditioned, further contributing strength to his learned chronic constipation.

Interaction of Age and Severity. This use of punishment probably interacts with the child's age in producing these results. It seems likely that the younger the child is when toilet training is begun, the more punishment is necessary to produce the desired eliminative habits because the child lacks sufficient language for verbal labels to mediate generalization of the punishment. The young child must be punished in every room of the house; the older child who has sufficient language need be punished only once. If he then is told that he will be punished for eliminating in every room except the bathroom, the words will mediate generalization of the fear of eliminating to all the other rooms, without it becoming necessary actually to punish him in each one. Thus the severity of the effects of punishment in toilet training probably varies with the age when the training is begun, as well as the extent to which the child receives love at other times during the day to offset the development of a "bad" self-concept.

The Anal Retentive Personality. Mothers who are severe in their toilet training (those who tend to employ punishment to produce a fear drive) have been found in general to be intolerant of aggression in their children, to be nonpermissive with respect to sex behavior in their children, to be generally restrictive in demanding that their children be orderly, neat, and generally conforming to adult standards of behavior. These mothers are also found to be high in their use of physical punishment and infliction of pain.[43] Such a mother is likely to use similar training procedures in a wide variety of situations in which the child is trained to inhibit his behavior. All of these situations are similar in that misbehavior in each training area is likely to be labeled as bad, with all of the implications of that term for attitudes related to morality. Thus it is that children who have been toilet trained through the use of punishment as described above tend not only to learn chronic constipation, but also fairly rigid morality regarding sex and modesty, and to react to dirt and disorder as bad. That is why there tends to be an identification of cleanliness and neatness with morality and being good, although there is little logic to support a connection between moral worth and goodness and cleanliness and neatness. The result is the aphorism that cleanliness is close to godliness, and the tendency for adults whose toilet training has been of the kind described here to react to dirt and disorder with strong feelings of disgust similar to their disgust for fecal material or of fear and emotional upset, as if punishment were expected. Such adults thus react with fear to dirt and disarray. As pointed out above, adults who react this way have been punished so extensively in childhood that they perceive themselves as bad, punishable, or guilty. To reduce the fear initiated by such labels, they have learned to be neat, clean, inhibited, and conforming to their parents' moral code. Thus there is a constellation of traits which go together in people who have been severely toilet trained (and severely trained in other areas of conformity to their parents' codes). These are the traits of constipation, rigid morality, inhibition, cleanliness, neatness, and passive conformance to the code of behavior approved in the individual's society. It was Freud who first discovered the relationships among these traits; he named them in terms of the common learning situation in relation to which they were acquired, and called them the "anal retentive" personality type.[44] Although this name may be an unfortunate one, research and clinical experience have testified to the existence of the relationship.[45, 46]

The extent to which the punishment-trained child acquires this constellation of behaviors is determined by the extent to which his mother was generally restrictive and demanding, and the extent to which she generalized her toilet training behavior to other situations. As it was pointed out above, such generalization appears to be common. Nevertheless, there are individual differences in the extent to which the mother reacts with distaste or horror to fecal material itself or similar conditions, to lack of privacy while eliminating, to the body organs involved in elimination, and so forth, and the extent to which these reactions are similar to the mother's reaction to incorrect elimination. It is variability in these things that is responsible for variability among people in their attitudes and responses to such stimuli.

The Anal Expulsive Personality. The training procedures employed in toilet training may have quite opposite effects; they can result in the learning of generalized disinhibition rather than inhibition, diarrhea instead of constipation, and pleasure from dirt rather than cleanliness. Theoretically there may be two ways in which these reactions might be learned. A child who readily learns to discriminate between the wrong and the right places and circumstances for defecation may derive so much drive reduction as a result of eliminating in the correct place that the response of correct elimination becomes very strong, and clearly greater in strength than the generalized inhibition produced by punishment for eliminating improperly. Should this happen, the reinforcement not only will reduce the relative importance or strength of the fear of disinhibition of the elimination response, but also will invest the stimuli associated with the drive reduction with secondary reinforcing capacities, so that defecation, fecal material, and nudity can become the goal objects of motivated behavior. Further, rather than fear producing an inhibition response, it should acquire the capacity to elicit a defecation drive (or, to generalize, a disinhibition response) as a learned drive, because the fear and punishment was characteristically great when the individual had high elimination drive, and he has learned to make eliminative responses to the drive. This should happen in the child who learns to attach fear to the cues of strong elimination drive quite readily, so that he suffers high fear when his bowels are full, but seldom gets punished *after* eliminating. The child who is punished frequently after eliminating, as we have seen, learns an inhibition response to fear; the child who is punished before eliminating may learn an eliminative drive as a response to the cues of punishment or pain. Such would be the case, for example, where the parent constantly warns the child in a threatening way not to soil himself while the child's elimination drive is growing but does not punish extensively or severely when the child does have an "accident." The cues of warning, threat, and disapproval thus may come to evoke the elimination drive characteristically high when these or similar cues were presented. And if in addition the child has received great reinforcement for defecating correctly so that the strength of the eliminative response is very much greater than the generalized inhibition response, then the child learns elimination responses to the cues of elimination drive (whether evoked by a full colon or by threat), and he will have acquired a tendency toward disinhibition, diarrhea, and the enjoyment of producing fecal and fecal-like material. Other stimuli which exist on the same stimulus generalization continuum — such as dirt and things labeled, as are feces, as dirty — also thereby may acquire positive aspects. It can be seen that the learning of these responses depends on the placement of punishment during the toilet training process, the ease with which a discrimination is established (which may be a result of such factors as the discriminability of the toilet from other rooms and the ability of the child's vocabulary to mediate stimulus generalization and discriminations, which may vary independently of each other so that they occur in different combinations in different families). It is obvious that the factors which determine the specific learnings which may occur as a result of toilet training are quite complex and very different effects may be produced by changes in only one of the variables.

There is a second training situation which may produce similar reactions. When a child first is introduced to the toilet, he may react with fear and discomfort; it may be the first time that he has ever sat on a seat so high off the floor or on one with a very large hole in it, big enough for him to fall through if he doesn't position himself carefully. This fear involving autonomic arousal tends to inhibit defecation responses as the child struggles to get off the toilet. His struggling may be increased by the tendency of young children to remain sitting still for only very short periods of time. Some parents attempt to force their children to stay on the toilet, so that a battle ensues which is so acrimonious that the mothers finally give up in disgust and allow the children off the seat even though they have not made the sought-after eliminative response. The children of these parents will have been rewarded for inhibiting and, in addition, their inhibitions will come to be associated with their own anger and hostility. These children may acquire the tendency to react to both pain and discomfort *and* the cues of their own anger with inhibition, refusal, and witholding. It is this kind of training which produces people who tend to be negativistic and denying in their relations with other people, or defiant in the face of laws and other demands placed upon them. Such a person is often coldly rejecting of others, expressing anger by closing himself off from others, denying them, and remaining aloof and uncooperative.

It also is possible that, despite the child's anger at his mother, he is required to remain on the toilet until he defecates. When he does so, he is permitted to get off the toilet and leave the bathroom. In this training situation, the cues of anger and resentment become associated with the child's eliminative drive and the elimination response. The elimination response which follows both the aggressive and the elimination drive is reinforced by the the defecation; the elimination response to the aggressive drive is reinforced by the reduction in anger which occurs when the child is allowed to leave the toilet. Thus the child learns to defecate when angry; the tendency to diarrhea in response to anger is not uncommon in adults and very likely is learned in this way.

These descriptions of the various ways in which the toilet training process may be conducted and the probable consequences of each method should not be taken as verified; certainly it is true that some adults respond to emotional upset and anger with diarrhea while others respond with constipation. It is equally true that one's position on the trait dimension of cleanliness is related to his position on the traits of orderliness and inhibition. Freud has implicated the toilet training process as the reason, an implication which gains strong support from clinical experience; what we have tried to do here is apply the laws of learning to toilet training in order to suggest how the socialization of the elimination drive *could* produce these behaviors and relationships.

Anal Symbolism. It has been mentioned that severity of toilet training is one aspect of a general tendency for the mother to demand conformity and adherence to adult norms in her children. Thus the responses the child acquires to adult demands and rules during toilet training are likely to be practiced in many other situations where rules and regulations are imposed, and the child is likely to receive reinforcement for his acquired responses long after toilet training has been accomplished successfully. As in the case of the learnings grounded in feeding training, toilet training alone is not responsible for adult behavior; rather, toilet training is involved because it is here that the child first acquires the responses which he will have many opportunities to learn even better later.

Because of the relationship between elimination and interpersonal drives of aggression, cleanliness, negativism, modesty, and conformity to rules, a relationship established by their being learned in the same training situation, a change in elimination control is expected to occur as a function of changes in the associated interpersonal drives and responses. It is in this sense that eliminative disturbances are symbolic of disturbance in the interpersonal drives. Diarrhea may be symbolic of anger, just as eating disturbances may be symbolic of difficulties in the individual's affectional drives.

Sex

An understanding of what is involved in the socialization of the sex drive requires some understanding of the nature of the drive and the extent to which the drive is modifiable. By no means may it be said that there is anything like a complete body of knowledge about sex, although it is one of the most thoroughly explored areas of behavior. The best that can be done at this point is to indicate the general lines along which present information runs.

Sex Drive, Sexual Reflexes, and Learned Sexual Responses. One must make distinctions among sex drive, sexual reflexes, and learned sexual responses. Sex drive refers to the autonomic arousing effect of the action of hormones on neural centers. The pituitary gland secretes a group of "gonadotropic" hormones which in turn stimulate the gonads to produce other sex hormones and to produce fertile sperm or egg cells. The pituitary secretes some of this gonadotropic hormone throughout infancy and childhood although at the beginning of adolescence it increases its secretion drastically. Sexual reflexes are those responses which are mediated by lower brain and spinal centers and over which the individual usually has little direct conscious control. Among such reflexes are those involved in producing erections in males and those involved in orgasm and ejaculation.[47] Reflexive erections are present from earliest infancy throughout childhood as well as in adulthood. There is some evidence that behavior similar to that of adult orgasm also is present (or at least possible) in young infants so that the orgastic reflexes also may be present at birth.[48] However, reflexive ejaculation does not occur until adolescence. Finally, "learned sexual responses" refers to the behaviors the individual must learn in order to produce the kind of stimulation which will set off the reflexive responses by means of which the sexual drive is reduced. Learned sexual responses include techniques of copulation, masturbation, and other ways of achieving orgasm, and those behaviors which lead up to orgasm, such as dating, courting, and marriage.

Infantile Sexuality. Freud was the first investigator to attach significance to erections occurring in young male infants, interpreting these erections as evidence for the existence in them of a sex drive related to the sexual interests of adults.[49] At the time of this discovery, the prevailing opinion among scientists, artists, and laymen was that infancy and childhood were sexless; for many people, the charm of youth lay in the assumption that children were without sex drive, and infancy and childhood were accepted symbols of purity and innocence in a culture where sexual knowledge was considered to be guilty, less than human, and a part of the "lower" or animal nature of man. Indeed, Freud's announcement of his discovery of sexual drive in infants was such a shock to his professional public that he was severely condemned and criticized even by scientists, not on the basis of the accuracy of his observations but rather because he violated strongly held prejudices against associating anything sexual with youth. It is of some interest that a common custom among nursemaids was, and still is to some extent, to massage gently the genitals of crying babies in order to sooth them. One only can imagine Freud's chagrin to discover that the scientific community rejected a notion which the nurses they employed were constantly applying in caring for their children.

It is not known whether Freud's interpretation of infantile erections as expressions of a sex drive is accurate. The specific nature of the stimuli necessary for the occurrence of this reflex is not yet known. Erections have been observed to occur in response to a full bladder, to interrupted feeding, to tactile stimulation of the penis, and to general physical excitement.[50] It is possible that initially these sexual reflexes may have nothing to do with a sex drive in the sense that they may not be dependent on the production of gonadotropic hormones. However, there is evidence that stimulation of the genitals is rewarding or reinforcing, even though a climax, or orgasm, is not achieved. Studies using naive white rats show that the animals will learn to make various kinds of responses where the only reward is that they are permitted to copulate with a female, even though copulation is interrupted before orgasm occurs.[51] It does seem that genital stimulation is drive-reducing in some way (although the operation of the goal gradient in experienced organisms results in an increase in the strength of copulatory responses as the organism approaches closer to the goal, so that genital stimulation has the net effect of increasing the drive to achieve orgasm, rather than being completely satisfying in itself.) It therefore seems likely that the erections observed in infants and genital stimulation of infants are reinforcing. If reinforcement means that a drive is reduced, then these studies suggest that a sexual drive is present in infancy.

Learned Sexual Responses. The aspects of sexual behavior responsible for the very great variability among humans are the learned sexual responses. The sexual drive itself is modifiable in only a very limited sense; like the other physiological drives, it can come to be elicited by new stimuli. But there is a great range of possible ways in which the individual might respond to a sexual drive or, in other terms, the number of ways in which a human may respond in order to obtain reinforcing stimulation of the genitals is very great. As far as the physiological drive and the nature of the innate reflexes are concerned, the genitals can be stimulated by mechanical means, and this stimulation is sufficient to be reinforcing to some degree regardless of the agent of the stimulation. Those agents the individual comes to use and how he uses them is a product of learning. Thus the sexual drive is reducible by self stimulation (masturbation), by stimulation applied by a like-sexed person (homosexuality), by stimulation applied by an opposite-sexed person (heterosexuality), by stimulation applied by lower animals (bestiality), and by other similar arrangements.

Our society has very strong prohibitions against several of these methods of obtaining stimulation; the only approved way is through heterosexual contact, and this also is highly restricted. One must be married and have sexual relations only with the one to whom he is married. In addition, the marriage partner must not be a close relation (the incest taboo), and less important but nevertheless present, the marriage partners are supposed to be of the same race, religion, and socio-economic background.

Our belief in the rightness of these restrictions is so strong that until very recently it was assumed that deviation from the approved way of obtaining sexual stimulation was a result of some pathological biological process. So for example, homosexual stimulation was considered to be a "perversion" or a twisting of the normal pattern. Part of this belief was the idea that normal people simply are physiologically or biologically not capable of stimulation by a like-sexed person. Here again it was Freud who exploded this myth. Freud found that he could not account reasonably for some of the behavior he observed in his patients in any other way except supposing that innately, at least, humans possess the capacity to be reinforced by both homosexual and heterosexual stimulation. This suggestion had been made to Freud by a friend some years before but Freud was so profoundly shocked by it that he rejected it out of hand. However, he was extremely honest and dedicated to empiricism, so that when he found his observations to be consistent with the hypothesis, and with no other, he accepted the assumption as part of his theory despite the personal discomfort it caused him. As was the case with the concept of infantile sexuality, Freud was not treated too kindly by the scientific community for this discovery.[52]

Much evidence has recently been acquired to support Freud's point of view. The famous studies of sexual behavior by Kinsey, Pomeroy, and Martin indicate that a very large percentage of American people have had and enjoyed homosexual stimulation at one time or another in their lives.[53] Thirty seven per cent of the men they interviewed admitted to homosexual experience; it is likely that this is an underestimate of the true incidence of such behavior. Comparable results have been obtained for women; the data indicate a sufficiently large number of people in our society have engaged in homosexual behavior to make it unlikely that homosexuality constitutes a genetic "sport" or perversion.[54] Other evidence is even more compelling. Clellan Ford, a cultural anthropologist, and Frank Beach, a physiological and comparative psychologist, have conducted an exhaustive cross-species and cross-cutural comparison of sexual behavior.[55] They have found that homosexual behavior is present in every mammalian species. In fact almost all lower animals including subhuman primates engage in both homosexual and heterosexual behavior. Masturbation is also found in every subhuman species capable of stimulating itself. Of the 76 human societies they investigated, 28 totally disapproved of homosexual behavior, as does ours, and anthropologists report that such behavior is either absent or carried on in secret. In 49 of the societies homosexuality is considered normal or desirable either for some members of the community or for all members at certain times (such as adolescence). The same general pattern emerges for masturbation and other arrangements for obtaining genital stimulation. Ford's and Beach's data indicate that either man is entirely different from all lower species or he is biologically bisexual in that, like lower species, he is capable of sexual behavior with both like- and opposite-sexed partners, as well as self-stimulation. Their data also indicate that one must either consider most human societies to be "perverted" from innate or "natural" sexual tendencies, or accept the proposition that the sexual pattern people display is determined largely by learning rather than by any innate or "natural" tendency. The latter position is obviously the more reasonable.

Of course, in no society was homosexuality found to be exclusively practiced, and similarly, in lower species, individuals are neither exclusively homosexual or heterosexual, most individuals seeming to "prefer" heterosexual behavior, in that they will more frequently attempt to copulate with opposite-sexed partners than with same-sexed. However, laboratory male rats have been observed to copulate with a female and then, with the female still available, mount another male. The Siwans of Africa talk about their masculine love affairs as freely as they do of their love of women, but they are more strongly heterosexual than homosexual in that marriage is expected and required, whereas homosexual affairs are not required. Similarly, persons who practice masturbation do not use it exclusively; it usually takes second place to heterosexual behavior. This suggests that there are differences among sources of stimulation in the degree to which they are reinforcing. It may be that heterosexual behavior provides stimulation which is in some way more effective or efficient in drive reduction than homosexual or other means of obtaining stimulation. On the other hand, it is possible that the preferences are learned. Social stimulation may be preferred to self-stimulation because it reduces not only sexual drive but also acquired gregariousness drive, and heterosexual contacts may be preferred to homosexual contacts not because of any difference in the quality of the stimulation but because of learnings which occur in relation to the socialization of the sex drive. Certainly all societies are more supportive of heterosexual behavior than of homosexual in that, though they may not proscribe the latter and may even encourage it, they must demand the former if the society is to continue to exist.

The Socialization of Sex Drive. Whether or not there are differences in the adequacy of stimulation from different sources, it is apparent that learning may overshadow completely any such differences. In our own society, children learn to inhibit completely all sexual responses, and they also learn to engage in heterosexual behavior only, when sexual behavior is permitted at all. Thus any possibility that homosexual behavior may prove satisfying is excluded by the training most children receive. In some children the reverse holds true: they learn to reduce their sexual drive by homosexual behavior exclusively, despite the possibility that heterosexual responses might be more biologically effective. The taboos against masturbation are not as great (or as effective) in our society as are the prohibitions against homosexuality, a situation which is reversed in some other cultures.

With these considerations in mind, it is the purpose of this section to discover the ways in which the sex drive is socialized in our society, and the consequences of various socialization procedures. These consequences lie in the domain not only of sexual behavior but include sex-linked behaviors, such as vocational and avocational interests, attitudes toward other people, and other such behaviors which are usually described as part of an individual's *sex role*.

It was indicated above that male infants have frequent erections. When children are old enough to use their hands effectively as manipulators, they readily discover that they need not wait for accidental stimulation such as that produced by clothing and bedding, but can stimulate themselves. When parents find their children playing with their genitals, their reactions will begin the child's earliest experience in sex training. In our culture, the child usually learns to inhibit sexual behavior completely, or so to disguise it that it is scarcely recognizable as sexual. Of the drives so far discussed, only the sexual drive can be so completely inhibited, because it is the only drive whose lack of satisfaction does not result in death. And unlike the other drives discussed, it is the only one in relation to which the object of training is the complete annihilation of the drive responses in our society. Sears, Maccoby, and Levin point out that parents typically use three methods to achieve this: they prohibit self-stimulation; they arrange situations so that the child will not be presented with social stimulation by making sure that the child does not play where the parents cannot see him or her, and by making other similar arrangements; and finally, they avoid sexual stimulation by not discussing sex before the child.[56] In general, these investigators found that most of the mothers they interviewed were nonpermissive regarding sexual behavior in their children but were relatively nonpunitive in controlling it. The typical response of a mother to the sight of her child's handling its genitals was to remove the hand gently or distract the child by proposing some interesting activity. Relatively few mothers reported using strong pressure such as threats of punishment or of unpleasant consequences for sexual behavior. Most of the mothers they interviewed made some efforts to avoid social stimulation —by not allowing their children to see the genitals of other children or to play with each other's genitals, as does happen in societies in which prohibitions against childhood sexuality do not exist. This is not meant to imply that the curiosity children display regarding genitals is motivated by a sex drive; it may be simple curiosity about normally hidden body parts, with the added interest which occurs when the child discovers that opposite-sexed children have genitals very different from his own. However, the training the child has in avoiding such exploration inevitably results in a loss of information about other people's genitals and may include fear of exposing one's own genitals, and by generalization, fear or shame of the genitals themselves. Of course, mothers differ in the extent to which they arrange to rid the child's environment of opportunities to observe others' sex organs. Some parents are very efficient, avoiding even the possibility that their children should view the parents' genitals. Others are more permissive in this regard. Parents are equally varied in the extent to which they satisfy their children's curiosity about sex. Some answer their children's questions while others refuse, occasionally even punishing their children for asking. The effect of such parental reactions on the child's tendency to continue to seek sexual information and to seek information in general, is obvious.

One of the most interesting discoveries made by Sears and his co-workers was the very general avoidance of labeling sexual parts and responses by parents. Mothers referred to the genitals as "it." A mother might say to her child, "Don't play with yourself *there*," or "Don't forget to wash *it* in your bath." It is probably a rare parent who labels an erection as an erection and, as the investigators point out, a mother might verbalize to her child her awareness that the child feels angry, but the parent is almost unheard of who will label her child's behavior or feeling as "sexy" in the child's presence. In general then, there is a strong avoidance on the part of parents of labeling stimuli, responses, and body parts associated with sex. This avoidance may be a result of the anxiety with which the parents themselves respond to sex-associated stimuli. From what has been said of the nature of thought in Chapter 5, it is apparent that this course of behavior must have important consequences for the child's ability to think about sex, to include sexual thoughts as part of his self-concept, and to be aware of his own sexual feelings and responses. Perhaps this is why the sex drive is so often unconscious in our society.

Sexual Inhibition. Children frequently learn to attach fear responses to their genitals, not only as a result of training against display of the genitals, but also through stimulus generalization of the attitudes acquired in toilet training. Parental training to avoid self-stimulation, usually occurring most strongly about the time of toilet training or shortly thereafter, will tend to increase the child's anxiety responses to his own genitals, in that parents frequently describe self-stimulation, like incorrect toilet functioning involving the same body parts, as "dirty" or "not nice." As such training increases in severity, the child's spontaneous and happy enjoyment of his genitals is replaced by fear, anxiety, shame, and inhibitions, which function to reduce the probability that the child will make sexual responses until they are appropriate in terms of the customs of his society. However, the childhood training may be so effective that the inhibitions are not readily extinguished. Thus severely trained people may find that their fear in relation to sex continues into adulthood and marriage. The embarrassment couples may feel on their wedding night and in some cases for years afterward is an expression of such generalized inhibition which may be so debilitating that it makes effective sexual performance impossible. The autonomic arousal of fear is incompatible with sexual excitement and the occurrence of sexual reflexes. The training in the avoidance of sexual responses in childhood is completely inclusive, allowing no exceptions to the rule. That is why the adult finds it difficult to make a discrimination between his or her previous experience when sex was punishable and his or her present status as a groom or bride, when sexual behavior is permissible and expected.

That sexual inhibitions in adulthood are related to childhood sex training is supported by the cross-cultural studies of Whiting and Child.[57] In our society, most people believe that they should abstain from sexual behavior when they are sick. Indeed, wives not infrequently use illness as an excuse for avoiding intercourse, and in one study, 66 per cent of the aged men studied indicated that the reason they ceased to engage in intercourse was poor health. This is one expression of the general feeling that sexual behavior is physically bad for the individual. In four of the societies which Whiting and Child studied, however, the situation was reversed, in that in these societies the belief was common that sexual intercourse was a good cure for illness. The investigators found that in the two of these societies for which they had data, parents are much more permissive of childhood sexuality than in the other societies in which sexual behavior was not believed to be efficacious in treating illness. In the two permissive societies, children are permitted to play with each other's genitals and even to practice intercourse and to engage in the complete sexual act whenever they have matured physiologically enough to do so. This early permissiveness presumably is what makes it possible for adults in those societies to be so free of guilt concerning sex that they see no physical harm but only benefit from it.

A not uncommon problem some parents experience is that of bed phobias in their children, in which the children show marked fright when they are put to bed at night. Clinical psychologists frequently find that such phobias occur in children who have been severely punished for masturbating. The fear is generalized to the bed and bedroom where the children have masturbated most frequently and the fear is increased by the close stimulus of the bed, which tends to arouse the tendency toward the punished behavior. The existence of bed phobias is one product of the sexually inhibited training of children in our society.

In general then, most children in our society learn to inhibit sexual responses to a great extent, and one of the common consequences of great inhibition is reflected in an inability to engage readily in sexual behavior in those situations in which such behavior is acceptable and expected. This inability or inhibition is worsened by lack of sexual knowledge, produced in part by the avoidance of labeling, punishment for questioning, and also by the embarrassment experienced in adulthood for asking questions about which one already is expected to know the answers. It is not uncommon to find that a woman who has borne several children knows almost nothing more than the superficial aspects of conception and childbirth. Her apparent lack of curiosity about a matter which has concerned her so closely and intimately is very likely a result of inhibition and inability to think about sex without experiencing the fear she has learned in response to sex-associated stimuli. To add to the difficulty of the sexually inhibited young adult, such a person has had little or no practice in making sexual responses so that his first attempts may be fumbling and ineffective, producing added anxiety about his sexual adequacy, a fear response which also will be associated with his sexual drive, producing further inhibition.

Sexual Facilitation. On the other hand, it also is possible for childhood learning to result in facilitation of sexual behavior; it happens not infrequently that sexual behavior, rather than being the stimulus for fear and inhibition, is in itself fear-reducing. Children are often able to masturbate frequently without incurring the displeasure of their parents, either because the parents are permissive, or more likely, because it is easy for a young person to avoid his or her parents long enough to masturbate. A child, after being punished or rejected by his parents for some misdeed, may avoid his fear-arousing parents and finding himself alone, masturbate. The erection reflex thus comes to be elicited by the cues of fear because it has occurred in close proximity to such cues frequently. This child may grow up with a tendency to seek sexual stimulation in response to fear or rejection by people important to him. Clinical psychologists have observed that children who are referred to clinics because of extensive or "excessive" masturbation usually are very anxious and fearful.

In sum, parents' responses to their children's self-stimulation is an important determinant of the extent to which sexual inhibitions or excitation will be present later. Where inhibition is taught, a common component of the teaching is an avoidance of verbal labeling of sexual objects and stimuli. This avoidance of labeling and lack of sexual information permitted the child may serve to reduce sexual stimulation; it also makes it difficult for the child, and later the adult, to think about sex drives and responses and thus to be conscious of their presence and informed about their nature.

Training in Goals of the Sex Drive. What are the conditions which determine whether a child will learn to seek sexual stimulation from males or females? In order to answer this question, we must examine some facets of the interaction between parents and their children.

Two related learning processes go on throughout childhood and, to a lesser extent, throughout the rest of the person's life: *sex role training* and *identification.*

Sex Role Training. Sex role training refers to the selective application of rewards to the child's behavior, depending on the extent to which that behavior conforms to the parental expectations or hopes for the kind of person the child should be. For example, a girl is being trained in a sex role when her mother and father reward her for behaving in ways which conform to the parents' ideal of appropriate feminine behavior. She even may be punished mildly for engaging in behavior inconsistent with the sex role the parents envision. In our society boys usually are rewarded for mechanical interests and athletic activities and at least are given greater freedom to be boisterous. Girls, on the other hand, are expected to be quieter and more sedate and are likely to be punished mildly more than boys for boisterousness, "unladylike" conduct, and being a "tomboy." Girls are rewarded more often for helping their mothers in household tasks, for looking pretty, for being interested in dolls, and for playing a nurturant or mother-type role, as in the care of pets or plants. It is in this way that children are rewarded for making specific responses which will conform to the larger society's norms for appropriate sex roles. One study very nicely illustrates the effect of such training. In this study, boys whose fathers were away from home (most of them were in the armed forces at the time) were compared with boys whose fathers were living at home for the amount of aggressiveness shown in their doll play. The experimenters hypothesized that it is usually father who reinforces a child for aggressive behavior, thus perpetuating the masculine trait of aggressiveness so that in homes in which the father is absent, the boys should show less aggressiveness than in those from homes in which the father was not absent. The predictions were confirmed.[58]

This kind of sex role training appears to start almost at birth. Baby boys often are given different kinds of toys with which to play than baby girls, so that very early they begin to get practice at some kinds of responses and not at others. Of course, parents differ in the extent to which they encourage such role-typing; some parents make clear differentiations between boys and girls, as far as toys and clothes are concerned, very early. The encouragement of early sexual differentiation is related to the parents' own anxieties. The more upset the parents are about sex and sex roles, the earlier and the more thorough is the training they give their children.[59] It is likely that such parents give more complete or more frequent training in sex roles than do those parents who do not differentiate their children in terms of dress or toys until much later. Such training interacts with sex differences present at birth. There is some evidence that even before such training begins, neonatal boys and girls are clearly different in their responses: boys tend to be more active and better coordinated and girls tend to have greater tactile sensitivity.[60] Such innate, sex-linked differences may form the basis for the greater probability that boys will try out, be rewarded for, and learn muscular skills, while girls will try out, be rewarded for, and learn responses which provide them with tactile stimulation.

Identification. Another very important determinant of whether the child will try out certain sex-typed responses and be rewarded for them is the extent of the child's identification with the parents.[61] Psychologists and nonpsychologists alike have noted that children tend to take after their parents. Freud attached the name "identification" to this tendency and described it as a process by means of which the child "internalizes" or "introjects" his parents' code of behavior, their prohibitions, punishments, and praises, so that their reactions now become his own reactions. When this occurs, it may be said that the child acquires a "conscience," or "superego," in Freud's terms, by means of which he no longer needs to depend upon his parents for further rewards and punishments with which to guide his behavior, but is now capable of rewarding and punishing himself. We already have seen how such identification and sex role training operate in the kinds of clothes children are dressed in to reduce their temperature drives.

Internalization. The core of identification lies in the process of internalizing. Freud did not spell out just what this process is and there have been several different hypotheses advanced to describe it. One explanation of "internalization" is that it is the result of learning by imitation. In an earlier section of this chapter an experiment was described in which children were taught to imitate by getting rewarded whenever they made the same response as the person who was to be imitated. As training progressed, the children more and more readily imitated the responses of the other person. In terms of this explanation, internalization occurs when the child has been rewarded for imitating his parents and as a result of extensive imitation acquires many of the responses or habits which are characteristic of the parents. By imitating his parents, the child not only gets a great deal of practice at making the same responses they do but also gets practice in imitating *per se,* thus further increasing the probability that he will acquire still more of his parents' traits. In this the child acquires not only his parents' mannerisms and traits but also practices responding to his own behavior in the same ways that they do. Thus he evaluates his behavior in the same terms as do the parents, acquiring a self-concept from them, and learns to punish and praise himself in the same ways they punish and praise him, and in response to the same cues — namely, the cues of his own behavior. When such evaluations have been well learned, the child will make such self-responses of praise or punishment to low-level cues such as the mere thought of behaving in certain ways. When this occurs, the child may be said to be inhibiting or facilitating his own behavior by means of an acquired "conscience," or by the internalized responses of his parents. The process of such internalizing may be observed readily in young children. At first, the parent must punish or scold the child every time the child touches a forbidden object. After a while, the child may be discovered touching the forbidden object and then withdrawing his hand, saying "no, no" or whatever else the parents habitually have said. The child even may slap his own hand. As training progresses further, the child will inhibit his touching response sometime after the response has started but before it is completed, so that he will reach for the forbidden object but not quite touch it. In the later stages of training, his "reaching" response will be inhibited while it is only a thought before any overt reaching has occurred. The child's training may be so thorough that he may come to inhibit even the thought itself, or at least his consciousness that he has such a thought or desire.

The Talking Bird Hypothesis. This example serves as a good introduction to another hypothesis about the nature of the "internalization" in identification. O. Hobart Mowrer has proposed that internalizing occurs in children as a process identical to that which he describes in talking birds, such as the mynah bird.[62]

Mowrer observes the following process in teaching birds to talk: The owner of the bird tends to talk to the bird whenever he feeds it. Under the influence of a hunger drive when alone in his cage and without the owner present, the bird makes trial and error responses. One of these includes vocalizing. The sound he emits is sufficiently like the sounds the owner makes when feeding the bird so that the sound the bird emits has some secondary reinforcing properties, because it or one like it on a gradient of stimulus generalization from the owner's voice was closely associated with hunger drive reduction. Thus the bird is reinforced for making a sound and tends to increase in the frequency with which it vocalizes. In the course of vocalizing the bird will make sounds even more like those made by the owner, which will be even more rewarding than the first sounds, because they are closer on the stimulus generalization gradient to those made by the owner with which reward is associated. Thus by a process of successive approximations to the owner's speech, the bird learns to talk with each approximation reinforced through secondary reinforcement, the reinforcement being stronger the closer the bird's sounds are to the owner's. In this way, the bird learns to reinforce itself in the owner's absence. Mowrer proposes that the same process occurs in children. They respond to themselves in the same ways as do their parents because these responses enable the child to reward himself in his parents' absence. Through practice at this, the child comes to "internalize" — that is, make as his own responses those which were originally his parents'. There are two sources of reward in this. The first is the direct reward he receives from the parents for imitating, in terms of praise and affection. The other is the secondary reward associated with the words the child tells himself in response to his own behavior. There also may be a third source of reward for this process: as the child internalizes, he becomes better able to do the right thing and avoid misbehavior, because it is no longer necessary for the parents to be present to tell him what is right and wrong. He no longer needs to resort to trial and error to discover if a response is praiseworthy or punishable. He therefore is better able to stay out of trouble, with a resultant decrease in fear of punishment which further reinforces the internalization process which led to this happy state of affairs.

Once a child has begun to make such internalized self-responses, he is able to reward his own behavior and punish his transgressions. The punishment he gives himself when he responds to his behavior with the words and sentences which his parents applied to him in association with the pain of punishment, is called "guilt." It is usually experienced as the expectation of punishment or the feeling of being punishment-worthy. However, because it is the guilty person himself who is responding negatively to his own behavior, there is no external agent of punishment such as a parent available. In a sense, by feeling guilty (which basically may be the same emotional state as that produced by the pain involved in the punishments the parents used), the person punishes himself. Psychologists working in clinics frequently come across people with such a pervasive sense of guilt that they do things in order to punish themselves in actuality by getting into trouble, picking fist fights which they are sure to lose, or turning themselves in to the police for crimes they did not commit. By arranging to get themselves punished, these people at least end the anticipation of punishment which their feelings of guilt involve.

Whiting and Child explored some of the conditions which encourage the development of internalization, and so the capacity for feeling guilty. They found that those societies in which people blame themselves for being sick, rather than some external agents such as unfriendly gods, are those which encourage internalization in their children. Whiting and Child interpret the self-blame for illness as an expression of the tendency to feel guilty, much as a person may blame himself for not being careful to wear the right clothes and catching a cold as a result. These investigators found that those societies where generalized guilt is common are those where the child is made independent of his parents relatively early —at a time when he is most in need of parental love and support and least able to make the kind of discriminations which would operate against a pervasive or generalized guilt.[63] Thus their evidence supports the idea that internalization occurs as a way of rewarding oneself when the needed parents no longer are constantly available to give rewards. Further support for this explanation is found in Whiting's and Child's discovery that guilt feelings are strongest in those societies where the usual modes of training children are those which they label as "love-oriented." These are punishments involving loss of love and affection as compared with punishments which involve physical pain. Where withdrawal of love is used as a punishment, the child is more likely to internalize as a means of regaining the feeling of being loved and he is more likely to be imitative of parents who love him (and only parents who love can withdraw it) than of parents who do not use withdrawal of love as a punishment, because they give too little to withdraw.

This extended discussion of the process and effects of the development of identification is important because of its implications for the development of a sex role in the child. It is apparent the sex role the child acquires and his attitudes toward sexual behavior will be determined by which parent the child imitates and internalizes and what that parent is like. As part of this sex role typing, the child acquires not only sex-linked interests, attitudes, and traits, but also the direction in which he looks for interpersonal and sexual rewards. Girls, imitating their mothers, learn to desire and seek rewards from men like their fathers. And all of this learning is powerfully controlled and maintained by the guilt which the person may experience —nameless, oppressive feeling of being bad or of being unloved —when he or she does not behave in terms of the role which has been acquired through identification and internalization, and by the positive rewards of being loved which the child receives when he behaves in terms of the approved role. It is quite difficult to change the nature of one's sex role even in relatively small details, because the rewards and punishments which attend sex-linked behavior come not only from the environment, but in the adult from his conscience; that conscience within himself which was acquired many years before and is itself very difficult to change because of the strength of the original learning, and the fact that it occurred before he was sufficiently skilled verbally to be aware of what he was learning. Thus an adult frequently is unable to explain why certain behaviors are wrong. He says that he feels it in his bones, by which he means that he cannot describe the learning experiences through which that particular standard of behavior was internalized nor can he see any logic in his feeling because it occurred before he was able to describe what was happening to him, and before he could think in terms of logical rules. There is much more to identification than this, and many other factors that influence the extent to which a child will "take after" his parents; we will return to identification in later chapters to discuss these other aspects.

Patterns of Identification. Let us examine some of the common family situations in order to point out how the sex role typing and identification of the children may be affected by them. In our society, children of both sexes usually have their closest early contact with their mothers. This is because the father typically works outside the home so that he is absent during most of the child's waking hours. It is the mother who administers most of the significant rewards and punishments during these early years.

However, boys come to identify with their fathers. Such identification usually begins during the child's second or third year. If identification of any kind has begun earlier, this means that the boy must change from the earlier identification, which most likely would be with the mother, to an identification with the father. However, it is not known whether the child is intellectually capable of developing an identification before this age, although many theorists, particularly those following Melanie Klein, have assumed that the child does identify with the mother to some extent at least before boys develop the patterns of identification with their fathers.[64] To the extent that the child learns by imitation will the young boy learn behaviors typical of his mother, at least until he begins to identify with his father. When this appropriate identification does develop, the boy usually modifies those responses he has acquired through imitation of the mother in terms of those he acquires through identification with the father.

The factors which determine that boys will develop identifications with their fathers, although the mother continues to be the more important parent in that she still gives most of the rewards and punishments and satisfies most of the child's needs in his day-to-day living, have not been extensively explored, although there has been much theorizing about them. It has been suggested that the boy begins to identify with the father rather than the mother when he is able to discriminate between the sexes and to note the essential similarity in sex between his father and himself. It also has been pointed out that a boy is more likely to be rewarded for identifying with his father than with his mother and that fathers tend to play a more important role as givers of rewards and punishments to a male child than they do to a female child who is more typically left to the mother to handle. There is evidence that the extent to which the father participates in family life, and particularly in the life of the children, determines to some extent the likelihood that the children will identify with him, so that if fathers increase their participation in the lives of their boys, this would account to some extent for the greater tendency of boys to identify with their fathers than with their mothers. Such participation implies, of course, that the father becomes relatively more active in administering rewards and punishments and is with the child relatively more frequently, thus giving the child the opportunity to imitate him and introject the father's standards.[65]

It probably is not correct to think that children identify exclusively with only one parent. It does seem more likely that children identify with both parents, acquiring traits from each, but with the balance of identification typically based on the like-sexed parent, at least as far as sex-linked behaviors in our society are concerned. Thus aggressiveness and physical activity in our society are linked with masculinity. A boy well may identify equally with both parents regarding such standards as honesty or such behaviors as the way he holds a fork, but will identify more strongly with the father in activities where aggressiveness or physical performance may play a role. This dual identification makes it possible for a child to be other than a carbon copy of his father or mother. As the child broadens his interpersonal contacts in the course of growing up, as a result of spending increasing amounts of time outside of the home in the neighborhood and in the school, he comes into contact with other models, including older children and the parents of his friends. He is also able to identify to some extent with these people, particularly if they are similar enough to his primary identification figure to elicit similar responses in the child, so that the habit of identification already acquired is evoked by these people. In this way the child still further modifies his response repertory, becoming even more different from the parent with whom he has his major identification. This is one of the many factors which contributes to variability in personality among generations, and among different children of the same parents.

The Oedipal Situation. In the typical family in our society, then, the boy comes to identify with his father and the girl develops an identification primarily with her mother. Thus the two sexes acquire traits, mannerisms, standards of conduct, and ways of doing things which are typical of their parents. To the extent that the parents display the behaviors which in the larger society are considered appropriate to their sexes, the children also will behave in ways considered appropriate to their sexes. This includes the tendency to seek interpersonal rewards and the satisfaction of affectional needs from the opposite sex. Thus boys expect to find rewards from a close association with females like their mother and girls come to expect to have their needs for affection and support filled by someone like their fathers.

This expectation is likely to be stronger in boys than in girls because boys have already had a great deal of experience in getting love and the satisfaction of all their other needs from a woman. Nevertheless, when identification is sufficiently developed to include a tendency to approach

the same person as does the object of the identification—when a boy
has identified sufficiently with his father to approach his mother for
interpersonal rewards like his father does, and when the girl seeks
affection from her father just as her mother does, the family situation
contains the possibility of developing rivalries between boy and father
for mother's attention and between girl and mother for father's. This
is the condition Freud described as the Oedipus situation. In Freud's
original formulation, it was thought that boys have an instinctive tendency to seek sexual contacts with the mother and that this was why
father-son rivalries develop. Freud also proposed that this rivalry
resulted in so much punishment and threatened punishment to the boy
that the boy ceased rivaling his father and came to identify with him
instead. However, few modern psychologists accept this formulation
and the evidence suggests that identification develops long before the
child is able actively to compete extensively with the father for the
mother's time, interest, and attention.

Nevertheless, some rivalry usually does develop; the child wants more
of the mother's or father's time and attention than the other parent is
willing to give up to the child. Children often make strenuous efforts
to attract the attention of one parent from the other when they are
engaged in conversation or other mutual activities. This competition
most frequently is settled by compromises. The child may learn some
behaviors which are rewarded by the attention he is seeking from his
mother, such as insisting, acting babyish, doing a stunt, or showing off
a new addition to his vocabulary or knowledge. Thus the child learns
some responses to competition, and a working relationship is stabilized
in which the child takes as large a share of the mother as she and
her husband are willing to give him. This development is reflected
in the child's fantasies. The period when such rivalries are strong
and as yet unstabilized is the period when children are most interested in fairy tales and stories about wicked stepmothers, ogre-like
fathers figures (every producer knows that Captain Hook, the pirate
in Barrie's *Peter Pan*,[66] should be played by the same actor who plays
the role of the father in the first and last scenes of the play), and boys
who save their widowed mothers from harm. These stories reflect
the child's perceptions of the parent who is his rival and the child's
wishes to play the role of that parent and have the exclusive possession of his love object, while the rival is either killed or is simply not
present.

In Freud's theory, the boy's demands on his mother are directly sexual. The boy seeks satisfaction of his sexual drive from his mother. Most theorists today agree that four and five year old children have no knowledge of sexual intercourse, the responses it involves, and the appropriate goal objects for intercourse. However, it is still possible that the boy, having sexual drive as was indicated earlier in this discussion, turns to his mother for help in finding relief of the drive, just as he has found that with most other strong drives, it was his mother who helped and thus was associated with drive reduction. To the extent that this is so, it follows that part of the boy's rivalry with his father is for sexual gratification although none may be forthcoming. Anecdotal evidence does suggest that, unless trained not to, young boys will report their erections to their mothers and even may have erections habitually at certain times when the mother is present, such as when she is dressing him or putting him to bed. However, there is no objective evidence based on studies of humans in this area at all. Some very recent work with monkeys, however, does bear on this problem. Harry Harlow has found that young monkeys can be raised having no contact with a real mother, but only with an artificial, terry cloth figure which crudely resembles a mature monkey, and that the infants respond to this figure in much the same way as other infants respond to their mothers. Now that the first group of infants raised this way are mature, it is found that the monkeys reared by artificial mothers are sexually unresponsive as adults to sexually mature partners; none of them thus far have copulated or attempted copulation. This gives support to the idea that there are some sexual implications to a child's relationship to his mother.[67]

In any event, it often does happen that the process of identification and the rivalry that may result from it occurs at about the same time that the child is being trained to avoid genital manipulation and sex play. It is often the father who participates in such training. Should the child be punished for sexual activity by his father frequently or severely enough sufficiently to produce avoidance of sex, sexual thoughts and the sexual apparatus, the boy may associate the punishment with his rivalry for the mother's attention, so that sexual behavior and the desire for the close and constant support of the mother become associated with each other in the boy's experience, in that both are punished by the father, perhaps often during the same day. This may be one of the ways in which the avoidance of incest and incestuous thoughts in human society is acquired in childhood — an avoidance found in all human societies (although there are some differences among societies in the range of relationships considered incestuous), but not in subhuman species. Further, should the mother withdraw from contact with the child, either out of distaste for his spontaneous sexual play or in order to minimize the rivalry with the father, loss of love may become associated with sexual activity in the child, or an effect like that found in Harlow's monkeys might be produced.

Sexual Object Choices. It can be readily seen that to the extent that the child is encouraged to imitate and identify with the like sexed parent,

Figure 10. Infant Monkey with Artificial Mother

Monkeys "reared" by artificial mothers are sexually unresponsive as adults.*

*Courtesy of Harry F. Harlow; Fred Sponholtz, photographer.

to that extent will the child develop a sex role which is like that of the parent, and to that extent the child will seek affection and attention from the opposite sex. This statement probably holds true except for a consideration of the possibility that too great an association between sexual avoidance and the avoidance of the mother or between genital stimulation and loss of maternal love may further modify the child's tendency to seek sexual and other rewards from the opposite sex (particularly through the process of stimulus generalization from the mother to other females). Although the child's turning toward one parent or the other for rewards may be for affection and love, this direction of seeking rewards will continue when as an adult he seeks rewards which are directly sexual in nature.

When imitation of and identification with the like-sexed parent is rewarded, the child will assume the sex role of that parent, and if that sex role is also approved in the wider, extrafamily environment, then the sex role assumed by the child will be appropriate in his culture. Where such like-sexed imitation and identification are but poorly rewarded, one may expect a corresponding tendency to develop a sex role which includes stronger components of the other parent and that parent's sex role; the child will have a less clear sex role which may range from some slight conflict over the "right" way to behave in sex-linked activities, to complete inversion in which the person takes a sex role very largely following that of the opposite sexed parent, and so comes to seek sexual rewards from people of his or her own sex.

Some Conditions Affecting Sexual Object Choice. Some of the conditions which might operate to interfere with the imitation of and identification with the like-sexed parent and thus increase the extent of identification with the opposite-sexed parent might be mentioned. It has been indicated already that the father's absence from the home may be a limiting factor in the case of boys, as well as any other condition which may deemphasize his participation and importance in the family life. Very likely the same conditions involving the mother may similarly affect girls.

A situation which is powerful in terms of its effects on identification is that of marital discord between husband and wife, or the failure to establish a marital relationship which sufficiently meets the parents' own needs for love, affection, and emotional support. These are the conditions which lead to a child being punished if he imitates the hated wife or husband, to efforts to put the child on the side of one parent against the other, and/or to attempts to gain from the child the love and the feeling of being needed the parents may not be getting from their mates. Such situations can lead readily to the development of identifications with the "wrong" parent.

Presuming that imitation and identification have followed their usual courses with the child acquiring the sex role typified by the like-sexed parent, it is still possible for the parents' handling of the Oedipal rivalry to create conditions which interfere with the child's learning to seek rewards from the opposite sex. Should the child experience punishment for sexual behavior in connection with rejection or punishment for monopolizing the opposite sexed parent's time, the child may learn an avoidance of both sexual behavior and of seeking the desired parent in such a way that the two are associated. Thus, although the boy may be primarily identified with his father, he may learn to avoid seeking sexual gratification from people like mother, particularly if she avoids contact with the child out of rejection for the child's sexual behavior or to avoid the hostility of a jealous husband. Where this occurs, the child may come to seek sexual gratification in adulthood with members of the same sex since the other is closed to him by being too strongly associated with punishment, fear, or the loss of love. In less severe cases, there may simply be less heterosexual interest without direct homosexual activities. In one study of college men, subjects with an Oedipal pattern like that described above were found to do less dating, to go steady less, and to have fewer heterosexual contacts, than subjects whose masculine identifications were more complete.[68] This kind of pattern may occur thus without the person displaying traits and characteristics of the opposite sex, because his primary identification and thus his sex role typing, are appropriate to his sex. However, where such a training situation is established, it is likely that the child will also come to avoid the punishing parent — the boy his father and the girl her mother — thus contributing to the weakening of the basic identification itself, and to the restriction of opportunities to further elaborate this identification.

It is generally thought that patterns of training such as these are responsible for the various types of sexual inversion which are found — homosexuality including attitudes and traits appropriate to the opposite sex, homosexuality in persons whose other behavior is appropriate to their sex, homosexuals who play the sex role appropriate to their sex (for example, a male who plays the male role in a sexual liaison with another homosexual male), and homosexuals who play the roles of the opposite sex (for example, a female who plays the male role with a female homosexual partner).

One other factor may play a part in determining the individual's learning regarding which sex he will seek for sexual drive reduction. This is the factor of sexual preference which appears to vary independently of sexual identification. There is much evidence that people vary in the extent to which they like being the sex with which they identify themselves. The evidence indicates, for example, that girls much more frequently than boys admit having wished at one time or another that they were of the opposite sex.[69] We will say more about this and its implications for cultural norms related to sex roles in a later section. Its importance here is to suggest that there may be family situations in which a child identifies with the like-sexed parent at an early age but later comes to respond with fear or avoidance to that parent, and thus to himself. This later fear or avoidance may come about as a result of changes in that parent's behavior, as during the Oedipal period, or of the child's increased realization of some aspects of that parent's behavior to which the child responds with avoidance. There also may be a growing awareness of the implications (and limitations) of his sexual role in the larger extrafamily society. If the early identification learning was strong enough, these later developments might not be sufficient to extinguish the learnings so acquired but they might produce a continued dislike or avoidance for behavior typical of the like-sexed parent, expressed through such sentiments as "when I grow up, I hope I'm not like that." Such a child may react with such strong avoidance of the like-sexed parent and the behavior associated with that parent that he cannot bring himself to behave in similar ways in sexual situations when he attains sexual maturity. A boy who does not allow himself to behave like his father therefore may not find it possible to seek sexual satisfaction from women as his father had done; if the alternative is less fear-arousing, homosexual object choice may result. Such a person probably would not appear or act like a member of the opposite sex, although he may be exclusively homosexual in his sexual life.

As was indicated earlier, sexual behavior includes sexual drive, sexual object choice (or learned cue), sexual reflexes, and the instrumental acts, or learned behaviors which bring the individual to the point at which the reflexive acts are stimulated. It is largely in adolescence that these instrumental acts are perfected, although the individual may have more or less vague ideas about what is involved before this. Most early social sexual performances are practiced first in adolescence. For the young adolescent, obtaining opportunity for such practice may often be in itself a trying experience which can arouse such great fear that the autonomic responses involved in the fear inhibit sexual arousal, frequently resulting in a failure of sexual drive, and thus a failure to cue off the sexual reflexes involved in orgasm. Correct performance (that which will result in drive reduction) in the realm of sex as in other realms, must be learned and it is not necessarily so that it will be learned in one trial. Imagine a young boy, perhaps somewhat frail and non-athletic, who enters adolescence feeling that he is generally inferior in the kinds of activities characteristic of his age sex group. Such a boy is likely to think of himself as generally inadequate as a boy. Although heterosexually inexperienced, the boy will tend to generalize his feelings of inadequacy to the sexual area, and so approach heterosexual experiences with trepidation, fearing that he will prove to be a failure in the male sex role. Such fear will tend to be incompatible with sexual arousal. The boy may well find that in his first experience with coitus, he fails to maintain an erection. This experience, especially if it is treated unsympathetically by the sexual partner, is likely to confirm further the boy's tendency to think of himself as inadequate and heterosexual situations thus will come to elicit still greater fear. Thus the boy may become motivated to avoid sexual experiences, producing shyness, loneliness, and tending to suggest to him that he may really be homosexual. Such a development is not uncommon and is responsible for much of the turmoil and unhappiness often found in adolescence, particularly among late-maturing boys[70, 71] whose feelings of inferiority are increased by comparison of their physical maturity with that of their friends. In one study it was found that men who were generally dependent on others, suggesting immaturity and feelings of inadequacy, tended to avoid "sexy" women, as measured by their ratings of photographs of women in which sexiness was expressed as breast size.[72]

In young girls, on the other hand, it seems to be more often the case that early maturity, rather than late, is responsible for much worry and anxiety. Our society tends to value early sexual maturity in boys, but to regard with disfavor the girl who early shows mature sexual characteristics. She is likely to be criticized as being too sexually precocious; the American ideal of a "nice" girl largely excludes sexual interests and activities. A young girl then, particularly one who already has acquired strong drives to win the approval of parent figures, is likely to respond to early physiological maturity with fear and self-devaluation, just as the people from whom she is anxious to win approval respond to "sexy" girls with devaluation. Many girls in these circumstances attempt to hide their sexual maturity even from their parents who are the people most likely to be able to reassure her and inform her about the bodily changes taking place, manifested in menstruation and breast development. Being sensitive to her sexual status, she may tend to interpret interest from boys as instigated by her sexual development. Such interpretation may arouse anxiety which the girl reduces by avoiding boys and the possibility of sexual contacts.

It would not be possible to spell out all the many constellations of learnings which can occur in relation to the sex drive. In general, it may be said that these learnings fall in the areas of specific sexual responses, sexual objects, sex-linked social roles, and self-concepts on the adequacy-inadequacy continuum.

Absence of Pain

It was indicated in the discussion of toilet training that the need for the absence of pain may be manipulated by parents through the administration of punishment in order to produce drives to avoid the pain stimuli, drives usually reduced by avoidance responses. The motivated avoidance of a pain-associated stimulus is called "fear."

The socialization of the pain drive will be discussed under two headings: those stimuli which acquire the capacity for eliciting fear responses, and the responses which people acquire in order to reduce pain.

Eliciting Stimuli. For most children, the most powerful fear evoking stimuli are those produced by their parents, as a result of the association between the parents and the punishment which they administer to the child. Through stimulus generalization, this fear also tends to be elicited by other adults, particularly those in positions of authority. Where parental punishment is high, the child may grow up with a pervasive fear of others. Such fear may take many different forms, depending on the nature of the situation in which it was acquired. A child who has been punished for self-assertive behaviors may become shy and withdrawn, while one who has been punished for getting into trouble while alone (as for example, when his parents discover him masturbating) may come to be fearful when he is without companionship or company, a fear which is really a reaction to what he might do when alone. A child who has suffered high drives and pain through parental neglect or as a result of being left alone a great deal of the time may also come to fear being by himself.[73]

Siblings and other children also may acquire the capacity to elicit fear if they have been frequent agents of punishment of the child, as in childhood fighting. Such fear is intimately associated with the nature of aggression, and will be discussed under that topic in the next chapter, which is concerned with some important acquired drives.

Guilt. Parents and other children as punishing agents play a major part in the development of what is popularly called "conscience," which is a part of what Freud called "superego," or the "higher me." These terms are abstractions referring to the body of drives and motives to avoid those behaviors that are unacceptable in one's society. Often, this social disapprobation is communicated to the child through the use of punishment following the performance of the disvalued act; however, more frequently fear and avoidance of behaving in certain ways is learned in connection with other drives which are usually acquired ones. That is, one learns not to do many things, not because of any real physical punishment associated with the behavior but because the behavior may be followed by a loss of love, or a failure to achieve some acquired goal. Parents in American society tend to use nonphysical punishments of these kinds, such as isolating the child for a period of time or depriving the child of a valued object. When an individual makes avoidance or fear responses to his own behavior — to his own responses and drives — these avoidance and fear responses are called "guilt." Guilt obviously is intimately related to the factors responsible for the constellations of learnings represented by the term "superego" and is a powerful and pervasive acquired drive among humans. The kinds of training experiences which produce guilt are those involved in the development of identification. Guilt, its origins and effects, will be discussed in Chapter 7; a discussion of the nature of "superego" and how it is acquired therefore will be postponed until that chapter. The main point to be made here is that not only may new environmental stimuli come to elicit fear (conditioned pain), but so may the person's own reactions and drives which are associated with those environmental stimuli. Thus fear of external events is often accompanied by internal guilt. Most significant are those fears evoked by other people or by their absence, or threatened absence.

The internal sources of fear are seen in the irrational fears of children. Childhood fears are quite common, typically appearing during the so-called Oedipal period. At this time the child is involved in discriminating his parents' roles and he is discovering that very often he should behave differently to his father than to his mother and differently to father when mother is present than when she is absent. This is a period of great ambiguity to the child (ambiguity which is increased as father and mother become more and more like each other in their roles, which seems to be the trend in America), and one in which he gets his roles mixed on occasion, is at a loss about what to do, and has a general fear that he is going to do the wrong thing. Add to this the more directly Oedipal fear of competing with a parent who can punish him, and the fears of not behaving properly as he is given more and more independence and self-responsibility in going about the neighborhood and playing with other children, and you have many factors inducing the child to be fearful of places and things which are associated with his tendencies or wishes to do the "wrong" thing. The result is that children at this age frequently and suddenly show fears of the basement, the attic, the garage, of being left alone, of the dark, of thunder and lightning, bogey men, and so forth. In each case, the fear usually represents an expectation of being punished for something—that is, guilt. The specific object to which the fear is attached—the basement, lightning, or whatever it might be—is the one the child has associated with his guilt, either because it serves as a cue for his guilty tendencies or because he has learned to think of the object as a punishing agent. Thus a child may fear a basement because he is tempted to do something wrong there, or the bogey man because his parents have threatened him when he was bad that the bogey man would "get" him, or a thunderstorm because his mother's fear of it has taught him that such things can be very painful and upsetting, and he expects a painful punishment.

Pain-Reducing Responses. The most readily acquired pain-reducing response is that of avoiding or moving away from the pain-producing stimulus. Such avoidance responses appear to be very high in the innate response hierarchy, and are so effective in drive reduction that they are very difficult to replace or supplant. Obviously, it is difficult to teach people to remain in contact with a painful stimulus unless the painful stimulus is of relatively low intensity and another very powerful drive which may be reduced by not avoiding is used. In such situations, one may be motivated to suffer pain without withdrawing in order to protect one's self-esteem or to avoid the disapproval or disesteem of others. Thus one hesitates before crying out with the pain of the dentist's drill. This suggests that there is some limit placed on the extent of withdrawal from pain stimuli. In a society which approves courage and bravery and defines these traits largely in terms of ability to suffer pain, the child is taught to endure pain and suppress avoidance responses as much as he can, with his ability to do so determined by the sensitivity of his nervous system and the strength of the conflicting drive. This probably is taught by increasing punishment when the child first tries to run away or avoid a threatened spanking, and by withdrawing love and approval when the child's response to pain is beyond the limits of the parents' standards.

The converse also may occur; an overprotecting mother may maximize the fear of pain in her child in order to motivate him to avoid dangerous situations through constant warnings of the painfulness of the consequences of adventure. Similarly this mother may behave in such a protecting fashion that her child rarely experiences pain when she is present and thus able to prevent accidents. Her child will therefore experience pain mostly in her absence. This, together with her frequent warnings and urgings to avoid hurt, will tend to produce a child generally fearful of being without his mother and one who expects to experience overwhelming pain whenever she is gone. Such a child will be met again in Chapter 7, in the discussion of dependency drive.

Of particular interest are the responses children learn in order to avoid the pain of threatened punishment. The avoidance of pain may provide one of the child's earliest experiences with rewarded lying. When accused of a transgression, a child is likely to discover that if he blames it on another child, he may not be punished at all, thus reducing fear and reinforcing the lie. Such a development depends on the child's mental maturity, which must be sufficiently advanced for him to distinguish between wish and reality and to "invent" a circumstance which does not and perhaps never did exist as such in his experience. This requires imagination and is one of the child's earliest creative mental acts. It also depends on the child's having observed the transgression committed by another and noting that despite his presence at the scene, he is not punished. He thus learns that it is not the fact of transgression which is punished, but rather the agent. It seems that these conditions are most likely to be fulfilled when the child is not an only child. Usually a child's first attempts at laying the blame elsewhere are quite transparent; nevertheless, many parents cannot help smiling at the child's ingenuousness or being impressed by the extent of his fear, so that they reduce the punishment greatly. By the time they become sufficiently annoyed at such behavior to begin to punish him for the lie as well as for the transgression, the child may have developed his skills so well that he is in fact able to convince his parents that he is not guilty. Thus lying as a way of avoiding punishment continues to be reinforced. Such learned lying may involve simple denial of guilt as well as blaming others for the crime. In older or brighter children it may include inventing sufficient mitigating circumstances to exculpate himself, as when a little girl explains to her mother that she accidentally spilled her milk because she was trying to hand baby sister a toy for which she was crying — an explanation which may appease mother on the first few trials, at least.

Such lies as defensive maneuvers provide the child with the basis for learning those anxiety-reducing behaviors which have been named "projection," "denial," and "rationalization." These behaviors will be described in more detail in a later chapter. However, in order to dispel the notion that the learning of lying is totally undesirable, it should be pointed out here that the acquisition of anxiety-reducing responses may have some important values, in that their presence may decrease the likelihood that more drastic and less socially approved responses to anxiety may be developed in the individual, such as those which form the symptoms of psychoses.

Sensory Stimulation and Activity

The socialization of these two needs will be treated together, partly because their status as independent needs is open to question and partly because in practice the two are almost inevitably confounded: any activity which reduces the drive state growing out of one of these needs is likely to reduce the drive arising from the other.

In early infancy, these needs are taken care of in connection with the satisfaction of the hunger drive. When infants are fed, they are usually cuddled, tickled, and exercised by their mothers. The implications of this practice regarding the development of social motives related to food and affection already have been discussed. Initially the helpless infant is entirely dependent upon others for satisfaction of stimulation and activity needs. However, as maturation proceeds and the child acquires the ability to move his limbs and change his immediate environment through locomotion on hands and knees and later on his feet, more and more responsibility to "amuse himself" is left to the child, who indeed does learn many responses under the impetus of these needs. It seems likely that the drive which sustains a child through the bumps and knocks sustained while he is learning to crawl and walk is one or both of these two. Rolling over, perhaps even falling may be more satisfying in terms of reducing these drives than they are painful, so that the "trying" to walk still receives more reward than punishment. The laughter of children when they play at falling further suggests this. Of course, the praise and affectional rewards parents give their young infants at these times also are powerful reinforcers.

In our culture, the main activity of childhood related to these needs is play, and it is through play that the child learns many perceptual-motor, social, and intellectual skills. He learns to use his body in many different ways, to use materials as tools, to solve the problems posed by toys and their operation, to discover new uses for familiar objects, to play with other children, share with them, keep faith with them, and agree on rules of the game. Play is not simply entertainment with no value beyond its ability to distract; the playground is a major training ground for the child.

The kinds of play permitted to a child, and encouraged by his environment through the approval of parents and the provision of appropriate materials, can play an important role in determining the direction of the child's interests and the kinds of skills which he will acquire. Parents who value highly intellectual attainment and define such attainment in terms of number and verbal skills, are likely to provide their children with "educational" toys and to encourage the child to obtain his stimulation and activity from them, rather than from other activities of a more physical or muscular kind. Others who value sensual stimulation more would tend to encourage, through their approval and through providing the equipment, muscular skills in climbing, swinging, and using the body in athletic exercises. Such differences in the way in which these drives are satisfied have been used to account for the very early appearance of differing interests between boys and girls (although we have seen that constitutional factors also play a part in determining these sex-linked interests), and for the differences among cultural groups in their skills and preferred leisure time activities. For example, Daniel R. Miller and Guy Swanson have found that one part of the middle class which they label as "entrepreneurial," because it seeks employment and status through individual achievement, tends to encourage its children to engage in play activities which are in some way useful for the future, whereas another section of the middle class in America, called "bureaucratic" because its members prefer to fit into larger social and economic units, is not as likely to require that play have future gains associated with it, and therefore is more likely to encourage social play or play whose value appears to be largely distractional, such as muscular activities.[74] The kinds of play activities a child practices also are associated with his identification with his parents; the kind of activities engaged in are to some extent determined by the identification process, and the play provides the child with practice in the role defined by the identification. The reduction of activity needs produced thus further reinforces the character of the sex and social role being acquired through identification.

As the child matures, play shades over into more and more routinized activities involving less and less dependence on the state of the child's needs for stimulation and activity. It becomes known as work, the nature of which certainly is influenced by the particular ways in which the child had learned to reduce these needs for activity and which continue to reduce these needs. It is almost axiomatic in public health work that the worst thing that can happen to an older person or one recovering from illness is for him to be deprived of work; part of the reason for this is that such deprivation makes it difficult for the person to remain active enough to satisfy his needs for stimulation. It even may be that the lack of such stimulation in retirement is partly responsible for the early appearance of the disorganization of thought which occurs in senility. It already has been established that similar disorganization of thinking occurs under conditions of sensory deprivation when the arousal functions of the brain stem, which require sensory stimulation in order to bombard the cortex with neural impulses to keep the cortex at an optimal level of efficiency, no longer operate.

In addition to this factor, the relationship between activity and one's role identification mentioned above makes enforced cessation of work particularly disturbing because of its implications for the individual's adequacy as an adult, and his ability to behave in the ways demanded by his introjected standards. There is more to work than stimulation and activity alone. These drives may account for the tendency to work, but identification and other learned factors participate in determining the kind of work done by a person (beyond the purely economic factors of job availability, income, and the like). For example, the very orderly person, whose emphasis on precision and accuracy is the product of the way in which he has learned to respond to parental standards, is more likely to enjoy the work of an accountant and to find such work more gratifying than a person who is more strongly oriented to finding gratifications through friendship relations. The orderly person finds the precision of numbers enjoyable while the socially-oriented finds numbers to be boring. In effect, a person's occupational choice is influenced strongly by the kinds of drives he has acquired and the kinds of things he has learned to do to obtain satisfaction of these drives.[75]

The role of personality factors in occupational choice has been demonstrated in a series of studies carried out at the University of Michigan Counseling Division. In these studies subjects whose occupational interests were in accounting, law, dentistry, psychology, social work, physics, and creative writing were studied by means of extended interviews and psychological tests. The researchers found that there were reliable differences among these occupational groups in those childhood experiences one would expect to play a part in influencing interests. Male social workers were found to have the kinds of experiences that incline people to enjoy providing help and emotional support to others; lawyers had more experiences in which questions of their fathers' authority were an issue. These studies point out that work, like any other activity, can be used by people to provide them with the kinds of personal rewards they have learned to value.[76, 77, 78]

Sleep

The newborn infant sleeps between feedings, which generally average out to intervals of three or four hours. Gradually the baby's parents delay the feedings usually given in the small hours of the morning until these late feedings are eliminated altogether and the child sleeps through the night. Thus the adult diurnal sleep cycle is established and the cues of darkness acquire the capacity to elicit sleepiness. These cues become so strong that many students find it impossible to remain awake during lectures illustrated by slides shown in a darkened room, even though it may be midmorning and they only recently had awakened from a night's sleep.

This diurnal cycle is the most common one throughout the world. It is not yet known whether this is so because of some innate process within the brain which responds to the presence or absence of light by producing sleep or waking or whether it is learned. Certainly there are innate processes which play a role, such as the absence of sensory stimulation at night which results in a loss of cortical arousal; it is equally certain that the cycle may be modified by learning, so that some people come to prefer working at night and sleeping in the day. It is likely that parents' practices in not feeding their babies at night and thus avoiding sensory stimulation and reward for awakening, play some part in establishing the sleep cycle which is characteristic of our society.

Before the full adult cycle is firmly established, young children are permitted to sleep sometime during the day — the particular time preferred varies with the child's need for sleep but soon becomes habitual. The most common nap time is after lunch, although there are many children whose naps occur earlier or later. When a mother is responsive to the child's need for sleep, she often will allow the child to cease his activities and take a nap. The desire to cease an activity may thereby become associated with sleepiness and fatigue, so that it acquires the capacity to elicit sleepiness. In this way the sleep drive comes to be elicited by boredom, ennui, imminent failure, or any other situation which involves a desire to desist from an activity. It is not uncommon to find healthy young college students sleeping twelve to fourteen hours a day, particularly toward the end of the semester when term papers and examinations are due; much of this sleepiness is a response to unverbalized wishes to escape or avoid the activities awaiting the student, rather than a real physiological need. That is, the sleepy state comes to be elicited by cues other than those arising from within the sleep centers of the brain, and this pattern may be established in childhood when the mother allows sleepiness to serve as an acceptable reason for not engaging in activity. As in the case of Lester, the response which is learned may come to produce even greater problems in the future (sleeping does not get the term paper written and in fact increases the probability that the student will fail), but such punishment occurs so much later than the response which is immediately drive-reducing, that it does little to reduce the strength of the response, particularly if the student fails to think of his imminent failure (and of course, he does not think of it directly when he falls asleep).

Why Infantile Learnings Are So Influential on Later Life

Although people have commented at length on some adult behavior as being babyish, it remained for Freud to make serious use of the observed similarity between adult and infantile behaviors. Freud used the concepts of *fixation* and *regression* to account for this. Fixation was said to occur when the socialization process is interrupted by some traumatic event, or a series of traumatic events, so that socialization does not proceed beyond that point. Or if it does, the new habits are acquired only superficially, so that the individual readily reverts to the level of social development at which the trauma occurred. Thus Freud would interpret such oral sucking activities as pipe and cigarette smoking as the adult product of some partial fixation during early infancy when the socialization of the hunger drive took place, probably the result of inadequate sucking experience or some other frustration during nursing.

In effect then, fixation refers to a strong tendency to perform a learned response, either because the drive motivating the response has reached great strength or because there have been many reinforcements of the connection between the drive and the response. Psychoanalytic theory uses another term, "cathexis," to refer to the connection between goal objects and the drives they reduce. Fixation refers to the strength of cathexes or, in nonpsychoanalytic terms, to the strength of connections among a drive, the response to it, and the cues that stimulate it.

Regression is said to occur when an individual begins to respond to situations in adulthood in ways in which he responded to them as a child or infant, rather than in the ways in which he has been accustomed to respond as an adult. Thus crying as a substitute for active problem-solving is a regressive response. Regression implies fixation: one regresses to behaviors characteristic of oneself at the time during socialization when fixation occurred, and one regresses when a problem arises which is related to the trauma that produced the original fixation. In the following section we shall present the factors that make possible the behaviors which Freud called fixation and regression and that account for the great endurance of habits acquired in infancy, compared to those acquired in adulthood, even when fixation and regression do not occur.

The first point to be made is that drives during infancy are stronger than those which occur in adulthood, so that responses which occur in connection with these drives are stronger than responses acquired later and therefore more resistant to extinction. The autonomic nervous systems of infants are more labile — they are more readily aroused and involved — than they are in adults. Thus the drive-associated responses acquired by infants have relatively great strength.

This factor interacts with another one: infantile learning occurs without verbal activity. Perhaps one of the reasons that drives are stronger in infants is that they do not have verbal skills which will allow them to think of the future when their drives will be allayed. Thus when an infant is hungry, there is no offsetting thought that he will be fed soon and no falling back on the memory of the last satisfaction. The lack of verbal activity also means that rewards during infancy are direct, rather than symbolic, thus producing more extreme drive reduction. The only thing that will stop a baby's hunger cry is food; an adult's hunger may be mitigated by the promise that he will eat in an hour. Such a set of verbal symbols does not have anywhere near the reinforcement value that the food has for the infant. This is another way of saying that the actual reduction of the need-produced drive occurs in infancy closer temporally to the infant's response to the drive, thus resulting in stronger reinforcement effects, than it does in adulthood.

The absence of verbal skills in infancy also means that the learning which occurs in the infant is unconscious. That is, the infant does not know what he has learned, in the sense that he could describe what he does. As such, he will often behave as an adult in certain ways without being able to identify the fact that he is so behaving. Without such verbal labels for his behavior, he cannot engage in the kind of verbally mediated discrimination learning which is so effective in producing extinction of unwanted responses. Thus infantile learning is long lasting because it is unconscious.

This suggests a further factor operating to make infantile learnings so enduring. The young infant lacks the ability to make the fine sensory discriminations which an adult can make. Thus responses acquired during infancy tend to be quite generalized, elicited by a wide variety of stimuli and therefore practiced far more than are adult responses. The young infant coos to his mother's face, to the faces of other women, and even to photographs of faces. In this way, infantile responses tend to be very pervasive.

When an adult learns a new response, it usually means that he must first unlearn an old, incorrect one which was higher in his response hierarchy. This is much less true for infants. Although the response an infant learns in a particular situation may not be the one which was first in his hierarchy, those which were stronger nevertheless were not very much stronger and thus extinguished readily. If it takes an adult let us say forty trials to acquire a certain response, twenty of those trials may have been largely spent in giving the wrong response and having it extinguished by nonreward. Only the twenty remaining trials increased the habit strength of the new response. However, of the same forty trials occurring in infancy, perhaps only five were spent in extinguishing a slightly more dominant response which may itself have had very little practice in the short history of the baby's life, with the remainder being responsible for increasing the strength of the new response. Thus trial for trial, the infant is more likely to acquire greater strength associated with the responses he learns than is the adult. In effect, the infant has less to unlearn. This is another way of saying that the response hierarchy in infants is more flexible than in adults.

infant : less to learn
unconscious
reduction in need
is closer in time

Two characteristics of reinforcement also are important in this connection. In some respects a wider range of events are reinforcing to a
baby than to an adult. Although food preferences do appear early, it
nevertheless is true that babies are less picky about what food will be
acceptable when they are hungry than are adults who get quite particular about the kind of food, its manner of preparation, how it is served,
and the physical environment, all of which could operate to reduce the
ability of the food to serve as a reinforcer, but most of which do not
operate to detract from the infant's feeding situation. Therefore events
tend to be less equivocal as reinforcers for infants, thus giving them
greater effect in producing habit strength. Secondly, reinforcements are
more likely to be partial or on a scheduled basis during infancy, and to
be more nearly on a 100 per cent schedule in adulthood. This is because
the adult can reinforce himself through his own thinking in which he
may congratulate himself on a job well done or through more direct
reinforcement, as when one treats himself to an ice cream soda in order
to reward himself for getting a good grade. Further, the adult can tell
others of his achievements if the achievement occurred when he was
alone, and those whom he tells will reinforce him with approval. On the
other hand, the infant who performs correctly when no one is looking
goes unreinforced on that trial. He cannot reinforce himself either
symbolically or directly nor can he induce reinforcement from others
by telling them about it. This is one of the implications of the lack of
verbal ability in infancy. The infant is then less likely than the adult to
be reinforced each time he responds correctly; we already have seen
that such partial reinforcement results in the acquisition of responses
which are much more resistant to extinction than is the case with responses acquired under 100 per cent reinforcement. And so responses
learned in infancy tend to be more enduring than those learned in adulthood.

Each response that an infant learns, through stimulus generalization
tends to be elicited by cues somewhat different from those to which the
response was conditioned. In a new situation, the infant then is likely
to behave in ways similar to those in which he had behaved in the past;
as he continues to emit responses until reinforcement ends the series,
he will give responses gradually decreasing in their similarity to past
behaviors. Thus the most dominant responses are those most like responses which already have been acquired. If the new situation permits
a number of different solutions, any one of which may work in the sense

of reducing drives, then it is more likely that the child will be reinforced for a response similar to past responses than for one which will be very different. That is, reinforcement will occur early in the series so that a very different response may not have the opportunity to appear in behavior at all. This is even more likely because the agents of reinforcement, the parents, remain fairly consistent in what they reinforce and so will tend to reward behavior in the new situation which is similar to behaviors they have rewarded in the past. In this way, each response an infant learns has a focusing effect by limiting the range of responses the infant may learn later in subsequent new situations. In other words, as learning progresses the response hierarchy becomes more and more restricted and the course of new learnings is profoundly determined by what was learned before. This then is one of the reasons for the importance and power of infantile learnings. Not only are the specific responses learned in infancy more resistant to extinction and of greater strength, but they also serve to influence the nature of later learnings which will be consistent with the earlier ones. This is the psychological background of the aphorism, "as the twig is bent, so grows the tree," and is an important factor in the consistency of personality over time.

Learnings in infancy occur in cue situations which are quite unique, in the sense that things never appear to adults in the same ways in which they appear to the child. Sometimes trick photography attempts to reproduce the world as it probably is seen by the child and one is impressed with how different it is. Adults are seen from the knees up and tables are seen only on their undersides, for example. These are part of the cue situations to which responses learned in infancy and childhood are attached. As the child grows older, these cues disappear; people are seen face to face and tables from the top. The responses which were associated with the childhood cues tend to disappear from behavior, replaced by newer responses which have been learned in relation to the new cues present in the environment of the older child and the adult. Thus behavior does change as one matures although the changes are consistent with earlier learnings, as pointed out above. However, the earlier responses which have disappeared have not necessarily been extinguished. They simply are not present in behavior because the cues which elicit them are not presented to the individual. Disuse itself does not produce extinction. Suppose that somehow the adult individual were faced with a perspective on his environment which he has not had since childhood. In such a situation, he would be more likely to present responses in his behavior acquired in relation to those cues, but responses which had not appeared in his behavior since childhood. His behavior would present the appearance of a sudden childishness, of a regression. This is what seems to happen with adults who are confined to beds in a hospital for the first time in many years. They are faced suddenly with cues which have not been present in their environment since they were children. They lie in bed for long hours, are taken care of by a sympathetic woman, the nurse, who is similar in this respect to their mothers, and they are subject to the orders of a dominating male who visits infrequently during the day and wields his authority. In this sense, the physician presents cues which are similar to those produced by the patients' fathers. And to add to the situation, there are other patients who, like siblings during youth, must compete with each other for the attentions of the mother-nurse and the favors of privilege. In such a situation, behavior characteristics of his childhood suddenly may appear in the adult patient. He becomes demanding, displays sibling rivalry, or becomes very dependent and docile, or complaining, depending on what behaviors were rewarded most frequently in his childhood —even though these behaviors may be very different from the ways in which he characteristically behaves as an adult.

In this way, situations which present themselves in adulthood which are similar to those which occurred in childhood will tend to elicit the behaviors characteristic of the individual's childhood and of his behavior in those childhood situations. This is particularly likely to occur if these situations are presented to the adult so infrequently that there is little opportunity to extinguish the earlier responses and acquire new ones more consistent with his changed status. In effect then, many childhood learnings do not extinguish at all but rather are always potentially present, simply waiting for the appropriate cues to elicit them.

Another consideration helps account for the great importance of infantile learnings. The infant and young child learn many things in order to avoid the pain of a spanking. Parents teach the child to fear, as we have seen earlier, and then manipulate this fear drive in order to teach the child responses which may produce increases in the strength of other drives, rather than decreases. A child may learn to delay satisfying a hunger drive, thus suffering an increase in hunger drive strength, if this delay produces a greater decrease in his fear of punishment. In many situations then, the fear drive must be stronger than need-produced drives, if learning is to occur as the parents want it to, and they use spankings and other physical punishments as ways of making sure that the fear drive remains at this usably strong level. This means that many of the things which children learn are means of reducing learned fear, and as we have seen, such acquired fear drives are extremely resistant to extinction and are very powerful drives. On the other hand, adults suffer relatively little direct physical punishment, so that their fear drives are probably much less strong than are the fear drives of children. The overall effect is to make responses acquired in childhood much stronger and more resistant to extinction than comparable responses acquired in adulthood.

These last two considerations combine in suggesting another factor which makes infantile learnings so important. Many responses learned in childhood are inhibited by parental punishment when the child has grown to the point when the responses are considered by the parents to be changeworthy. The inhibition of a response is itself a response, associated with the cues of the parents and their disapproval. However, the parents and cues similar to those they produce may not be present in many situations in the child's adult life. Therefore the inhibition they produced is not elicited, so that the response which used to be inhibited appears again in behavior, looking like a return to childishness. For example, a child may learn to inhibit temper tantrums because of parental disapproval, but in adulthood, if no parent or parent-like people are present, the inhibition will not occur so that the temper tantrums reappear in behavior. The man who as an employee was nonassertive and passive may turn into a tempestuous boss when he is top man and has no authoritarian superiors like his parents over him.

Finally, imprinting has been used to account for the importance of infantile learning experiences. Imprinting refers to a process in which infants become irrevocably oriented toward whatever moving stimuli are present at a certain crucial stage of development.[79] This process has been studied extensively in birds, but it has not yet been established as a fact of human life. Imprinting will be discussed in more detail in the next chapter, in connection with some aspects of identification.

We have seen that, for several reasons, responses acquired in infancy are stronger, more resistant to extinction, unconscious, often hidden but potentially present, and exert a focussing effect on later learnings. That is why infantile learnings are stressed, and that is why adult personality is often interpreted or explained in terms of childhood events. It is for reasons such as these that fixation, which we understand as very powerful learnings produced by some traumatic event or series of related traumatic events, leads to regressive (childish) behaviors in adults when a new situation similar to the ones in which fixation occurred presents itself. We will have more to say about regression in Chapter 9, when we discuss reactions to frustration and conflict.

REPRISE. In this chapter we have examined the more important needs with which an infant is born, looking at the kind of training which the child undergoes in relation to these needs, in order to discover the implications of this training. The major point is that the ways in which a child is permitted to reduce his drives reduce the infinite variety of behavior of which he is capable to the more limited variety which he will consistently display as characteristic of himself and of his society, and that further, the methods of training have profound implications for the acquisition of important skills, attitudes, and learned drives.

Among the significant points of this chapter are the following:

1. Infantile feeding is related to the development of attitudes toward food and oral activities, and toward people and the external environment in general.

2. Toilet training begins the child's education in conformity, aggression, cleanliness, and compliance to other's demands, which become related to bowel activity. Guilt is learned in such situations.

3. Modesty, attitudes toward sex and toward the self may also be related to toilet training.

4. Training related to clothing may be associated with status, with sexual identification, the self-concept, and modesty.

5. Play activities, imitation, and introjection comprise a constellation around the child's sex role identification and the socialization of sex drive, in connection with which extent of sexual inhibition, the direction of sexual behavior, and the development of sex-linked role behaviors are established. The satisfaction of needs for stimulation and activity combine with these in determining interests and occupational choice.

6. Pain as a drive is manipulated by socialization agents to counteract prohibited reduction of other drives. Pain may come to be elicited by other people, or by their absence. As a result of identification, self-administered pain (guilt) is acquired.

7. Pain is readily reduced by avoidance which may lead to the discovery of lying.

8. Sleepiness and fatigue may be elicited by desires to withdraw or avoid unpleasant activities.

9. Many factors combine to make infantile learning very strong, highly resistant to extinction, and unconscious.

10. Infantile learnings operate in the direction of producing consistency in personality development.

11. Fixation and regression are among the products of infantile learnings.

12. Traits and drives are acquired in the course of socialization of primary drives, so that connections between these acquired traits and drives and the primary ones are established. In this way, primary drive behaviors may serve as symbolic of the traits and drives associated with them.

13. Situations in adulthood which are similar to those present in childhood and thus symbolic of childhood events, may elicit the behaviors acquired in relationship to those childhood events. In other words, learnings acquired during the socialization of primary drives generalize to similar situations.

7. The Socialization of Some Acquired Drives

The last chapter presented a discussion of some of the learnings which occur in the course of socializing the primary drives, as this socialization may be carried out in different families and in different cultures. For this chapter we have selected some of the acquired drives of particular interest in our society. We will explore the conditions under which they are acquired and the products of their socialization.

It was pointed out in Chapter 4 that secondary drives may be classified and named in terms of the primary drive states which provide them their motive power, the cue situations which elicit these non-need-produced primary drive states, or the general classes of responses which result in the reduction of the drive states so elicited. This last is the common practice in psychology. Some of the drives so named in these terms are aggression, guilt, achievement, affiliation, dependence and counter-dependence, and sex. These are the drives presented in this chapter.

Aggression

In our discussion of the laws of learning, it was pointed out that response strength increases as one nears the goal. An organism exerts more effort in making responses close to the goal than it does in making responses further from the goal. If a child approaches a goal such as a toy and he is blocked from further progress by the presence of another child, the energy involved in his approach will stand in opposition to the child that is blocking him, and he will tend to try to continue toward the goal. If he is putting forth more energy than the barrier can withstand, the barrier may be overcome and he will achieve the goal. When this happens, he is reinforced for all the responses which preceded the attainment of the goal, although the strengthening effects of the reinforcement decrease with distance from the goal response. Therefore one of the responses reinforced is the one which removed the barrier and the closer this was to the goal, the more strongly it was reinforced. The child is learning to be aggressive. Repeated occasions on which responses that remove barriers from before a goal are reinforced operate to increase the readiness to make aggressive responses again when barriers are again present; repeated occasions make these responses more efficient, more resistant to extinction, and so forth. In other words, aggressive behavior is learned just as are other kinds of responses and is more or less characteristic of an individual's behavior depending upon his past practice and reinforcements. The situation responsible for this kind of learning is the presence of reinforcement for responses which result in the elimination of barriers to a goal; that is, frustration tends to elicit aggressive behavior, and the learning of aggressive responses depends on how successful the aggressive behavior is.[1] The closer to the goal the frustration occurs, the more likely that the individual's response strength will be sufficient to overcome the frustration and thus produce reinforcement for the forceful response society calls "aggressive." At greater distances from the goal, the child's tendency to approach has a greater chance of being too weak to overcome the obstacle so that the force exerted in tending toward the goal is relatively small, no reinforcement for such mild forcefulness occurs, and an aggressive response is not acquired. Or if a frustration occurs close to a goal and if the energy in the child's approach (which should increase as frustration—that is, deprivation—continues) is insufficient to achieve the goal, then the aggressive or forceful behavior is not reinforced, and again does not increase in response strength.

The learning of aggressive behavior was illustrated neatly in an experiment by Neal Miller who taught one rat to strike another who was between himself and the food cup. The animal was not allowed to eat until he had, as a result of trial and error behavior, struck another rat in the cage with his paw. The other rat recoiled from the blow, and not being under a hunger drive himself, allowed the aggressive rat to eat. After several trials, the aggressive rat came to strike the other rat in the cage smartly as soon as he entered the cage.[2]

Thus there are several factors operating to determine the learning of aggression. When a barrier occurs far from the goal, the probability of an aggressive response occurring is low and the probability of such a response resulting in reinforcement also is low, so that little learning of aggressive behavior is likely to occur. If the barrier occurs closer it is more likely to evoke aggressive behavior because of the greater response strength producing progress toward the goal, and this greater strength is more likely to overcome the barrier, thus producing reinforcement for the aggressive behavior. If aggressive responses occur because of a frustration close to a goal but are not reinforced, such as when the child's parents refuse to give in, then the lack of reinforcement for both the responses leading toward the goal and for the strength of the response at the barrier is likely to result in extinction of both. In this way, the failure to be reinforced on many different occasions may result in general traits of passivity and lack of striving, particularly when the frustration occurred close to the goal.

Training in frustration-produced passivity seems to be typical of the socialization of Balinese children. The anthropologist Gregory Bateson has noted that Balinese adults are extremely nonaggressive and tolerate long periods of delay and interruption with no anger at all. Bateson points out that this probably results from the fact that Balinese parents engage in extensive frustration of their children in which the aggressive responses which the children make to the frustration are not permitted to result in reinforcement.[3] Thus aggressiveness and annoyance when barriers are presented tend to be reduced, becoming so low in the Balinese response hierarchy that they do not appear in overt behavior.

Closeness to the goal has been mentioned as an important factor because response strength close to a goal tends to be high. However, the same factors operate when response strength is high for other reasons. For example, the frustration of well-learned responses, or responses resulting from a high level of drive because of great deprivation, also will elicit forceful responding. In effect, any condition which increases response strength also tends to increase the probability that an aggressive response will occur when a barrier or frustration is imposed between the organism and the goal. This is why parents find it easier to keep tempting but forbidden objects out of the way of children, rather than attempt to take them away from the child once the child has started for such an object or even begun to play with it. And this is why parents also find it easier to take something new away from a child than to take away from him something which he is so accustomed to having that he has high response strength in connection with it.

Threat. Frustrations of very strong drives — those which are most deeply a part of the individual, such as drives for affection and achievement, are particularly potent in instigating aggressive responses (which, incidentally, are most likely to result in the still further frustration of these drives in our society). Such frustrations are commonly referred to in psychology as "threat"; where great aggression is found, one frequently can infer the existence of threat to some of the individual's strongest drives.

In a child's trial and error forceful activity at a barrier, he may kick, bite, knock objects down, and scream or cry. While all of these behaviors may become fairly typical of a child's aggressiveness, the one which gradually becomes most dominant in our society is that of hitting with one's hands and fists. There probably are many reasons for this. Parents tend to punish other kinds of aggressive behavior more than they do hitting which they even may condone when they interpret it as "standing up for one's rights" or "self-defense" *vis-a-vis* a playmate. But American middleclass parents condemn biting and kicking much more strongly. This was shown in a study in which groups of parents were asked to rank aggressive behaviors in terms of "how bad" each was; they consistently ranked biting and kicking as "worse" than hitting.[4] Another factor which probably favors hitting is that it is less likely to produce pain in the aggressive child. That is, he is more vulnerable to painful counterattack when he attempts to bite another child. His balance is precarious enough when he stands on both feet and kicking is likely to down him completely, leaving him quite accessible to injury from the opponent. These aggressive behaviors are therefore more dangerous to the angry child than is hitting. Further, hitting is effective with many more kinds of frustrating agents than is biting, the effectiveness of which is limited to living barriers. Thus hitting is likely to be reinforced more frequently than biting.

The Learning of Hitting in Anger. However, the situation most likely to result in greater strength associated with hitting than with other aggressive responses occurs at home with parents. In our society, the punishments parents administer to their children that are most easily learned by the children are physical ones. It is difficult for a child to learn to imitate his parents' punishment when they deprive him of some desired object, but it is quite easy for the child to imitate his parents when they strike him. We have seen that imitation learning occurs in the development of identification with the parents, particularly the like-sexed parent. Just as a child learns to imitate his parents' mannerisms, so he is likely to imitate his parents' hitting behavior. This is one of the reasons that boys learn to hit more than girls; since fathers usually are assigned the task of spanking children and boys tend to identify with their fathers, boys learn to make "spanking" responses more readily than girls, and as we have seen, such aggressive responses are quite likely to be reinforced, even by parents themselves who often regard such first imitations with amusement and affection. And of course, parents are more likely to reward aggressive behaviors in their male children than in their female children. Girls, on the other hand, tend to develop more verbal forms of expressing aggression. This difference between boys and girls is not present at age two but is clearly marked by age four, according to a study by Gesell, who counted and categorized the aggressive behaviors of large groups of children (an average of one aggressive act every five minutes!)[5] The period between two and four is the time when parental identification develops most rapidly. Thus many factors operate to make boys more overtly aggressive than girls.

The practice of spanking as a punishment is particularly potent in teaching children to be aggressive, not only because it gives the child an opportunity to learn aggressive behaviors by imitation, but also because the spanking itself provides an instigation to aggression. That is, spanking constitutes a frustration of the behavior for which the child is being punished, as well as frustration of drives for affection and positive regard. And through its effect in producing fear, punishment creates the conditions for internal frustrations in the child, as when he wishes to do something but dares not for fear of being punished. If the child has learned aggressive responses to frustration, his reaction to such fear will continue to be aggressive, although because the source of the frustration is internal, his aggressive behavior will have no apparent cause to others who may consider it to be unwarranted "orneriness."

Thus physical punishment is quite effective in teaching aggressiveness to children. This was seen in a study in which mothers who were rated as being high in the extent to which they used physical punishment on their children also reported that their children tended to be more aggressive than the children of mothers who seldom used physical punishment.[6] Further evidence comes from a doctoral dissertation by Beverly Allinsmith. She had a group of boys write endings to stories in which a boy is frustrated by someone whom he highly regards. One such story started off by describing a boy, Jack, who has a great deal of respect and admiration for the basketball coach. Jack tries out for the team but does not make it, and feels that the coach did not give him a fair chance. The boys in the study wrote endings for the stories, and their endings were classified in terms of how much direct aggression was shown against the frustrating figure. Allinsmith also had a great deal of information about the mothers of her subjects and about their child rearing practices. She found that mothers who favored physical punishment had sons whose story endings were classified most often as showing direct aggression. She further found that mothers who tended to lose control over their anger when disciplining their children had boys whose story endings also showed more direct aggression. Friends of these boys also rated them as more likely to get angry and talk back to teachers than boys whose mothers did not favor corporal punishments. These same boys, when asked if they felt that spankings were particularly necessary, felt more strongly that they were necessary than did boys who were not physically punished. Allinsmith comments, "It seems that the children whose mothers have beaten them to discourage them from beating others will, when they are fathers, probably beat their own sons to discourage them from beating others."[7]

A Punishment Paradox. However, there is a paradox involved in the use of physical punishment, when it is used to punish the child for his own aggressive behavior. A child who is characteristically punished for behaving aggressively is placed in what is called conflict; on the one hand, the instigation to aggression is heightened by the punishment, and on the other hand, he is fearful of behaving aggressively. This consideration makes it necessary that a distinction be made between aggressive drive and aggressive behavior. The punishment will continue to produce increments in the *instigation* to aggression — that is, in the aggressive drive, although direct acts of overt aggression may be reduced at the same time. In a sense, the aggression goes underground to appear in either disguised forms or more socially acceptable forms or to appear only in moments of reduced self-control, such as in alcohol intoxication.

American middleclass parents tend to disapprove very strongly of overt aggressive behavior and to punish such behavior by means of the many techniques of punishment commonly used, including the use of physical punishment which has the paradoxical effect noted above. Thus a child will learn to suppress overt anger and temper tantrums and will replace them with more acceptable expressions, such as negativism (particularly if this is effective in such important training situations as toilet training, as discussed in Chapter 6), passive resistance, "lording it over" other people, competitiveness, achieving some apparent superiority over the frustrating agent which will make the agent feel badly, teasing, and verbal attack or "sassing," if the parents have arranged the rewards and punishments for such behaviors appropriately. It is of some interest to note that temper tantrums are most common where verbal means for expressing aggression are absent, as in the very young child or the deaf child. Thus a very wide range of responses may come to substitute for the less acceptable but more direct acts of physical aggression. These responses themselves may become further socialized, as when negativism, occurring in a child of sufficiently high intelligence, develops into an interest in developing new and unique ideas to oppose older and more accepted ones, and verbal attack develops into sharpened powers of criticism and analysis. It is even possible to teach children "positive" or "constructive" reactions to frustration, rather than aggressive ones.[8]

It has been found that middleclass parents, particularly those who value independence and self sufficiency of the type that characterizes the family in its own private business, teach their children to control angry outbursts earlier than do lower socio-economic groups. As one sociologist has put it, the middle class teaches its sons: (1) To fight when attacked by another boy, (2) not to attack a boy unless he has been struck, (3) not to attack girls or supervisory adults under any circumstances, but also (4) not to withdraw when in a normal, approved, competitive situation. In a word, the middleclass boy is taught to be quite careful about when, where, and against whom he expresses anger."[9]

Substitution of Objects of Aggression. In addition to the development of new responses to express aggression, socialization also can result in the avoidance of expressing aggression toward prohibited objects, with a comparable increase in aggression toward other, but perhaps less appropriate ones. It has been found that American middleclass parents regard aggression against parents as the most intolerable direction in which aggression may be expressed, while aggression against playmates is much more acceptable to them. If such parents arouse aggressive drives in their children but do not allow the children to behave aggressively toward themselves, it is likely that the children will increase in their hostile behavior toward their brothers and sisters or playmates or toward their toys or other objects. In the study in which rats were trained to strike other rats, the aggressive animals attacked a toy doll in the cage when the other rat was not available. Similarly, American middleclass children and adults are more likely to express aggression directly against their peers than they are against people who are close to their parents on a stimulus generalization continuum, such as teachers and other authorities. Aggression usually is expressed most directly against objects not likely to retaliate, such as younger brothers and sisters or minority groups.[10] The child not only acts to avoid retaliation in the form of physical punishment; he also acts to avoid losing love from those people whose love is important to him. The fear of loss of needed love constitutes the guilt a child feels when he is angry with his parents, and it is this guilt that sends him to seek other objects for his ire—objects that mean so little to him that he doesn't care if he loses their love. In a famous study, boys in a work camp in the western United States showed more unfavorable attitudes toward Mexicans and Japanese after a frustration than before, even though the frustration had nothing to do with Mexicans or Japanese.[11] There was a time when increased economic problems in the southern United States, with the increased frustration this implies, were associated with an increase in the number of lynchings of Negroes.[12] The mechanisms by means of which these substitutions of objects of aggression occur will be discussed more fully in Chapter 9, which deals with how people behave when they have conflicts such as those between aggressive drive and an avoidance of aggressive behavior against the frustrating agent.

Permissiveness for Aggression. Children of middleclass parents tend to express their aggression much more indirectly than children of lower class parents. Obviously there are differences in the extent to which parents permit their children to behave aggressively in an overt manner. This variable may be referred to as "permissiveness for aggression." It has been found that children whose homes were rated as high in permissiveness for aggression were more aggressive in their doll play than children whose homes were not permissive, and that mothers rated as permissive describe their children as more aggressive than those rated as being less permissive.[13] In effect, the permissiveness of parents allows children the opportunity to practice overt aggressive behaviors and be rewarded for them. When permissiveness is combined with high instigation to aggression, as in families rated high in physical punishment, then overt aggression is likely to be fairly characteristic of the children. In one study, two groups of children were observed in a free play situation, but one group was handled less permissively than the other, in that each time a child in the group expressed aggression, he was told that "nice children don't do that:" After two sessions like this, both groups were then observed in a free play situation in which neither group was handled less permissively than the other. In this session, the group that had less permissiveness in the previous two sessions showed less aggression than the other group, which in fact increased in aggression throughout the three sessions, again because of the great permissiveness.[14]

Physical and Psychological Punishments. The use of physical punishment by parents as a way of reducing aggressive behaviors in their children has the effect of increasing direct aggression, as noted above. Such physical punishments are more often used by lowerclass mothers than middleclass mothers, who place higher value on their own self-control. Middleclass mothers instead favor "psychological" punishments, such as those which attempt to make the child feel guilty or ashamed of his behavior. As you would expect, children whose mothers use this kind of punishment show less direct aggression than children whose mothers use physical punishment. A mother who punishes a child's aggression by hitting him in anger at the same time is teaching the child to hit in anger and also provides him with a justification for his anger against his mother. However, more predominantly in the middle class where psychological punishments are used, the child really can't get angry at his parents because they have not really punished him; they tell him that they are "teaching" him how to behave, and that they are doing this with his best interests at heart, and that the punishment hurts them more than it does the child. A child told this would be an ingrate to react with aggression, although his behavior has been frustrated just as effectively. The effect is to produce an increase in indirect expressions of aggression.[15] It also has been found that this effect, though characteristic of middleclass boys, is not a direct result of class membership, but is rather a result of the child training practices commonly used in that class. Thus, where a lowerclass mother also uses psychological punishment and avoids loss of self-control in her own anger, she has a child who, like middleclass children, expresses his aggression indirectly. These findings illustrate a general principle that it is not social class membership *per se* which accounts for differences in behavior, but rather the things done by members of the social class — the particular stimuli which exist in that class and the particular behaviors which it characteristically reinforces.

Intropunitiveness. Where aggressive drive is stimulated but aggressive responses are totally prohibited, the aggressive behaviors may be directed against the angry person himself. This is called *intropunitive-ness,* and is most likely to occur in people who are internalizing strongly standards of conduct, including prohibitions. In such children it is no longer the parents or parent-substitutes such as authorities and teachers who frustrate most of their goal-directed behaviors but rather themselves. In an experiment in which sensitivity to pain was measured, it was found that the subject characteristically most expressive of overt aggression hurt himself least, while the subject least overtly expressive of hostility hurt himself most on the pain test.[16] The subject who hurt himself most may be described as intropunitive (directing punishment inwardly) rather than expressing it outwardly in overt aggressive behavior. People who have become intropunitive readily blame themselves when things go wrong rather than blame others. They may punish themselves by working extra hard (a response likely to be highly reinforced in our society), or by exposing themselves to danger by selecting risky occupations. Temper tantrums in which the child bangs his head on the floor are an early intropunitive response, occurring when other, more direct expressions of aggression have been prohibited.

In his doctoral dissertation, Leonard Lansky measured intropunitiveness by having boys make up endings to stories in which aggression against a loved person is aroused. He counted as intropunitive any story ending in which the angry person in the story has something bad happen to him. For example, in one story a boy wants to play football very badly and the coach wants him for the team, but the boy's mother, afraid of injury to him, refuses to give her consent. If a subject ended the story by saying that the boy goes against his mother's wishes anyway but turns out to be a second-rate player, flunks his courses because of the time he devotes to football, or is injured or killed while playing football, then the ending was classed as intropunitive. Lansky found that such intropunitiveness increased after frustration in boys who, because of difficulties in completing the process of identification, still were trying to stop themselves from doing forbidden things, such as expressing aggression directly, by punishing themselves, much as a two-year-old child slaps his own hand after he has touched something that he usually is punished for touching, and says, "No, no," to himself.[17]

Because it is the middleclass parent who is most concerned with teaching a child to avoid aggression, it is not surprising that middleclass boys more frequently feel bad or guilty when aggression is aroused — a form of self-punishment — than feel angry. That is, they themselves become the objects of their own aggression and they interpret their frustrations as being their own fault, a violation of their own internalized standards. Sometimes the learning of intropunitive guiltiness may be so strong that when under high instigation to aggression such people confess to crimes they did not commit. This is most common in connection with sensational crimes. Often the kind of crime for which the person claims guilt reveals something of the nature of the frustration which aroused his intropunitive aggressive drives.

The Relationship Between Aggressive Drive and Overt Aggressive Behavior. To summarize: Given an instigation to aggression, the occurrence of direct overt aggressive behavior against a frustrating agent depends largely on the extent to which parents permit their children to behave aggressively and on their techniques of socialization. Thus, where parents permit the expression of aggression, there ought to be a greater correlation between the extent to which aggression is aroused and the extent to which it is expressed. In one study it was found that this in fact is so. The children of parents who permitted aggression were reported by their friends to behave about as aggressively as one might expect from a measure of how aggressive they felt or wished to be; the children of parents who did not permit such direct aggressive behavior were rated by their friends as being opposite in their behavior. That is, the more aggressive these children wanted to be, the less aggressive they actually were, according to their friends who knew them well.[18] In addition, the technique of socialization affects the extent to which aggression occurs; children whose parents use physical punishment were rated by their nursery school teachers as more overtly aggressive than children whose parents did not use physical punishment.[19]

The overall effect is that children of parents who are moderate in punitiveness are more overtly aggressive (in doll play, at least) than children of low punitive or high punitive mothers. The low-punitive mothers do not arouse aggression; the high punitive mothers arouse aggression but also punish direct aggressive behavior. The moderately punitive mothers apparently frustrate their children enough to arouse aggression but do not punish them enough to block overt aggressive behaviors.

Parents are not the only ones responsible for the extent of aggressive behavior in their children. Teachers and other parent substitutes also play a part. In a study on different kinds of leadership patterns, it was found that boys in a club led by a very authoritarian leader who told the boys just what, when, and where they could do things were much more aggressive toward each other than were boys in clubs led in less authoritarian ways. This is very likely because the authoritarian leaders were much more frustrating to the boys than were the other leaders.[20] This may also be why it is often said that the most disciplined (used to frustration) armies are those in which their members are also high in expressing aggression.

Aggressive Interaction. There is another paradox in connection with aggression. Because aggression always tends to breed more aggression, it is a large scale social problem, one for which we have not yet found an adequate solution. The problem is that the reinforcement for aggressive behavior — the state of affairs that will end the aggressive behavior and reduce the drive — is the admission by the object of the aggression that he has been hurt. The child fights until his opponent has given way to tears or run away. Adults use verbal attack and they gauge their effectiveness by whether they have been able to wound their opponent psychologically. The evidence for such wounding, however, lies in whether the aggressed-against person becomes angry. One has struck a telling blow if he makes his opponent mad (rival politicians often actively seek to anger each other). In other words, one feels that he has effectively frustrated another person, which is the goal of one's aggression, if the other responds with aggression — the usual response to being frustrated. Thus aggression demands aggression in return, as evidence that the attack was successful. But — and here lies the problem — the returned aggression, although needed by the instigator to prove that his attack was effective, also may be effective in wounding or frustrating the instigator, leading him to further attack and then his opponent to further aggressive responses, and so on. It is in this way that aggressive interactions tend to spiral into more and greater aggression, with each round becoming more fierce. The tendency to spiral in this fashion makes it easier to stop such an interchange early than late. The problem is worsened by the fact that in many situations the opponents stay together long enough for this spiralling to develop because they need each other to serve as objects for aggression. This is particularly likely when the opponents seem to come together time and again, only to have each interaction result in an argument and ill will. Their need for each other may be the result of a number of factors: if each has had aggressive drive stimulated by someone against whom they dare not express the aggression or by some impersonal event that cannot serve as an object (such as the social "system"), then they need each other as the only available objects; the guilt stimulated by aggressive feelings may make the antagonists need each other's aggression as punishments to alleviate their guilt; finally, they may need each other in a very positive way. That is, they may have strong feelings of mutual attraction for each other. But these feelings may be either so uncomfortable and guilt-arousing that they cannot be expressed directly (and so frustrating that they stimulate aggression against the other as the "cause" of the frustration) or the antagonists may be so inhibited in expressing tender feelings that they cover them up with gruff and aggressive words. How conflict between aggression and love can produce such behaviors will be discussed in more detail in Chapter 9. The main point to be made here is that a continued aggressive interaction often implies some positive motivation that holds the antagonists together. If they did not have such motives they simply would avoid each other, rather than come together to have a fight. Marriage counselors often have found that the couple that fights continuously does not seek a divorce even where there are no children and no strong moral convictions about divorce (except as a reasonable excuse for continuing what is really a satisfying relationship). The reasons the marriage counselors point to are those we have been discussing here—the warring husband and wife cannot do without each other's service as an object of aggression and a punisher.

Aggression—Innate or Learned. Is aggression innate and inevitable? Freud proposed that aggression was an instinct. It has been compared by psychoanalysts to catabolism. They say that if the life- or growth-instincts (broadly speaking, sex) are anabolic, then catabolism should produce a death instinct which is shown in aggression. For Freud, instincts (or drives, to use more modern language) are psychological representations of physiological states; in such a theory it is quite reasonable that catabolism—the breakdown of body cells—should be represented as a death or destruction drive.[21] If aggression is such an innate feature of man, then there is a limit to the extent to which there can be a society without aggression in some form or other. Most theorists today do not accept the idea of aggression as an innate instinct. Nevertheless, from what has been said here about aggression, it seems likely that it is acquired very readily, and that given the inevitability of frustrations, the learning of aggression is close to inevitable. And frustrations are inevitable. Every child has experiences with barriers to goals, with delays of gratification, and every child learns some ways of getting rid of the barriers—a learning that applies to living as well as inanimate barriers. Thus it seems likely that everyone acquires at least some potential for aggressive behavior simply because it is so easy to learn. It also should be kept in mind, however, that such potential can be socialized into acceptable forms, and that the same learnings that result in the acquisition of aggressive potential also result in problem solutions and their acquisition. It may not be possible to do without one without also doing without the other.

Guilt

In the socialization of some drives we have seen that it is often the practice of societies to attempt to modify the responses which the infant most readily makes when the drives are present. That is, responses initially high in the response hierarchy must be replaced by responses which are lower rather than merely delayed. This is true for the sexual drive in our society, the responses to which are at first completely eliminated by parents, and of elimination drive to some extent in that the infant's accustomed response to this drive comes to be changed during toilet training, and also of aggression. In this section we shall examine the implications that the mechanisms for producing such modifications have for the development of guilt drives and behaviors.

Three Ways of Eliminating a Habit. In general there are three ways in which an organism's habitual mode of behaving may be changed. One is by restricting him in some way that prevents the behavior from occurring. For example, parents often see to it that their children do not play for long periods out of their sight with opposite sexed playmates, to make sure that the children do not have an opportunity to make and practice sexual responses. Similarly, tempting objects around the house usually are removed to higher ground when the young child begins to toddle around and reach for things.

A second way is to apply punishment when the response is performed so that it is inhibited or extinguished. We have seen how this usually is done in connection with toilet training, to teach the child to discriminate between right and wrong places in which he may eliminate and in the socialization of aggression, so that direct overt aggression against parents often is eliminated from the child's response hierarchy or at least driven down much lower in the hierarchy. Obviously, this method has a great advantage over the first, in that it can continue to work even when the child's mother is not immediately present to prevent the undesirable behavior by removing temptations. However, this method will not serve completely; it will not cover the case in which it is not possible completely to extinguish a forbidden response. Some drives and drive responses may be almost impossible to extinguish because no reasonable substitutes for the drive are permitted (this is the case with the sexual drive in American society), or because there are so many occasions on which the response is reinforced and permitted that it is not possible to extinguish it, or because the association between the drive and the undesirable response is so strong that the response is always potentially present when the drive is present. This last seems to be the case with aggression; whenever frustration is present, aggressive drive is sure to be aroused as a consequence of the laws of learning — laws which are not repealable.

In situations such as these, a child must be taught to resist temptation, and so tolerate a high level of drive that he does not reduce by making the forbidden response. Resistance to temptation becomes something like a control within the person, so that he need not have an authority figure constantly present to remove temptations from his path or to punish him whenever he errs. The child is taught that failing to resist temptation is followed by an even greater increase in drive than he must tolerate by resisting temptation. That is, while resistance to temptation may be somewhat punishing to the child, failing to resist must be even more punishing, and this punishment must be of such a nature that the individual administers it to himself to cover those situations in which his parents and other controlling people are absent. The drive to punish himself which must be learned is called "guilt"; how guilt is learned is the subject of this section.

The Generalization of Punishment Effects. When a child is consistently punished after performing some action, such punishment goes a long way toward insuring that the child will not again commit the same or similar actions. The response tends toward extinction. In a very young child who is not able to make meaningful discriminations, this may mean that the punished response may never appear in behavior; he is too young to learn that there may be occasions on which it is justified or permitted. Thus a child learns not to strike his parents and authority figures at an age at which it is not possible to teach him to distinguish between justified authority and authority which even his parents would want him to violate, such as that of an enemy society. Furthermore, the conditions of such punishment add to its generality. The young child often learns that he may be punished for committing a certain act, whether or not his parents are there to see him perform the act. That is, the act is punished, rather than performing the act publicly. This is likely to occur with the very young child, during the first three years perhaps, when children often leave the evidence of their misdeeds around to be discovered later by their parents who then punish them. To the child whose parents were not present at the commission of the crime, but who nevertheless know about the crime, his parents must seem to be indeed godlike, with eyes present even when they are not. Such a child is likely to grow up with the feeling that parental prohibitions simply cannot be violated safely; parents are sure to know about it, and punish. The performance of the act then becomes a stimulus for the fear drive, so that its commission results in an increase rather than a decrease in the child's drive state, and so tending to inhibit the punished response. Later on, when the child is old enough to "cover his tracks" and distinguish between occasions when parents are present and when they are absent, the learning to avoid the forbidden behavior is not nearly so effective; it becomes a learning to avoid doing the act when it will be discovered and fear is aroused by the discovery of the act, rather than by the commission of it. A fear of such discovery is often described as "shame"; it is the increase in drive state following the discovery of a forbidden response and is manifested by such behaviors as avoiding the eyes of the discoverer, so that one does not see that he sees, staying out of his sight, and attempting to be inconspicuous, to minimize the cues which arouse the fear drive (fear of punishment). Thus shame has reference to the discovery of a forbidden act, while guilt has reference to the commission of the act itself regardless of whether it is discovered by someone.

These developments are not restricted to the use of physical punishment in order to associate pain with the act or its discovery. Withdrawal of love, rejection, isolation —any reaction to the forbidden act which will produce a greater increase in drive level after it is performed (or discovered) than would occur if the response were not made —will serve to inhibit the response and produce shame or guilt.

These processes apply not only to the doing of the act but also to its substitute, thinking it. Because thoughts of the act occur at the same time that it is punished, the punishment tends to extinguish the thoughts and make them cues for shame. However, because such thoughts often occur without the act, they are practiced successfully more often, and are punished a smaller percentage of the time that they occur. Being thus intermittently reinforced, they are more resistant to extinction, so that many people who never do anything of which they might be ashamed have thoughts of which they are ashamed. One sees this quite clearly in the suspiciousness which people show when in the presence of a psychologist. They often are afraid that he will discover or infer their shameful thoughts, and in order to prevent this, become much less open and frank in their conversation than they would be with a stranger who is not a psychologist. On one occasion, a middle aged woman began a conversation on a train with a man sitting next to her, and in the course of an hour began to confide in him secrets about herself, her marriage, and her family she would certainly not relate to her neighbors. However,. when she asked the man for his occupation, and he indicated that he was a psychologist, conversation almost ceased after she first attempted to deny the truth of the things she had said, out of fear that the psychologist would infer from them thoughts of which she is ashamed.

The ability to produce shameful thoughts thus makes it possible for people who are correct in all of their behavior to feel ashamed of themselves nevertheless; it is not that there is no reason for the shame. Rather, the reason is there but on a private level, not readily discerned by others who therefore consider the person's usually apologetic behavior and hang-dog look to be inappropriate.

While shame learning is an important first step in the establishment of internal controls, it has definite limitations by itself. It only can produce avoidance of responses the child has already tried and similar responses. This is a fairly narrow range, compared to the many restraints an adult usually exercises. How do behaviors new to the individual fit into his scheme of permissions and prohibitions which we call conscience? Secondly, shame learning for most responses occurs after a child is able to discriminate between the occasions on which he is discovered and those on which he is not. Such learning would not account for the exercise of self-restraint when no one could discover the transgression. To be sure, there is more transgression in secret, but there are many occasions when even in secret, people respond to their consciences. Finally, many more behaviors become a matter of conscience than parents directly teach through direct rewards and punishments. A child does not have to be rewarded for going on to college or punished for not doing so for him to feel that he "should" as a matter of obligation. Whence comes such a sense of obligation?

Much recent research indicates that, as Freud had postulated, the sense of what one should and should not do is developed through the process of identification with those who teach the child shame and the avoidance of behaviors considered undesirable. Identification was described in our discussion of the socialization of the sex drive. Let us see how it pertains to the development of internal standards of behavior.

Identification With the Shame Teachers. We have seen that the child comes to make responses to himself which are imitations of his parents' responses to him, and that this serves to bring the child rewards from his parents, both directly for the "cuteness" of the imitation, and for its effects. Learning to copy the parents' behavior is one of the functions of the imitation games (peek-a-boo, clap hands) in which parents and infants delight. In imitating his parents' responses to his behavior, the child is able to avoid doing those things to which the parents respond with their usual form of punishment; when he does do such things, he may even punish himself in imitation of his parents by slapping his hand or calling himself a bad boy. When he is making initial responses to a prohibited object, he may repeat to himself the things which his mother said to him when she observed him approaching the object, "No, no —mustn't touch," etc. When he does this, the child avoids the punishment which would come to him if he did commit the proscribed act. In this way, his imitation of his parents is rewarding. In addition, it was noted that there are sex differences in the usual direction of identification wherein boys are encouraged to identify with their fathers and girls to continue identifying with their mothers.

This process of identification becomes a common feature of children's play. They become quite elaborate in making believe that they are their parents in familiar situations, doing what they have seen their parents do, and saying what they have heard their parents say (much to the chagrin of their parents when a neighbor overhears this play). Such play is called "role playing," and through it the child practices his identification, practicing both the process and its contents. That is, he acquires more and more skill at imitating and also at the particular responses he is imitating. Here we see that several processes occur in the child at the same time: while he is satisfying his need for sensory stimulation and activity, he also is confirming his sex role behaviors and is acquiring a broad spectrum of behaviors he is taking over directly from his parents. Included in these behaviors are the parents' likes and dislikes, their prohibitions and their rewards —in short, their standards of behavior. We have seen that this is a highly rewarding process for the child. It has an additional value to him. It enables the child to reward himself for behaviors when his parent is not watching or is not inclined to reward him. That is, the child now can tell himself that he is a good boy and reproduce in his own behavior many of the stimuli which his parents usually present to him as rewards because of their close association with drive reduction. He can say nice things to himself and cuddle himself. Conversely, the child also can punish himself, tell himself that he is bad, slap his own hand (or his doll's) and isolate himself when he has done something to which parents would respond in the same way. Thus internal standards of behavior are established, and the set to continue internalizing parental norms.

Identification with the shame teachers — that is, with those who reward and punish the child for his behaviors — works in several ways. First, it gives relatively greater practice, through role playing in fantasy, to those responses typical of the parents, so that in this sense the parents' norms (whether conscious or not) become established as preferred responses in the child's response hierarchy. Second, it establishes the conditions which will produce an increase in drive state when the child does something his parents do not do or for which they punish him, through self-administered disapproval and its ability to elicit the fear which parental disapproval and punishment customarily elicit. This increase in drive strength with its overtones of vague fear is what we experience as feelings of guilt or pangs of conscience. As increased drive it has motivating properties, and so may be referred to as a guilt drive. To it the individual may attach responses which may reduce the drive. The response of guilt may be attached to both an overt response and to the thought of the response. When the thinking elicits guilt, it serves to prevent the occurrence of the overt act itself. The guilt reaction to the thought tends to extinguish the thought. If the thought is a cue for the overt response and the thought fails to occur, the overt response itself fails to be elicited. And of course the overt response itself is relatively low in the individual's response hierarchy anyway, because of the punishment it has received and because of its lack of practice. This is what is meant when someone remarks that a certain behavior is so foreign to him as to be "unthinkable."

It is of great importance that learning through identification tends to be largely unconscious. That is, while playing the role of his parents, the child is not necessarily able to verbalize what it is he is doing or what he is learning. Acquired in this way, moral strictures in adults are usually very difficult to verbalize and to account for. In one study of adolescent boys in which they were asked how they know when they should not do something, most of the boys' answers indicated that they simply didn't know how they knew. They just "felt" that something was wrong to do or they referred to a "voice" inside which told them.[22] This is why it is often said that moral strictures are not intellective; people do not necessarily know why they believe that certain things are bad, although they are deeply convinced that they are bad in fact. This is one of the things that makes it so difficult for people of one culture to understand and accept those of another, who may have just as strong consciences but with different content, so that their behavior is seen as immoral, bad, and anxiety-arousing. Observing others engaging in behavior which the observer feels is immoral is anxiety-arousing because it serves as a cue for the observer to behave in the forbidden way, thus stimulating his guilt drive.

To summarize: there are two processes which account for the development of internal controls. The first is the learning of shame, or fear of punishment from the parents when they discover the child's transgressions. The second, the learning of a guilt drive, is based on the first but depends on the operation of the conditions which favor identification with the teachers of shame. In this second process, the individual responds to himself in the same way as did his significant parents, and thus comes to evaluate his own behavior in their terms, responding to forbidden behavior and to failure to conform to desired behavior with an increased drive called guilt.

Guilt Behaviors. The cues which elicit guilt drive therefore are behaving in a manner inconsistent with norms internalized from parents or thinking of behaving in such ways. The drive may be reduced in several ways, leading to various kinds of guilt behaviors. One way is to remove the eliciting cues as much as possible by either undoing the act, making restitution, ascribing the act to some other agent, or doing things to make sure that one does not produce the guilt-arousing cues, such as avoiding temptation. The second way is to be punished. Though perhaps painful, punishment is associated with a renewal of love and affection by parents, and so is drive reducing. The punishment may be done by the individual himself, he may arrange to have others punish him, or he simply may expect and perceive punishment in events which, while unfortunate and discomforting, may not have any intrinsic connection with the transgression he has committed. This second general method obviously is related to intropunitive aggression and interacts with it.

Internal standards are frustrating. Aggression in response to such frustration is intropunitive because it is the self that is the frustrating agent and direct aggression has usually been inhibited by parental training.[23] When a temptation to violate internal standards occurs and guilt is aroused, this guilt drive may be reduced by self-punishment not only because such behavior has been rewarded in the past but also because such behavior also has been learned as an intropunitive response to frustration. The stronger the tendency to intropunitive response to frustration, then the stronger will be the tendency to punish the self in response to guilt. Further, if the guilt-inhibited behavior is itself an aggressive reaction to some instigation, the likelihood of intropunitive self-punishment for the guilt is increased still further. The self-punishment often will be related to the transgressed-against norm. Just as a parent often punishes the child in a way related to his crime, such as slapping the hand which touched the prohibited object, or depriving the child of the toy which he was mishandling, so the self-punishment which the individual either inflicts upon himself or expects from the environment is often appropriate to the crime he has committed. In this sense it is symbolic of his violated standard and can be used diagnostically to infer the standard of behavior which he has violated. These various ways of reducing the guilt drive will be described in detail in the next section.

Eliminating the Cues for Guilt. There are several different ways in which the cues which usually elicit guilt drive in the individual may be removed, thus reducing the drive and reinforcing the action which resulted in the removal of the cues. One of these behaviors is called "undoing," in which some effort is made to right the wrong which one has committed. A college student, studying in a liberal arts curriculum although he knew that his parents very much wanted and expected him to study in the sciences, would start off each semester doing well in his courses but then would fail to meet course requirements such as term papers or would find that he couldn't bring himself to study for his final exams, so that he would invariably receive poor grades. This behavior could well be a way of undoing his enrollment in a curriculum which aroused guilt in him. A more typical kind of undoing, however, is making restitution. People often contribute money to charity as a restitution for some antisocial behavior they have engaged in, but which never was discovered. It is not unusual for people who have acquired a good financial position through unethical or "shady" practices to attempt to relieve their consciences by reversing their earlier acts through trying to do more good than the bad they feel they have done. It is possible that this kind of response to guilt may be acquired in the kind of child training procedure in which the mother of a child who has violated a rule requires that the child right the wrong before he can be accepted and loved once more. He must clean up the mess he has made with his paints, mop up the spilled water, and the like.

Guilt also may be assuaged if the behavior for which the individual feels guilty can be ascribed to someone else. If it is not his fault or if he can point to the compulsion of extenuating circumstances, this may be sufficient to end the heightened drive of guilt. Another way of doing this is to ascribe the guilty action to some praiseworthy motive. One may say that he cheats on his income tax out of a desire to make life more secure for his family; the child tells his mother that he spilled the water because he was trying to get a drink for his younger sister who was thirsty. If a good explanation is sufficient to restore love and lessen punishment, this kind of response to guilt will be readily acquired. In a sense, the child learns that actions themselves are not punishable; what is punishable is action that stems from a bad reason. Similarly, if one can ascribe the guilt-stimulating behavior to someone else ("He made me do it," or more extremely, "I didn't do it — he did.") the cues eliciting guilt may be eliminated, if the child training situation was such that emphasis was put on the agent rather than the crime. Spilled milk is punishable if Johnny does it, not if his mother does it, and tramping through the flower beds is not punished if it was the dog rather than Susie.

Finally, a person who has learned well to respond with guilt to actions which are contrary to those of the parents' ideals which he has internalized may avoid guilt by keeping away from temptation. In a person with high potentiality for responding with guilt and who has strong drives which motivate guilt-arousing behavior, such as sexual or aggressive drives, guilty thoughts and actions can be eliminated if he stays away from those cue situations which tend to elicit the behavior for which he would feel guilty. Just as one who does not trust his self-control when on a diet refrains from entering a candy shop, so may one avoid sexual guilt by staying away from sexual situations. As we have seen, when drive strength is very high, a wide variety of cue situations on the stimulus generalization continuum are able to elicit the learned response to the drive. When a drive which results in guilty behavior is particularly strong as a result of past frustration or deprivation, many situations which do not ordinarily do so may serve to elicit the guilty response. For example, a person with a very strong sexual drive who responds to his sexual behavior with guilt may feel very upset when he sees others engaging in sexual behavior, when he reads about sexual activities, or sees pictures of nudes. These are stimuli which elicit sexual behavior in himself, to which he responds with so much guilt that he feels great tension composed of his implicit sexual responses and his guilt. In addition, because of his high drive he is very sensitive to perceiving such stimuli. This high drive state, made even higher by the cues for sexuality which are present, may be reduced and the guilty feeling eliminated if he sees to it that such stimuli are removed from the environment. He is likely to disapprove of "risque" movies, books with sexual themes, and to be in favor of banning them in order to be sure that they are not in his environment as cues which could elicit his own sexual behavior. Those things an individual violently opposes on moral grounds often indicate, then, his own guilt and the nature of his own frustrated, guilt-arousing drives, and in this sense are symbolic of the situations in his childhood which led to his guilt and inhibitions.

Guilt Reduction Through Punishment. Once the learning of guilt has started in a young child, his guilty drive state may be reduced by confessing his crime to his parents, acting sorry, receiving his punishment, and returning to a state of acceptance and love. The more quickly the punishment is over, the more quickly does reward follow upon the confession, thus reinforcing the confession somewhat and reducing the guilt. Where punishment is greatly delayed, as when a guilty child is told that his father will deal with him when he comes home, the child has many opportunities to recall his crime, thus increasing the cues which elicit guilt, and the deprivation of love which continues until the punishment is over increases the child's drive for love throughout the day. When the punishment is finally administered, it therefore produces very powerful drive reduction. Where this kind of pattern has been established, the child learns that relief from guilt occurs in connection with punishment, so that the guilty child may actually expect and seek to be hurt. This reaction may be seen in such behaviors as "unintentionally" giving oneself away when he has done something which arouses guilt, so that by being discovered he may be punished. Occasionally people who commit crimes leave some obvious clues to their identity although they are clever enough to have been expected not to. Often this "slip" may be a reaction to the criminal's guilt which may be relieved only if he is punished. Returning to the scene of the crime, despite the high probability of being caught there, also may be such a response. Although the main reason for returning may be to admire one's work, the person usually feels that the risk involved is of relatively small consequence — that is, it wouldn't be so terrible if he were caught and punished. Another expression of the same kind of response to guilt is to become engaged in some dangerous occupation which could result in death or injury. The soldier who feels guilty over the death of a friend with whom he used to argue and compete may accept risky assignments or even volunteer for them, partly out of the feeling that if he were to be hurt, he might actually feel better about the death of his friend — that is, he would no longer experience guilt if he were punished appropriately.

Even if the individual does not actively seek punishment through confession or one of its modified forms, he may still expect punishment. As we have seen, perceptions are strongly influenced by drives, so that an individual with a high guilt drive is more likely to respond to stimuli as punishment because feeling punished is so high in his response hierarchy as a result of the high drive. Such a person may then interpret events as punishing which really are not intended as such. A thunderstorm which spoils a Sunday picnic is a punishment for not going to church; the illness of one's child is interpreted as a punishment for failing to love the child enough. At the very least, the guilty person may feel that unfortunate events which occur are somehow his fault, and of course, he can always find things for which he is guilty — mistakes he has made or occasions on which he has failed to live up to his internalized ideals — and he always can find reasons for feeling that his self-blame is justified. The child would not have gotten sick if he had been dressed warmly or if one had taken greater care that he did not play with other children who might be sick. Frequently, these justifications for self-blame are not the real reasons for the guilt drive; the individual cannot think the real reasons because such thoughts, as cues for further guilt, are too upsetting. They are inhibited because they are cues for higher drive, rather than for drive reduction. The reasons given (and they are often given publicly in a breast beating manner in which the person calls upon everyone to witness how terrible he has been and how sorry he is for it) are ones which can be thought about and talked about by the person. That alone suggests that they are not guilt-arousing enough to be the real reason for the person's punishment-seeking. If he can talk about such things publicly, chances are they are not really very anxiety- or guilt-arousing to him. The breast beater often is really seeking reassurance which he receives because the things to which he ascribes his guilt are usually minor. The things that really are making him feel guilty are unconscious because they are too upsetting to think about.

Whiting and Child made use of this tendency to blame oneself for unfortunate events as a measure of guilt in a very interesting way.[24]

Studying primitive cultures which were without scientific knowledge, they reasoned that in a culture where guilt was characteristically high as a result of the kind of child training procedures typical in that culture, there should be a greater tendency to interpret illness as the fault of the sick person than in cultures with lower levels of guilt. In these latter cultures, illness may be interpreted more readily as an arbitrary act of the gods or of one's enemies. This reasoning even holds true in such scientific cultures as our own. Some people are more inclined to say they became ill because they didn't take care of themselves properly or should have taken more precautions, while others may be more likely to blame their illness on the lack of consideration of others who spread their germs around.

Using self-blame for illness, Whiting and Child gathered information from the cross-cultural files of Yale University to study the relationships among various kinds of child-training practices typical of a culture and that culture's guilt. They found, as would be expected from the theoretical discussion presented above, that self-blame for illness was more prevalent in societies in which socialization practices were severe, involving relatively more punishment of the children. They found that this was particularly true in the case of the socialization of aggression: the more severely a society proscribed aggressive behavior, the greater was the tendency to take blame on the self. As we have seen, this is to be expected, in that self-blame is not only a reaction to guilt *per se*, but particularly to guilt for aggressive tendencies because there is an element of intropunitiveness as part of the self-blame. Such training in intropunitiveness of course is most likely to occur in societies with relatively strict rules about the expression of aggression.

We have seen that socialization practices involving punishment account for only a part of the development of guilt, and that the process of identification also contributes to the development of conscience. Thus it is reasonable that societies which encourage identification should have greater guilt than societies in which the factors favoring the development of identification are not present. Whiting and Child tested this in a number of ways. They reasoned that techniques of child training which maximized that child's dependence and love for his parents would be most effective in producing strong identifications and therefore proneness to guilt. They labeled such techniques as *love-oriented;* they include denial of love, punishment by threat of denial of reward, and punishment by threat of ostracism. These techniques are love-oriented in that they keep the child oriented toward his parents even when being punished, rather than driving him away. The effect is that the punishment is over when the child receives love, reward, or companionship. These techniques were contrasted with physical punishment, threats of physical punishment, and ridicule, which have the effect of turning the child away from the parents, since there is nothing to be gained by remaining oriented toward them. Love-oriented techniques should encourage identification because the child remains in close enough contact with his parents most of the time to use them as models for himself, because imitating them is likely to reduce punishment, and because he can give himself the same kinds of rewards they gave him, even when he is being punished, and the fact of punishment increases the child's drive to give himself such rewards. Whiting and Child found that in fact, greater emphasis on love-oriented techniques of punishment was more characteristic of cultures with high guilt than of cultures with low guilt. These investigators also found that in societies in which married people live away from their parents' homes and so do not have relatives nearby to help in the care of their children — relatives who would be more inclined to be kindly disposed toward the children and thus use love-oriented techniques which would encourage identification — in such societies there is less self-blame for illness as a result of less identification.

Finally, Whiting and Child found that in societies in which socialization began fairly early, particularly socialization of sex, food, and independence drives, there was greater potential for guilt as evidenced by the tendency to blame the patient for his illness. They explain this by pointing out that the use of love-oriented techniques of socialization, which encourage identification and thus the potential for guilt, are probably more effective when applied early rather than late, because when the child is very young, he is particularly dependent upon his parents for love and has not developed the self-reliance which would enable him to tolerate punishment without identifying with his parents.

Another study, in this case of American children and their parents, supports the emphasis on identification as a major source of guilt. In this study, the investigators rated children as prone to guilt if the children were described by their mothers as tending to confess their misdeeds, feeling bad when they had done something wrong, acting as if they wanted some extra signs of love as reassurance, or in general showing the kind of guilty "look" that young children get when they have done something wrong.[25] They considered children not prone to guilt if the children committed misdeeds with apparent impunity, and did not seek any means of returning to a state of parental love and acceptance. That is, these children did not seem to have characteristically high guilt drives because they did not seem to display usual guilt-reducing behaviors. In this study which was largely based on interviews with several hundred mothers, it was found that mothers who were rated as rejecting of their children — a condition which should operate against identification — had fewer high guilt children than mothers who were rated as more accepting. They also found that children who were more dependent on their parents showed more guilt behavior than children who were not so dependent, confirming Whiting and Child's reasoning that dependency favored the development of identification and therefore of proneness to guilt.

In the interview study, the investigators paid particular attention to the sex differences which we have found to play such an important part in identification. As was pointed out in the discussion of the role of identification in developing sex roles, both boys and girls first identify with their mothers but boys come to switch their identification to their fathers. The development of behaviors typically masculine in a particular society depend on making this switch to a masculine identification as exemplified by the father. Because boys make a switch, it would be expected that their identification would be more uncertain than that of girls who do not make such a switch. If their identification is less certain, then boys should show less guilt. This is exactly what was found: boys showed less behavior indicative of guilt than did girls, as rated from the interviews of their parents. This is one of the reasons for the stereotype of the mischievious boy, whose relative lack of guilt allows him to engage in deviltry.

Other evidence comes from boys who are rated as being rejected by their fathers. Rejection of a boy by his father should have a more profound effect on his identification than would a girl's rejection by her father. Thus it was found that boys rejected by their fathers had less guilt than boys not rejected, but that there was no difference with girls. Rejection by their father had no effect on their main identification with their mothers, and so had no effect on their guilt.

These studies confirm the importance of identification in the development of internal controls which are signified and powered by guilt, and point out some of the factors which influence the adequacy of such identification: the use of love-oriented techniques of socialization during the child's most dependent years. In addition, these studies also suggest the complex nature of guilt, in its connections with the socialization of aggression into intropunitiveness and in its relationship to the factors which also influence sex role typing.

Guilt may not be a general trait. That is, a person who responds with strong guilt to one action may not necessarily respond in the same way to another act which some people would consider equally wrong. In other words, the cues which elicit guilt are not the same for all people. Certainly the nature of the models which parents present for their children to identify with determines to a large extent what the child will come to feel guilty about and what he will not. And as we have seen, the specific types of punishment used also play a role. One other factor also may operate. A parent may stress the socialization of certain kinds of behavior but if the child has not begun to identify with the parent, the child may acquire little guilt in connection with that type of behavior. In other words, the age at which identification occurs may determine what the child will come to feel guilty about; he is likely to feel guilty about the behaviors being socialized at the time that the identification begins to "take hold," but less guilty, if at all, about behaviors which may have been socialized earlier and since that time no longer stressed by the parents.

Sex

Although the socialization of the sex drive was discussed in Chapter 6 as a primary drive, it must also be discussed in somewhat different ways as a secondary drive. In this section we will be interested in how new stimuli come to elicit sexual drive and the kinds of responses acquired to reduce this drive. We shall see that often these stimuli have little intrinsic connection with sexual behavior itself, and that many responses which reduce the drive so elicited do not appear to be sexual at all. These are the factors which make sex important as a secondary as well as primary drive.

It has been pointed out that in our society efforts are characteristically made by parents to eliminate sexual behavior completely from the child's repertoire, although the process of identification may still give the child the opportunity to develop a sexual orientation toward people. That is, through identification the child can still learn to seek rewards from men or from women, even though he may not engage in any strictly sexual behavior with them at the time. The completeness of the inhibition of sexual behavior and of the acquisition of an appropriate sex role based on identification may be seen in childhood play groups, in which the children gradually segregate themselves into like-sexed groups and exclude children of the opposite sex to the point where the two sexes appear actually hostile to each other, simply on the basis of their sexual identifications. This development is probably the result of two processes: on the one hand, boys and girls through their play are confirming their role identifications to themselves and to their parents who reward them for being what the parents expect of children of their sex and such confirmation would be threatened by playing in mixed sex groups, which would involve play activities not completely appropriate to the sex role being developed. On the other hand, children are still young enough to be relatively uncertain of their sex roles and their interests in appropriate play activities. There are still some residual interests in activities which are considered by their parents as more appropriate to the opposite sex. This is more likely to be true for boys than for girls, because boys have changed their identification from mother to father to some extent at least, and this change means that their identifications with their fathers are not as well established as the identifications of girls with their mothers. Thus boys tend to have stronger interests in feminine activities than girls do in masculine activities. This was demonstrated in a doll play study, in which the experimenters made father and mother dolls available to boys and girls and then observed the extent to which boys and girls played with each doll. They found that boys played with father dolls more than mother dolls and girls played with mother dolls more than father dolls; but they also found that boys played with the mother doll almost as much as with the father doll, reflecting their uncertain identification, while girls did not play with the father doll anywhere near as much as they did with the mother doll.[26] This suggests that one reason that children's groups tend to be of the same sex is that they avoid the opposite sex in order to avoid temptations to step out of the sex roles they are developing. The temptation is likely to be greater for boys. That is, the habit strength associated with opposite activities is likely to be greater with boys, so that the cues created by the play of girls would tend strongly to elicit responses which would compete with the boys' uncertain sexual identifications with their fathers. Thus the boys become irritated with girls' play, belittle it, support each other in their rejection of it, convince each other of the superiority of boys, swear never to marry, and even become aggressive in their relations with girls, partly out of the frustration which the cues of girls' play acting on their own inhibited inclinations produce, and partly because by being aggressive they drive the girls away, thus eliminating the upsetting stimuli from their environment. Thus boys tend to be more rejecting of girls than girls are of boys. However, the fact that there is an interest in girls, although inhibited, is evidenced by the way in which boys will go out of their way to fight with girls, which means that they must get close enough to them to fight and incidentally to observe the girls' play. If they simply didn't care about girls, they would merely leave them alone and ignore them. It requires some positive interest to go out of one's way in order to have a fight. We have already seen how some positive approach drives may be involved in aggressive interactions among adults. The same thing also happens with children.

Latency and Adolescence. Thus the segregated childhood play groups continue, gradually acquiring greater skill at their sex roles and more self-assurance in their sexual identity. Freud called this age the *latency period* because it is so superficially nonsexual in Western society. But the advent of adolescence changes all this, much to the relief of those who successfully have crossed this bridge and to the dismay of those who have not yet arrived at it.

Drastic changes in the physiological systems of boys and girls at puberty include a greatly increased secretion of gonadotropic hormones, which appear to play a major role in sexual drive. The result is a sudden huge increase in sexual drive state occurring in people who, in our society, have learned few or no sexual drive-reducing responses, although they have a vague idea of where to look for help as a result of their identifications. They have similarly little ability to label and thus identify their drives, and so discriminate them from others which may be similar in the stimuli which they produce.

Typically at this time the adolescent begins to broaden his interests and activities widely, perhaps deriving some energy from his high, unrelieved sex drive, and perhaps seeking for some activities which will reduce his drive state. He will find that contact with girls is no longer frowned upon by his colleagues as much as it used to be, although some wariness remains. The adolescent in our society is likely to feel quite confused about his heterosexual contacts. On the one hand, he is still quite used to thinking of girls in an aggressive and rejecting manner, but on the other hand, he finds that with his new social status and physical maturity his identification with his masculine models is rapidly approaching its fulfillment in reality, and he can and is expected by his models to enjoy the company of girls. And to further confuse matters, he has had little practice at developing responses to girls which are appropriate. The same problems exist among early adolescent girls.

Sexual Cues. Masturbation is rediscovered usually some time around puberty, and is so highly reinforcing because of the high drive present that it is difficult for the adolescent's guilt to inhibit it. Even with fairly rigorous training in guilt and sexual inhibition by his parents, most adolescent boys masturbate and suffer with guilt, rather than abstain and suffer from their high sex drive. Such masturbation usually takes place in secret and seclusion, often in the dark, so that the cues of secrecy, particularly combined with seclusion and darkness, often thereby acquire the capacity to elicit sexual drive. Frequently pubertal boys also masturbate in small groups, usually as a result of sharing their new found pleasure with their friends and in an effort to learn from their friends more about sex. Later in adolescence and young adulthood, boys who have had such experiences with mutual masturbation or group masturbation and who have encountered difficulty in making satisfying heterosexual contacts begin to interpret these childhood experiences as signs of homosexuality, thus raising the fear and guilt associated with such a label. In situations such as this, the cues of being alone with people of the same sex, particularly in settings similar to those which often are associated with sexual activities — settings in which the people are nude, as in a locker room, or in which they are sleeping in close proximity to each other, as in an Army barracks — are likely to stimulate sexual drive and the fear and guilt associated with homosexuality, producing intense fear of such situations, sometimes even to the point of panic. A very large portion of psychiatric breakdowns of men still in basic training in the Army is a result of this process. The ability of such situations to elicit sexual responses is increased by the prevalence of sex-related conversation and sex-related activities in the locker room and barracks, such as discussion of sports and physical prowess among men, which serve as further cues for sexual responses. These situations and reactions probably are more common among American men than among women, possibly because of the greater training in modesty which women receive so that they do not present as many sex cues to each other in their behavior and talk, and possibly also because there is less fear associated with close contact among females than among males in our culture. There is less fear of this because such close contact does not exist beyond the realm of acceptable behavior among women in our society, as it often does among men. It is not interpreted as homosexual in nature, so the girl who has such close contact is not as likely to think of herself as homosexual, and therefore is less likely to react with fear and guilt to her attachments to other girls. Intimate friendships among girls exist within the pattern set by the girls' identifications with their mothers, who frequently also have intimate women friends, while it more often does not exist within the pattern set by boys' identifications with their fathers who, while having good friends, are seldom as intimate in their friendship relationships as women are.

Although the adolescent is expected to establish heterosexual contacts and is not permitted to reduce his or her sex drive through self-stimulation or homosexual behavior, restrictions on heterosexuality are still present in our society — restrictions which often exist as the internal controls of conscience — that is, as products of identification. Thus the adolescent knows that actual sexual responses with an opposite sex partner leading to coitus are not permitted except under the highly restricted conditions of a monogamous society which the adolescent is not yet able to enter fully because of his immaturity and lack of financial independence. The inhibitions imposed during the socialization of the sex drive in early childhood are only slowly relaxed, often only enough to further stimulate sex drive but not enough to allow drive reduction; only enough to stimulate further guilt about sex but not enough to relieve the guilt through the elimination of the restrictions. Kissing, which usually starts as imitation with but little sexual component as far as arousing the participants, becomes one of the few heterosexual behaviors permitted to adolescents, and because of the high sex drive elicited by the close contact with an appropriate partner kissing readily acquires the capacity to elicit sexual drive and rapidly becomes a form of sexual activity and stimulation for adults (of course, with much contributed by the experiences of childhood years in which kisses were associated with the reduction of drives for love and affection and even earlier in childhood, when oral activity was so important in producing powerful hunger drive reduction). In this connection it is noted that kissing is an accepted sexual activity in relatively few human societies and is seldom observed in lower primates, leading to the conclusion that its association with sex is learned rather than intrinsic.

Dancing is one of the few other heterosexual activities permitted to adolescents and it too acquires strong sexual characteristics as a stimulus for sexual responses. Obviously dancing involves, in our culture, two people of opposite sex moving in rhythm with their bodies in close contact; at the same time that dancing has such obvious sexual significance, it is highly enough stylized that its sexuality is not blatant and so fails to arouse guilt. It is thus a highly rewarding activity for adolescents, with their great energy and high sex drive. That dancing has such sexual significance is obvious from the fact that boys — who, as we have seen, have more extensive inhibitions of homosexual behavior than girls — never dance together and would feel terribly uncomfortable if they were to do so, even as a joke. Were dancing strictly an artistic or sociable activity, there would not be such a restriction on the sex of the dancing partner. As in kissing, dancing rapidly acquires sexual significance for the adolescent because of its heterosexual nature, and because of the rhythmical movement which approximates the rhythmical stimulation that releases the sexual reflexes. And as was seen in Chapter 2, while such stimulation further increases drive, it also is reinforcing even when orgasm does not occur, so that kissing and dancing become highly reinforcing sexual activities for the American adolescent. In fact, in those who are not able to extinguish their strong acquired inhibitions against activities which result in orgasm, necking and dancing may serve as the only available means of behaving sexually.

Other situations which become capable of eliciting sex drive are more obvious: the sight of a part of the body of an opposite sexed person, particularly a part usually seen only in connection with actual sexual activities; the sight or touch of an item of clothing which is sex-linked, such as women's underwear; pictures of people behaving sexually or of sexual body parts; verbal symbols for sexual activities; in short, any set of cues which is similar to those usually present during actual sexual behavior or which come to represent such cues, can acquire the capacity to elicit sexual drive. In addition any activity which is carried on in stealth, secrecy, or darkness, and which violates the individual's standards of behavior by such characteristics would be sufficiently like sexual behavior such as masturbation or premarital intercourse to serve as cues for heightened sexual drive. In this way illegal activities such as thefts often acquire some element of sexual excitement for the offender. And all of these activities may be engaged in exclusively for their sexual satisfactions by people whose inhibitions against those practices which lead to orgasm in socially acceptable manners are too strong to allow them to reduce their sexual drives in more complete and direct ways. In such people, these erotic cues are often followed by masturbation, as a learned response producing relief from the high drive so induced. Less commonly, they induce spontaneous orgasm through the association of such cues with the orgastic reflex in people under very high drive states. This is the process which accounts for burlesque, for the sale of salacious literature and pictures, for the use of field glasses trained on the bedroom windows of people who could serve as sexual partners, for fetishism (receiving sexual gratification from the touch or sight of objects or clothing associated with an appropriate sex partner), for compulsive shoplifting (usually of sex-connected items such as lingerie), and for such behaviors as "indecent exposure" in which the person exposes his or her genitals to an opposite sexed person. These behaviors are highly complex, and there are many more determinants which influence their occurrence than those mentioned here, but such determinants are little known, and it would be beyond the scope of this book to explore such problems. The main point is that a wide range of stimuli are capable of eliciting sexual drive, and such drive may be reduced by a wide variety of activities, other than heterosexual intercourse, in people for whom this method is not available.

In addition to these, there are two other situations which may often come to have sexual implications. These involve aggression and dependency. Freud suggested that sex and aggression always act together.[27] A connection between aggressive and sexual behavior is often apparent in American society. One notes, for example, that lynchings not infrequently include castration of the victim; that rape often includes more physical assault than is necessary merely to obtain the cooperation of the victim, and that seduction often is considered to be an appropriate form of punishment for excessively haughty girls by their male peers. There is the implication that intercourse is demeaning to females, rather than something which reduces their sex drive state, and a seduction is thought of as a triumph over the female by many men, even when the female is more than cooperative. Further, sexual intercourse in such situations not infrequently includes the administration of real physical pain to the participants, as in sexual sadism. These facts make it apparent that for some people, usually men, sexual behavior includes a large element of aggression, and indeed, may be engaged in more for its ability to reduce aggressive drive than sexual drive. While little is known about this connection between sex and aggression, it does suggest that the cues for the instigation of aggression acquire the capacity, in some American men, to elicit sexual drive, rather than the more direct forms of aggressive behavior. There are probably several factors which may account for this. It is part of the typical belief of people in our society that sexual activity, while appropriate for males, is somehow unfeminine and against the best interests and desires of females, who are considered to be "above" sex. This provides the possibility that subjecting a female to sex can be punishing to her when she and the aggressor accept this belief. Another factor which may also operate is hostility against women, either as a result of generalization from a rejecting mother, or as a consequence of severe frustration of the sex drive through rejection by females who have been sought as sexual partners. Frustration of sexual drive, like any other frustration, may instigate aggressive drive; and just as the form in which aggression is expressed and the object against which it is directed may be related to the nature of the frustration in other kinds of aggressive behavior, so too is it where the frustration leads to sexual aggression. Finally, it was noted in Chapter 6 that some child training practices may lead to an association between aggression and sexual behavior, as when a child is punished by his parents and as part of his punishment is isolated from them. In his isolation the child may masturbate, which through its reduction of the sex drive present reduces the child's overall drive state which was heightened by the punishment. The aggressive drive stimulated by the punishment then becomes a cue for sexual behavior, particularly in the child who feels that by behaving sexually he is getting back at his parents who punished him, by violating their norms and standards.

There is another factor which may be related to this connection between sexuality and aggression, and which also is responsible for other complications in relation to sex. This is the fact that sexual performance plays a major role in the extent to which the individual feels adequate as a person. Particularly among men, evaluations of oneself as an adequate person to a large extent are based on one's success in sexual activities, including the ability to have frequent sexual intercourse and the ability to produce sexual pleasure in oneself and one's partner. When the adolescent is concerned, as he usually is, with whether or not he is the kind of person which his internalized standards demand that he become, this includes a concern about whether he can in fact do the things that adults do; his realization of adult status then becomes contingent on his being sexually successful, since sex is the main privilege permitted adults and denied to sub-adults. Whether the boy is as good as his father, and as much a man, and whether the girl is as feminine and attractive as her mother thus often depends on whether the adolescent is able to behave sexually as an adult.

Sometimes sexuality and aggressiveness become connected through a person's efforts to enhance his masculine status. Behaving sexually and aggressively are both masculine stereotypes; the man with an uncertain identification may intermix both in his efforts to avoid feelings of failure as a man. The frustration produced by his feelings of inadequacy lead to aggression while he attempts to prove his masculine prowess by behaving sexually. Thus the same drive produces both sexual and aggressive behavior, which therefore are elicited together by the same cues. To the extent that most men have some feelings of not completely reaching the ideal of complete and successful identifications with their fathers (which is impossible), to that extent do most men have a potential for intermixing sexuality and aggression. Thus we find that while the connection between these two drives may not be innate as Freud postulated, such a connection is nevertheless common in our culture because it is so readily acquired.

While sex as aggression is often found in men, sex as a means of maintaining a dependency relationship is found more typically in women. That is, a woman sometimes responds sexually when her dependency drive is aroused, so that sexual behavior becomes a means of attracting and holding a man on whom she can be dependent, and who can be expected to take care of her in a nurturant way. Even less is known about the dynamics of this relationship, although it has been pointed out that the customary forms of sexual intercourse in our society include a passive and submissive role for the female, so that by being a sexual partner, a woman is in effect behaving dependently. It also has been pointed out that by offering and withholding sexual satisfaction to males who are more active seekers of sexual gratification than females in our society, it being a more accepted part of the male sex role, a female can control very powerful reinforcements, and through their administration can control the behavior of her sexual partner in the same way as any other reinforcers can be manipulated to control the behavior of organisms in states of high drive. Thus a female with strong dependency drive can control men through sexual behavior to make them behave in ways that will reduce the female's dependency drives.

A confounding of sex and dependency is particularly likely to occur when the marital partner plays the role of a parent. A woman whose love for her husband is based on his approximation to her father and who places her husband in a parental role in their relationship, is likely to respond to her husband in a dependent fashion and this dependency may be expressed through their sexual relationship. Similarly the man who uses his wife as a nurturant substitute for his mother will show an amalgamation of sexual and dependency drives.

In Chapter 6 it was pointed out that in some family situations, the avoidance of sexual behavior is taught at about the same age that the boy is taught not to compete with his father for his mother's attention, and the girl is taught not to compete with the mother for her father's attention. This situation encourages the learning of an association between sex and the opposite-sexed parent wherein sex is strictly prohibited in relation to such family members. This occurs at the same time that the child is identifying with the same-sexed parent in order to avoid the punishment which nonconformity with that parents' standards may involve. The associations among these kinds of learning create a difficult situation for the adolescent who is anxious to achieve sexual adequacy as an adult, but who has acquired strong inhibitions against sexual behavior toward people like his or her parents. With stimulus generalization from the parents, any potential sex partner may be excluded. This situation is made even more complicated by the adolescent's identifications which, if strong, may require that the boy love people like his mother, just as his father does, and *vice versa* for girls. This encourages a split between the idea of love and that of sex, so that adolescents often are attracted to girls who are similar to their mothers in such matters as appearance, mores and behavioral standards, religion, and social class, and then find that sex with such a partner is unthinkable. Further, the association between the genitals and elimination produces a generalization of the idea of dirtiness from feces and urine to the genitals and sexual behavior. A typical solution to this problem for middleclass boys is to seek sexual gratification which will reassure themselves of their masculine adequacy with lower class girls, or girls of foreign nationality — that is, with girls who are sufficiently different from the idealized mother for their inhibitions to be too weak to interfere with sexual behavior. Such a liason also includes a release from inhibition of aggression for the same reason, and carries with it an element of contempt for the sexual partner who is still considered to be beneath the sexual purity of the mother and "nice" girls. This kind of thinking is aided by the prevalent notion in Western society that females tend to avoid sex, so that one who does not so avoid is thought to be less than an acceptable human, and unfeminine. This pattern often continues through marriage, in which the husband may avoid sexual activities with his wife or be uninterested in such a relationship, particularly if he has married a girl who approximates his image of a "good" woman—that is, one like his mother, but he may continue to have sexual affairs outside of his marriage. The custom in some European countries of wealthy married men keeping mistresses who tend to come from lower social classes has been ascribed to these factors.

Such a marriage is often a difficult one, perhaps largely because it involves continued sexual frustration of the wife whose inhibitions in our society are greater than her husband's, and who therefore does not seek sexual gratification elsewhere. The presence of marital dissatisfaction in the wife may serve to threaten the husband's feeling of adequacy as a man who is able to satisfy and make his wife happy, and these feelings, serving as cues for further sexual activities outside the marriage, will tend to confirm the pattern.

In summary then, it appears that sexual drive may be elicited by the cues of frustration, inadequacy, kissing, dancing, being alone and secretive, committing forbidden acts, seeing body and clothing parts which are associated with sex, and hearing talk about sex, depending upon the conditions of learning. And once elicited, sexual drive may be reduced by avoiding the situations which elicit it, masturbation, homosexual activities, preliminary sexual activities such as dancing and necking, as well as by sexual intercourse with approved or disapproved partners. Finally, it should be added that unrelieved sexual drive may be tolerated because it is not inimical to physical health as is the case with other unrelieved biological drives. Unrelieved sex drive simply may contribute to the individual's over-all level of drive which can motivate many activities other than sexual ones. These activities may be reinforced by the reduction of other drives also present. For example, a writer or artist with high sex drive together with a high achievement drive will be particularly motivated to write, and any success he achieves will be reinforcing by reducing at least part of the total drive state. Where sexual drive contributes to such motivation, the product or the work may be expected to reflect the fact; the artist with strong sex drive may specialize in nudes or in painting great lovers and the writer may concern himself with themes about love because these subjects are high in their response hierarchies as a result of the high sex drive.

Much of what has been said here is based on theoretical considerations and on inferences from clinical studies of people with sexual problems. This area has been but little explored by controlled experimental investigations. Obviously it is difficult to get many people with atypical sex habits together for experimental work; even if it were possible, it would still be difficult to obtain from the subjects valid information about their sexual activities because of the great guilt often associated with sex. There is no disputi ng the fact that people do show the sexual behaviors described here but so far accounting for the behavior is more a matter of logical and reasonable hypothesis than it is of established fact.

Interpersonal Approach Drives

There are several different interpersonal drives which are related in that they involve a motivation to approach other people, to be with others, to have relationships with them. Various investigators have used different names, but many of them seem to overlap. Some psychologists refer to affiliation drive and some to gregariousness. Drives to receive affection or positive regard from others are more complicated variants of affiliation or gregariousness, because they involve not only motivations to be with other people but also for these others to present some evidences of having reciprocal approach drives, which include affectionate or accepting behavior. Dependency drive also is a variant of gregariousness and affiliation; it differs from affectional drives in that it includes the use of others' resources by the person to solve his problems or to dispel fear and anxiety. In this section we will explore some of the situations that contribute to the character of these approach drives, and the consequences of these learnings for the individual's behavior.

Learned Drives and Reinforcements in Infancy. We already have explored the relationship between early infantile feeding experiences and the development through secondary reinforcement and learned drive of attitudes toward the feeding agent. It was indicated that the development of such attitudes was influenced by the consistency with which one person—usually the mother—is closely associated with reduction of the baby's drives, and the extent to which that person provides a variety of stimuli for the child through holding, fondling, cuddling, and singing to the child.

An experiment in which college students' attitudes toward certain musical and art works were changed through secondary reinforcement provides an analogy to the way in which attitudes toward the mother are established when stimuli presented by the mother are coupled with her feeding of the infant. In this experiment, subjects rated their liking for little known works of art and musical selections. Weeks later the subjects were invited to meetings at which lunch was served. The works of art were on the walls of the meeting room and the music was played softly as a background during lunch. No attempt was made to draw the subjects' attention to these stimuli and the subjects were unaware that they were continuing in an experiment which had started with their ratings of the stimuli. However, as a result of the association between hunger drive reduction and the background stimuli, attitudes toward the stimuli changed. When these attitudes were tested again, there was a general shift toward more positive evaluations than the subjects had given at the first testing.[28]

The role of stimuli associated with infantile feeding has been underscored by a number of studies. One very famous group of studies is that being carried out in Harry Harlow's primate laboratory at the University of Wisconsin.[29] In these studies, infant monkeys were raised by inanimate substitute mothers, rather than by their real ones. "Dummy" mothers were constructed of chickenwire with round wooden blocks for heads and buttons for facial features. It was found that the infant monkeys would cling to these dummies much as naturally reared animals cling to their mothers. They were fed by the dummies through an arrangement in which a baby bottle and nipple were inserted so that the nipple protruded from the dummy's front. Some of the dummies were covered with soft terry cloth. Although the infants would go to the plain wire ones when hungry, if that was where they were usually fed, they spent a great deal more time clinging to the softer cloth-covered ones. One of the most interesting findings of the early phases of these studies was that the dummies served very similar functions to real mothers. If the infant monkeys were put in a strange room with many "frightening" objects in it, such as mechanical toys that moved around and made noises, they generally reacted with great fear. Those infants put in the room alone simply cringed and whimpered, and tried to stay as far away from the toys as they could. If the dummy mother was then introduced into the room, the infant would run to it and cling much like a frightened child clings to its mother. Infants without the dummies never did any exploration of the strange room. However, those with the dummies present would cling for a short time and then leave the mother to walk around the room and engage in some explorations of the objects in it. Apparently the dummy mothers served as cues that reduced fear sufficiently for the animals to engage in this more independent exploration. Further research supports the importance of the presence of the mother (or some mother substitute): in one, it was found that it is virtually impossible to produce neurotic behavior in lambs put into an impossible discrimination experiment if their mothers are present, but they are made neurotic very easily if the mother is absent.

These reinforcing capacities of the mother or mother-substitute have been interpreted to be the products of secondary reinforcement resulting from the mother's (or dummy's) close association with very important drive reductions on many different occasions. It also was suggested in Chapter 5 that the drive to be near the mother may be a learned one in which the absence of the mother serves as a cue for hunger drive or pain, because these drive states are usually higher when the mother is not present and that when the mother is present and the infant is in close contact with her, these drives are reduced. This was offered as an explanation for the close connection between food and hunger and affectional drives.

It is appropriate here to offer an alternative explanation for these phenomena, an explanation that is receiving increasing attention from psychologists. This explanation involves the concept of *imprinting*. It has been discovered that there is an age in many animals (most notably in chicks and ducklings) which is such that any moving object (usually an animal) which is larger than the baby chick or duck, and which is present within the animal's visual field becomes imprinted in the chick or duckling. That is, from that time on the baby chick or duckling always will follow that object around, will attempt to nestle up to it, and in general respond as if the object were its mother. In most situations, the object which is imprinted is in fact the mother, because it is she who is most usually present when the baby is at the optimal age for imprinting to occur. This optimal age is a few days after hatching. However, if the mother is taken away, any other large moving stimulus, including a human, may be imprinted, and thenceforth the baby will follow that stimulus.[30] Several years ago, *Life* magazine published a delightful picture of a whole brood of ducklings paddling after Konrad Lorenz, the distinguished German scientist who has extensively explored imprinting, and who had arranged the situation such that it was he whom the ducklings imprinted.[31] The age of the animal is crucially important as far as imprinting is concerned. If an appropriate stimulus is present earlier than the optimal time for the particular species, but is not present when that species imprints, then imprinting will not occur. Similarly, if an appropriate stimulus is presented beyond the optimal age, again it will not be imprinted.

Imprinting occurs not only in fowl; there are some breeds of dogs that show imprinting behavior quite obviously (those which are popularly known as "one master" dogs, such as the sporting breeds). It has been found that lambs deprived of their mothers at an early age do not herd with the flock even when danger is present, as non-deprived sheep do, suggesting that imprinting occurs in lambs also.[32]

These studies suggest that perhaps the reason for the presence of gregariousness in most humans is that they are imprinted in infancy. In Chapter 6, imprinting was suggested as one reason for the importance of infantile learnings. If humans imprint, such imprinting hardly could fail to occur, because the very survival of human infants is dependent upon there being some more mature and bigger person present to provide the materials necessary for reducing the child's hunger drive, needs for a proper temperature, and similar conditions. However, whether or not there is some optimal age for imprinting in humans, what that age might be, and how necessary it is for there to be extensive contact with some *one* adult is so far a matter of speculation. Much of the research on institutionalization of children, and on maternal deprivation and its effects is relevant to these questions and will be presented later in this chapter.

Imprinting itself is not very well understood. It is possible that the phenomenon is a special case of secondary reinforcement. Enduring secondary reinforcement, like imprinting, first occurs when the organism's sensory and central nervous capacities are sufficiently developed some time after birth for the stimuli occurring in proximity to drive reduction to be associated within the organism in the form of a neural trace. In the same vein, the persistence of the effects may be because it is the first such learning experience; we already have explored some of the reasons for the fact that the earlier a response is acquired, and the less inhibition that exists from earlier competing responses, the more long lasting it is. Thus there is reason for thinking that imprinting may be a result of secondary reinforcement occurring at a particularly appropriate time in the infant's development.

Effects of Maternal Deprivation. Human infants who are reared in an impersonal environment such as foundling homes provide natural experiments, albeit unfortunate ones, for the study of the development of interpersonal attitudes and their relationship to the interaction between child and mother.[33] When these studies are examined there is found a situation very much like that which obtained in the question of infantile sucking. It was concluded, you may remember, that sucking is not an innate drive, but rather is one which is established through early sucking experiences, and once established leads to various kinds of reactions when it is frustrated through weaning. Similarly, social approach drives are not innate, but apparently are acquired through experience. Infants separated from their mothers and brought up in institutional environments during the first six or nine months of life apparently do not acquire such drives.[34] They remain unresponsive to emotional relationships with adults, their abstract thinking remains below that of children not institutionalized during this period, they appear withdrawn and unexcitable.[35] In Chapter 6 we mentioned the studies by Goldfarb that demonstrated this. In addition other investigation has shown that children evacuated from their homes and separated from their parents during wartime reacted differently to the separation, depending on the character of the relationship they had with their mothers in the first six months of life before the evacuation. Those who reacted violently to the separation were largely those children whose relationships with their mothers had been close, involving a great deal of comfortable interaction. However, the children who did not become depressed and anxious by the separation were almost entirely from a group whose infantile experiences had not been happy ones.[36] That is, these latter children had not established strong interpersonal approach drives toward their mothers, and so had no strong drives to be frustrated by the separation. However, the absence of the capacity for affectionate relationships which typified these latter children has serious consequences in the development of schizophrenia, as was mentioned in Chapter 6. Some further information comes from Harlow's infant monkeys reared by dummy mothers. While these animals did develop strong affectional drives toward their substitute mothers and behaved towards them in situations of insecurity much as other monkeys behave toward their real mothers, there nevertheless were observable differences of far-reaching consequences. Because the dummy mothers were not in fact real, the infants apparently did not generalize their affectional reactions from the dummies to other monkeys. The first group of monkeys raised with the dummies now are physically mature and show gross differences in their behavior compared to normally reared animals. In particular, they show absolutely no interest in other monkeys and are completely unresponsive to them. They do not mate, even when paired with the most gentle and the most experienced partners. They do not engage in mutual preening or any body-contact play with other monkeys. These animals thus look very much like human schizo-phrenics.[37] (had dummy mothers)

These studies suggest that the first six or nine months of human life are crucial for the establishment of drives to approach others. Whether this is imprinting or secondary reinforcement so far is not definitely known. But it has been well established that maternal deprivation during these months produces rather different effects from maternal deprivation at later ages. Further, there is some evidence that extensive deprivation of close contact with a mother figure during these months produces irremedial results. Even extensive mothering later on does not result in the establishment of reliable affectional drives in the child.[38]

Later Deprivation. Once interpersonal (or inter-monkey) approach drives are established during the first six or nine months of life, the infant has acquired an orientation to other people and events outside himself. However, the drive so acquired must continue to be satisfied. Maternal deprivation after this early period produces some distinctive consequences. Most typical is severe depression including loss of appetite, weight loss, sleeplessness, lying stuporous, and a slowing down of development. Just about 50 per cent of a group of mother-deprived children (almost all of those whose relationships with their mothers had been happy ones) reacted in this manner in one study.[39] Death is not an infrequent event if the separation lasts much longer than several months, particularly if during the separation the child is given no opportunity to form a stable relationship with a mother substitute. This kind of consequence was illustrated in an experiment by Prof. Lidell of Cornell who worked with goats. He put twin goat kids into a situation which is known to be frightening to these animals — sudden periods of darkness during a 40-minute experimental session. One kid was allowed to stay with its mother during the experimental period, while the other was separated. The separated kids "froze" when the lights went out and acted terrified, while the others, though apprehensive, continued to sniff around and explore. One separated kid ceased suckling after the experimental session and died of starvation shortly thereafter.[40]

The effects of short separations are reversed when the child is restored to its mother, except that frequently the child becomes very clinging and reacts with terror on future occasions which he interprets as leading to another separation. The longer the period of separation, the slower is the recovery and the stronger is the dependency reaction.

Some investigators report that the consequences of separations in excess of three months during the second half year of life are never completely reversible.[41]

Children separated from their mothers after six months of age frequently react in one or more of the following ways when they return home: they become very dependent and react fearfully to even temporary absences of the mother; they become hostile and suspicious, expressing this by not engaging in affectional interchange but not letting the mother out of sight and by violating many of the prohibitions which had been established within the home. One child, who had been hospitalized for surgery, would not allow his mother to be near him for a day or two after returning home, but followed her wherever she went at a discrete distance. He had not simply forgotten her, because he paid much more attention to her than he did to strangers. On his first day at home he committed a number of minor crimes; he emptied the sugar bowl, played with the radio, spilled his milk, and soiled his pants. All of these were things which he had already learned to avoid doing. This kind of behavior is called "testing the limits." It usually represents an attempt by the child to find out if home still is the same place it was before he left it with the same rules and regulations. The child is comforted to find that the same old rules still apply (even if he must be chastised to find this out) because it means that he has really regained the secure and trustworthy place that he missed during his separation. It also means that even though they sent him away, his parents still care about him and what he does, a thought which further reassures the child. Without such limits, he would be perpetually fearful that he might do something that would produce another separation and loss of love. By testing and so rediscovering the limits, the child also reminds himself of what he can and cannot do, the knowledge of which is important if he is to behave well and thus reduce the fear of incurring further punishment.

A third type of reaction also may be evident, particularly after long separations. The child may either remain quite withdrawn from the mother emotionally, engaging in conversation, but without any affectional warmth, or he may be quite friendly, but on a superficial level. That is, he seems pleasant and positive in his feelings, but he makes no effort to be with his parents, accepts absences from them "like a little man," and does not react to shows of affection and warmth as reinforcers. The dependency and affectional drives have not been extinguished in these children. Rather, it seems as if they avoid situations which would arouse their affectional motives out of fear that they will be hurt again as they were hurt by the separation before. In other words, for these children the longing to be near another person on whom they relied and who was the source of so many rewards has become a cue for fear and tension, such as that which occurred when the child was separated from the mother. In effect, the child is afraid to love.[42]

Many children react to separation from parents as if it were a punishment. They may respond with great anxiety because they cannot figure out what the punishment is for. As a result, such children act in a very restrained and circumspect manner when they are reunited with their parents, as if they were trying to avoid doing anything which might be punished by separation again. Children who have been hospitalized for some period not uncommonly threaten their dolls in their imaginative play that they will be sent to the hospital if they do not behave, thus demonstrating their interpretation of the hospitalization as a punishment. In general, when dependency drives are high or are stimulated by some event such as maternal deprivation, there is a tendency for aggressive behavior to be reduced. In most situations, dependency drive and aggressive drive conflict, so that either one or the other is expressed only very indirectly. This was demonstrated in a study on nursery school children who were given a doll play interview in which the experimenter acted out a situation with one doll and each child then acted out with another doll how that doll would react to the situation. It was found that when dependency drive was aroused in the children by telling them a story about a little dog that couldn't find any friends with whom to play, the amount of aggression ascribed by the child to "his" doll in the doll play interview was less than when dependency drive was not aroused.[43]

Despite these reactions to separation, it is not the separation itself which is of significance, but rather what is learned as a result of the child's reaction to it, and what is not learned as a result of the absence of the child's main teachers, the parents. Children separated from their parents after they have developed interpersonal approach drives develop patterns of personality which are related to the kind of response they had to separation, if these responses were reinforced. For example, the child who upon restoration to his home behaves in an aggressive attention-getting manner, which is reinforced by eliciting the parents' attention, is likely to continue in this vein. This kind of development is most likely to occur when the parents' own feelings of guilt for the separation and pity for the child's unhappiness force them to be more solicitous and more yielding to the child's demands than logic decrees.

Often, the child's reaction may have a distinctly anti-social cast to it, in which lying, truancy, and even stealing are present. A number of related factors play a part in this. Such behavior often represents both the child's hostility toward the parents who sent him away (and is particularly likely to occur in the child who interpreted the separation as a punishment), as well as a way of gaining attention from the parents. This kind of re-action is particularly likely to occur in a child who has been punished frequently in the past, so that the separation is readily interpreted as a punishment and indeed becomes the last straw for the child. Not know-ing why he is so punished, he acts as if there is little he can do to avoid punishment, so there is no longer any value to restricting his behavior and inhibiting himself. Further, if the separation has been long, the child has lost many opportunities to develop identifications with the par-ents, and so has not internalized their standards adequately. As a result, he does not react with guilt to his transgressions. Upon restoration to his parents he may be past the age when such identifications can develop. That is, he may be past the age when he spends many hours a day in close contact with the parents, and instead may spend more time with other children in the streets. Add to this his hostility toward his parents and his feeling that they punished him without cause, and all the factors are present which lead to the development of anti-social behavior pat-terns, such as those involved in psychopathic or sociopathic personalities. The situation may be worsened by the fact that as the child commits transgressions because of the lack of internalized standards, and is pun-ished by the parents for them, he is driven even further away from the parents so that identification with them is made even less likely. The re-sult is often a person who chronically steals, is sexually promiscuous, does not respond with guilt, fails to develop any stable interpersonal re-lationships, and one who does not inhibit or restrain himself in order to win the regard or affection of other people.[44] As a consequence, such personalities are quite irresponsible, because most responsibilities in our society are enforced by the withdrawal of affection and regard when they are not met, and this does not serve as a punishment to the psycho-pathic person. The role of redeeming secondary reinforcers in the devel-opment of this kind of personality was described earlier in Chapter 4. Psychopaths are quite unresponsive to treatment, largely because psy-chotherapy requires that patient and therapist enter into a mutual re-lationship of shared regard and trust and the psychopath does not have the affectional drive for such a relationship. Psychopaths often are still responding to interpersonal approach drives but they do so by trying to avoid the situations which will evoke such drives and the anxiety associated with them. Thus they avoid therapy, and in fact react with aggression to therapists who are perceived by them as similar to the parents who sent them away. That the drives for affectional relationships are nevertheless present in many such people is seen in their frequent thefts and sexual promiscuity. Often the thefts are of objects having little direct value, except as status symbols which are evidences that they are highly regarded (loved) by others. Sometimes the psychopath may work much harder at committing the theft and run much greater risks, than if he worked to earn enough to buy the object. However, the fact that the object was stolen, that it once had belonged to someone else, makes it a token of that other person and of a connection with him, in the same way as a child highly values even the most worthless object if it was his father's. The object is a symbol of the person to whom it belonged, and the child who is strongly motivated to have a close relationship to his father responds with the same approach drive to the objects associated with him. Similarly the psychopath wants objects from people he would want to be near if it were not for his fear of his affectional drives and his hostility toward them. The psychopath's sexual promiscuity also is often interpreted as a near substitute for having affectional relationships with others. In one study of delinquent girls, it was found that those whose behavior improved after treatment were largely those whose delinquency was not a result of deprivation of satisfaction of affectional drives in childhood. Those delinquent girls who had such a history, on the contrary, were not modified by therapeutic efforts.[45] This latter group clearly illustrates the psychopathic personality as a consequence of prolonged maternal deprivation.

Psychopathy is not the only consequence of maternal deprivation. Extreme dependency in adulthood, characterized by clinging relationships with other people, frequent requests for help from others, for direction and support from other people, excessive "borrowing" of objects from friends and neighbors, a great deal of socializing and joining of clubs, or extraordinary efforts to win the regard and/or attention of others are characteristics of adults with strong dependency drives which have not been adequately satisfied. In the backgrounds of such people are frequently found forced separations from parents for short periods of time or a great deal of shifting around from one set of substitute parents to another, often after the age of five or six years. Processes of internalization which prevent the development of antisocial patterns have begun by that age, but the child is still too young to have "grown out" of his strong dependency on his parents by relying on his own introjected standards. That is, these people have not had the gradual socialization of affectional drives in which they learn to become more and more independent of the parents and to derive greater satisfaction from being able to be self-reliant and adult than they get from more infantile relationships with others. As a result, being independent for such children is a deprivation without the rewards consequent upon being self-reliant. To them, self-reliance means loneliness and absence of affection, and they respond to these conditions in whatever ways they have learned to bring attention, support, and care from others, and continue into adulthood their search for a stable affectionate relationship like the one taken away from them in childhood.

Separation from parents is an extreme form of deprivation of affectional rewards, even when the separation is from a very bad home. In one study, the proportion of children who had been reared in an institution and who developed socially undesirable behavior patterns was much larger than was the case even for children who were reared in homes which had been rated as being very poor from a health, economic, and psychological point of view.[46] Nevertheless, events within the homes of children who are never separated from their parents for any significant periods of time still influence the course of the interpersonal approach drives. As one would expect, children without siblings have stronger such drives and are described by their parents as being more dependent than children with siblings.[47, 48] The amount of satisfying interaction with parents also is related to dependency. Children whose dependency drives were frustrated by severe weaning were rated as more dependent in their behavior in nursery school, for example.[49] Further, parental demonstrativeness has also been found to be related to dependency; the more overtly demonstrative of affection parents are, the more seeking of affection are the children. It is of interest that in the study that showed this, ratings of mothers' "warmth" of attitudes was not related to dependency. Apparently warmth is not enough; it must be shown overtly to have an effect.[50]

Sex of the child also is a factor in the development of affectional or interpersonal approach drives. It is a commonplace observation that females in our society are more responsive to social stimuli and are more highly motivated to have affectional relationships than are males. Girls respond more than boys to efforts to invoke drives to be socially acceptable.[51] They also tend to be more accepting of and seeking for help from others and are more likely to modify their own behavior to match the standards of the social environment. In one study on suggestibility it was found that female high school students accepted a higher proportion of prestige suggestions than did boys. In this study it was found that dependency, as implied by accepting suggested "right" answers to difficult problems, decreased with age and high school year level, that more dependency was evidenced in relation to high prestige people than to low prestige "authorities," and that at all of the age-grade levels studied (tenth, eleventh, and twelfth years of high school), girls accepted more suggestions than boys and were more responsive to both low and high prestige authorities than the boys.[52]

The highly dependent adult was mentioned earlier as a frequent product of maternal deprivation in childhood. But paradoxically, we see that maternal demonstrativeness and status as an only child also have been found to increase dependency. To add to the paradox, parental rejection of their children also leads to dependency, if the rejection is expressed through either doing too much for the child or doing too little. The mother who is highly protective of her child leaves the child without adequate skills to do things for himself, so that he must continue to have mother or other adults do them for him. We saw in Chapter 6 how the socialization of pain by a very protective mother leads to fearfulness, feelings of inadequacy, and a fear of being independent. Such protectiveness in a mother is sometimes a reaction to her rejection of the child. She may do so much for the child because she lacks the patience to tolerate the child's fumbling attempts to do for himself, and she does not tolerate the less than perfect results of the child's own efforts. In this sense such protectiveness may be considered a rejection of the child.[53] Sometimes the mother rationalizes her behavior by explaining to herself and others that she wants to take very good care of the child and she is afraid for the child's safety and health if he is left to do many things for himself. Such great readiness to interpret things in terms of the child's physical welfare often is motivated by feelings of hostility toward the child and by reactions of guilt which make the mother expect punishment through the child for her unacceptable feelings. That is, she takes such good care of the child in order to reduce her fear that she might be neglecting him. This fear is stimulated by her drives to avoid the child and she responds to such avoidance with guilt. We already have seen how motivations influence perceptions in this way.

On the other hand, the mother who does too little for the child places the child in a position very much like those of maternally deprived children. In addition, the child who receives little help from his parents

must frequently face failure as a result of his inept efforts. As a result
he may learn that the only way in which things may be done successfully is if his parents (or other adults) do them. That is, he learns to be
dependent.

In effect then, both the rejection of dependency by parents and also
their reward of dependency result in the development of high dependency in children's behavior. The paradox may be resolved in much the
same way as was the paradox of aggression, in which it was found that
some factors contributed to the development of the drive, and others
affected the extent to which the drive was expressed in behavior directly.
Similarly, parental protectiveness, demonstrativeness, rewards for dependency, and focusing on an only child contribute to the development
of dependency drive and overt dependent behavior, while severe weaning, rejection, withdrawal of help, and maternal deprivation after the
first six months of life are events which produce frustration of the drive,
leading to disguised dependency, increased demands for attention, and
resistance to the development of more mature and independent ways
of behaving. In other words, some situations affect the strength of the
drive, and others affect the extent to which dependent behavior will be
displayed overtly.

Counter-Dependency. It is in relationship to the socialization of
dependency that enduring drives or attitudes toward other people develop, largely through stimulus generalization from the parents to others, as well as through the learning of interpersonal skills which will
elicit approval and affection from others. It is for these reasons that we
have examined in some detail early parent-child relationships, and it is
for these reasons that adult behavior indicative of drives to affiliate with
others, to share affection with others, and/or to depend on others are
the outgrowths of such parent-child relationships. In addition, the
opposite trends in adulthood, involving antisocial behavior and the lack
of affectional responsiveness also are related to infantile and childhood
events connected with dependency. These opposite trends were characterized as apparent lack of emotional responsiveness as in schizophrenia, or the avoidance of affectional involvement together with
antisocial behavior in psychopathy. One further opposed trend in adulthood may be mentioned—the behavior characterized as counterdependent. The counterdependent adult is one who does have affectional
relationships with others, but who excludes from these relationships
any traces of dependency on the other person. Such a person reacts with
anxiety whenever he is in a position of asking for or receiving help,
comfort, or succor from another. He frequently is highly sensitive to the

presence of such things, and reacts by refusing the relationship or the help or by going out of his way to demonstrate that he neither needs nor profits from the proffered help. His sensitivity to the cues of dependency provides the psychologist with the clue that such a person does have very strong dependency drives. Such an inference is based on what is known about the effects of motivations on making people perceptually sensitive to cues associated with their drives. However, the rejection of such relationships indicates that being dependent is associated with punishment or fear in the person. That this in fact is what happens was demonstrated in one study in which children were characterized as over-dependent, neutral, or counterdependent on the basis of their story completions about seeking help from other people.[54] The mothers of the children were extensively interviewed, and it was found that the mothers of the counterdependent children were much less likely to help their children in various situations and remained aloof from their children more often than did mothers of the other children. It is quite reasonable that this aloofness included a rejection of the child's requests for help and thus a punishment for behaving in a dependent fashion. In this study, the mothers of counterdependent children also more often indicated that they would wait to help their children in problem situations until the child already had gotten into trouble or had clearly failed when he did things by himself. In other words, the counterdependent adult is one for whom receiving help is associated with failure, with rejection, and with pain.

Dependency is just one of several modes of "moving toward people," to use the expression of Karen Horney, a psychoanalyst who led a movement away from many of Freud's theories toward a theory based on characteristic ways of relating to people.[55] In addition to dependency, there are modes of relating to others in which one plays a protective, nurturant, or helping role (as in the helping professions of psychiatry, clinical psychology, and social work). There also are modes of relating based on power in which a person derives satisfaction from influencing another, as in sales work. Erich Fromm has classified and explored some of these orientations toward people, which he categorizes as receptive (the dependent receiver of love and its substitutes), marketing (the use of one's self to influence others), and hoarding and exploitative styles which he calls nonproductive orientations.[56] These varieties of interpersonal approaches reflect the ways in which people have learned to elicit rewards from others, and the kinds of drives whose satisfactions have been dependent on the actions of those who control the reinforcements — namely, the parents.

Achievement

Achievement motivation has been defined by David McClelland, the psychologist who has most extensively explored it, as "competition with a standard of excellence."[57] McClelland started out by trying to test some ideas of Max Weber, the social economist who hypothesized a relationship between the rise of Protestantism and the growth of mercantilism through the industrial revolution.[58] Weber had reasoned that one of the fundamental aspects of Protestantism was that salvation was an individual matter, rather than being ensured by the church. Therefore it was necessary for each person to be responsible for his own salvation. This individual responsibility to do good works and to prove one's freedom from sin was said to have led naturally to the Protestant ethic of hard work, frugality, independence, and individual enterprise which in turn led to the development of business economies, inventiveness, and the growth of commercial establishments which comprised the industrial revolution. McClelland first began by testing to see whether in fact there was more modern industry in Protestant nations than in non-Protestant ones. He roughly matched various Protestant and non-Protestant nations for natural resources and population, and then used measures of annual consumption of electricity in the two groups as an index of industrialization. He found that in fact the Protestant nations such as the United States, Germany, and England did use more electric power than countries such as France, Spain, Portugal, and others. The next step in the research program was to discover if Protestant individuals were more strongly oriented toward achievement than were non-Protestants. In order to do this, McClelland developed a measure of achievement motivation in which subjects were asked to make up stories to four pictures shown to them, with the stories composed of answers to four questions for each picture: What is happening? Who are the people? What led up to the situation? How does it turn out? It was reasoned that people with strong drives for achievement would make up stories in which the characters were solving some problems or working toward some socially valid goal having achievement aspects, such as inventing, manufacturing, or performing. A method for scoring the stories was worked out to give objective scores to each subject. This method included scoring points for the presence of an achievement theme and additional points for the specific presence of other elements such as mention of how the goal would be reached, mention of whether the work would be successful or not, indications of positive feelings about achievement, and several others. The next task of the experimenters was to discover if such stories could be taken as valid measures of motivation. They had found that people under hunger drive tended to increase the number of food references in the stories they told to pictures, so there was some evidence that imaginative productions of this kind did measure some aspect of motives.[59] In testing the achievement motivation pictures, the experimenters found that some people increased their achievement motivation scores if the pictures were shown to them after some experience that could be safely assumed to stimulate achievement motivation. For example, subjects might be given what seems to be an intelligence test and told that a group of successful business executives scored very high on that test. In general, scores on the achievement pictures increased after such arousal of achievement motivation. The authors also found that subjects who got high scores on the achievement motivation test generally did better in other performances than did subjects with low scores, if achievement motivation was aroused by setting some standard of excellence. That is, subjects with strong achievement drives would work harder than subjects without such drives, if achievement drives are aroused. One study showed that children whose scores on I.Q. tests increased in successive testings were those with high achievement motivation, and those children whose scores got lower were those with low achievement drive.[60] One of the interesting findings was that achievement imagery scores increased in males when the experimenter invoked competition with a standard of excellence, but this did not affect the achievement motivation scores of females. However, if the experimenter invoked social acceptability motives, the achievement motivation scores of the females increased, but not the males. Social acceptability was invoked by having the subjects indicate which of the other subjects they would like most to have as friends, and then having each subject guess how often he or she was chosen by others as a desired friend. This kind of procedure seems certainly to be one in which the subjects become highly motivated to be liked and wanted by others. The finding that girls respond to this by increases in achievement motivation fits well into much other evidence that females in our society are in general more responsive to social approach motives than are males.

Thus evidence began to accumulate demonstrating that the pictures and scoring scheme were valid measures of achievement drive. The next step was to test whether in fact Protestants got higher scores than did non-Protestants. In several studies it was found that Protestants had a higher average score than did Catholics (and that Jews had higher scores than both). However, more recently these data have been called into question, and the weight of the evidence suggests that in fact religious affiliation alone does not account for differences in achievement motivation. Thus the main hypothesis that stimulated McClelland's work has received only ambiguous support, but the methods used in testing the hypothesis, the development of fantasy tests of motivation, and the exploration of achievement motivation in general have been important contributions in methods and content in psychology. Although Protestants may be no more achievement motivated than other religious groups, there are nevertheless individual differences in achievement motivation which includes such things as individual differences in the extent to which a person will work hard on a task, and the extent to which he will profit from certain types of instruction which places heavy reliance on individual initiative, and McClelland's work has shown us how to measure such individual differences.

As we have pointed out before, group affiliation or classification as such is not a psychological determinant. As far as achievement motivation is concerned, the important consideration is the kind of child training practices which may or may not be characteristic of a particular group.

Perhaps of greatest interest here is the research of Winterbottom, in her doctoral dissertation, on the factors that contribute to the development of high achievement motivation. Winterbottom reasoned that if Protestantism resulted in achievement orientation through its emphasis on individual responsibility and independence from a salvation-granting church, then parental training practices that emphasize the rapid development of independence from the home might be the things that produce the achievement motivation. She tested this by asking parents to go over a list of "developmental tasks," things that children eventually must learn to do for themselves, and to indicate next to each item at what age they expect their children to accomplish that item. The children of the parents then were tested for achievement motivation, and it was found that the parents who had indicated expectations that their children would be able to do things for themselves at early ages (become independent) had children with higher achievement motivation scores. In other words, parental attitudes that favor early independence training apparently lead to high achievement motivation. One of the very interesting findings in this research was that some items on Winterbottom's scale turned out to be unrelated to achievement motivation, and that these items were different from those that were so related in a particular way. Those items that were not related to achievement motivation were the ones in which the child was encouraged to learn to do something not because it made him more independent from the parents, but rather because it saved the mother some work. One such item, for example, was "making his own bed." Obviously making up one's own bed is not a particularly important skill so far as becoming independent of the parents is concerned, but it is the kind of thing that some parents encourage early because if the child makes his bed, the mother is saved some work. The items that were related to achievement motivation were those in which the parent was in fact encouraging a skill in the child that enabled the child to get along without his parents, such as selecting his own clothing, and choosing his own friends.[61] Other evidence that independence training is related to achievement drive comes from a study in which it was found that deaf children whose parents encouraged early independence had social maturity scores much closer to their capacities than did deaf children whose mothers did not encourage early independence. These latter mothers had children whose social maturity was far below what they were capable of achieving, judging from their intelligence. In other words, the deaf children whose independence was encouraged were in fact using more of their capacities to achieve independent goals and to solve problems than were the children whose parents encouraged greater dependency.[62]

The encouragement of early independence by parents can be done in a number of ways. Praise for independent actions, producing affectional rewards for self-reliance, is one way. Or the parent simply may leave the child to his own devices, so that he must do without those things that he cannot obtain for himself. If he wants a cookie, he must get it himself or do without it. Parental rejection and severe punishment can create a situation in which the child's fear of his parents and hostility toward them prevents him from asking for help, so that he must do things for himself. This situation can also contribute to early independence and thus achievement motivation. Each of these various methods probably colors the nature of the child's achievement drives. One would expect the punished child to show a great deal of hostile competitiveness in his achievement striving, while the ignored child might be more likely to strive for achievements that satisfy him rather than for achievements related to others' standards of excellence. The child who has been selectively rewarded for achievement is perhaps more likely to seek achievements which are public—those that are visible and can elicit applause or praise from others.

What looks like achievement motivation also may be produced by parental punishment for failure, rather than praise for success. However, people with this kind of experience behave in ways somewhat different from those who were rewarded for early independence. Those punished for failure may be thought of as motivated not by achievement, but rather by a fear of failure. They compete with standards of excellence not because this produces some positive rewards, but rather because if they did not compete they might fail and this is associated with fear and anxiety. Characteristically these people start out on a task with a burst of energy, but as they near the end of the task, which has been associated with punishment in the past when the end revealed their failure, they grow anxious and slow down, as if from a feared goal. They even may cease striving in order to avoid the end of the task completely, and this cessation reduces their anxiety. One frequently meets students who withdraw from their courses before the end of the semester or fail to take the final examination, so that actual failure does not occur, and the outcome of the student's efforts remains forever ambiguous. In effect, such a student avoids the crucial test because of his fear that when the chips are down he will fail. In contrast, the achievement motivated person starts out more slowly than the "fear failure" person and speeds up as he approaches the goal which has been associated with rewards for him.

These considerations indicate that the conditions under which achievement drives are acquired are intimately involved with the conditions that produce and modify other drives, such as aggression, affection, identification, and guilt. It is because of the many possible different combinations and interactions of these drives that there are so many different kinds of personalities. The relatively unique combinations of these conditions lead to the unique constellations of characteristics in individual people. These various combinations also lead to the development of conflicts such as those which will be discussed in Chapter 9. For example, in one person achievement motivation may stimulate and add to affectional drives in which outstanding performance becomes a way of satisfying both drives. But in another person the two drives may compete, as when the achievement takes the form of aggressive competition that drives away people and thus reduces the possibility of satisfying affectional drives. It is because of the possibility of these interactions among drives that individual people must be studied individually, and generalizations about any one feature of their personalities are likely to fail to do justice to the complex interplay of all of the features. Because of the many possible interactions among drives it is not possible to spell out in a single work all the varieties which are commonly found. However, the last section of this text will be concerned with some of the laws that govern interactions and a few of the main patterns that emerge from such interactions. But before getting to this last step in the analysis of personality, it is necessary to discuss the contributions of one other set of factors—those that influence the nature and content of thought.

REPRISE. In this chapter we have explored some of the drives that are acquired during the socialization process. Although there are individual differences in the extent to which these drives may be aroused and in the kinds of behaviors displayed when they are operating, these drives are apparently nearly universal because the learning situations in which they are acquired are nearly universal. There are also individual differences in the "slants" given to guilt, aggression, sex, interpersonal approach, and achievement drives as a result of variations in the socialization practices which have produced them, as well as individual differences in the kinds of situations that elicit the drives once they are acquired. Finally, there are differences in the extent to which these drives become interrelated and confounded among themselves and with the drives described in Chapter 6. Some of these sources of individual differences were explored in this chapter, which focused on the following:

1. Aggressive drive is a learned response to frustration, and responses to this drive range from overt aggression to aggression directed against the self (particularly when the frustration is internal) and to inhibition of aggressiveness.

2. Aggression is socialized through parental permissiveness for aggression, and the extent to which they frustrate the child. Use of physical punishment was cited as an important determinant of aggression. Socialization determines the direction of aggression, the range of prohibited and permitted objects of attack, and the kind of attack.

3. Guilt is a product of identification with the teachers of shame which operates such that violation of internalized standards produces anxiety and fear of punishment. Guilt elicits responses which are reinforced either by the elimination of the cues that elicited the guilt through undoing, making restitution, and avoiding temptation, or by obtaining

punishment through confession, self-injury, or through perceptual interpretation of events as punishing.

4. Sex roles are acquired through identification and practiced in childhood play. Conflict over sex practices and role adequacy leads to the development of disguised forms of sexual activity such as dancing and kissing, and to the ability of various nonsexual cues to elicit sexual drive. Oedipal conflicts also produce a split between the ideas of love and sexual behavior.

5. Sexual drive readily becomes confounded with dependency and aggression as a result of interconnected socialization practices, particularly those affecting the individual's confidence in his sex role status.

6. Interpersonal approach drives are the result of learned drives and reinforcements in infancy, and possibly of imprinting. The effects of maternal deprivation on these drives vary with the timing of the deprivation, its length, and the parent-child relationship before the deprivation. The effects of such deprivation include absence of interpersonal responsiveness, dependency, aggression and antisocial patterns, and superficial friendliness.

7. Maternal protectiveness and/or rejection are determinants of dependency and counter-dependent reactions.

8. Achievement motivation is a result of early independence training, which may be linked to cultural and religious norms. It is evoked by competition with a standard of excellence in boys and by arousal of affiliation drive in girls.

9. Achievement drive is different from fear of failure, producing different patterns of performance.

8. The Socialization of Thinking

We saw in the last chapter that the manner in which certain secondary drives such as sex, achievement, and aggression are acquired and the ways in which these drives are socialized are related to the ideas which are common in a society. In addition, it was noted that some socialization practices have the effect of inhibiting thinking about prohibited topics, as when parents avoid labeling sexual activities and body parts. Further, people vary in the extent to which they engage in thought about themselves, their guilts, hostilities, and their sexual drives. It is the purpose of this chapter to discuss the socialization of thought with reference to these topics: How are individual differences in the extent of thinking and/or fantasizing established? Why is the thinking and/or fantasy of some people less realistic than that of others? What are the common ways of thinking in our culture and how are they transmitted to children? And finally, how are general "styles" of thinking established, such as the tendency to direct one's thoughts and perceptions to other people, or the tendency to think more exclusively about one's self?

The Extent to Which Thinking Is Done

It will be recalled from Chapter 5 that thinking is a process of producing symbols which are associated with external events, and to which one may react as he reacts to the external cues themselves. As responses, we have seen that they follow the same laws as do motor responses: they are influenced by levels of drive, reinforcements, and cues. People differ in the extent to which they characteristically respond with thought. Some people tend to spend a great deal of time and effort in thinking and fantasizing about themselves, their experiences, or their environments, while others tend more toward action and to the direct expression in motor behavior of their responses, rather than to covert responding in thought. Thus one person thinks and worries a great deal about his problems, or engages in extensive planning of future actions, while another avoids thinking, often by distracting himself in other activities, or by sleeping, and plunges ahead toward his future, making do with events as they occur rather than planning, or acting out his responses instead of thinking them. What are the factors which make for these differences?

Infantile Experience and the Growth of Thinking. It appears likely that a major source of these differences is the extent to which the production of symbols about events is rewarding or at least is not punishing. We have seen that an infant who suffers from very high levels of drive which are not reduced in a reliable fashion and who lacks stimulation from his environment suffers from a disorder known as marasmus, characterized by progressively decreasing interest in the environment, and a decrease in responsiveness to it and to himself and his own drive states. Such an infant shows no interest in eating, although hunger drive may be very great. This suggests that the making of responses to the environment depends on having an environment which contains more reward than punishment in it. Stimulation from the environment which is associated with drive reduction may well be necessary for the arousal and functioning of the cortical neurons involved in thought. Where environmental stimuli are associated with increased drive, rather than decreased drive, the production of covert symbols for such stimuli similarly would be followed by increased drive, thus operating against the development of the habit of producing such stimuli. When these conditions prevail in early infancy, the child fails to establish what is referred to as reality contact; there is a more or less permanent lack of responsiveness to stimuli which are presented.

It was noted in Chapter 5 that some of the energy for thinking comes from a need for stimulation. The operation of the need involves the activation of cortical neural traces. However, what objects and events will be symbolized through the activation of traces and thus thought about, depends on the relations between these objects and the individual's drives. When the environment is punishing, thinking will be concerned with internal events, with an imagined pleasant environment, or with the memory of a pleasant event. If the environment has been chronically punishing, there will be few such memories to occupy thought, with the result that a greater portion of thought will be devoted to an imaginative elaboration of the few pleasant events that had occurred.

It also is possible that the need for cortical stimulation can be fulfilled by sensory stimulation produced by activity, through feedback to the cortex from the sense receptors in the muscles. When symbolization of events is unpleasant because the events are associated with punishment and drive increase, thinking may diminish greatly to be replaced by motor activity and overt responding, usually called "acting out." "Acting out" thus is an alternative to thought as a means of producing cortical stimulation.

If frustration and punishment become characteristic of the environment, one therefore would expect relatively little learning of the habit of thinking. There is some recent evidence to support this. It has been found that when faced with a difficult problem which arouses anxiety, boys who tend to not think about the problem are those whose early socialization was marked by greater environmental stress, such as arbitrary demands for obedience, few rewards, and harsh discipline.[1] When habits of responding to and thinking about external stimuli are ill established, thoughts may still be produced, particularly if early infantile experiences have not been punishing to an extreme. But these thoughts are likely to have little correspondence to the reality stimuli. This kind of thinking was labeled as fantasy in Chapter 5, in which it was pointed out that such fantasy may be rewarded if it changes a potentially punishing cue situation into one in which reinforcing cues are produced in thought. Thus fantasy may come to be elicited by environmental stimuli, but the content of the fantasy may not correspond to the environmental events, and may indeed be quite opposite from it. For example, when the cues of failure are presented to a person with strong achievement drive who has not established habits of thinking about his situation, he is likely to engage in fantasy in which he produces cues that reduce his achievement drive, rather than think about the environmental stimuli that are associated with an increase in drive. His fantasy still will contain an achievement theme, but in a manner reversed from the reality state of affairs. This fantasy therefore can be used diagnostically for inferring something about the situations which motivate people and their experiences in such situations. Similarly, fantasies about sexual adventures may indicate strong sex drive and frequent sexual frustrations. Because of inadequacy in his perceptual processes, the very young infant probably has most of his cortical stimulation arising from his own drive states. This is a parallel to what Freud called "primary process" thinking, referring to thought dominated exclusively by drives, rather than by the nature of environmental reality. As the infant matures and is socialized, more and more of his thought is determined by external cues. This kind of reality dominated thinking is called "secondary process," in psychoanalytic language. As we have seen, the extent to which secondary process thinking develops at the rate made possible by increasing maturation depends on how attractive and nonthreatening socialization has made the environment.

The socialization of thinking continues throughout childhood. Parents teach children how to look at things so that they are right side up (as late as four years old, children have an easier time perceiving common objects in upside down pictures than adults), children learn to respond to the cues of depth, to discriminate objects from their backgrounds by reference to their outlines, form, and color, and later by their surface textures, and to make accurate verbal reports. As one would expect, parents differ in the extent to which they encourage such learning; some parents are particularly concerned with their children's acquisition of verbal symbols and cognitive concepts, and reinforce their children for developing skill in conceptual behavior, while others place greater emphasis on muscular coordination and dexterity. Elton McNeil has found that there are class differences in this, with lower class children and their mothers favoring motor activities and responses, and middle-class children and their mothers doing better at encouraging conceptual acitivities.[2] He tested this by having boys engage in various activities such as playing statues and doing abstract paintings. Lower class boys were more expressive in taking poses with their bodies to communicate various emotions, while middleclass boys were more spontaneous in their abstract paintings. Through interviews with the boys' mothers, McNeil found that lower class mothers valued hobbies and jobs for their sons which involved muscular activities, while middleclass mothers valued jobs and hobbies which were more conceptual in nature. This difference in emphasis during socialization has been used to account for the fact that lower class people tend to be more overtly expressive, preferring activity rather than thinking and using language. There are several possible reasons for these class differences. Lower class people more frequently earn their livings through occupations requiring extensive muscular activities, while middleclass people more frequently are employed in jobs requiring verbal and conceptual skills. Child training practices may therefore be geared to the children's occupational outlook. Another possibility is that middleclass people may have greater innate potentiality to acquire and use concepts. There is a great deal of evidence that the middle class has higher verbal intelligence than the lower class; the child training practices in the two classes thus may be determined by what the parents and the children *can* do. It has been found that lower class children of high verbal intelligence are more conceptually oriented and less oriented toward muscular responses than lower class children of lower intelligence.[3]

These class differences extend to the kinds of behaviors characteristically acquired as responses to fear and anxiety; lower class people tend to respond muscularly and thus overtly, while middleclass people more frequently respond verbally and in thought. There are several different responses which may serve to reduce anxiety. Although these will be discussed in detail in Chapter 10, two will be mentioned here. One anxiety-reducing response involves extensive inhibition of the muscles whose responses are cues for anxiety. The other response involves a great deal of ruminative thought, in which the person continues to think anxiety-arousing thoughts but in such a ritualized and stylized way that they no longer elicit anxiety. Both these kinds of responses may become elaborated and generalized to form the symptoms of neuroses and psychoses. It has been found that those neuroses and psychoses in which motor activities are most directly involved (hysteria and catatonic schizophrenia) are found more frequently in lower class people, and those behaviors which rely on thought forms to reduce anxiety are found in the symptom pictures of neurotic and psychotic people from the middle class (paranoid schizophrenia, obsessive-compulsive neuroses).[4]

Situational Factors. While socialization practices play a major role in determining the extent to which an individual characteristically responds with thought, situational factors are also important. A person who has developed relatively good reality contact and who has usually been reinforced for making thought responses by finding solutions to problems, making successful plans and rehearsing actions may find himself in an environmental situation which is so punishing and so difficult to solve intellectually, that after trying to solve it through thought and finding only increases in punishment rather than drive reduction, he may continue to give responses from his response hierarchy until he stops responding with thought; stopping thinking will be reinforced by the reduction in fear or anxiety which follows when the thought cues for these drive states are no longer produced, and he may begin to behave in ways which are characteristic of people who have not developed close reality contact. The continued stress of front line combat may be one such situational factor which can be so stressful that established habits of thinking fail and are abandoned. The failure of thought to solve such environmental problems may provide a very powerful additional source of anxiety. Such failure places the person in a position of almost complete helplessness to understand and act on the environment successfully — in other words, in the position he was in as an infant. But there is a difference: protecting parents are no longer present, and the individual may react with the terror of an infant whose parents have (to him) mysteriously disappeared. This terror adds still further to the environmental stress. It may be said then, that there is a reciprocal relation between early training and current stress, in their ability to produce inhibition of thinking; the less favorable to cognitive activity the former is, the less of the other is necessary to reduce thinking.

The extent to which thinking occurs is then, to some extent dependent on the extent to which childhood experiences have been conducive to thought. To summarize some of the variables that have an effect on thought: Deprivation of stimulation may inhibit the development of thought habits; the encouragement to engage in physical exercise play *vs.* imaginative and thought play (which also has been found to vary with class status of parents), and the extent to which the child is exposed to problems which are challenging enough (that is, are frustrating but obviously capable of yielding reinforcement) and at the same time not so difficult that the child cannot solve them through thought.[5] Finally, it appears likely that intelligence is a limiting factor on the extent to which a child will be reinforced through overcoming frustration and reaching a goal, for making thought responses rather than direct "acting-out" in motor activity.

Cognitive Style

It is not only the strength of the tendency to engage in thought which is influenced by socialization experiences. The direction or "style" of thinking also is acquired. Interest in studying cognitive styles is quite recent, perhaps dating from the late 1950's, when emphasis shifted from personal adjustment to intellectual mastery as major goals of education. Such study is still in the stage of trying to discover meaningful dimensions or ways of classifying cognitive styles which ultimately will lead to the discovery of the factors which determine an individual's position on each of the major dimensions. We will discuss here some of the styles which have been proposed and which seem to be significant.

Tolerance-Intolerance of Ambiguity. Elsa Frankel-Brunswik became interested in one dimension of thinking which she has called "tolerance *vs.* intolerance of ambiguity."[6] She began work on this subject as a result of some discoveries she made during the course of extensive research on how prejudice is established in children. She found that highly prejudiced children tended to evaluate things as falling into well-defined categories which were internally consistent, even in situations in which such categorizations are over-simplifications.[7] Such children do not see things as being partly good and partly bad; they do not observe that parents are sometimes loving and sometimes not, sometimes happy and sometimes sad. Rather, they describe things as entirely one or the other. Frankel-Brunswik called this "intolerance of ambiguity" because, when presented with vague or poorly defined visual stimuli, these children tended to make an interpretive response to the stimuli earlier than did children low in prejudice, and to maintain their interpretations longer, despite evidence which conflicted with them. She has described this dimension as the extent to which a person thinks in terms of uncertainties or absolutes. Although Frankel-Brunswik has discovered a relationship between intolerance of ambiguity and authoritarian home atmosphere, the specific factors which determine a child's position on this dimension have been explored only cursorily. It has been suggested that a tendency toward intolerance of ambiguity is found in children who have conflicting response tendencies in which a motivated response potential is opposed by a guilt drive. This creates an uncertainty in the child or adult; the uncertainty is reduced by not thinking about one side of the conflicting response tendencies, thus producing a "black-or-white" kind of thought. When this response to conflict becomes widely generalized and characteristic of the person, as a result of stimulus generalization from a large number of situations in which conflicting responses are aroused, it defines a general trait of the person's thought.

The presence of conflict alone is not sufficient to account for intolerance of ambiguity. As we have seen in Chapter 6, conflict between initial response tendency and social norms is inevitable. It seems likely that specific training in being definite and avoiding ambiguity also plays a part in establishing this trait. It has been suggested that parents themselves may see things as black or white and so punish their children for explanations and accountings which are not sufficiently unambiguous. Thus a parent might ask a child how he feels about a certain topic or person and reject any of the child's responses which report mixed feelings or doubt with a characteristic "Make up your mind. Do you or don't you?" Frankel-Brunswik says that this is likely to be the case in authoritarian homes in which only one position on any issue is tolerated, and in which issues are clearly dichotomized in order to reduce doubt and ambiguity, even if such dichotomization does violence to the real state of affairs. In addition, the child's identification with such models would reduce tolerance of ambiguity. Discipline tends to be harsh in authoritarian homes, requiring prompt obedience which may leave the child little time to think of responses and alternatives which, although complex, would permit him to satisfy both conflicting response tendencies. From her interviews with the parents of such children, Frankel-Brunswik also has concluded that they tend to emphasize overt appearances and behaviors in their socialization practices, rather than how their children feel or think. This suggests that such parents are more likely to encourage frustration and denial of their children's desires, even if this produces a great deal of tension in the children, in order to produce conformity to parental standards. Such denial of the child's response potential thus inclines the child to not think of one alternative response in a situation in which such an alternative conflicts with the parents' expectations. The child gets a good deal of practice in rejecting his own desires.

One of the features Frankel-Brunswik found to be characteristic of the parents of children who were high in intolerance of ambiguity was uncertainty about their socio-economic status. The parents tended to be marginal middle class; Frankel-Brunswik theorized that their emphasis on conformity, particularly in appearances, reflects their striving to maintain a middleclass identification, by being sure that their children behave like middleclass children. It also has been suggested that threats to their status are interpreted as the fault of others, rather than a reflection of their own failures. Such an interpretation obviously serves to reduce anxiety about one's achievement. The others who are blamed are usually those who are outside the group with which one wishes to identify; in the case of the marginal middle class, minority outgroups thus frequently become the object of displaced aggression, producing the prejudice which goes along with intolerance of ambiguity.[8]

Cognitive Simplicity-Complexity. Another cognitive style which has been investigated recently is concerned with the extent to which people characteristically try to reduce complex phenomena to simple terms.[9] A cognitively simple person is one who tends to evaluate various people all in the same terms or by reference to the same dimension, such as power, or prestige, or beauty; a cognitively complex person tends to use more dimensions and traits in characterizing others. It seems likely that cognitive simplicity-complexity is allied closely to tolerance-intolerance of ambiguity, and they may be in fact the same traits, although this has not been clearly demonstrated.

The cognitively simple person, in his grouping of a larger range of phenomena on the same stimulus generalization gradient, frequently fails to note the differences among the phenomena; the cognitively complex person, on the other hand, makes many discriminations and fewer generalizations, and responds more strongly to differences among events than to similarities. These styles have been illustrated in several experiments. In one, subjects were shown drawings which contained incongruous elements and after a period of time were asked to reproduce the drawings. The cognitively simple subjects tended to eliminate the incongruity in the drawing in their reproduction of it, while the cognitively complex tended to emphasize or "sharpen" the incongruity.[10] Sometimes these reactions are referred to as *sharpening* or *leveling*.[11] In another experiment, subjects took personality tests, and then were asked to take the same tests again, except that this time they were to answer the items as they thought another person, whom they had met for a while, would answer them. It was found that the cognitively simple subject predicted that the other person would answer the items in the same way he did more often than did the cognitively complex. In other words, the cognitively simple person did not ascribe as many differences between himself and the other person as did the cognitively complex person.[12] These two studies also illustrate the generality of the simplicity-complexity trait; it plays a role in thought about visual stimuli such as drawings, and in thought about interpersonal stimuli.

Acquiescence. When Frankel-Brunswik did her work on prejudice, intolerance of ambiguity, and authoritarianism, she developed a test known as the California F (for Fascism) Scale which measured authoritarianism. This test was made up of a number of aphorisms, such as "War is inevitable," and subjects were asked to indicate the extent to which they agreed with each item. It since has been discovered that, when the items are all turned around and made opposite in meaning, people who agreed with them in the original still tended to agree with them.[13] A person who indicated agreement that war is inevitable also tended to agree with the statement "War is not inevitable." This led to the discovery of what is called the acquiescent response set — the tendency to agree, regardless of the content of what is being agreed to.[14] It was also found that people who got high scores on the F Scale, and who were thought to be highly prejudiced and authoritarian, tended to be high on acquiescent response set. While some psychologists think that the F Scale was not really measuring authoritarianism but was instead measuring acquiescent response set, it seems more likely that acquiescence is one of the habitual responses which characterizes the authoritarian personality. High acquiescence seems to be a general trait in which responses of conforming to or agreeing with other people have great strength, probably as a result of training in conformity during socialization, training which was perhaps not very different from that described as typical of children who are intolerant of ambiguity.[15]

There also is some evidence that high acquiescence is found in people who describe others as being like themselves, and low acquiescence is more often found in those who describe others as being different from themselves. These relationships among cognitive styles and various perceptual and thought responses thus seem to suggest that there are many similarities among the traits of tolerance-intolerance of ambiguity, cognitive complexity-simplicity, and acquiescence. It is not yet known whether they are all related, but distinct traits, each having its own causes or antecedents, or whether they might really be different ways of describing and measuring the same general response tendency, in which case the conditions which are found to favor the development of one such style will also be found in the histories of those with comparable positions on the other traits. So far at least, this field is no place for someone who is high in intolerance of ambiguity.

Field Dependence-Independence. The situation is further complicated by two other styles which also seem to be related. These are called field dependence-independence, and inner-other directed.

The field dependence-independence dimension is best described by one of the basic measures which went into the research by Witkin who has investigated this topic.[16] In his research, he placed subjects one at a time in a special chair in a dark room. In front of the subject was a luminous bar inside a luminous square frame. The job of the subject was to turn a knob that would rotate the luminous line until the line was perpendicular. The frame around the line was tilted somewhat. If the subject straightened the line by reference to the frame, he would set it at a different position from the one that it would be set at if he used his own body as a reference point for the perpendicularity of the line. Subjects who used their own kinesthetic senses as the reference point for the line were found to behave differently from those subjects who used the external frame as a reference point, on other measures which were made. In general, Witkin has concluded that those subjects who used themselves as reference points were more independent, self-directed, thoughtful, and introspective than those who used the external frame of reference.[17, 18] He therefore has called the former group field independent, in the sense that their behavior is determined by events within themselves rather than by external environmental influences, and the latter group as field dependent. There is evidence that these are pervasive styles of attending and perceiving, such that the field independent person is more likely to act on his own principles rather than expediently, to behave as he thinks right rather than in terms of others' expectations for him, to think more about himself than about others, and to be less influenced by customary modes of behavior. The field dependent person, on the other hand, is likely to be more responsive to other people, more socially graceful, and more alert to the expectations of others, more likely to seek their support and approval, and more appreciative of custom.

Although no unambiguous evidence has been collected about the factors which determine the extent to which an individual may be field dependent or independent, it seems reasonable to expect that the adequacy or completeness of identification may be an important variable. The individual who has internalized standards for behavior which have been rewarded when acted upon is more likely to be field independent than one who has had to continue relying upon signs of parental approvals and disapprovals for cues for his own behavior. Supporting this is the finding that field dependent men have closer emotional ties with their mothers than do field independent men, indicating that they have not developed as strong an identification with their fathers.[19] One also might expect that parents who place relatively greater emphasis on rewarding their children for independent and creative actions and problem solutions than on reserving rewards for only the customary and most socially acceptable solutions are more likely to have children who would be characterized as field independent.

Inner Directed-Other Directed. Field independence-dependence appears to be quite similar to a dimension of cognitive style described in a dramatic criticism of American society by the University of Chicago sociologist, David Riesman.[20] He categorized people who are highly responsive to social expectation, custom, and group pressure as *other-directed*, in that their behavior is primarily oriented toward receiving rewards from the social community. Occupations in which getting along with co-workers and superiors and inferiors is a prerequisite for success are congenial to the development and elaboration of other-directedness. You will recognize this as part of Miller and Swanson's bureaucratic integration setting, in which parents typically stressed interpersonal skills, techniques of cooperation, adherence to group norms, and permissiveness for temporary enjoyments, rather than stressing the need to make all activities contribute to the establishment of future security, independence of judgment, competitiveness, and strong internalized standards. These latter characterized the child training practices of those in the entrepreneurial integration setting.[21] The entrepreneurial group is more like Riesman's inner-directed, in which the individual engages in activities more directly for his own needs, rather than because of the expectations of others, and he uses his own fulfillment as a criterion for his evaluation of events, as against the other-directed who refers to the social norms. Essentially, the inner-directed person is one who is responsible for his survival through his own activities, while the other-directed person is more dependent on rewards from others. Riesman suggests that different kinds of societies encourage one or another of these styles, with the economic system of society playing a major role. A culture made up of individual producers and merchants whose consumption is almost exclusively limited to their own success and what they can make for themselves is more likely to employ the child training techniques which result in the inner-directed personality, while societies in which complex social organizations exist in order to regulate the behavior of its members — societies in which the means of survival involve the cooperation of various segments and specialist groups of the population — these "business" societies are more likely to emphasize the socialization practices which lead to "other-directedness."

These are some of the dimensions of cognitive style which have been of recent interest to psychologists. It is obvious from the lack of information about the determinants of the various styles, about the extent of their generality, and from the apparent large areas of overlap among the dimensions that research on cognition is in its infancy, although its potential contribution to an understanding of the thoughts, ideas, and habits of thinking found in people is great.

Ideas

These styles of thinking represent attempts to discover patterns of thought which can be investigated without regard to the content to which they are applied. That is, it should be possible to study intolerance of ambiguity in different cultures, even if ideas and beliefs differ among the cultures. Similarly, the extent to which people in a culture are characteristically field dependent or independent may be compared with similar measures derived from a different culture, even if the ideas or thought contents found in one are not found in the other. However, the study of personality does not stop at these general dimensions; there remains to be explored the question of the content of the thought which is present in the members of a society. What are the ideas found in people, and how are they acquired? In general, an idea may be thought of as a way of construing experience. Such constructions, or schemata, include the phenomena or objects which are their subjects and the ways in which these are evaluated and related to other phenomena. In effect we are asking the question: How do people come to symbolize their experiences in the ways they do in our society?

It would not be possible to summarize and explore all the thoughts and ideas which may be found in a society such as our own — a list of such ideas would be as extensive as the state of knowledge and belief (both true and false) which exists in the society. Below are some examples of ideas mentioned by McClelland as characteristic of a college student subject who was studied extensively by him.[22] These ideas are just a few of those held by the subject, obviously, but they seem to be quite typical of people in our society, particularly males like McClelland's subject, and they are the ideas which came out of the subject most readily; they were high in his response hierarchy.

1. A well rounded education is valuable since it opens up all areas of knowledge to the person.
2. Bigness is valuable.
3. The future is very important.
4. The growth of knowledge presents problems to men.
5. Nature can be conquered if we understand human nature.
6. Knowledge is not so important in itself but as a means to the higher value of happiness.
7. Empirical explanations are to be preferred to nonempirical, religious ones wherever possible.

8. The individual is on his own and must make a living by his own efforts.
9. The primary goal of work is money.
10. Competition is an inherent part of economic life.
11. Competition promotes selfishness and is not conducive to the welfare of all.
12. Formal artistic experience is of relatively little importance in life.
13. Achievement does not bring happiness.
14. Life is rather painful, full of suffering and worry.
15. All men are equal.
16. Power and authority are essentially suspect and undesirable.
17. Authority is also good and desirable.
18. Power should be exercised only if subordinates wish it and ask for it.
19. I am without strong, solidary, affiliative ties.
20. Love, especially through marriage to a woman I love, is the key to existence.
21. Lack of courage is the most serious vice.
22. One's occupation should involve service to people.
23. The individual must seek salvation (happiness) on his own.

We already have mentioned some other ideas common in our culture: homosexuality is bad; sexuality is inconsistent with femininity; direct aggression is wrong; cleanliness is a mark of goodness; males can fight but females cannot; girls can have intimate relations with other girls, but boys should not have similar relations with other boys; males should compete, and females should be passive; mothers and fathers should love their children.

Direct Learning. We could not track down each of these ideas to the kinds of situations in which they were acquired. However, we can review here the general psychological determinants of thoughts. Children typically are taught to label events, to report causal relationships and explanations acceptable to their parents in terms of the parents' thought habits, and to relate experiences through agreed upon language forms. That is, the direct learning of ideas and thoughts occurs through the reinforcements administered by parents, teachers, and peers. We have seen that the structure and vocabulary of the language has a selective influence on the kinds of phenomena and relations which form the content of thought. Extensive research has been done on the development of ethical ideas and basic concepts of physics (such as that two objects cannot fill the same space at the same time, and that if an object such as a ball is not in a certain place — the toy chest — at a particular time, and does not move to that place, then it will not be there at a later time).[23, 24] This research has been the life work of Jean Piaget, the Swiss child psychologist who has a genius for developing research methods appropriate for use with children. Piaget's research presents convincing evidence that such ideas are acquired by children when their intellectual maturation and their background of experiences in being rewarded when they make the correct responses are extensive enough for the child to develop generalized expectations about how objects and people behave and should behave.

An example of this kind of learning is the way in which a child learns that objects he cannot see have not disappeared. It is through games like peek-a-boo that the child discovers that even when he is not looking his mother is still there, and all he need do is open his eyes for the object to be visible again. In this way the child comes to tolerate his mother's absence, because he has learned that even when she is not immediately present to his senses, she will be present again. Deaf and blind children do not learn this as readily because they lack the sense modalities through which such learning takes place. The result is that deaf and blind children are much more intolerant of separation from their mothers.

Probably the most potent sources of rewards for thinking and for schematizing experiences are parents. Parents, through talking to their children, teach them what to think about, what is good and bad, and how to evaluate events. More subtly, parents impart ideas to their children by the connections they make between the child's responses and rewards and punishments. All of the parental socialization practices described in Chapters 6 and 7 present the conditions for the child to verbalize relationships among events and evaluations of traits and behaviors. In other words, the responses which parents teach to their children become ideas when the child develops sufficient verbal skills to label them and think about them. Thus children come to believe that sex is shameful, that toilet activities require privacy, and that it is only justifiable to fight when it is in self-defense against age mates.

Even more subtly, the parents themselves serve as models for behavior, models which the child may internalize through his imitation and identification with them. Thus children readily learn that fathers are the final authorities, that mothers should be housewives, and that a man is one who behaves in the way father does. In this way the child acquires his ideas about the behavior appropriate to his sex role, to marriage, to handling other children, relatives, guests, neighbors, shopkeepers, and in all the social situations in which the child may observe his parents.

To a lesser extent, other adults serve the same function. Important among other adults are teachers, relatives, and the parents of friends. Imitation and identification occur in relation to these people also, as was pointed out earlier. Even teachers, who make direct efforts to teach children specific verbal responses, rely heavily on the student's identification with them in order to transmit attitudes toward learning in general and subject matters in particular.[25] Teachers, relatives, and other adults broaden the scope or range of behaviors which the child may observe in various social situations, label, and associate with the persons and the situations in order to produce constructions or schematizations regarding appropriate and permissible behavior.

Age mates are another particularly important group of teachers in our society. Wayne Dennis' study in which he found that American children appear to regard praise from playmates as more important to them than do children of several other cultures, demonstrates this.[26] Age mates continue parental instruction in sex role behaviors, by expecting the members of the play group to behave in certain ways, deviation from which may be corrected by the group or punished. The norms for behavior in social groups vary from class to class (as we have seen, physical activity is more characteristic of lower class adolescent males, and conceptual activities of middleclass adolescent boys); so also does the instruction of group members in acceptable behavior which, through imitation and labeling, becomes transformed into ideas about what is good or bad, right or wrong, or appropriate. In addition, the activities of age mates serve to focus the child's attention on what age mates consider to be phenomena of note, thus teaching the child what to think about, as well as how to evaluate the phenomena.

Institutions. To a great extent, the conceptualizations which a child will acquire are presented to him readymade through the institutions which are a part of his society. To think of youth as a time of irresponsibility and of learning is inevitable in a society whose institutions are so arranged that productive work is not expected of children, and in which education is directed almost entirely at youth. Similarly, the nature of our society's marriage institutions presents to the child a readymade conception of the relationship between adulthood and marital status, the breadwinning responsibilities of men, and the nurturant role of women. Economic institutions provide set patterns and ideas regarding ways of accumulating wealth and providing the necessities of life.[27] Finally, the cultural artifacts which exist in the society into which a child is born play an important part in directing his attention to activities and events considered important in the society. As a specific example, the institution of advertising does much to influence children and adults to develop an acquisitive orientation, and to see relationships between possessions and prestige, power, or personal adequacy. Similarly, the great number of gadgets available and used in daily life in America communicates our society's high valuation of efficiency and inventiveness.

Institutionalized Communications. A particularly important determinant of one's ideas lies in the characteristics of communications to which one exposes himself — the newspapers, books, magazines he reads, the art he looks at, the music and radio programs he hears, and the movies and television productions he watches. These media are powerful reflections of the society's mores and folkways, and provide models for the child to imitate, identify with, and learn from. For example, many newspapers still mention the race of the offender when describing a crime committed by a Negro but do not mention race in connection with Caucasians. Thus readers have their attention focused on "Negroness" as an important subject of thought. As another example, the typical rags-to-riches plots of many movies, television productions, and novels focus attention on upward-mobility and success measured in terms of economic class membership and conspicuous consumption. Still further examples: McClelland reports an analysis of British and American crime movies which shows that in British films the police or Scotland Yard frequently solve the crime, while in American movies the police are more often pictured as bumbling people who only get in the way of the private individual who eventually solves the crime. This reflects the societies' attitudes toward legal authority and the power of the private individual; one's ideas and expectations regarding the behavior of police and private citizens must be strongly influenced by which type of movie one has been exposed to. Mention should also be made of a study of children's books reported by McClelland; in such books, females are very frequently described as playing nurturant and supportive roles, while males are presented as the problemsolvers, courageous, protecting of the females, and successful if they are honest.[28] In a similar vein, analysis of the plots of radio, television, and movie stories reveals that heroines are often presented as modest, delicate, sensitive, and guided by their hearts, while villains are cold, highly intellectual in a scheming sense, and thus able to outwit the innocent (who are simple and not-so-intelligent folk). Young lovers are commonly pictured as opposed by their oldfashioned and cruel parents. Such common plots communicate information and expectations regarding the behavior of people, the values which are rewarded, and the role behaviors appropriate to many different situations as construed in the culture. As such, they are powerful sources of ideas about the nature of people, events, and societal institutions. A recent study showed a high correlation between the frequency of achievement themes in elementary school reading texts and the number of patents issued by the U. S. Patent Office over a period of almost 150 years, indicating that the themes common to the texts were reflected in individual resourcefulness, inventiveness, and achievement.[29] It is part of the task of social criticism and literary criticism in particular to isolate and explore the ways in which these institutionalized media conceptualize experience and communicate their conceptualizations.

Culture. What we have been saying about the determinants of thoughts is that in many different ways, culture is a major factor; how parents, neighbors, peers, and teachers behave, what institutions exist and how they function, and the ideas that inform the mass media are all expressions of culture. However, it is not sufficient to say only that the ideas held by people are products of the culture in which they live. We have tried to indicate some of the ways in which these ideas which are a part of the culture in abstract are concretized and communicated within the experiences of the people who comprise the culture. These methods of communication include direct teaching by adults and age mates, as well as through imitation and identification, and more indirect teaching through the representation of already existing ideas in the institutions and institutionalized communications within the society.

Roles

Within a society people occupy or fit into social positions which have connections with other positions in the society of such a nature as to define the individual's position and the behaviors which are permitted in it. For example, the position of being a child in our society carries with it a range of behaviors which others related to the position of the child such as the parents, teachers, legal authorities, and peers expect of those who fill the position. Children are expected to be subservient to adults, to play, go to school, have the smaller bedrooms in the house, and not join in adult conversations. The position of a guest in our society involves being very thankful to one's host, praising him, asking for nothing, and declining special favors. The behaviors which are characteristic of a position within a society are referred to as role behaviors; they represent the ways in which a society has schematized relationships among people and in this sense, are ideas held in common by the people of a culture. They are transmitted in the ways described above for the acquisition of ideas —direct teaching, identification and imitation, institutionalized guides for behavior, and the mass media. Children thus learn the behaviors appropriate to the various positions which they may occupy. We have seen that much of this learning and practice goes on during children's imaginative playing at roles, such as playing house and playing school, in reducing activity and stimulation needs and developing their identifications. In addition, role performance is maintained by the responses of others to the individuals occupying positions. When one meets a school teacher, one expects him to behave in certain ways as a teacher, and is likely to respond favorably or unfavorably to him in terms of how well his behavior matches one's ideas of what is appropriate to the role. Thus one's responses to the teacher serve to maintain and enhance correct role performance. It has been noted for example that in our society males are expected to marry once, selecting their partner from an appropriate social and economic class, whereas in at least one primitive society, males are expected to continue having love affairs with other males during the course of their heterosexual marriage.[30] In our society, the male who marries outside of his social and economic class is held suspect —he is a social climber if he marries above and a failure if he marries below. In the other society, the male who does not have a homosexual affair is considered to be strange and untrustworthy. These expectations regarding the behavior appropriate to a role are called role prescriptions.

People occupy many different positions which have role prescriptions associated with them. A person is a male, a son, a husband, a father, an employee, a supervisor, a friend, customer, salesman, driver, pedestrian, traveler, native resident, middleclass. Each of these roles may involve responses which are different from those involved in the others. The stimuli arising in connection with a position are the cues for the role behaviors which one has learned for that position. This makes it possible for an individual to behave in different ways on different occasions; aggression which may not be expressed in one role may be expressed in another, and dominance, inappropriate in a son, may be fairly marked in the same person when he is in the position of a father. In effect, hierarchies and groups of responses which go together within a role thus are evoked by the cues of a position, once the roles have been acquired. The classification of positions is culturally determined, and different cultures classify positions differently. We have no position of "shaman" in our society, but many other cultures do.

Role prescriptions include the range of behavior acceptable to others by a person in a position. Usually these ideas are invoked by simply labelling the position which one occupies. There is, for example, fairly wide agreement among people in our society about how a person described simply as a businessman behaves. In this sense, role prescriptions have somewhat the nature of cultural stereotypes, in that the label invokes an already learned set of responses without much regard to the nature of the particular person who is so labelled. Such stereotypes of occupational and social roles also serve as symbols for various kinds of behaviors. A priest appearing in a dream frequently is a symbol for self-denial, and a nurse is often a symbol for nurturance, because these behaviors are generally accepted as part of the prescriptions for such roles.

We are accustomed to thinking of stereotyping as morally bad, because of the association between stereotyping and prejudice. It should be pointed out, however, that a stereotype is basically an acquired set of responses evoked by the cues arising from a person's position. As such, they permit a great deal of economy in behavior, and reflect the individual's repeated experiences with the behavior of people so labelled. They are generalized ideas based on common elements in events which all bear the same label, and follow the laws of stimulus generalization. On the average, therefore, they can be expected to be fairly accurate, though they must also be inaccurate because they do leave out the individual differences among the phenomena bearing the same label. The particular events which are grouped together under a common label, and the particular elements which define the commonality among the various events are a product of one's habits of thinking developed within a culture. Different cultures may be expected to group or categorize events differently, but grouping and categorizing goes on in all people in all cultures. There is some reason for thinking that it would not be possible to do without stereotyping, in the same way as it would not be possible to avoid stimulus generalization.

Factors in Role Performance. There is a difference between role prescription and role performance. Role prescriptions are the general behavioral definitions for a position held in common agreement by members of a society. They are the commonly held systems of selectively rewarding and punishing certain behavior, the system varying with the position class in which the behavior occurs. Role performance refers to the behavior which an individual actually displays in response to the cues arising from the position he is occupying. It is not uncommon for role performances to vary considerably from role prescriptions, and within a role prescription there usually is considerable room for individual differences or styles in the role performance. Some of the discrepancies between role prescription and role performance may be the results of the following factors.

Conflicting Roles. An individual may find himself in a situation which elicits incompatible responses or role behaviors. For example, the man who is a business partner of his father is in a situation of conflict between the subordinate role of the son and the more equal role of a business partner. Similarly, the boy who brings his girl friend home to dinner may experience a role conflict between his dominating role toward the girl and his subordinate role in his relations with his parents. Role conflicts of this sort are responsible for much of the awkwardness, hesitation, and tension which arises in such situations. Confusion is particularly likely to arise when the situations occur but seldom and then suddenly, so that the individual has not had an opportunity to develop some integration of his competing responses in a way that will satisfy the behavioral demands of both role prescriptions. It is a favorite comic device for authors to place their characters in a situation in which they are suddenly faced with role conflict, as when Mozart had his Count Almaviva woo a girl whom he thought was his chambermaid, only to find that she was his wife in disguise. The comedy often lies in the use of roles that include conflicting motives.

Role conflicts may be intensified by attempts to sharpen the conflict, as when a parent attempts to extend his role prescription for his daughter in order to reduce her performance of a role which he considers undesirable. This is a common source of difficulty among adolescents, who are at an age in which role conflicts are prevalent. The adolescent, in moving from the well learned and practiced role of a child into the new position of an adult for which there has been only vicarious practice and conflicting models available, typically experiences difficulty in defining his role and integrating his competing tendencies in a manner which will satisfy the expectations of parents, who are inclined to continue the role prescriptions of childhood, and those of peers (and to some extent of parents also) who are likely to prescribe more adult roles for the adolescent. It is a difficult task for the adolescent to find role behaviors which will satisfy his established drives for dependency and affection, and also for independence and achievement. These conflicts are further intensified by the lack of explicit, widely accepted role prescriptions for adolescence. In our society, adolescents are literally people without a purpose. The task of childhood is to grow to adulthood; the task of adulthood is to work. But for the adolescent, it is no longer appropriate to behave as a child and play continuously, while many characteristics of adult roles which could serve as cues for adult role performances, are denied to the adolescent. He cannot be self-supporting nor can he engage in adult sexual patterns nor is he given opportunity to embark on a life work. He has limited financial and legal responsibility and privilege. As Margaret Mead has shown in her pioneering anthropological study of adolescence, such ambiguity in role prescriptions is not a necessary consequence of adolescence. She demonstrated this through her study of adolescence in Samoa in which such ambiguity does not seem to be present, as a consequence of which adolescence is not the period of stress which it is so often described as in America.[31]

It is important to note that it is not the conflicting role prescriptions *per se* that confuse the adolescent in America; it is the fact that the youth is motivated by his identifications to conform to the conflicting demands on his behavior. He is not a passive recipient of pressure, but rather participates quite directly in his problems through the part his own motives play in making the pressures capable of influencing him.

Another source of ambiguity in role prescriptions should be mentioned. Within a society, there may be conflicting role prescriptions for the same role with the alternatives of nearly equal strength over all, although within segments of the society one or another set of prescriptions may be dominant. This may be seen most graphically in the public's images of movie personalities, which are frequently expressions of the society's role prescriptions. Three available models of femininity may be distinguished. There is the demure, happy-go-lucky, morally pure and nearly asexual youth, perhaps typified as everyone's kid sister. She is neat, modest, well-mannered but somewhat unpolished, and is thought of as sincere and highly ethical, though perhaps often confused. She is a girl "just like Mom." Another image of femininity is that of the aggressively sexual girl, rougher in manners than the first, usually presented as independent of any family connections, passionate, and one who can inspire a man. She is presented as a person whose life is not smooth, though it may reach heights of emotion not found in the first girl described. She is the woman desired, though perhaps not often married. The third set of role prescriptions available to the adolescent girl is that of the quiet, reserved, but highly sophisticated "woman of the world." She has impeccable manners, dresses in the height of fashion but not gaudily so, appears to be in complete command of herself, is socially very graceful, and hobnobs with presidents and princes. She is the strong woman behind the achieving man. Each of these roles has its own wardrobe and style of behaving. It is not surprising that adolescent girls find it difficult trying to discover which of these women they are, nor is it surprising that they frequently suffer feelings of inadequacy arising from the fact that no matter how well they fit one of these models, they must fail at the alternatives which may be equally stylish. This is one of the factors which accounts for the typical inconsistency of adolescents, who are often described by their parents as "acting" too much. In fact they are acting, rehearsing their performance of the role prescriptions which are presented to them and which they idealize. It should be added that the same ambiguity poses difficulties for adolescent boys, who frequently find it difficult to decide which feminine model is the most desirable to them. Obviously, a boy's choice will depend to a large extent on the characteristics of his mother, his attitudes toward her, the extent to which the role prescriptions are enforced by the social pressures of rewards and punishments administered by his peer group, and the nature and comparative strengths of his own drives for independence, achievement, dependency, and sex. These drives are satisfied differentially by the different models. Similarly, ambiguities exist in other role prescriptions present in our society, although the extent of ambiguity varies with the nature of the position.

Another factor which may operate to create disparity between role prescription and role performance exists in the individual's acceptance of the role prescription. We have seen in our discussion of sex role identification that after habits of identification have been established, new events may occur which make the identified sex role undesirable. Girls often discover as they grow older that there are frustrating limitations placed on their behavior by the sex role prescriptions of society, so that they may reject their sex role in whole or in part. In one study, girls reported much more often than boys that they have wished at one time or another that they were of the opposite sex.[32] A boy who has identified with his father may come to reject the masculine role, either as a result of learning things about the father to which he has already learned to react with aversion, or as a result of changes in the father's behavior which produce the same reactions, or because of the emergence and domination of motives which are incompatible with sex role prescriptions as enforced by the customs of society, such as achievement drives in females or dependency drives in males.

This kind of process occurs quite commonly. The individual who has identified with a particular person so far as one segment of that model's behavior is concerned, may respond with anxiety to the cues of his own behavior in performing a role as the model did if there are other aspects of the model's behavior which he has rejected. The more he behaves like the model, the more fully are cues presented for avoidance of the undesirable aspects of the model's behavior. Thus a boy may experience satisfaction when he notes that he is strong and dominating like his father, but feel fear when he thinks that he also might be cruel or irresponsible "just like your father." It is not always easy to integrate partial role identifications; the extent of the difficulty depends, of course, on the extent of incompatibility in the alternative models available, as well as on the individual's intellectual resources in finding common grounds or successful compromises.

It was implied above that an individual may have acquired the responses necessary for a role performance, but suffer confusion about role prescriptions and thus be unsure of the cues which should elicit his acquired responses. Or he may be presented with conflicts among competing role prescriptions which result in a failure to behave in the ways he has learned or in the manner expected by others. The alternative problem also exists; the individual may be highly motivated to assume a role and occupy a position for which the role is prescribed, but he may not behave as prescribed if he has not already acquired the habits of which the role is composed. Examples of this abound in our literature in descriptions of the difficulties encountered by people whose financial success places them in a new and higher social position for which role prescriptions are available, but which the newcomer cannot perform because of lack of training, and perhaps also because of the interfering presence of habits of role performance appropriate to the former position. Daytime radio serials and rags-to-riches movies and novels frequently concern themselves with these problems, as would be expected in a society as mobile as ours, and as oriented toward upward revision of one's social position. This problem also is found in the adolescent who is moving into adulthood but has not had sufficient practice in adult behaviors, perhaps as a result of too great restrictions imposed on him by parents. It is also the situation found in the person who is attempting to play a role for which he has not been prepared, as when a man acts as if he were of a higher social class than the one in which he was socialized, either because he has learned that rewards are based on others' impressions of one's social class, or because he has actually moved into the higher class by virtue of achievements or marriage. Finally, parents may specifically discourage the practice of certain role performances, such as independence of parents as part of the adult role. Foreign born parents may discourage their children from acquiring behaviors prescribed by their new country. In both cases, the reason is that the discouraged role behaviors imply rejection of the parents' own role performances.

The clarity of role performance in the upwardly mobile is further complicated by role conflicts. While parents may encourage upward mobility in their children and contribute to the development of strong achievement drive, they may fail to teach the child responses appropriate to the higher class out of fear of rejection of their own role habits. Thus an ideal frequently expressed in our literature is that of the person who achieves great success and renown but who remains "true to his class" and modest, rather than becoming "snooty," acquiring the role performance of his new position. Frequent expression of this occurs when the children of poorly educated parents are graduated from college; the parents often will try to reassure themselves that the child has not rejected them through such expressions as "Remember, you've been to college, but you're still my boy," or through attempts to test the boy's continued interest in and fondness for activities, foods, and clothes which are characteristic of the lower position. This situation not infrequently creates embarrassments and tensions for all concerned.

In this discussion of role prescriptions and performances, mention has been often made of the role of society in establishing and enforcing role prescriptions. A word of caution is in order. "Society" is an abstract term which does not refer to any real physical event or phenomenon which is capable of movement or action in the usual meanings of these terms. When we say that society does something, it is meant that individuals within a society — those who compose it — act in certain ways in common. When the focus is on the particular situations and people who transmit or express the cultural norms, one is made aware of the range of individual differences which occur in the transmission and acquisition of cultural forms. No parent teaches his child to behave in exactly the same way as the majority of the people in a culture would prescribe. In other words, our discussion of what our society characteristically does is normative. It refers to the central tendency or average of what people within the society do and it should be kept in mind that the person who is absolutely average in all aspects of his behavior does not exist. Further, the range of variation around the model role prescriptions may vary from one position to another. That is, some roles are more explicitly and narrowly defined than are others.

Conformity Pressures. The narrowness or explicitness of the role prescriptions transmitted to new members of a society plus the extent to which reinforcements are made contingent upon the accurate performance of the role prescriptions and the power of the reinforcers (the strengths of the drives which usually are reduced or increased) define the extent of coerciveness toward conformity and similarity among the behaviors of people within the culture. The role prescriptions for the behavior of a corporal toward a major are quite well defined and narrow in their range. If rewards and punishments are used readily which are of great importance to the individual, then the society using them will be one which may be described as valuing conformity. Social acceptability, love, and to a great extent money are manipulated in our society in the enforcement of role prescriptions, in the sense that the person who does not behave appropriately may lose friends, the regard of others, or opportunities for financial success. If the drives which may be reduced by these things are characteristically strong, as they are in our society where there is extensive training in the establishment of such drives, then these things operate as powerful reinforcers of conforming behavior.[33] Social acceptability is, by its very nature, a major tool of controlling behavior; but where conformity to role prescriptions is not a value, there are likely to be few and loose role prescriptions so that social acceptability is not made contingent upon any particular way of behaving, and/or there is likely to be less emphasis on socialization practices which lead to strong drives for social acceptability.

These points are illustrated in a study by Read Tuddenham, who studied conformity in an experiment in which subjects were asked to make judgments of such perceptual objects as line lengths, areas, and figure sizes, and on opinion items.[34] Each subject was made to believe that he was part of a larger group and that he was the last of the group to make each judgment. However, the experimenter had arranged things so that the judgments the subject thought were made by other group members were really fake and far out of line with the stimulus. In this way Tuddenham was able to study the extent to which the subject modified his judgments in the direction of the fake group norm. The greater the modification, the greater the conformity of the subject as inferred from his modified judgments. In this study Tuddenham found that those subjects who conformed the most to the influence of the supposed group were those who were more conventional in many areas, and had higher scores on several measures indicating strong motivations to be liked and accepted by others. Thus we see that conformity goes hand in hand with needs for affectionate interpersonal relationships. These conforming subjects also were described as being "highly socialized."

Earlier in this chapter, it was indicated that the cognitive styles of inner- or other-directed seem to be related to socio economic conditions of the society. It is apparent that the extent to which conformity to role prescriptions is valued and enforced is related to these styles. One would expect pressures toward conformity to be greater in a complex interdependent society where drive reductions of the people are to a great extent dependent upon the responses of others. Pressure toward conformity is one way of making sure that the others behave in such a manner that one will be able to reduce his drives. Thus one would expect conformity to be associated with other-directedness, an expectation that the Tuddenham experiment supports. Reisman, the University of Chicago sociologist who has explored these cultural cognitive styles, presents convincing evidence that those societies which are more likely to enforce conformity to established role prescriptions are those in which the birth rate is high relative to the death rate. These are complex societies in which there is a constant influx of new members requiring socialization who must be carefully trained to behave properly if the society is to continue to function in its accustomed ways.[35]

Finally, it should be mentioned that conformity and other-directedness (and similar cognitive styles) appear to be related to the extent to which identification and internalization of parental norms are encouraged. In a society in which parental practices usually are such that identification is not as strong as in other societies, it would be likely that conformity pressures and other-directedness would be high. Where internalization of standards occurs minimally, the individual has few inner guides for his behavior and so is likely to be other-directed, thus permitting the pressures toward conformity to operate. The reverse also holds: Where parents are other-directed and encouraging of their children to behave in socially approved ways, they are likely to employ those socialization practices which minimize the extent of identification. In Miller and Swanson's study of the bureaucratic and entrepreneurial social orientation in Detroit, a study mentioned earlier for its relevance to socialization practices, it was found that parents of the bureaucratic orientation used child training techniques which encouraged conformity and the relative absence of internal controls, while the entrepreneurial parents similar to Reisman's inner-directed operated in such a way as to encourage internalization of parental standards.[36]

Relationships Among Roles. Although one individual may behave in many different role performances more or less according to his role prescription, some thread of continuity seems to run among the roles. The behaving person in one role is fairly readily identified as the same person when in a different role. A woman's behavior as a mother usually bears some similarities to her behavior as a wife or teacher (although important differences also are present). What are the similarities among the role performances, and how do they occur?

Common Elements Among Roles. First it may be indicated that there is usually room within the various different role prescriptions for the several positions an individual may occupy for variation which permits freedom for idiosyncratic ways of behaving. The same mannerisms, cognitive styles, and traits may occur in most, if not all, of the roles an individual engages in. He may have a drawling speech which is permitted in most positions, or a tendency to take the initiative in most interpersonal situations. Even in roles in which taking immediate initiative is discouraged, the individual with a generalized trait in this direction may show relatively more initiative than others would in the same role, though it may still be less than in roles in which such behavior is more acceptable. In other words, the extent to which an individual behaves in certain characteristic ways may vary from one of his roles to another but he will tend to maintain his rank, relative to the behavior of others. As an example, Werner Wolff of Bard College has found in his study of motion pictures of expressive behavior that a person who is highly expansive and active in sports (a role in which activity is highly appropriate) also is likely to be more active or energetic even when walking casually down the street than people who are characteristically less expansive, even though the role of a pedestrian does not include an expectation of high activity.[37] In general, role prescriptions refer to what a person should do, rather than to how he will do it. Most role prescriptions are quite permissive about the "how," leaving a great deal of room for individual style which then may be common to all of the individual's role performances, producing a consistency in his behavior.

Common Teachers. Another source of similarity among an individual's various role performances are his teachers. A parent who rewards energetic performance in one situation also is likely to reward energetic performance in another. And of course, to the extent that much of an individual's behavior in many different roles is a result of learning through imitation of parents, to that extent will there be consistencies among his various role performances since they are based on the same models. Finally, the role performance which an individual acquires, even later in life, is conditioned or modified by the responses he has acquired earlier. As we have seen, early learned behaviors tend to be quite generalized and without discrimination as to the various cue situations which occur. In other words, in early learning, role discrimination is poor, if present at all. As discrimination ability and behavior grows, as responses become more specific to particular cue situations and develop into the groups of related responses which we call roles, they are differentiated out of the more generalized behavioral traits already established. The way in which a role prescription new to the individual becomes translated into his performance is a function of the habit strengths already acquired. That role performance will be acquired which, within the limits set by the role prescriptions, is most like other performances in other, already acquired roles by the person. And if new role prescriptions are transmitted primarily by the parents, those same persons who taught the child his earlier acquired traits, it is even more likely that the new role prescription will include behaviors similar to those which the child has acquired already as part of other roles. These factors all operate to produce consistency among performances of different roles by the same person, within the limits permitted by the role prescriptions as the individual has learned through past training to accept those limits.

Common Motives. A third source of consistency in behavior across role performances lies in the consistency of an individual's drives. To the extent that the same drive states are evoked by the cues of different positions, to that extent will the learned responses to the drive states occur in the role performances. An individual with readily aroused achievement motivation will respond with competitiveness in his role as a student, as an employee during his summer vacation, as a team member in sports, and as a determined follower of his career after his graduation from college, thus lending consistency to his performance of these various roles.

The Self-Concept

The commonality which exists among an individual's various role performances is related to his self-concept. Let us examine here some of the factors which determine the nature of an individual's self-concept, and how it relates to this commonality among role performances.

Initially the young infant responds to the cues presented to him with little or no ability to make discriminations among the cues, as was pointed out above. In his responses, one of the first and most important discriminations he will make is that between cues arising from himself and those arising from everything else, which is not-self. The baby mouths his crib and the objects in it, he thrashes around and waves arms and legs which strike the crib and objects. Sometimes these responses will produce sensations in other parts of the body. When he mouths his arm, sensations are produced both in the mouth and the arm, whereas when he mouths a doll, sensations are produced only in the mouth. It is through experiences such as these that the infant comes to discriminate between stimuli arising from the self and those from the not-self. This is one of the infant's first steps in construing his experiences and discovering some aspects of reality.[38]

As the infant experiences rewards and frustrations, he comes to discriminate the location of the stimuli of drive reduction and production as being within himself, making stimuli arising from himself a salient focus of his attention. In a sense, the self becomes an object of greater and more enduring attention and interest than other stimuli in the environment, further encouraging the discriminations between self and not-self.

We already have seen that an unfavorable early environment may operate so that the infant fails to develop an interest in his environment and that when this occurs, a fundamental weakness in reality contact and thinking is established. It should be added here that in such situations it also is true that stimuli arising from the infant himself are also likely to be painful or uncomfortable, in the sense that they will be the stimuli of strong drive levels and only seldom will they be stimuli produced by drive reduction. Thus the infant is as unlikely to focus attention on himself as on the environment. In this case, a discrimination between the self and the not-self is not readily established. Bizarre and unrealistic behavior in schizophrenia may serve to illustrate this failure to develop a discrimination leading to the establishment of a self-concept. The schizophrenic sometimes responds to external stimuli as if they were part of himself, as when he receives thoughts from inanimate objects, the thoughts obviously being his own. Conversely, he often responds to his own body as if it were an external object. The schizophrenic occasionally may describe his body as rotting away, as behaving independently of himself, and may even perform acts of self-mutilation.

These early experiences with rewards and punishments lay the groundwork for the establishment of the self-concept, although it could not be said that they are sufficient for the development of the concept. They influence the extent to which there is discrimination of the self as an object or stimulus of particular importance and interest to which responses may be directed which are different from the responses which might be made to external stimuli.

During the ensuing years of early childhood, the self becomes enlarged and extended, in the sense that objects are further discriminated as being part of or related to the self, or not-self related. This elaboration is manifested in the discovery of "my, mine" that children make during their second year and in the increased exploration of their bodies.

It is about at this time that early training experiences which contribute to the establishment of identification and the potentiality for guilt are begun, as in toilet training and in all the other little matters of child control in which the toddler is rewarded or punished for his actions. The character of the reactions to the child by the reinforcing people in the child's environment produces the content of the child's concept of his self. Whereas up to this time the self was only a particularly important object, repeated experiences of rewards and punishments for his behavior add to the reactions to the self a set of evaluations based on the actions of parents and significant other people. As language skills also develop, a set of descriptions or labels attached to the self are developed. It is at this point that one may say a self-concept exists, which includes an attention to the self as an object together with evaluations (that is, increases or decreases in drive in response to stimuli arising from the self) and communicative labels. As E. R. Hilgard of Stanford University has pointed out, the presence of a self-concept implies the presence of the capacity for guilt, in the sense that guilt includes a perception of the self as an active agent capable of being rewarded or punished for its behavior.[39] That is, rewards and punishments intended to alter the behavior of the child usually communicate to him that he can change his behavior, that his self as the agent of the punished behavior is free to change, upon which rewards are contingent. The feeling that one has free will thus is a consequence of the development of a concept of the self as rewardable or punishable.

When rewards and punishments are administered selectively in an effort to establish the kinds of behaviors desired by parents, "conditions of worth" are established, as Carl Rogers terms it. Rogers, a leading psychotherapist and psychotherapy researcher, has based his theories of behavioral change on a theory of the self-concept in which he points out, on the basis of his intensive study of thousands of therapy cases, that conditions of worth are established when the parents' behavior is such as to reward or punish the child in an effort to produce conformity to their demands.[40] Those punishment techniques which have the greatest weight in establishing conditions of worth are those which usually are called "psychological discipline" involving the manipulation of love and regard for the child, shame, embarrassment, pride, — in other words, the techniques in which the attitudes of acceptance or rejection of the child by others are involved. These are the techniques which focus on interpersonal relations as sources of approval and disapproval, rather than on institutions, a deity, or the presence of pain regardless of the administering agent. They are the ones which operate on the child's already acquired drives for affection and the approval and regard associated with affection. They are the techniques which we already have seen to be the ones that encourage introjection and identification — the inclusion within the self of standards of conduct.

As the child develops his symbolic abilities, he begins to attach verbal responses to the self in terms of the extent to which he is rewardable or punishable. He thinks of himself with approval and pleasure when the self is associated with drive reductions, and in negative terms when the self is associated with increases in drive and with pain. As his identification with his parents develops, he begins to respond to himself with the same evaluative and descriptive terms which characterize their responses to him. As he expands his repertoire of role performances, he is able to make responses to the self in its various roles in terms of the way in which his role performances are evaluated by those whose approval or disapproval serve as important reinforcers to him. In this manner a description and evaluation of the self is built up, composed of responses to one's own behavior based on the extent to which that behavior is rewardable or punishable.

Because the self and one's own behavior and feelings are so intimately "alive" to the individual, the self becomes the object of very strong emotional responses. This was demonstrated in an ingenious experiment by Werner Wolff in which photographs were taken of subjects' hands without their knowledge. When several photographs of hands were shown to the subjects, including their own (which most failed to recognize), the experimenter asked them to evaluate the personalities of the people whose hands they saw. It was noted that most of the subjects tended to go to extremes in evaluating the personality that they thought went with the hands which were really their own. They became highly emotional in rejecting or praising their own hands, even though they did not consciously recognize them as their own.[41]

Basically then, the self-concept includes symbolized responses to both good and bad behavior, as these are defined by the agents of socialization. The impetus for such labelling responses comes from the child's training in making correct verbal reports and descriptions. But distortion and inaccuracy enter the self-concept, so that it is not a faithful symbolization of all the person's behavior. Those symbols or descriptions which are associated with punishment and punished behavior become stimuli to which the child's avoidance responses to the punishment may become attached. He learns to fear the thought that he is a person who does certain punishable (or in his terms, bad) things. The fear invoked by thinking such thoughts may be reduced by not thinking them, so that these parts of the self-concept are reduced in the frequency of their occurrence. In effect, the child and later the adult fails to symbolize or think about that aspect of his behavior which he has come to evaluate as bad. The punished behavior itself also will tend toward extinction, so far as overt performance is concerned, although covert tendencies to make the forbidden responses may still remain. Or the punishable responses may remain overt, but the explanation − the labels associated with them − may be changed so as to reduce the fear which more accurate labels would invoke. For example, it is bad to fight with others, but if one labels his behavior as self-defense, the fighting may continue with the self-concept of "I am not aggressive, but I defend myself against other's aggression." At this point, the self-concept has begun to be distorted, in that its nature is determined not only by the behavior which the individual displays, but also by anxiety or fear drives which can be reduced by changes in thought resulting in biased or even clearly inaccurate interpretations of the behavior of the self. In this way unacceptable aspects of one's behavior either may be unsymbolized, in which case they are referred to as part of the individual's unconscious self, or they may be distorted in the self-concept.

Distortions enter in another way. It is obviously not possible for a person to include within his self-concept a description of every aspect of his behavior, of every response to every stimulus which has occurred. If symbolization and thought are to be at all economical, the thinker must summarize. He will include responses which have high habit strength — usually those associated with strong drives — and will think but seldom if at all in terms having low response strength. What is left out in summarizing, then, will be those responses which are either of little consequence or which produce unpleasantness in the form of worry or fear.[42]

This discussion leads to the conclusion that people vary both in the extent to which they have a developed self-concept, (that is, how "large", developed, or differentiated the self is *vs.* not-self stimuli), and in the extent to which the self-concept that exists is conscious or unconscious, as well as in the contents of the self-concept.

The Unconscious Self-Concept. On a ward in a psychiatric hospital a patient sits, staring attentively into space as if listening to something. He becomes agitated, and starts talking aloud, saying "Leave me alone. I am not. Go away." A nurse approaches and asks him what the matter is, and he tells her that "they" are talking to him again. They are vilifying him, calling him dirty names, and accusing him of terrible things. He tells the nurse that what they are saying is not true, and that he always has tried to be good.

The "voices" the patient apparently is hearing may be said to be expressions of his unconscious self-concept. Consciously he describes himself in one way — as trying to be good. But he hears voices, obviously expressions of his own ideas about himself, which accuse him of things which he consciously denies.

In this example, it is easy to observe the operation of unconscious self-responses. However, when hallucinations are not present, it is more difficult to infer the existence of such a thing, although psychologists believe that people do make self-reactions of which they are unaware. Wolff's study on evaluations of personalities from photos of hands including those of the subjects illustrates the operation of an unconscious self-concept, because the subjects did not recognize their own hands. In one study, Sears had college men rate themselves and their fraternity brothers on various traits in a study on self-concepts. Those subjects who rated themselves as low on stinginess but whose brothers rated them as high on this trait (suggesting that their conscious self-concept was not accurate) ʋehaved differently from those subjects whose brothers did not rate them high on stinginess. The latter group may be said to have fairly accurate conscious self-concepts as far as stinginess is concerned. The inaccurate self-concept subjects tended to rate their brothers as stingier than the average subject did. In effect, they were ascribing their own trait (according to their brothers' ratings) to others, and not seeing it in themselves.[43] This tendency to see others as stingy provides some inferential evidence for unconscious self-perceptions. Although the stingy subjects did not include stinginess in their conscious self-perceptions, they must have been responding to their "tight" behavior somehow or other, as evidenced by their out-of-the-ordinary tendency to see stinginess in others.

A large part of one's self-concept is unconscious, in that one may not be verbalizing many things about the self, either overtly or covertly, at a particular moment in time. At that time, the unverbalized portions are unconscious. But many of these aspects of the self-concept may be verbalized at a later time, when they become salient — that is, when the appropriate cues elicit them. On the other hand, there may be some portions of the self-concept which are chronically unverbalized, as in the hallucinating patient and the stingy fraternity brothers. Nevertheless, these are part of the individual's self-concept; they represent some response to his own behavior, as indicated by the fact that other behavior of the individual reflects a concern about or reaction to those very aspects of his behavior which are not represented in his conscious self-concept. He is responding to it, but does not make direct symbolic self-responses to it.

It appears likely that those aspects of the self-concept which remain unconscious, even when appropriate cues for eliciting them are presented (as when the boys were asked to rate themselves on stinginess), are those which themselves serve as cues for anxiety. When the avoidance of anxiety-producing stimuli occurs, it indicates that the cue for anxiety was present, at least at some level of intensity. When an individual chronically avoids including certain aspects of his behavior in his self-concept, it usually means that the avoided self-responses are present but at very low intensities, perhaps only as partial symbolizations which are sufficient in strength only to cue off anxiety which in turn inhibits further symbolization. It already has been indicated that autonomic responses can be elicited by cues which are of too low intensity to elicit verbal responses. This means that the autonomic components of anxiety can occur in response to perceptual cues, such as to one's undesirable or disapproved behavior, which are too vague to elicit conscious (that is, verbal) self-responses as part of the self-concept. The anxiety thus produced can serve to motivate an avoidance of further thinking about the upsetting behavior, in that the anxiety can be reduced by stopping thinking.

In sum then, the chronically unconscious self-concept consists of those conceptualizations about the self or about one's behavior, which have come to serve as cues for anxiety which in turn motivates an avoidance of thinking about that portion of the self.

Conditions of Worth. We have already mentioned some of the factors Rogers calls "conditions of worth" which can operate in such a way that some aspects of the self-concept become cues for anxiety and thus tend to remain unconscious. If one has been disapproved, punished, or lost affection or regard for behavior which is described by the punishers as stingy, then the conditions have been established which permit the word "stingy" to elicit fear or anxiety, or heightened drive for affection and approval which may be reduced by not thinking about "stinginess."

Carl Rogers has interpreted this process as the major cause of the unhappiness which brings people to clinics for help. One college man described it like this: "I've always done what people wanted me to, I try to act like I'm supposed to. I'm really putting on an act when I do this — in fact, I'm always acting. I act so much that I don't even know what the real me is like. I just don't know myself anymore." In effect, the patient is saying that so much of his self-concept is unconscious in order to give role performances according to the role prescriptions which have been presented to him, that he is not able to discriminate between a temporary role performance and his self-concept. Rogers has developed a system of counseling to cope with such a situation, in which he emphasizes that the counselor must establish an atmosphere of such "unconditional positive regard" for the patient that conditions of worth disappear. In effect, the counselor attempts to create a situation in which anxiety is no longer elicited by aspects of the self-concept, which therefore can be verbalized (become conscious). The counselor further assists by trying to clarify (label) the self-conceptions which are implicit in the patient's talk about himself.[44] As a result of this kind of process, Rogers has noted that patients gradually increase in the number of negative self evaluations as they continue in counseling, indicating increasing freedom from anxiety and anxiety-motivated avoidance of the disapproved portions of the self-concept. Finally a point is reached in the course of the counseling when presumably the patient has made conscious all the feared unconscious ideas he has had about himself, and then begins to make more positive self-reactions.[45] This probably occurs partly as a result of the counselor's implied approval of him so that the patient also begins to conceptualize himself in positive terms, and partly also because the fear responses are no longer present to interfere with more complete self-reactions in which the desirable as well as undesirable features of the formerly unconscious traits can be thought about. In confirmation of this, James Dittes of Yale University charted a subject's GSRs during the course of counseling and found that responses indicating anxiety reactions to sexual topics extinguished during the counseling, and that the rate of extinction was greatest in those counseling sessions in which the counselor was most accepting of the patient and of what the patient said.[46, 47] Those were the sessions in which the counselor was best able to respond to the patient with the unconditional positive regard which operates against the conditions of worth that had been imposed on the patient during his growing up years. During this kind of counseling, the psychologist, unlike the parents, reinforces even the socially or parentally disapproved descriptions of himself that the patient gives. He may do this in such subtle ways as merely saying "Hmmhmm" or "Good" in response to something the patient has just told him, as in the experiment reported earlier that demonstrated the reinforcing effects of such comments. Thus the counselor teaches the patient through the use of reinforcement to say whatever he is stimulated to say about himself, in this way making more of the self-concept conscious. When the patient says something to the counselor to which his parents had reacted with rejection or punishment, he finds that the counselor does not so react, and in fact approves him for saying it. In this way, the patient's fear of conceptualizing his behavior into a self-concept are extinguished.

In his theory, Rogers has emphasized the withdrawal of love as expressed through parental rejection as the factor which imposes conditions of worth and thus limitations on consciousness of the self-concept. Previous discussion indicates that the use of love-oriented techniques keeps the child oriented toward the parents as role models and encourages the acceptance of conditions of worth through identification. However, it should be pointed out that any parental reaction to the child which results in an increase in drive, rather than a decrease, will serve to inhibit further responses of the kind to which the parents have responded. For example, a child with an already acquired achievement drive of great strength may not conceptualize overtly those aspects of his behavior or experience which indicate failure. This is likely to occur in a child whose parents hold such high standards for him that they do not accept any failures; any inadequacy is responded to with rejection or increased pressure to achieve.

The conditions of worth become part of the child's internalized standards through his identifications with his parents. In effect, limitations on a person's consciousness of his self-concept are inherent when standards are internalized; behavior or even tendencies to behave in ways which fail to match these standards will be part of the unconscious self-concept. Such failures produce guilt, as we have seen, and guilt inevitably includes reference to the self as agent of the "wrong" behavior. In this way guilt supposes a self-concept, albeit an unconscious one.

In effect the dynamics of the self-concept involve a playing out on the verbal-symbolic level of all the forces which we have observed as determinants of behavior, including their complex interrelationships. It involves the conceptualization of all the drives and drive-responses which have developed during the socialization of the child, including their internalization as standards of behavior and the internalized evaluations of the extent to which those standards are met.

The Ideal Self. The ideas which characterize a culture include generally agreed-upon standards for behavior which we have seen are organized into role prescriptions. An individual's conceptualization of these role prescriptions as they have been interpreted to him by the significant figures in his environment, and particularly through his identifications with such figures, is referred to as his ideal self, or ego ideal. The ego ideals complement internalized parental prohibitions; both prohibitions and ideals make up the "superego" in psychoanalytic theory. The example was given of the behaviors expected of a person labelled as a school teacher. When one considers the inherently conceptual nature of role prescriptions, it becomes apparent that there is a relationship between the development of verbal skills in a child and the development of his ideal self. It is not possible for a child to have very much of an ideal self as a set of thoughts or standards for his performance of role prescriptions, until he has developed enough language ability to form the verbal concepts and respond to the verbal cues which elicit role behaviors. However, the acquisition of drives and responses is begun before verbal skills are acquired. This has the consequence that there may be no close association between the ideal self which a person internalizes as his standard and the drives and behaviors which he already has acquired. His behavior therefore may be inconsistent with, if not quite contrary to the ideal self which he holds. A child already may have acquired a strong dependency drive before he develops the ideal of an independent, responsible adult. Another example, perhaps more common in our society, is of the child who already has acquired a strong aggressive drive by the time he adopts the ego ideal held in our culture of non-aggression.

Ordinarily because the people who are responsible for the child's early learning of drives are the same ones who later are the models and teachers of the ideal self, gross discrepancies do not occur. However, there are some situations which favor the development of such discrepancies.

One of the most interesting of these situations is that in which the milieu outside the family in which the individual lives is so different from the culture of the family and is so overpowering in its teachings that a conflict between what is learned in the family and what is learned outside of it develops, expressed often through a self-ideal at great variance with the self-concept. This is particularly apt to occur among members of minority groups. For example, the first generation American-born children of the Italian immigrants who flocked to New York City in the 1920's often showed this kind of conflict between their American ideals, which they were exposed to through movies, radio, and the zealous Americanizing activities of their teachers in the schools, and the learnings which occurred in their earlier years within their families, which tended to operate on the European model of paternal dominance and European customs and manners. These conflicts frequently involved extreme ambivalence and confusion in the self-concept, hostility toward the parents, and a great deal of guilt fostering still more negative self-concepts, *vis-a-vis* the ideal selves.

A similar problem is presented to American Negro children, whose ideal selves are based on their experiences with movies, radio, TV, newspapers, cartoon characters, and in the schools. These teaching agents invariably are dominated of Caucasians, and the heroes and heroines who express the culture's ideals are almost never Negro. Negroes are more often presented as stupid, brutal, or clowns constantly in need of the help and guidance of their Caucasian intellectual superiors. The models presented to the children, including the teachers in the schools, hold jobs and occupy social positions which are likely possibilities for only a very few Negroes. The ideal selves which Negro children develop are therefore very often at variance with their self-concepts, having the result of producing either rejection of the ideal and of the controls on behavior which such standards involve, or of the self. This discrepancy was noted in a study by Kenneth B. Clark and Mamie P. Clark, in which Negro children were asked to select either brown or white dolls in answer to questions about which they preferred, which was nice, which was good, and which was like them. It was found that although almost all the children clearly were aware of which was the Negro doll, many of them did not select the brown doll as being most like them, and the majority of the children selected the white doll as a preferred play companion, as nice, and as good, while the brown doll was selected as bad. Some of the children even denied their own self-identification ("I burned my face and made it spoil").[48] In this remark made by one of the children is clearly implied a rejection of his social characteristic, together with self-blame for his Negro identification.

A second situation which seems to be responsible for self-ideal discrepancies is that in which major inconsistencies exist within the family's training practices. Such inconsistencies could be produced by drastic changes occurring within the family's structure, such as through sudden social mobility, or through the death of a parent or the introduction of a new parent-figure, as when a grandmother takes up permanent residence with the family. More common is the situation in which the confusion is built into a child's self ideal by parents whose child training practices are at variance with their own ideals, or whose behavior as models for the child's identification differs from the demands they make on the child. This is the "do as I say, not as I do" problem, and is particularly apt to occur in the highly mobile American middle class in which a popular ideal is for the children to "do better" than their parents. Thus the standards imposed on the behavior of the children are often higher than those which guide their parents' behavior. To the extent that the child's standards and role performances are acquired through identification, they will be based largely on the parents' behavior. Some portions of the child's standards however will be based directly on the ideals which the parents transmit to him through direct teaching and pointing out of approved models: these standards will conflict with the earlier acquired role performances and standards. A frequent consequence of this conflict is the presence of guilt as a result of behavior in accordance with the ideal which conflicts with the internalized standards based on identification. This kind of guilt is frequently expressed as embarrassment over surpassing the parents in economic and social achievements (an embarrassment which it should be noted, may be reduced by failure to achieve, although the achievement drive itself may be strong, thus producing motivated failure in people who nevertheless continue to strive until they are near the goal of their striving). The nascent fears and resentments of their childrens' greater success in the parents further may add to the development of this pattern of behavior, through the subtle rewarding of failure or inconsistency in rewarding achievement.

Inconsistency between parents' behavior and their standards for their children also can produce the opposite effect, depending on whether the child's identification is weaker or stronger than the effects of the parents' standards. When the identification is strong, compared to the learning of standards for behavior which differ from the behavior of the parents themselves, the child is likely to behave in terms of his identification, producing guilt for not living up to his ideal self. This is particularly likely to occur if the ideals held by the parents for their children are very high and unrealistic.

Alternatively it may happen that the parents encourage their children to identify with them in large segments of life, but punish the child for behaving completely in terms of such an identification. The child may be expected to be "grown up" and responsible in most things like the parents, but he may be punished if he also uses bad language or smokes like the parents. This produces confusion in the child's ego ideal, and creates a situation in which the child fears to behave in accordance with the introjected standards and performances he has acquired.

One last situation should be mentioned: the ideals transmitted to a child may be impossible in themselves of achievement. As ideals, they frequently may be unrealistic, in that they are not true to human potentialities and the dynamics of behavior. For example, a common ideal is that one is never aggressive except under certain circumstances such as in defense of one's self, family, or possessions, and then only against certain objects. When permissible, the ideal person is sufficiently aggressive to be victorious. It is, in fact, quite difficult to translate such an ideal into reality. In order for aggressiveness to occur at all, the child training situation must be such as to reward this kind of behavior at an age in which discriminations are difficult for the child to make. Thus the general trait of aggressiveness may be established, even though the ideal is that of a generally nonaggressive person. On the other hand, training in the inhibition of aggression is likely to leave the child without the ability to behave aggressively when such behavior is appropriate and expected in the ideal.

The idealized pattern which is presented to parents and their children even has appeared in psychological writings. The "normal" person has been defined, for example, as one who likes and is liked by others and has positive feelings and skills in his social relations, but who also can enjoy being alone and communing with himself; as one who can express aggression when to do so is justified, but who is nonaggressive in his social behavior; as one who is "wellrounded" in his interests and activities, and also an expert in some areas; as one who is responsible and reliable in his work, but happy-go-lucky and carefree in his recreation; as one who loves his wife but enjoys male companionship and still can maintain objectivity with his family; as one who is completely honest but not foolhardy, and one who weighs the consequences of his actions and speech; as one who never lets passion get control over his behavior, but who is capable of intense emotional experience.

The contradictions are obvious, making this statement of ideals impossible of fulfillment, and thus inevitably producing a gap between the ideal and the self-concept.

Interpersonal Perceptions

Much of the discussion in this chapter has been concerned with the ways in which people in our society construe their experiences, with particular attention devoted to their experiences with their selves. Now let us turn to the ways in which they construe their experiences with other people.

The variables which operate in a perceptual situation may be summarized as follows: We can begin with the responses which an individual has acquired, including those aspects of his responses which we have called his "style," and the stimulus generalizations inherent in the acquired responses. These responses or habits, as we have seen, are organized into groups which we have called role performances, the learning of which has included the directing of attention to the perception of the social positions which serve as cues for role performances. These response potentials comprise the behavioral repertoire which a person carries with him. Included in this habit structure are his usual ways of schematizing and grouping events and stimuli, ways which are based to a large extent on the ideas which characterize his culture, as these ideas have been transmitted to him by his parents and the other media mentioned earlier. Attention to those stimuli which are indicative of social status and sex are examples of these schema-habits. One has learned so well to respond to certain cues when they occur together that he has a strong tendency to react to those cues when they are present, rather than to other cues which may also be present. He is "sensitive" to such cues.[49] In our society we learn to respond to those aspects of another's behavior which vary from one social class to another, from one occupational level to another and also from one sex to another, so that we are sensitive to the cues denoting socio-economic class and sex. The ideas of our culture produce habits of schematizing or construing events in certain ways by making some stimuli important as cues for role performances and leaving other stimuli without cue functions of any importance, in that few if any responses are characteristically associated with them.

These response potentials form the "givens" which are present when the individual is confronted with a situation in which perceptual stimuli are present. The nature of these givens has been influenced, of course, by the motives in connection with which the responses were acquired. These include not only the innate need-produced drives which are responsible for the learning of simple habits and of acquired drives, but also learned drives like those for acceptance, regard from others, and avoidance of guilt which were operative in producing identification-based behavior, role performances in particular. Thus the behavioral repertoire of a person bears the stamp of the drive states which have existed in him. In addition, the drive states operating in the person at the time he engages in an interpersonal perceptual situation operate to make salient some response potentials and role performances (those associated with the drive) and not others (those not associated with it).

Given this repertoire, when a stimulus situation is presented to the person, some aspects of the event serve as cues which elicit from the behavioral potential certain responses, among the first of which are those which label or symbolize the event. At this first stage of the perceptual process, selectivity in terms of the responses which are available to the person operates to bias the perception, making it less than completely perfect.[50] Those stimuli are ignored which do not serve as cues, because they are irrelevant to the perceiver's hierarchy of available responses. One notes another's clothes, but seldom the shape of his ear lobe, for example, and perception occurs partly in terms of the reactions we have acquired to such clothes and not at all in terms of his ears, unless by chance they too have become cues because of their similarity to the ears of a significant person with whom responses have already been associated such that the ears "remind" one of someone else.

In this manner the stimuli are identified and the identification made in itself serves as a cue for further behavior, particularly for one's role performance. Thus one's response to the stimulus situation is determined both by the initial cues of the situation and by those which are produced by the perception of the event which the initial cues elicited. In addition, responses also are made to cues which, for various reasons already suggested do not elicit labelling or identification responses. One may respond to cues of which one is unconscious. Perception of the stimulus situation involves all of these responses, although some part of the perception may be unconscious.

Among the very important response tendencies which are brought to the perceptual situation are those which are elicited by cues of the self — those which comprise the self-concept. Stimuli produced by another person are often sufficiently like one's own behavior so that one evaluates and categorizes the other's behavior in the same terms as he has categorized his own. The result is that in most cases, people tend to assume similarity between themselves and others. In a study in which subjects were asked to sort test items in terms of how well each item applied to themselves, and then to sort the items the way they thought the average person would sort them, it was found that most subjects sorted the items in the same way on both occasions, producing high correlations ranging between .89 and .98 for the two sortings.[51] This indicates that people usually perceive others and themselves as being quite similar. However, there are consistent individual differences in this, with some people tending to "assume similarity" to a greater extent than others who, conversely, have stronger tendencies to assume differences between themselves and others. It already has been indicated in the discussion of reality-testing in Chapter 5 that these initial perceptual response tendencies do not change readily with more experience with the perceived person. It seems that one's tendency to assume similarities or differences is a fairly stable behavioral trait which is activated or elicited more strongly, the closer one is to the cues arising from another person.[52]

One's position on this perceptual trait dimension contains within it the possibility for inaccurate perceptions of others. While the assumption of similarity between self and others is probably usually the safest one because most people living in a common culture are in fact quite similar in many ways, thus confirming the assumption of similarity and strengthening one's tendency in this direction, it also is true that there are many differences between people which therefore will go un-noted, and the research cited earlier suggests that continued experience with others is not likely to remedy the misperception. As has been pointed out, interpersonal stimuli are sufficiently ambiguous so that reality-testing is quite difficult, and frequently results in confirmation of even an erroneous perception. The mechanisms of perception described in Chapter 5 help account for the processes which permit such selective perception to occur.

There is another important self-concept factor which contributes error to interpersonal perceptions. It was pointed out earlier that the self-concept inevitably involves inaccuracies. When one assumes similarity between himself and others, he may be similarly inaccurate in perceiving their behaviors which are like those of his own which are cues for anxiety. One either may tend to note particularly those behaviors in others which are excluded from one's self-concept and to ascribe such behaviors to others, or he may fail to note the same things which he fails to note in himself. The research already has been mentioned in which it was found that some psychotherapists who had personality problems tended to be very responsive to the same problems in their patients and over-diagnosed the problem while other therapists with similar problems went in the other direction, failing to note the problem even when it obviously existed in the patient.[53] When the former behavior occurs, it is called projection. Projection seems to occur in those who are high in assumed similarity so that they ascribe their own characteristics to others, but whose self-concepts are distorted by their avoidance of anxiety-arousing labels attached to themselves.

When projection occurs, one may therefore generally infer guilt in response to one's own behavior, for it is guilt which often provides the motivation for not including the behavior in one's own self-concept. Thus the behaviors ascribed to others in projection are usually those which impute offensive behavior to the others, usually either sexual or aggressive in nature since these are the behavioral systems to which guilt is usually most strongly attached in our society. Further, when many other people are perceived as having "negative" traits, these traits may come to appear less undesirable so that anxiety associated with the traits in one's own behavior is reduced.

The consequences of misperceiving the behavior of others are complex. When one reacts to another in terms of the misperception, he is likely to find his behavior inappropriate and so fail to find rewards from the misperceived others. The misperceiver may come to feel that he does not understand other people, or that they are in general contrary and unpredictable or even hostile to him, because they do not react to him in the ways he expects. Misperception therefore further contributes to the frustration of the person's drives, including those whose great strength is responsible for the misperception occurring. For example, one may have such a strong dependency drive that he tends to interpret another's behavior as maternalistic. The perceiver then reacts with even greater dependency on the other who, unwilling to play the role of mother, finally withdraws and rejects the dependent perceiver whose dependency drive is thereby further frustrated, and continues to increase in strength because of lack of drive reduction.

Misperception even may have the effect of producing the very behavior erroneously ascribed to the other person. This is particularly likely to happen when aggressive or sexual motives are imputed to another person. The perceiver, interpreting the other person as aggressively or sexually motivated, responds with defensive aggression or with the seductive behavior which formed the cue for the projection in the first place. The other person is then likely to respond to the aggression or the seduction with hostility or with sexual advances, confirming the original projection. This is a case in which the projection itself produces the behavior which forms the content of the originally erroneous projection. A man, when he misperceives another person as aggressive, may respond to him with rejection and resentment — a response tendency which is already high as evidenced by the fact that he projected it — which in turn elicits sarcastic or aggressive behavior in the misperceived person. In this way, the expectation of being rejected often brings about rejection, and people's fears about others' attitudes toward them are made to come true. Because the projector has excluded from his self-concept the traits which he ascribes to others and which are present in his own behavior, he is unaware of the part that his behavior has played in producing the actual aggression or rejection. This tends to further confirm the tendency to project, because the projector feels that the other person is in fact completely at fault, and the experience adds strength to his assumption that people in general are hostile. Thus projection tends to have a spiralling effect, in that the more one projects unacceptable behavior onto others, the more one is likely to perceive them as behaving in socially unacceptable terms.

Guilt not only leads to the occurrence of projection, but it is also a determiner of the content of the projection. A person who responds to his own behavior or thoughts with guilt (defined as a fear of punishment) continually may punish himself for his forbidden behavior by blaming himself, telling himself that he is bad or inferior. However, if this self-punishment is excluded from his self-concept as it usually is — people do not generally think of themselves as punishing themselves — the punishment may be ascribed to others. Thus the guilty person feels that other people are aware of his misbehavior and blame him or condemn him for it. A beginning driver usually feels that every motorist on the road is thinking of him as stupid for making the errors he has made, although most of the motorists have not even noticed it. Similarly, the clumsy person who drops his fork at the table blushes with embarrassment, feeling that everyone at the table is laughing at or criticizing him. This projection of guilt is responsible for the interpretation of events as punishing, although the events may have no connection with the misbehavior at all. A child may think that his tonsillectomy operation was a punishment to him for having been a bad boy, just as the people in the cultures studied by Whiting and Child perceived their illnesses as punishments for misbehavior. In the most extreme cases the delusions that people are against him or are plotting his death that are frequently found in the paranoid schizophrenic and the hallucinations of voices blaming and warning of terrible punishments which often are found in the severely depressed patient, are projections of guilt in people whose reality-testing habits are but poorly developed.

A Note on Ego Strength

In Chapter 5 it was mentioned that the processes of thinking, perceiving, and conscious knowing are often referred to by psychologists as ego functions, the ego being the name given by Freud to that part of the organism's functioning which is concerned with cognition of the self and the environment. The term "ego strength" has been used to describe the adequacy with which cognitive functioning occurs, particularly when strong drives of the kind that often produce distortion in cognition are present. Thus a person who thinks and perceives relatively clearly despite the presence of great fear and anxiety is said to have high ego strength. Similarly, the person whose self-concept is fairly accurate despite the fact that to recognize much of his behavior produces discomfort is said to have high ego strength. Those who are conceptually oriented, rather than motorically, also are described as having more ego strength, as are those whose reality contact is relatively good despite great frustration and pain in the environment. From these examples it readily can be seen that ego strength refers to many different kinds of behavior, although they are all related in that they involve symbolic processes by which phenomena are conceptualized or schematized. Just as we have avoided using the concept of the ego because it lumps several different functions together and so obscures differences which are important, so is "ego strength" eschewed for the same reasons. To describe both the nonconformist who does not behave in accordance with the strong pressures of role prescriptions, and the guilty person who does relatively little projection by the same term — high ego strength — appears to be too much of a simplification that may tend to shift attention away from the differences between the processes involved in role performance and those involved in projection, although there is a family relationship between the two.

REPRISE. In this chapter we have discussed various aspects of cognitive functioning including its extent, its style, content, and organization into roles and concepts. We have paid particular attention to the factors that interfere with complete and accurate cognition, partly because such incompleteness is so inevitable and characteristic that most often we are not even aware of it. We are so accustomed to thinking that our behavior always is realistic and rational that we fail to recognize how complex the forces are that operate in this area and how readily they produce inaccuracies in our higher mental processes. Our emphasis on these forces points up the fact that extensive and valid thinking and conceptualizing is rather more of an achievement than a natural endowment, although the potential for such thinking is a natural endowment in man. This discussion of the factors that bias or limit thinking does not necessarily mean that the forces making for pathology are overwhelming; they are explored here mostly to highlight the ways in which thinking is socialized, and to emphasize the processes involved by studying these processes in their most exaggerated forms. It is important to keep in mind that the same processes that account for inaccurate perception also account for perceptual speed and efficiency. The strong drive that makes one sensitive to drive-related stimuli also makes one prone to misinterpretations of stimuli not related to the drive. Similarly, the cognitive style in which attention is directed away from inner experiences is the same style that makes one sensitive to other people.

The major ideas of this chapter are:

1. The extent to which thought or acting-out are established as patterns depends on the reinforcement value of these two modes in the infant's environment.

2. Realistic thinking depends on a rewarding environment to encourage the shift from primary to secondary process thought.

3. Style of thinking also is acquired. The styles discussed were tolerance-intolerance of ambiguity, cognitive simplicity-complexity, acquiescence, field dependence-independence, and inner-other directedness. These styles are not independent of each other, and in fact they may describe essentially the same phenomena.

4. Specific idea contents are acquired through direct learning and identification with parents, teachers and agemates, through institutionalized schemas, institutionalized communications that transmit the culture's values and typical ways of organizing experience, and through cultural forms and artifacts.

5. Roles and role prescriptions comprise an important source of schemas which serve to organize behaviors into culturally defined patterns dependent on the position being occupied.

6. Role performance can vary from role prescriptions, depending on many learning factors and on the extent of coerciveness to conformity. Role conflicts constitute a major source of inappropriate behavior and personal discomfort.

7. A thread of consistency runs through an individual's performances in various roles. This consistency is made possible by a looseness in role prescriptions, by common elements among roles, by the fact that the same teachers foster the learning of diverse roles in the child, and by the existence of common motives operating in the several different positions a person may occupy.

8. The self-concept is an important feature of behavioral consistency across roles. The self-concept is developed through the ability to discriminate self from non-self, and to internalize parental norms as self-norms.

9. Conditions of worth limit the accuracy of the self-concept. Conditions of worth are products of socialization.

10. Conditions of worth operate to make a large part of the self-concept unconscious.

11. A concept of the ideal self containing the individual's acquired standards and valued ideals may differ from the self-concept as a result of inconsistencies in socialization and within the culture.

12. There are styles of perceiving interpersonal stimuli, these styles being related to the self-concept and to the schemas which the individual brings to the perceptual situation.

13. Guilt and conflict produce projection and other distortions such that interpersonal misperceptions occur, leading to poor social relationships and the frustration of interpersonal approach drives.

IV. Consequences

We have now completed what might be called the anatomy of personality. It remains for us to put the pieces together to form the functioning individual. This last section is concerned with the ways in which these pieces are put together, and the results of the combination. Here we will be discussing the interaction of drives and their associated responses, and the behaviors which these interactions generate. After that, we will discuss personality patterns, involving the cumulative operation of all the factors which play a role in personality functioning as they are found in people. The section will be concluded with a discussion of the major implications of human personality as it has been presented in this text so far as theory of behavior is concerned.

9. Conflict

At many points throughout the last section reference has been made to situations in which opposing forces operate. Parents use fear as a counterforce against their children's free elimination in toilet training; aggression is met with counteraggression in an effort to reduce overt aggressive behavior; sexual drives are made the cues for guilt by opposing rejection to sexual responses in children; children's interests are sometimes in conflict with their sex role identifications; performance of one social role may conflict with performance of another role; the ideal self may be inconsistent with the self-concept, which may itself be inconsistent with one's behavior. The time has come to study in more complete detail the general form and operation of conflicts.

A Scheme for Expressing Conflict

Conflicts have been roughly grouped into three main types, identified in terms of the directions of the competing forces: approach-approach, avoidance-avoidance, and approach-avoidance.

Approach-avoidance conflicts are generally considered to be the most important, in terms of their behavioral effects. Conflicts are classed as approach-avoidance when there is a response tendency to approach a particular goal which also elicits avoidance responses, or to perform responses which have been punished in the past. Such a conflict exists, for example, when strong sexual drives motivate a person toward a sex object which has, however, acquired the capacity to elicit fear responses, perhaps as a result of stimulus generalization from a punishing parent. Approach-avoidance conflicts are those that arise whenever the same goal state is both desired and feared. The classic cases of this kind of conflict involve the wedding-day upset of the groom who loves the bride but is afraid of "losing his freedom," the adolescent who hungers for sexual experience but is afraid to reveal his ignorance, the child who wants the fun of a roller-coaster ride but is afraid of its speed. When the person in conflict is aware of his conflicting tendencies, he experiences what is called *ambivalence*. The figure of Hamlet has become a symbol of such ambivalence.

A second type of conflict is the approach-approach; this occurs when a person is motivated toward two mutually exclusive goals. Common approach-approach conflicts are those of the college girl who wishes both to have a career and to have a husband and family, of the adolescent boy who wants to adopt the role performances of both the suave intellectual sophisticate and the rugged outdoors he-man, and of the student who wants to get good grades but also wants to live his ideal of a carefree college life. It is generally felt that approach-approach conflicts are not of great psychological interest, because the behaviors to which they give rise are relatively simple and without the complications of anxiety. Usually these conflicts are readily solvable. The hungry ass standing midway between two haystacks does not starve to death; he goes to the one that seems nearest (if only because he chances to look at it, so that it occupies his visual field while the other is only on the periphery if it is present at all in his vision), and afterwards he may go to the other. In general, there seem to be few pairs of goal states which are really mutually exclusive. Often integrations of the two may be arranged, as when a girl marries and takes a part-time job. Or the competing goals may be scheduled; the college student reserves his "wild" periods for weekends and vacations, and the working man sets aside some hours of the week for his hobby. Approach-approach conflicts may become more important when they are converted into approach-avoidance conflicts. The married woman who has put off a career until her children are grown may come to resent and hate her position as housewife because she is not enjoying that of a career woman, at the same time that she loves her family too much to leave it. She is then in the kind of approach-avoidance conflict already mentioned, the consequence of which will be explored more fully below.

The third conflict type is that of avoidance-avoidance. Conflicts are so classified when one is faced with a two-choice situation in which he wishes to avoid both goal states, but must make a choice. An example might be that of the young man who wishes to avoid military service but also wishes to avoid arrest for draft-dodging, and of Nanki-Poo in Gilbert and Sullivan's *Mikado* who must marry Katisha or die. An avoidance-avoidance conflict is implied when one is on the horns of a dilemma. Like the approach-approach conflicts, these are not of great psychological interest, again because there are few goal states which are so exclusive that there is not some third way out. Also, the occasions are few when one is compelled to choose between two undesirable goals. When this does occur, a decision forced, and a goal state achieved, it usually turns out to have its compensations and to be less painful than it initially appeared. Most important, these conflicts are not usually internal, in that they are not conflicts of motives within the individual, but are rather situational, and situations can be readily changed compared to motives. When real problems seem to be presented to a person by avoidance-avoidance conflict, it is because it is really an approach-avoidance conflict; one of the feared or undesired goals is also, if only unconsciously, a desired one. One does not fear having to do something which is distasteful unless there is some drive present which can be reduced by performing the otherwise distasteful act, thus producing some motivational tendency to approach the undesired goal. One does not fear doing something that there is no probability of his doing. One has no fear that he will commit suicide, if he has no drive to do so. When such a fear is present, it thus denotes the presence of a tendency toward the feared behavior, albeit an unconscious one. Similarly, a strong fear that some terrible event might happen, such as a fear that a tree might fall on one, suggests some unconscious desire for punishment which makes the event something not totally undesirable. In avoidance-avoidance conflicts, some third alternative is usually available; if this alternative is rejected, or fails to be considered, then it suggests that the person may really have some positive tendencies toward at least one of the "feared" goal states. In fact, avoidance-avoidance conflicts may be maximized by a person so as to force him to do something which he really wishes to do, but which he would feel guilty about admitting if he could not appeal to the force of circumstance and the impossible choice as an excuse, thus avoiding the responsibility for the choice. Acts of aggression "in self defense" may often be motivated acts of hostility by a person who is able to convince others that he was in an avoidance-avoidance conflict which left him no third way out. This was one of the techniques used by Shakespeare's Richard III to get rid of possible sources of opposition to his throne. Similarly, one often claims that he could not do something expected of him, because he was so busy doing some other "undesirable but necessary" task. Thus a student may apologize for not doing his assignments by claiming that he has so little time for them because he must work on an outside job many hours in order to remain in school; upon investigation, it often happens that the student is working on the outside job more hours than he really must to stay in school, indicating that there is some approach drive toward his job, rather than simply a desire to avoid poverty. He avoids an undesirable alternative—doing assignments—by claiming the necessity of choosing another undesirable alternative which masks an unacceptable approach motivation toward that goal.

The Significance of Conflicts. One of the important things about conflicts is that there are two or more drives which cannot be satisfied, because of their mutually exclusive nature. Therefore conflicts involve more frustration than that which exists when a simple barrier is placed between a motivated subject and the goal. Further, the more the conflict is based on the nature of the individual's motives, rather than on circumstances of the individual's environment, the more difficult it is. This is true for two reasons: when the conflict is of motives, there is no escape by leaving the source of the frustration and seeking elsewhere for the opportunity to make responses which will be rewarded. Thus the conflicted person must face continued lack of reward, and continued punishment through the further increase in drive strength, wherever he turns. The second reason is that motives have been historically established, and so cannot be eliminated by any simple direct means, whereas environmental blocks present in the contemporary situation may be circumvented or even removed entirely through intelligent problem-solving behavior. These are the same factors which make approach-avoidance conflicts so important, because these are the conflicts most likely to involve competing motives within the individual, rather than some arbitrary limitation placed by the environment on the individual. The avoidance-avoidance conflicts mentioned above, for example, were the results of legal restrictions imposed on the individual which operated only against those responses which initially appeared most likely to reduce drives. Other responses are readily discovered in connection with the same drives—young men do solve the draft situation by getting married and obtaining exemptions, or by going to school, and Nanki-Poo is not beheaded. Approach-avoidance conflicts, however, do not admit of third alternatives; the goal which is desired and which elicits motivated behavior as a result of past learning is the very same goal which also elicits avoidance as a result of past learning. Any choice the individual makes in this situation inevitably involves frustration of one of the drives, and there is little he can do in his environment to overcome the frustration, the source of which resides in his own experience.

Anxiety. Anxiety is a consequence of conflict. Fear and anxiety have been mentioned in many places in this text; it is now necessary to consider more carefully what is meant by these terms. Fear has been defined as a conditioned pain drive. What is its relationship to anxiety? A number of answers have been proposed.

One answer is that anxiety is a general state of fear, in which either the cues for fear are so ubiquitous that the drive state is almost continuously present, or the consciousness of the source of the fear is not present, so that the state of anxiety is one of a nameless fear, in which the individual does not know what to avoid in order to reduce the state. Thus all cues are potentially anxiety-arousing. The source of a fear may be unconscious either because the fear was established before symbolic processes were sufficiently well established for the individual to be able to think about the feared object, or because thinking about the object itself serves as a cue for further fear and is thus avoided. It has been suggested that anxiety is particularly associated with internal cues— those arising from the individual's drives. These are most likely to be unconscious, because of the difficulty in making discriminations among drives, and because these drives are so frequently established before verbal skills are acquired. In this sense, anxiety is a fear of one's drives —those which have been disapproved by the parents—and so its source is even more likely to be unconscious. Fear of external objects can be interpreted, in this theory, as the result of an attempt to identify the source of the anxiety, to externalize it in such a way that the person can think about it and avoid the external event, without having to suffer the increase in anxiety which would occur if he thought about the forbidden drive. When this occurs, the environmental objects avoided are those which in some way serve as cues for the feared drive. Thus feared external objects have a symbolic value, in that they suggest the nature of the internal source of the fear. In the extreme case in which the objective justification for the fear is low, in terms of the probability that the object will in fact produce pain, the fear is called a *phobia.* In this interpretation, anxiety is a generalized state of fear, out of which specific fears develop. Furthermore, it is closely associated with the presence of approach-avoidance type conflicts, because it involves fear-evoking drives, or objects which elicit both approach and avoidance behavior.

Another interpretation of anxiety is that it is a component of all drives, becoming more and more apparent as the drives increase in strength. In this interpretation, anxiety is the physiological state producing tension and arousal which accompanies the more specific physiological motive components. As such, it is an autonomic function, and is usually manifested by galvanic skin responses, in heart and breathing rate, blood pressure, and other autonomically mediated reactions. As was mentioned in Chapter 2, there is good reason for suspecting that there are individual differences in which reaction systems are the surest indicators of the physiological arousal defined as anxiety.

In any case, anxiety operates as a response and as a drive; it is conditionable, and its reduction can reinforce the acquisition of responses. It appears to be a particularly strong drive, which is one of the things that makes it seem likely that even if it is interpreted as the physiological accompaniment of drives, it is in some way connected with pain and fear, which have been shown to be so powerful.

Regardless of which interpretation of anxiety is eventually demonstrated to be the more nearly correct, it is apparent that anxiety is present in approach-avoidance conflicts, either as an accompaniment of both drives, or of the avoidance component only.

The Effects of Anxiety on Performance. Anxiety, when it is conscious, is experienced as an objectless but pervasive apprehension. It has been described as a feeling of some impending disaster. Physiologically, states of anxiety may include any or all of the following effects: sweating, trembling, rapid heart rate, exaggerated "startle" responses. Feelings of nervousness, irritability, upset stomach, headache, and "jumpiness" may also be present. There may be reported inability to concentrate, sleeplessness, and difficulty in thinking. Obviously, anxiety is a very upsetting state, the reduction of which is a very powerful reinforcement.

Experimentally it has been demonstrated that mild anxiety facilitates performance on laboratory tasks,[1, 2] but that high anxiety lowers performance. When anxiety is mild, it serves as an additional drive energizing behavior, shortening latencies and response times, thus producing better performance. However, when anxiety is great, the responses which are evoked by the cues of anxiety compete with those involved in the task performance, producing a decrement in accuracy or speed. Similarly, anxiety facilitates performance in simple tasks in which the opportunities for competition among responses is minimal, such as in pressing a key when a signal light is turned on, but in complex tasks, such as pressing one key when one light goes on, and giving a different response when the other light is flashed, anxiety is associated with poorer performance.[3] It is because of these effects of anxiety that psychological examiners make extensive efforts to place subjects at their ease, thus reducing anxiety, before administering their tests.

Responses to Anxiety. The most important of the effects of anxiety are those produced by the responses people acquire to reduce anxiety. These responses may be classified into two groups. Some are *instrumental* in the sense that they produce anxiety reduction through the elimination of the conflict or frustration. In other words, instrumental responses are those which produce a reduction in one or both conflicting drives. The other group of anxiety-reducing responses is that usually called *defenses,* a concept borrowed from Freud who first became interested in the behaviors people displayed when anxious and conflicted. Freud called these behaviors *defense mechanisms* because of the way they served to reduce anxiety or defend the individual from anxiety, without resulting in any change or improvement in the conflict conditions which underlay the anxiety. While we will be discussing some of the same behaviors first identified and named by Anna Freud as falling within this group,[4] we shall avoid using the term *defense mechanism,* because it implies that these behaviors are like automatic reflexes, rather than learned, and at the same time suggests, by the term *defense,* a purposiveness in the selection of the behaviors which may not exist. Further, the word "defense" tends to elicit value judgments about such behavior which are usually oversimplified and often obscure a more objective study of the behaviors themselves. One can hardly avoid thinking of a defense as somehow bad. Instead, we shall call this group by the general term *noninstrumental anxiety responses.*

Instrumental Responses to Anxiety

Behavioral Variability. One of the most apparent consequences of conflict is variability in behavior,[5] when the anxiety produced in the conflict is not great. There is a casting about for a response which will satisfy the conflicting drives. Often, out of such variable behavior comes a response which resolves the conflict and reduces the drives involved. Variability is most likely to occur when the conflicting drives are not too intense; when they are intense the already learned responses they elicit are too resistant to extinction for new trial-and-error to occur. Behavioral variability is thus not found in highly anxious people, when the anxiety results instead in a restriction of behavior known as rigidity. Rigidity will be discussed more fully below, as one of the noninstrumental responses.

The conditions under which responses were learned are, as we have seen, factors in determining resistance to extinction, and thus are also factors in determining whether new problem-solving trial-and-error will occur under conditions of conflict. One would expect, for example, that the 100 per cent reinforcement which is approximated by consistency in parental behavior should be more likely to produce the kinds of conditions which facilitate the occurrence of new trial-and-error behavior when the child is frustrated by conflict. There is some evidence that inconsistency in parental behavior is more common in the backgrounds of rigidly neurotic and psychotic people than it is in "normal" people.[6] Another factor which probably influences the extent to which variability in behavior occurs is the range of problem solutions which the parents have found acceptable and worthy of approval. Parents who insist that things be done one way only are more likely to have children whose instrumental trial-and-error responses will be minimal, if they occur at all. It has been found, for example, that children coming from homes which have been rated as high in permissiveness—a condition which probably fosters the development of freedom and variability in the child's problem-solving experiences—tend to persist in obviously unsuccessful task solutions less than do children whose homes were rated as low in permissiveness.

It is important to distinguish between ambivalence and instrumental variability as reactions to conflict. Ambivalent behavior involves a vacillation between the behaviors elicited by the competing motives. Such vacillation can result in no new responses or compromise solutions. This kind of ambivalence is, in fact, opposite to instrumental variability, because of the stereotypy or rigidity of the alternative behaviors which the ambivalent person alternates between. On the other hand, the behavioral variability which is instrumental is that which involves the trial of new responses until one, which meets the needs of the situation, is emitted and reinforced by a reduction in the conflict-produced anxiety through the satisfaction of the competing drives. Leonard Lansky in a doctoral dissertation has found that college men whose psychological tests indicate the relative lack of traumatic experiences in childhood respond to conflicts with increases in realistic problem-solving endings to the stories they completed as part of the experiment; college men whose tests suggested difficulties in their relationships to their parents made up story completions notable for their absence of any problem-solving attempts and for indications of withdrawal from the problem.[7] Another study has shown that children can be taught to respond to frustration by increased problem-solving.[8]

Great variability may not always result in an effective problem solution, if the conflicted person rattles through a large number of alternatives without giving any of them a fair chance. Some responses whose reinforcement value might not be readily apparent could be passed by when there is great variability. Some stick-to-it-iveness, together with sufficient thinking ability to assess the consequences of the various response alternatives, is necessary for behavioral variability to result in success.

Instrumental Aggression. A second kind of instrumental response to frustration is that of increasing efforts to make the frustrated responses and reach the goal. This kind of response, however, is not likely to be successful where the frustration is produced by a conflict, rather than by some block in the environment. A by-product of increased vigor in response to frustration is, as we have seen in Chapter 7, the learning of aggressive behavior. Such aggressive behavior may be considered to be instrumental if it is directed against the barrier to the goal, or against the restrictions which oppose the individual's drives. However, aggression may also be noninstrumental, as when it is directed against some substitute object. Noninstrumental aggression has been discussed in Chapter 7, and will be mentioned again in the section on noninstrumental responses to anxiety. When the frustration is the result of internal conflicts, aggression must be noninstrumental, because it cannot eliminate the frustration or the barrier from the person's psychological environment.

Instrumental Regression. There is a third type of instrumental response to frustration. Suppose that a barrier has been placed across a road commonly used for traffic between a suburb and the downtown area. Motorists approaching the barrier are likely to do either one of two things. They will either seek out a new route, or they may try a route which they have on occasion used in the past. The former solution is an example of behavioral variability. When the latter solution occurs, it is called *instrumental regression*. This term simply means that when a response fails to be reinforced (as, for example, because of the imposition of a barrier to the goal, or because of the appearance of a force conflicting with the already acquired response), the organism will give the response which is next strongest in its response hierarchy, and this next strongest response is likely to be one which was once learned but later replaced by an even stronger one. A response that has been successful in the past occurs when a better learned response is no longer reinforced, and thus tends toward extinction.

Regression can be readily observed in young children, in whom alternative responses are so often nearly equal in strength that the child easily slips back to a former response when frustrated. A little boy, desiring some ice cream, gives the "best" response he can to the situation and asks his mother, *"Please,* may I have some ice cream?" If this fails of reinforcement, the child may regress to the earlier, "I want ice cream!" and may quickly run through that stage to the still earlier temper tantrum, which used to bring results in the past. If he puts up enough fuss, his mother may modify her position and promise ice cream after dinner, a response which will reinforce not only the temper but also the regression sequence, thus increasing the probability that regression will occur in response to later frustration. Nevertheless, such regression is instrumental, so long as it involves the giving of a response which has, in the past, been followed by a reduction of the drive presently motivating the person. Like instrumental variability, such regression may in fact result in a good solution to the problem, if the conditions of the problem permit such a solution. However, regression may also be noninstrumental. Once learned as a response to frustration, regression may occur as a means of reducing anxiety, even though no previously acquired response is produced to the conflicting drives. Such regression will be discussed in more detail below.

These various instrumental responses may all be combined in a creative problem solution in which some responses are discovered that resolve the conflicts with minimal if any frustration of the competing drives. Conflict provides motivation for creative thinking; behavioral variability provides the possibility of discovering a uniquely useful set of responses; increased effort provides the persistence for working at various solutions; and regression in the service of the ego permits a temporary return to the earlier, less conventionalized thinking from which a creative idea may emerge.

Noninstrumental Responses to Anxiety

Rigidity. The behavior which has drawn the greatest attention from psychologists as a response to conflict and anxiety is that called *rigidity.*[9]

In general, this term refers to a resistance to change in behavior and/or to change in the environment which might, through the presence of new cues, elicit behaviors in the individual which represent a change from previous behavior. Such rigidity is manifested in stereotyped responding, even when the response is patently inappropriate, in a resistance to changing one's "set," or attitude, to changing plans on short notice, to breaking routine, to trying new ways of doing things, or to allowing others to change accustomed features of the environment. Rigidity may also be manifested by slowness to change perceptions when the initial perception is in error, and by a tendency to insist on rigorous definitions, criteria, and instructions, with adherence often being more in terms of the letter rather than the spirit. Extreme orderliness may be one way in which such rigidity is satisfied.

Rigidity in response to the anxiety involved in conflict was demonstrated by Norman R. F. Maier in the experiment described in Chapter 3 as an example of the use of an impossible discrimination problem to produce experimental neuroses in animals. Maier used rats that were trained to jump from a platform to a goal box in which food was placed behind a door. There were two goal boxes facing the animal, but only one of them had food in it; it was signified by a different colored door from the "wrong" one. When the animal jumped to the correct door, it popped open and let the animal enter the compartment; if he jumped to the wrong door, it remained closed so that the rat bumped his sensitive nose and fell into a net below. The rats readily learned the discrimination between the two doors, but Maier gradually altered the colors of the doors until the rats could no longer discriminate between them. The rats refused to jump under these conditions, but Maier arranged for an unpleasant blast of air to be administered to the animals' hind quarters, which forced them to jump. A large number of the animals developed very stereotyped or rigid jumping habits under these circumstances. Some of them jumped abortively, so that they always fell into the net. Others jumped to either the right or left door consistently. These "rigid" rats would not even alter their responses when the experimenter removed the door of the correct compartment so that the animals could actually see the food inside and the absence of the nose-bumping door.[10] This demonstration of the source of rigidity in conflict is a pioneering one, and one of the earliest experiments in which conflicts were produced for laboratory work.

Jules Masserman has also demonstrated rigidity in response to conflict, but he used cats in a somewhat different situation.[11] His cats were very hungry, and were taught to press a bar in order to obtain food from a feeding cup in the side of their cage. When this bar-pressing response was well-learned, Masserman arranged to have a blast of compressed air delivered to the cats' whiskers whenever they approached the food box. Thus the cats were placed in a fear-hunger conflict. Following this, several of his cats showed rigid behavior. They would go to the far corner of the cage and cower whenever they were placed in the apparatus. They refused to eat, even when the food was held in the experimenter's hand, and despite extreme starvation. When a movable wall was used to force the animals to approach the food cup, they resisted with all their strength.

The rigidity illustrated in these experiments refers to stereotyped behavior in response to frustration—the repetitive performance of a response even when the response is manifestly inappropriate, and despite efforts to alter the response—efforts which would presumably be successful in organisms not suffering frustration. There are two questions psychologists face in using the concept of rigidity. Is it a response automatically or innately produced by conflict, having no goal and thus no reinforcement, or is it learned or learnable? And does rigidity always presuppose frustration?

Psychologists have not yet resolved these questions. There are those like Maier who interpret rigidity as goalless behavior in response to frustration,[12] and others who are so impressed with the necessity for reinforcement that they are unwilling to agree with Maier.[13] These theorists suggest that the rigidity observed in consequence of frustration is simply an overlearned response which reduces anxiety. It may be pointed out that rigidity is not a response per se, but is a quality of a response. In Maier's experiments in which the rats jumped to the wrong window even when the discrimination was made obvious to them, the response was that of jumping to the "wrong" window; its persistence earns it the label of rigid. In this sense, any well-learned response which is highly resistant to extinction may be called rigid. The question still remains, however, of whether reinforcement is needed to produce such rigid responses, or whether the condition of frustration is sufficient. In Maier's experiment, the rats were obviously reinforced for jumping by escape from the airblast, even when the jump was to the wrong door. When the discrimination between the two doors was impossible, the rat had little choice but to jump to one or the other, or abortively so that he bumped his nose on neither. In such a situation, it seems reasonable to suppose that the response of jumping was reinforced by escape from the airblast. Similarly, in the experiment on cats, it is likely that the cats' avoidance of the food cup was powerfully reinforced by a reduction in anxiety, thus becoming overlearned and apparently "rigid." In general, responses such as those which are motivated by pain, fear, or anxiety and which are reinforced by avoiding the stimuli which arouse the drive — that is avoidance responses — are more "rigid" than approach responses. This greater resistance to extinction may be an aspect of the very great strength which we found was characteristic of pain and fear drives.

Now for the second question. In order to answer the question of whether rigidity always presupposes conflict, we must review some of the factors which may be responsible for responses which are highly resistant to extinction and highly consistent from one occasion to another.

Overlearning. We have seen that responses which are learned in relation to high drive, are frequently reinforced, and on a scheduled basis, are very resistant to extinction. In childhood, it is likely that those responses are overlearned which the parents are particularly desirous of teaching their children. Parents differ, we have seen, in the importance they attach to toilet training, or to inhibition of sexual behavior, for example. It is likely that the more important such training is to the parents, the more likely that they will use powerful drives and significant reinforcers on many occasions to produce the desired learning. Such parental "pressure" is even more likely to be applied in those child-training situations in which the child's behavioral tendencies are markedly different from the behaviors required by the parents. Again, elimination and sex are response areas in which this condition is likely to prevail in our society. In effect, this means that rigidity is most likely to be a characteristic of those responses which are the more extreme modifications of innate behavioral tendencies. In this sense, such rigidity is a product of conflict — conflict between the child's original response and the prohibition imposed by his parents and later internalized, particularly in children whose parents have considered such training to be of great importance. A further implication is that those habits acquired in the course of socialization of elimination and sex are most likely to be characterized as rigid. One need only observe the reactions of Americans to suggestions that they change either their defecation or sexual habits to appreciate the rigidity associated with their learning in these areas.

Avoidance Learning. We have seen earlier that in some areas of socialization, parents often use fear to counter the child's strong response tendencies, in order to advance the learning of responses — usually inhibitory—whose performance involves an increase, rather than decrease, in the drive being socialized. Young children seem to be more responsive to punishment as a way of managing learning than are older children. In addition, it has been noted that responses learned in relation to fear and punishment tend to be more resistant to extinction (and less variable in their performance) than approach responses. These factors thus contribute still more to the development of rigid response patterns in those whose socialization may be considered to be severe, in the sense of involving relatively high punishment and other parental pressure occurring relatively early in life. To the extent that the training the child received in the control of his hunger, elimination and sex drives generalizes to similar situations in adulthood may we expect him to respond with rigidity in adulthood. For example, situations which arouse sexual drives are likely to elicit the inhibitory responses acquired in childhood—responses which are not readily modifiable or extinguishable. The more strongly the prohibited drive is aroused, the more strongly will the inhibition be aroused which was associated with the drive in childhood. The result is increasingly rigid inhibition in a situation of conflict between the aroused drive and the learned inhibitions. In this sense, the resultant rigidity is a reaction to conflict.

Specific Training in Rigidity. In our discussion of the cognitive style of intolerance of ambiguity, it was pointed out that children may be trained to reduce ambiguity and conflict by rigid adherence to simplified, socially acceptable interpretations, rather than by thinking in terms of compromise and complex resolutions of competing response tendencies. In effect, this is training in rigidity, in the sense of producing behavior which is not amenable to compromise and modification; it results in the learning that there is only one "right" behavior in an ambiguous conflict situation—the socially acceptable one, usually—and this "right" response itself may be overlearned, further contributing to its rigidity.[14] Investigators report, on the basis of their interviews with the parents of "high intolerant of ambiguity" children, that the parents did in fact tend to employ these child-training practices. As would be expected, they made much use of punishment and fear, whose capacity to produce rigid responding has already been noted.[15]

Hidden Reinforcements. A response may seem impervious to extinction and thus rigid, despite repeated failure of the response to be followed by apparent reinforcement, when in fact subtle reinforcements are present. A young man who was being seen in a psychological clinic once mentioned that he and his wife often got into arguments over his habit of putting his cigarettes out in his coffee saucer. He reported that there was no reason for him not to use the ashtray, and his wife had pointed out to him that when he is visiting others he always uses the ashtray. The patient was annoyed at his wife's irritation with him, because he felt that it was a small matter, and he really tried to remember to use the ash tray, but just couldn't. He said he would automatically put the cigarette out without thinking, although every time he did so, his wife complained. During the course of this man's therapy, it became apparent that there were many different things he did which were just the things that irritated his wife, and it rapidly became apparent to his therapist that the patient was getting some satisfactions from getting his wife angry; he himself never started an argument with her, and he was quite inhibited in expressing direct aggression. However, he could justify his own unconscious resentment of her on the basis of her constant criticism of his behavior, and he could claim, in defense of his resentment, that his wife was a nag.

In this example, the patient's behavior was seemingly very resistant to extinction, even though it was frequently followed by punishment and blame from his wife. However, upon closer analysis, it is seen that there are in fact positive reinforcements present, in that some of his motives of which he was unaware were being rewarded, thus reinforcing rather than extinguishing the behaviors. Of course, conflict is implied in such a situation, in that one motive is hidden rather than directly expressed, making the patient's behavior appear to be unreasonable and unmotivated. When a motive is hidden, and is only indirectly expressed, one can assume that some conflicting, stronger drive, such as the fear of expressing aggression or need for social approval, is present.

Limited Availability of Alternative Responses. Mention should be made of one other source of rigidity, particularly in experiments on conflict. An animal may continue to make an obviously bad response, in the sense that either no reinforcement, or even punishment follows, if the animal is placed in a situation in which it must respond but has no alternatives except the "bad" response. For example, Maier's rats were forced to jump by the blast of air directed against their rumps; without the ability to discriminate between the two doors facing them, there was no alternative but to jump anyway and fall into the net. The number of alternatives may be limited by the particular situation, by the capacities of the subject, or by previous learning which makes alternative responses so low in the response hierarchy that the probability of their being tried is very low. All of these factors are illustrated in a study on problem solving under stress, in which university students were used as subjects. Each student was put in a room by himself, with a number of doors in the room leading to other rooms. Suddenly a blast of water was released at the student. Most subjects ran around the room, frantically trying one door after the other, but all of them were locked. Instead of seeking other solutions, most of the subjects continued trying the same doors which they had already tried, although this was obviously a "bad" response.[16] However, there were few other responses available to them; there were only a few objects in the room, so that the availability of alternative responses was limited, and the previous learning of the subjects was such as to make the response of exiting through a door extremely high in their response hierarchies, and one not likely to be extinguished very rapidly. To be sure, the same subjects would not have continually tried, in this rigid fashion, to open doors already found to be locked, if they were not under stress. But it is also likely that, if they were not under stress, they would either not have continued to try to leave after discovering the doors to be locked, or they would have felt free to spend time in symbolic thought activities which might have resulted in the discovery of a workable alternative — time which they did not have when they were being doused with water.

There are, then, several mechanisms which may be responsible for rigidity. While conflict is usually involved in these mechanisms, it seems to be an oversimplification to think of rigidity as a direct response to conflict. There are many other conditions which play a role, as we have seen, and these should be considered in making a complete accounting of rigid behavior.

Fixation. It was Freud who proposed the concept of fixation. He suggested that it was possible for some aspect of an individual's development to be arrested by severe emotional difficulties, such that at later ages the individual would show in his behavior, either subtly or obviously, some traces of the kind of behavior he displayed at the age at which the difficulty occurred. In this sense, he is "fixated" at the earlier age. Difficulties during the socialization of the hunger drive, for example, result in the persistence of "oral" behaviors beyond this age, as in thumb-sucking, excessive drinking, smoking, or mouth twitches, stuttering, or in the drives acquired in connection with the socialization of hunger (strong dependency, high need for displays of affection). The emotional difficulty which creates the fixation was said usually to involve some intense conflict. Freud hypothesized that some amount of "libido," or psychic energy, remained attached to the body organs involved in the conflict, so that this portion of behavioral energy was always expressed through that organ. Although nothing has been discovered in the human body which is coordinate with Freud's concept of libido or psychic energy so that this explanation of fixation is not generally accepted today, the idea that later behavior may be related to early conflicts or emotional upheavals is unquestioned. We have already seen how the conditions under which various response systems are socialized have marked effects on other aspects of the individual's behavior, and on subsequent behavior involving the socialized response system. We have seen, for example, how the conditions of socialization of the hunger drive, involving the mouth and digestive activities, can result in a relationship between eating and affection, such that eating is often symbolic of love. In this sense, Freud's insight into the relationship between early experience and later behavior, as expressed in the concept of fixation, was a notable and apparently valid one, although the means by which this relationship occurs may not be the one suggested by Freud. The processes which mediate fixation may be observed in the following case.

When she was two years old, a little girl was hospitalized for a tonsillectomy. She had not been prepared in advance for the hospitalization. One day her mother told her they were going for a ride in the car, an activity she always enjoyed. The car stopped in front of a large building and her parents took her out of the car, into the building, and up in an elevator. A lady in a white dress met them when they got out of the elevator and held out her arms; her father put her in the nurse's arms, who carried her down the hall, away from her parents, as she began to cry. The nurse took the little girl's clothes, put her in strange pajamas and into a strange crib which had a net on top of it so she couldn't climb out. The little girl's parents came in, but she could not be held by them, and then they went away, leaving the girl alone in strange surroundings for the first time in her life, and terror stricken. The next day she was anesthetized, becoming even more terrified when the suffocating mask was held over her mouth and nose. When she awakened, nauseous and frightened, her throat burned intolerably. The next day her parents took her home. When they put her to bed that night, she became terrified that they would leave her again as they had left her in the crib in the hospital. She screamed, cried, and kicked so violently, that her parents, fearing that she might hemorrhage from the surgery, allowed her to sleep in their bed. The same pattern was repeated on successive nights, and ultimately crystallized into a customary procedure in which the girl was allowed to sleep with the parents every night for the next several years.

This pattern is a focused example of the many ways in which the little girl developed strong habits of dependency on her parents, literally not allowing them out.of her sight, as a result of her hospitalization. In Freud's terms, the hospitalization constituted a trauma as a result of which the child became fixated at a dependent level of development. The learnings at this age were subject to all the considerations listed in Chapter 6 as contributing to the importance of infantile learnings. One of the most important of these was the way in which the things learned as a result of the trauma focused or limited later learnings which were, of course, consistent with the earlier responses acquired as a result of the trauma. As an adult, the girl showed many social behaviors which were obviously related to dependency and fear of desertion, in which she arranged things so that she could always count on not being left out by the people on whom she depended. As an adult she was described as immature and fixated. During adulthood, when her husband made plans for a business trip, she became insistent on going along with him, cried and became so hysterically emotional about his going away that he gave in. As a result, she always accompanied him, even though this created great inconvenience. His business trips could be considered symbolic of the early trauma, and her emotional reaction a regression to the behavior in infancy which was reinforced by allowing her to sleep in her parents' bed.

This case describes a general pattern in which trauma leads through the learnings it produces to fixated behaviors and in turn yields regression to the fixated behaviors when events symbolic of (that is, existing on a stimulus generalization gradient with) the trauma occur.

When the conditions of socialization have resulted in the development of behaviors which are symbolic of earlier events, or which are the unmodified result of earlier experiences, these behaviors are usually called immature. When the lonely man eats excessively, his eating may be considered an immature way of reducing his affectional drives. Although wanting to be fed by the mother was valid as a response to loneliness in infancy, it is less valid in an adult's situation, and in fact may have no success at all as a means of achieving love, even though it may reduce the drive state initiated by loneliness. Because neurotic and psychotic behaviors are often of this nature, the neurotic and psychotic are often described as immature and fixated.

This discussion of fixation may be summarized as follows: later adult behavior is modified by the conditions existing at earlier ages, and particularly by important conflicts which may have existed earlier, in such a way that the adult will respond with the behaviors he learned in the earlier situations, and these behaviors will be related in their nature to the conditions under which they were acquired so that they serve as "symbols" of those conditions. This much follows from the way in which learning and performance occurs. However, fixation as an attachment of psychic energy to a response system as a result of conflict, so that the fixated response or remnants of it occurs repetitiously from that time on, is an explanation which is too simple and too much lacking in scientific support to handle all the details of the learning process which produces "fixated" behavior. We thus arrive at Freud's conclusion about the immaturity of some adult behavior, and its symbolic value, but by a different path, one which stresses the acquisition of a connection between a drive and a goal state which is so strong that a very specific goal is required to reduce the drive. We will have more to say about fixation and immaturity when we again deal with the topic of regression later in this chapter.

Aggression. We have already dealt extensively with the origins of aggressive drives and aggressive responses in frustration. It is only necessary to point out here that frustration produced by conflict operates very much like the frustration produced by some block in the path toward a goal, so far as serving as an instigation to aggression is concerned. However, when frustration occurs as a result of conflicting drives within a person, rather than from some external barrier, then the frustrated person is also the agent of his own frustration, and as such is also the likely target of his aggressive reaction. Thus conflict-instigated aggression has a high probability of being intropunitive in its direction. Nevertheless, even in this situation, extrapunitiveness may occur, as a result of the operation of displacement and other response substitutions to be discussed in the next section.

So far we have discussed rigidity, fixation, regression, and aggression as noninstrumental responses to conflict and frustration. These should not be thought of as entirely independent kinds of responses, but rather as different ways of looking at the same behaviors. For example, a particular aggressive reaction may well involve rigidity, fixation, and regression to the fixated age of temper tantrums. Every response has a force associated with it, an origin, a set of psychological processes relating the stimuli present to the response and to its origin, and every response is more or less modifiable. Each of these aspects has its parallel: force may be strong or weak aggression, origin refers to time of fixation, the evoking processes are more or less regressive and the modifiability may go from high to low rigidity. Thus any response to conflict may be examined in terms of its aggressiveness, its reflection of fixated learnings, the relationship between the cues that elicited the response and past experiences of the person, and the modifiability of the reaction. Two other aspects of noninstrumental responses are yet to be considered: their content, and the nature of the environmental stimuli (or cathected objects) involved. These will be discussed under the heading of "substitutions." In what follows, keep in mind that every response involves all of these aspects, although we discuss each aspect separately from the others.

Substitutions

Freud identified a number of noninstrumental responses to conflict which are similar to each other in that they are all substitutions, in one way or another, for the competing responses involved in the conflict. Let us see how such substitutions occur.

Figure 11 facing is a graphic illustration of an approach-avoidance conflict.[17] At the left side of the figure is the goal of the response, the strength of which is shown by the broken curve. The figure illustrates the goal gradient discussed in Chapter 4, in which, the farther away from the goal, the less is the strength of the response. In an approach-avoidance conflict, there is also a drive to avoid the goal or the goal response; usually this avoidant drive is in the nature of fear or anxiety associated with the goal state or the goal response. A conflict between an aggressive impulse and a fear of punishment for behaving aggressively would be an example of such a situation. In the figure, there is an avoidant drive graphed—the solid curve—which is highest at the goal, and which decreases in strength the further one goes away from the goal. At the goal, in the conflict illustrated, the avoidance drive is stronger than the approach drive, as indicated by the greater height of the avoidance gradient at that point. However, you will note that the approach drive is not as steep as the avoidant gradient; it seems to be a characteristic of avoidance drives that drive strength falls off more rapidly than is true for approach drives as one goes away from the goal. This difference in slopes has been demonstrated in several experiments in which the speed with which rats ran toward a goal was charted at various points along the runway or alley leading to the goal.[18] It was found that a decrease in speed of running toward an aversive goal where shock had been administered occurred more strongly and closer

Figure 11. Goal Gradient Conflict Model

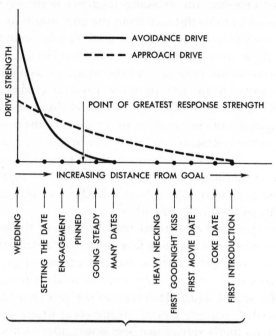

POINTS ALONG THE PATH FROM
FIRST MEETING TO MARRIAGE OF A HYPOTHETICAL
SUBJECT WHO DIDN'T MAKE IT TO THE WEDDING.

to the goal than did increases in speed of running toward a positive goal in which the animals had been fed. These experiments therefore indicate that the gradient of response strength for an avoidance or aversive response is steeper than is the gradient of approach, in that the gradient of avoidance falls off more rapidly as a function of distance from the goal. However, the reason for this difference in slopes remains obscure. It may simply be in the nature of aversive drives to have steep gradients, or it may be because pain receptors are more discriminably and directly stimulable than hunger or other appetitive need receptors, so that the learning of pain drives is to a narrower range of specific stimuli than is the case with slower acting and diffuse appetitive need-stimulation.

The point at which the two gradients cross is the point at which the strength of the tendency to approach the goal is exactly equal to the strength of the tendency to go away from the goal. To the right of that point, the tendency to approach is stronger than the other tendency, so that the subject should continue to go toward the goal. To the left of the point of crossing, the avoiding tendency is stronger than the approach; a subject at this distance from the goal would then be more strongly motivated to go away from the goal than he would be to approach it. It can be seen from the figure that a subject at the extreme right of the figure would move toward the goal, increasing in his speed or force as he moves to the left, until the avoidant gradient begins to rise above zero. From that place on, he would decrease in speed or strength of response until he comes to the crossing of the two gradients. If he should, in the course of random behavior, go even closer to the goal than this, he will backtrack because of the greater strength of the avoidant drive, until the point is reached at which the approach drive is again dominant. In effect, the subject is likely to vacillate around the point of equality of the two gradients.

Behaviorally, this kind of conflict may be seen in the actions of a little girl whose mother is about to take her to see a department store Santa Claus. The little girl is very excited and anxious to go; when they arrive at the store, she runs to where the Santa Claus is situated, and runs toward the seated figure. However, as she gets closer to him, her fear of the bearded stranger mounts to the point where she suddenly retreats to her mother's side. Then she slowly approaches the Santa Claus, cautiously, lest she get too close, but she stops some distance before him. Her mother cannot urge her closer, but neither will she leave as she enviously watches the other children sit on the Santa's lap and talk to him. The little girl has, in effect, stabilized at the point at which the gradients cross.

A similar situation is seen in the behavior of the shy college man who is anxious to make a date with a coed, but is also somewhat fearful that she might turn him down. When he is away from her he longs for her presence, but when she is near, he retreats, too fearful to broach the subject. When he is in his dormitory, he is strongly approach motivated, and may call her on the phone, but when her roommate answers, and he is presented with cues which are in close proximity to his goal, his fear may become so great that he is relieved to find that the object of his call is not in, although once he hangs up he may again experience his longing for her, perhaps expressed in elaborate fantasies about where she might be and what she might be doing.

Illustrated below is a graphic presentation of another conflict, but in this one, the approach drive is always higher than the avoidance drive although it is only very little higher at the goal. This conflict might be a model of the experience of disappointment. Throughout the journey toward the goal, the approach drive is stronger than the avoidant drive; as the individual starts out, it is with great ambition, but the closer he gets to the goal, the more he slows down. Stronger and stronger fear or anxiety occurs until at the point of completion—at the goal—there is so little excess of approach drive over avoidance that the goal is only minimally rewarding, because it involves great increase in avoidance drive. The *net* effect is only a very small reduction in drive. This is the situation in which one continues toward his goal, but when

**Figure 12. Representation of the
Attainment of a Disappointing Goal**

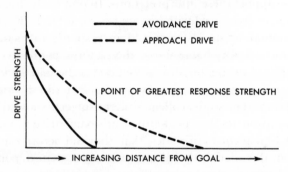

The approach gradient is higher than avoidance all along the way, so the subject continues to the goal, where he receives relatively little net satisfaction.

he arrives there he wonders if it was really worth it, because of the small net satisfaction he receives considering all the negative drive strength, although at the beginning of the sequence there was only approach drive operating to make the goal appear unequivocally desirable. This model may describe the person who, visualizing a lovely garden around his home, commits himself to a program of gardening which he discovers to require more and more arduous work and heavy expense. Although he continues his program until his goal is reached, he may wonder whether the results were really worth all the negative factors he had to endure.

Another implication of this model is that as a person is moved toward a feared goal, he may show a reduction, rather than an increase, in goal-relevant behaviors. For example, a person who is subject to conflict between aggressive drive and fear or anxiety concerning the expression of aggression will tend to become relatively *less* aggressive, rather than more, when his aggressive drive is aroused by an increase in the cues for aggressive responses, or by an increase in arousal of aggressive drive. As these conditions move him toward the goal, his avoidance of aggression increases faster than his tendency to behave aggressively, so that there is less and less excess of approach drive over avoidance drive, producing a net reduction in aggressive behavior. This is what seems to happen in people who are afraid of what they might say or do when they are intoxicated. As they drink more and more, they become more and more constricted and restrained in their behavior, the net effect of which is that they sometimes become more "sober" when drunk than when not. Experiments support these interpretations. In one study, highly aggressive subjects were compared with low aggressive subjects in terms of the aggressive content to stories they told in response to pictures which they were shown. Before being shown the pictures, aggressive drive was aroused by the experimenter. It was found that the initially low aggressive subjects then told more aggressive stories than did the high aggressive ones.[19] In another study, college student subjects showed less direct sexual fantasy in stories they made up after sexual drive was aroused by having them view pictures of nudes, than they did before the arousal.[20]

Note that in this model, the direction of movement depends on the relationship between the two gradients—away from the goal when avoidance is greater than approach, and toward the goal when approach is the stronger—and that the strength of the movement tendency is dependent on the size of the discrepancy between the gradients. Strong approach occurs when the approach gradient is far above the avoidance gradient, and strong avoidance occurs when the two are reversed. However, the *total* amount of drive strength, in terms of the amount of motivational arousal occurring in the subject is expressed by the *sum* of the two drives. The total amount of drive strength existing in the individual at a particular point on the continuum from the starting place to the goal is made up of the total amount of approach drive which is present at that point plus the total amount of avoidance drive present. Thus the total motivational arousal which exists close to the goal is much greater than the motivational arousal existing far from the goal. In Figure 11, a person who is at the point at which the two gradients cross may show no greater movement toward or away from the goal than a person who is so far away from the goal that neither gradient is above zero, but he will be in a much higher state of drive, perhaps experienced as severe tension, indecision, and anxiety. Thus the closer to the goal that the two gradients cross, the greater will be the anxiety which is present. This is probably one of the reasons why conflicts are more productive of severe anxiety than simple frustration resulting from the blocking of the path toward the goal by some external agent. In simple blocking, only one drive is present and unsatisfied, while in conflict there are two drives which are frustrated, each by the presence of the other.

In this model, distance from the goal as represented by the baseline of the figures need not be taken literally as referring to distance in space. The model may apply just as well to situations in which distance is used figuratively to refer to sequences of events or hurdles which lead to some goal. For example, passing a course in introductory psychology is further away from a goal of becoming a psychologist than is the writing of a dissertation, and asking a girl for a date is further away from the goal of marriage than is becoming engaged. These events exist in culturally established sequences which do not exist on a dimension of length, although they do involve a dimension of time. Nevertheless, they describe points which mark a progression toward the goal states and may be represented by the same model as that used to describe linear distance from the goal of a maze used in animal experiments.

Along with these processes may be others based on another variable of the learning process, describing behavior toward goals more or less similar to the conflicted one. The goal gradient model of conflict, based on the gradient of reinforcement, may also be derived from conflicting gradients of stimulus generalization, in which approach and avoidance responses are elicited by the same cues, or by different aspects of the same cue situation. Thus one may make approach responses to some of the cues produced by a particular female—perhaps the cues closely associated with her sexual nature—and at the same time be repelled by other aspects of her behavior, such as her tendency to dominate, or by cues that she is sufficiently like a dominating mother to elicit generalized avoidance. As long as one assumes that the avoidance gradient of generalization is steeper than the approach, an assumption which is in accord with the experimental evidence which exists, then one may make similar predictions from a stimulus generalization conflict model as from the goal gradient model, except that instead of talking about distance from the goal, one deals with distance along a dimension of similarity to the originally conditioned cues.

It is this model which best accounts for certain kinds of substitution responses to conflict. In general, substitutions can be divided into two types: those in which there is a substitution of a different response for those which are conflicting, and those in which the feared response remains unchanged, but it is made to substitute cues instead of to those which elicit the fear. Let us look first at these latter substitutions in terms of the conflict model.

Displacement. As you look at the conflict model in Figure 13 in terms of the relationships between the two gradients at various points on the stimulus generalization gradient, you will note that the greatest excess of approach strength over avoidance response strength occurs at some distance to the right of the intersection of the gradients. At this point, and to the stimuli whose extent of similarity to the original stimulus places them this far out on the stimulus generalization gradient, will

**Figure 13. Displacement of Aggressive Response
from the Father**

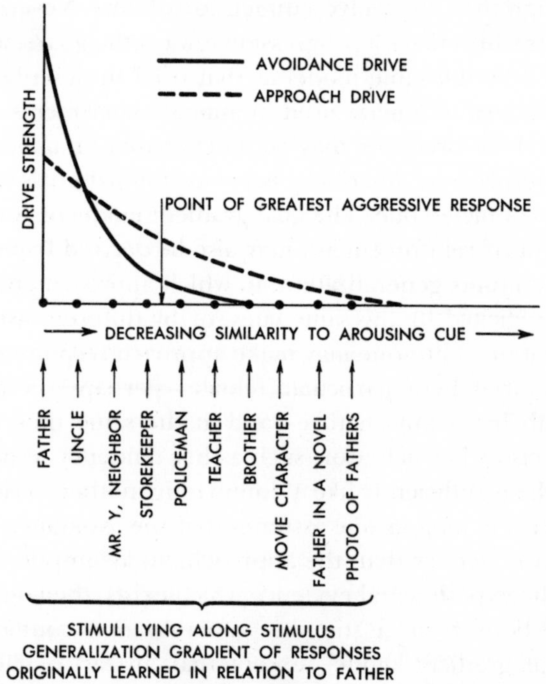

AVOIDANCE DRIVE

APPROACH DRIVE

DRIVE STRENGTH

POINT OF GREATEST AGGRESSIVE RESPONSE

DECREASING SIMILARITY TO AROUSING CUE

FATHER
UNCLE
MR. Y, NEIGHBOR
STOREKEEPER
POLICEMAN
TEACHER
BROTHER
MOVIE CHARACTER
FATHER IN A NOVEL
PHOTO OF FATHERS

STIMULI LYING ALONG STIMULUS
GENERALIZATION GRADIENT OF RESPONSES
ORIGINALLY LEARNED IN RELATION TO FATHER

For this subject, anger stimulated by the father will be expressed most strongly against shopkeepers and policemen.

the strongest response be made. It is here that the approach response has its greatest strength, relative to the inhibiting effects of the avoidance response. Thus the response potential, really evoked by the stimuli with which it was originally associated but not given to such stimuli because of the stronger avoidance also evoked by them, is given to the stimuli which are at this distance from them on the continuum. For example, aggressive responses evoked in a child by his father cannot be made to the stimuli of the father because of even stronger learned fear of attacking the father. However, stimuli arising from a strange male adult walking down the street are sufficiently like the father to evoke fairly strong aggressive responses by means of stimulus generalization, but yet not so similar that the avoidance gradient is evoked in sufficient strength to inhibit the aggression. As a result, the child behaves aggressively to this man, although not to his father, perhaps by teasing or throwing snowballs. This, although the stranger has done nothing to stimulate aggression. In this example, the aggression is said to be *displaced* from the father to the stranger. Teachers and impersonal authorities such as police are frequent objects of hostility displaced from parents, and wives and children are frequently the objects of hostility displaced from one's employer. The paradoxical thing about displacement is that the object of the displaced response receives much greater hostility (or sexuality or dependence, depending upon the responses involved in the conflict) than does the object which is arousing or eliciting the feared response. Thus one occasionally reads of some young person who surprisingly commits a dramatic or sensational crime, seemingly unprovoked, even though the offender has had apparently very "ideal" relationships with his parents and people close to them.

Provocation for Displacement. Frequently a displaced response is not made without some "provocation" which is, however, inadequate by itself to account for the magnitude of the response, so that the displaced response appears inappropriately strong. A husband, boiling with rage as a result of a severe dressing-down by his boss returns home, acting grumpy, but may not displace his aggression to his wife or children until they do something, however minor, which can serve as an excuse for the hostility and as a further cue for its expression which, once begun, becomes very great because of the displacement. This is the "straw that broke the camel's back" effect. Such a pattern of displacement is so common that in general, whenever a response appears to be much greater than seems warranted by the provocation, one should ask if there is not some conflict producing a displacement.

Displaced responses are stronger than are the same responses to the orginally eliciting cues, not only because there is less avoidance at the point of displacement, and often a little provocation which heightens the·response, but also because the frustration of the conflicted drives has allowed them to become particularly strong. A child who displaces his dependency from his parents to his teacher, because of fear of parental rejection, becomes extremely dependent on the teacher not only as a displacement, perhaps even aided by the teacher's warmth and acceptance, but also because the dependency drive has become very strong as a result of not being satisfied by the parents.

Aggression in Displacement. In displacement, there is likely to be an element of aggression added to the displaced response as a result of the frustration implicit in the inhibition of the response to the stimuli which are really evoking it. Therefore a displaced aggression may be even greater than it would be against its true object if it were not inhibited by the conflicting avoidance. In a conflict between sexual drive and a generalized fear of parental punishment for sexual behavior, the displaced sexual response may be made to stimuli which are sexual enough to elicit sexual response, but different enough from the mother that the avoidance is not too great. Such stimuli are often found in females of lower class or of different race. This is how it comes about that middle-class young men often seek sexual gratification in slum areas, although they do not attempt to make sexual advances to girls of their own class, a phenomenon pointed out in Chapter 7. When this occurs, an aggressive cast may be given to the sexual relationship, not only by contempt for the girls with whom the conflicted boys consort, but also as a response to the frustration of their sexual drives toward girls with whom they have closer contacts in their daily lives.

The net result of displacement is a highly complicated affair, including not only the original displaced response, the arousing effects of the minor provocation, the addition of aggression, but also factors based on the direction of aggression which has already been established in the conflicted person. As we have seen, aggression may be expressed against the self, if extrapunitiveness has been punished. Intropunitiveness is itself a product of approach-avoidance conflict, still further complicating the displacement. An example is a dependent response, displaced from rejecting parents to a teacher; the aggression which is also likely to be present as a result of the frustration of the dependency by the parents may operate in such a way that the dependent person controls the teacher through appealing to her pity, to her own desires to dominate, and to her professional responsibility to the student. The dependent student may then make excessive demands on the teacher in an extrapunitive way which in fact do punish the teacher. Or, if the student has developed intropunitive aggression, his dependency may take the form of self-abasement and an excessive display of his inferiority and need for external support, thus becoming dependent on the teacher and at the same time blaming himself for his failure to win the support of his parents. It should be noted that in these examples, there is also a substitution of the aggressive response itself; if one assumes that the aggressive response originally is one which directly injures or removes the object of the aggression, it will be seen that self-castigation and controlling dependency are both substitutions for this more direct aggression. Response substitution will be discussed in more detail below.

Learning Displaced Responses. There is one other factor which further complicates the picture of displacement. The displaced response is itself subject to learning, so that although initial displacements may be given to several different stimuli at various distances from the evoking stimulus, with various results so far as drive reduction is concerned, the conflicted person finally "hits" on one which reduces his conflicted drive with a minimum of punishment, and so reduces the anxious tension of the conflict. He learns to displace to that object the next time the conflict is aroused. This process may result in the learning of a discrimination between the object of the displacement and the evoking stimuli. For example, a boy who displaces aggression from his father to a teacher is likely to discover that the teacher does not punish him very much at all for his aggression, compared to his father. There are few people who are likely to react to aggression directed against them by a child as strongly as do the child's parents. The failure to be punished by teachers and other authority figures produces the feeling in the child that he can "get away with it" which itself may be a further justification for his contempt for the teachers who appear helpless to stop his attacks. The child's avoidance of aggression toward these figures, already low enough to permit the expression of aggression, is further reduced by the lack of punishment and the extinction of fear generalized from the father, so that aggression directed against the teachers becomes even stronger, relative to the amount of inhibition, than it was before the learning occurred. Teachers then become habitual targets of aggression as a result of the learning, so that a more stable response to the aggression conflict occurs after the initial trial and error.

Projection. There is another kind of substitution of cues which may also be based on the stimulus generalization model. Referring again to Figure 13, imagine that the baseline of degrees of similarity refers to degrees of similarity to the self, and that the gradients refer to the strength of the tendency to attach verbal labels or descriptions to behavior. Thus the figure describes the strength of the tendency to have certain thoughts about behavior, which conflicts with an avoidance or fear of thinking such thoughts. It can be seen from the model that the strongest tendency will be to ascribe conflicted behavior and thoughts to people who are sufficiently like the self to evoke the thoughts, and yet sufficiently different that the fear aroused by the thoughts is low. In other words, conflicts over thinking about behavior lead to the response of ascribing socially unacceptable behavior and ideas, elicited by the cues of one's own behavior, to other people who are somewhat like the self, and to not make such thought responses to one's own behavior. This kind of substitution in conflict is what is involved in *projection*. One can observe projection of aggression in the unreasonable fear of strangers, which implies that strangers are expected to behave aggressively. People who have such fears are usually not aware of aggressive feelings in themselves, but instead ascribe them to others, and therefore react with fear of others. Different social classes and races are frequently the objects of projection, in that the projector ascribes his unacceptable impulses and traits to them. To ascribe them to members of one's own race and class would be to say that people with whom one identifies himself behave in the unacceptable way; such a thought would evoke great anxiety. But people of other classes are sufficiently different so that a perception of unacceptable behavior in them does not evoke very much anxiety. Projection to other races and classes seems most likely to occur in people whose self-concept includes very strong definitions of one's class and racial indentification. This kind of projection is one source of prejudice. As in other frustrations, aggression is present and usually plays a role in the projection; the projector may either direct his aggression against the minority groups or prejudiced-against groups who are presumed to be so ill-behaved, or the aggression may also be projected, in the form of a fear that the minority group members are trying to "take over" one's society, or in secret ways are trying to harm one's own group.

Culturally Stereotyped Projection. Some projected ideas may become established ways of thinking in a culture. Whiting and Child in their study of several primitive societies found that some of them — those in which training in guilt was strongest — had folk myths in which the cause of an individual's illness was ascribed to hostile gods, ghosts, or spirits.[21] In American culture, the Negro is a stereotype of the primitive so far as aggression and sex is concerned; conflict over these drives is well established in our middle-class society, and the strong tendency to perceive Negroes as being primitively sexual and aggressive is probably at least in part attributable to projection of these common conflicts. As mentioned earlier, therefore, lynchings (of American Indians in the West, as well as of Negroes in the South) often included injury to the genitals of the victim, including castration.

Projection and Interpersonal Perception. Projection seems to occur particularly in conflicts concerning aggression and/or sex, and the guilt which these drives may produce. The anxiety-arousing thoughts may themselves be projected, as when a husband, irritated by his wife, feels that it is she who is being nasty or ill-tempered, or when the sexually aroused female interprets the behavior of others as "making passes." In our discussion of interpersonal perception in Chapters 5 and 8, we have seen how readily such misperceptions may occur; it was pointed out that misperceptions readily occur when drives are strong and the stimuli ambiguous; here we see that conflict can create the conditions under which drives become strong, and in addition, in which the individual fails to perceive his own drive state.

Not only may anxiety-arousing, drive-related thoughts be projected, but the guilt with which the individual may respond to his own drives may also be projected. That is, he may expect punishment from others, and may tend to misperceive others as intending to punish him. We have already discussed the development of this expression of guilt. What is added here is that the individual may fail to perceive his own guilt reactions as a result of the operation of conflict. Projection of conflicted drives and guilt may occur simultaneously, as in unfounded fears of being sexually assaulted, or in "magical thinking" such as that of the student who expects that his professors are simply waiting for an opportunity to pounce on him when he is unprepared — a fear that tends to occur when the student feels guilty for not having adequately done his work. The ironic aspect of projection is that the conflicted person who projects tends to behave in such ways as to confirm his projections. The man who preceives others as being unfairly competitive as a product of his own conflicts between achievement and dependency drives will respond to the perceived competition of others in the manner he has learned in the past — probably by vacillating between dependent passiveness and competitiveness, which will in turn either stimulate the competitiveness of others, or provide opportunities for them to secure advancements at his expense. This kind of interaction is most obvious where aggression is projected; perceiving others as aggressive, the conflicted person becomes defensively pugnacious, now able to express his aggression because it is justified as self-defense, and thus without evoking strong guilt and fear. The result is that he insults the objects of his projection who in turn react with counteraggression, thereby confirming the original misperception based on projection. As you can see from this example, interpersonal relations where conflicts are involved are quite fluid, and the operation of projection as a response to conflict is subtle; what looks like a case of simple hostility between two people often includes projection, and may be very difficult to distinguish from interpersonal antipathy arising from other causes. In both cases, enough justification for the hostility is likely to be produced.

Perhaps less dramatically, projection of guilt can be seen or inferred in such situations as when a mother has the feeling that she has failed in some way when her child has had an accident or become ill, or when people have the vague feeling that their good fortune or great fun will be punished in some way by an unexpected misfortune. The mother, who has almost certainly felt irritated and angered by her child on many occasions, is ready to interpret events as punishments for her anger. In this example, the projection operates in another way also: the illness of her child is an occurrence in reality of what her own aggressive drives against the child would have produced. The child's illness is thus seen as a product of her aggression, and she feels guilty for it. The child's illness is then seen both as an expression of her past anger at the child and as a punishment for it.

The relationship between projection, assumed similarity, and the self-concept was discussed in the last chapter. From what has been said here about the conflict model for projection, it is apparent that this kind of substitution is likely to occur most strongly in people whose thinking involves a stimulus generalization gradient extending from the self through other people of various degrees of similarity to the self. In other words, projection depends on the presence of assumed similarity, which means that the person operates on the stimulus generalization gradient that projection involves.

Reaction-Formation. Projection as a response to conflict usually is associated with another response to conflict known as *reaction-formation*.

This is a psychoanalytic concept referring to the observation that people sometimes go very far in behaving in ways which are directly opposite to the drives which are motivating them. The woman who has great hostility and contempt for her husband, which conflicts with her avoidance of aggression and her own drives for affection may behave in such a way as to give the appearance of being a very doting and loving wife, and the young man who is stingy but is afraid that others would reject him for it, spends his money overly freely and behaves as if he did not care at all about money. In reaction-formation, there may also be a tendency for the person to make frequent protestations of his feelings. The wife will frequently tell her husband and her acquaintances about how much she really loves her husband, and the young man may often say things like "It's just money," or "Money is not important to me." These protestations themselves are evidence for the conflict; they indicate that the subjects of loving one's husband or spending money are frequently in the thoughts of the "reaction-former," and we have already seen how such thoughts are motivated. Further, the character of the thoughts suggests their source. One does not protest his innocence unless he suspects that someone believes him guilty. Neither does one disclaim his generosity unless he suspects that he is not generous, any more than one walks across the street to avoid meeting someone who is not approaching.

Reaction-Formation and Projection. In projection, as we have seen, thoughts which occur to an individual as a result of his own drives are ascribed to others, rather than the self. In reaction-formation, the individual behaves in a manner opposite in character to those behaviors which are elicited by his feared drives. The two behaviors are usually combined in that while the thoughts aroused by the drives are projected, the projector displays nothing of the unacceptable drive in his own behavior, appearing highly virtuous relative to the others on whom he projects. The reaction-formation is itself a product of the conflict of drives, in which stimuli arising from one's own responses to his conflicted drive, stimuli which would arouse intense guilt or anxiety, are eliminated, thereby reducing the guilt or anxiety, by studiously avoiding such responses and responding instead in ways which are as different as possible from the anxiety-arousing responses.

The phenomenon of reaction-formation was observed in a study by Irving Sarnoff, who exposed one group of habitual reaction-formers to a situation designed to elicit strong feelings of sympathy and compassion, and another group to a situation designed to elicit milder feelings of the same nature.[22] Sarnoff had the first group see some excerpts from Saroyan's moving drama *Hello Out There*. The other group only heard the same excerpts in a recording. The experimenter reasoned that people whose reaction-formation was a result of affectional drives that conflict with anxiety over affectional behavior should be cynical, the cynicism serving as an opposite for their feelings of sympathy and affection. Therefore reaction-formers whose tender feelings are aroused should show more cynicism after the arousal than those whose conflicted feelings are only mildly aroused. This is what he found in the experiment: the group of reaction-formers who saw the Saroyan excerpts gave more cynical responses to test items after the arousal than the group that only heard the excerpts.

Aggression in Reaction-Formation. As in other frustrations, aggression is typically present as a part of reaction-formation. It may be manifested very subtly, however. Aggression may be implied, for example, in the boasts of the free-spender which implies an invidious comparison of his own virtuous behavior with that of other people, whom he tends to perceive as stingy as a result of his projection. Gossiping about the presumed socially unacceptable behavior of others is another form that this aggression may take. Less subtle is the aggression which is expressed through efforts to curb the activities of the objects of the projection. Overzealous attempts to restrict individual freedom in the interests of protecting people from the immorality which the projector is ready to perceive in them and not in his own reaction-forming behavior often has a note of triumphant aggression mixed with piety, not unlike the aggression apparent in the witch-hunts and religious inquisitions of bygone days.[23]

Reaction-Formation As a Response Substitution. Reaction-formation illustrates another important point: the stimuli which lie along the baseline of the conflict model need not necessarily be those external to the person. They may be internal stimuli produced by his own responses and thoughts to which anxiety is associated, with the points on the baseline referring to degrees of similarity to the response or thought with which the avoidance was initially associated. Reaction-formation occurs when the greatest response strength resulting from the action of approach and avoidance tendencies is at a point sufficiently removed from the conflicted response that the response at that point on the baseline produces very different stimuli—opposite in nature—from those which are produced by the response occurring at the left end of the figure.

Figure 14. Model of Response
Substitution for Aggression

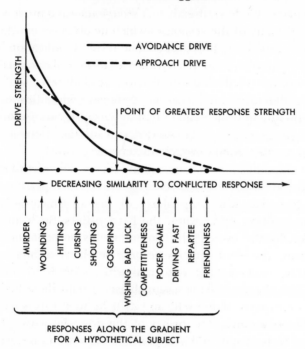

When the subject's impulse to destroy the object of his anger is aroused, so too is his avoidance of such an act. For him, gossiping and wishing bad luck for the object of his anger receive the greatest net response strength.

It can be seen that there is an important difference between reaction-formation and the other two conflict responses described, displacement and projection. In reaction-formation it is the response itself which evokes the avoidance drive, whereas in the other two it is not the response itself, but the object of the response which must be avoided. Thus in displacement, the individual may still behave aggressively, but not to the object which elicits avoidance. In projection, one may still have the anxiety-arousing thoughts, so long as they are ascribed to someone else. But in reaction-formation, it is the occurrence of the response itself, without regard to its object, which arouses the avoidance gradient. Displacement and projection are examples of cue substitutions, whereas reaction-formation is a response substitution. However, before presenting other kinds of response substitutions, one other cue-substitution should be mentioned.

Identification. We have already met *identification* as a process by which a child learns many of the responses which he observes in other significant people, particularly his parents. The term identification is used in psychology in another, but related, sense, to describe a particular response to anxiety. To distinguish the two, we shall refer to the anxiety response as defensive identification. Defensive identification is, in a sense, an opposite to projection, in that defensive identification involves ascribing to one's self the characteristics of another person or object, rather than ascribing one's own characteristics to others.

Defensive identification may take many forms. The identifier may act as if he shared in the traits or prestige of another person, and may therefore feel glad when the object of his identification has good fortune, and sad or upset when the hero suffers. Such an identifier takes personally the events which occur to his hero; if the hero is a national figure, the identifier may become defensive or angry when he hears his hero attacked. Another form in which identification is revealed is that in which the identifier reacts to objects, usually those he possesses, as if they were parts of himself, and as if he therefore shared in the traits of the possessions. The owner of the dog who wins a fight with another dog feels proud, and acts as if his dog's strength were a reflection of his own strength. Similarly, young men often go to great expense and trouble to make their cars more powerful than those of other people, and to demonstrate the superiority of their automobiles at every opportunity, as if the power of the car meant that the owner too possessed such power. If his car is criticized, even though it is a stock model exactly like several hundred thousand others manufactured during the same year, designed and built by people unknown and unrelated to the owner, he may nevertheless react as though he himself had been insulted.

A third form of identification is that in which the identifier attempts to behave exactly as if he were the object of his identification. This kind of identification is illustrated by a young man who began to model himself after the dead movie actor, James Dean. The youth wore the same kinds of clothes that Dean had worn in his movies, wore his hair the same way, and spent many hours a day before a mirror practicing smiles, facial expressions, and the gait of his hero. Although a very mild-mannered person, he began to behave in the antisocial ways typical of his hero's movie roles, and was eventually apprehended by the police who sent him for psychiatric treatment. During the course of his treatment it became apparent that the patient was a very shy man, greatly lacking in self-confidence and self-esteem. However, since acting like James Dean, he found that girls responded very favorably to him, as did other men his age, so that his role-playing operated to increase his self-confidence; it became the task of treatment to maintain the self-confidence while efforts were made to produce a reasonable integration of what he had learned in the role with the more socialized role performances which he had developed prior to this identification.

From this discussion it is apparent that identification often occurs in people who perceive themselves as lacking in characteristics which they value or which they feel they ought to have. Unable to behave in the admired ways themselves, either as a result of inhibitions or of lack of the personal resources, such as strength, intelligence, etc., they reduce their failure, and the anxiety associated with it, by including within their self-concepts the attributes of the object of their identification. The man who identifies with his car is one who very likely feels that he does not have as much personal power as he would like or ought to have, just as the patient's identification with James Dean grew out of a rejection of his image of himself as shy and socially inept. The people who are most likely to identify, because they so obviously lack the characteristics valued in their society, are children; we have already seen that identification with parents constitutes a major segment of the child's development, and forms the backbone of a large variety of his play activities. This suggests that developmental identification and defensive identification are closely associated, and in fact they may be merely different aspects of the same psychological process. It should be pointed out that identification is frequently an unconscious process; the identifier becomes like his model even though he may be unaware that he is doing so.

Defensive identification involves seeing as one's own the strength, power, or beauty of the hero, someone who is different but also not too unlike the self. The identifier cannot see these things in himself often because of earlier training in perceiving himself as inadequate or inferior, or because of strong guilt expressed intropunitively. The object and nature of identification provides some insights into the nature of of the underlying self-concept. One who identifies with a political figure, for example, is usually responding to unconscious feelings of personal powerlessness.

Identification, Projection, and Reaction-Formation. Identification and projection are alike in that they occur in situations in which the individual's perceptions of himself arouse anxiety, identification occurring where the self-perceptions would not include traits and characteristics which the individual requires, and projection occurring where self-perceptions would include traits and characteristics which the individual must not have. Just as projection often involves reaction-formation, so is identification close to reaction-formation in that the identifier acts as if he were the opposite of what he would otherwise see himself as. It is therefore not surprising that identification and projection often go hand in hand, such that the individual adds desirable characteristics to himself through identification and subtracts the undesirable through projection. The young woman who does not perceive herself as being as beautiful as she must be in order to receive affection and regard identifies with a movie star whose beauty is renowned, imitates her mannerisms and her styling, and projects by perceiving her peers as lacking grace and good looks, and resorting to sham and tricks in order to attract the attention of men. Both of these reactions involve a stimulus generalization gradient of similarity to the self, so that both are likely to be found in conflicted people in whom assumed similarity constitutes a salient dimension or schema for organizing their experiences.

Response Substitutions

Under the heading of substitute response, several related behaviors should be discussed, aside from the already mentioned reaction-formation. Included here are compensation, sublimation, regression, and rationalization.

Compensation. *Compensation* occurs when a person, frustrated by conflict, devotes his energies to behaving in ways similar to the frustrated behavior, but different enough so that avoidance is not aroused. The compensatory behavior is thus a substitute for the frustrated responses. However, the substitution is not necessarily on the basis of similarity of the responses involved. It is more usually related to the frustrated response as a result of the institutionalized progressions toward certain goals which are a part of the culture. In discussing the goal-gradient model, it was mentioned that distance from the goal is not necessarily in terms of linear measurements, but may be in terms of the hurdles which must be passed, the hurdles being the accepted sequences characteristic of the culture. In compensation, the individual may substitute for the feared goal response, a response which usually leads to the goal, but is far enough away so that it does not evoke the fear. A young man afraid of marriage may compensate by specializing in dating and courting, becoming a "man about town." Sometimes the substituted response is one which is symbolic of the goal because it occurs so frequently in connection with the goal, serving thus as a secondary reinforcer. This is illustrated by the compensatory emphasis on dancing skill in a woman who is fearful of intimate social contact with men. Another example of this is that of the youth who strives for athletic prowess because such success is associated with heterosexual success. And finally, the substitution may be a result of response similarity. The unmarried woman who provides room, board, and mothering to college students illustrates such a compensation. Dancing in the example of the compensating sexually inhibited girl can also involve similarity of response to the feared goal; dancing is a rhythmic heterosexual activity bearing very obvious similarities to sexual intercourse. In the same way the compensating athlete mentioned as an example might specialize in body contact sports, such as football or wrestling, because of the similarity between such activities and the conflicted responses.

Compensation and Fantasy. These examples of compensation may remind you of the discussion of fantasy in Chapter 5. There is a connection. Compensation may be thought of as acted out fantasy, in the sense that the person creates situations and stimuli in the real world which are inconsistent with and contradictory to those arising from his own thoughts, feelings, experiences, and cues denoting inferiority and failure, which arouse anxiety and self-blame.

One of the most apparent characteristics of compensation is that it seems obviously overdone. The man whose interests in athletic activities are the product of compensation seems to put forth much more energy and interest in such activities than the man whose interest is only a product of the way in which his activity and gregariousness drives have been socialized. The compensator often acts as if he were trying to prove something to himself, and as if the only way to do it is by proving it to the world. In a sense, there is more than the apparent rewards and punishments dependent on the success of the activity, when compensation is present. The young woman devotes so much attention to her dancing, not only because success brings her the usual compliments, but also because failure would mean that she was incapable of being desirable to a man. To take another example, let us compare the reactions of two amateurs to losing the local baseball tournament. One of them, whose interest and enjoyment of playing is the result of past reinforcements for athletic skill, together with a high activity drive, feels sad about the loss, but nevertheless enjoyed the game and the season, and accepts the implication that he is not the best ballplayer in the locality. He plays ball not in order to establish self-esteem where it is lacking, but for other reasons. The other player, however, is compensating; being a successful ballplayer would end the doubt he feels and he suspects others feel, that he may be inadequate as a male—a sissy. He reacts much more emotionally to the loss of the game, because to him it means not only that he is not the best player, but also that he is not adequate as a man. It is this sense that one may say that more than the usual rewards are riding on the success of a compensatory activity, because more than the usual motives are involved. In effect, the compensator has unusually high motivation for the activity, and this becomes apparent in what would otherwise be a strangely gross overreaction to the failure of the compensatory activity. Indeed, one indication of compensation is the massiveness of the emotional response when the activity results in failure.

Compensation as a Social Value. Compensation occupies a particularly valued place in our society. The belief is frequently expressed that everyone can excel in some activity, and teachers are often urged to find for each student the thing that he can do best, not only in order to encourage the best utilization of talent but also in order to help each student compensate for his failures and avoid feelings of inadequacy. Both Theodore Roosevelt and Franklin Roosevelt are cultural heroes at least in part because they compensated so successfully, and their compensations are held up to children as models for them to emulate. As a result, the successful compensator is likely to be highly rewarded, not only by the reduction of his own anxiety as a result of the success he has achieved, but also by the approval of others simply for the fact of compensating. Indeed, we are often tempted to accord success where it is not strictly deserved, if the individual is obviously compensating for a physical defect.

Obviously people develop interests in those activities in which they are most consistently rewarded, usually by achieving success. The student who does well in mathematics comes to prefer it over his other courses (and by so doing, increases the likelihood of further success, because he will tend to study math more). However, when the activity comes to have other values associated with it, because it serves as a substitute for drive-instigated responses which are frustrated, then it may be called a compensation. In practice, there is no sharp line between a "normal" interest and compensation; most people discover, as they become interested in some occupation or hobby, that the activity brings rewards which they had not expected. The student who enters into extracurricular activities because he has learned to find interpersonal rewards of approval and friendship in this way may find, as he becomes involved, that through such activities he can feel that he is getting much of what college has to offer, even though he gets low grades in his courses. Some compensatory values have thus become attached to his extracurricular interests which may become more and more significant as his school work declines in quality and his need to avoid the cues for feelings of failure increases.

Sublimation. We have already noted a connection between compensation in the real world and compensation in thought. When compensation occurs through the socialized and creative expression of fantasy in the real world — that is, through writing, acting, painting, and other creative pursuits which involve the translation of imaginative activity into shared social terms, it is called *sublimation*. Sublimation, then, is a kind of compensation in which artistic production is the compensatory *activity*; the content and nature of the artistic production itself is a product of the compensatory *fantasy* of the artist.[24] This is not to say that all art is the produce of conflict, and all artists are sublimating. It is possible that where creative activities in a talented person have been reinforced in the past, art naturally becomes a preferred occupation which makes use of the artist's habits of problem-solving through thinking. It is an old controversy, as yet unsolved, as to whether all art is sublimation; the most that can be said here is that artists, like all other people, are conflicted, making it highly probable that at least to some extent, their art involves sublimation. Like the fantasies discussed in Chapter 5, the artistic product reflects the creator's motivations. However, it would be foolish to think of art, or any other human behavior, as having only one "reason" or "cause." There are usually a large number of variables operating to determine any particular response, and each response usually includes several different sources of reinforcement, as indicated by the complexities which exist in displacement, projection, identification, and the other behaviors already discussed.

Regression. We have already discussed one aspect of *regression* as an instrumental response to frustration. It was said to occur when a later learned response to a stimulus, if not followed by reinforcement, is extinguished and an earlier learned response which had been lower in the response hierarchy occurs during the unreeling of trial-and-error responses, as the individual continues to emit responses until some drive reduction occurs. Regression in this sense can, however, become non-instrumental. The individual may find that an earlier learned response may not solve his present problem, but that it does involve other values or reinforcements. For example, after trying to solve a difficult problem, a student may engage in instrumental regression by asking someone —a classmate or a teacher—for help. Dependent asking for help is, of course, a response learned earlier than the intellectual skills the student had been using in his unsuccessful efforts to solve the problem alone. So long as this regression results in a solution, it may be considered to be an instrumental response. However, should the student find that by asking for help from the teacher, he receives also the attention and interest of the teacher, and his "moral support," any existing anxieties associated with "being on his own" may be reduced, and noninstrumental values have been thereby added to the regressive behavior. In addition, the fact of appealing for help produces cues in the student which are similar to the cues which characterized his earlier, more dependent life. These cues are likely to elicit other responses which were characteristic of earlier times, adding further to the reduction of anxiety associated with his more mature but more problematical existence. Thus regression in one response is likely to spread to include larger and larger segments of the individual's response repertoire.

Variables in Regression. The occurrence of regressive behavior seems to depend on a number of things. It presupposes greater avoidance associated with a later response than with an earlier one. It also suggests that mature ways of behaving do not bring more reinforcement than did earlier responses.[25] Finally, regression requires the presence of cues to which earlier responses were learned.

Regression is particularly likely to occur when earlier responses are highly resistant to extinction as a result of partial reinforcement, and later-learned responses are only slightly stronger, so that relatively few failures of the later response may result in the barely less strong regressive response appearing in behavior.[26] Of course, partial reinforcement implies that the individual did not always meet with success when he gave the response in childhood. This means that regression is more likely to occur in people whose childhood included enough reinforcements to maintain the response, but not enough to permit its extinction when conditions changed. It is not surprising, then, that regression usually occurs where the background of childhood includes much evidence of inconsistency and frustration of the person's drives.

Coupled with this is the principle that regression is more likely to occur where an earlier learned response was not extinguished, but rather was inhibited because of fear associated with it. When a parent punishes her child for crying, because she feels that he is old enough for more mature reactions, there is likely to be a reduction in crying. However, the reduction is not an extinction of the crying, but is rather an inhibition—usually one in which some response incompatible with crying is attached to the cues of the beginning crying response. Thus the crying response must begin before the incompatible response, which blocks its continuance, can occur. In adulthood, conditions may arise which elicit the inhibited response, and in which the conditions which support the inhibitions themselves are not present. Instead of a mother ready to punish, the individual may be in the presence of a sympathetic and accepting peer. Or the inhibition itself, such as an attitude of bravado, may in adulthood be punished instead of rewarded, so that it is weakened. Similarly, temper tantrums and rages in children may be inhibited by punishment from the parents, which results in associating fear or other incompatible responses to the cues of incipient temper outbursts. In adulthood, when anger is aroused in the presence of business subordinates, who are totally unlike the superior parents who punished the temper tantrums in childhood, the inhibition response may not be elicited, and the regressive temper tantrum will appear in behavior.

From this discussion it can be seen that regressive behavior is more likely to occur in people whose childhood may be characterized by inconsistent discipline in which inhibitions associated with childish responses were established. Regression will thus occur in the adult when the inhibiting responses are either no longer elicited or are in fact punished, while the cues for the childish responses are presented.

Rationalization. The last response to conflict which will be discussed is that of *rationalization*. At its simplest, rationalization refers to the giving of inadequate explanations of one's behavior. Like projection and identification, it is a response involving thought, rather than a conflict response in overt muscular behavior. As such, it may exist on the cognitive level along with any of the conflict responses which occur on the overt behavioral level. As identification and projection involve altered thoughts about the self, so does rationalization. In rationalization, the basic conflict is between an individual's drive to avoid behavior the labeling of which would result in anxiety, and the drive to engage in the conflicted behavior. Usually rationalization has reference to the motives with which responses are associated; it consists of ascribing an acceptable motive to behavior which is motivated by drives which are unacceptable as a result of past training. This suggests that rationalization is likely to occur where inhibitions in childhood have been attached to accounts of why certain responses occur, rather than to responses themselves. For example, a child may learn that it is all right to break his brother's toys if it was an accident resulting from his efforts to teach his brother how to play with them, but it is punishable to break toys in anger. Such a child is learning that the behavior is acceptable if a "right" account in words and thoughts is attached to it.

A person is often thought of as rationalizing when he consistently accounts for his behavior in terms of inescapable environmental pressures, failing to include in his account the personal motives which also play a part. However, rationalization has more to it than that. Let us first note that it is impossible for anyone to give a complete accounting of all the determinants of any particular behavior. He would have to include in such an accounting a statement of all the cues which were present when the behavior occurred, the nature of the learning he has had in relation to those cues, a description of the nature and origin of the various drives which were present in him at the time, a statement about the training practices of his parents which resulted in his acquisition of the response and motives in question, and then an accounting of the historical and social roots of the beliefs and values which guided his parents in their training. Obviously, no one goes into such an involved and detailed explanation, partly because he does not have the necessary information, and partly because it involves more of an answer to the question "why" than anyone expects or wants of him. What gets left out of this complete explanation when an answer is given to the question of "why"? What determines what gets left out? Most obviously, what gets left out includes those determinants that the responder doesn't know about. He may not know about them either because he has not learned them, and perhaps no one else has, considering the lack of completeness of our knowledge about the determinants of behavior. He may also not know about some determinants because to learn about them—to put them into words—may involve the production of verbal cues to anxiety. He has failed to learn such information because the learning produces an increase, rather than a decrease, in drive level. Other things get left out of the explanation because the responder does not think that his questioner is interested in them; they are irrelevant. In effect, when he learned to give answers to the "why" question to his parents, he did not learn to include such details. In addition, some items are excluded because the responder suspects that to communicate them might alienate his hearers; he might tell them things about himself which he knows are socially undesirable, and his hearers might reject him as a result. Finally, some things are left out because the responder cannot put them into words; to do so would be to produce cues to which anxiety is attached. In other words, some of the full answer is excluded from the self-concept. Naturally, those parts of the full explanation get left out which are most anxiety-arousing. The result is an incomplete answer, and therefore necessarily a rationalization. In this sense, rationalization is not an occasional thing. It exists whenever explanations are given, and particularly for responses whose motives are not quite socially acceptable. When asked why he entered the contest, no one answers, "Because I have a very strong achievement drive as a result of the way my parents made affection dependent upon doing things for myself." The more typical answer is, "Because the prize is really something I could use." In other words, rationalization does not necessarily involve the telling of untrue things, except in the sense that anything less than the whole truth, hardly to be expected from anyone who is not omniscient, is untruth. Rationalization is more often a partial truth, in which that which is unsaid is the part that would elicit anxiety.

As was mentioned above, rationalization often exists in company with other responses to conflict. The displacing husband who explodes in response to a relatively slight cue for aggression rationalizes his anger by pointing to provocation by his wife. The identifier rationalizes his imitation of his hero by pointing to the social good which would exist if everyone were like the hero.

Repression and Inhibition

In these responses to conflict, nothing has been said about the conflicted individual's knowledge or awareness of what he is doing, although the implication is apparent, particularly in projection, rationalization, and identification, that he is not conscious of what he is doing. To be conscious would mean that he would necessarily be producing the very thoughts and ideas about himself which the high avoidance gradient makes it impossible for him to do. The avoidance of such thoughts is called *repression*. It is also true in displacement, reaction-formation, sublimation, compensation, and regression, although to a lesser extent, that thought about the conflict and the response to the conflict is lacking or incomplete. However, it may not necessarily be so in these cases; one may be quite aware that he is displacing (and feel guilty about it, which usually contributes to the frustration which results in still further displacement). However, a process akin to repression enters into these behaviors in a different way; the response which is blocked by the higher avoidance gradient may be said to be *inhibited*. When a response becomes conflicted because it is followed by the pain of punishment, or guilt, the response becomes a cue for avoidance motives. It is the conflicted response itself which serves as the stimulus for the avoidance which results in the inhibition of the response, and the occurrence of the displacement, reaction-formation, sublimation, compensation, or regression. Thus it may be said that the original response has been inhibited; thought about the response may or may not be repressed in these cases. Conversely, in projection, rationalization, and identification, thoughts are repressed, but the responses which serve as the cues for the thoughts are not necessarily inhibited. The man who ascribes his hostile drives to others may behave in an aggressive manner, and the rationalizer usually makes the punished response, but distorts the reasons for it. In other words, repression of thoughts or inhibition of actions is present in all of the conflict responses mentioned, and both may be present at the same time.

Repression was very likely Freud's most important contribution, and the exploration of the concept of repression is a cornerstone of psychoanalytic theory.[27] Freud noted two types of repression. Primary repression was used to describe the situation in which the individual fails to become conscious of stimuli which are present, although unconscious responses may be made to them. Freud designated as secondary repression, or after-expulsion, the situation in which ideas, once conscious, are no longer conscious, although they continue to influence behavior. We have already noted the kinds of experiences which led Freud to the concept of unconsciousness; repression is the means by which he accounted for the existence of unconscious phenomena, and is therefore based on the same clinical experiences that led him to investigate "the unconscious." Freud did much of his clinical work with neurotic patients who are diagnosed as being hysterics, a neurotic behavior pattern in which some normal function of the individual becomes inoperative, such as the responses of an arm or leg, or the memory, although no physical pathology in the response system is found. Freud explained behaviors such as amnesia, nonorganically caused paralyses, seizures, and anesthesias as the results of repression of certain thoughts which serve as cues for these body functions, which are therefore inhibited.

Mechanisms of Repression and Inhibition. Several of the mechanisms which account for Freud's observations of primary and secondary repression have been presented in various sections of this book. These mechanisms will be reviewed briefly here.

We have seen that repression may play a role in perception through a number of mechanisms: these include the failure to perceive accurately because the perceiver may not have acquired the appropriate perceptual responses, either as a result of a simple failure of opportunity to acquire them or because they were associated with pain, so that they were not learned as a way of avoiding fear. In addition, it has been noted the perception may fail to occur correctly because of fear that might be elicited by the already acquired correct perceptual responses. It was also noted that discrimination of perceptual stimuli at low intensities can occur through autonomic responses, even though verbal recognition does not occur. Finally, the process of sensory gating, in which peripheral neurons fail to transmit impulses reporting environmental events to which the organism is not "set" or "attending," because its motivational state is eliciting other, incompatible responses, may account for the operation of failures to perceive.

In the domain of thought, we have seen that a person may fail to think certain thoughts because he has not acquired the symbols for thinking, or because to think them would produce anxiety. In addition, it was seen that the manifest content of dreams is a disguise for the latent content which cannot be dreamed directly. These are examples of repression in thought.

It has also been noted that many events which occur in childhood are unconscious, in the sense that the child cannot think about them later because they occurred when he was too young to symbolize the events adequately. An example of this is the failure of parents to label sexual body parts and activities, leaving their children unable to think about sex. This seems to be very much like what Freud meant by primary repression.

Finally, thoughts about the self may be repressed and thus not included in the self-concept, because they are stimuli for fear or anxiety, and so are not produced. There are thus many ways in which thoughts may be repressed, in the sense that when they fail to occur, the individual does not suffer the anxiety with which he would respond to the stimuli of the thoughts.

In the realm of nonthought responses, we have also seen operating the factors which produce inhibition. For example, we have noted that aggression may be turned inward, if extrapunitiveness was punished.

This is an example of the inhibition of hostility toward the frustrating agent. Sexual responses may be inhibited because they come to serve as cues for fear, as a result of punishment for sexual behavior. And in this chapter, we have explored in some detail the ways in which responses become modified under conditions of conflict. In Freud's terms, it could be said that these responses are inhibited.

A Model of Repression. These mechanisms clarify the meaning of the term repression. Repression appears to refer to a failure to make a particular response of labeling one's behaviors, wishes, and drives, a failure which is reinforced by the reduction of anxiety or fear which occurs when the thought response does not occur. In this sense, repressing is itself a response—a response of not responding. In operation, the repressive response is a reaction to the cues of fear or anxiety which are elicited by the initial cues of a punished response. The model in Figure 15 may make this clearer.

Figure 15. Repression and Inhibition

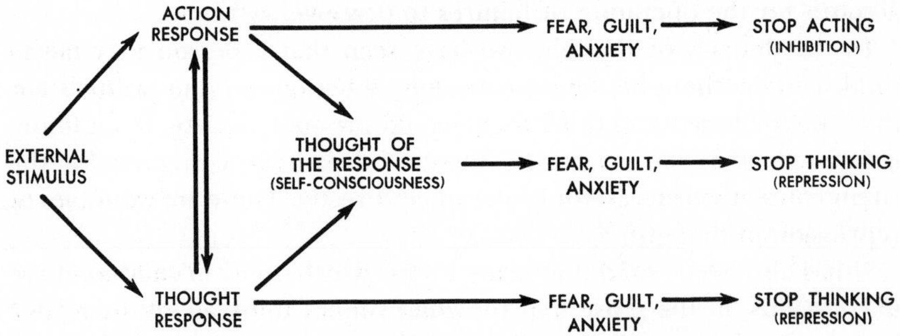

THE ARROWS GO FROM STIMULI TO RESPONSES;
EACH STEP IN THE CHAINS, EXCEPT FOR THE FIRST AND
LAST, INVOLVE CUE-PRODUCING RESPONSES.

An external stimulus might cue off either an action response or a thought response, or both. An action response may in turn cue off a thought response, and vice versa. Either the thought or the action can also cue off an awareness or consciousness of the response. Any of the three (action, thought, or awareness) can stimulate fear, guilt, or anxiety, which in turn cues off the "stop acting" or "stop thinking" responses, which therefore reduce the fear, guilt, or anxiety. Thus the presence of inhibition or repression always implies a tendency toward the inhibited act or repressed idea, and fear, guilt, or anxiety in connection with the act or idea.

It can be seen in the figure that the final repressive-inhibitory response cannot occur unless at least some anxiety is present, for it is the anxiety which serves as the cue for the final response of "not responding." When this final response occurs, it eliminates the stimuli of the thoughts or actions which cue off the anxiety. When these stimuli no longer occur, because of the "stop thinking or acting" response, the anxiety is reduced, thus reinforcing the repression and/or inhibition responses. Note that the thought or the action does not have to occur in its entirety in order for the repression-inhibition chain of events to occur; if only the initial phases or preparatory muscle tensions of the punished response occur, these may be enough to cue off the anxiety, which in turn cues off the repression. Thus the anxiety produced may seem very great in comparison to the magnitude of the abortive response that elicited it. Similarly, it may be sufficient, once overlearning has occurred, only for very slight anxiety to occur—again, only the preparatory tensions—to cue off the response of repressing. In slow motion, this chain of events may be observed in a conversation that chances to touch upon an unpleasant subject which raises anxiety in the participants, anxiety which is then reduced when one of them makes some effort to change the topic in order to avoid the discomfort he feels.

The "not responding" response may in itself be complex. One may arrange to stop thinking about something unpleasant by engaging in some activity which necessarily diverts his attention and occupies his thoughts with other, non-anxiety-arousing, ideas. This is what is implied when the conversationalist mentioned above suggests a game of tennis as a way of staying away from the upsetting subject. One of the functions of a hobby is to occupy one's thoughts with things in such a way that one cannot produce upsetting thoughts. In this sense it may be said that engaging in a hobby is a means of repressing. The same process may be seen in the compensatory fantasy described in Chapter 5, in which one imagines situations which are different from the one he finds himself in, the process being reinforced by a reduction in anxiety that occurs when the anxiety-arousing cues are blotted out by the fantasy. Figure 15 describes how it is that an aroused response potential fails to occur; our discussion of the substitute responses tells us how it comes about that other responses occur in place of the aroused response potential. Thus all the substitutions, of which compensatory fantasy and activity are examples, serve as means of repressing.

Repression As a Response to Internal Events. There is one other point that should be stressed in connection with repression: it may be seen from the figure that repression is a response to one's own behavior, rather than to environmental stimuli directly. Where repression occurs, one can then infer the potential for making a response that has been punished in the past. One does not repress a response which he is unlikely to make just as he does not fear events that are not likely to occur. This is what is meant by the statement that repression always implies a motivation to perform the repressed response. This is suggested by experiments on conflict in animals. In such experiments it has been found that the anxiety displayed by the conflicted experimental animals is much more resistant to extinction than are simple conditioned fears, or fears in response to environmental frustrations. The reason seems to be that in conflict situations it is the animals' own behavior that serves as the cue for fear or anxiety. These cues may be produced by the animal even in extinction trials without the experimenter knowing it. In simple conditioned fear, the cues for fear are probably presented much less frequently, and the animal can avoid such external cues, whereas he cannot readily avoid those produced by his own internal drives.

Individual Differences in Repression. This presentation of repression suggests that repressing is a response which people may learn to various degrees, depending in part on the frequency with which they respond with anxiety, and the strength of their habits of thinking anxiety-arousing thoughts, and perhaps also depending on childhood training practices which encourage this kind of response to anxiety. It is also a response which is readily overlearned. In other words, repression may be a trait that some people show to a great extent, while others may repress very little. There is much evidence to support this. It has been found that some people have strong tendencies to "forget" verbal material that has been associated with punishment, while others seem to remember such material well, although they may have stronger tendencies to forget non-anxiety-arousing material. In other words, given sets of words, some of which are cues for anxiety, the habitual repressor and the nonrepressor may remember about the same number of words, but the former will remember more of the non-anxiety-arousing words than the latter, and the latter group may remember more of the anxiety-arousing ones.[28] A person who represses on one list is also likely to repress in other situations, indicating that repression is a fairly reliable general trait.

Symptoms of Repression. As was pointed out above, repression is a feature of responses to conflict which result in either cue-substitution or response-substitution. In addition, repression may include the acquisition of responses which function as ways of maintaining the repression by keeping the person occupied with behaviors that are inconsistent with those that arouse anxiety. Hobbies have been mentioned as one kind of repressing response. Others might include reading as an escape through fantasy, or engaging in some simple mechanical task to which one may devote his attention and which does not arouse anxiety, such as cleaning silverware, washing the car, or playing cards. Withdrawal from the cues which elicit the anxiety-arousing response may also serve to maintain repression, and this withdrawal may vary from simple flight to very complicated life patterns which result in the isolation of the individual from the situations which are likely to arouse fear or conflicted drives. The selection of an occupation that takes one away from his usual environment, or in which one works in a narrowly prescribed area which allows for little contact with other people may be rewarding in part at least through the avoidance of anxiety which might be stimulated by people or by familiar situations and environments. Of course, the selection of occupations involves many other factors, such as those involving identification with the parents, the nature of the job market and the social and financial rewards involved, the successes the individual has found in various related activities, and his aptitudes and abilities. But it is also true that considerations of anxiety and avoidance may also play a part in how rewarding a person finds various kinds of activities. In sum, there is a large variety of behaviors which indicate the presence of repression; such behaviors may be referred to as symptoms of repression.

Latent and Manifest Anxiety. Repression and the other responses to anxiety and conflict described in this chapter all function to keep anxiety at a low level. When these responses are well learned to the cues of anxiety or fear, the amount of anxiety which actually occurs is very small, because only minimal cues are necessary to elicit well-learned responses. However, if the individual is prevented from reacting in these learned ways to the cues of anxiety, either because of the interpersonal situation in which he finds himself (as when a companion points out that he is displacing or rationalizing, or he is not permitted to "forget" uncomfortable ideas by being constantly reminded of them by others), or through hypnotic intervention in which the hypnotist makes suggestions that prevent the response, the anxiety may occur with its full force, and be manifested in overt behavior through perspiring, nervousness, jumpiness, and feelings of panic. This appearance of the otherwise avoided anxiety provides the reason for referring to the anxiety which motivates repression and the other behaviors described as *latent.* This does not mean that the anxiety is present, hiding in some manner, when the individual represses or projects; rather, it means that he is potentially capable of suffering a high anxiety drive if he is deprived of his anxiety-reducing response. This was demonstrated in clinical studies of fear in World War II in which it was found that fear and anxiety seemed to be greatest in those situations in which there was nothing the men could do about the situation; when they had to be idle while in danger, or could not fight back when being attacked, they reported much more fear than when they could do something that could reduce the fear.[29] In laboratory experiments it has been found that sheep that have been exposed to conflict situations do not show "neurotic" behaviors if the conditions of the conflict allow the animals plenty of room in a large pen, so that they can do things that will reduce the conflicting forces.[30] In general, animal research has shown that the breakdown of learned behaviors as a result of fear and conflict occurs mostly when the experimental animals are closely confined in such a way that they cannot make anxiety-reducing responses.

Some people, however, are deprived of anxiety-reducing responses to conflict simply because they were not given the opportunity to learn them. A parent who forbids her child from displacing aggression, but also continually reminds the child of its "badness" so that repression cannot occur, and who at the same time prevents projection by presenting herself as a model of perfect morality, is arranging conditions in such a way that her child cannot learn the responses described in this chapter. Such a child is likely to experience anxiety directly. It has already been indicated that people differ in the extent to which they characteristically respond to anxiety with repression; those who are low in repression are people who experience anxiety without being able to avoid it. Another factor that determines the extent to which anxiety will occur directly is included in the term *ego strength.* The individual who has learned to perceive, think, and respond to himself accurately, and whose habits of reality testing are very strong would find it difficult to repress, displace, project, and so forth, because all of these behaviors involve a misperception or a failure to label events correctly. In some sense, they are all distortions of reality. The person whose reality testing is too good to permit such distortions, even though it means that he will experience anxiety, is described as one with high ego strength. There are, then, several variables which operate such that many people experience anxiety directly when the appropriate cues are present, and reveal it in their nervous behavior. And like the animals in the experiments on conflict whose confinement prevents the occurrence of anxiety-reducing responses, these people also show a breakdown of learned habits and a deterioration of motor skills in complex tasks. It has already been indicated that the reason for this seems to be that in complex performances, all the responses which occur, both relevant and irrelevant to the task, become greatly strengthened by the high drive state until they interfere with each other, producing a decrement in performance. Among the responses which probably increase in strength and which interfere with performance are self-responses. The highly anxious subject becomes overly self-conscious and attends too much to internal cues to do a good job. As a person who has learned to respond in thought and perception accurately to cues, the cues produced by high anxiety drive become the focus of his attention, unlike the repressor who stops thinking about his internal responses. As we have seen, anxiety is a reaction to one's own incipient responses. While the repressor therefore ceases to produce the incipient responses, and is not aware of their existence, the nonrepressor is aware of the incipient responses that produce anxiety responses which he does not stop by repressing. As a result, the highly anxious person who does not repress tends to be introspective, self-doubting, self-conscious, and inept in complex tasks when he is anxious. This does not mean that such a person is perfectly aware of the conditions in his experience which are responsible for his acquisition of fear responses to certain ideas and responses; he may have no more insight into the development of his personality than one who represses, because the significant events which shaped his personality may have occurred before he had the verbal skills to label them or understand what was going on. And further, repression is a readily learned response. One may be very low in the tendency to repress, but this does not mean that repression never occurs. It may simply be less frequently and less strongly given in response to the cues of anxiety.

Determinants of Choice of Conflict Response

It has been implied in this discussion of responses to conflict and anxiety that people vary in the extent to which they show the responses described. Why one person is a habitual rationalizer, while another tends to develop strong identifications, a third represses extensively, and a fourth experiences his anxiety overtly is a question of the conditions in which these alternative responses are learned. Each is capable of producing a reduction in anxiety, either through avoiding the anxiety-arousing cues, or through a substitute response which reduces the high drive states produced by conflicting motives. Thus all of these behaviors can be reinforced. Where then do individual differences in reactions to conflict and anxiety originate?

Social Class and Related Factors. It must be admitted at the outset that there has been very little research in psychology on the parental training practices which lead to the development of particular responses to anxiety. There is some recent work by Miller and Swanson who found that more severe parental training practices (arbitrary demands for obedience, physical punishment, severe discipline in combination with few rewards) result in a tendency for high-school age boys to repress quite completely references to failure, after failure anxiety was created in them experimentally.[31] The boys were made to believe that they had failed aptitude tests related to their occupational aspirations, after which they were asked to compose endings to stories about failure. The boys who had had the severe disciplinary background frequently ended the stories in such a way as to ignore completely the failure of the character. For example, a story about a boy who, after practicing his music very hard, is told by his teacher that he lacks talent, might be ended by the severely disciplined boys by making the boy suddenly into a musical success with a concert at Carnegie Hall. Miller and Swanson call this kind of massive repression of the cues of failure *denial*, and point out that such a reaction does a great deal of violence to reality. They reasoned further that denial should be great in people whose conditions of life are so difficult that the factors conducive to good reality testing would not be operating; such conditions probably exist more often in the lower socioeconomic class than in the middle class, and in fact they did find that among boys of comparable intelligence, the lowerclass boys showed denial more than the middleclass boys. This finding is of particular interest because it points out the role of intelligence in responding to anxiety. The lowerclass boys of high intelligence showed denial no more frequently than did the middleclass boys. Apparently intelligence helps either in developing reality testing, or by permitting the child to respond to a bad environment in a way that does not involve massive withdrawal or denial.

In contrast to lowerclass boys who have experienced harsh discipline, middleclass boys and those whose discipline has been relatively benign (little punishment, many rewards, and reasonable requests for obedience) show more restricted repression which does less violence to reality. This was shown in an experiment using the Zeigarnik effect, named for the psychologist who first developed the procedure.[32] In the experiment, boys were given a large number of tests which they thought were tests of their aptitudes for the occupations they wanted to have. The boys were allowed to finish some of the tests, but were not permitted to finish others, giving them the impression that they had failed the uncompleted ones. The subjects were later asked to recall the names of all the tests. It was found that repression, defined as the tendency to remember the completed tasks more than the uncompleted ones, was more common among the middleclass boys whose discipline had been nonphysical in nature.[33]

Training Situations. It has already been mentioned that the way in which punishment is administered, or more correctly, the particular behaviors punished, may determine whether a child will tend to displace, identify, or project, or respond with one of the response substitutions. If the child is punished, not for a particular act, but rather for selecting a forbidden object for the act, he is likely to learn to displace. For example, if a child is punished for hitting only when his anger is directed against his parents, but not when it is directed against playmates (a likely experience, because many fights among children take place without the parents' knowledge), one would expect that he would learn displacement more easily than the child who is never permitted to hit, regardless of the object.

Rationalization. On the other hand, a child's punishment might be more dependent on his motive than on the act itself. That is, a child might perform the same act on several different occasions, but be punished only at those times that his motive is one which the parents consider reprehensible, and not at the times that he has an acceptable motive. The parents might chastise a boy for fighting in general, but if he claims self-defense, or tells his parents that the other boy hit him first, or was trying to take away his bike, he would not be punished by them. In repeated situations like this, the boy will learn a discrimination between when fighting is acceptable and when it is not, and the difference will depend on the motives involved. In other words, the child learns that he is punished not for bad acts, but for bad motives or reasons. Such a child is more likely to learn to rationalize than would a child who is punished for his acts regardless of the motive.

Projection. Suppose that a child has "gotten into" things that he is not supposed to touch, and is punished by his mother, and that on another occasion he observes his sister do the same things, with the consequence that she is punished but he is not. These may be the conditions for the child to learn that it is not the act or the object of the act which is punishable, but rather the agent. It seems reasonable that this kind of experience would incline the child toward projection, in which bad things are blamed on others. Such training would also lead to identification, in which the self as agent is rejected and another self acquired, at least in part. We have already seen how identification functions to prevent the child from being the agent of punishable actions.

In the example given above, of the boy who escapes punishment for fighting when he can give a good reason for the fight, we may also see training in projection, in that the child is ascribing the forbidden behavior to the other child and thus escaping punishment. Such a situation therefore involves multiple learnings, and it is apparent that many reactions to conflict and anxiety, learned in such complex situations, are themselves mixed, involving several of the kinds of reactions discussed.

Another factor which may play a part in both projection and rationalization is the practice an individual has had in lying in childhood. Although there is no evidence on this, it seems reasonable to suppose that the child who has been reinforced for blaming his transgressions on others, or for making up a valid excuse for his transgression, would have acquired some of the skills involved in rationalization and projection. He would have developed a sensitivity to the presence of "possible" excuses, or to the presence of any evidence he could seize to support his claim — a sensitivity which might then shade into actual conviction that others are really to blame, or that one's stated motives are in fact the only ones. Such commonality of training in rationalization and projection may be the reason that these two behaviors go together, in that rationalization implies a denial of blame, and projection puts the blame elsewhere.

The training situations described above account for the maintenance and development of projection. But there is some reason to think that the basic phenomenon on which these training situations build is an innate thought pattern. In the discussion of the self-concept in Chapter 5 it was mentioned that young infants go through a process of learning to discriminate themselves from the nonself environment, which includes the mother. This process alters the primitive lack of differentiation between self and significant others that characterizes the infant's behavior. Projection represents a return to this primitive kind of thinking, implying as it does a failure to discriminate when drives belong to the self or to others. Thus projection might be thought of as an elaboration of this primitive mode of thought, or a representation in more sophisticated terms of what may be basically a very infantile ego-function. As we will see in our study of schizophrenia in the next chapter, severe regression in chronic schizophrenics goes along with very primitive projections, supporting the idea that the mechanisms involved in projection occur early in the infant's cognitive development.

Identification. Defensive identification is very likely an outgrowth of developmental identification. Although there are no experimental data on this subject, it seems reasonable that a child who has been rewarded extensively for identifying with its parents, and who has therefore learned the response of identification, is likely to engage in defensive identification when conflict and anxiety are present. This is particularly likely to occur when the motivation for the child's identification with his parents is heavily weighted by defensive processes. That is, the more the identification is rewarded by a reduction in feelings of inadequacy or fear vis-à-vis the parents, and the less it is motivated by the direct rewards and secondary reinforcements already described in Chapter 6 as contributing to developmental identification, the more likely that defensive identification habits will be acquired and will be elicited by conflicts in adulthood.

Identification tendencies may be so strong that the individual may identify even with those who oppress him, provided they are more powerful than he. In the concentration camps of Germany during World War II, it was noted that many Jewish prisoners modeled themselves after their German guards in speech and action. This has been called "identification with the aggressor."[34] The same phenomenon has been observed in many American Jews and Negroes who show anti-semitic and anti-Negro prejudices. We have already seen how the ideal self (involving one's internalized standards) is influenced by the dominant social group, as in the Negro children whose ideals involved a rejection of their own skin color.[35] This identification probably depends in part on acquired habits of identification with parents and other culturally approved figures and types, and also on the presence of standards of behavior enforced by a strong aggressive person or group who thereby define the range of acceptable behavior. Anna Freud has argued that identification with parents is itself a manifestation of the identification with the aggressor, particularly when the identification is a way of reducing fear of punishment by a parent-figure who defines the range of acceptable behavior, and with whom the child is competing for the attention of the other parent.

Like projection, identification is a primitive response in that it is based on the infantile lack of differentiation between the self and the parents.

Compensation. It has been pointed out that compensation is a behavior which receives much social reinforcement and encouragement in our society, probably as part of our stress on individual achievement and enterprise. It is a response that is likely to be encouraged by both parents and teachers. Sublimation, as a type of compensation, would seem to depend not only on this kind of encouragement, but also on the presence of outstanding skill or talent occurring in an environment which permits the development of creative activities, and in the several processes described earlier as contributing to creativity, including negativism, flexibility of response, and so forth.

Regression. Regression may depend upon the presence of gratification in childhood and the tolerance of childish behavior by parents, in a person who does not find such gratifications in adulthood, or on parental inhibition of childish behavior which later is expressed when the inhibitions are extinguished or not evoked. In young children, regression occurs easily, because the child's new "mature" behaviors are so recently acquired that they are relatively weak. Typically, regression occurs in response to the situations produced by the birth of a sibling. An older child observes the attention and care the new baby gets, and notes that the baby gets that attention even though he is behaving in very babyish ways — ways which he himself has been encouraged to give up, and perhaps even been punished for. To this child, growing up means the giving up of comfortable and habitual relationships with his parents, lessened satisfaction of his established dependency drive, and competition with a baby sibling for the attention he used to get. He is very likely to show some regressive behaviors in this situation, either as a result of the great strength of earlier habits compared to the weak new ones which are found to be so little rewarding, or out of imitation of the baby sibling in an effort to obtain the rewards the sibling gets. The regression may take the form of a loss of toilet training, an increase in clinging and crying, or a demand to be treated more like a baby, as in requests to be given a bottle, to be carried, or to ride in a baby carriage. The response which the parents give to the regressing child will be crucial in determining whether regression per se will come to be an habitual mode of responding to anxiety and conflict. Parental ridicule or punishment for regression is likely to inhibit overt regressive behavior, but will not reduce the child's desire for a more infantile status, which may then be revealed in very subtle ways, such as in increased resistance to acquiring more adult ways of behaving as the child grows older, or regressive behavior when away from the parents. Parental ridicule of regressive behavior actually makes regressive wishes stronger, because it puts the child in even greater need of love and regard from parents, such as being received by the baby. Ridicule, as a love-oriented technique, also fosters identification, often producing a conflict between regressive wishes and strong internalized standards for mature behavior. This is not an uncommon conflict, and often leads to inconsistent behavior and any of the other conflict responses discussed in this chapter. On the other hand, excessive reward for the regression may reinforce it. A middle ground in which the parents permit the child to exercise his regressive desires without overly rewarding them by giving the child great attention only when he shows regressive behavior, is likely to be effective in allowing the regression to extinguish. As the child comes to realize the privileges and rewards of greater maturity which he gives up when he regresses, a realization which can only occur if the child is permitted to engage in regressive behavior, the regression is likely to extinguish.

Regression is naturally associated with conflicts involving dependency, because regression results in the production of behavior similar to that associated with the cues of dependency and dependency-gratification in childhood. Thus regression automatically gratifies dependency and is the obvious response to the presence of high dependency drive.

An individual may regress to the overt actions characteristic of earlier years; there may also be an ego-regression, in which he returns to the mode of thinking characteristic of children. The appearance of primitive projections, with its implied loss of discrimination between self and not-self, is an example of such an ego-regression to the kind of thought present in the infant.

Reaction-Formation. Reaction-formation, the only remaining substitution discussed in this chapter, appears likely to occur and to be learned when the child has been punished for performing a forbidden act, regardless of the motives, agent, or objects of the act. The act itself must be inhibited completely. Where parental control over the child's day-to-day activities is great, so that little or no opportunity is provided for displacement to occur, there seems little left for the child to do but to exercise great caution that he does not behave in the forbidden way at all. Additionally, reaction-formation seems to occur particularly in people whose childhood was marked by very strong emphasis on narrowly defined morality, in which the child was made to suffer great fear for any but the most acceptable thoughts and actions. Where such an environment exists, and when the conditions favoring the development of strong identification with the moralistic parents are also present, a tendency for reaction-formation responses is acquired.

Most people show more than one of these responses to conflict in their behavior; the conditions of their socialization experiences frequently permit the learning of several different ways of responding to anxiety. However, it is also true that in each person, the relative strengths of the responses vary such that one seems to be "preferred" or is dominant, compared to the others. Psychologists often use this as a means for describing personalities, when they categorize people in terms of their most typical or usual response to conflict.

Situational Factors. It is also true that people learn to make one kind of response to conflict in one situation, and another when the conflict or the social situation is different. That is, while one kind of response may appear in behavior most frequently, most people do learn to vary their reactions to conflict in terms of the appropriateness of the various reactions to the situation. Although one person may tend to identify strongly, he may resolve his conflict in a different manner, perhaps through reaction-formation in a situation in which no appropriate model for identification is found. This is another way of saying that factors in the conflict situation and the environment may make some responses more rewardable than others, and these factors will therefore influence the response which the individual tends to make in that and similar situations. This may be illustrated by what happens in a family structure in which both partners displace any hostility that arises between them onto their children. Such displacement is likely to be rewarding, because it permits the marriage relationship to continue, with the rewards inherent in it. However, when the children eventually marry and leave the parental home, the displacement can no longer occur, and the partners have to find other ways of responding to their hostility-inhibition conflicts. These considerations suggest that the effectiveness of a particular response to conflict depends in part at least on the reactions it elicits from other people. Regression in a husband will be reinforced, and will be effective in controlling hostility which conflicts with dependency needs, if his wife is one who engages in reaction-formation when hostility toward her husband is aroused, so that she responds to his regression and dependency by becoming protective and maternal. Their responses "mesh" and are likely to be effective. However, if the wife instead projects or rationalizes hostility, so that she expresses it against her husband quite directly, he will be stimulated to more and more regression until neither partner can stand the relationship, and it dissolves with each feeling that the other doesn't understand him. This means that the stability of a close relationship, and the effectiveness of anxiety-reducing responses, depends in part on the extent to which those used by the participants are mutually compatible or incompatible. This is true not only for relationships between husbands and wives, but also for those between parents and children, teachers and students, employers and employees. Something like this mutuality was described earlier in our discussion of relationships which are relatively stable and enduring despite the fact that the participants argue or fight whenever they are together. One of the important implications of this mutuality is that when one discovers a case in which one kind of reaction to conflict seems to occur with very great frequency, perhaps to the point where the individual can no longer function effectively in many situations, it is not sufficient to work only with that individual in order to modify his behavior; the behavior of those significant people in his life which is supportive of his way of responding to conflict must also be changed if permanent improvement is to occur. This may be one of the reasons why it sometimes occurs that after psychotherapy, previously effective relationships with significant people may no longer "work" because the patient has greatly changed his habits. The marriage partner of a person who has shown extensive change as a result of therapy must himself make new adjustments, or the relationship may no longer be as satisfying as it once was, and may tend toward dissolution. Imagine, for example, what would happen in the marriage between the regressing husband and reaction-forming wife if the husband were to extinguish his regressive habits and instead assert his independence. His wife would find that her reaction-forming protectiveness and maternal domination would create difficulties and resentments, rather than making things go easier, and unless she too were to change, the marriage might well become quite unstable as communication breaks down, misunderstandings arise, and both partners fail to find satisfactions from their relationship with the other.

Nature of the Conflict As a Determinant. The kind of response made
to conflict and anxiety is not only a result of past learning and the
opportunities and restrictions present in the individual's social environment; it also depends on the nature of the conflicting forces. We have
already seen that both fantasy and reaction-formation are compensatory, so that one may frequently infer the motives involved from a
knowledge of a person's fantasy or reaction-formation. When someone
goes out of his way to avoid any interpersonal commitments or "entan-
gling alliances," when he rejects even usual assistance (as, for example,
when a woman refuses to allow a man to hold a door for her), and
shows resentment when he is offered special considerations—in short,
when strong counterdependent attitudes are revealed, one may suspect
a reaction-formation response to conflict involving dependency drive.
This is illustrated in the description a patient gave of his wife's behavior
after they had an argument. He reported that at such times, she would
refuse to allow him to do anything for her around the house, and rejected his attempts to continue with his usual household chores, such as
drying the dishes. When they went out in the evening in the aftermath
of an argument, his wife would rush to get to the car ahead of him so
that she could open the car door herself and get in before he could offer
his customary gentlemanly assistance. The patient could see that his
wife was trying to show him (and perhaps herself) through such counterdependent behavior, that she was not really dependent on him, reflecting a fear which would of course not exist if she were not motivated to
be dependent in fact. It was further noted that there may have been
some aggressive component to the wife's behavior, judging from the way
in which she tried to "rub in" her independence from her husband. This
suggested to the therapist that the wife may have been aware that her
husband had fairly marked motivation to be dominant; her reaction-
formation could only really work if her husband was encouraging dependency in their relationship. Her behavior was a way of punishing
him by frustrating his drive, thus making him resentful of her independence. Later in the course of therapy, the hypothesis of strong domination tendencies in the patient were confirmed by subsequent events. In
short, the content of the reaction-formation response of the patient's
wife provided information about the conflict which produced it, and
about the interpersonal situation which maintained it. From this information, it would then be possible for the psychologist to reconstruct
some of the likely training situations in the wife's history which could
account for her conflict concerning dependency, in terms of the kinds of
socialization procedures discussed in Chapter 7 which have been found

to produce dependency conflict, and in addition, the psychologist could have made some inferences about the kinds of training situations in the wife's background that led to the development of reaction-formation as a response to conflict. In the sense that this reaction to conflict therefore provides rich information for the making of inferences about the wife's background, it may be said that her behavior was symbolic of its determinants. That is, her behavior expressed directly the factors which contributed to it, and these factors could be inferred from the behavior by those whose knowledge of the causes of such reactions enables them to make the inferences, or translations of the symbol into its "meaning." So it is with other reactions to conflict. One may frequently detect in the art productions growing out of sublimation the nature of the artist's conflicts. The sublimating artist who writes novel after novel about lonely men is expressing something about the nature of his conflicts. Similarly, the object of displacements may be symbolic of the conflicted goal of the response. The fact that authority figures frequently exist on a gradient of stimulus generalization from a tyrannical father allows the psychologist to infer from displaced aggression directed against teachers, policemen, Army officers, and the like, that the displacer had a frustrating father who inhibited the direct display of aggression. In this example, authority figures are symbolic of the father. The diagnostic value of projection is even more apparent; one can infer from the projection that the projector has the same drives or traits which are imputed to others, and is also motivated to avoid recognizing their existence in himself.

Although the content of responses to conflict may therefore provide rich information for drawing inferences about the individual's conflicts, the socialization practices which may have produced both the approach and avoidance drives, and the practices which led to the particular conflict-response displayed, these inferences must of necessity be in the nature of hypotheses. There are individual differences which must be recognized. It is possible that for one subject, authority figures are stimuli on a generalization continuum not from a father, but perhaps from an older brother, and even possibly from a dominating mother or grandparent.

It is the goal of clinical psychology, the branch of psychology concerned with applications of knowledge about personality, to achieve an accurate translation of behavior into an understanding of the factors which are responsible for it in the individual case. And although such translations cannot yet be made with certainty, and many people behave in ways whose determinants are not yet known, it is nevertheless true that responses to conflicts are not "accidentally" learned, as if one is as good as any other. It is not purely chance that a person learns to respond in one way rather than another. Once psychology has gained a clear understanding of how they are learned, the "symbolic value" of responses to conflict will be firmly established.

This point is stressed because it applies not only to conflict responses, but more importantly to symptoms. That is, when severe conflict is present, responses to conflict become elaborate, automatic, and occupy significantly large portions of the individual's time and effort, often to the point where he is so busy reducing anxiety that he cannot solve the conflict and satisfy the drives that are involved. So much of life may be devoted to conflict responses that the individual does not function adequately in his job, family, and social environment because of the large distortions of reality which his behavior involves. When this occurs, the person may be considered to be neurotic or psychotic, and the behaviors which he displays, largely his elaborate responses to his conflicts, are looked at as symptoms of his disturbance. Symptoms, as extensions of the conflict responses presented in this chapter, are, like those responses, symbolic. They can be used as sources for interpretations of the nature and determinants of the patient's difficulty. The symbolic nature of conflict responses therefore becomes of great interest in the diagnosis and treatment of what is commonly called mental illness.

Psychophysiologic Reactions

So far, we have dealt with only the overt behavioral consequences of conflict. It must be remembered that conflicts are conditions in which at least two drives are involved, neither of which is completely reduced by noninstrumental responses to conflict, and further, that drives include states of physiological arousal. This means that the conflicted individual is in a more or less continuous state of physiological arousal—a condition which has important consequences for his physiological health. Prolonged arousal can have a debilitating effect on body structures, such that physical impairment of the structures can result. When this happens, the individual is said to have a psychosomatic illness—that is, a real physical illness which is related to the psychological factors involved in the production of the physiological states influencing the illness and its course.[36]

The best-known example of psychosomatic illness is that of stomach ulcers. Ulcers are wounds in the wall of the stomach, produced by the action on the tissue of the wall of the hydrochloric acid in the stomach.

Normally coated by a protective layer, the wall may be exposed directly to the action of the stomach acid which can produce wounds ranging from slight tenderness to a complete perforation.

Our stereotype of an ulcer case is that of the driving, ambitious businessman, striving to keep moving forward and gain greater security. This stereotype, like others, is an abstraction, or modal description, of the common features of a large proportion of examples, and therefore has a great deal of truth in it. Clinical work with ulcer patients reveals with surprising regularity intense conflicts between competitive striving for more and more achievement and strong dependency drives.[37] The ulcer patient is characteristically a person whose driving competition inevitably means further frustration of his drives to be liked, cared for, and passive. It is of some interest that ulcers, formerly almost restricted to men, are found with increasing frequency in women, which many people interpret as a result of women's greater entrance into the competitive world of business life. Frequently, to the ulcer patient, getting ahead is a response acquired as a way of acquiring the love and regard which his dependency drives require, but which at the same time he must forego if he is to be as competitive and aggressive in his getting ahead as he feels he must be.

The ulcer itself is caused by the oversecretion of hydrochloric acid; when the stomach contracts without food matter being present for the interaction with the acid which results in the breaking down of the food tissues and the neutralization of the acid, the high secretions are constantly exerting an abrasive and corrosive action on the stomach lining, wearing it away and producing the ulcer. The question is, how do competitive achievement-dependency conflicts act so as to produce this more or less constant stomach secretion and contraction? The answer to this question is not yet known, although one can think of reasonable explanations. Remembering that these conflicting drives include physiological states, it is possible that one of the drives involved is differentiated out of hunger. It seems likely that the dependency drive involves a conditioned hunger drive which comes to be elicited by the cues of other people who exist on a stimulus generalization continuum from the mother. Constantly aroused by the presence of other people, but not reduced because the patient does not behave in a dependent manner which would elicit the love and protection that would in turn reduce the drive, and yet forced by his achievement drive to remain in close enough contact with others so that he cannot escape the cues which elicit the dependency drive, the drive continues to operate, producing the ulcer. The direct effect on the stomach of fear and anxiety about rejection by others has been watched by scientists, who have seen the stomach contract, the lining and walls become reddened, and the acid secretion increase when their ulcer patients experience these emotional states.[38]

The fact of the ulcer, of course, requires medical and sometimes surgical treatment—the wound is real and painful. However, continued cure and the prevention of further ulcerations obviously requires psychological treatment to correct the conditions which give rise to the ulcers—a requirement of therapy which physicians increasingly recognize in their practice, although they may not always know how to go about obtaining psychological treatment for their patients that goes beyond a well-meant but ineffective injunction to stop worrying.

The beginning of an alternative explanation of the psychosomatic disorder of ulcers has recently been announced by Joseph Brady, a comparative psychologist who works at the Army's Psychology Laboratory in Washington. Brady found that he could reliably produce ulcers in monkeys when he put them in the decision-making position of an executive.[39, 40] He did this by strapping two monkeys into a frame which limited their freedom of movement. The two were side by side, and the apparatus was arranged in such a way that at prearranged intervals both animals received an electric shock. However, one of the animals, the "executive," could press a button which would eliminate for both of them the shock which was to be administered next. In this way, both animals were shocked equally often and at the same times, but only one could do anything about it. Brady found that in this arrangement, the executive monkey developed stomach ulcers, but the dependent monkey, who got the same shocks, did not. This experiment suggests that decision-making in a situation in which pain is the consequence of failure may be the essential ingredient of ulcers, and that factors of conflict, ambition, and dependency may not be directly involved at all, except insofar as they are influential in establishing the punishment-value of failing to act or decide in the social world. There is some reason to think that these drives are involved in "executive" ulcers. It has been noted that ulcers occur with greater frequency among junior or subordinate executives than among those at the top level. Those at the lower level obviously have more riding on their decisions, so far as their personal careers are concerned, than those who have reached the top.

Even in the kind of situation that stimulates the development of ulcers, different members of a species are likely to develop the disorder at different rates, with some apparently quite resistant, and others readily becoming incapacitated. While general level of autonomic responsiveness undoubtedly is one of the reasons for this, there are very likely other physiological differences which also affect the development of ulcers. It has been pointed out that the structure and shape of the stomach, and the nature of the lining of the stomach walls, differs among individuals, and its seems reasonable that some shapes and structures are more liable to result in ulceration than others. This factor of individual differences in organ structure affecting the development of psychosomatic disorders is referred to as "somatic compliance." It has been proposed that in any conflict, somatic compliance plays a part in determining whether a psychosomatic disorder will be produced, and also what organs will be involved. There is another aspect to somatic compliance, one which was mentioned earlier in Chapter 2. There it was pointed out that people differ in the effects of autonomic arousal, such as that which is present in states of drive. In some people the heart is very responsive, while in others sweat gland activation is the more prominent effect. In general, people differ in the extent to which different organs are involved in motivational states. These differences may be part of the reason that one person develops ulcers, another develops a heart ailment and a third has a skin rash as a result of persistent motivational arousal following from unresolved conflict.

Ulcers are not the only disorder in which psychological factors participate. In recent years it has been more and more widely accepted among the health professions that every emotional state, involving as it does the physiological components of drive, is capable of interfering with the healthy functioning of the body, and conversely, any disorder of the body has its psychological implications. These implications lie not only in the patient's learned responses to illness and his self-concept, but also in the altered emotional or drive states which malfunctioning of the physiological systems involved can produce. A man who is ill, for example, often simply lacks the ability to develop a strong achievement drive.

These principles have resulted in a greater appreciation of such factors as the patient's personality structure in assessing prospects for cure. A very anxious person is not as likely to develop or recover from a heart ailment as readily as one who is less anxious. Similarly, a tubercular patient whose personality is such that he cannot relax as completely and as long as the usual treatment for the disease requires will find the disease lingering longer than it may in other patients. In the sense of these related principles, then, there is no such thing as a nonpsychosomatic disorder.

Psychologists have been engaged in extensive investigation to discover if there might not be many illnesses which have been ascribed in the past to system inferiority or unknown disease organisms that might have large components of psychological factors in their cause. While somatic compliance is generally recognized, the question is whether many disorders might not be produced indirectly perhaps by the biochemical and physiological consequences of emotional or drive states, rather than by malignant organisms. In addition, they are exploring the possibility that these psychological factors might spell the difference between succumbing to or resisting the assault of disease organisms. Finally, psychologists are investigating the possibility that there might be very specific relations among particular disorders and particular psychological events.[41] We have already seen that ulcers have been ascribed to an achievement-dependency conflict. Migraine and other headaches, the immediate cause of which is dilation of the blood vessels in the region of the head, have been ascribed to repressed and intropunitive hostility as the cause of the blood vessel dilation. This was illustrated very dramatically by L. R. Wolberg, a psychoanalyst. He had a patient who suffered from migraine headaches, but who believed that they were caused by some organic factors and so resisted consulting Wolberg when it was recommended to him by his physician. Wolberg hypnotized the patient and made him believe, while he was hypnotized, that someone had insulted him. He told the patient that he would not remember what happened under hypnosis, and then awakened the patient, who shortly after developed a migraine headache. Wolberg repeated the same procedure on several occasions, varying the nature of the hynotically implanted "cause" of the migraines, except that it was always some situation that would arouse aggression. Each time, the patient developed a headache after the hypnotic procedure. After several repetitions, Wolberg hypnotized the patient and told him that when he awoke, he would remember what happened in all the previous hypnotic sessions. When the patient remembered, he could see the relationship between his headaches and aggression-arousing situations, and was then willing to begin exploring psychological factors as the cause of his difficulty.[42]

It is not yet known why anger specifically affects certain blood vessels in the head. It has been demonstrated that muscle tensions at the back of the head occur in response to stress among people who have frequent headaches.[43] It was mentioned earlier that experiments on sham rage in decorticate cats point to the hypothalamus as the integration center for aggressive reactions. It may be that there are innate connections between the hypothalamic structures involved in rage and the muscles in the neck and head, so that these always react when the hypothalamus is involved in a rage response. However, this has not yet been empirically demonstrated so that thus far the mechanisms relating headaches and their physiological components to anger are only a matter of hypothesis.

Among the disorders which many investigators have identified as having important psychological factors as their causes are warts, hives, asthma, and other allergies, many of the various skin disorders labeled as dermatitis, arthritis and rheumatism, head colds and cold sores, and often such symptoms as upset stomachs, coughs, chronic vomiting, diarrhea, and constipation.[44, 45, 46] Aside from those behavioral factors which affect the extent of the patient's compliance with the physicians' directions in the treatment of these disorders, and thus indirectly the speed of recovery, and aside from those physiological, emotional, and drive states which influence the extent to which the diseased structures will be released from stress that would aggravate the condition, psychologists have identified these disorders as more or less directly produced by various specific psychological factors. There is evidence on both sides of the question, but the question is not likely to be settled until investigators are able to identify the mechanisms that mediate between a psychological state and the physical disorder. For example, until someone is able to identify the particular physiological processes which produce warts, and can then show how these physiological processes are affected by emotional and motivational states, the status of warts must remain ambiguous. It is not sufficient, for example, to show that there is a correlation between dermatitis and proneness to embarrassment, or concern with one's appearance. Which is the cause of which? The answer can only come from an analysis of the intervening processes.

More obviously psychological than the disorders discussed above are such physiological responses to emotional states as blushing, turning pale, cold extremities, erections in males, hand tremors, perspiring, increased heartrate, rapid breathing, and muscle tensions. Should these reactions become chronic because of the out-of-the-ordinary endurance of the emotional states that produce them, or should they occur in conjunction with other factors such as assault by disease-producing organisms or weakened body structures, long-lasting physiological dis-orders may be developed. Obviously, strong and persistent fear may precipitate a coronary attack, and chronic blushing can result in some more or less permanent changes in the skin as a result of too rich blood supply.

Simple conditioning can produce some physiological reactions which, if repeated often enough, may result in permanent structural damage. This is seen in the case of a twenty-year-old girl who was brought to the hospital because of pain in her chest. She was found by the examining physician to be emaciated and to have several lesions in her upper di-gestive tract. The girl's mother reported that her daughter was unable to keep food down, vomiting several dozen times a day, a condition that had been in existence for many weeks. Investigation of the case revealed that the girl was in great conflict about a young man with whom she had had sexual relations and whom she felt she had to marry. Her mother opposed the marriage and the girl herself had strong dependency needs which would not allow her to leave her mother. Her symptoms started after she eloped with her lover, married him, and then left him to re-turn home. It was also learned that her relationships with her mother had been stormy throughout childhood and into adolescence, and that there were many occasions on which she had violent arguments with the mother which ended with the daughter becoming so aroused by aggres-sive drive that it interfered with digestion, and she would vomit, upon which her mother would usually relent and become very solicitous. These arguments usually started when the mother tried to deny her daughter's needs and wishes. The vomiting probably also represented her conflicted wish to be with her husband and to be made pregnant (and "morning-sick") by him. It therefore was concluded that the pa-tient's condition on admission to the hospital was the indirect result of a learned response to conflict involving dependency needs, aggression toward the mother, and frustrated sexual drives. Medical therapy was obviously necessary to repair the damage, as well as psychotherapy. Incidentally, the oral component of this girl's reactions are obvious, indicating that her difficulties had begun very early in life, in conjunc-tion with her infantile feeding experiences. This inference was further confirmed by the observation that the patient's conception and testing of reality was relatively weak, as would be expected when very early experiences with external stimuli were negative and painful.

This case may be compared with another in which a forty-five-year-old man suffered the same chronic vomiting. By means of hypnosis, it was suggested to the patient that he would not vomit. This produced a marked reduction in the frequency of vomiting, but it did not cease altogether, so the psychologist who worked with the patient suggested that there may have also been other, nonpsychological factors in the disorder. Upon full physical examination, it was discovered that the patient had a tumor in an area of the brain which integrates the vomiting reflexes. It was concluded from this case that while an organic factor may have first produced the vomiting, the patient's life situation, including marital and financial difficulties, was such that the vomiting was rewarded by sympathy from his wife and escape from financial responsibility. In this way, the symptom was learned as a response to his personal difficulties, although it originated as a physiological disorder. That part of the vomiting which was learned could be treated psychologically, but the part that remained was a medical problem.[47]

Before closing this discussion of psychosomatics, it should be mentioned that schizophrenia has been extensively investigated in an effort to explore the roles of physiological and psychological factors, and the terms of their interaction. It was mentioned in Chapter 5 that there is much evidence for the presence of altered biochemical functioning in schizophrenics. Although there is no way as yet of knowing whether this is a cause or an effect of the schizophrenic process, some theories have been proposed which attempt to integrate psychological factors in infancy with physiological events to produce a picture of the schizophrenic that includes his poor reality contact and his conflicts stemming from early infantile experiences, and his distinctive physiological functioning. Schizophrenia will be discussed at length in the next chapter; it is sufficient to indicate here that it may be another disorder having particularly prominent psychosomatic aspects.

It can be seen that psychosomatics is a confusing and still confused field of investigation. While the principles involved are widely accepted, their working out in the case of any particular disorder is still much of a mystery. Among the factors mentioned in this section were the nature of the conflict, individual differences in somatic compliance (including organ susceptibility and individual differences in the effects of autonomic arousal), specific conditioning, the chronicity of effects of emotions and motives, and the interaction of all these factors in determining the occurrence of real physical disorder, its severity, and its amenability to treatment.

Some General Remarks About Conflict and Conflict Responses

This discussion of conflict and its consequences leads to some important conclusions that should be stressed.

Conflicts Involve Drives. The noninstrumental responses to conflict are reactions to anxiety produced by the individual's own desires, wishes, or motivations. They are not so much barriers to the environment as they are barriers to the individual's own behavioral potentials. In this sense, the presence of these responses to conflict in a person's behavior signifies a war within him, and this war is the basis and meaning of his skirmishes with the environment. He may fear the power and authority of his boss, but at bottom his fear is a reaction to his own anger or resentment of the boss, and of what that anger might do to his career, to the boss' attitudes toward him, and to his own attitudes toward himself.

Conflicts Are Usually Unconscious. The noninstrumental responses to conflict are based on repression and inhibition and are largely replacements for the repressed or inhibited responses. This means that when these responses are present in a person's behavior, some of that person's behavioral potential has been diminished — the range of his thoughts has been diminished by repression, and/or the range of action has been diminished by inhibition. The cue and response substitutions based on repression and inhibition prevent him from recognizing a motive, from thinking about it, or from executing it overtly; the cue and response substitutions may therefore be considered to be defenses of the individual's self-concept which excludes the conflicted thoughts and behaviors.

Conflict Responses Are Reinforced. Along with the function of the cue and response substitutions in defending the self-concept through repression and/or inhibition, they also provide some gratifications for the conflicted drives. Displacement of aggression does permit the expression of aggressive behavior; rationalization permits the conflicted behavior to occur, as does projection, and so on with the others. The form of the behavior may be changed, or the individual's recognition of what he is doing may be distorted to make the behavior acceptable to him, or the object of the behavior may be altered — but these tactics permit the motivated behavior some overt expression. This provides the reason for the fact that conflicted people are often quite unaware of the meaning or intent of their behavior, although these meanings and intentions may be quite apparent to observers. In effect, the cue and response substitutions are self-deceptions which permit unadvertised gratifications.

Conflict Responses Are Self-Defeating. At the same time as they allow some gratifications, the cue and response substitutions are not completely satisfying because they distort or disguise motives. Displacement does release aggressive behavior, but it does not hurt the true instigator of the aggression and so it is less than completely satisfying to the displacer. He hurts someone he doesn't care about, rather than the person with whom he is really angry. This is why it is that although the substitutions allow for "cheap" gratifications (because they avoid anxiety and danger to the self-schema), they also create a feeling of unhappiness, misery, dissatisfaction, or ineffectuality, because complete satisfaction of one's desires is lacking.

What we have said in the above paragraph is an elaboration of a point made earlier that drives are reducible, and their associated behaviors reinforceable, without there necessarily being any alteration of the conditions eliciting the drive, whether these conditions be stimulation by innate need-sensitive mechanisms, or by environmental events eliciting learned drives. The displacement of anger reduces aggressive drive, but it does nothing to affect the behavior of the true object of the anger, the one who aroused the aggression in the first place. It is this ability of drive states to be reduced without altering the eliciting stimuli that makes possible partial gratification for conflict responses, together with the lack of complete gratification.

Conflicts Involve Stimulus Generalization. Most of the noninstrumental responses involve stimulus generalization, which provides the mode of operation or the mechanism for these responses. Which particular response occurs depends on the nature of the generalization continuum involved, which in turn is a function of the schemas or ways of grouping events that the individual has acquired. A complete understanding of responses to conflict therefore requires a knowledge of the conflicting drives, the individual's schemas, the operation of stimulus generalization, and of the partial gratifications or reinforcements maintaining the behavior.

Conflict Is Inevitable. It is as inevitable as socialization which opposes the innate or acquired drives, an opposition which is necessary if the child is to give up his infancy and become a mature and civilized adult. It is as inevitable as inconsistency in parental behavior which makes socialization both enduring and conflictful. Similarly, the substitution responses to conflict are as inevitable as stimulus generalization. This means that everyone has conflicts; everyone has acquired some non-instrumental responses to his conflicts; everyone is therefore his own enemy to some extent; everyone has some repression-inhibition-based restrictions on the range of his thoughts and actions; everyone receives some partial gratifications, and by the same token blocks himself from receiving complete gratification. This fact of the universality of conflict is what makes possible the human drama — both tragic and comic — as each person goes through life balancing his drives and gratifications as best he can. The inevitability of conflict may seem discouraging in that it precludes the possibility of a completely perfect life and world. But it should be kept in mind that the factors responsible for this inevitability of imperfection — socialization, stimulus generalization, and so forth — are also the factors that make civilization and culture possible. To an extent, then, conflict and its substitution responses are the cause and the means for the development of science, art, and all enculturated human enterprises. Incompleteness and indirectness of gratification is the price we pay for these.

REPRISE. This chapter has been concerned with the nature and consequences of frustration. The great bulk of the discussion was concerned with frustration by conflicts, because these are the frustrations which participate to a significant extent in the formation of the responses that become important components of personality. These responses include both instrumental and noninstrumental reactions. Several varieties of conflict were presented — the approach-approach, avoidance-avoidance, and approach-avoidance conflict, which is the condition of ambivalence. The ways in which conflict produces a variety of cue and response substitutions was presented. It was noted that these responses may become habitual, as anxiety-reducing behaviors, and that they are influenced by the nature of the conflict, the nature of the individual's socialization experiences, and by his interpersonal environment. These influences operate in such a way that a person's response to conflict is of great symbolic and diagnostic value. Finally, the effects of conflict on physiological functioning, as expressed in the concept of psychosomatic illness, was discussed. The considerations presented in this chapter further attest to the complexity of personality, pointing up the many factors which participate in determining a particular response to conflict, the many "meanings" which such a response may have in terms of the variety of reinforcements which influence its performance and the interrelationships among the responses, and finally, the complexity which is presented by the effects of conflict on the performance of habits, on perception and thought, (particularly in the interpersonal realm), and on physiological functioning. Having seen how these things operate, we now may turn to a consideration of personality in a more integrated fashion. The next chapter will be concerned with the dominant features of several kinds of complete personalities, presented as a kind of summing up of the effects of all the factors which have been presented in this book up to now, and a fitting together of them into the composite which forms a complete individual.

10. Patterns of Behavior

In this chapter we will examine some of the interrelationships among drives, habits, and thoughts, particularly with reference to their action in conflict, thereby integrating the preceding material. In order to do this, we will be concerned primarily with a description of several kinds of abnormal or unusual patterns. It is a reflection of the historical origins of personality psychology that while there is no widely accepted independent taxonomy, or classification, of "normal" personalities, there is one of abnormal personalities. Nevertheless, much can be learned from a study of abnormal patterns, extreme cases of behavior which, because of their extremeness, stand out in sharp focus. Even so, they are closely related to normal behaviors in the sense of being exaggerations of processes and events which take place in all people. As such, they shed a good deal of light on the "nonabnormal" personality.

The novelist may exaggerate some salient characteristics of his characters in order to focus on them, and although this exaggeration makes his characters different from real people, his intent is to show the similarity between his characters and the less exaggerated but nevertheless similar attributes which exist in reality. So it is with the study of abnormal behavior, interpreted as an oversized portrait of processes in normal people. The fundamental assumption involved is that there is a continuity between the normal and the abnormal, such that the personality processes which account for abnormal behavior are exactly the same as those which account for normal behavior. The qualitative differences observed among the neurotic, the psychotic, and the normal are mostly appearances based on quantitative differences in the extent to which particular drives, habits, and ideas have been acquired and are evoked. This theme will be stressed over and over again in this chapter.

Classifications of Patterns of Personality

Many more or less successful efforts have been made to classify abnormal behaviors; however, no completely acceptable scheme has been developed. The present categorizations or diagnostic groupings are largely the result of historical precedent, modified here and there by modern viewpoints but basically unchanged since Freud's day. There have been attempts to classify on the basis of the kind of response to conflict which is predominant. There also have been attempts to classify in terms of the nature of the most important conflicts. Similarly, there have been efforts to classify according to the stage or time of life when the conditions leading to the abnormal behavior were established. The problem of classification is very complicated because any particular experience may precipitate different neuroses in different people, depending on the motives affected by the situation and the responses learned. For example, the death of a parent may be followed by a severe disorder characterized by intense depression in one person, by a neurotic paralysis of an arm in another, and by severe attacks of nervousness and panic in a third, depending perhaps on whether the death of the parent produced guilt over hostility toward the dead one, or frustration of strong dependency needs, and whether the individual had acquired habits of intropunitiveness or repression in response to conflict and anxiety, or had acquired no such habits at all. To classify in terms of the precipitating incident would mean lumping together people of very different behavioral propensities. On the other hand, to classify in terms of overt behavior may also lead to inefficient groupings; it has been pointed out by psychologists that the same symptom in two different people may be the result of very different experiences. For example, severe attacks of anxiety and panic in one may be a reaction to aroused homosexual response tendencies, while in another they may be reactions to projected fears of aggression.

The traditional groupings have been made in terms of similarities in overt behavior, a scheme subject to the criticism pointed out above. There have been attempts to save such a scheme from criticism by discerning common elements of experience in the etiology or development of all cases of the same disorder. One of Freud's greatest contributions to the understanding of abnormal behavior was his fairly successful effort to do just this. It is implied in such a search that similar "causes" must have similar effects. That is, if the determinants of behavior are identical, or nearly so (a condition which, of course, can prevail only approximately, because of the diversity of each person's experience and the uniqueness of each person's life situation, even among children in the same family who are separated in time, sex, and physical attributes from each other), then these determining conditions should give rise to the same, or nearly the same, behaviors. Where different behaviors occur, it can only be inferred that different determining situations existed. It must be remembered that cause, in the sense of determining conditions, is never simple. It includes not only the immediate event which precipitates or elicits symptomatic behavior, but all the factors which rendered that event capable of serving as a stimulus for the symptoms, and all the experiences which determined what symptoms would be acquired as responses to such an event. In Freud's theory, a synthesis of behavior with its determinants was achieved by his discovery that the important conflicts which underlie symptomatic behavior usually are acquired in particular kinds of life situations, situations which also incline the individual to acquire the particular responses to the conflict which form the basis for his symptomatic behavior. For example, conflict over conformity to societal extensions of parental rules has its first major development in connection with toilet training, so that strong guilt over breaking taboos may be manifested through an emphasis on cleanliness and orderliness. These habits usually are acquired in association with toilet training. All symptomatic behaviors which include such an emphasis, such as excessive handwashing, fear of germs and infections, and rigid orderliness therefore may be grouped together without the danger that such a grouping will obscure differences either in "cause" or in overt behavior.

With the above considerations in mind, we will review the major syndromes or groups of abnormal behaviors, a grouping based on similarities in overt behavior with inferred similarities in their determinants.

One reservation is in order: the symptom pictures to be described are abstractions drawn from many similar cases. Such abstraction necessarily ignores differences which exist among examples of the same disorder. This results in "textbook cases" — cases in which the disorder is crystal clear and unambiguous, but which almost never occur in such a pure form in reality. There is almost always some mixing of the categories in the particular case. A personality dominated by trends established in connection with infantile feeding also may show prominent features resulting from harsh socialization of aggression, while another with a very similar "core" may have had fairly typical and unremarkable experiences in connection with aggression but serious difficulties arising out of the socialization of achievement drive. In effect, the behavior of a neurotic (and a nonneurotic) person is the product of all his experiences, although some parts of it may have produced the more dramatic aspects of his behavior. While different people may have had fairly similar experiences in certain areas, so that they are alike in the main features of their behavior, they are likely to differ in many other experiences, producing subtle but nevertheless important differences in their behavior, even though they both may be considered to fall into the same diagnostic category. Unlike the physical sciences, psychology does not and cannot, because of the nature of its human material, deal with purified samples.

Psychosis

Psychosis is the general name for patterns of behavior which are at such variance with the physical and social environment that the individual usually requires a protected environment and legal recognition of his inability to function in society. The psychoses are divided into two groups, the *organic* and the *functional* psychoses. An organic psychosis is one in which a large portion of the individual's behavior can be accounted for on the basis of structural changes in the glandular and central nervous system. Examples of organic psychoses are those which are the result of progressive diseases attacking the brain, such as general paresis (a syphilitic infection of the frontal lobes), or the destructive effects of brain tumors which, in growing, crush and kill brain cells, or brain damage produced by accidents, wounds, and other physical mishaps.

Functional psychoses, on the other hand, have been considered traditionally to be those psychotic states in which no neuropathology in the central nervous system has been demonstrated. Such psychoses are often assumed to be acquired as the products of the individual's social experience, although many scientists suspect that there may be an organic basis, as yet undiscovered, for the disorders currently considered to be functional.

There has been much questioning of the dichotomy of organic *vs.* functional. A great deal of evidence indicates that so-called functional psychosis, such as schizophrenia, includes organic changes in the body which are traceable to the action of neural centers in the brain. Conversely, many investigators have claimed that not all the symptoms in organic psychosis can be accounted for only on the basis of the destruction of some percentage of the brain cells. For example, some symptoms may be interpreted as the products of anxiety aroused by the gradual, fearful discovery by the individual that he can no longer understand things as well as he used to, that his judgment is no longer as reliable as it once was, and the frustrations produced by the loss of acquired habits.[1] The emotional meaning of symptoms is observed perhaps most clearly in senile psychosis, considered an organic psychosis resulting from the progressive starvation of brain cells because of the hardening of the arteries (arteriosclerosis) in the brain which so often accompanies aging. The variety of symptoms shown by the senile psychotic covers the range of symptoms seen in the functional psychoses. Psychologists suspect that the symptoms are the products of earlier-learned ways of responding to anxiety, responses which are exaggerated by the great anxiety which the senile person suffers, and perhaps also by the loss of self-restraint and judgment which may be a direct result of the brain pathology. This hypothesis seems to be confirmed by study of the premorbid history of senile psychotic patients, which indicates that the symptoms are related to premorbid personality.[2] It also has been observed that the more the premorbid personality was dominated by noninstrumental reactions to frustration and anxiety, the sooner symptoms of senile psychosis appear.[3] It is hypothesized by many clinicians that a similar interaction between personality and organic factors exists in other organic psychoses. On the face of it, it seems reasonable to recognize that the person struck by some organic disease involving the central nervous system has had a personality —a set of learned drives and responses —before the disorder, and that this previous learning does not simply disappear when organic disease develops.

Functional Psychoses

The functional psychoses usually are divided into two classifications —the schizophrenias (further subdivided into paranoid, catatonic, hebephrenic, and simple schizophrenia) and the manic and depressive psychoses.

The Schizophrenias. The common element that runs through the various kinds of behavior classified as schizophrenic, and which has become therefore the main definitional element of schizophrenia, is poor contact with reality. The unrealistic thinking and/or perceiving may take the form of hallucinations, delusions, bizarre interpretations of events, inability to comprehend events, or the presence of ideas which bear little relationship to the nature of the physical and social environment. As would be expected where thinking and perceiving are disordered, there also is frequently peculiar use of language, in which words are used more in terms of their personal and atypical meanings than in terms of meanings shared with other people. Others therefore find it difficult to understand the schizophrenic's verbalizations. An example of such personal meanings is seen in one man who refused to drink the coffee served him by his wife in a cup with a broken handle. He was sure that the coffee was poisoned, as indicated by the broken handle. It was learned that the first letters of the words *broken handle* were the initials of a man who had been the patient's rival for his wife in their courtship many years previously, and the patient was fearful that his wife did not love him as much as she had loved B. H.

Associated with schizophrenic thinking are, as one would expect, emotional states which are equally incomprehensible to the outsider. The schizophrenic often appears oddly unemotional and "colorless" —a state which is referred to as "flattened affect" —but he also may show on occasion very strong feelings of rage, guilt, fear, or elation, although these feelings may seem to have very little relationship to the person's environment or the apparent content of his thought as revealed by his verbalizations. This discrepancy between thought and feeling is the basis for the name *schizophrenia,* which means "split mind." This is not the same as multiple personality, often spoken of as "split personality," which refers to a very different personality type not usually classed as a psychosis.

An older name for the schizophrenias is "dementia praecox," which means early loss of intelligence. This name was applied because of the observation that the thought disorder now known as schizophrenia usually appears early in life—most often in the early twenties. There are many cases in which the first onset occurs much later —even in the forties and fifties —and similar behavior has been noted as early as two and three years of age; nevertheless, the most frequent age of onset is in the decade between fifteen and twenty-five years of age.[4]

Usually associated with the thinking and feeling aspects of schizophrenia are avoidance of interpersonal relationships and strong fear felt merely in the presence of others, gesturing and posturing and in extreme cases, loss of bladder and bowel control, loss of interest in food (to the point where the schizophrenic might starve to death if left to his own devices), self-mutilation, playing with fecal material, and a preoccupation with magic, the occult and mystical (or, more modernly, in mysterious powers operating through electronic "waves").

Before exploring the various theories about the nature and development of schizophrenia, we will examine the distinguishing characteristics of the various subtypes.

Paranoid Schizophrenia. The paranoid schizophrenic is marked by intense suspiciousness of the motives of others with whom he comes in contact. Delusions of persecution frequently take the form of a belief that a large number of people are involved in some coordinated plot against him. The patient may ascribe his hospitalization to the machinations of these others. He also may believe that they are influencing his behavior through their control of his thoughts. Hallucinations may also be present. Many paranoid schizophrenics also believe that they have some special distinction, such as being a nationally or internationally noted person in disguise. The stereotype of the patient who believes himself to be Napoleon is based on the paranoid pattern. Frequently, topical references are present; there have been more and more paranoid patients claiming that they have found the cure to cancer, and are the objects of plots against them by the medical profession. Another common paranoid delusion is that the patient is an agent for the FBI with important government secrets, and he is a victim of a gigantic communist conspiracy. Thus delusions of grandeur often are associated with the delusions of persecution. The paranoid schizophrenic also may tend to be quite precise regarding his rights and privileges, and sensitive to power and authority relationships, often being legalistically inclined. The legalism, secretiveness, and suspiciousness are obviously related to his picture of himself as requiring and deserving of the protection of the law from his enemies.

The delusions of the paranoid schizophrenic usually are interrelated to some extent; in some cases, the various delusions are so well articulated or organized that they form a coherent body of belief which may appear to be completely rational, and may be quite difficult to prove or disprove in the legal sense. Obviously, such a patient is likely to be of very great intelligence; it requires no little intellectual ability to reconcile all aspects of his delusional experience into a coherent scheme. This extreme is illustrated by a middle-aged man who entered a hospital seeking a complete psychiatric diagnostic examination. He was a successful businessman but suspected that his wife and brother-in-law were trying to wrest control of the business from him by claiming that he was mentally incompetent by reason of insanity. To forestall this, he sought the examination by physicians of his own choosing, rather than those his wife might select, in order to get a "clean bill of health." When asked what evidence his wife might use against him, he gave as an example the fact that she did not believe that he was really partly Negro. He did not know his true father, who died before he was born. His mother was not Negro. He did not believe that his last name (an Italian name) really was the name of his father. The patient's complexion was somewhat swarthy but he had no apparent negroid features. However, there was little doubt in his mind of his Negroness, which he felt accounted for the cold and unfriendly stares he received from white patrons in restaurants he entered. On the basis of this information alone, of course, the psychiatrist must become something of a detective, if he is to discriminate between a delusion —a false belief —and a realistic problem. The patient *could* be partly Negro, and his wife *might* be plotting against him with her brother. Such things have happened before. However, in this case, the diagnostic problem became simplified when the patient, detained in the psychiatric ward for further examination, began to show more and more marked delusions, such as interpreting a TV commercial by an investment company as part of his wife's plot to tease him.

At the other extreme of systemization of delusions are those patients with more or less isolated delusions having little connection with each other, and diffuse suspiciousness of others. In general, the better organized the delusional system, the older is the patient at the time of his first hospitalization; the younger and the less intelligent the patient, the less organized his delusions tend to be.[5]

Often paranoid delusions are frankly sexual; the patient may believe that others are plotting to make homosexual assaults on him, or that others are putting homosexual thoughts in his mind, or that "they" make him masturbate so that he will lose his mind or be eternally damned.

Catatonic Schizophrenia. The catatonic schizophrenic is one who tends to use a great deal of symbolic movements. It is not known whether the posturing of the catatonic are intentionally communicative or are only expressive.[6] The patient appears vacant and detached from his social environment. In classical cases, the patient's body is so passive that for long periods of time and without apparent effort it will maintain the fairly distorted positions into which a physician may place it. This characteristic is known as "waxy flexibility." More frequently, the catatonic state is marked by extreme inertia and rigid posturing which offers resistance to attempts to change the position of the body or limbs. On occasion, the catatonic may suddenly change from this extremely passive state to one of intense rage and fury in which the vigor of his attacks on other people and objects disregards physical pain produced in the patient in his attack as completely as the catatonic stupor disregards physical comfort. Because of this disregard of pain, catatonic rage exceeds the rage of a normally excited person. The inhibition produced by pain and restraint where there is danger of injury are absent.

The catatonic frequently appears to be hallucinating, responding to his hallucinations with gestures and occasional verbalizations. It is quite difficult to establish verbal communication with the patient, who appears not to hear verbal stimuli and who, after his catatonic state has been present for a long period of time, is simply not in the habit of speaking.

Hebephrenic Schizophrenia. "Hebephrenic," a word of Greek origin meaning "youthful mind," describes a schizophrenic state in which giggling, playfulness, and overt acting-out is very similar to play characteristic of childhood. The hebephrenic may enjoy playing with dolls, toy airplanes, and other playthings. His activity usually is solitary, and his only relationships are those with the objects with which he plays. The hebephrenic patient frequently talks to himself, grimaces, even becoming emotionally excited by his hallucinations, in a manner reminiscent of the way in which a young child entertains himself with acting out his fantasies when he is alone. The hebephrenic may show similar interest in or delight in his excreta, and may act coy and irreverent, particularly regarding sex. He may be naively frank in his sexual behavior, making giggling references to his genitals. Speech is likely to be incoherent, with the patient's associations and responses seeming to be incomprehensible and irrelevant to any shared reality. In general, the hebephrenic shows extreme disorganization of personality, in the sense that very little of normal functioning remains intact. Despite the apparent childish pleasure, the hebephrenic's laughter often seems forced and tense, and may be interrupted by fearful hallucinations in which voices are described as calling him vile names, accusing him of immoral acts, and the like.

Simple Schizophrenia. This variety of schizophrenic behavior is characterized by unemotional solitariness in a person who appears to be almost completely without interest in objects, persons, or events. There seems to be no motivation to do anything. The patient simply may sit and stare vacantly into space; he may not feel that eating, getting dressed in the morning, or any of the other routines of life are important enough to engage in. Relationships with other people are quite distant, with an apparent lack of real emotional responsiveness in the patient who often acts as if he cannot understand other people and cannot feel any companionship with them. Although thinking may not be as impaired as in the other forms described, the patient often seems "vague" and "abstracted." The patient does not respond to his work or family responsibilities and sometimes appears not to understand why they are considered important by others. The patient is difficult to arouse emotionally, seemingly nonaggressive and apathetic. The content of the patient's thinking reflects a "what's the use" attitude, a kind of resigned lack of pleasure in life, in which the best that the patient can say about anything is that it is "not so bad."

Onset and Development of Schizophrenia. The first onset of schizophrenic behavior may occur suddenly and dramatically in many cases, usually involving some obviously bizarre or inappropriate act. In other cases it has a slower development in which the individual seems to drift into more and more loneliness and withdrawal, with the gradual appearance of mumblings to himself, then talking to himself, and eventually clear-cut hallucinations. Withdrawal and indifference to events and people in his surroundings, seclusiveness, fearfulness in the presence of others, and suspiciousness, may have a similarly gradual onset. Bizarre thinking may be the culmination of a long development, beginning with "odd" interpretations of events which have enough reasonableness in them to appear acceptable, gradually becoming more and more magical, mysterious, or absurd. At first the person may be only "not with it," tending to be shy and lonely, with few interests in his social environment. He may be thought of by others as a "grind" or merely "odd." As the seclusiveness continues and grows more intense, as there is less and less social participation and a sharing of ideas, thinking becomes more and more disoriented. The person goes from being "square" to "odd" to "eccentric" to "crazy." Where the onset is apparently sudden, however, there usually has been clearly present to the trained observer an established pattern of isolation, emotional indifference or apathy, and inability to deal intellectually and realistically with ideas and problem situations. This prodromal pattern of extensive fantasizing, weak reality testing, and difficulty in understanding emotional relationships with other people is described as *latent schizophrenia.* It may include some extra efforts to understand those events which the person finds initially incomprehensible, efforts manifested by unusually close attention to details, intensive efforts to figure out things which most people simply accept at face value or ignore, or unusual concern with paradoxes and inconsistencies which confuse the person and which he focuses on as the basis of his difficulty in understanding reality.

Sudden onset characterizes "reactive schizophrenia" while the gradual development produces "process schizophrenia."[7] In reactive schizophrenia the thought disturbance is almost all in the area of perception, with relatively little disturbance of logic or language. It is quite possible that this kind of schizophrenia is the result of sudden intense stress, involving very high drive levels. We already have seen that perception is quite sensitive to drive; the effects of drive on perception forms the basis for hallucinations. However, habits of logical thinking and speaking are less sensitive to sudden changes in drive level. When these functions are disturbed, as they are in process schizophrenia, it seems more likely that there has been a long history of poor reality testing and withdrawal from the environment. As you would guess, the reactive schizophrenic usually makes a more rapid recovery than does the process schizophrenic.

As schizophrenic behavior progresses, the patient's life situation usually deteriorates. Inability to support himself, and the straining of whatever reliable personal relationships he had, create more and more problems for him, further overburdening his limited problem solving skills. Eventual hospitalization constitutes a major trauma, as the patient becomes isolated from his accustomed environment and is placed in the hospital world in which even those few situations and relationships which he has been able to feel comfortable in are changed drastically, or are entirely absent. As hospitalization continues, with its relative lack of inhibitions against infantile and unrealistic behavior, and as the patient has more and more practice at schizophrenic behaviors, it becomes more and more difficult to produce effective personality change. It is not surprising that a patient who has been hospitalized for twenty years as a chronic schizophrenic, with the first hospitalization occurring relatively early in life, is completely inaccessible to treatment; such a patient has had more practice at not communicating, at using private language, at engaging in fantasy and regressive behavior, than he has had in logical thinking, reality testing, and problem solving. Obviously, the earlier in the schizophrenic process that treatment is begun, the greater is the opportunity for success, even though the early schizophrenic may be more eruptive, dramatic in his symptoms, changeable in his behavior, and overtly bizarre than the chronic, stabilized patient who had reached the stage of well-confirmed habitual schizophrenic behavior. The early reactive schizophrenic is still in the stage of behavioral variability in which he is trying out various responses to his conflicts; the process schizophrenic is past this stage and shows rigid ambivalence which is less modifiable than the reactive's flexibility.

Theories of Schizophrenia. Because of the severity of the social and individual problems posed by schizophrenic behavior (it accounts for 20 to 30 per cent of first admissions to hospitals, and because of the great length of hospitalization involved, usually is responsible for over half of the population of psychiatric hospitals),[8] great efforts in research and theory have been directed at understanding its nature and causes. However, it is the kind of social problem which does not receive widespread social support, compared with physical illnesses which do not arouse as much fear and avoidance in the people who donate money for charity, and compared with economic, political, and military problems. As a result, there is a multiplicity of theories, with too little research data available to be sure which of the theories are most likely to be confirmed. A further problem is the variety of behaviors which are included as schizophrenic; this makes it likely that no single theory will adequately account for all schizophrenic manifestations. The result is that there are different theories appropriate to different aspects of the problem. An attempt will be made here merely to mention the salient features of what seem to be the most promising theories.

Physiological Predisposition. Some theorists have addressed themselves to the important question of who is likely to become schizophrenic. One answer that has been proposed is that schizophrenics are people with some innate, usually inherited biological predisposition toward the development of such behavior when sufficient stress is present. Two lines of evidence are cited: schizophrenia tends to run in families, such that the child of two schizophrenic parents is more likely to become schizophrenic than the child of one schizophrenic parent, or the one whose parents and grandparents have not been so diagnosed; the identical twin of a schizophrenic is much more likely to be schizophrenic than the nonidentical fraternal twin of a schizophrenic.[9] Secondly there are demonstrable differences between schizophrenics and nonschizophrenics in blood chemistry, autonomic functioning, and anatomical details of the body organs.[10, 11] In addition, there is considerable evidence that schizophrenia is diagnosed more frequently in people from the lower socioeconomic class, and in people from marginal status and socially disorganized neighborhoods, than in people from well established middleclass groups.[12] Obviously, there are alternative interpretations possible for these data; schizophrenic parents may provide experiences for their children which result in the acquisition of schizophrenic behaviors, and the nonschizophrenic children of schizophrenic parents nevertheless may have enough tendency toward such behavior to provide schizophrenogenic experiences to their children. The physiological changes present among schizophrenics could well be the results of the schizophrenic process, particularly of chronic, unsolved, conflicting drive states. And schizophrenia may actually exist no more frequently in certain segments of the population. It may only be more apparent, or less well hidden by friends and relatives, in such groups. Alternatively, schizophrenics may tend to "drift" into lower class areas because of their failures in their usual environments.

Variations of the biological predisposition theory have been proposed. One is that schizophrenia is a potential characteristic of all humans, as evidenced by the behavior of two- and three-year old children. Their behavior is very similar to that of schizophrenic adults, involving a great deal of fantasy, difficulty in understanding the physical and social environment, lack of respect for the nature and limitations of reality, loose associations, and even bizarre ideas. This theory suggests that as one grows up he learns *not* to be schizophrenic, and the failure of such learning results in adult schizophrenia. It has already been indicated in our discussion of thinking that reality contact is more of an achievement of the socialization process than it is an innate property of people. In effect, this achievement means that infants usually learn to grow out of their "natural schizophrenia."

Nevertheless, not everyone becomes schizophrenic — not even all the children of schizophrenic parents. The biological theorists suggest that there is an interaction between environmental stress and innate predisposition, such that where predisposition is low, stress must be great to produce even the most transient schizophrenic episode, and where predisposition is great, relatively minor stress is sufficient to produce a longlasting schizophrenic pattern. The environmental theorists, on the other hand, argue that all schizophrenia can be accounted for on the basis of psychological factors in the experience of the individual. A compromise position between the two has been suggested: emotional stress may produce changes in the autonomic centers of the brain which in turn produce a physiological predisposition toward schizophrenic behavior. This theory was mentioned in Chapter 3.

It should be noted here that recent work with mescaline drugs and LSD-25 has provided some support for a physiological theory. It has been found that when these drugs are taken by normal people, they produce behavior which is very similar to schizophrenic, thus suggesting that schizophrenia may be the product of some similar biochemical substances produced in the body.[13]

Learned Factors in Schizophrenia. Many psychologists have concerned themselves with the environmental factors which may affect schizophrenia, either as the whole cause, or as catalysts for some innate predisposition resulting in the activation of the behavior. The impaired reality contact in schizophrenia has focused attention on early infantile experience, occurring at the age at which interest in and responsiveness to the social and physical environment is first established or fails to be firmly established. It has been suggested that difficulties in the early feeding relationships between the infant and the mother — the child's first interaction with reality — may be crucial in determining how much reward or punishment will result from the child's responses to external stimuli. Studies on institutionalized children, and on the relationships existing between the parents and their children who later become schizophrenic suggest that these relationships are marked by a failure to establish reliable mutual satisfactions, lack of consistent maternal warmth, and inability of the child to be assured of the gratification of established drives for affection.[14] Generally it is felt that the trauma responsible for schizophrenic withdrawal from reality must be one which occurs before the child has developed sufficient mental functioning to acquire reactions to frustration and conflict less drastic than the massive denial of reality involved in shizophrenia.

The environmental theorists thus suggest that a basic weakness in reality contact is early established, one wherein later stress can easily result in the unrealistic thinking and acting which characterizes overt schizophrenia. In addition, the early difficulty in paying close attention to and solving reality problems can have a snowballing effect. As the child grows older, he leaves more and more problems inadequately solved, thus further increasing the difficulty he has in understanding and thinking about his situation in realistic terms.

Some support for this viewpoint is inferred from the relationship between the age at which the first overt schizophrenic behavior appears and the degree of impairment of thought which is present. The earlier the schizophrenia occurs, the more bizarre, illogical, and distorted are the patient's ideas. Paranoid schizophrenia, which has the latest age of onset (usually about forty years) is the type in which logical and reasonable thinking is least impaired, and within this type, the later the paranoid pattern emerges and the more intelligent the patient, the better is his reality contact. This suggests that the longer the person has had practice at reality testing and logical thinking in shared social terms, the more resistant to extinction such thinking becomes when the severe stress of conflict occurs.[15]

Schizophrenic Thought. There has been some exciting recent work on the nature of schizophrenic thought which attempts to answer the question of how the bizarre associations and inappropriate responses become established. This work, done largely by Sarnoff Mednick and his students, suggests that schizophrenic thought may be the product of extreme stimulus generalization resulting from extraordinarily high drive.[16] As was pointed out in Chapter 3, increases in drive result in an increase in the overall height of the stimulus generalization gradient, so that more and more tenuously related stimuli become included under the gradient. Mednick suggests that the odd associations of the schizophrenic are the results of giving responses initially learned in relation to one cue —responses which in that cue situation appear reasonable —to cues which are very different from the initially learned one, but which exist far out on the stimulus generalization gradient. Responses to such distantly related cues occur because of great increases in the height of the stimulus generalization gradient as a result of extremely high anxiety drive. It has been further hypothesized that the widening of the stimulus generalization gradient may itself become habitual. In the chronic schizophrenic, odd responding is rewarded by a reduction in anxiety which occurs when the schizophrenic thus is able to avoid responding to the originally learned cue, or those which are closely similar to it —cues which may be associated with fear and punishment. A wide stimulus generalization gradient may become habitual as a result of the operation of learning set (see Fig. 16, p. 480). Because of numerous learning experiences in which wide generalization is reinforcing, succeeding learning experiences produce wider and wider generalization gradients than they would if they had not been preceded by the experiences that produced a "set" for wide generalization. In the schizophrenic, then, the extreme stimulus generalization which occurs even in new learning situations is a product of his already acquired "set." This set has probably been acquired through the repeated exercise of the substitution responses to strong and persistent conflicts evoked by a stressful environment. It will be remembered that the substitutions are based on stimulus generalization. It is likely that the schizophrenic, whose conflicts are intense (that is, the competing gradients are very high), is one whose substitutions occur far out on the gradients. While these substitutions are reinforced, thus establishing the learning set for wide generalization, the conflicts grow more intense and the substitutions less capable of reducing anxiety, pushing the schizophrenic to substitutions further and further away from the realistic response to the reality cues. This process weakens reality contact, and when it occurs in a setting of poor reality testing habits, greater and greater violation of reality occurs and the individual becomes a deteriorated chronic schizophrenic. A return to the discussion of reality testing (Chapter 5) will remind the student that weak reality testing is a product of the same factors that interact with the dynamics of conflict and poor reality contact.

The schizophrenic's habitually wide generalization also may be related to two other factors: inconsistent parental training may teach the child to make the same response to a wide range of parental behavior, in effect teaching the child to generalize his responses to a wide variety of stimuli (and such inconsistent parental behavior is a typical feature in the childhood backgrounds of schizophrenics);[17, 18] and the categories for perceptual definitions of objects widen in the developing schizophrenic because a highly punishing or nonrewarding environment makes fine discriminations among external objects and events unnecessary and unrewarding, so that discrimination learning that would counteract stimulus generalization does not occur.

The overinclusive generalizing of schizophrenics, upon which this theory is based, has been noted by many investigators. As an example of this kind of thinking, a schizophrenic may use the word "door" to mean "whore" simply because they sound alike, this being the basis of generalization from one to the other word. This is called "clang" associating. Familiarity with the illness known as gall stones may lead a schizophrenic to think of his stomach as stone, and to react to stones as parts of his stomach. The patient who responded to a broken handle as a symbol of his wife's rejection is an example of schizophrenic generalizing. The poor judgment involved in such overinclusive thinking, which represents an extreme form of *schizoid thought* (in which connections between events may be slightly tenuous but not clearly bizarre), is a result of the schizophrenic's poor reality testing, and his inability to assess and understand the responses of others to his ideas. The nonschizophrenic usually interprets such responses as having relevance to whether

Figure 16. Stimulus Generalization and Learning Set

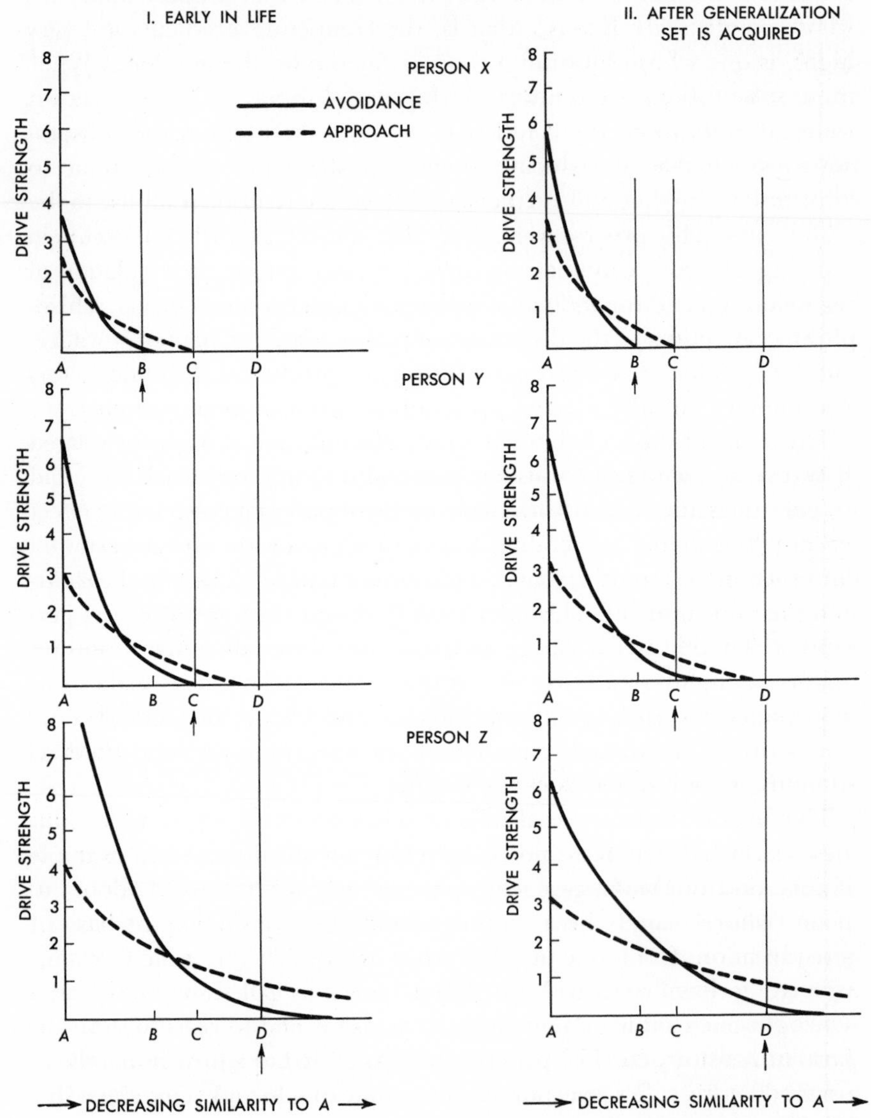

The arrow marks the point of greatest net response strength. Stimuli at that distance from *A* evoke the strongest displaced response.

Person *X* has small conflicts in early life, displaces to *B*, and develops a generalization set that produces habitually close displacements to *B* even when stronger conflicts occur after the set has been acquired. Person *Y*'s early conflicts are stronger, producing displacements to *C* and a generalization set to displace as far as *C*. Person *Z*, with intense conflicts early in life, displaces quite distantly to *D* because of the heights of his conflicting gradients. He thus develops a generalization set so that even with milder conflicts later, he displaces distantly to *D*. The result is that after generalization sets have been acquired, if *X*, *Y*, and *Z* experience conflicts of exactly the same intensity, *X* displaces narrowly to *B*, *Y* displaces to *C*, and *Z* displaces very widely to *D*. Early in life, the extent of displacement depends on the intensity (height) of the conflicts experienced; after these displacements have become habitual as a result of the growth of a set, the extent of displacement remains about the same regardless of the intensity of the conflict. Person *Z* is most like the schizophrenic, in that his set to generalize widely produces distant displacements even under mild conflict, while other people like *X* and *Y* do not displace so widely under the same conflict conditions. Thus *Z*'s response to *D* seems bizarre and inappropriate.

his thoughts and ideas are reasonable; the schizophrenic, who does not understand others so well, or the meanings of their behavior, does not have this avenue of feed-back to use in checking his ideas.

The motivation which produces over-inclusive thinking is anxiety of great proportions, anxiety which is readily stimulated and evoked by a large variety of cue situations. The seclusiveness of the schizophrenic, his fearfulness of others, points to the presence of other people as the cues which evoke this strong anxiety. Some research on the learning performance of schizophrenics supports this theory: it is found that schizophrenics learn simple responses as readily as nonschizophrenics when the reinforcement used is nonpersonal (such as a light flashing after the correct response), but they learn more poorly when the reinforcement is interpersonal (the experimenter saying "Yes, that's right"). The fearfulness and anxiety evoked by other people is probably the result of the same factors which account for the schizophrenic's poor reality contact — the early infantile feeding situation, which we already have seen has important implications for the development of positive feelings towards others. It is not surprising then that many schizophrenics show in their behavior feelings of trememdous rage and hostility toward others, feelings which form part of the schizophrenic's conflict between his hostility, his fear of being hostile, and his affectional drive.

Conflict Responses in Schizophrenia. Many psychologist have been concerned with an analysis of the behavior of the schizophrenic in terms of his reactions to conflict and anxiety. The basic pattern of the schizophrenic is interpreted to be denial of reality and compensatory fantasy — a denial which probably is established early in life before contact with reality is well enough developed to make denial difficult, and before less drastic responses to anxiety are made available by the child's intellectual development. Delusions and hallucinations, occurring in a setting of weak reality contact, are extreme forms of primitive projection. The content of the schizophrenic delusions and hallucinations frequently seem to serve as rationalizations for the schizophrenic's behavior, or for his unsatisfying life situation. Thus the delusions of the paranoid that he is an important person rationalize the hostility which he projects onto others. A common delusion among schizophrenic women is that they are the long lost daughters of either royalty or some wealthy persons, stolen from their parents by enemies or gypsies. The particular content of these rationalizations (their self-glorifying nature) point to the schizophrenic's preoccupation with his self instead of a positive interest in external objects. His own fantasy is more rewarding than are people in his environment.

The childish behavior, the loss of social graces, and the deterioration of habits of eating, dressing, and elimination which is present in many schizophrenics, often are interpreted as a massive regression to the infantile state at which the original fixating trauma presumably occurred. We have already discussed the concept of regression; it is an extremely complicated behavior pattern. Very likely the schizophrenic is one whose learning after infancy has been relatively weak, so that more infantile responses may readily appear in behavior when later learned responses tend toward extinction through lack of continued reinforcement. The denial and withdrawal of the schizophrenic contribute to his fear of the interpersonal environment. The denial and withdrawal combine with the fear to make later learning less strong than that which was present before the schizophrenic process was begun in infancy. Further, the continued frustrations of the schizophrenic, in part due to his ineffectual ways of responding to reality and to his problems, create a situation in which regressive responses are likely to occur. The cues arising from regressed infantile or childlike behavior act as secondary reinforcers because of their association with feelings of safety and security. The contrast between the security feelings evoked by infantile behavior, and the insecurity and fear which marks the schizophrenic's life situations contributes to the regressive tendency. This regression removes some of the inhibitions placed on behavior by the social environment's enforcement of its role prescriptions for adult behavior. Thus the fantasy of the schizophrenic is likely to be of a very immature and naive quality, and to include the kind of personal or private images characteristic of children's fantasy. The regression theory of schizophrenia fits into the theory that childhood represents a "normal schizophrenia" which people grow out of.

Some Unanswered Questions. There are obvious lines of continuity among the various theories of schizophrenia presented here. However, and despite the plausibility of these theories and their mutually supporting nature, there are many many unanswered questions. Why do certain drugs seem to produce a remission in schizophrenic behavior? Why does electroshock treatment seem to "snap" some patients out of schizophrenia? Even more pressing problems exist in the area of therapy. Schizophrenic behavior is such as to make efforts to reverse the process particularly difficult. Such efforts usually must be made by people, to whom the schizophrenic responds with avoidance, withdrawal, and denial, thus making communication almost impossible. Why is it, then, that many recovered schizophrenics can report quite accurately many of the things that happened around them at a time when their reality contact seemed so obviously poor? We can only conclude that schizophrenia is still largely a mystery, though not as mysterious as it must appear to the lay person. It is becoming one of the most researched behavior patterns today, and continued advances are likely to provide some of the answers.

Affective Psychoses. Extreme states of mood, as in severe depression or intense elation, are included as affective psychoses. These also may be known as manic or depressive psychoses, and sometimes when they occur in the same person, they are known as manic-depressive psychosis. Although it is the popular belief that the swings of mood included here go from elation to depression and then back again in a full cycle fashion, this does not in fact happen in most patients. One patient may become depressed, swing back to a relatively normal mood, and then go back into a depression; or a manic state may give way to a normal pace, and then reappear. It is less frequent for a depression to be followed by a manic state. These mood states are usually temporary, although they may be repeated. Many patients may have only one episode, others may have two, and still fewer have three or more episodes.

The depressive psychosis may be one of two kinds: the patient may show a severe slowdown in behavior, becoming almost mute, moving slowly, minimally responsive to others, and appearing profoundly sorrowful. He may sit for long hours silently weeping or simply sighing. The other kind of depression is an agitated state of severe anxiety, in which the patient paces back and forth, is very jumpy and fidgety, and seems to have to keep moving, perhaps moaning aloud, accusing himself, uttering prayers for salvation, and behaving impulsively in his motor activity, responding with dramatic fear to his hallucinations.

In either state the patient may have hallucinations of voices accusing him of terrible crimes against morality, or warning him of horrible punishments and tortures in hell awaiting him, or simply telling him what a terrible person he is. The patient usually feels that he is beyond help, even though he may plead for someone to do something, saying at the same time that he is too bad, too far gone in evil ways, for anyone to help him. The patient also may feel that he is unworthy of help. While appreciative of interest shown in him by others, the patient nevertheless may tell them to go away and leave him because he is not worth their interest or attention. Suicide is a potential danger in both types, with the agitated depressive patient more likely to be impulsive in his suicide attempt, and the retarded patient more deliberate and planful.

The manic state is essentially the reverse of the depressive. It includes a tremendous speedup in activity and associative processes, a great deal of overt activity, feelings of great euphoria and elation, an expansive mood which looks toward the future as containing everything good within it. The patient anticipates some great event that will "set everyone free," or will provide everyone with riches, love, and beauty. Frequently this expectation is expressed through a religious delusion in which the patient believes either that the second appearance of Christ is imminent, or that God will reveal himself to the world. The general tone of the patient is of great confidence in himself and in his powers. There may be the belief that he possesses magical powers of insight. The patient may be full of confidence in some worldshaking or ambitious plans which "can't fail." His generosity is unbounded as he promises others that they will share in the fruits of his plan. The patient may hear God talking to him, or may hallucinate contact with famous dead people. The patient usually plays the role of a hero in his delusions.

The patient's thought processes as well as his motor behavior seem to be greatly speeded up. He associates so rapidly that it may be difficult to follow him. He cannot stay on one topic long enough to explain but is already thinking about other things. He shows quick humor and a sharp wit, which may have a distinctly hostile tone to it, through its effect of poking fun at or belittling others. On occasion the patient may talk in rhyme for extended periods, so rapid is his thinking. His motor behavior may be similarly excited, so that he will attempt ambitious physical feats and show apparently great endurance and "bounciness," to the point where he may physically wear himself out and produce real physical problems by trying feats of which he is physically incapable. Needless to say, his judgment is greatly impaired.

Between episodes, and before the patient has ever had a psychotic episode, his behavior may show marked similarity to either manic or depressive patterns. Normally he may be subject to fairly marked mood swings, either given to mild depressions, or to a capacity for excitement, joking, and activity. The depressive patient is often described as having been particularly concerned with matters of religion and guilt before his psychotic episode, to be a very sincere, serious person, perhaps given to extensive worrying about the human condition, or about particular people. He is often described as scrupulously honest, and frequently sacrificing of his convenience, time, and energy, in his devotion to others. The premorbid personality of the manic is often that of a wise-cracking, life-of-the-party kind of person, one who frequently is developing new schemes or plans for getting rich, a fountain of optimism and fun. He tends to talk and act rapidly, although his impulsiveness may be well within normal limits.

Manic and depressive psychoses do not constitute the kind of social problem created by schizophrenia. Spontaneous remission of symptoms frequently occurs, and the pattern of behavior is readily modified by drugs and electroshock therapy. As a result, there is much less experimental and theoretical investigation of the affective psychoses than there is in schizophrenia, so that much less is known about these patterns of behavior. It seems likely, from a consideration of the symptoms of depression, that guilt plays a central role in producing the severe anxiety which is seen, and that intropunitiveness is the primary mode of its expression. The retarded and the agitated depressives may differ in that one represents a depressive state in a conceptually-oriented person, while the other is a depressed motorically-oriented individual. The factors influencing the growth of habits of responding in thought *vs.* responding in action were discussed in Chapter 8.

Depressions apparently occur in people who have not acquired any responses to anxiety which reduce it. Thus anxiety is experienced directly, and as would be expected, has a large component of fear of punishment in it. The hallucinations which are present are exaggerated projections of the patient's guilt.

Of what is the patient guilty? As noted above, frequently such patients are described as having led very moral and upright lives. The depressed patient frequently cites some relatively minor action as the cause of his impending punishment — a childhood prank, or a lack of proper respect for a distant relative who later died. Should one attempt to convince the patient that that is really not a very bad thing, and had no dire consequences, the patient is likely to reply that there really is a great deal of evil in his heart. This kind of behavior suggests that the patient's guilt is aroused by punished drives of which he himself may be only barely aware; the small crime to which he ascribes his condition may be an effort to find something to justify his feeling of guilt — something which is, however, not so terrible that he cannot think of it. The crime to which the patient admits may be the result of efforts to think of something of minor importance in order to avoid thinking of the real guilty idea. In this sense, a depressed patient is one who is repressing the source of his guilt.

This explanation suggests that the depressive person is one who has had particularly extensive training in guilt, and in the intropunitive expression of hostility. That is, the person who tends toward the depressive personality structure is one who is highly prone to develop strong guilt; he is one whose standards for his own behavior are very moralistic. Even mild hostility in response to frustration arouses intense anxiety. The depressive episode has been interpreted as the failure of reaction-formation to maintain repression of aggression aroused in the person. Violent aggressive impulses frequently are the basis of the patient's feeling of being a very terrible person.

The reaction-formation which seems to characterize the depressive person's usual behavior often requires that he do things to demonstrate his goodness. It is not sufficient to refrain from committing wrongs; rather, it is necessary to do good works, in order to reduce the presence of any cues which might elicit anxiety and guilt. It often happens that the personal sacrifice made in such reaction-formation is not fully appreciated, and does not bring overt rewards aside from the reduction of guilt to the person. The increased hostility which such failure to find appreciation may arouse, stimulating still further reaction-formation and even greater disappointment and frustration, sets the conditions for the possible breakdown of the reaction-formation as a means of reducing the cues of aggression. Thus an acute depression is precipitated. It is possible that the great passivity of the depressed patient may itself be a reaction to the impossibility of doing more, as well as an expression of the patient's aggression which is too much to permit him to continue doing good. In a sense, the depressed patient is immobilized by his conflicts.

In many depressed patients the failure to feel appreciated seems to be a very important feature. One is struck by the patient's strong dependency drives, particularly as they are expressed in his extreme passivity. It is often found that the patient as a child failed to have his dependency needs satisfied, because of his identification with parents who prohibited "childish" behavior or affectional displays. This is illustrated by one fairly typical depressed patient. His mother was a very self-contained woman who seldom initiated affectionate interactions with her children. His father, on the other hand, was a stern man who required the patient to act grown up and to inhibit his childish dependent behavior. The patient identified strongly with his father, and so was in a position in which he was given little affection by his mother, and could not ask directly for satisfaction of his affectional and dependency drives. Very likely the patient's reaction-forming "goodness" was a subtle way he had learned to get attention and support from other people as partial satisfactions of his dependency drive.

This strong dependency, together with the aggression mentioned earlier, provides the depressed person's basic conflict. Obviously his aggression would create no problems if it were not so dangerous so far as satisfying dependency and affectional needs is concerned; similarly, dependency by itself would not produce the turmoil which ensues were it not threatened by the fear that aggression might destroy the object who satisfies the drives for love and regard. It is a key feature of depressions that there has been a loss of the object of the patient's dependency and affectional drives — either a real or a psychological loss of the object.[19] And it is this loss which produces the guilt over the hostility that the patient feels is responsible for his loss, the pervading grief and sadness, and the lack of interest in life and the world. It is in this sense that psychotic depressions are extensions of mourning sadness.

The manic state has been interpreted as a reaction-formation to the depression, as a denial of the anxiety and worthlessness which the patient is likely to experience if he should slow down and stop thinking thoughts incompatible with this feeling. Many investigators have noted the combination of disguised hostility in the patient with a desire to do good for others in a moral sense.

Affective psychotics vary in the extent to which reality is violated in their hallucinations and delusions. Some workers have suggested that to the extent there is such violation, to that extent may the patient be considered schizophrenic. This interpretation makes psychosis, schizophrenia, and weakened reality contact coincidental in having a common core, a position that seems to have some merit in it.

A discussion of manic and depressive states would not be complete without mention of associated physiological factors. The extent to which physiological factors are determinants of the mood state is still a matter of uncertainty. It is well known that glandular factors affect activity level. Thus some theorists have suggested that the slowdown in depression and its reverse in manic states are the result of some disorder of the glandular balance. The similarity between the behavior of the depressed patient and involutional psychosis, a depression precipitated during the "change of life" in which there is marked change in hormonal production (as well as in psychological and social factors), between depressive episodes and the feelings of depression which often accompany menstruation, and between depressive states and the dysphoric feelings which mothers sometimes experience shortly after they have given birth (postpartum depression) again presumed to be the result of the hormonal changes occurring, all suggest a contribution by physiological factors to these psychoses. It should be pointed out that all of these similar reactions with which depressions have been compared can also be explained on psychological grounds, even though hormonal factors obviously are present. On the other hand, we have already seen that there are individual differences in both the ease of autonomic arousal and in the extent of such arousal, which could operate such that some people are physiologically more capable of the great retardation found in depression than are others. It also should be mentioned that the physiological anomalies found in depressed patients could just as well be the effects of the physical retardation, as the causes of it. One who sits passively all the day long is likely to breathe more shallowly, to have a slower pulse, and less oxygen provided to the brain and the muscles, which in turn makes it even more difficult for the patient to move and engage in activity. Finally, it is possible that what may start out as a physiological reaction becomes functionally psychotic when the physiological processes involved are learned and become chronic and habitual. Something like this was seen in the case of the man with the vomiting symptom, described in Chapter 9.

There are other psychotic states which have not been mentioned or elaborated in this section: involutional melancholia, postpartum psychosis, childhood autism, senile dementia, alcoholic hallucinosis, and dementia tremens, to name a few. However, a more complete study of such behavior would constitute a course in abnormal psychology. The main effort here is to indicate some of the major problems in the area, and to stress the pertinence of the study of personality to these problems (and vice versa).

The main distinguishing feature of the psychoses is extensive loss of contact with reality, particularly as expressed in hallucinations and delusions; this poor reality contact may be the product of both inadequate learning and the development of responses to anxiety which involve a turning away from reality, as in denial and restitutive fantasy. Both these elements are present in the premorbid personality before some precipitating incident occurred to increase the display of such habits in a person with an already tenuous orientation to reality. They also exist in people who do not ever become actually psychotic, either because they have just enough training in realistic thinking to prevent psychotic thought, or because they lack the stress which results in extensive denial, withdrawal, and fantasy. Such nonpsychotic people may nevertheless be referred to as having schizophrenic or manic-depressive tendencies or schizoid, manic, or depressive character structures, by which is meant that their main pattern of personality is similar in its features to the personalities which include psychotic behavior under certain circumstances. We will discuss in greater detail this continuity between psychotic and nonpsychotic behavior later in this chapter.

The Psychoneuroses

The psychoneuroses (or, more commonly, neuroses) have been differentiated traditionally from the psychoses on the grounds that the neuroses do not involve such extensive loss of reality contact. The neurotic is usually thought to be a person whose responses to anxiety and conflict are more focalized, and do not result in such extensive violation of realistic thinking as that expressed in delusions and hallucinations. Because of the good reality contact in neurotics, communication is adequate to permit effective psychotherapy. As a result, the neuroses have been more extensively and intensively studied than the psychoses. Thus the major portion of this chapter will be devoted to the main neurotic patterns and their causes.

Obsessive-Compulsive Neuroses. An obsession is a dominating, insistent idea or symbolic content that is so everpresent that the obsessed person's thoughts are frequently quite inappropriate to his social situation. A compulsion is similar to an obsession, except that it exists in overt motor acts, rather than in thinking. Like an obsession it is insistent and inappropriate, and repetitive.

The contents of obsessions and compulsions usually are apparently odd or meaningless, or inconsistent with the person's ideas about himself and others. Some common obsessions are the thought by a father that some terrible thing will happen to his children, or that he might do something to harm them; the thought aroused in a young man every time he saw a girl that he might attack and rape her; the feeling in a middle-aged mother that she was unclean and was spreading infectious germs to everyone and everything she touched; an insistent idea in a religious person that he will commit a sin or a blasphemy. The obsessed person often feels literally haunted by the thought, which seems to have some independent existence that comes and goes without the person being able to control it in any way. There is a suggestion that the sufferer does not feel responsible for the thought as being *his* idea, and he is often genuinely puzzled about why he should have such thoughts. The person often is afraid of his obsessional thoughts, becomes depressed by them (sometimes to the point of suicide as the only escape), and is particularly terrified by the feeling that his thought might "take hold" of him so that he actually commits the act suggested by the idea, that he might lose control of himself and in fact do something horrible. Many patients attempt to protect themselves from such a possibility. The father afraid that he might do something to his children may make elaborate arrangements to insure that he is either never left alone with his children, or that there are never any objects around that might serve as weapons: scissors, table knives, hammers, letter openers, razors, etc., are banished from his environment. Such efforts obviously extend the significance of the behavior pattern in the patient's life, because they involve more efforts at self-control, and restrictions on the person's normal course of life. These efforts to avoid or reduce the power of the obsessive idea may become the dominant feature of the person's behavior and become the most significant source of interference in his relationships with others and himself.

Compulsions seem to be more varied and elaborate than obsessions. They may range from repetitive washing of the hands with strong soap (perhaps twenty to thirty times a day) through elaborate rituals which include most of the person's day. Some typical minor compulsions are: the requirement by a businessman that his desk be arranged in a particular invariant way by his secretary, a repetitive gesture which seems apparently meaningless, such as pulling out a strand or two of his hair several times a day by a grade school boy, repeated checking that the brake on the car was properly set, or that the front door was locked, or that the water was turned off in the sink, with recurrent doubt that such details were properly taken care of, or a regularity in performing usual routines which becomes so perfect that the routines become like rituals. For example, the routine of getting dressed in the morning may become so ritualized that the person feels he must put on his undershirt before his underpants, must put on the right sock before the left, the right shoe before the left, and his shirt before his trousers. The person usually tolerates no change in the order of these performances; should he make an error, he usually begins all over again, sometimes feeling that to do so is a just punishment for his carelessness and therefore a way of training himself to be more careful next time. Rituals of this kind often spread to other activities. The dressing ritual may come to include the order in which he bathes, cleans his teeth, shaves, and eats breakfast, and can become so elaborate that it soon becomes difficult for him to get to work on time, or meet his social obligations.

Other compulsions include counting fenceposts as one walks on the street, or avoiding stepping on the cracks in the sidewalk, or an irresistible impulse to steal an object from a store (usually an object which is not needed and which would probably never be bought by the person), stealing items of women's clothing and masturbating with them, setting fires, or revealing one's sex organs in a public place. The compulsive person often feels that his compulsion is peculiar and nonsensical, and one that he finds very disturbing and unpleasant. He makes frequent vows to resist performing the act, and may take steps to remove himself from temptation. However, he usually experiences a buildup of tension and anxiety and worry which becomes intolerable, and which he knows can be reduced only by performing the act, so that resistance usually gives way to the need for relief. Sometimes the compulsive person feels little control over the action, which seems to go on almost outside of self-awareness, as in well ingrained habits. The person even may seek some external controls to prevent himself from repeating the action, such as asking to be placed in jail or in a hospital where others will not permit him to give in to his need to perform the compulsive action. In others, the compulsive act is regarded as of minor importance, and not worth fighting against, although it is recognized as being silly and irrelevant. This reaction is not unlike that of the person who walks around a ladder, knowing that his superstition is silly, but still feeling that it is easier to walk around than to feel the discomfort and anxiety which he knows would be his if he walked under it.

Both obsessive and compulsive people have many traits in common. They are usually highly intolerant of ambiguity, are orderly and neat,

and tend to be habit bound, in the sense that they are resistent to changing their accustomed ways of doing things. This trait is referred to as
rigidity. Such people tend to be precise in words and action and seem
to seek and demand perfection in themselves and others. Their resistance to change is present in their attitudes toward social and political
processes, which are usually conservative and respectful of the authority
of the past. As part of the intolerance of ambiguity which is characteristic of this kind of personality is the trait of concreteness — an avoidance
of abstract and/or vague ideas, percepts, and concepts, with a strong
preference for the tangible, the concrete, the specific. The orientation
toward dealing with details which is implied here is sometimes so
strongly present that the obsessive-compulsive patient is not able to fit
the details into general principles or relationships which might be quite
obvious to others.

It is apparent from these traits that obsessive-compulsive patterns
are clearly related to the kinds of learnings begun in relation to the
socialization of elimination responses, and continued in the course of
training the child to extinguish behaviors inconsistent with the society's
mores. It is therefore not surprising that obsessive and compulsive
people are usually quite unquestioningly committed to their society's
moral and ethical structure, and in our society, put a great emphasis on
cleanliness.

Dynamics of Obsessions and Compulsions. Because of the range and
variety of obsessive and compulsive behaviors, it is not possible to
present any simple explanation of all the traits and characteristics which
are involved. However, the main outlines of the processes as they are
understood today may be briefly indicated. Such an outline includes
some discussion of the kind of conflict involved, how such conflicts are
established, the kinds of reactions to these conflicts which result in
obsessions and compulsions, and how these reactions are acquired.

That conflict is an essential of obsessive and compulsive behavior is
suggested by the presence of rigidity, and the intolerance of ambiguity
which we have seen to be a habitual manner of resolving inconsistencies.
The morality and striving for perfection, as well as the emphasis on
cleanliness and order, suggest that the obsessive-compulsive person is
one who has had such extensive training in conforming to parental
standards that even relatively minor deviations from their standards
arouse anxiety. The contents of the obsessions and compulsions provide further clues; they frequently are related to disapproved or antisocial drives, such as hostility in the fear of doing harm to one's children,

sex in the rape obsession, and in the sexual compulsions. Although the patient may act as if these obsessions and compulsions are not part of himself, they are obviously expressions of drives which are unacceptable to the person. It therefore seems reasonable that the obsessive and compulsive person is responding to conflicts between very high moral and ethical standards and his human drives which are considered to be largely socially unacceptable. It has been suggested that the moral standards are so high and rigid in this kind of personality that even "ordinary" or relatively acceptable feelings, such as occasional hostility toward one's children or mate, or sexual desires toward forbidden persons — feelings which most people have on occasion and dismiss as unimportant and "only human" — become part of very strong conflict with the person's moral training, and are capable of producing relatively high anxiety. The background of learning which can produce such sharp conflict already has been suggested in the discussions of toilet training, training in intolerance of ambiguity, and the conditions of internalization of parental standards, which are such that conformity to parental models is the only condition which can produce satisfaction of the need for acceptance and love, and the absence of punishment. Thus guilt usually is identified as a main factor in obsessive-compulsive neuroses.

The content of the obsessions and the compulsions, therefore, often are interpreted as expressions of guilt; this is particularly the case with compulsions which stress cleanliness. Such behaviors also may have an element of self-punishment in them. Certainly compulsive hand washing or cleaning of the house several times a day can be punishing. One patient scrubbed her hands with strong soap and a scrub brush so often during the day that she inflamed her skin to such an extent that it was extremely painful for her to continue the compulsive behavior. Despite the pain, she continued her hand washing compulsion. Lady Macbeth has come to be a symbol of the guilt meaning in hand washing compulsion.

Other obsessions and compulsions are expressions of the patient's conflicted or guilty drive, rather than of the guilt itself. In these cases, the obsessive thought or compulsive action is looked upon by the patient as something outside of himself, somehow disconnected from his real feelings or intentions. Thus the expression of the anxiety-arousing drive is disowned from the self. This seems to be the case with the anti-social compulsions, the sexual compulsions, and such obsessions as the thought that one is likely to do harm to one's wife or children. The restitutive behavior which often accompanies such behavior, as in the father who arranges to avoid being alone with his children, may have an element of self-punishment in it, as well as an avoidance of the cues which are likely to elicit the dangerous drives.

Many obsessions and compulsions may be thought of as anxiety-reducing responses which produce cues incompatible with the cues arising from thoughts which would arouse anxiety. Counting fence posts, avoiding the cracks in the pavement, serial and ritual compulsions such as those in which the person must go through daily routines in a particular invarying manner, often are interpreted as efforts to so engage the thoughts by paying close attention to unimportant details that there is no opportunity for the person to begin thinking about anxiety-arousing desires. With his mind so occupied with minor details, nothing can happen which might elicit the upsetting ideas. This may be one of the functions of the concreteness and attention to details found in obsessive-compulsives. In this sense, such behavior serves as an aid to repression and is reinforced by the freedom from anxiety, however temporary, which is created. Such behavior is not unlike picking up some simple occupation as a hobby as a way of freeing oneself from the cares and worries of the workday. The compulsive requirement to repeat the ritual when an error is made may be a way of insuring that the person will pay closer attention to what he is doing, and thus be more effective in avoiding anxiety-arousing thoughts. It also has been suggested that the emphasis on routine and the absence of change which often is found in obsessive-compulsive persons reduces anxiety by avoiding the possibility that some untoward event which might arouse the feared thoughts or desires would occur. Thus many obsessive and compulsive behaviors may be viewed as responses which permit an avoidance of anxiety cues.

The obsessive and compulsive behaviors themselves may therefore be thought of as anxiety-reducing responses; some are apparently reaction-formations with reference to guilt; some are compensatory. Compulsive rituals also may serve as rationalizations for avoiding anxiety-arousing situations, and it already has been indicated that the maintenance of repression also is involved. Finally, any obsession or compulsion may function in several of these ways at the same time. The more functions such a behavior fulfills, the greater will be its economy and effectiveness in reducing anxiety, and so the more stable such a behavior will become in its resistance to extinction. However, as the conflict continues unresolved, the competing drives may become stronger and stronger, cueing off the anxiety-reducing behavior more and more frequently, until the person may be seriously involved in personal and social difficulties. It often happens, when such a progression of severity occurs, that the end is reached in a schizophrenic episode and hospitalization, as the compulsive or obsessional behaviors become less and less adequate to reduce the anxiety of unresolved conflicts. The residuals of such obsessions and compulsions are often observed in schizophrenic patients.

This discussion of the obsessions and compulsions suggests that obsessive and compulsive behavior occurs in particular kinds of people — those whose background of learning has stressed rigid morality, denial of conflict and ambivalence, cleanliness and respect for parental authority, — the socialization experiences which produce a readiness to develop strong conflicts involving guilt, and a readiness to respond to such conflict with the particular anxiety-reducing behaviors which are classified as obsessive or compulsive, when the person's life situation is such that conflicts are strongly aroused. Many people who have had the same kind of socialization experiences as the obsessive and compulsive patients may never show actual obsessive or compulsive behavior, at least not in important ways, although some tendencies toward rigidity, orderliness, and strong morality may be present. Such people may be thought of as having the same personality pattern as obsessives and compulsives. They may not develop overt obsessions or compulsions which become obvious in their social environment either because they never develop sufficiently strong conflicts which would elicit such behavior, or because their training in this pattern has not been quite as rigorous as those who do develop the neurosis. It also sometimes happens that the neurotic behaviors are present, but are not thought of as neurotic because they fit in so well with the person's environment, rather than interfering with his relationships to others. A man whose job it is to clean and restore valuable works of art, for example, can become far more meticulous, careful, precise, and restrained on the basis of a neurotic obsessive-compulsive development, without it being noticed or thought of as neurotic, than can one whose work or life situation would be seriously interfered with by such traits, such as a short order cook, or a house painter who might never finish a job because of his meticulousness. Some obsessive-compulsive people do manage to find occupations congenial to the pattern of their personalities, and in such cases, their occupational success may further reinforce their neurotic behaviors. However, many do not have the opportunity to make such nice occupational choices, getting into whatever line of work is most available to them at the time that they begin their occupational career, so that the making of an inference of personality pattern from a person's occupation is at best a risky procedure. On the other hand, experience in an occupation can produce the conditions in which neurotic responses are learned. A person in an occupation requiring ritualistic and meticulous attention to details may acquire these traits on a neurotic basis should strong anxiety and conflict occur. If these anxieties are reduced when he is at work, the compulsive behaviors demanded by the job may spread to situations outside of the job when conflict is aroused. In other words, there is a complex interaction between personality and occupational choice, such that some of the rewards of an occupation aside from the obvious economic ones lie in the extent to which it fits in with the person's drives and habits;[20] and conversely, a worker's personality is modified by the kinds of responses he acquires in his work, when these responses are reinforced by rewards both on and off the job. Thus it is that many pre-psychotic persons are attracted to jobs in mental hospitals and once on the job, their thresholds for behaving in psychotic ways are lowered by their close contact and identification with psychotic patients. Similarly, the stereotype we currently have of the advertising executive is probably based in part on the characteristics of people who find a career in advertising particularly attractive or reinforcing, and in part on the traits fostered and learned through daily immersion in the particular mores and folkways of the society which advertising agencies form.

There remains much to be learned about obsessive and compulsive neuroses. One of the most interesting problems is understanding how it is that there seems to be little anxiety associated with what should be upsetting obsessional ideas. The compulsive housewife who works fifteen hours a day insuring that her home is clean often seems but little concerned about the kind of life such behavior forces her into. One such patient weekly cleaned the motor and underside of her family car, without apparent concern about how atypical and non-functional as far as disease is concerned such behavior is. It has been suggested that the compulsive person is isolating the emotional component of his behavior, which involves a repression of the association between a thought and its associated emotional-drive response and between the thought and other ideas connected with it, so that the thought seems to have a disconnected and independent existence.[21] It is not possible to repress directly the action of the autonomic system, although it may be prevented from becoming aroused indirectly through avoiding arousing cues; however it is possible to repress awareness of drives. Other theorists have suggested that the person is unconcerned about his behavior because the behavior is highly reinforced by the reduction of anxiety, and so is not perceived as undesirable by the patient. There has been much speculation about the nature and meaning of obsessive and compulsive behaviors, but there are still many issues to be resolved.

Phobias. Phobias are the main symptoms of a neurosis now called "anxiety hysteria," although phobias used to be classed with the obsessive-compulsive neuroses under the heading of "psychosthenia." Phobia, a kind of obsessive fear, really stands midway between the obsessive-compulsive neuroses and hysteria, having features of each. A phobia is a fear which is determined by past experiences, rather than by the danger inherent in the person's contact with the situation which frightens him. Often the fear is greatly out of proportion to the danger, as in a phobia of closed places, although in many cases the phobic person can rationalize his feelings by exaggerating the real danger which is present. A housewife with a phobic fear of knives can justify her fear by indicating that many people are hurt accidentally by knives. However, such a fear may legitimately be called a phobia if close analysis of the case shows that the fear can be more adequately accounted for on the basis of factors in the personality of the person than it can on the basis of the actual extent of the danger from knives.

Phobias are usually experienced as strong apprehension and anxiety when in the presence of the phobic object or situation, a fear that can develop into panic proportions in which the person blindly flees in a loss of self-control from the phobic situation. Objects associated with the phobic object acquire the capacity to elicit the fear, through stimulus generalization. The phobic person usually takes steps to avoid the phobic situation, and these steps often produce a restriction on his life which makes it more and more difficult for him to engage in the usual social interactions. As the phobia spreads to associated objects, the restriction becomes more and more severe, until the person is no longer able to function in society at all. The restriction may spread to include those situations in which the phobic object accidentally might be encountered. Thus a phobic fear of locomotives spread in one case to a fear of going out of doors at all. It is possible that the phobic person may be in the kind of occupation and life situation in which his phobia does not interfere. If the man who was afraid of going out at all were an artist who could do his work at home, his phobia might seldom become apparent and his perseverance in staying home and working may be interpreted by others as evidence for his artistic dedication, rather than the result of a phobic neurotic development. The similarity between these considerations and those in obsessive-compulsive neuroses are apparent. In fact, the housewive's fear of knives may go along with the obsessive thought that she might kill her husband. And as in the obsessions and compulsions, the phobia can serve as a means of reducing the anxiety that would occur if conflicted drives were elicited by cues in the environment by restricting the person from contact with the eliciting cues. In many phobias, the fear is not directly related to the phobic object, but is a reaction to the conflicted drives which are cued off by the phobic object which has been associated with the upsetting motive in the past. This is seen clearly in the case of a young woman who developed a phobia of syphilis, marked by an intense fear of contracting the disease. The phobia kept her away from the heterosexual contacts which would arouse her conflicted sexual drive.

Phobias can develop in many ways. They may be acquired directly from a phobic parent. A child whose mother becomes tense and frightened in the presence of a dog is likely to develop a fear of dogs. The mother's tension and anxiety frightens the child, who seldom sees his parents so upset, and who has come to look upon them as sources of strength and protection from fear. Further, in her anxiety, the mother is likely to be irritable and unloving, thus associating punishment with the sight of dogs. The fear which the child then habitually experiences in the presence of dogs can therefore be reduced by the fearful avoidance of the animals, an avoidance which naturally makes it impossible for the child to discover that dogs are not necessarily dangerous. And because the fear is not based on any direct experience with dogs, the child cannot conceptualize what it is about dogs that frightens him. He therefore cannot learn to discriminate what in dogs is to be avoided. His fear thus takes on the character of a generalized anxiety evoked by anything having to do with dogs.

Some phobias are learned directly as a product of generalization or secondary reinforcement from a traumatic experience. A child who has been punished severely for playing with his genitals in bed may associate his punishment with the cues of the bed, which is one of the cues which stimulates his drive to play with his genitals, thus developing a phobia of the bed. Many children's phobias, which are quite common in the four-to-six-year age range, develop in a similar way. One little boy who was terrified of the cellar steps was responding to some threats that a bogey man was awaiting him down there, made on an earlier occasion by his mother to keep him from playing on the stairs. Such threats are not likely to produce phobias in children who have not already had experiences with intense anxiety and threat.

In many phobias of objects or situations associated with a traumatic experience, the memory for the experience itself may be repressed, so that in later life the phobic person is at a loss to explain the fear which he recognizes as irrational. Thinking about the traumatic experience would produce intense anxiety because the thoughts themselves are cues for the fear; thus the thinking of the experience fails to occur, with the phobic person left only with the thoughts of his fear of the trauma-associated object.

In many cases, the phobia is not the result of any direct trauma associated with the phobic object. In such cases, the phobic object is often one which would elicit either anxiety-arousing conflicted drives, or anxiety-arousing memories. Such phobias therefore serve as aids to repression. In such cases, the phobia itself may be a displacement from the real anxiety-arousing cue. Thus a fear of crowds may be a displacement from a situation in which homosexual desires were aroused in the course of an attempted homosexual seduction of the patient. Another example is that of a young man who developed a fear of closed places such as his small business shop, as it became more and more likely that the business would fail. In this case, the fear of a business failure was displaced to a fear of the physical properties of the shop. This phobia also served as a rationalization for the eventual failure: the proprietor had to close the business, not because of the failure of the venture, but because of his "nervous condition."

The development of a phobia is well illustrated in a case reported by C. Scott Moss, a psychologist who was asked by a forty-five-year-old woman for help in overcoming a phobic fear of dogs which she had always had since her childhood.[22] She wanted to be able to buy a dog as a birthday present for her adopted daughter, but could not because of the extreme fright she experienced in the presence of dogs. Before beginning hypnotic explorations of her experiences with dogs, in the hope of finding some childhood experience in which some dog might have bitten her, she suggested to the therapist that he also try to find out what it was her physician had said to her on one of the three occasions on which she had given birth, only to have the child die. She had the feeling that she wanted to remember what he said at the time, but she could not. In the course of treatment she was able to recall that he had told her that the baby's neck had been broken, which was a different cause of death than in the earlier two pregnancies. As treatment progressed, she recalled under hypnosis an occasion when her young sister was knocked over by her own little dog, received a cut on her face which became infected, and died shortly thereafter. At the time that the sister was cut, the patient was blamed for the incident by her mother, who had not seen the dog knock the sister down. Later another sister was born, and in the course of therapy the patient told of an occasion on which this new sister was knocked down by another dog, which produced such fright in the patient, who was about seven years old at the time, that she lost her affection for her dog, and gave it away. The patient also reported a dream in which her daughter was holding a doll with a torn dress — a doll which on closer inspection turned out to be a dead infant. Under hypnosis the meaning of this dream became clear when the patient told that on the day of the funeral of her young sister, she was in the room alone with the body and, not knowing about death, picked her up to play with her. While holding the tiny body, her dog jumped on her and tore the baby's dress. Her mother then entered the room, and blamed the child for tearing the dress as part of her horror of the sight of her little girl, whom she held responsible for her sister's death, holding the dead baby. The patient was not able to recall these experiences outside of hypnosis even when she was told of them by the therapist, but she was able to find supporting evidence from her relatives. She also reported another occasion when her older sister died, when she was blamed for not having nursed her sister during her last illness. In this case, the patient's pervasive feeling of being inferior and inadequate, together with her great hostility toward her parents and others for unjustifiably blaming her became associated with dogs, the death of her sisters, of her own children, and her relationship to her own daughter. All of these thoughts were repressed, but dogs served as symbols, or cues which might elicit such anxiety-arousing thoughts, and were thus feared. This case is described here in detail to point up the many inter-relationships among the patient's experiences, and how all contributed to her fear of dogs, and to show the complex associations among the patient's experiences and ideas. Such complexity is usually the case. Phobias are seldom simple conditioned fears based on a single experience. Most often, the phobic fear is built up of many mutually supportive experiences which are intense enough to produce a strong phobia. Thus a phobic reaction is often powerfully reinforcing, because so many different sources of anxiety are connected with it. It is in this sense that behaviors such as phobias are described as *over-determined*. Another interesting feature of this case is that seemingly disconnected topics, such as her experiences in childbirth and her desire to get rid of her phobia really were closely connected, and this connection was what made her bring up such apparently irrelevant subjects in the course of treatment, even though she was not aware of the connections.

Dynamics of Phobia. Several points about phobias may be summarized. They are usually started by experiences occurring in childhood before the child is able to make logical causal connections among events, such as those between irrelevant stimuli and a traumatic experience which occurred in association with such stimuli. Further, it has been pointed out that where anxiety is a result of conflicted drives of which the person is afraid, a displacement of the fear to some concrete object which is only distantly related to the real source of the fear is especially likely, because such an object can serve to "explain" the fear which otherwise cannot be explained because it is caused by repressed drives. One can fear an object and avoid it in a way which is not possible when one is afraid only of one's own hostility. Such *concretizing* of fear is especially likely to occur in a person whose socialization has been similar to that which was described in relation to obsessive-compulsive neuroses.

There is a general model that describes the basic operation of many phobias, and that interacts with the points made so far about the development of phobias. The general model is as follows: when a conflicted or feared drive is elicited by environmental events similar in some ways to earlier experiences in which the drive was punished, the individual responds with fear to the eliciting events. The feared drive remains repressed, partly because it is not strongly enough evoked by the stimuli present which are only approximately like the earlier ones, and partly because to be aware of the drive would create even greater anxiety. Since fear was associated with the drive in past learning, fear will be elicited by whatever elicits the drive. The forbidden or dangerous drive is the mediator between the stimuli and the fear, much as verbal labels can mediate responses to different cues. It is only through arousing the feared drive that the environmental stimuli, not in themselves dangerous, can elicit the fear. However, because the person remains unconscious of the feared drive itself, he experiences only the fear which he connects directly in his thinking to the external cues. Thus what is really a fear of one's own desires comes to be elicited by stimuli only

Figure 17. Operation of Phobias

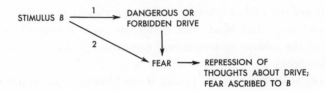

Phobias may occur via Route 1, in which avoidance (fear) is cued by a forbidden drive aroused by stimulus *B*, or via Route 2, in which stimulus *B*, through secondary reinforcement based on the association between *B* and *A*, directly elicits the avoidance.

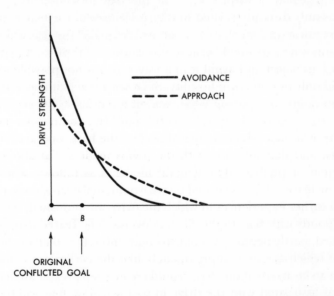

In either case, when *B* occurs, high approach and higher avoidance are produced either because the forbidden approach drive stimulates avoidance (Route 1), or because *B* arouses the avoidance (Route 2). Because avoidance is higher than the approach, the subject avoids *B*, which he thinks is the cause of his fear, and doesn't think about his forbidden approach drive toward *A*.

indirectly related to these desires, through similarity of the stimuli to experiences in which the fear was learned as response to the drive. The result is an unreasonable fear of events which are not necessarily inherently dangerous, and which seem to the observer not at all logically connected to the phobic person's main concerns.

A phobic behavior may embody several of these responses to anxiety: displacement of fear from its eliciting cues, projection of guilt to some external object which is feared as potentially punishing, rationalization, and as a means of repression, and it may be all of these things at once, as an overdetermined behavior. The phobic object may be thought of as symbolic, in the sense that it stands for the anxiety-arousing situation which is the real source of the fear. In the case of the dog phobia described above, the dog became a symbol of several of the woman's experiences of blame for the death of children, and served as a substitute cue for the feelings associated with those experiences. Often, as in that case, the symbol is private; it is created out of the individual's unique past experience, so that its meaning—the events for which it stands—is not apparent to external observors. However, many symbols are conventional in a society, so that one can frequently guess correctly at the meaning of the phobic object. For example, the tolling of church bells is a common symbol of death because it is used that way in literature and the mass communications, and because the association between such bells and death is one which many people have experienced in essentially similar ways. A phobia of bells readily may be interpreted as based on experiences involving death and the interpretation is likely to be correct. Nevertheless, many people have quite unique experiences with bells, which therefore could be a private symbol. Evidence confirming the interpretation of the symbol always should be sought before the interpretation can be made with much certainty.

The Hysterias. The hysterias include phobias (anxiety hysteria) as well as a large variety of neuroses marked by malfunctions of the person's physical and psychological equipment. In this section will be discussed those hysterias which are distinguished from anxiety hysteria by being called "conversion reactions" or "conversion hysteria." Hysteria is the neurosis which has been studied most extensively and contributed the most to knowledge of personality. Freud's earliest discoveries were based largely on his clinical experiences with hysteric patients. The term itself is the oldest in the field of psychopathology. It comes from the Greek "hystera," meaning womb. The Greeks thought of hysteria as essentially a woman's disease and ascribed it to the breaking loose of the womb, which in the course of its wanderings through the body got lodged in various places, producing disfunctions of the body part where it was lodged. Although hysteria is not by any means a woman's disease (it was the most common neurosis in the United States Army during World War II), in most cases it does involve some disorder of various body functions. Among the hysterias are such things as paralysis of part or all of a limb, anesthesia of some part of the body, loss of visual responses or auditory responses, sexual impotence or frigidity, amnesia, tunnel vision, rigidity of some part of the body, inability to digest food, and occupational cramps such as writer's cramp or telegrapher's cramp. Other hysterical disorders are chronic sleepwalking (somnambulism), suffering a loss of identity associated with leaving one's customary environment and staying away as a "different person" for varying periods of time (fugue state), multiple personality, seizures, and various automatic movements such as tics, habitual blinking or grimacing, or muscle twitching. It has been suggested that these various behaviors be grouped into two categories: hysterical inactivations, in which there is a loss of responding in some function; and hysterical autonomy, in which a part of behavior occurs in some way disconnected from the rest of the individual's behavior, or without the person's apparent intention or control.[23]

Hysterical Inactivations. In the inactivations, there is a loss in bodily functioning which cannot be accounted for entirely on the basis of organic pathology of the structures involved. A typical example of this is in the following case of hysterical blindness. A forty-five-year-old assembly line worker reported to a veteran's hospital extremely upset about the fact that while driving that day, his vision became cloudier and cloudier until he had to stop the car and ask at a nearby house that the police be called to take him to the hospital. By the time that he arrived, he was completely without visual responses. During therapy, the following circumstances became known: the man had an extremely boring routine job in which his eyes were exposed to periodic bright flashes of light. He worked in a room in the factory in which there was a blinding glare from the windows. He had complained about the glare unsuccessfully. He worked six days a week, and had worked for several years without a significant vacation. He was afraid to take a vacation because of an unstable employment situation and he was afraid, with so many men laid off, that he might not have a job when he came back from a rest. He was married and in financial difficulty. His car was almost unrepairable but he did not have enough money to buy another one (under hypnosis, when instructed to dream about the most wonderful thing that could happen to him, he dreamt that he had a newer used car). His landlord was requiring that he move out of his rented home and he was upset about having to find a new place as economical as the one in which he was living, and about the expense of moving. His mother, who had been chronically ill for years, was dying and he was the only relative who would do anything about having a funeral and burying her, which was a further financial drain. His older son was doing poorly in school, and he was disappointed in him, although the patient had not done well in school himself. It was in such circumstances that the patient's blindness occurred. Medical examination revealed no pathology of the eye or the neural pathways involved in vision. Under hypnosis he was told that he could see and he then was able to make visual responses. However, the next day, although he could see when his eyelids were held open, he could not seem to open his eyes. There had been a shift in the patient's symptom, when the first one was hypnotically removed, indicating that whatever was the source of anxiety which was being reduced by the blindness, that source had not been removed, so that when the blindness was removed, another related anxiety-reducing response developed.[24]

The patient in this case was one who had never been able to make decisions adequately and deal with his problems directly. He was chronically unable to set a course for himself and follow through on it. He had drifted into his assembly line job and though he hated it, had made no efforts to get out of it, and was afraid to take any step that would jeopardize his position. He was compliant to demands made on him, such as taking care of the expenses of his mother, and was unable to demand that his siblings share the expenses. He was anxious about having to decide about renting another house. He had tended to let things slide, so that he had saved no money on which he could fall back for another car, although he was earning an adequate wage. With all these things oppressing him, he seemed to focus on his job as the worst, although he probably would not have been so upset with it if he had not the other things – the need for money soon so that he could not leave his job without being considered a shirker of his responsibility to his family and his mother, and the anxiety created by having to look for a new rental, select one, and make arrangements for moving. At work on the day that the hysterical blindness began, the glare was particularly strong. He was worried and upset and had the feeling that so much weight was on him that it was not good for his health, and certainly his work was not good for his eyes. The repeated flash of light bothered him, and he half fearfully thought that if he lost his sight, he would not be able to work at that job any longer. He recalled hearing about people who had been blinded by bright flashes, as from explosions, and spent much of the day thinking about the possibility that his eyes might be affected. While driving home that day, after looking at another house for rent, he felt particularly fatigued, especially in his eyes. When he closed them for a moment, they were somewhat hard to open again. When they did open, things seemed grayer. He thought about what he would do if he were to lose his sight. He would ask someone to take him to the veterans hospital, which was free, and they would take care of him. He imagined himself lying in a clean hospital bed, with people taking care of him, and with his relatives visiting and being very worried about him. When he next paid attention to how he was driving, he noticed that things seemed very gray. He throught more strongly that he might be losing his sight. It was at that moment that he stopped the car and asked to be taken to the hospital. When he arrived at the hospital he was sedated and put to bed at once. The next day he began to feel strong fright that his blindness might be permanent and although the hospital was nice, it wasn't what he had expected it to be. He was hypnotized, and was much relieved, when he awakened, to know that his sight was not lost permanently. However, he was afraid that there might be more wrong with him than appeared at first glance, and he was afraid that going back to work right away might make things worse. He was sure there was still something wrong with his eyes — that his job was simply not good for his sight. Upon awakening from a nap, he found that that he could not open his eyes, and although he was relieved that he still could see when he opened his eyelids with his fingers, he realized that he still had much recuperating to do before he had to go back to work. He could get a sick leave which would not jeopardize his job. His wife simply would have to move without him. Perhaps friends would help her.

This case well illustrates the reinforcement value of hysterical symptoms as anxiety-reducers which function by taking the person out of his usual environment, or by changing his status in his environment so that he is relieved of demands on him to act in ways which create anxiety for him. The patient had a fairly typical hysterical personality pattern — a strong drive to live up to the demands and expectation others made on him, and a fear of rejection and criticism from others for failure to do what was expected, even though to do so was a great burden on him. This is very frequently the basic conflict found in hysterics — between strong drives for approval, and forces which make it difficult for the person to continue to conform to demands made on him. In addition, there was a well established habit of repressing, of not thinking about problems, which was why he seemed simply to "let things slide." Such habits of repression are the essential components of the hysterical response; the lack of visual responses in the patient was a repression of responses to visual cues, so that the patient acted as if he saw nothing, and indeed was not aware (that is, not making symbolic responses to visual stimuli) of light, dark, and color. The patient also illustrates another common component in hysterical neurosis: a longstanding concern about his health and his body functioning, together with vague and incorrect ideas about how the body operates and what can go wrong with it.

Another hysterical inactivation is illustrated by the case of a soldier who was in severe combat for an extended period of time, constantly in danger of being killed, and seeing friends killed almost daily. The soldier was desperately afraid that he too would be killed and was at various times tempted to flee. However, he looked upon his fear as cowardice and was very guilty about wanting to escape, so that he stayed where he was. However, his desire to escape was so strong that he often had the feeling that at any moment he would start running. It took almost constant inhibition of his leg muscles to keep himself from fleeing. One day, while under very heavy enemy bombardment, he saw many men wounded and carried back to medical attention, from where he knew that they would be transferred to a large army hospital in a distant city to which his comrades were sometimes sent for leaves. He felt sorry for the wounded, but also a twinge of envy for what he was sure was their feeling, that they may be hurt, but they weren't killed, and now they could get away from the constant danger and still feel that they had given their best to the battle. While thinking thoughts such as these, an enemy shell exploded nearby, knocking him down. He hit his head on a rock, and was unconscious for about half an hour. When he awoke, he found blood from what turned out to be a superficial shrapnel wound on his leg. He realized that he was wounded. His leg was twisted into an odd position, in which it apparently had lain for the time that he was unconscious, in the cold winter air. He tried tentatively to move it. It felt stiff and difficult to move. The soldier realized that he had been wounded in the leg, seriously enough perhaps to paralyze the leg. He called desperately for an aidman, who eventually found him and made arrangements for him to be carried back to an aid station on a stretcher.

On the way back, the soldier felt a great relief that he was going back and he was appreciative of the encouragement and solicitousness of the stretcher bearers who carried him. From the aid station he was sent further back behind the lines where he was examined by a physician who looked at his leg and then asked him if he could move it. The soldier interpreted the question to mean that such injuries often result in inability to move the leg, and so was not surprised when he found out that the leg did not move. Eventually the soldier was returned to a large general hospital where he was diagnosed as hysterical paralysis. During an interview conducted while he was sedated with sodium pentathol, a drug which seems to release inhibitions, the soldier began to talk about his fear and terror in combat, and about the sight of his friends being killed. The psychiatrist frequently reassured him that he was safe, that he would not be sent back into combat, and that he had performed his duty well and that the Army was proud of him, that he had stood more than anyone could expect, and that his shattered nerves would be better after a rest. When the patient awakened, he found that he could walk.

This case illustrates another important feature of hysteria: the symptom is often cued off by some traumatic event which in itself is frightening, and which strongly activates the unresolved conflicts which have been present, and which also is interpreted by the patient as a cause of the physical disorder which the patient considers to be really on an organic basis. Further, both cases illustrate the fact that the particular symptom developed is usually symbolic of part of the patient's conflict, in that it is a repression of that function of the body which, if it continued to operate, would leave the patient in very strong conflict. Often the precipitating incident, such as the explosion near the soldier, occurs as an accident which provides the patient with a learning situation in which he discovers the anxiety-reducing consequences of his symptom, as a result of his misinterpretation of the effects of the trauma. We already have seen how drives can increase the probability of such misinterpretations. In the case of the soldier, the paralyzed leg is symbolic of his motivation to flee from combat, and of the conflicting guilt about this desire which he interpreted as cowardice. The repression prevented him from fleeing as a coward.

Thus it can be seen that the hysteric is one who has an already established conflict, and has already acquired strong habits of repressing which produce physical symptoms when an appropriate stimulus, related to the conflict, occurs. Where a phobia represents a fear of one's

own drives and impulses, an hysterical inactivation represents a blocking of the means by which such drives and impulses might be expressed
in overt behavior. It should be pointed out that the learning of the symptom usually is not immediate; although the soldier had only one occasion on which his leg was hurt, he had had many prior experiences, in
his imagination, of what it meant to be wounded, an imaginative activity
which was motivated by the same factors involved in his conflict. So too
with the factory worker; he had done a great deal of thinking about his
eyes and what would happen if they were impaired. Thus it was not surprising that the factory worker asked immediately to be taken to the
veterans' hospital (although he had never been there before). It was
something that he had rehearsed in fantasy before.

One of the factors favoring the development of physical symptoms
such as these is our cultural orientation to illness. In general, illness is
rewarded in our society. Children often receive more care and attention when ill than when healthy, and in addition, are permitted to escape from the anxiety which school often involves for them, without
any guilt in their escape being involved. In military life, it is not unusual
for the incapacitated soldier in the hospital to receive more rewards
than the one who remains on duty. The incapacitated soldier is likely
to be greeted by the civilian public as a hero, in contrast to the man who
stays on duty until the end of the war only to find that he cannot find
employment when he is only one of the millions discharged after doing
their job. It is very likely that the hysteric with physical symptoms such
as the two cases discussed is one who already has experienced rewards
for being incapacitated, usually from an oversolicitous mother who had
done so much to take care of her child that the child had never had
much opportunity to develop ways of solving conflicts on his own. The
dependency implied here is one of the features commonly found in
hysterics, often expressed as a fear of rejection by others. In the soldier,
this was in the form of a fear of being considered a coward; in the
factory worker, it was a fear of not doing what others expected him to
do. In both cases, a strong dependence upon the attitudes of others is
implied. We already have seen that the repressor, such as the hysteric,
is one who tends to think of himself as being like other people, and to
have his attention directed to the cues coming from others, rather than
to the cues coming from within himself. These traits are part of the
hysteric's dependency, and are very much a part of repression, which
itself involves not responding to internal cues arising from his own body
or thoughts. The escape drive which is part of the hysteric's conflict

is apparent in both cases presented, and is based on the patient's previously rewarded experiences in which illness and disability resulted in the avoidance of anxiety. These factors point to a particular period of childhood as the age at which the learnings of their personality patterns are established. This is the age at which the child's already established dependency drive comes into conflict with his life situation in which further and further independence from the home rapidly occurs, as when the child begins to go to school and must make decisions without his parents' constant presence. The strongly dependent child finds reality outside the circle of parental protection unpleasant; he is motivated to avoid such independence, often through illness, and often through fantasy such as that in which he later rehearses and imagines his physical symptoms. Thus hysteria often indicates a particular kind of socialization experience starting about age four or five in our society, when children begin to go to school.

Conversion Symptoms. Hysterical inactivations in which a body part fails to function such as in the two cases discussed, are referred to as conversion hysteria, as a result of the since-discarded idea that mental conflict becomes "converted" into physical symptoms. Naivete about body functioning is an almost necessary prerequisite for the development of conversion symptoms. The hysteric believes that the precipitating event did in fact cause a real physical disorder. Without such belief, the symptom could not function as a rewarded escape, and so could not be reinforced. The hysteric believes that his disorder is really organic. Concern over physical functioning is characteristic of the personality pattern which gives rise to hysterical symptoms when conflict is great and precipitating events occur. This concern with body functioning is an outgrowth of the person's previous experience with rewarded illness. It also contributes to the misinterpretation of bodily functioning. It has been pointed out that the more one pays attention to his physiological processes, the more likely it is that he will discover evidence to support the fear and the expectation that motivated the paying of attention, thus further contributing to the cycle of misperception leading to further confirmation and further misperception. It is not surprising that hysterics have long medical histories of seeking consultations for a large variety of disorders. In one study it was found that the case folders in a general hospital of those medical patients whose personalities were essentially like the hysterical pattern were much larger and heavier than the case files on nonhysterical patients.[25]

Conversion symptoms are usually fairly easy to distinguish from organic disorders. Usually the hysterical paralysis does not follow the anatomical distribution of nerve supply to the affected limb, so that in fact, such a paralysis on organic grounds is quite impossible. The same is true of hysterical anesthesias. The hysteric's naivete about such matters is too great for his symptoms to be realistic imitations of organic pathology. Perhaps it is the spread of information about human biology which is responsible for the decrease in frequency of hysterical conversion symptoms since before World War II. In cases of hysterical blindness of one eye, diagnosis often can be made by the use of a prism which bends light in such a way that the patient believes the light to be going into his "good" eye, although it is really going into his blind eye. The patient then reports that he sees the light.

One of the things that distinguishes hysterical paralyses from organic paralyses is that in hysteria, the bed sores that often develop in organic paralysis are absent. This is because the patient really moves the affected limb very slightly throughout the day, so that the continued contact with the bed clothing that provides the warm moist atmosphere for the growth of the organisms that create bed sores is absent. Further, the hysteric often magically recovers the use of his affected part (which usually has not atrophied very much, because muscle tone is maintained, unlike in organic paralyses) under certain circumstances, such as some sudden danger which can only be escaped by the use of the affected part, or by religious conversion or the performance of a miracle or faith cure. Thus many of the stories about bedridden patients who are able to run to safety when their homes are on fire, and the stories about miraculous cures by oracles or magicians are cases in which the disorder was hysterical, rather than organic. Behind such cures and recoveries is usually a complex process in which the patient, who believes his symptoms to be organic, has been discovering that the symptoms are perhaps more incapacitating than he cares for, or that the original conflict creating the anxiety which is reduced by the symptom is no longer operative, so that the reinforcement value of the symptom has been greatly reduced. Yet it does not occur to the patient that his symptom is not real, so that he may not discover that he can in fact use the affected body part. And further, he is committed to the symptom. To simply recover would indicate to everyone including himself that the disorder was not real, and the hysteric who is so sensitive to others' reactions to him could not do that. Thus frequently a socially accepted excuse for recovery is required, even after the central conflict is no longer operative. However, as long as the conflict is present and the symptoms are reinforcing, the hysteric is not motivated to recover, and is usually slow and reluctant to consult physicians, rationalizing his reluctance by casting doubt on the honesty or ability of physicians, etc. This reaction to his symptom has come to be called "la belle indifference" — beautiful indifference to the disability. When the patient does seek help, it is usually from someone in physical medicine, rather than a psychiatrist or psychologist, and he is often highly upset, defensive, and anxious if he is referred to a psychiatrist or psychologist because of the meaning such a referral suggests to him about his symptoms.

In the occupational cramps, discrimination between hysterical and organic disorders is readily accomplished, because the occupational cramps are usually only present when the patient is faced with the cues which activate his conflict. Thus the inability to grasp a pencil (or to relax one's fingers for typing) which characterizes writer's cramp only occurs when a pencil and paper are present. The patient can grasp pencil-like objects such as the handle of a screwdriver, or of eating utensils. The symbolic significance and the nature of the motivating conflict is apparent in such cases.

Often hysterical symptoms are precipitated by real but temporary physiological events occurring in people who already have established the kind of personality pattern which is necessary for the development of this kind of neurosis (dependence, emphasis on body functioning, conflicted escape drive, rehearsal in fantasy, and skill in repressing). Impotence, for example, not infrequently occurs in the first attempt at intercourse in the nervous adolescent or young adult, as a physiological effect of the interference of strong autonomic arousal in anxiety. The conviction that one has a weak heart can develop from real organic symptoms mediated by the autonomic system produced by intense fear. These temporary physiological states are misinterpreted by the person with the appropriate personality pattern, as a consequence of his conflict and high drive, and are thought to be permanent, which they do become as an hysteric represses the responses involved after the physiological factors which started the symptoms are no longer operating.

It nevertheless should be kept in mind that hysterics, like other people, do develop illnesses on an organic basis. As Norman Cameron has pointed out, even hysterics die of demonstrable physical pathology, so that medical attention to symptoms is always necessary, even where the symptoms are grossly exaggerated by the hysteric's repressive tendencies.[26] Often hysterical symptoms are founded on real physical pathology, which is added to by the reinforcement which such pathology provides to the conflicted person with this kind of personality pattern, so that the patient's real disorder is magnified by the addition of repression and resistance to cure.

Amnesia. Amnesia is a very dramatic hysterical symptom, in which the person seems to lose his memory more or less completely. We all are more or less amnesic for many experiences in our past, but hysterical amnesia is more massive, usually including loss of memory for one's identity, address, occupation, and family. However, memory for other things more distantly related to the self remains, such as for the layout of the city in which the patient lives, how to drive a car, for things learned in school, and so forth. Amnesia alone is fairly rare, and is usually not long-lasting, because it involves such a large scale denial of reality. Where there is such denial, reality contact usually has been characteristically weak, so that psychotic symptoms also are present; amnesia in conjunction with schizophrenia is not uncommon. Where reality contact has not been weak, and the patient remains in his usual environment, the cues which elicit memory are so ever present in the patient's attention that he finds himself making his habitual responses quite readily, including those of naming and identifying himself. Further, the amnesia is so dramatic that it usually is quite effective in reducing the conflict-produced anxiety quite readily. The dependency drive which is part of the conflict immediately is reduced by the attention which such an unusual symptom immediately brings. Further, the loss of satisfactions from pleasant memories, and from associations with members of one's family and one's friends, a loss which is inevitable when there is repression of all aspects of one's identity, becomes too great a loss, so that the symptom is punished, rather than reinforced. Nevertheless, even a temporary amnesia indicates that large parts of the patient's life are so anxiety-arousing that he can no longer think about them. We shall see later that under certain circumstances amnesia may be more long-lasting when it is coupled with an hysterical autonomy.

Hysterical Autonomy. The hysterical inactivations are generally responses which inhibit the expression of conflicted drives; the autonomies, on the other hand, may be thought of as either partial repressions of the conflicted drive, or more importantly, repression of cognitive responses to the self, so that the conflicted drive is expressed in behavior, but in such a way that the individual is not aware of it directly.

Somnambulism. Somnambulism is a good example of this. The sleepwalker usually engages in some motivated behavior such as acting out an incident which aroused strong but conflicted drives. While doing this, his eyes are open and he is responsive to the physical features of his environment, although he may ignore onlookers. His face is usually expressionless. When he returns to bed, he falls into ordinary sleep, and when awakened in the morning, fails to recall his sleepwalking. This kind of behavior is not too different from that described earlier in which one turns off the alarm clock and goes back to sleep and later wakes up with no recall of his behavior. Frequently the "failure" of the alarm is blamed for missing class or getting to work late. In this sequence, the person has acted out a motivated sequence of fairly skilled responses, seemingly in his sleep. The conflict between the desire to sleep, and the desire to avoid censure for failing to respond to one's commitments, for being lazy, is apparent in this not atypical incident. Similarly, the conflicting factors in hysterical somnambulism usually are equally apparent from the content of the sleepwalker's behavior.

Seizures and Faints. Hysterical seizures are very much like somnambulism, except that they usually occur while the person is awake, and they represent a sharp break in the flow of his behavior, in which he suddenly falls to the floor and acts out in pantomime the conflicted behavior in a manner that looks very much like the epileptic seizures produced by organic brain pathology. However, some differences are often apparent. Whereas the epileptic often injures himself during the course of his seizure, because he cannot control the violent movements of his muscles which make his limbs and body parts strike hard objects that might be present, such injuries are seldom part of hysterical seizures, indicating that the hysteric is responding to the features of his physical environment, although he may not know it himself. Further, hysterical seizures seldom occur when the patient is alone and not likely to be discovered, whereas epileptic seizures can occur at any time. Interpersonal situations usually are the cues which elicit hysterical seizures, by creating intense anxiety associated with conflicted drives which are stimulated by the interpersonal environment. Further, there is no reinforcement for the hysterical seizure if there is no one to observe it. Hysterical seizures are essentially like hysterical fainting spells. These differ from the faints produced by a loss of oxygen to the brain cells in organically produced faints, in that the hysteric seldom hurts herself when she falls, she usually utters a warning cry which brings attention to the faint, and instead of falling in a heap, the hysterical faint is more like the faints in the movies and on the stage in which the fall is graceful and dramatic. Hysterical fainting may be precipitated by a slight cerebral anoxia which is one of the autonomic components of severe anxiety in response to environmental cues, but such anoxia is not sufficient to account for the severity of the hysterical faint. Such fainting shades off into seizures imperceptibly, in that the fainter may act out, if ever so slightly, some aspects of the conflicted drive. Cameron has described the case of a girl who, in a faint seizure, habitually acted out the responses she had made on an occasion when she was the victim of a rape attack, an experience that produced very great conflict in her regarding her own sexual drive.[27] Even without such symbolic acting out, the faint is quite obviously a response whose major reinforcement comes from the passive avoidance of contact with anxiety-arousing cues in the environment. Such hysterical behaviors often interfere greatly with the course of treatment, because when upsetting material is discussed, the patient often avoids it by having a seizure or a fainting spell as a result of the learning of such responses to the cues of anxiety.

Fugues. Seizures and faints also are very much like fugue states. In a fugue state, the person leaves his usual environment, often under an assumed name, and travels to some distant point, where he may continue to live and work under his "new" identity, or where he more typically suddenly awakens, confused, and not knowing how he got to where he is. The development of a fugue is seen in the following case: the patient was a married man living in a small western town. His wife was somewhat extravagant and frequently complained about the level of support which he was able to maintain for his family. The patient was a relatively passive and dependent person who never became angry with his wife, and who responded to her complaints by working harder and harder, in order to make more money so that his family could live in the style which he felt they should have, if he were to be an adequate husband and not a failure. His dominating wife frequently invoked the needs of the children as her reason for wanting her husband to work and earn more, and the children usually felt that their mother was more responsive to their desires than their father, so that the patient got relatively little support from them. He failed to find support in his job, because of his great discomfort with his supervisor. Although he hated his work and his employer, who treated him with contempt as a man without any gumption (as the patient perceived it), he never thought of leaving, and complied with the demands made on him by his employer in order to win a more favored position for salary raises, and as part of his general passivity. One day while walking downtown, he noticed one of the main passenger trains which travels across the country pulling into the station and he caught a glimpse of the passengers sitting in the dining car and club car. He saw some groups of men lounging in the club car with drinks in their hands and laughing. He admired the freedom from care which he ascribed to them, and thought a little bit about the romance of traveling to far off places, of the independence and freedom from external demands which such traveling implies, and he imagined himself as one of those men, buying a ticket at the station, having a polite porter carry his bags to the car, and settling himself in a comfortable lounge chair as he watched the country speed by on his way to S_____, several hundred miles distant. As he had these thoughts, he was jostled by a passerby, and then continued on his errand, without even being able to recall what he had been thinking about. Throughout the next several days, he had essentially the same preconscious fantasies, particularly after an unpleasant interchange with his employer, and after his wife made some disparaging remarks about his earning power. Some days later, while he was on an errand for his boss —a task which he always resented, because it made him feel as if he were thought of as no more than a lackey or office boy— he went near the railroad station. He crossed to it, as the regularly scheduled passenger train for S_____ entered the station, walked to the ticket counter, wrote out a check for a one-way ticket to S_____, and boarded the train. On the trip he talked to a man sitting next to him, swapping stories about life as a salesman (he told his companion that he was a salesman for one of the large paper manufacturing companies, which recently had built a processing plant in his home town) and then got off at S_____. He entered the station, had a snack in the station dining room, and went outside and took a cab to the main hotel. When he entered the room to which the bellhop took him, he began to feel a little lonely —the room seemed so much less fancy and comfortable than he had expected. He thought a bit about contacting potential paper customers in the morning, but couldn't think of who they might be. He lay down and fell asleep. When he awakened some hours later, he experienced a period of confusion. He was surprised at his surroundings, and unsure about how he, a bookkeeper from R _____, had gotten into what was obviously a hotel room. The man went down to the desk and asked to see the manager, to whom he explained his plight —he didn't know how he got to where he was, but he wanted to go home. A physician was sent for, who examined him and tentatively diagnosed his behavior as hysterical fugue.

This case shows some of the usual features in hysterical fugues: the patient's behavior during the fugue appears quite natural and socially oriented, revealing the rehearsal in fantasy that had preceded it. During the fugue, the patient displays an identity which is different from his usual one. Upon arrival at his destination (or before, if no destination had been imagined and unconsciously planned before), there is usually a brief period of confusion as the patient doesn't know what to do and finds situations that do not fit into his fantasy rehearsals, and which are more unpleasant than had been expected. At this point there is usually a return to the pre-fugal identity, with amnesia for the events intervening from the time that the patient interrupted his activity to escape from his environment in the fugue state. It sometimes happens that the fugal hysteric does not recover his former identity, but continues, sometimes for several years, in his new environment and with his new identity, even developing a new occupation, hobbies, and interests, although remarriage seldom occurs. However, such continued fugues are quite rare, although their drama often results in a great deal of publicity when such a case is discovered. There is some reason to believe that such long term fugues occur in highly intelligent people whose pre-fugal fantasies have been complex enough so that the new situations which present themselves in the new environment can be met fairly adequately. Often the new occupation stands in strong contrast to the person's previous way of life. A fairly typical pattern is for a restrained, cognitively-oriented person, such as a teacher or minister to engage in a less socially acceptable and less restraining occupation in the fugue, such as working as a circus hand or dance band musician. The character of the change suggests the nature of the patient's conflict, which usually involves a resentment of the demands made upon him by his occupation, family, and way of life, so that the new occupation is one with freedom from such demands.

Multiple Personality. Complex fugues such as this, while rare, shade off into hysterical multiple personality, an even more dramatic and even more rare neurosis. In multiple personality, the person may or may not go far from his environment, but he usually develops an identity and ways of behaving consistent with his new identity which stands in sharp contrast to his usual role. He may shift back and forth from one personality to another, each referring to the other as if it were another person, or sometimes with the various personalities amnesic for behavior in the other states. There may be three or even more personalities, although more than two during the same time span are seldom encountered. Multiple personality has received a great deal of public interest as a result of a recent extensive case study by Thigpen and

Cleckley whose book was made into the movie *The Three Faces of Eve.*[28] The movie is quite faithful to the facts of multiple personality, and clearly shows how Eve, as a fairly typical, submissive, perhaps dowdy southern housewife, developed alternate personalities first as a sexy and seductive vamp, and later as an intellectually-oriented and sophisticated young woman. Each of the "faces" reflects a different ideal of femininity in American society, and each contrasts with the others. Each involves satisfactions not found in the others. The extensive fantasy life in which these alternative orientations is rehearsed is shown in such things as Eve's lonely play with her dolls as a child in which elaborate fantasy plots were developed, and in Eve's reading poetry while playing the housewife role, poetry which she did not understand in that role, but which became incorporated in the later-appearing role of the intellectual sophisticate. This points up a fact which is often overlooked by the public: in multiple personality, no one reveals a skill in the "new" personality which did not exist, perhaps hidden in the old. One who has never learned to speak German cannot assume the role of a German translator, with a knowledge of the language mysteriously appearing. A long-forgotten language suddenly may be recalled (where the forgetting was of a repressive nature), or skills may appear which had been acquired in such an incidental way that the person himself may not have been aware of it. In the case of Eve, although there were marked differences among the several "faces," there was also a thread of continuity. In each of the three roles, her very strong sexual inhibitions which formed part of her conflict continued, so that even though in the role of the seductive tramp, she arranged to avoid actual sexual intercourse with the men she picked up.

The role conflicts, resulting from the desirability of disparate role performances in a person who has not been able to integrate them, usually because of conflicts connected with the roles (conflicts often based on conflicting identifications with different parent figures each of which required exclusion of the characteristic associated with the other parent), is apparent in multiple personality. The escape function of the role alternatives is seen in the fact that the patient usually switches out of a role when events in that role create anxiety for the patient. The role that is adopted after the switch usually is related to the anxiety in an indirect way. When passivity in one role begins to produce anxiety, then the patient is likely to switch to a role of dominance and assertiveness. The hysteric's skill at repression is involved in the amnesia for the alternative roles which is usually present, and in the absence of the responses characteristic of one role while the patient is in another one. In addition, like the complex fugues, multiple personality tends to occur only in people of sufficiently high intelligence to permit them to learn well several different styles of behaving in a wide variety of social situations.

When the repressive behavior involved in hysteria is well learned, such behavior is readily cued off by ever lower levels of anxiety, so that the well developed hysteric displays symptoms in response to anxiety at levels which non-hysteric people tolerate without cuing off anxiety-reducing responses. This often is referred to as the weak ego-strength of the hysteric, or alternatively, as low frustration tolerance. It is such overlearning which produces symptoms in the hysteric's response to conflicts which other people experience directly.

Tics. Habitual, automatic muscular twitches and gestures, referred to as tics, also are included as hysterical autonomies. Repression is apparent here too, in that the response often occurs without the person being aware of it. Like the other autonomies, the hysterical behavior involves a repression of self-responses, because the person does not include the hysterical behaviors within his responses to himself. It is generally thought that hysterical tics are gestures or highly abridged versions of some action resulting from a repressed and conflicted drive. In this sense, the tic is symbolic of the unconscious motivation, often left as the residue of an action taken during some extremely traumatic experience, the memory of which has been repressed. The anxiety-reducing effect of the tic is suggested by the fact that it usually increases in frequency and magnitude when the individual is under great tension, and may quite disappear during relaxation. Like stuttering, which many psychologists consider to be a kind of tic, the response disappears when self-consciousness is reduced greatly by the person's close attention to other stimuli. Tics acquire this ability to reduce anxiety, it has been theorized, because they lower drive by expressing symbolically the conflicted response (many tics are interpreted as expressions of hostility as in sneering or spitting), or because they are residuals of a response which was closely related to anxiety-reduction. An example of the latter is a tic which is the remains of a response made by the patient at the time that he almost drowned, and which was followed almost immediately by being discovered and dragged from the water almost unconscious by a passerby. At the time, the patient was a five-year-old child, and the memory of the drowning was quickly repressed, with the aid of the parents who avoided talking about it in the child's presence after they noticed that when they did, the child involuntarily made frantic gestures.

Dynamics of Hysteria. So far, little is known about what kinds of experiences determine what type of hysterical symptom will be developed. While it seems reasonable to expect that there are differences in the socialization experiences between the child who later develops hysterical paralyses and the one who later develops a fugue state in response to conflict, such differences are so far a matter of speculation. However, the common features among the personalities of hysterics are fairly well established. To summarize, these include well-developed skill in repression, conflict including drives to escape from the present situation and its demands without incurring social disapproval, an emphasis on living up to the expectations of others, with the consequent repression of desires and drives considered to be socially unacceptable, and a great deal of fantasy activity. In addition, interest in and naivete about physiological functioning, together with training experiences in which illness is associated with the reduction of anxiety through the avoidance of anxiety-arousing situations, are found in conversion hysteria. In general the repression which occurs in hysteria involves an exclusion of responses to the self, or an exclusion from the self-concept of the conflicted drives. The situation which precipitates hysterical symptoms in the person who has acquired the necessary skills is one which is related to the conflicted drives, by being a cue which arouses the drive and thus creates anxiety. Further, the symptom is symbolic of the conflicted drive, and of the situations which led to the development of the conflict. The precipitating situation may be considered to be symbolic of the situations which led to the conflict, through its similarity to those situations. It is this similarity which makes the precipitating situation so capable of arousing anxiety.

Finally, the learnings that produce the personality pattern which results in hysterical symptoms when conflicts are aroused and precipitating situations occur seem to be related to the socialization practices typically arising after four years of age. It is then that the established dependency drives are threatened and disturbed by the child's moving out into a wider social community. It is from this time on that the child is subject to external demands which he is motivated to avoid through dependent behavior on parents who have already established a pattern of permitting and encouraging such dependency, and who themselves may be reluctant to see the child grow up and face what they often consider to be an unpleasant world from which they would like to protect the child for as long as possible. We have seen that strong dependency encourages identification, which flowers at about this age. Disturbances in the pattern of identification, such as those which characterize fugue states and multiple personality, may be related to the setting of standards by the parents which involve great denial by the child of his own drives, or to conflicting models for identification, such as would be involved where the parental relationships are strained and each parent attempts to make the child like himself and unlike the other parent. These difficulties in identification are seen in the hysteric's anxiety concerning his sexual status. This anxiety, coupled with his dependency which makes him so anxious to please others and to live up to social standards, results in severe conflict and repression regarding sexual drive. Such repression also involves an avoidance of thinking about unpleasant realities, often encouraged by the overprotecting parents, an avoidance maintained by the hysteric's drive to be like what he thinks socially acceptable people are. This drive uses as models the cultural stereotypes of nice people that are present in the society; in America, these stereotypes exclude sexual and aggressive behavior, bad thoughts, and unfriendly attitudes quite completely. Thus the hysteric is usually very friendly and socially skilled, has his attention directed toward other people and toward pleasing them, and has a superficial and rosy view of life colored by a conformity to whatever social definitions of niceness are currently in vogue. It has been found that when people purposely answer personality tests in the direction which they think is the most socially desirable, the results are very much like the results obtained from testing hysterical patients.[29] The hysteric's answers to the test therefore reveal his exaggerated responsiveness to social desirability, and his repression of behavior which does not conform to this standard. Another study on yielding to group norms showed that those who yielded the most, showing their passive dependence on external standards, had the constellation of traits that are usually associated with the hysterical personality pattern: conventional in behavior and values, conscientious, conforming, good natured, anxious to help others, and highly motivated to be with and be liked by others, denying of psychological symptoms (repression), and feeling less anxious and tense than those who yielded least.[30]

From about four years of age on, children's role-playing fantasy becomes quite elaborate and well developed as a regular part of play, particularly in dependent children who find reality more upsetting than their parents had led them to expect, who avoid a great deal of social communication outside the home and so have few friends with whom to engage in shared play, and who have strong needs to practice social roles in fantasy because of their strong needs to identify. This experience in fantasy role-playing establishes the habits of fantasy rehearsal which provide the means by which hysterical behaviors may arise when conflict becomes great and precipitating situations arise.

These learnings that go into the formation of the hysterical personality pattern all occur during the childhood period of which the Oedipal conflict is an outstanding feature. Psychoanalytic theory directly implicates the Oedipal interaction as the basic motivational conflict in hysteria. The theory is that hysterical neuroses represent an inhibition of sexual impulses which were originally directed toward the opposite-sexed parent, or of aggressive impulses directed against the rivalry of the like-sexed parent.[31] In this theory, all later occasions which arouse either sexual or aggressive drives are responded to as if they were similar to the Oedipal situation, producing fear and inhibition of sexuality and aggression, and continued frustration of these drives. Thus the person is attracted to situations like the Oedipal one (the hysterical girl is attracted to older men like her father, the hysterical man to older women like the mother), tends to interpret situations as sexual and seductive, to have Oedipal fantasies, and even unconciously to behave in a seductive manner, although conscious sexual performance is inhibited and awareness of sexual drive is repressed. The theory also suggests that the hysterical symptoms, like all responses to conflict, provide some partial satisfaction of the conflicting drives at the same time as they function to maintain repressions. This theory is illustrated by Brenner's interpretation of a case of chronic vomiting in a young woman.[32] His analysis indicated unconscious wishes to be made pregnant by her father just as her mother was. This desire was firmly inhibited by the parental reactions and by her own desire to avoid arousing her mother's resentment. However, when much later her parents were divorced, a situation that reduced the inhibitions against her sexual wishes, the conflict became intensified as her sexual drive became more and more strongly aroused. The result was the hysterical symptom of vomiting, like the morning sickness of a pregnant woman. Brenner points out that the symptom, through its intropunitive effects, also functioned to punish the woman for her guilty drive, although the substitution of vomiting for the conflicted behavior enabled her to remain unconscious of the real motives that were operating.

Clinical evidence from patients in psychoanalytic treatment strongly supports this interpretation. However, there also seem to be many cases in which this explanation does not work well (as in the combat veteran with the paralyzed leg, described earlier)—particularly in the kinds of cases that do not come into the analyst's private practice. Nevertheless, even in these cases there is usually a clear conflict regarding sex role. One usually finds inhibitions and fears associated with playing the sex role that was acquired through identification during the Oedipal years and maintained by social role prescriptions, with the hysterical symptoms serving as a partial expression of both the desire to meet the role standards and at the same time to avoid the prescribed sex role behaviors. Stimulus generalization from the parents to other possible love objects is clearly present and participates in the conflict over behaving sexually with such love objects. This theory points not only to the Oedipal period of life as an important determinant, but also to adolescence, in which for the first time in the person's life the full implications of his sex role standards are clear to him. We have already noted that in addition, the adolescent is exposed to inconsistent role models and prescriptions, adding further to his conflict and anxiety over how he shall behave and how well he shall meet the standards without at the same time being forced into behaviors that he has learned to feel are repugnant.

It can be seen that many of these factors are interrelated in complex ways, such that repression, identification, fantasy, escape drives, dependency, and naivete about the world are all mutually supporting of each other and interconnected. It would be well for the student to re-read the cases of hysteria presented in this chapter with these considerations in mind, and to attempt to see how the effects of these various processes are present in the adult hysteric.

Hypochondriasis. Hypochondriasis is so similar to conversion hysteria that it is frequently included with it, rather than as a separate neurotic entity. The distinguishing feature of hypochondriasis is that the person is greatly concerned over the possibility of developing a physical disorder, and may be sure that one has already started; it differs from hysteria in that there is in fact no alteration in the functioning of the body parts. Although the hypochondriac may expect that his leg will become paralyzed, the paralysis does not actually develop. However, in other respects the hypochondriac is very like the hysteric. He is a dependent person with conflict concerning the expression of drives which are anxiety-arousing, and shows an interest in and attention to physiological functioning against a background of learning that illness brings important rewards to the dependent person through having others care for him, and through avoiding situations which arouse conflicted drives. The hypochondriac avoids such situations with the rationalization that his delicate health would not permit participation. In this way his life becomes more and more restricted.

The expectation of impending physical illness has several other important components. The projection of guilt concerning forbidden drives is often found as one of the determinants of the expectation that one will be punished by ill health. Such projection of guilt provides the basis for hypochondriacal symptoms not only in neurosis, but also in the psychoses, in which the fears of becoming ill may be quite bizarre (e.g., my stomach is being devoured by snakes). In addition, ill health serves as a means by which the dependent person can receive the solicitation and care of friends, family, and physicians. There may be an element of disguised hostility, in a reaction-forming way, in the relationship between the hypochondriacal invalid and those on whom he is dependent. The patient often behaves in such an overtly compliant, submissive, and grateful manner, that others are forced to take pity on him, and to allow themselves to be dominated by the needs of the invalid. In this way, the invalid can become quite a controlling influence on those about him.

Hypochondriacal self-concern may sometimes involve a displacement of solicitous concern from others to the self. A parent whose dependency drives were reduced by the return in affection and solicitousness received from the children on whom the parent has lavished a great deal of love and care may find that when the children reach maturity, marry, and leave the parental home, their life-long habits of caring for somebody, habits which are reinforced by an increase in status, approval, and regard from their children, no longer have an object, and there is a consequent increase in the feeling of being unloved, uncared for, and unneeded. Coupled with such feelings is the idea that one is, after all, growing older and toward death, that one's health and vigor are no longer what they used to be, further focusing concern on one's own physiological functioning which adds to the displacement. So it is that hypochondriacal behavior is often found in middle-aged parents who have been particularly dependent upon their absent children. There may also be some projection of guilt over aggressive thoughts about their children, an aggression stimulated by the parent's feeling of having been cast off by the children. Sometimes this aggression takes the form of a secret hope that something will happen to the children's marriages so that they will return to the parental home. The projection of guilt for such thoughts adds to the expectation that punishing illness and disability is imminent.

Narcissism. The great self-concern involved in both hypochondriasis and conversion hysteria, together with the relatively low frustration tolerance in which symptoms are easily produced to relatively low level anxiety cues, plus the motivation to avoid the demands made by the social and economic environment all participate in defining a characteristic which Freud identified as *narcissism*, named after the boy in the Greek legend who so admired and doted on himself that he was condemned to the life of a flower that grows by and bends over pools, where it may always see its own image.[33] Freud described the infant as narcissistic, in the sense that the infant responds quite exclusively and directly in terms of his own drives and their relief. It is only through identification with the parent-model that the child begins to behave in ways which are only very indirectly rewarding to himself. One of the products of identification is that the person begins to direct his interest at satisfying the needs and desires of others, and his main source of reward in this is the reinforcement involved in successfully internalizing parental standards and playing the social and sex role that they have approved. At least this seems to be the case in American culture, in which the mature person is expected to be generous and interested in others for their sake rather than for his own personal gain. Freud has defined such behavior as the essence of mature love, as compared to immature love in which the main reinforcement comes directly from the return of love and the reduction of one's own sexual drive. The narcissism in hypochondriasis and hysteria thus further points to learnings connected with identification and the end of infantile narcissism as a major formative process in creating the adult neurotic personality.

Unrelieved narcissism therefore participates in the formation of the personality pattern from which overt hypochondriacal symptoms emerge when conflict and precipitating experiences occur. It has already been indicated that loss of love is one such precipitating incident, and one which is anxiety-arousing partly at least because of its similarity to childhood experiences in which the child's strong dependency drive was frustrated. Cameron has pointed out that where narcissistic interests have included an emphasis on one's physical strength and beauty, a chance illness or the normal depredations of time and age may constitute serious threats to the person's way of maintaining a feeling of being loved and desired.[34] Such a threat may precipitate hypochondriacal interests as a means of reducing anxiety stimulated by the cues of approaching ill health. By taking very good care of oneself, by responding with medications and therapy to the slightest symptom, the hypochondriac can feel that he is holding off real illness and disability. Thus he continues his narcissistic devotion to himself.

A not uncommon consequence of such behavior is that the patient becomes a burden to his physician, who is called upon to treat the slightest imagined irregularity in the patient's physiological functioning, and often to respond as if to a dire emergency. In this way the great demands made by the hypochondriac can further contribute to his rejection by those on whom he tries to be dependent. This is well illustrated in Edith Wharton's *Ethan Frome* in which the wife's hypochondriasis is one of the factors that drives Ethan to an adulterous relationship with another woman.[35]

Of course, when one constantly expects and seeks for signs of physical illness, he usually finds some evidence to confirm his expectation. This is particularly likely when anxiety, with its physiological components, is great. Among these components, for example, are increased breathing and heart rate, related to a deficiency of oxygen in the central nervous system. These effects are likely to be interpreted by the hypochondriac as supporting evidence for his delusion, although these symptoms are really evidence for a psychological rather than strictly organic disturbance.

Hypochondriasis is, in the long run, a self-defeating behavior, because of the inevitability of illness and death. It is obviously impossible for the hypochondriac to hold off serious illness forever, so that anxiety is increasingly aroused as the patient ages, contributing to more and more desperate hypochondriacal efforts to seek cure and protection — efforts which are often seen in the bizarre delusions and fears in senile psychosis that the body is rotting away. This kind of development is aided by the American emphasis on youth and vigor, and by the commercial practices of drug manufacturers who attempt to create the idea that one owes it to oneself to take every possible step that anyone thinks might contribute to longevity and health, such as the many patent medicine and vitamin preparations for aging people which deluge and delude the market. Advertising stresses that continued social acceptability rests on maintaining, at all costs and with money no object, one's youthful beauty and vigor. Illness and physical decline are often presented as punishments (fitting in with the already existing cultural idea that illness is a result of misbehavior)—with the added idea that the punishment is for not taking proper care (that is, a vitamin pill every day) of oneself. It is in this way that the culture supports the learning of hypochondriasis as an anxiety-reducing response. Nevertheless, such cultural factors are probably not sufficient themselves to account for hypochondriasis; they interact with already existing personality patterns to have their effect. It is as unlikely that such advertising practices would exist without an already prepared audience for them, as it is that such an audience could exist without giving rise to these commercial practices and cultural ideas. As in other institutionalized practices, interacting cultural forces and individual personality are reflections of each other, and it would be oversimplifying to see one as the exclusive cause of the other, although each contributes to the development of the other in a mutually symbiotic fashion.

Fatigue State. This syndrome, characterized by chronic feelings of fatigue, used to be called neurasthenia because of the then current theory that it was the result of fatigued or weakened nerves, a theory since discarded. In many respects, fatigue state is very much like hypochondriasis, except that instead of expecting severe illness from which the person must protect himself, the neurasthenic expects to be excessively fatigued, and takes steps to protect himself from such an eventuality. The neurasthenic usually feels too tired to do anything and so restricts and schedules his activity as much as possible and spends frequent periods throughout the day resting in bed. Often even passive occupations such as reading, watching a movie or television, or having a visitor, prove to be exhausting, so that even these events are carefully scheduled and prepared for. Insomnia usually goes along with fatigue state. The patient has spent so much of the day resting in bed, dozing off and on, that his physiological need for sleep has been fairly well met by nightfall, and he finds himself unable to fall asleep. Turning and tossing for hours, he arises in the morning even further fatigued by the belief that he has not slept a wink all night.

A number of factors play a part in fatigue states. Probably one of the most important is the presence of actual fatigue produced by conflict, in which the enervation of muscles leading to motivated responses is counteracted by inhibitory enervation of opposed muscle groups as a result of the operation of drives which conflict with and oppose the excitatory one. The constant muscular tension produces physiological fatigue in the same manner as does hard work. Furthermore, the anxiety involved in the conflict, with its elevation of blood pressure, rapid heart beat, and so forth, adds to the fatigue by the elevated metabolic rate.

In addition, fatigue is reinforced by being a socially acceptable reason for not participating in activities which raise anxiety, or which the individual is motivated to avoid. Fatigue may be defined as the disinclination to continue an activity, whether that fatigue be on a physiological or psychological basis, or more usually, both. Even where physical fatigue is great, most people are able to find the energy to engage in some activity that they find enjoyable, particularly if it is different from the activity which generates reactive inhibition, as well as the fatigue products in the muscles. The neurasthenic, like the hypochondriac and the hysteric, is one whose conflicts typically involve a desire to avoid some activity or set of cues, a desire which conflicts with a fear of social disapproval for "escapism" or irresponsibility. He has learned, usually in childhood from an oversolicitous mother, that fatigue is something to be avoided, and that the avoidance of fatigue is an acceptable way of withdrawing without incurring disapproval. Being careful not to tire oneself has been reinforced by the avoidance of the anxiety that would be produced by the conflict-arousing activities. This attention to the cues of fatigue finds support in the presence of cues which are readily interpretable as fatigue in one who is motivated to find such cues. The cues interpreted as fatigue are those that are produced by the tension of conflict, by reactive inhibition, anxiety, and by the avoidance drive itself. As the fatigue symptoms occur more and more frequently, they lend stronger and stronger support to the patient's self-perceptions of himself as frail. He finds more and more reinforcement which in turn leads to lower frustration tolerance and a failure to deal with problems that arise as a result of the withdrawal, problems which add to the motivation to withdraw and avoid further anxieties. The fatigue symptoms therefore are elicited ever more frequently, so that the withdrawal becomes more and more generalized until the patient is almost a complete recluse and entirely dependent. The social acceptibility factor in fatigue is supported by the fact that such neuroses occur much more frequently among women than men (further indicating also that the theory of a physiological basis in excessive work is false), and that it tends to occur in those women whose social class is most inclined to look upon such frailty as natural and expected in their sex as a mark of femininity. These attitudes were particularly strong in the American upper middle class and the upper class. Thus it is paradoxical that those women who had servants and maids, and had the least work to do, were the ones most likely to develop fatigue states.

As the fatigue syndrome becomes established and restriction on activity has been maintained for some period of time, there is an adjustment of metabolic functioning to the low activity level of the patient, which operates in such a way that the person does in fact become less and less capable of expending "normal" amounts of energy, and tasks which are not physically fatiguing to others come to be quite tiring to the patient because of the relatively greater drain on his physiological resources.

The insomnia which is frequently present in this syndrome may be increased by the motivation to avoid dreams which are likely to be disturbing because of their conflict-laden content.

There may be another important factor involved in fatigue states. It has been suggested by many theorists, particularly the psychoanalysts, that fatigue is often an intropunitive expression of guilt over masturbatory activity. It is widely believed in our culture that sexual acitivity is fatiguing, particularly autoeroticism. Because sexual inhibitions are usually involved in the conflicts of the dependent, narcissistic person, sexual drive is likely to be very strong, giving rise to almost compulsive masturbation which the person simply cannot inhibit enough, despite his many efforts to do so. The guilt which follows is therefore expressed through the expectation of becoming physically debilitated, an expectation which finds support from the other factors that contribute to the development of fatigue state. The process is encouraged by the restriction of the neurasthenic to his chambers. Alone much of the day and in bed, frequently too tired even to dress, the opportunities and stimuli for masturbation are many and great. Some theorists have further suggested that the avoidance of social participation and of the stimuli of the wider world outside the home expressed through fatigue may in many female cases arise from a fear that she will be either sexually aroused by stimuli encountered outside the confines of the home, or a fear that others whom she meets may be able to guess that she has been masturbating. This fear is obviously based on projected guilt which leads readily into misinterpretations of the behavior of others.

Anxiety Neurosis. The neurotic and psychotic behaviors described in this chapter thus far have all involved various means by which anxiety is reduced, means which become the behaviors defined as symptoms. However, in anxiety neurosis the person experiences anxiety directly, without the anxiety leading to any habitual responses except repression of thoughts about the conflict which produces the anxiety. Thus the anxiety neurotic does not know why he is anxious, or what are the cues which stimulate it. Not knowing, he is unable to avoid the stimulating situations, so that he is chronically suffering and experiencing tension and upset. All of the characteristics of anxiety are present, as described in Chapter 9: sweating, heart palpitations, fatigue, stomach upset, digestive disturbances, rapid pulse and labored breathing, a sense of extreme nervousness, tremors, the withdrawal of blood from the extremities producing cold feet and hands, frequent headaches, and the feeling that one is unable to think, concentrate, or remember things. These are the same effects which the hysteric interprets as physical disability, the hypochondriac as signs of impending ill-health, and the neurasthenic as fatigue.

The cognitive symptoms of being unable to think, concentrate, or remember are very likely aspects of the repression of symbolic activity which prevents the patient from thinking about the cause and nature of his problem, because to do so would increase still further his anxiety. Thus the anxiety neurotic is frequently cognitively depressed, showing a restriction of association and imaginative activity. What thoughts or imaginings he does have are frequently unpleasant, frightening, or of black and forbidding mood.

The anxiety neurotic is prone to anxiety attacks —sudden outbreaks of symptoms, cued off by some situation which arouses the underlying conflicting drives, or which is like the severely traumatic but repressed experience in the patient's past from which the generalized anxiety stems. In such attacks the patient may break down in tears, become extremely frightened and appeal for help, and become terribly over-reactive to the slightest unexpected sounds or sights. These are very much the same kinds of experiences which precipitate symptoms in the hysteric, the hypochondriac, and the neurasthenic; they are also the experiences such neurotics have when their symptoms fail to effect an avoidance of conflict-arousing situations, or when the symptoms are removed without there being any change in the conflict processes giving rise to them.

The cognitive symptoms in anxiety state and anxiety attack are themselves frequently further sources of worry to the person, and can contribute to his ineffectiveness as a worker, marriage partner, and parent, thus further worsening his situation and creating more sources of anxiety. Such symptoms can become chronic, particularly in one whose reality-contact and problem-solving skills have not been very strong. Anxiety states thus often shade off into psychosis. The hysteric who is prematurely left without his anxiety-reducing symptoms often develops new symptoms, as did the hysterically blind worker described earlier. In the hypochondriac and the neurasthenic, such experiences with intense anxiety usually are followed by a further development of symptoms, but in the anxiety neurotic, anxiety attacks can often result in further deterioration in thinking and the development of delusions and hallucinations characteristic of the schizophrenic or the depressive patient.

When anxiety attacks have become more and more frequent, so that the patient's general level of anxiety is quite high, he is susceptible to a full-blown panic attack. In a panic attack, stimulated by some situation which, like other precipitating events, further activates conflicts through its similarity to past traumas, the person may blindly run or attack those who impede his running or who are intimately connected with the precipitating incident. The intense fear may produce projected expressions in the form of hallucinations. In every respect such a panic attack resembles a psychotic episode, and it frequently happens that when the flight is over, the patient continues to manifest psychotic thinking, requiring hospitalization. In panic attacks, impulsive suicide as the only means of ending the tension is an everpresent possibility.

These factors are strongly suggestive of intropunitive expressions of hostility and many theorists have suggested this as the source of the anxiety in such cases. The anxiety is interpreted as self-punishment which may reach its climax in either a psychotic depression or suicide. The intropunitive hostility is apparent in the almost obsessive ruminations of the anxiety neurotic in which he blames himself for everything that has gone wrong and is sure he cannot handle every new task that comes his way. Even when things are going very well he anticipates a decline and ascribes the good state of his affairs to luck. The anxiety neurotic seems bound and determined to find fault in himself, in the face of all kinds of evidence that may contradict his self-perception. In an earlier chapter we mentioned such a patient, a straight A student in college, who later made Phi Beta Kappa and successfully went on for a Ph. D. He ascribed his good grades to chance, to the fact that his teachers liked him, and to the fact that he was lucky enough to take only easy courses in which the competition was very poor, much poorer than that faced by other more able students who did not get such good grades. This student was able to turn everything against himself.

Such intropunitive hostility, we have already seen, can be related to inhibitions arising from restrictive internalized standards for behavior, so that the individual is frustrated by his own self. The anxiety neurotic is often a highly inhibited person as a result of too restrictive standards for behavior set by parents who expected more from the child than the child could really deliver. Coleman cites as typical of the history of the anxiety neurotic one patient's report that his father once gave him a model airplane to assemble at an age at which the child could not possibly do it, so that the father had to help him extensively.[36] Such an experience further contributes to the child's own feeling of inadequacy, that there is nothing he can attempt successfully, and that he can never be as competent as his father and other adults. Such feelings are part of the symptom picture in the adult who later develops anxiety neurosis, often as a result of some experience with a difficult or challenging job, or with a critical employer or wife which is enough like the earlier childhood experiences to arouse the great anxiety and fear of rejection and failure that was characteristic of the childhood experiences. Thus the feelings of failure or impending failure and inadequacy that are found in anxiety neurosis are the products of intropunitive hostility in greatly inhibited personalities together with training in the expectation of failure and inadequacy which produces a fear of trying anything which is at all challenging.

Impossibly high standards set by parents further contribute to anxiety neurosis in another way. Because the standards are so high, the child cannot successfully live with and satisfy his introjected demands. He thus hates the part of himself which cannot meet his internalized standards, and he hates the standards themselves which, as part of himself, can be hated in a way that the father, the real author of the standards, could not be. This forms the background of the intropunitiveness of the anxiety neurotic. This process suggests the narcissism that underlies the anxiety neurotic's intropunitiveness; it is the narcissism implied in the feeling of outrage and resentment that he should be made to meet such high standards. Because the process of identification has been prevented from full development by the child's ambivalence toward his demanding parents, his infantile narcissism is not fully replaced by the introjected parents. These developments form the basis for the clinical observation that the anxiety neurotic's great self-deprecation goes along with an unusually great amount of self-concern and solicitousness about his own feelings. This self-concern is what remains of the unreplaced infantile narcissism.

Anxiety neurotics often act as if they actually feared success, or feared to label themselves and interpret their lives as successful. Some theorists have seen in this an expression of conflict over the patient's adoration for his parents and for their high standards, and of hostility toward them. To become successful would be evidence of successful competition with the parents, and as such, would be an aggressive triumph over them. Such aggression arouses strong fear of loss of parental attention which the child learned was gotten only when he needed help —that is, was unsuccessful. Added to this process may be a fear of being successful like the parents because such success might result in the exposure of his deeply felt inferiority and moral weakness (which is the way such a person interprets his feeling of ingratitude toward his parents), a weakness which he may find confirmed by his awareness of disapproved sexual desires. The anxiety neurotic therefore feels that he is worthless and undeserving of success and good fortune, and may behave in such a fashion that when success seems within his grasp, he bungles—he impulsively quits his job, fails to study for the final examination, etc.

Personality Disorders

There is another group or diagnostic category, beside the neuroses and psychoses, which should be mentioned, although it will not be gone into in detail. This is the group often referred to as "personality disorders" (or "character disorders") in which the behavior observed is not the result of conflict producing various kinds of noninstrumental behaviors and symptoms, but is rather the result of the way in which the individual has learned to reduce his drives more or less directly. However, because of atypical socialization experiences, these ways of reducing the drives are such as to run counter to the demands and expectations of the individual's society. These are, then, personality patterns which conflict with the individual's society, and which result in a great deal of conflict between him and social forces, conflict which is bred out of the individual's failure to play the kind of social role demanded of his position and status. They are considered to be disordered personalities rather than neuroses or psychoses, although one could make a strong case for suggesting that the shoe be on the other foot, and that one refer to society disorders in which certain kinds of human phenomena are produced but not tolerated. Among the personality disorders are listed psychopathic, or more modernly, sociopathic personality (in which the inhibitions which have been acquired by most people in our society are lacking), those kinds of homosexuality which are not displaced responses resulting from conflict, passive-aggressive and passive-dependent personalities, "inadequate" personality, and a host of sexual patterns which are considered immoral in the individual's society. Alcoholism, juvenile delinquency, and drug addiction are often considered to be part of this group, particularly when these behaviors seem to be more clearly determined by a lack of the customary social standards and inhibitions, than by neurotic needs to avoid cues that arouse conflicts. In the personality disorders such behavior may be anxiety-reducing, but the anxiety is usually situationally caused, rather than resulting from the activation of conflict by environmental cues. For example, threatened loss of a job and income can create realistic anxiety in its own right, to which an inadequately or atypically socialized person may react by becoming chronically drunk. Or such a situation could activate conflicts relating to achievement, internalized parental standards, or drives for social approval, based on childhood learning experiences, which in turn involve great anxiety avoided by becoming intoxicated. In the latter case, the alcoholism would be considered to be largely neurotic, whereas in the former it might be considered to be more of a personality disorder. Obviously there is great room for overlap and confusion between neuroses and personality disorders. However, therapists generally report that they have much greater success with neurotics than with personality disorders, possibly because the neurotic's conflicts can be resolved thus eliminating the symptom-formation process, whereas in the personality disorders it is impossible to rid the environment of anxiety-arousing situations sufficiently to prevent the occurrence of the antisocial or asocial anxiety-reducing behaviors.

One of the most interesting features of the personality disorders is the fact that the individual does not seem to learn, in adolescence and adulthood, that his mode of behavior is punishable by law and society. Guilt is seldom present (although fear of being caught and of being punished is), and there seems to be little ability to develop an internalized moral code which is consistent enough with that of his society to keep the individual out of trouble. It seems as if once the period of major identification and internalization in childhood is passed, if internalization has not taken place then, it simply cannot occur later. This is essentially an explanation based on imprinting, such as was discussed in Chapter 8 in connection with the interpersonal approach drives, and maternal deprivation during the period in which identification with parents develops. The failure to respond to secondary reinforcers was mentioned in Chapter 4 as another aspect of psychopathic behavior.

Some thinkers in this area have suggested that the personality disorders represent some failure of reality testing, because of this apparent inability to learn later a set of acceptable standards, even though not doing so often means that the individual will spend a great deal of his life in jail, or unemployed and without money, or without achieving a stable marital relationship. This failure has been ascribed to some lack in ego functioning (sometimes considered to be an organic defect) not unlike that present in psychosis.[37] There is thus an area of confusion between the personality disorders and the psychoses, and it is often difficult to distinguish between the unsocialized and uninhibited rage of the psychopath and the bizarre delusional behavior of a schizophrenic. At any rate, the personality disorders are but little understood, largely because they respond so poorly to therapy that clinicians who have contributed most to our understanding of neuroses and psychoses have relatively little contact with the personality disorders.

The difficulties in understanding the personality disorders has involved many confusions in diagnosis. The confusion arises from the fact that there are no specific symptoms such as obsessions or conversion features, and the same apparent overt behavioral patterns may exist with or without a neurotic background. We therefore distinguish among *sociopathy*, as described in this section (including antisocial personalities, sexual perversions, alcoholism and addiction—all of the patterns involving a basically infantile narcissistic orientation toward direct drive gratification, but without significant conflict and anxiety), *neuroses* and *psychoses* having similar behaviors but in which the behaviors represent noninstrumental responses to conflict (they may be obsessive-compulsive as in many perversions, or schizophrenic, as in many kinds of asocial and antisocial behavior), and *character neuroses*, which are personality structures identical to those involved in the neuroses and psychoses, but without overt specific symptoms. This last group will be dealt with in the next section.

But before leaving the sociopathic personality, a few remarks about social attitudes toward this kind of personality are in order. Because of his lack of apparent anxiety and the readiness of the sociopath to violate social norms in order to gratify his drives and wishes, the sociopath arouses strong feelings in other people. They respond either with intense anger and resentment, or they idolize and idealize him, making him a hero of folklore, such as Bluebeard, Morgan the pirate, Jesse James, and others. These reactions occur because the sociopath does what most of us would like to do but cannot because of the inhibitions and conflicts that we have but he lacks. Thus we admire him and keep him in our fantasy as a folk hero, and at the same time reduce our own guilt and control our own drives by trying to eliminate him and his arousing effect on us from our environment. These reactions are complicated by the fact that the sociopath often is a charming and socially graceful person, again because he lacks inhibitions and anxieties cued off by other people. He thus seems both more admirable and more dangerous to our own self-control. In effect the sociopath is so much of what we would like to be and fear to be.

A further complication arises because the sociopath's relative freedom from interpersonal anxiety and from desires to conform to social norms provides some of the conditions for original and creative activity. Thus some creative sociopaths become literary and artistic heroes, and criminals in general are sometimes perceived as symbols of the creative artist rebelling against the constraints of a philistine society. Some novelists owe at least part of their fame to the public's response to their sociopathic personalities and to their colorful histories of having committed violence and defied convention. Similarly, there are many fictional heroes who serve as symbols of the free (and criminal) spirit. People often have a feeling of awe before a really flamboyant criminal, a feeling that he has somehow transcended to a new and ideal dimension the confines of our humdrum world. He has had experiences that go beyond our (conscious) imaginations—experiences that touch our own repressed drives sufficiently to attract us and to mix our rejection of his behavior with an odd attraction, a combination that produces our feeling of awe.

We recognize the relationship between creativity and asocial or antisocial behavior, and the extent to which we will tolerate the latter as the price of the former represents a real problem for our ideas about justice and the social good. This is one of the meanings of Dostoevski's Raskolnikov, who asks if a superior person can violate social prohibitions against murder.[38] Thus far we have not found an enduring solution to this problem.

The Relationship Between Abnormal and Normal Behavior

This completes our brief review of the various diagnostic categories, and of representative examples of the major ones. There are many syndromes which have not been mentioned, and many subvarieties of those discussed which have not been included. To go into detail on this aspect of personality would be beyond the intention and scope of this book. One of the main reasons for including a discussion of the neuroses and psychoses was to present total personality patterns in an effort to throw some light on the integration of socialization practices, habits and drives, thinking, perception and consciousness, conflict and response to present pictures of unified personality patterns: to answer the question of how the various processes discussed come to life in individuals operating in their environments. The following discussion of the syndromes presented is aimed at answering this question in terms of current thinking.

The first point to be made is that neurotic and psychotic behavior involves the expression of previously learned, practiced, and established noninstrumental responses to anxiety in response to stress. The stress is the anxiety produced by the activation of already acquired conflicts by environmental stimulation which is related on a stimulus generalization dimension to the learning situations in which the conflicts were acquired. Stress is thus based on an interaction between environmental events and the effects of past experiences. The symptoms which are developed are massive elaborations of the noninstrumental responses to anxiety which had already been learned before the neurosis was precipitated. These noninstrumental responses to anxiety are essentially like those acquired by people who never have overt symptoms precipitated to a noticeable extent, and so are never diagnosed as neurotic. In this sense, the neurotic and the psychotic are normal people who have been exposed to stress. However, some qualifications on this point are in order.

The first qualification is that the person who later develops symptoms is one who has usually had the kinds of learning experiences which make him susceptible to intense conflict. That is, the conditions for conflicting drives have already been established during the socialization process, so that such a person is perhaps more likely than others to have conflicts activated by later experiences. We have seen that the conditions for acquiring such conflicts in childhood, usually referred to as "traumatic" experiences, really involve many many occasions on which the conflicting drives are elicited and reinforced until they have become quite well established. Although there may have been a single traumatic event in the person's history, it has been pointed out that it is not the trauma itself that is important, but the learnings which grow out of it, and which take place over a long period of time. In this sense, the person who later develops a neurosis or psychosis is one who differs from "normal" people in having acquired the potentialities for fairly strong conflicts. Of course, conflicts exist in everyone, but it is usually very intense conflict that is responsible for symptom development. Innate individual differences in the ease and the extent of autonomic arousal participate by influencing the extent and strength of the conflicting drives mediated by the autonomic system.

The second qualification is that those who develop neurotic or psychotic symptoms when conflict is activated are those who have had a solid background of learning the anxiety-reducing responses to their conflicts which form the character of their symptoms. While all people have usually learned some noninstrumental responses to their conflict-anxieties, people do differ in the extent of such learning, or in the strength of such habits, and in the extent to which instrumental problem-solving responses have been acquired. Thus it may be said that those who develop symptoms differ from "normals" in the extent to which they have acquired the skills or habits which form their symptoms.

The third qualification is a most important one. It is that there is a complex interaction among strength of conflict, strength of noninstrumental responses to anxiety, and strength or frequency of environmental cues which activate conflict, in producing symptoms. That is, relatively few conflicts and little strength of the tendency to engage in anxiety-reducing behaviors (both of which go hand in hand because if there are few conflicts, there are few occasions on which to practice anxiety-reducing responses) can be compensated for by extremely stressful conditions. One who is relatively unlikely to become neurotic or psychotic can nevertheless have symptoms precipitated by sufficient stress, as shown over and over again during wartime in which great ranges of stress were produced. Some men "broke" under relatively minor stress, indicating that strong conflicts and strong habits of noninstrumental anxiety responses were established and readily elicited, while others developed symptoms only after prolonged and very intense stress. World War II was responsible for the development of the concept of the "breaking point"; it became apparent that that point, defined as the amount of stress necessary to precipitate symptoms, varied from one man to another as a function of the extent of previous training in conflict, instrumental, and noninstrumental responses to anxiety. Each person actively participates in determining what is stressful for him, through having conflicted motives that can be aroused by environmental events. Some learning histories are such that a wide range of events are stressful, and others are such that stress is minimal.

In the light of these considerations, the earlier statement about the difference between "normals" and neurotics and psychotics may be revised to mean that a normal is a person whose level of conflict, and strength of noninstrumental responses to anxiety are low enough so that symptoms are not precipitated by the stress that person is exposed to, and/or whose instrumental responses to anxiety are strong enough to solve the problems produced when conflicts are activated by stress.

The important point here is that normals do not differ from neurotics and psychotics in the kinds of elements in their personalities, but rather in the extent to which various components have been acquired. Normals differ among themselves just as do neurotics and psychotics in the particular kinds of conflicts and responses acquired, and in fact, most normal people are very much like one or another neurotic or psychotic in the type—though not in the extent—of behaviors displayed. For example, there are many college students who tend to sleep extensively at such crucial periods as exam time, or term-paper writing time, a response very much like that made in fatigue neurosis, and having essentially the same meaning, although the student may not be considered to be severely neurotic. Similarly there are many people, not diagnosed as neurotic, who "forget" and deny unpleasant experiences and drives, but who develop mild conversion symptoms such as occasional headaches, when conflicts are aroused. Again, there are "normals" who, like the manic patient, are full of wit and cleverness, have spurts of great activity and ambitious plans, although they may never become quite as unrealistic and extravagant as the psychotic. So also are particularly fussy or pedantic people who are "bugs" on neatness and orderliness responding in ways similar to the obsessive-compulsive patient, although they may never have such overt symptoms as repetitious rituals or obsessive thoughts, beyond mildly chronic worrying about truth, justice, or other abstract ideas. The lonely eccentric who follows his narrow interests almost without regard to the world around him has a personality pattern basically like the schizophrenic; strong inferiority feelings mark the personality type which in its more extreme representation is called anxiety neurosis, and superficial gregariousness, modishness, and sincere conventionality of interests and attitudes mark the hysterical character type. The nonsymptomatic personalities, which all of us approximate to some extent, however subtly, are what we referred to as *character neuroses,* although neurosis may be too strong a word for them. In other words, each diagnostic category may be used to describe a personality pattern that exists without symptoms of neurosis or psychosis. In this sense the hysterical personality structure (or *hysterical character structure,* as some writers refer to it) exists both within and without hysterical neuroses; all hysterical neurotics were once only hysterical personalities or hysterical characters, but the person with an hysterical personality pattern may never become an overt neurotic. He has an hysterical personality because he has acquired very similar conflicts and similar repressive defenses, attention to physiological functioning, drives to avoid without losing social acceptability and dependency, etc. — in short, the same processes occur in him, although to a lesser extent, as occur in the hysterical neurotic. This is why psychologists refer to the continuity between the normal and abnormal, with normality at one end and one of the neuroses or psychoses at the other end of each continuum. With this situation there is no clear point at which one can place the start of neurosis or psychosis. The presence of any noninstrumental responses to anxiety may be considered neurotic to some extent, so that many writers refer to the "normal" as the "average neurotic" because most people show some such behaviors, if only in relatively minor and unimportant ways. Other writers reserve the use of the diagnostic labels for people who have overt symptoms. However, we have seen that in some life situations, symptoms may fit in so well with the individual's work or family structure that they are never considered to be noninstrumental responses to conflict because of their great instrumental value as far as the occupation or family life is concerned. Such people would then not be considered neurotic so long as their occupational and family lives remain stable and unchanged. Those writers who use symptoms as the criterion for neurosis or psychosis then resort to a social definition of these diagnostic conditions; one is neurotic or psychotic if his behavior is in some way dissonant or inappropriate to the norms or standards of his social environment. Such a definition, however, runs into a great deal of trouble because of its implied definition of normality as conformity, and because the criterion for what behavior is nonneurotic and nonpsychotic shifts from one culture to another. In any event, it seems to be irrelevant whether a certain type of behavior is labeled as neurotic or psychotic; what is important is the nature of the behavior, how it occurs, and what its consequences are for the individual's life. Whether therapy or change in behavior is desirable should depend on considerations other than whether the behavior is labeled as neurotic or psychotic, such as the extent to which responses to conflict fail to solve the individual's important problems and contribute to further frustration and anxiety. It is, therefore, a moot question as to whether everyone should be considered more or less neurotic, depending on the presence of noninstrumental anxiety-reducing responses, or whether diagnostic labels should be reserved for those with disabling or interfering symptoms. However, in thinking about the problem one should keep in mind which definition of neurosis and psychosis is being used.

One should avoid thinking that a necessary implication is that neurotic behavior is bad. It has been pointed out that rationalization is unavoidable, that compensation and sublimation are responsible for much valued political, social, economic, scientific, religious, and artistic activity, and that various responses to anxiety may be of particular value in certain kinds of occupations and social settings. The attention to interpersonal cues which characterizes the hysterical personality can result in a sensitivity to the needs of others, as well as in symptoms, and the ruminative activity of the obsessive personality type can lead to theoretical discoveries, as well as to obsessional symptoms, providing intelligence and not too great conformity to current modes of thinking are present. It might even be argued that displacement of hostility can serve as a means of maintaining adequate interpersonal relationships. These are implications of the point made in Chapter 9 that responses do not occur in an interpersonal vacuum, that the social environment participates in differentially rewarding or punishing the various kinds of responses to anxiety. Finally, many reactions to conflict may shape the character of great advances in knowledge and thought. For example, the direction of Freud's theorizing was undoubtedly influenced by his own personality structure,[39] but in such a way that many of the products of his thinking have been found to be valid truths, even though it may well have been a neurotic process which led him to them. Knowledge is not limited to creation only by the most conflict-free people. In short, diagnostic terms such as *neurosis* and *psychosis* should be used descriptively, rather than evaluatively, and the behavior they label may be studied without reference to value judgments. Evaluations of the behavior so labeled must depend on the use of frames of reference outside of the behavior being studied. While valuing is itself a psychological process, and may be studied psychologically, knowledge may exist about events regardless of how those events are valued. The question of what constitutes a sound basis for valuing is a subject for philosophical discussion which cannot be dealt with in this book although it is one with which all of us must ultimately deal, particularly when we are familiar enough with the details of the phenomena whose value is being considered.

So far we have been discussing the difference between normality and nonnormality. A few words are in order about the difference between neurosis and psychosis. It was said, in introducing the neuroses, that they differ from psychoses importantly in that there is no failure of reality contact or cognitive functioning in the neuroses. However, we have seen that in many ways the anxiety-reducing responses which include symptom formation involve some denial of reality—denial of the individual's conflicting motives, or of the cues in the enviroment which stimulate conflicts and anxiety. To the extent that this is so, then to that extent must the neurotic also be considered to have weakened reality contact, at least in those areas related to his conflicts. Reality contact is therefore an unfirm basis for dividing the psychoses from the neuroses. Some theorists have suggested that neuroses are marked by anxiety, while anxiety is only peripheral or unimportant in the symptom picture of psychosis. However, psychotic behaviors are quite apparently responses to anxiety, although the patient's fantasy and his other symptoms may be adequate to avoid, at least temporarily, the arousal of anxiety. The same may be said of neurosis, at least of those whose responses to anxiety are effective enough so that they do not experience anxiety directly, and so seldom feel the need for therapy to end their discomfort. Thus a differentiation on the basis of anxiety is not wholly adequate. It must be admitted that so far, no completely adequate criterion for distinguishing between the two has been widely adopted, so that one may have reason to question the utility of both classifications. It might be more logical to distinguish only between those patients who require hospitalization and those who do not regardless of diagnostic category.

The Concept of Mental Illness. We have seen in this chapter that neuroses, psychoses, and the "personality disorders" are complex products of learning which includes socialization conditions in which conflicts are established and anxiety-reducing responses to the conflicts are learned, and precipitating stress which activates the conflict because of its similarity to the situations in which the conflict was acquired and which elicits the anxiety-reducing responses acquired at that time. The process operates in such a way that the precipitating situation and the reactions to it may be considered symbolic of the earlier learning situations and of the conflicting drives. In this sense, the behavior displayed may be thought of as a regression to a fixation produced by the early learning experience. Finally, the behaviors revealed in response to the precipitating condition constitute what are looked upon as symptoms of the significant learning history of the individual.

Then what has happened to the concept of mental *illness*? The picture we have is that of an individual with a given set of experiences which are such that he behaves in particular ways as logical and necessary consequences of that set of experiences. The question of illness, with its implication of a necessarily pathological state of the organism, does not seem to be appropriate as a way of describing this process, at least if illness is used in its usual meaning of referring to some debilitating state caused by pathogenic agents.

The term "mental illness" was originally introduced primarily as a device for changing the public's conceptions about neurosis and psychosis from one in which such behavior was thought to be the result of moral or constitutional defect and inferiority in the person, to an attitude of greater permissiveness, understanding, and sympathy for patients which would encourage more people to seek the therapy they need, without incurring social stigma. However, the term seems to have outlived its usefulness, does not seem appropriate, and in fact introduces some other problems of its own. It suggests that the patient and his behavior play no part in the process, but that rather, illness is something that happens to one. Thus many people seek therapy under the misapprehension that the doctor will administer things to cure the illness, in a manner analogous to treating an infection. Further, it suggests that the neuroses and psychoses are the province of specialists in disease, rather than of specialists in those processes of learning which are involved in personality formation and functioning. It also suggests that, like an illness, the processes involved have no connection with the life goals, and the selfhood of the person "afflicted," whereas it is these very things that are most directly involved.

When a person has difficulty getting along in his environment, it may be presumptious to assume that there is something pathological or sick in him, rather than in the environment which produced his personality in interaction with his biological nature, or in the environment to which he does not conform. The concept of "mental illness" has made the hospital a cultural symbol for the place in which happiness and love is supplied where these are lacking. Finally, the concept of "mental illness" necessarily implies a disvalued phenomenon, and in the light of the discussion above, it seems likely that such a frame of reference for values attached to human behavior may be unjustified oversimplification of the problem of worth, and of good and evil.[40] It introduces confusion into our understanding of the determinants of human behavior.

It would be well to avoid disvaluing a phenomenon by definition when under a different label, the same phenomenon might not be disvalued. That is, values should not be involved in diagnosis, which is really an elaborate description and explanation; they should be reserved for consideration in connection with what is to be done with the knowledge given in diagnosis, rather than becoming confused with the diagnosis itself. And unfortunately, the use of the term "illness" automatically brings a value judgment into the description of whatever is diagnosed as an illness.

There are, then, good reasons for abandoning this outmoded concept, and there is a strong trend in this direction among the professions concerned with personality.

Overdetermination. This review of the major personality types points to a unity existing within the personality despite the fact that so many different drives, psychological processes, and habitual responses are involved. This unity comes about through the coalescing of these elements into a consistent character structure, the maintenance and enhancement of which becomes an important motivation because it is so important to many underlying processes.[41] For example, all the processes in the socialization of cognitive and activity drives may go into an interest in mathematical work; culturally acquired schemas regarding productivity, and conflicted attitudes toward other people producing an avoidance of interpersonal relationships, may combine with the mathematical interest to produce a character structure in which bookkeeping and accounting work are highly valued activities because they fulfill these several underlying functions.[42] The main mechanisms underlying this coalescing of various parts into a single multipurpose structure are those discussed in Chapter 3 as producing efficiency in behavior — those that operate so that the person acquires behaviors that produce the maximum reinforcement or gratification with the least effort. The person then has strong motives to maintain and enhance the resultant character structure. He now wishes to be a very good and successful bookkeeper. This desire is a derivative drive which is really secondary to his motives to avoid people, to have enjoyable cognitive experiences, to meet his internalized standards, and to play the role he has accepted. That is, all of these sources participate in his desire to be a competent bookkeeper.

For this person it would be said that bookkeeping is an *overdetermined* occupational choice. Overdetermination refers to a number of related processes. It refers to the fact that any resultant behavior is the product of the coalescing of several motivational sources, as in the example of the bookkeeper. It also means that any resultant behavior depends on the complex interaction of learning experiences, the presence of the appropriate drives, the availability of reinforcements for the behavior, and the occurrence of cues similar to those present in the original training experiences, so that they have the capacity to elicit the behaviors learned then as a means of reducing the motives present. Each one of these elements determines the occurrence or nonoccurrence of the behavior and the nature of the behavior. Thus the behavior is multiple or overdetermined.

Many of these determining factors, including the various drives that are coalesced in the resultant behavior, are usually unconscious. The behaving person cannot adequately verbalize them, either as a result of repression, lack of knowledge, and/or because they were acquired before adequate language for labeling them was developed. A man is a bookkeeper because he "enjoys" the work, and further explanations are usually unavailable. Indeed, many people find it difficult adequately to account for their interests, giving them the feeling that interests are determined by mysterious internal forces. Frequently students report that they do not know what their interests are, suggesting the unconscious status of the determinants of their choices (and also the lack of familiarity with an occupation that would sufficiently satisfy these determinants to precipitate their coalescence). The main point here is that all resultant behaviors are overdetermined in the sense that they satisfy many different motives, they are products of complex interactions among psychological processes, and there are usually unconscious as well as conscious reasons for the behavior.

REPRISE. In this chapter we have presented some of the most common behavioral patterns as represented in their extreme forms in the psychoses, neuroses, and personality disorders. The following topics were explored:

1. The psychoses are traditionally divided into the organic and functional, although there are reasons for questioning the validity of such a division.

2. The functional psychoses include schizophrenia and its several subtypes, and the manic and depressive psychoses.

3. The psychoneuroses, involving less distortion of reality than the

psychoses, were explored in obsessive-compulsive reactions, phobias, hysteria and its subtypes, hypochondriasis, and fatigue and anxiety states.

4. In each syndrome the resulting behaviors are associated with the learning conditions in which the underlying conflicts were acquired and are exaggerations of noninstrumental responses to conflict.

5. Personality disorders, as distinguished from neurotic patterns having similar behaviors, include patterns marked by unsocialized drive reduction and a lack of inhibiting anxiety.

6. Character neuroses, or more appropriately, character structures, are coordinate with the diagnostic groups presented, but exist without symptoms. Character structure refers to personality types in non-neurotic and nonpsychotic people, types similar to the neuroses and psychoses but without the exaggerations of the processes involved.

7. The complex interactions of strength of conflict, strength of responses to the conflict, and strength and frequency of environmental cues which activate the conflict determine whether sufficient stress is present to move a character structure toward neurotic or psychotic symptoms.

8. The distinctions between normality and psychopathology may rest on the extent to which noninstrumental responses to conflict are present. Since most people show such behaviors, most people are psychopathological. If the distinction is made on the basis of whether symptoms are present, the range of normal behavior becomes wider, but this distinction produces problems in avoiding an implied agreement between social conformity and normality.

9. Diagnosis is separate from valuing; neurotic and psychotic behavior is good or bad depending on one's frame of reference in evaluating the actual behaviors which the diagnosis merely names and summarizes. A diagnosis is not a value judgment.

10. There is no adequate conceptual base for separating neurosis from psychosis, although in practice this distinction is usually made.

11. The concept of mental illness is outmoded when behavior is seen as the product of reasonable and logical developments based on the individual's experiences and the psychological processes that transform these experiences into personality. Illness implies a value judgment, but that which is to be valued in some frames of reference is not necessarily nonneurotic, nonpsychotic, or nonsociopathic, nor is all disvalued behavior always neurotic or psychotic, or sociopathic. Hospital treatment for a person whose behavior does not quite fit his society is

not always the most just or appropriate course for producing the needed or desired changes. It may be the society which ought to change to accommodate the individual.

12. All behavior is overdetermined in the sense that every action involves the complex interplay of many forces and processes, and of several different drives, and in the sense that behind the conscious reasons for any action there are also unconscious determinants of the behavior.

11. Human Nature and Value

Having explored many of the basic phenomena of human behavior in the last ten chapters, we are ready to point up some general principles, and to bring the material together into a summary of the meaning of the study of personality. In this, we will discuss some of the value implications of personality as it has been explored in this book.

Man's Behavioral Potential

Human beings have a tremendous potential for behavior. At birth, the range of behaviors which he might acquire includes all the behavior ever displayed by man in any age of human history, past, present, and future. There are limits on his potential, however: he is limited by his biological structure, and by the laws of behavioral acquisition (the relationships among drive, cue, response, and reinforcer). These factors do constitute limits. We cannot smell as well as dogs, climb like flies, or carry burdens as large, relative to our size, as ants. Nor can we have knowledge of that which we have not experienced in one way or another, or behave without energy being mobilized by drive states. These limitations have far-reaching consequences for the kinds of behaviors which humans display; shelters are usually made with entrances accessible from the ground, we arrange things in such a way that our means of gathering information rely heavily on sight and sound rather than smell, and the artifacts of our cultures are made to a scale appropriate to our need and ability to manipulate and transport them.

548

On the other hand, humans have some characteristics which make possible behaviors that are denied to other organisms, such as fine control of the organs of speech and of prehensile hands. The most outstanding feature of the human is his brain, which because of its high development and elaboration makes it possible for man to invent alternative ways of doing things that the rest of his physiology would make impossible. Thus man can detect odors even better than dogs, with the aid of apparatus whose existence is made possible by man's intellectual resources. He can carry burdens larger than can ants, and he can climb and fly when he needs to. Man's brain thus permits him to accomplish almost every behavior that any living thing can accomplish, and much that no other animal can.

That his brain is man's most distinctive asset suggests that if man is to maximize his humanness he must maximize the use of his intellectual functions, including his ability to both arouse and inhibit bodily processes, to combine a tremendous number of neural traces in such myriad ways as to allow arousal and inhibition to be made dependent on very subtle differences among stimuli, and to develop integrations between the demands of his biological status and of his social environment. In effect, the brain is the main organ permitting culture. To think as little as possible, to allow one's life to be exclusively and directly controlled by physiological processes and drives, to avoid all physiological discomforts without regard to the social environment—to live such as to protect and maximize those aspects which do not differentiate man from other animals, is to reduce one's humanness.

The Control of Behavior

Out of the multitude of potential behaviors, only a small proportion are selected to be actualized in any particular person's behavior. This selection is governed by the same processes which provide man with the limits discussed above: the nature of his physiological structure and functioning, and the laws of behavioral acquisition. The same laws that make some behaviors impossible, by the same token make other behaviors possible. The structure that prevents people from bending their elbows backwards also permits them to bend their elbows forward. The laws of learning that make knowledge without experience impossible also make possible the acquisition of knowledge through experience. Thus it is of no use to be dismayed by the limits on man's behavior discussed above, because each factor which has the ability to limit him thereby has the ability to provide him with a possibility.

Physiological Determinants

One source of limits and possibilities is man's biological status. It is this source which frees him from rigid determination of behavior by instincts and reflexes, through the brain's ability to excite and inhibit lower centers. We have seen that man can therefore eat when he is not hungry, and love without hormonal excitement, and he can also refuse to eat although hungry, and refuse sex although sexually excited. These are capacities which make man very different from other animals. However, this difference does not mean that man, unlike other animals, is but little influenced by his physiological structure and functioning. Rather, these biological factors are of central importance in providing man with his freedom from direct hormonal and chemical control. Many people regard man's body as representing his "lower" nature, as the aspect of him which is animalistic, uncivilized, and therefore not humanistic, an indignity to his highly civilized and cultured intellect. Such thinking results in an effort to underplay and de-emphasize the role of physiological determinants of behavior. But the paradoxical thing is that these very disvalued physiological components are what make possible man's "higher" intellectual nature. For it is in the functioning of the brain that inhibition and arousal of lower centers are made possible, and it is through the socialization of physiological drive states that people acquire their social attitudes. Many of society's most valued social institutions including marriage, government, concepts of law and justice, etc., owe their existence to the socialization of drives.

Physiological drives participate in defining man's higher mental functions not only through their socialization, but also because these drives include those that contribute directly to the desire to think and to create. These are the stimulation-activity-curiosity drives which were referred to in the text as the "reaching-out" drives that are centered in the reticular formation of brain. The appetitive drives such as hunger and thirst operate in such a way that the organism behaves until it produces a cessation of stimulation in the need-sensitive receptors. These appetitive drives thus act as if organisms constantly tend toward some Nirvanalike state of the absence of stimulation, seeking always a return to its condition before the arousal of need-sensitive receptors. But the reaching-out drives can achieve this state of rest only through the creation of activity and stimulation. These "proactive" drives thus operate to increase activity and stimulation as a means of reducing needs. In this sense, these drives impel people to create sensations, to be active, to think, to act on the environment for the pleasure of acting itself. Thus these drives participate in determining the existence of thought and activity which finds its socialized forms in play and work, intellectual pursuits, scientific and artistic searches—in short, in all those activities that are part of what people mean by man's "higher" nature. Thus we see that here too man's physiological nature clearly participates in his intellectual life, and we find the paradox to be true that though behavior tends constantly to turn him back to a state of rest, it does this by turning him forward and outward to his environment, seeking more as well as less stimulation. The fact that thoughts and fantasies are motivated by physiological drive states and reflect this in their contents does not mean that such thoughts and fantasies are necessarily crude, animalistic, and undignified; this depends on how they have been socialized, not on the source of the motivation.

Social Determinants

Out of the limits and possibilities posed by man's biological status, specific behavioral potentials are selected and become actualized into behaviors that become more or less characteristic of the individual, and of individuals collected in societies. This selection is controlled by the interaction of physiological functions and environmental events, an interaction according to the laws of learning and performance. That is, the way in which people learn, together with the kinds of stimuli presented to them, interact with what is already given within the organism (his physiological status, including whatever alterations have been made in it by the action of past experiences in producing neural traces) to determine what they shall actually learn and do. Social and environmental situations do participate in determining behavior, but the individual is not simply a passive recipient of environmental control and direction, completely at the mercy of external stimuli. He brings his internal processes and the fruits of his past to the environment, and these things control what the environment can do to him in modifying his behavior. Thus man participates actively in his own fate. On the other hand, he is not impervious to an external reality that exists independently of himself. Some aspects of this environment—those that are related to forces within him—participate in determining his significant experiences through which he learns and further modifies the state and nature of the internal processes that he brings to the next set of environmental stimuli that present themselves. Thus we see that man is neither completely subordinate to social controls, nor is he completely independent of them with his social environment serving only as an external projection of his personality.

The complex interaction among physiological, social, and learning determinants is a difficult concept with which to work, and personality theories tend to emphasize one or another of these sources of determinants. Social psychological theories tend to emphasize the modification of behavior by social forces, and often overlook those factors within people that render social stimuli capable of affecting them. Thus group pressure is investigated as a determinant of conformist yielding to influence, but the investigators neglect to consider the drives within their subjects whose reinforcements by the social group make the individual responsive to the group and its selective rewarding or punishing of his behavior, through increasing or decreasing the individual's drive states.[1] One does not simply succumb to social pressures; rather, he participates in the process by deriving satisfactions from conforming, satisfactions which he wants because they reduce his drives, or he does not conform. Conformity is a two-way street.

On the other hand, clinical theories tend to err in the other direction. Impressed by the extent to which perceptions and actions are determined by the individual's past experiences and his present motives, such that he perceives only certain aspects of his environment, and interprets those aspects according to his own personality, these theorists tend to think of the social environment as a passive reflection of the individual personality. They point out that the individual naturally seeks the environment which best meets his needs, and distorts through perception whenever his psychic processes require it. A physically existent and determining environment is thus almost irrelevant to such theories, and personality is seen as modifying the environment, rather than being modified by it. This is the kind of theory that maximizes the use of unstructured and ambiguous perceptual stimuli, such as the Rorschach and Thematic Apperception Tests.

These two orientations, although incomplete by themselves, complement each other, and only through their interaction can a more realistic view of the complexity of behavior be attained. However, such an integration is difficult, because these views are encouraged by the two prevalent models of psychological research, the model of experimental research, and the model of clinical research. In the experimental model, the researcher manipulates environmental stimuli and observes the way in which the subject's behavior varies with these manipulations. In a sense the researcher's major interest is in the environment as a determining force, for it is the environment which he studies most closely, rather than what goes on inside the organism. For such research, the rat and other nonhuman animals are appropriate subjects. This research does yield valuable knowledge about control of behavior by environmental stimuli, but as long as the investigator fails to ask what it is within his subjects that make these stimuli capable of modifying their behavior, and as long as his research methods and subjects do not lend themselves to this kind of question, his theory and account of behavior will be onesided and incomplete.

The clinical method, on the other hand, attempts to keep environmental stimuli fairly standard, through the use of standard interview situations and tests that are fairly alike for each subject. Within the framework of the interview, the clinician explores the life histories, the fantasies, and the motives of his subjects, and correspondingly deemphasizes the contributions of external stimuli. He too, is therefore onesided and incomplete in his view.

To see man as a passive plaything of social forces is to see him as an automaton, something less than human. Conversely, to see personality as existing independently of the social environment, and therefore often opposed to it, is to see personality as something spiritual and superhuman, and to see behavior controlled by factors other than those which establish cognitive contact with an external reality. One says that behavior is controlled by the senses that receive environmental stimuli—man's cognitive functions symbolized by the head. The other says that behavior is controlled by his emotions, desires, and instincts—the nonrational passions symbolized by the heart and the gut. Thus the mind-body dualism continues. Neither, then, presents a human view of man's constant balancing of internal and external forces, each of which is dependent on the other, and each of which has its ability to influence behavior only through its action on the other. A morsel of food can only tempt if hunger can be aroused, and an achievement drive can only result in behavior if it is elicited by cues and if there are present the possibilities for a standard of excellence to be achieved. This is what is meant when it is asserted that internal forces can only influence behavior through the participation of external ones, and external factors can only have influence when they are related to internal forces. The head and the heart, mind and body, constitute a single action system. Just as the brain cannot function without its supply of oxygen from the lungs and heart which in turn depend on the brain for their neural stimuli, so do social and the internal forces operate as a single complex system in producing behavior. Thus man participates in his own fate, but the terms of the fate depend on the nature of the environment as well as on the nature of the man. A recognition of this interaction is necessary if a description of personality is going to include within it those processes which alone can account for human drama, human tragedy, and human comedy, which are only possible if man is neither a god nor an automaton.

The Relationship Between the Individual and His Society

The interactional nature of behavioral control has a number of important implications. One of these is that the idea of an opposition between the individual and his social environment is a false concept. This idea rests on the notion that society inhibits the potentials for development within the organism, through its pressures and its socialization practices. It is a carry-over of the old idea that mind and body are opposed. Neuroses and psychoses are ascribed to the opposition of a restricting environment to human needs and desires. As was pointed out above, this is a onesided view, and fails to take into account the extent to which these needs and desires provide social stimuli with their powers to affect behavior. It also fails to note that it is only through socialization that innate behavioral dispositions and potentials can become selected and actualized. At birth, the human infant has the potential for becoming saint or sinner, a murderer and rapist, as well as a philanthropist, scholar, and artist. All of these are potentials which people have actualized in their behavior over and over again in the history of the species, as a result of the selective rewarding and punishing of motivated responses by their social environments. It is therefore oversimplifying to assert that social inhibitions account for only the existence of behavior disvalued by our particular culture, and that anything which inhibits man's potential dehumanizes him. Part of his potential is a potential for evil, and each society must and does make efforts to maximize those potentials which it values and to inhibit those which it disvalues. To value indiscriminate actualization of human potentialities is to value larceny and love together. In effect, a civilized human being is an achievement of the socialization process, rather than what is left when social pressures, with their inhibitions and facilitations of behavior, are removed. To seek for the uninhibited and completely free and spontaneous man who is also not simply an animal like the new-born infant or the child who is reared without human contact, is to seek for a culture that does not frustrate, socialization process that does not teach inhibitions and facilitations, a coin that has only one side.

Social institutions do not exist without a corresponding element within individuals, nor can there be demands within people without social institutions developing to meet these demands. The existence of hypochondriasis provides a market for patent medicines and their advertising, and the existence of these products and services contribute to the development of hypochondriacal demands in people by making these ways of responding capable of yielding satsifactions, as was pointed out in Chapter 10. This suggests that there tends to be a consanguinity between individuals and their society. That is, societies become modified in the direction of providing satisfactions of the drives of its individuals, and on the other hand, socialization practices and the presence of social institutions produce personalities and actualize human potentials that require the institutions, folkways, and mores of that society for their expression and satisfaction. It is in this sense that it may be said that people in a society deserve the institutions they have, and a society deserves the kind of people who comprise it. Thus there are no innocent victims of society. Victims there are, but they are without innocence because it is their own drives, if only the innate physiological ones in the most tender baby, that create the possibility for them to be victims.

This mutuality between society and the individual also makes possible a national character, composed of the common elements in the personalities of the people who share the same institutions and culture, who share similar conflicts, and who have acquired similar ways of responding to their conflicts. Similar experiences produce similarity in behavior.

Such similarity of experience has also been pointed to as the source of some personality traits that are common to all humans regardless of the nature of their institutions. Thus all societies have marriage institutions, authority structures, roles of conduct, and forms for the relations between parents and children. This is because all societies must socialize their children, and particularly sexual and aggressive drives, if the society is to remain stable and reliable enough for learnings at any one time to be useful at some future time. If a villager's learning how to participate in the fishing team of his village, upon which depends their supply of food, is to have an enduring benefit for his continued smooth working with the team, the team's association and society must not be susceptible to being split apart and reconstituted at frequent intervals by the disruptions of unsocialized sexual and aggressive impulses. Thus all societies socialize these drives, and thus there are invariants among people regardless of culture. As was pointed out in Chapter 3, these invariants are those based on learnings that exist wherever people exist. Such learnings are those that are most intimately connected with man's biological status, because this is about the only aspect of man that exists everywhere, regardless of the state of his civilization.

We have been centering our discussion on the social environment. But the nonsocial physical environment also shapes behavior, and produces commonalities among people that transcend cultural borders. Thus there are regional personalities, climatic zone personalities, as well as national personalities and common elements in pan-human personalities. The fact that sound travels around objects whereas light does not means that crying by infants will more readily stimulate others than will waving legs. Thus crying is more likely to be selected as a rewarded behavior by the infant's society, and so almost all babies learn to cry, regardless of the nature or status of the culture into which they were born. These constants participate with man's physiological structure and the laws of behavior in defining the contents of a basic human nature.

Finally, we can point to one other implication of the interactional determination of personality. This is that cultural institutions and practices can provide insights into the personalities of the individuals who live in that culture. This is the basis for the study of cultural beliefs about illness that provided Whiting and Child with tests of their hypotheses about the effects of socialization practices. It is also one of the most important values of cultural anthropological research. This research tells us not only how societies differ, and how behavior is relative to the society in which it occurs, but it also tells us how human potentials are actualized by different experiences, and so broadens our knowledge of the determinants of behavior.

All that has been said here about the interaction between the individual and his society applies with equal force to the interaction between one individual and the society of as few as one, two, or three others. Here too, there is a consanguinity of needs and offerings, as we saw in Chapter 9 in our discussion of the mutual reinforcements existing between people who maintain a stable relationship.

The Ambivalent Nature of Behavior

Much of what we have been saying points to the ambivalent nature of behavior, the fact that a psychological process in itself is capable of yielding both desired and undesired behaviors, and that what behaviors are desired depends on who and what culture is doing the desiring. For example, we have seen that the same processes that make for prejudicial stereotyping also make it possible for people to generalize, which is a valued and necessary intellectual activity in our culture. Similarly, one cannot be trained to inhibit aggression completely without also being trained in such a way that he cannot defend himself against attack. The same neurotic process that produces symptoms can also produce sublimations, and the displacement of aggression from a punishing father can produce readiness to revolt against a tyrannous regime. One cannot eliminate frustrations and conflicts without also eliminating the compromises and problem solutions that generate art, intellectual pursuit, and social institutions. This suggests that there can be in fact no such thing as the completely wellrounded personality who is capable of behaving in whatever way that conditions may make appropriate, for by being socialized, he inevitably becomes inhibited for some behaviors and specialized in others. Each gain through socialization involves losing something that someone in some society might value. It involves giving up that which was involved in the behavior which the socialization has replaced with a more culturally approved behavior. Thus one loses while he gains. In general, each society's values are usually such that what is lost is not valued as highly as what is gained, and socialization practices within a culture tend toward those which produce the gains most highly valued by the culture while sacrificing the least valued.

This also means that there is little use in despairing over the psychological processes that produce behavior. One may despair of a particular behavior which is displayed, but it must be remembered that the processes that led to that behavior are also the processes that can lead to valued and socially desired behavior.

The Function of Experience and the Significance of Past and Present

These relationships between the individual and his society are mediated through the individual's experience. Each experience provides learnings that modify the behavioral potential that he brings to succeeding interactions with his environment. Thus his behavior in each new situation recapitulates his past history; the past lives in the present, in which the seeds of the future are formed. This does not mean that man goes blindly through his life, compulsively and repetitively acting out his infantile experiences. Each new experience alters the representation of the past that exists in his neural traces. And further, the past only operates as it is elicited by some contemporary state, including present motives and present cues which exist on a stimulus generalization gradient with past experiences involving similar motives. The present and the past must work together to elicit behavior, and one would no more wish to be freed of the influence of either than he would wish to lose his already acquired knowledge of reading or his contact with present reality. Finally, the future tense also participates through the representations of possible future events in thought, representations which provide anticipations that can stimulate future oriented drives and behavior.

Our discussion of the variables influencing perception did show that the past is so able to dominate that perceptions are distorted. However, such a situation reflects not only the strength of previous learnings, but also the failure to discriminate present cues from past events. Thus it is not simply the existence of influences from the past which create difficulties; rather, these difficulties reside in the relationship between past and present forces.

Rationality and Irrationality

The participation of the past does not mean that human behavior is dominated by irrational forces, even though past learnings influence present perceptions. Indeed, there is nothing more rational than the fact that the similarity between present and past stimuli should elicit behavior that was successful and reinforced in the past. Generalizing from one situation to other similar stimuli is a most rational way to generate constructs and abstractions, and to fit new situations into an orderly arrangement with what has preceded them. And responding with fear to cues that have been associated with punishment in the past is a most rational use of signals of danger. Too much has been made of irrationality in human behavior. While it is true that overdetermination operates to freight each behavioral situation with many meanings and many sources of satisfaction, many of which are unconscious, what could be more reasonable than that one should tend to behave in the way that provides the most gratifications for the largest number of his

needs? Behavior often appears irrational, it is true, but this is so because the observer fails to take into account some of the hidden sources
of satisfactions that may be involved. It is unreasonable for a person to
engage continually in the same aggressive and acrimonious interactions
with another; but when one considers how this interaction may provide
satisfactions of which even the subject is unaware, then his behavior
appears quite reasonable, given the terms in which he has learned to
find satisfactions. A particular item of behavior may appear irrational
when it is observed only in its contemporary context; for example, it
may seem quite irrational for a young man to respond to girls as if they
were his mother, and to seek satisfaction of dependency drives from
them. But the process underlying such behavior is reasonable: it is quite
understandable that strong responses acquired in relation to the cues
of mother should have such a wide generalization that they are evoked
by similar cues, such as those arising from girls. Thus given the process
and meaning of an item of behavior, it becomes reasonable although
on the surface it might seem like an unaccountable hiatus in the person's
ability to function as a reasonable and realistic human being.

Many people have the impression that the irrational is coincidental
with the unconscious, creating the image of a world of violent and selfish
forces hidden within the person, hidden even from his own intelligence,
a world which his intelligence and mental functioning must control.
However, this is a false image, again left over from an outmoded mind-
body dualism, and based on an oversimplification of the psychological
processes involved. We have seen, in our discussion of thinking, perception, and consciousness, that these emotional drives are not simply
opposed by the brain with its cognitive resources. Rather, the two realms
of intellect and passion mutually support each other, with cognitive
functions serving to locate opportunities for satisfaction of one's drives
and impulses, and with the drives and impulses motivating cognitive
and intellectual pursuits and influencing the nature of these pursuits.
That the behaving individual may have little awareness of these processes and their operations does not make them necessarily irrational.
The reduction in one's knowledge that repression produces does limit
the use of one's intellectual resources, and may make one's behavior
appear irrational, as the example of the aggressive interaction illustrates, but this does not mean that the behavior is nonsensical. Man is
not manipulated by mysterious and seething forces that arise within
him; rather, he functions as the coordinated operation of motivational
and cognitive resources which serve and express each other, whether or

not he knows it. One need not be frightened when told that his behavior is influenced in ways of which he is ignorant, for such is the way of behavior, although the factors that maintain his ignorance of their operation are the same ones that produce his fright upon their discovery.

The Important Drives

Repeatedly we have stressed the operations of sexual and aggressive drives. There are two reasons for this. First of all, these are the drives of which we are most ignorant, because they are the ones most subject to repression, so that their influence is but little apparent to most people. This reason relates to the second one: because these two drives are the ones which are most disruptive of social organization, defining as they do the two extreme poles of human relationships of love and hate, life and death, they are the ones which are most extensively and strongly subjected to socialization. As a result of this socialization, many learnings are produced based on these drives, and the final socially accepted forms of sexual and aggressive behavior are such a far cry from their origins in the unbridled emotions of the infant and the animal that careful analysis is required to discover the relationships between these forms and the material which was molded to produce them. These two drives are therefore the ones which are most likely to be repressed in most human societies (although societies do vary in the extent to which they characteristically elicit sexual and aggressive behavior, in the range of sexual and aggressive behaviors which they will permit, and in the kinds of learnings which their socialization practices encourage). It seems likely that the extent to which these potentially dangerous drives are socialized depends, at least in part, on the extent to which the factors in the social and economic life of the society which contribute to its stability are capable of being disrupted by these drives. A loosely organized group in which the conditions of life allow the group to continue with fairly few interdependencies is more likely to permit the direct expression of these drives, while a society in which close coordination and interpersonal proximity are necessitated by its economic and geographic structures is more likely to inhibit these drives and through socialization turn them in directions away from the sensitive segments of the group.

Their subjection to repression training makes these two drives the most potent stimuli for anxiety, and therefore sources of neurosis and psychosis, in our society. By the same training practices that make of these drives the underpinnings and reason for being of our institutions of marriage, law, ethics, and national sovereignty, so do these drives also constitute our most insoluble personal problems. That is why they appear over and over again in this text.

But this does not mean that they are the only human motives or the strongest. We must keep in mind that other drives, which may create less difficulties for people in our society, are nevertheless important influences on human behavior, including the drives for sensory stimulation and activity, for food, for interpersonal relations, and for achievement. Any emotional state of arousal that can be paired with distinctive cues can form the basis for motivated behavior whose expression is subject to the administration of rewards and punishments.

Symbolism

The subject of symbolism is often associated with mysterious, irrational, and unconscious psychic events. We have used the term "symbol" in several different but related ways in this book. At its simplest, a symbol is a stimulus which stands for something else. This is why words are called symbols. However, it has been indicated that the relationship of "standing for" comes about through several learning processes. An event stands for another through secondary reinforcement, so that mother and the cues she produces become symbols of the feeding and nurturant care which were associated with those cues she produces. Stimulus generalization also produces symbolism, in that events which exist on the same generalization continuum, and thus tend to elicit the same response, can all symbolize each other. Typically, those cues to which the response was first learned serve as symbols for the others, because they came first, and later stimuli are perceived in terms of the earlier. Responses also produce cues which exist on generalization gradients with other responses, so that responses may also serve as symbols for other events. The same is true of the cues produced in thought, which in turn is symbolic of external stimuli. In this connection it should be noted that generalization gradients are not only defined in terms of the similarity of the physical properties of cues. We have seen that these gradients may be constructed out of the culturally determined order of progress toward goals, and out of the schemas that individuals develop. The result of these processes is that in any behavioral situation, the cues that elicit behavior may be interpreted as symbolic of the earlier events in which the behavior was learned, and the response may be understood as symbolic of the reinforcements which confirmed the response and the motives which gave these reinforcers their drive-reducing abilities.

These symbol-forming processes take place whenever symbols are used, whether their use is intentional or not, and whether they are parts of a work of art or a dream.

Anxiety, Conflict, and Problem Solving

Anxiety provides one of the most difficult theoretical problems in psychology. It was indicated in earlier chapters that it is not yet known whether anxiety represents a general high drive state, or whether it is a state of generalized and diffuse fear. However, it is known that it has drive properties, and that responses cued off by anxiety can be reinforced by a reduction of anxiety. Therefore, people are motivated by anxiety, and they behave in ways which either extinguish the drive or avoid its elicitation. There is a temptation to think of the presence of anxiety, in the form of human unhappiness, as a valid indicator of the need for efforts to change behavior, such as psychotherapy. Certainly this kind of misery constitutes a grave concern in our society. There are many who feel that our age is becoming increasingly characterized by anxiety, which leads to large scale and society-wide efforts at anxiety reduction involving the noninstrumental responses of repression, rationalization, and projection —and, that these responses are becoming increasingly inadequate to handle the magnitude of the problem. It is both the blessing and curse of our affluent society that other forms of human misery —hunger, disease, and poverty —have so paled in importance that our psychological problem of anxiety has developed and assumed pre-eminence. As our fund of material misery decreases, the problems of an increasingly complex and achievement-driven society increase our fund of psychological misery manifested in repressed hostilities, guilt projected onto "enemy" societies, and increasing feelings of no longer being masters of our own lives, less able to make our own decisions and more susceptible to threats to our well-being from a myriad unsuspected forces.[2]

In thinking about anxiety, it is well to keep in mind the distinction between its overt and latent forms. Overt anxiety involves the manifest feeling of misery, but latent anxiety represents the existence of traces controlling anxiety reactions, traces which can be activated by appropriate stimuli but are not so activated at the moment. The noninstrumental responses to conflict, including their elaborated form in symptoms, are behaviors which operate to reduce the extent to which this latent anxiety is elicited, through producing an avoidance of the cues which arouse it, whether these cues be those arising from the environment or from one's own impulses and wishes. Ultimately, as we have seen, it is the presence of such feared drives and responses that gives to a stimulus its ability to elicit anxiety. In this sense, anxiety represents a fear of oneself, producing the paradox that man is his own worst enemy, the source of his own misery.

This rooting of anxiety in our own forbidden impulses implies conflict; in this sense, the existence of manifest and/or latent anxiety may be thought of as a sign of the conflicted person's inability to commit himself wholeheartedly to a choice. The existentialists have made us aware of the fact that anxiety implies the possibility of making a choice —that is, of resolving a conflict —and that the presence of anxiety signals the fact that a choice involves giving up some gratifications in order to obtain others. By being in conflict, the individual has an opportunity to choose. What we have described as the noninstrumental conflict responses may be interpreted as a failure to choose through an effort to make the most of both sides of the conflict, thus ensuring both partial gratification and partial frustration. This is particularly so for the conflicts between a positive drive and the anxiety it awakes; the noninstrumental responses make it impossible for the conflicted person fully to realize the frustrated approach drive as a part of himself, and to either live out the drive or discard it.

The latent anxiety present indicates that the person is failing to make a choice and is denying a part of himself. He is using his resources to diminish himself either through inhibiting his drives, and/or through the reduction of his cognitive functioning produced by repression. When anxiety-reducing responses are present, he is further fooling himself by reducing the manifest anxiety which indicates that he has the possibility of choosing, although his latent anxiety continues and increases through continued frustration. Thus he cannot make a choice. The existentialists, therefore, see value in anxiety for it means that man has the possibility of making choices, and its absence in manifest behavior (that is, when it is made latent by the anxiety-reducing responses) means that the individual has avoided this possibility and the choices involved, and in so doing, has diminished himself.[3, 4, 5]

It is for reasons such as these that the presence or absence of anxiety cannot serve as a signal of the need for therapy. It is argued that anxiety is necessary for human choice, and therefore should not be done without, and further, the absence of anxiety, as through symptoms, obviously cannot by itself mean that the individual is behaving in such a way that psychotherapy is unneeded or undesirable.

This argument points to the problem-solving nature of conflict behavior. The existence of conflict defines the presence of a problem, and the instrumental and noninstrumental responses comprise strategies for dealing with it, either through active and enduring solutions or through temporary escapes from it. It may be argued that it is only through the solution of problems that people grow in their ability to master themselves and their world, and deal consciously with their own human characteristics. (Remember that anxiety is a reaction to one's own impulses.) To seek for the elimination of problems, or to hold as a value the avoidance of problems by noninstrumental responses that reduce anxiety without solving them, may thus be interpreted as a strategy that dehumanizes. Since conflict is inevitable, it seems reasonable that the best we can do is to educate and socialize children and adults so that conflict-problems provide the occasion and opportunity for them to seek solutions whose strategies are both effective and consistent with the most valued aspects of human nature.[6]

Normality and Adjustment

The most unambiguous meaning of "normal" is that something conforms to the norm or statistical average. Thus the normal length of pregnancy in humans is 280 days. However, seldom is anyone exactly at the norm. Although it is true that if one averages the length of pregnancy of people with short pregnancies and those with long ones, the figure of 280 days best expresses the length of pregnancy which one is safest in expecting, relatively few women actually give birth on the 280th day. In one study, only 3.7 per cent of the women delivered their infants on that day, with somewhat less than half the remaining mothers studied giving birth in less than that time, and slightly more than half after that day.[7] Thus relatively few mothers can be considered to be precisely normal, in the statistical sense. The same is true of most physiological structures. No one, or close to no one, has a heart whose dimensions are exactly at the norm for human hearts. It is equally true for personality; no one has exactly the normal personality, in the sense of showing precisely the average number of responses, of precisely average strength, for each item of behavior represented in people. In this sense, there is no such thing as a normal personality, and if there were, it would be so rare, like giving birth on exactly the 280th day, that we would hardly hold it up as a standard for all people to emulate.

Of course, one can talk of *degrees* of normality in the statistical sense. A woman who has her baby on the 275th day of pregnancy is more normal, or closer to normal, than the woman whose baby is born on the 270th day. In the realm of personality, it might be said that the person whose behavior more closely approximates the norm is more normal than one who deviates more.

The problem with this conception is that it makes no distinction between normality and conformity. Such a distinction is not necessary so long as people keep in mind that they are using the term "normal" in a strictly defined statistical sense. Unfortunately, it is almost impossible for people in our society to use it in that sense, because it immediately evokes drives to be like other people. Thus one cannot be abnormal (that is, different from most people) without becoming concerned, and feeling that one ought to be less different. We have already talked about assumed similarity and other-directedness in American culture, which places a value on being like others. The implication is that it is good to be normal. There are three problems with such an orientation: first, it implies that it is always the abnormal individual who is at fault, rather than those with whom he was compared in determining that he was different from the norm. Thus he is blamed, and his behavior is considered to be changeworthy. Social forces are set into motion (education, therapy, hospitalization) to make his behavior more like the behavior of others which, from other frames of reference, might be considered to be no more desirable. Today the pacifist is considered abnormal in American society; at best he is called a crackpot, and at worst legal and social sanctions are placed upon him in an effort to make sure that he does not influence others to become so unwilling to kill people. Should the abnormal pacifist or the norm-defining society be changed?

The second problem with normality is that as a value, it implies the disvaluation of unique and individual achievement, for these necessarily imply that one does things that others do not do. We would disvalue the painter of a masterpiece, the creator of a new scientific theory, the man who sells more insurance, because in each case his performance is out-of-the-ordinary and unusual, and therefore abnormal in the statistical sense. And the more unique his performance the more abnormal. A society that operated in this way could not long survive, because it would not produce new solutions to its problems.

The third problem is more of a theoretical one. Suppose that a person were perfectly "normal" in competitiveness, compared to his society, but that he emigrates to another society which is much more competitive than his former one. Compared to his new society, he is now abnormally noncompetitive, and he is urged to do something about it, even though he has not changed his way of behaving one bit. If we were to define personalities in terms of the extent to which they were normal, we would then have to say that this man's personality changed when he emigrated, although his behavior did not. This would make personality a very slippery concept with which to deal.

The very same problems apply to the use of the term "adjustment." This word has had two main usages. One refers to adjustment in the sense of having a smooth and integrated relationship to one's surroundings, and to the demands and expectations of society. This usage is, like normality, indistinguishable from conformity, and automatically evokes a high value for a good adjustment and a disvaluation of maladjustment. Shall we say that a man who fits in well and comfortably to his prison environment is well-adjusted, and the prisoner who continually chafes at the restrictions which he cannot change is maladjusted and should be made less rejecting of his state? The other meaning of adjustment refers to the relationship between an individual's drives and what he does to reduce those drives. It would be said that when a response results in frustration of the individual's drives, that response is maladjustive. The only situation in which it is possible for such responses to occur is that of conflict, in which a response that reduces one of the conflicting drives further frustrates the other. Conflict is inevitable because it is a necessary aspect of socialization, in which the infant's behavioral propensities are opposed by the parents through their selective rewarding of responses which are inconsistent with the changeworthy ones. Thus, maladjustment in this sense is inevitable. On the other hand, we have seen that responses to conflict involve partial gratification of the conflicting drives, and therefore are at least partially adjustive. An hysterical symptom, such as a paralysis of the arm, usually involves some gratification of dependency and attention-getting needs together with a repression of fear-arousing impulses. In the sense that the paralysis "works" and is effective, we would say that it is adjustive. However, to the extent that the paralysis is a disvalued way of reducing these drives, it might be called maladjustive. We might say that there are other ways of reducing this person's drives, ways of which our society approves more than it does of hysterical symptoms. In other words, we find that even this use of the term adjustment can be reduced to a statement of social values, which means that other societies might value the behavior differently. In our society, a psychotic episode is disvalued, and so is considered to be a maladjustive way of satisfying some human needs. But in some cultures, the psychotic is believed to possess magical and religious powers, and the psychotic occupies a high status. We cannot therefore say unequivocally that psychosis is maladjustive or maladaptive. If one were to study the causes of maladjustment in our society, he would include psychosis, but he would not include its study in the study of maladjustment in those societies that value psychosis. Imagine how these studies would produce entirely different theories of behavior in the two cultures. The situation becomes more confused when we note that many of the noninstrumental responses to conflict, such as compensation and sublimation, can result in highly socially valued products which we would be loath to do without. Since such responses are maladjustive in the sense that they provide only partial gratifications of the conflicting motives, and if maladjustment is bad, as we inevitably think it is, then we would be in the position of having to change those behaviors which yield some of our most cherished benefits. Efforts to rationalize sometimes result in the development of explanatory theories that advance science considerably, and projection can aid in the preparation of defense against an expected enemy attack. This does not mean that such benefits are necessarily and always the by-products of conflict. But it does suggest that the values associated with adjustment and maladjustment can and do conflict with other values which we might hold. Values placed on the processes involved in behavior can conflict with our values for the behavioral outcomes. Finally, it seems somewhat unfair to place the source of disvalued maladjustment within the person, when it is his society which is doing the valuing. If you do not like my behavior, perhaps it is you who are maladjusted, rather than me. Of course if there are more of you than there are of me, it lends weight to your argument, but it is the weight of force rather than of truth, for we have seen that forty million Frenchmen can be wrong; in the history of their nation, as well as of our own, the majority has been wrong.

Mental Health and Social Values

The tendency to value and disvalue behaviors according to our moral and ethical standards led to difficulty in the psychological treatment of people who wanted help in changing their behavior. Interpreting an item of behavior as immoral or unethical, they were not able then to admit such behavior in themselves and so could do nothing about getting help from others in changing themselves. And if their societies interpreted behavior in such moral terms, then people shied away from those that they considered immoral, rejected them, and tried to punish them, all of which are precisely the things least likely to be effective in helping the individual change his behavior and live more effectively. In order to avoid public disapprobation of disvalued behavior, the concept of mental illness was developed. But we have seen that this concept can no longer be considered to be an appropriate or valid one.[8, 9] The processes involved in producing "ill" behavior are the same processes that produce "healthy" behavior, and if some behavior is disvalued, it seems unreasonable to say that the behaving person is pathological in the medical sense when it is the valuing society that is unhappy about it. One of the problems with the concept of mental illness is that it puts medical and psychological science in the position of upholding social values, and makes the hospital the conservitor of majority opinion and prejudice; this operates against the development of increased knowledge, because events are labeled in terms of the society's values rather than in terms of their actual properties. For example, if items of behavior become labeled as signs of illness or maladjustment, the labels obscure the close analysis of the behavioral items themselves and the study of their meanings and consequences which may or may not be valued. When this happens phenomena are grouped and classified according to external criteria rather than according to factors intrinsic to the behaviors themselves, producing a culture-bound science having no relevance to phenomena occurring in different societies and different ages.

Students of personality almost inevitably ask if such and such a behavior is "normal." They ask what is the "right" way to bring up children. And they are sometimes dismayed to discover that almost every behavioral process is capable of yielding consequences which they desire as well as some of which they disapprove, giving them the feeling that "one just can't win" against the forces that make for problematical behavior. But there is no single "right" or "normal" way, valid for all people in all societies, and the anxiety stimulated by consideration of these values interferes with the student's ability to examine the behavior itself without bias as to what he shall find — without the need not to find some things, and the desire to find others. One must accept the ambivalent nature of psychological processes, realizing that the question of value has little to do with the nature of the behavior itself (except, of course, when one studies the valuing behavior of people), and that it is not possible for a person to be all things to all men. One loses something whenever he gains something from socialization, and while it is true that every socialization process, and every conflict and its response, is potentially capable of yielding disvalued behavior, it is also capable of yielding something of value to someone or some society, and that it would be impossible to have any society at all, or any values, without socialization and its inevitable production of conflict. These are the reasons that this text has been concerned with the analysis and description of personality, no matter how the elements, processes, and consequences involved may be valued by any particular culture at any particular point in time, and these are the reasons for our avoidance of labels such as normal and abnormal, labels that classify behavior not in terms of its intrinsic character, but rather in terms of a particular time-and-place-fixed value system. A knowledge of behavioral phenomena must be independent of our evaluation of them, if we are to learn enough to be able to deal wisely with them according to any framework of values which we might bring to bear. Thus we come full circle to our definition of the study of personality as the study of the processes, contents, and consequences of behavior, whenever behavior occurs, and in whatever setting, without regard for distinctions based on systems of assigning utilitarian, aesthetic, religious, or social merit to these behaviors.

Notes and References

Chapter 1: **1.** Edwards (1954). **2.** Shaffer and Shoben (1956). **3.** Cannon (1932). **4.** Allport (1937). **5.** Rank (1929). **6.** McClelland (1955).

Chapter 2: **1.** Taylor (1958). **2.** Hall (1938). **3.** Chess, Thomas, Birch, and Hertzig (1960). **4.** Chess, Thomas, and Birch (1959). **5.** Thomas, Chess, Birch, and Hertzig (1960). **6.** Katz (1952). **7.** Carmichael (1954). **8.** Dennis and Dennis (1940). **9.** Cannon and Washburn (1912). **10.** Cannon (1929). **11.** Morgan and Morgan (1940). **12.** Tsang (1938). **13.** Hoelzel (1927). **14.** Wangensteen and Carlson (1931). **15.** Goodenough (1931). **16.** Keys, Brozek, Henschel, Mickelsen, and Taylor (1950). **17.** Wilkins and Richter (1940). **18.** Montgomery (1931). **19.** Adolph (1939). **20.** Adolph (1941). **21.** McGraw (1940). **22.** Sheffield, Wulff, and Backer (1951). **23.** Beach (1956). **24.** Butler (1953). **25.** Harlow, Harlow, and Meyer (1950). **26.** Harlow and McLearn (1954). **27.** Bexton, Heron, and Scott (1954). **28.** Heron (1957). **29.** Solomon (1961). **30.** Hull (1943). **31.** Ribble (1944). **32.** Wang (1923). **33.** Hill (1956). **34.** Edwards (1941). **35.** Nauta (1946). **36.** Malmo (1957). **37.** Dollard and Miller (1950). **38.** Berlyne (1960). **39.** Hebb (1958). **40.** Samuels (1959). **41.** Harlow (1953). **42.** Stellar (1954). **43.** Lacey, Bateman, and Van Lehn (1952). **44.** Lacey and Van Lehn (1952). **45.** Ax (1953). **46.** Cameron (1947). **47.** Ford and Beach (1951). **48.** Tatz (1956). **49.** Bruner (1957a). **50.** Golambos, Sheatz, and Vernier (1956). **51.** Hernandez-Péon, Scherrer, and Jouvet (1956). **52.** Bard (1928). **53.** Cannon (1927). **54.** Stellar (1954). **55.** Wheatley (1944). **56.** Duffy (1957). **57.** Fries and Woolf (1953).

Chapter 3: **1.** Schlosberg (1954). **2.** Cohen (1961). **3.** Estes (1958). **4.** White (1959). **5.** Estes (1954). **6.** Noble and Taylor (1959). **7.** Prokasy (1956). **8.** Rheingold, Gewirtz, and Ross (1958). **9.** Verplanck (1956). **10.** Murdock (1937). **11.** Inkeles and Levinson (1954). **12.** Hull (1932). **13.** Dollard and Miller (1950). **14.** Mowrer (1940a). **15.** Hull (1943).

Chapter 3, continued
    16. Guthrie (1952). **17.** Hovland (1937). **18.** Secord and Jourard (1956). **19.** Maier, Glaser, and Klee (1940). **20.** Watson and Raynor (1920). **21.** Humphreys (1939). **22.** Jenkins and Stanley (1950). **23.** Kellogg (1939). **24.** Light and Gantt (1936). **25.** Morgan (1943). **26.** Lashley (1935). **27.** Krechevsky (1936). **28.** Goldstein and Scheerer (1941). **29.** Hanfmann and Kasanin (1937). **30.** Olds (1955). **31.** Olds (1956). **32.** Hilgard (1956).

Chapter 4: **1.** Skinner (1938). **2.** Weingarten (1962). **3.** Goldfarb (1947). **4.** Wolfe (1936). **5.** Cowles (1937). **6.** Dollard and Miller (1950). **7.** Rotter (1954). **8.** Harlow (1949). **9.** Spence (1947). **10.** Zimmerman (1957). **11.** Miller (1949). **12.** Kimble (1955). **13.** Brown, J. (1948). **14.** Sidman (1955). **15.** Mowrer (1939). **16.** Mowrer (1940b). **17.** Mowrer and Lamoreaux (1942). **18.** Farber (1954). **19.** Meehl and MacCorquodale (1953). **20.** Calvin, Bicknell, and Sperling (1953). **21.** Lacey (1950). **22.** Michigan State Department of Mental Health (1953). **23.** Stauffer and Lumsdaine (1947). **24.** Campbell (1960). **25.** Hunt (1941). **26.** Allport (1937). **27.** Siegel and MacDonnell (1954).

Chapter 5: **1.** Koehler (1925). **2.** Hunter (1913). **3.** Hebb (1949). **4.** Mednick (1962). **5.** Penfield and Rasmussen (1950). **6.** Goldstein and Scheerer (1941). **7.** Head (1926). **8.** Jacobson (1932). **9.** Hunter (1913). **10.** Hemingway (1952). **11.** Hunter and Nagge (1931). **12.** Munn (1950). **13.** Max (1937). **14.** Scott (1957). **15.** Brown, R. (1958). **16.** Dollard and Miller (1950). **17.** Hunter (1913). **18.** Osgood (1953). **19.** Whorf (1956). **20.** Brown and Lenneberg (1954). **21.** Ghiselin (1955). **22.** Freud, A. (1937). **23.** Feshbach (1955). **24.** Grotjahn (1957). **25.** Schachtel (1959). **26.** Mednick (1962). **27.** Schachtel (1959). **28.** Kris (1952). **29.** Sanford (1936). **30.** Sanford (1937). **31.** McClelland, Atkinson, Clark, and Lowell (1953). **32.** Murray (1943). **33.** Henry (1956). **34.** Williams (1962). **35.** Klein (1930). **36.** Clark and Sensibar (1955). **37.** Freud (1900). **38.** Nachmansohn (1951). **39.** Freud (1904). **40.** Tepas (1962). **41.** Dement (1960). **42.** Rapaport (1958). **43.** Hartmann (1939). **44.** Noble and Parker (1960). **45.** McCleary and Lazarus (1949). **46.** Lazarus and McCleary (1951). **47.** McGinnies (1949). **48.** Cowen and Beier (1951). **49.** Howes and Solomon (1951). **50.** Thorndike and Lorge (1944). **51.** Goldstein and Barthol (1960). **52.** Bruner (1957b). **53.** Siipola (1935). **54.** Postman, Bruner, and McGinnies (1948). **55.** Allport, Vernon, and Lindzey (1960). **56.** Golambos, Sheatz, and Vernier (1956). **57.** Bruner (1957b). **58.** Gilchrist and Nesberg (1952). **59.** Cutler (1953). **60.** Toch and Schulte (in press). **61.** Proshansky and Murphy (1942). **62.** Freud (1911). **63.** Gordon (1957). **64.** Gordon (1959a). **65.** Rorschach (1942). **66.** Freud (1909). **67.** Gordon, Martin, and Lundy (1959). **68.** Greenspoon (1955). **69.** Lecky (1945).

Chapter 6: **1.** Spock (1946). **2.** Netter (1953). **3.** Freud (1905a). **4.** Kelley, E. (1955). **5.** Bernstein (1955). **6.** Erikson (1950). **7.** Dollard and Miller (1950). **8.** Marquis (1941). **9.** Sears, Maccoby, and Levin (1957).

Chapter 6, continued

10. Sears, Maccoby, and Levin (1957). **11.** Newton and Newton (1950). **12.** Bowlby (1958). **13.** Levy (1934). **14.** Sears and Wise (1950). **15.** Davis, Sears, Miller, and Brodbeck (1948). **16.** Whiting and Child (1953). **17.** Davis and Havighurst (1946). **18.** Sears, Maccoby, and Levin (1957). **19.** Whiting and Child (1953). **20.** Sears, Maccoby, and Levin (1957). **21.** Sears, Whiting, Nowlis, and Sears (1953). **22.** Goldfarb (1947). **23.** Goldfarb (1943). **24.** Piquer y Jover (1946). **25.** Hoagland (1952). **26.** Klatskin, Lethin, and Jackson (1950). **27.** Escalona (1945). **28.** Radke and Trager (1950). **29.** Miller and Dollard (1941). **30.** Whiting and Child (1953). **31.** Sears, Maccoby, and Levin (1957). **32.** McGraw (1940). **33.** McGraw (1943). **34.** Spock (1946). **35.** Sears, Maccoby, and Levin (1957). **36.** Whiting and Child (1953). **37.** Sears, Maccoby, and Levin (1957). **38.** Sears, Maccoby, and Levin (1957). **39.** Sears, Maccoby, and Levin (1957). **40.** Freud and Burlingham (1944). **41.** Sears, Maccoby, and Levin (1957). **42.** Ferenczi (1950b). **43.** Sears, Maccoby, and Levin (1957). **44.** Freud (1908). **45.** Stagner and Kraut (1940). **46.** Sears (1936). **47.** Ford and Beach (1951). **48.** Kinsey, Pomeroy, and Martin (1948). **49.** Freud (1905a). **50.** Ford and Beach (1951). **51.** Sheffied, Wulff, and Backer (1951). **52.** Jones, E. (1957). **53.** Kinsey, Pomeroy, and Martin (1948). **54.** Kinsey, Pomeroy, Martin, and Gebhard (1953). **55.** Ford and Beach (1951). **56.** Sears, Maccoby, and Levin (1957). **57.** Whiting and Child (1953). **58.** Sears, Pintler, and Sears (1946). **59.** Sears, Maccoby, and Levin (1957). **60.** Brownfield (1956). **61.** Levin and Sears (1956). **62.** Mowrer (1960). **63.** Whiting and Child (1953). **64.** Klein (1948). **65.** Gold (1961). **66.** Barrie (1928). **67.** Mason (1960). **68.** Winch (1950). **69.** Lynn (1959). **70.** Jones, M. (1957). **71.** Jones and Bayley (1950). **72.** Scodel (1957). **73.** Schachter (1959). **74.** Miller and Swanson (1958). **75.** Hendrick (1943). **76.** Segal (1953). **77.** Nachmann (1957). **78.** Galinsky (1961). **79.** Hess (1959).

Chapter 7: **1.** Dollard, Doob, Miller, Mowrer, and Sears (1939). **2.** Miller, N. (1948). **3.** Bateson and Mead (1942). **4.** Walters (1959). **5.** Jersild and Markey (1935). **6.** Sears, Maccoby, and Levin (1957). **7.** Miller and Swanson (1960). **8.** Keister and Updegraff (1938). **9.** Davis (1947). **10.** Berkowitz (1959). **11.** Miller and Bugelski (1948). **12.** Hovland and Sears (1940). **13.** Sears, Maccoby, and Levin (1957). **14.** Hollenberg and Sperry (1950). **15.** Miller and Swanson (1960). **16.** Sears, Hovland, and Miller (1940). **17.** Miller and Swanson (1960). **18.** Lesser (1957). **19.** Sears, Whiting, Nowlis, and Sears (1953). **20.** Lewin, Lippitt, and White (1939). **21.** Brenner (1955). **22.** Miller and Swanson (1960). **23.** Rosenzweig (1944). **24.** Whiting and Child (1953). **25.** Sears, Maccoby, and Levin (1957). **26.** Sears (1953). **27.** Freud (1920). **28.** Razran (1955). **29.** Harlow (1958). **30.** Hess (1959). **31.** *Life Magazine* (1955). **32.** Scott (1945). **33.** Goldfarb (1944). **34.** Bowlby (1953). **35.** Spitz (1945). **36.** Freud and Burlingham (1943). **37.** Mason (1960). **38.** Spitz (1946). **39.** Bowlby (1953). **40.** Liddell (1944). **41.** Bowlby (1953). **42.** Levy (1937). **43.** Cohn and Gordon (in press).

Chapter 7, continued

44. Glueck and Glueck (1950). **45.** Bowlby (1953). **46.** Bowlby (1953). **47.** Schachter (1959). **48.** Sears, Maccoby, and Levin (1957). **49.** Sears, Whiting, Nowlis, and Sears (1953). **50.** Sears, Maccoby, and Levin (1957). **51.** McClelland, Atkinson, Clark, and Lowell (1953). **52.** Patel and Gordon (1960). **53.** Levy (1943). **54.** Townsend (1958). **55.** Horney (1945). **56.** Fromm (1947). **57.** McClelland, Atkinson, Clark, and Lowell (1953). **58.** Weber (1958). **59.** McClelland and Atkinson (1948). **60.** Kagan, Suntag, Baker, and Lester (1958). **61.** Winterbottom (1953). **62.** Gordon (1959b).

Chapter 8: **1.** Miller and Swanson (1960). **2.** Miller and Swanson (1960). **3.** Miller and Swanson (1960). **4.** Miller and Swanson (1960). **5.** Fraiberg (1959). **6.** Frenkel-Brunswick (1949). **7.** Block and Block (1951). **8.** Frenkel-Brunswick and Sanford (1945). **9.** Kelly, G. (1955). **10.** Berkowitz (1957). **11.** Holzman and Klein (1954). **12.** Bieri (1955). **13.** Jackson and Messick (1958). **14.** Berg (1959). **15.** Couch and Keniston (1960). **16.** Witkin (1959). **17.** Witkin (1949). **18.** Witkin (1950). **19.** Witkin, Lewis, Mackover, Meissner, and Wapner (1954). **20.** Riesman, Glazer, and Denney (1953). **21.** Miller and Swanson (1958). **22.** McClelland (1951). **23.** Piaget (1926). **24.** Inhelder and Piaget (1958). **25.** Adelson (1961). **26.** Dennis (1957). **27.** McClelland (1961). **28.** Child, Potter, and Levin (1946). **29.** De Charms and Moeller (1962). **30.** Ford and Beach (1951). **31.** Mead (1928). **32.** Gallup (1955). **33.** Walker and Heyns (1962). **34.** Tuddenham (1959). **35.** Riesman, Glazer, and Denney (1953). **36.** Miller and Swanson (1958). **37.** Wolff (1935). **38.** Ferenczi (1950a). **39.** Hilgard (1949). **40.** Rogers (1961). **41.** Wolff (1933). **42.** Janis and Feshback (1953). **43.** Sears (1936). **44.** Rogers (1951). **45.** Butler and Haigh (1954). **46.** Dittes (1957a). **47.** Dittes (1957b). **48.** Clark and Clark (1952). **49.** Wallerstein (1954). **50.** Bruner (1951). **51.** Gordon (1961). **52.** Gordon (1959a). **53.** Cutler (1953).

Chapter 9: **1.** Spence (1954). **2.** Farber (1954). **3.** Mandler and Sarason (1952). **4.** Freud, A. (1937). **5.** Lepley (1954). **6.** Henderson and Moore (1944). **7.** Miller and Swanson (1960). **8.** Davitz (1954). **9.** Luchins and Luchins (1959). **10.** Maier and Klee (1941). **11.** Masserman (1943). **12.** Maier (1961). **13.** Wilcoxon (1952). **14.** Shroder and Rotter (1952). **15.** Adorno, Frenkel-Brunswick, Levinson, and Sanford (1950). **16.** Patrick (1934). **17.** Dollard and Miller (1950). **18.** Miller and Kraeling (1952). **19.** Hokanson and Gordon (1958). **20.** Clark and Sensibar (1955). **21.** Whiting and Child (1953). **22.** Sarnoff (1960). **23.** Bandura, Lipsher, and Miller (1960). **24.** Grotjahn (1957). **25.** Barker, Dembo, and Lewin (1941). **26.** Martin (1940). **27.** Freud (1926). **28.** Gordon (1957). **29.** Shaffer (1947). **30.** Liddell (1954). **31.** Miller and Swanson (1960). **32.** Zeigarnik (1927). **33.** Miller and Swanson (1960). **34.** Bettelheim (1947). **35.** Clark and Clark (1952). **36.** Dunbar (1955). **37.** Kapp, Rosenbaum, and Romano (1947). **38.** Wolf and Wolff (1946). **39.** Brady (1958). **40.** Brady, Porter, Conrad,

Chapter 9, continued
and Mason (1958). **41.** Dunbar (1954). **42.** Wolberg (1948). **43.** Malmo and Smith (1955). **44.** Anderson, Parmenter, and Liddell (1939). **45.** Miller, M. (1948). **46.** Wolff (1953). **47.** Brownfain (1961).
Chapter 10: **1.** Ferenczi and Hollas (1925). **2.** Wagner (1944). **3.** Rothschild (1944). **4.** Brown, J. (1940). **5.** Cameron (1947). **6.** Krout (1954). **7.** Mednick (1962). **8.** Coleman (1956). **9.** Kallman (1938). **10.** Hoagland (1952). **11.** Hoffer and Osmond (1959). **12.** Faris and Dunham (1939). **13.** Kety (1959). **14.** Freeman and Grayson (1955). **15.** Cameron (1947). **16.** Mednick (1958). **17.** Lidz and Lidz (1949). **18.** Gerard and Siegel (1950). **19.** Fenichel (1945). **20.** Menninger (1942). **21.** Fenichel (1945). **22.** Moss (1960). **23.** Cameron (1947). **24.** Brownfain (1961). **25.** Welsh and Dahlstrom (1956). **26.** Cameron (1947). **27.** Cameron (1947). **28.** Thigpen and Cleckley (1957). **29.** Messick and Jackson (1961). **30.** Tuddenham (1959). **31.** Freud (1905b). **32.** Brenner (1955). **33.** Freud (1914). **34.** Cameron (1947). **35.** Wharton (1922). **36.** Coleman (1956). **37.** Cleckley (1941). **38.** Dostoevskii, F. (1947). **39.** Jones, E. (1957). **40.** Szasz (1961). **41.** Snygg and Combs (1949). **42.** Galinsky (1961).
Chapter 11: **1.** Helson, Blake, and Mouton (1958). **2.** May (1950). **3.** May, Angel, and Ellenberger (1958). **4.** Kierkegaard (1944). **5.** Camus (1955). **6.** Mowrer (1952). **7.** Guttmacher (1950). **8.** Szasz (1960). **9.** Szasz (1961).

Adelson, J. (1961). "The teacher as a model," *The American Scholar,* **30,** 383-406.
Adolph, E. (1939). "Measurements of water drinking in dogs," *American Journal of Physiology,* **125,** 75-86.
——— (1941). "The internal environment and behavior: Water content," *American Journal of Psychiatry,* **97,** 1365-1373.
Adorno, T., Frenkel-Brunswick, E., Levinson, D., and Sanford, R. (1950). *The Authoritarian Personality.* New York: Harper.
Allport, G. (1937). *Personality, A Psychological Interpretation.* New York: Holt.
———, Vernon, P., and Lindzey, G. (1960). *A Study of Values: A Scale for Measuring the Dominant Interests in Personality.* Boston: Houghton.
Anderson, O., Parmenter, R. and Liddell, H. (1939). "Some cardiovascular manifestations of the experimental neurosis in sheep," *Journal of Psychosomatic Medicine,* **1,** 93-100.
Atkinson, J. and McClelland, D. (1948). "The projective expression of needs: II. The effect of different intensities of the hunger drive on thematic apperception," *Journal of Experimental Psychology,* **38,** 643-658.
Ax, A. F. (1953). "The physiological differentiation between fear and anger in humans," *Psychosomatic Medicine,* **15,** 332-433.
Bandura, A., Lipsher, D. H., and Miller, P. E. (1960). "Psychotherapists' approach-avoidance reactions to patients' expression of hostility," *Journal of Consulting Psychology,* **24,** 1-8.
Bard, P. (1928). "A diencephalic mechanism for the expression of rage with special reference to the sympathetic nervous system," *American Journal of*

Bard, P. (1928), continued

    Physiology, **84,** 490-515.

Barker, R., Dembo, T., and Lewin, K. (1941). "Frustration and regression: An experiment with young children," *University of Iowa Studies in Child Welfare,* **18,** No. 1.

Barrie, J. (1928). *The Plays of J. M. Barrie.* New York: Scribner.

Bateson, G. and Mead, M. (1942). *Balinese Character.* New York: New York Academy of Sciences.

Beach, F. A. (1956). "Characteristics of masculine 'sex drive.'" In Jones, M. (ed.), *Nebraska Symposium on Motivation.* Lincoln: University of Nebraska Press.

Berg, I. (1959). "The unimportance of test content." In Bass, B. and Berg, I., *Objective Approaches to Personality Assessment.* Princeton: Van Nostrand.

Berkowitz, L. (1957). "Leveling tendencies and the complexity-simplicity dimension," *Journal of Personality,* **25,** 743-751.

Berkowitz, L. (1959). "Anti-Semitism and the displacement of aggression," *Journal of Abnormal and Social Psychology,* **59,** 182-188.

Berlyne, O. (1960). *Conflict, Arousal, and Curiosity.* New York: McGraw.

Bernstein, A. (1955). "Some relations between techniques of feeding and training during infancy and certain behavior in childhood," *Genetic Psychology Monographs,* **51,** 3-44.

Bettelheim, B. (1947). "Dynamics of anti-Semitism in gentile and Jew," *Journal of Abnormal and Social Psychology,* **42,** 153-168.

Bexton, W., Heron, W., and Scott, T. (1954). "Effects of decreased variation in the environment," *Canadian Journal of Psychology,* **8,** 70-76.

Bieri, J. (1955). "Cognitive complexity-simplicity and predictive behavior," *Journal of Abnormal and Social Psychology,* **51,** 263-268.

Block, J. and Block, J. (1951). "An investigation of the relationship between intolerance of ambiguity and ethnocentrism," *Journal of Personality,* **19,** 303-311.

Bowlby, J. (1953). *Child Care and the Growth of Love.* London: Penguin.

———— (1958). "The nature of the child's role to his mother," *International Journal of Psychoanalysis,* **39,** 350-373.

Brady, J. (1958). "Ulcers in 'executive' monkeys," *Scientific American,* **199,** 95-100.

————, Porter, R., Conrad, D., and Mason, J. (1958). "Avoidance behavior and the development of gastroduodenal ulcers," *Journal of the Experimental Analysis of Behavior,* **1,** 69-73.

Brenner, C. (1955). *An Elementary Textbook of Psychoanalysis.* New York: Doubleday.

Brown, J. (1940). *The Psychodynamics of Abnormal Behavior.* New York: McGraw.

———— (1948). "Gradients of approach and avoidance responses and their relation to level of motivation," *Journal of Comparative and Physiological Psychology,* **41,** 450-465.

Brown, R. (1958). *Words and Things.* Glencoe, Ill.: Free Press.

———— and Lenneberg, E. (1954). "A study in language and cognition," *Journal of Abnormal and Social Psychology,* **49,** 454-462.

Brownfain, J. (1961). Personal communication.

Brownfield, E. (1956). "An investigation of the activity and sensory responses of healthy newborn infants," *Dissertation Abstracts,* **16,** 1288-1289.

Bruner, J. S. (1951). "Personality dynamics and the process of perceiving." In Blake, R. and Ramsey, G. (eds.), *Perception—An Approach to Personality.* New York: Ronald.

———— (1957a). "Neural mechanisms in perception," *Psychological Review,* **64,** 340-358.

———— (1957b). "On perceptual readiness," *Psychological Review,* **64,** 123-152.

Butler, J. and Haigh, G. (1954). "Changes in the relation between self-concepts and ideal concepts consequent upon client-centered counseling." In Rogers, C. and Dymond, R. (eds.), *Psychotherapy and Personality Change.* Chicago: University of Chicago Press.

Butler, R. A. (1953). "Discrimination learning by rhesus monkeys to visual-exploration motivation," *Journal of Comparative and Physiological Psychology,* **46,** 95-98.

Calvin, J., Bicknell, E., and Sperling, D. (1953). "Establishment of a conditioned drive based on the hunger drive," *Journal of Comparative and Physiological Psychology,* **46,** 173-175.

Cameron, N. (1947). *The Psychology of Behavior Disorders.* Boston: Houghton.

Campbell, B. (1960). "Effects of water deprivation on random activity," *Journal of Comparative and Physiological Psychology,* **53,** 240-241.

Camus, A. (1955). *The Myth of Sisyphus, and Other Essays.* New York: Knopf.

Cannon, W. (1927). "The James-Lange theory of emotions: A critical examination and an alternative theory." *American Journal of Psychology,* **39,** 106-124.

———— (1929). *Bodily Changes in Pain, Hunger, Fear, and Rage.* New York: Appleton.

———— (1932). *The Wisdom of the Body.* New York: Norton.

———— and Washburn, A. (1912). "An explanation of hunger," *American Journal of Physiology,* **29,** 441-454.

Carmichael, L. (1954). "The onset and early development of behavior." In Carmichael, L. (ed.), *Manual of Child Psychology.* New York: Wiley.

Chess, S., Thomas, A., and Birch, H. (1959). "Characteristics of the individual child's behavioral responses to the environment," *American Journal of Orthopsychiatry,* **29,** 791-802.

————, Thomas, A., Birch, H., and Hertzig, M. (1960). "Implications of a longitudinal study of child development for child psychiatry," *American Journal of Psychiatry,* **117,** 434-441.

Child, I., Potter, E. and Levine, E. (1946). "Children's textbooks and personality development: An exploration in the social psychology of education," *Psychological Monographs,* **60,** No. 279.

Clark, K. and Clark, M. (1952). "Racial identification and preference in Negro children." In Swanson, G., Newcomb, T., and Hartley, E. (eds.), *Readings in Social Psychology.* New York: Holt.

Clark, R. and Sensibar, M. (1955). "The relationship between symbolic and manifest projections of sexuality," *Journal of Abnormal and Social Psychology,*

Clark, R. and Sensibar, M. (1955), continued
  50, 23-32.
Cleckley, H. (1941). *The Mask of Sanity.* St. Louis: Mosby.
Cohn, F. and Gordon, J. (in press). "The effects of affiliation drive arousal on aggression in doll interviews," *Journal of Abnormal and Social Psychology.*
Cohen, B. (1961). Paper read at University of Michigan Psychology Colloquium, Ann Arbor, April 14.
Coleman, J. (1956). *Abnormal Psychology and Modern Life.* Chicago: Scott.
Couch, A. and Keniston, K. (1960). "Yeasayers and naysayers; agreeing response set as a personality variable," *Journal of Abnormal and Social Psychology,* **60,** 151-174.
Cowen, E. and Beier, E. (1951). "The influence of 'threat expectancy' on perception," *Journal of Personality,* **19,** 85-94.
Cowles, J. (1937). "Food-tokens as incentives for learning in chimpanzees," *Comparative Psychology Monographs,* **14,** No. 5.
Cutler, R. E. (1953). *The Relationship Between Therapist's Personality and Certain Aspects of Psychotherapy.* Unpublished doctoral dissertation. Ann Arbor: University of Michigan.
Davis, A. (1947). "Socialization and adolescent personality." In Newcomb, T. and Hartley, E. (eds.), *Readings in Social Psychology.* New York: Holt.
Davis, H., Sears, R., Miller, H., and Brodbeck, A. (1948). "Effects of cup, bottle, and breast feeding on oral activities of newborn infants," *Pediatrics,* **2,** 549.
Davis, W. and Havighurst, R. (1946). "Social class and color differences in child-rearing," *American Sociological Review,* **11,** 698-710.
Davitz, J. (1954). "The effects of previous training on postfrustration behavior," *Journal of Abnormal and Social Psychology,* **47,** 309-315.
De Charms, R. and Moeller, G. (1962). "Values expressed in American children's readers; 1800-1950," *Journal of Abnormal and Social Psychology,* **64,** 136-142.
Dement, W. (1960). "The effect of dream deprivation," *Science,* **131,** 1705-1707.
Dennis, W. (1957). "A cross-cultural study of the reinforcement of child behavior," *Child Development,* **28,** 431-438.
——— and Dennis, M. (1940). "The effect of cradling practices upon the onset of walking in Hopi children," *Journal of Genetic Psychology,* **56,** 77-86.
Dittes, J. (1957a). "Galvanic skin response as a measure of patient's reaction to therapist's permissiveness," *Journal of Abnormal and Social Psychology,* **55,** 295-303.
——— (1957b). "Extinction during psychotherapy of GSR accompanying 'embarrassing' statements," *Journal of Abnormal and Social Psychology,* **54,** 187-191.
Dollard, J., Doob, L., Miller, N., Mowrer, O., and Sears, R. (1939). *Frustration and Aggression.* New Haven: Yale.
——— and Miller, N. (1950). *Personality and Psychotherapy.* New York: McGraw.
Dostoevskii, F. (1947). *Crime and Punishment.* New York: World.
Duffy, E. (1957). "The psychological significance of the concept of 'arousal' or 'activation,'" *Psychological Review,* **64,** 265-275.
Dunbar, F. (1954). *Emotions and Bodily Changes.* New York: Columbia U.P.

Dunbar, F. (1955). *Mind and Body: Psychosomatic Medicine.* New York: Random.

Edwards, A. (1941). "Effects of the loss of one hundred hours of sleep," *American Journal of Psychology,* **54,** 80-91.

—————— (1954). *Edwards Personal Preference Schedule.* New York: Psychological Corp.

Erikson, E. (1950). *Childhood and Society.* New York: Norton.

Escalona, S. (1945). "Feeding disturbances in very young children," *American Journal of Orthopsychiatry,* **15,** 76-80.

Estes, W. (1954). "Individual behavior in uncertain situations; an interpretation in terms of statistical association theory." In Thrall, R., Coombs, C., and Davis. R. (eds.), *Decision Processes.* New York: Wiley.

—————— (1958). "Stimulus-response theory of drive." In Jones, M. (ed.), *Nebraska Symposium on Motivation.* Lincoln: University of Nebraska Press.

Farber, I. (1954). "Anxiety as a drive state." In Jones, M. (ed.), *Nebraska Symposium on Motivation.* Lincoln: University of Nebraska Press.

Faris, R. and Dunham, H. (1939). *Mental Disorders in Urban Areas.* Chicago: University of Chicago Press.

Fenichel, O. (1945). *Psychoanalytic Theory of Neurosis.* New York: Norton.

Ferenczi, S. (1950a). "Stages in the development of a sense of reality." *Sex in Psychoanalysis.* New York: Bramer.

—————— (1950b). "Psycho-analysis of sexual habits." *Further Contributions to the Theory and Technique of Psycho-analysis.* London: Hogarth.

—————— and Hollás, I. (1925). *Psychoanalysis and the Psychic Disorder of General Paresis.* New York: Nervous and Mental Diseases Publishing Co.

Feshbach, S. (1955). "The drive-reducing function of fantasy behavior," *Journal of Abnormal and Social Psychology,* **50,** 3-11.

Ford, C. and Beach, F. (1951). *Patterns of Sexual Behavior.* New York: Harper.

Fraiberg, S. (1959). *The Magic Years.* New York: Scribner.

Freeman, R. and Grayson, H. (1955). "Maternal attitudes in schizophrenia," *Journal of Abnormal and Social Psychology,* **50,** 45-52.

Frenkel-Brunswick, E. (1949). "Intolerance of ambiguity as an emotional and perceptual personality variable," *Journal of Personality,* **18,** 108-143.

—————— and Sanford, R. (1945). "Some personality factors in anti-Semitism," *Journal of Psychology,* **20,** 271-291.

Freud, A. (1937). *The Ego and Mechanisms of Defense.* London: Hogarth.

—————— and Burlingham, D. (1943). *War and Children.* New York: International Universities Press.

—————— —————— (1944). *Infants Without Families.* New York: International Universities Press.

Freud, S. (1900). *The interpretation of dreams.* In *Standard Edition,* Vols. IV and V. London: Hogarth, 1953.

—————— (1904). "The psychopathology of everyday life." In Brill, A. (ed.), *The Basic Writings of Sigmund Freud.* New York: Random, 1938.

—————— (1905a). *Three Essays on the Theory of Sexuality.* London: Imago, 1949.

—————— (1905b). "Fragment of the analysis of a case of hysteria." In *Collected Papers,* Vol. III. London: Hogarth, 1925.

—————— (1908). "Character and anal eroticism." In *Collected Papers,* Vol. II.

Freud, S. (1908), continued
   London: Hogarth, 1924.
—— (1909). "Analysis of a phobia in a five year old boy." In *Collected Papers,* Vol. III. London: Hogarth, 1925.
—— (1911). "Formulations regarding the two principles in mental functioning." In *Collected Papers,* Vol. IV. London: Hogarth, 1925.
—— (1914). "On narcissism: An introduction." In *Collected Papers,* Vol. IV. London: Hogarth, 1925.
—— (1920). *Beyond the Pleasure Principle.* New York: Liveright, 1950.
—— (1926). *Inhibition, Symptoms, and Anxiety.* London: Hogarth, 1936.
Fries, M. and Woolf, P. (1953). "Some hypotheses on the role of the congenital activity type in personality development." In Eissler, R. et al. (eds.) *Psychoanalytic Study of the Child,* Vol. 8. New York: International Universities Press.
Fromm, Erich (1947). *Man for Himself.* New York: Holt.
Galinsky, M. (1961). *Personality Development and Vocational Choice: A Study of Physicists and Clinical Psychologists.* Unpublished doctoral dissertation. Ann Arbor: University of Michigan.
Gallup, G. (1955). *Gallup Poll.* Princeton: Audience Research, Inc.
Gerard, D. and Siegel, J. (1950). "The family background of schizophrenia," *Psychiatric Quarterly,* **24,** 47-73.
Ghiselin, B. (ed.) (1955). *The Creative Process.* New York: Mentor.
Gilchrist, J. and Nesberg, L. (1952). "Need and perceptual change in need-related objects," *Journal of Experimental Psychology,* **44,** 369-376.
Glueck, S. and Glueck, E. (1950). *Unravelling Juvenile Delinquency.* New York: Commonwealth Fund.
Golambos, R., Sheatz, G., and Vernier, V. (1956). "Electrophysiological correlates of a conditioned response in cats," *Science,* **123,** 376-377.
Gold, M. (1961). *A Social Psychology of Delinquent Boys.* Unpublished doctoral dissertation. Ann Arbor: University of Michigan.
Goldfarb, W. (1943). "Effects of early institutional care on adolescent personality," *Journal of Experimental Education,* **12,** 106-129.
—— (1944). "Effects of early institutional care on adolescent personality: Rorschach data," *American Journal of Orthopsychiatry,* **14,** 441-447.
—— (1947). "Variations in adolescent adjustment of institutionally reared children," *American Journal of Orthopsychiatry,* **17,** 449-457.
Goldstein, K. and Scheerer, M. (1941). "Abstract and concrete behavior: An experimental study with special tests," *Psychological Monographs,* **53,** No. 2.
Goldstein, M. and Barthol, R. (1960). "Fantasy responses to subliminal stimuli," *Journal of Abnormal and Social Psychology,* **60,** 22-26.
Goodenough, F. (1931). "Anger in young children," *University of Minnesota Institute of Child Welfare Monograph Series,* No. 9. Minneapolis: University of Minnesota Press.
Gordon, J. (1957). "Interpersonal predictions of repressors and sensitizers," *Journal of Personality,* **25,** 686-698.
—— (1959a). "The stability of the assumed similarity response set in repressors and sensitizers," *Journal of Personality,* **27,** 362-373.

Gordon, J. (1959b). "Relationships among mother's *n* achievement, independence training attitudes, and handicapped children's performances," *Journal of Consulting Psychology,* **23,** 207-212.

—— (1961). Unpublished research.

——, Martin, B., and Lundy, R. (1959). "GSRs during repression, supression, and verbalization in psychotherapeutic interviews," *Journal of Consulting Psychology,* **23,** 243-251.

Greenspoon, J. (1955). "The reinforcing effects of two spoken words on the frequency of two responses," *American Journal of Psychology,* **68,** 409-416.

Grotjahn, M. (1957). *Beyond Laughter.* New York: McGraw.

Guthrie, E. (1952). *The Psychology of Learning.* New York: Harper.

Guttmacher, A. (1950). *Having A Baby.* New York: New American Library.

Hall, C. S. (1938). "The inheritance of emotionality," *Sigma Xi Quarterly,* **26.** 17-27.

Hanfmann, E. and Kasanin, J. (1937). "A method for studying concept formation," *Journal of Psychology,* **3,** 521-540.

Harlow, H. (1949). "The formation of learning sets," *Psychological Review,* **56,** 51-65.

—— (1953). "Motivation as a factor in new responses." In Jones, M. (ed.), *Current Theory and Research in Motivation.* Lincoln: University of Nebraska Press.

—— (1958). "The nature of love," *American Psychologist,* **13,** 673-685.

——, Harlow, M., and Meyer, D. (1950). "Learning motivated by a manipulation drive," *Journal of Experimental Psychology,* **40,** 228-234.

—— and McClearn, G. (1954). "Object discrimination learned by monkeys on the basis of manipulation motives," *Journal of Comparative and Physiological Psychology,* **47,** 73-76.

Hartmann, H. (1939). *Ego Psychology and the Problem of Adaptation.* New York: International Universities Press, 1958.

Head, H. (1926). *Aphasia and Kindred Disorders of Speech.* London: Cambridge University Press.

Hebb, D. (1949). *The Organization of Behavior.* New York: Wiley.

—— (1958). "The motivating effects of exteroceptive stimulation," *American Psychologist,* **13,** 109-113.

Helson, H., Blake, R., and Mouton, J. (1958). "Petition-signing as adjustment to situational and personal factors," *Journal of Social Psychology,* **48,** 3-10.

Hemingway, E. (1952). *The Old Man and the Sea.* New York: Scribner.

Henderson, J. and Moore, M. (1944). "The psychoneuroses of war," *New England Journal of Medicine,* **230,** 273-278.

Hendrick, I. (1943). "Work and the pleasure principle," *Psychoanalytic Quarterly,* **12,** 311-329.

Henry, W. (1956). *The Analysis of Fantasy.* New York: Wiley.

Hernandez-Péon, R., Scherrer, R., and Jouvet, M. (1956). "Modification of electric activity in the cochlear nucleus during 'attention' in unanesthetized cats," *Science,* **123,** 331-332.

Heron, W. (1957). "The pathology of boredom," *Scientific American,* **196,** 52-69.

Hess, E. (1959). "Imprinting," *Science,* **130,** 133-141.

Hilgard, E. (1949). "Human motives and the concept of the self," *American Psychologist,* **4,** 374-382.

—— (1956). *Theories of Learning.* New York: Appleton.

Hill, W. (1956). "Activity as an autonomous drive," *Journal of Comparative and Physiological Psychology,* **49,** 15-19.

Hoagland, H. (1952). "Metabolic and physiologic disturbances in the psychoses," In Milbank Memorial Fund, *Biology of Mental Health and Disease.* New York: Hoeber-Harper, 434-449.

Hoelzel, F. (1927). "Central factors in hunger," *American Journal of Physiology,* **82,** 665-671.

Hoffer, A. and Osmond, H. (1959). "The adrenochrome model and schizophrenia," *Journal of Nervous and Mental Diseases,* **128,** 18-35.

Hokanson, J. and Gordon, J. (1958). "The expression and inhibition of hostility in imaginative and overt behavior," *Journal of Abnormal and Social Psychology,* **57,** 327-333.

Hollenberg, E. and Sperry, M. (1950). "Some antecedents of aggression and effects of frustration on doll play," *Journal of Personality,* **1,** 32-43.

Holzman, P. and Klein, G. (1954). "Cognitive system principles of leveling and sharpening: Individual differences in assimilation effects in visual time-error," *Journal of Psychology,* **37,** 105-122.

Horney, K. (1945). *Our Inner Conflicts.* New York: Norton.

Hovland, C. (1937). "The generalization of conditioned responses with varying frequencies of tone," *Journal of General Psychology,* **17,** 125-248.

—— and Sears, R. (1940). "Correlation of economic indices with lynchings," *Journal of Psychology,* **9,** 301-310.

Howes, D. and Solomon, R. (1951). "Visual duration threshold as a function of word-probability," *Journal of Experimental Psychology,* **41,** 401-410.

Humphreys, L. (1939). "The effect of random alternation of reinforcement on the acquisition and extinction of conditioned eyelid reactions," *Journal of Experimental Psychology,* **25,** 141-158.

Hull, C. (1932). "The goal gradient hypothesis and maze learning, *Psychological Review,* **39,** 25-43.

—— (1943). *Principles of Behavior.* New York: Appleton.

Hunt, J. (1941). "The effects of infant feeding frustration upon adult hoarding in the albino rat." *Journal of Abnormal and Social Psychology,* **36,** 338-360.

Hunter, W. and Nagge, J. (1931). "The white rat and the double alternation temporal maze," *Journal of Genetic Psychology,* **39,** 303-319.

Hunter, W. S. (1913). "The delayed reaction in animals and children," *Behavior Monograph,* Vol. 2.

Inhelder, B. and Piaget, J. (1958). *The Growth of Logical Thinking from Childhood to Adolescence.* New York: Basic Books.

Inkeles, A. and Levinson, D. (1954). "National character: The study of modal personality and sociocultural systems." In Lindzey, G. (ed.), *Handbook of Social Psychology.* Reading, Mass.: Addison-Wesley.

Jackson, D. and Messick, S. (1958). "Content and style in personality assessment," *Psychological Bulletin,* **55,** 243-252.

Jacobson, E. (1932). "Electrophysiology of mental activities," *American Journal of Psychology*, **44**, 677-694.

Janis, I. and Feshbach, S. (1953). "Effects of fear-arousing communications," *Journal of Abnormal and Social Psychology*, **48**, 78-92.

Jenkins, W. and Stanley, J. (1950). "Partial reinforcement: A review and critique," *Psychological Bulletin*, **47**, 193-234.

Jersild, A. and Markey, F. (1935). "Conflicts between preschool children," *Child Development Monographs*, No. 21.

Jones, E. (1957). *Life and Work of Sigmund Freud*. New York: Basic Books.

Jones, M. (1957). "The later career of boys who were early- or late-maturing," *Child Development*, **28**, 113-128.

——— and Bayley, N. (1950). "Physical maturing among boys as related to behavior," *Journal of Educational Psychology*, **41**, 129-148.

Kagan, J., Suntag, S., Baker, L., and Lester, S. (1958). "Personality and I.Q. change," *Journal of Abnormal and Social Psychology*, **57**, 131-139.

Kallman, F. (1938). *The Genetics of Schizophrenia.* New York: J. J. Augustin.

Kapp, F., Rosenbaum, M., and Romano, J. (1947). "Psychological factors in men with peptic ulcers," *American Journal of Psychiatry*, **103**, 700-704.

Katz, B. (1952). "The nerve impulse," *Scientific American*, **185**, 55-64.

Keister, M. and Updegraff, R. (1938). "The behavior of young children in failure; an experimental attempt to discover and to modify undesirable responses of preschool children to failure," *University of Iowa Studies in Child Welfare*, **14**, 27-82.

Kellogg, W. (1939). "'Positive' and 'negative' conditioning without contraction of the essential muscles during the period of training," *Psychological Bulletin*, **36**, 575.

Kelly, E. L. (1955). "Consistency of the adult personality," *American Psychologist*, **10**, 659-681.

Kelly, G. (1955). *Psychology of Personal Constructs*. New York: Norton.

Kety, S. (1959). "Biochemical theories of schizophrenia," *Science*, **129**, 1528-1532.

Keys, A., Brozek, J., Henschel, A., Mickelsen, O., and Taylor, H. (1950). *The Biology of Human Starvation*. Minneapolis: University of Minnesota Press.

Kierkegaard, S. (1944). *The Concept of Dread*. Princeton: Princteon U.P.

Kimble, G. (1955). "Shock intensity and avoidance learning," *Journal of Comparative and Physiological Psychology*, **48**, 281-284.

Kinsey, A., Pomeroy, W., and Martin, C. (1948). *Sexual Behavior in the Human Male*. Philadelphia: Saunders.

———, ———, ———, and Gebhard, P. (1953). *Sexual Behavior in the Human Female*. Philadelphia: Saunders.

Klatskin, E., Lethin, A., and Jackson, E. (1950). "Choice of rooming-in or newborn nursery," *Journal of Pediatrics*, **6**, 878-889.

Klein, D. (1930). "The experimental production of dreams during hypnosis," *University of Texas Bulletin*, No. 3009.

Klein, M. (1948). *Contributions to Psycho-Analysis, 1921-1945*. London: Hogarth.

Koehler, W. (1925). *The Mentality of Apes*. New York: Harcourt.

Krechevsky, J. (1936). "Brain mechanisms and variability," *Journal of Com-*

Krechevsky, J. (1936), continued
parative Psychology, **23,** 121-138.

Kris, E. (1952). *Psychoanalytic Explorations in Art.* New York: International Universities Press.

Krout, M. (1954). "An experimental attempt to determine the significance of unconscious manual symbolic movements," *Journal of General Psychology,* **51,** 121-152.

Lacey, J. (1950). "Individual differences in somatic response patterns," *Journal of Comparative and Physiological Psychology,* **43,** 338-350.

———, Bateman, D., and Van Lehn, R. (1952). "Autonomic response specificity and Rorschach color responses," *Psychosomatic Medicine,* **14,** 256-260.

——— and Van Lehn, R. (1952). "Differential emphasis in somatic response to stress," *Psychosomatic Medicine,* **14,** 71-81.

Lashley, K. (1935). *Brain Mechanisms and Intelligence.* Chicago: University of Chicago Press.

Lazarus, R. and McCleary, R. (1951). "Autonomic discrimination without awareness: A study of subception," *Psychological Review,* **58,** 113-122.

Lecky, P. (1945). *Self-Consistency.* New York: Island Press.

Lepley, W. (1954). "Variability as a variable," *Journal of Psychology,* **37,** 19-25.

Lesser, G. (1957). "Relationships between overt and fantasy aggression as a function of maternal response to aggression," *Journal of Abnormal and Social Psychology,* **55,** 218-221.

Levin, H. and Sears, R. (1956). "Identification with parents as a determinant of doll play aggression," *Child Development,* **27,** 135-153.

Levy, D. (1934). "Experiments on the sucking reflex and social behavior of dogs," *American Journal of Orthopsychiatry,* **4,** 203-224.

——— (1937). "Primary affect hunger," *American Journal of Psychiatry,* **94,** 643-652.

——— (1943). *Maternal Overprotection.* New York: Columbia U.P.

Lewin, K., Lippitt, R., and White, R. (1939). "Patterns of aggressive behavior in experimentally created 'social climates,'" *Journal of Social Psychology,* **10,** 271-299.

Liddell, H. (1944). "Conditioned reflex method and experimental neurosis." In Hunt, J. (ed.), *Personality and the Behavior Disorders.* New York: Ronald.

——— (1954). "Conditioning and emotions," *Scientific American,* **190,** 48-57.

Lidz, R. and Lidz, T. (1949). "The family environment of schizophrenic patients," *American Journal of Psychiatry,* **106,** 332-345.

Life Magazine, August 22, 1955, 73-78.

Light, J. and Gantt, W. (1936). "Essential part of reflex arc for establishment of conditioned reflex. Formation of conditioned reflex after exclusion of motor peripheral end," *Journal of Comparative Psychology,* **21,** 19-36.

Luchins, A. and Luchins, E. (1959). *Rigidity of Behavior.* Eugene, Ore.: University of Oregon Press.

Lynn, D. (1959). "A note on sex differences in the development of masculine and feminine identification," *Psychological Review,* **66,** 126-135.

Maier, N. (1961). *Frustration.* Ann Arbor: University of Michigan Press.

———, Glaser, N., and Klee, J. (1940). "Studies of abnormal behavior in the rat,

Maier, N., Glaser, N., and Klee, J. (1940), continued
   III. The development of behavior fixation through frustration," *Journal of Experimental Psychology,* **26,** 312-346.
—— and Klee, J. (1941). "Studies of abnormal behavior in the rat, VII. The permanent nature of abnormal fixations and their relation to convulsive tendencies," *Journal of Experimental Psychology,* **29,** 380-389.
Malmo, R. (1957). "Anxiety and behavioral arousal," *Psychological Review,* **64,** 276-287.
—— and Smith, A. (1955). "Forehead tension and motor irregulatities in psychoneurotic patients under stress," *Journal of Personality,* **23,** 391-406.
Mandler, G. and Sarason, S. (1952). "A study of anxiety and learning," *Journal of Abnormal and Social Psychology,* **47,** 166-173.
Marquis, D. (1941). "Learning in the neonate. The modification of behavior under three feeding schedules," *Journal of Experimental Psychology,* **29,** 263-282.
Martin, R. (1940). "'Native' traits and regression in rats," *Journal of Comparative and Physiological Psychology,* **30,** 1-16.
Mason, W. (1960). "The effects of social restriction on the behavior of rhesus monkeys: I. Free social behavior," *Journal of Comparative and Physiological Psychology,* **53,** 582-589.
Masserman, J. (1943). *Behavior and Neurosis.* Chicago: University of Chicago Press.
Max, L. (1937). "Experimental study of the motor theory of consciousness. IV. Action-current responses in the deaf during awakening, kinaesthetic imagery and abstract thinking," *Journal of Comparative Psychology,* **24,** 301-344.
May, R. (1950). *The Meaning of Anxiety.* New York: Ronald.
——, Angel, E., and Ellenberger, J. (eds.) (1958). *Existence: A New Dimension in Psychiatry and Psychology.* New York: Basic Books.
McCleary, R. and Lazarus, R. (1949). "Autonomic discrimination without awareness," *Journal of Personality,* **18,** 171-179.
McClelland, D. (1951). *Personality.* New York: Sloane.
—— (1955). "Some social consequences of achievement motivation." In Jones, M. (ed.), *Nebraska Symposium on Motivation.* Lincoln: University of Nebraska Press.
—— (1961). *The Achieving Society.* Princeton: Van Nostrand.
——, Atkinson, J., Clark, R., and Lowell, E. (1953). *The Achievement Motive.* New York: Appleton.
McGinnies, E. (1949). "Emotionality and perceptual defense," *Psychological Review,* **56,** 244-251.
McGraw, M. (1940). "Neural maturation as exemplified in achievement of bladder control," *Journal of Pediatrics,* **16,** 580-590.
—— (1943). *The Neuromuscular Maturation of the Human Infant.* New York: Columbia U.P.
Mead, M. (1928). *Coming of Age in Samoa.* New York: Morrow.
Mednick, S. (1958). "A learning theory approach to research in schizophrenia," *Psychological Bulletin,* **55,** 316-327.

———— (1962). "The associative basis of the creative process," *Psychological Review,* **69,** 220-232.

Meehl, P. and MacCorquodale, K. (1953). "Drive conditioning as a function of latent learning," *Journal of Experimental Psychology,* **45,** 20-24.

Menninger, K. (1942). "Work as sublimation," *Menninger Clinic Bulletin,* **6,** 170-182.

Messick, S. and Jackson, D. (1961). "Desirability scale values and dispersions for MMPI items," *Psychological Reports,* **8,** 409-414.

Michigan State Department of Mental Health (1953). *Michigan Picture Test.* Chicago: Science Research Associates.

Miller, D. and Swanson, G. (1958). *The Changing American Parent.* New York: Wiley.

———— ———— (1960). *Inner Conflict and Defense.* New York: Holt.

Miller, M. (1948). "A psychological study of a case of eczema and a case of neurodermatitis." In Alexander, F. and French, T. (eds.), *Studies in Psychosomatic Medicine.* New York: Ronald.

Miller, N. (1948). "Theory and experiment relating psychoanalytic displacement to stimulus-response generalization," *Journal of Abnormal and Social Psychology,* **43,** 155-178.

———— (1949). "Studies of fear as an acquirable drive: I. Fear as motivation and fear-reduction as reinforcement in the learning of new responses," *Journal of Experimental Psychology,* **38,** 89-101.

———— and Bugelski, R. (1948). "Minor studies of aggression: II. The influence of frustrations by the in-group on attitudes expressed toward outgroups," *Journal of Psychology,* **25,** 437-442.

———— and Dollard, J. (1941). *Social Learning and Imitation.* New Haven: Yale U.P.

———— and Kraeling, D. (1952). "Displacement: Greater generalization of approach than avoidance in a generalized approach-avoidance conflict," *Journal of Experimental Psychology,* **43,** 217-226.

Montgomery, M. (1931). "The role of the salivary glands in the thirst mechanism," *American Journal of Physiology,* **96,** 221-227.

Morgan, C. (1943). *Physiological Psychology.* New York: McGraw.

———— and Morgan, J. (1940). "Studies in hunger: II. The relation of gastric denervation and dietary sugar to the effect of insulin upon food-intake in the rat," *Journal of Genetic Psychology,* **57,** 153-163.

Moss, C. (1960). "Brief successful psychotherapy of a chronic phobic reaction," *Journal of Abnormal and Social Psychology,* **60,** 266-270.

Mowrer, O. (1939). "A stimulus response analysis of anxiety and its role as a reinforcing agent," *Psychological Review,* **46,** 553-565.

———— (1940a). "An experimental analogue of 'regression' with incidental observations on 'reaction formation,'" *Journal of Abnormal and Social Psychology,* **35,** 56-87.

———— (1940b). "Anxiety reduction and learning," *Journal of Experimental Psychology,* **27,** 497-516.

———— (1952). "Learning theory and the neurotic fallacy," *American Journal of Orthopsychiatry,* **22,** 679-689.

———— (1960). *Learning Theory and the Symbolic Processes.* New York: Wiley.

Mowrer, O. and Lamoreaux, R. (1942). "Avoidance conditioning and signal duration: A study of secondary motivation and reward," *Psychological Monographs,* **54,** No. 247.

Munn, N. (1950). *Handbook of Psychological Research on the Rat.* Boston: Houghton.

Murdock, G. (1937). "Comparative data on the division of labor by sex," *Social Forces,* **15,** 551-553.

Murray, H. A. (1943). *Thematic Apperception Test.* Cambridge: Harvard U.P.

Nachmann, B. (1957). *Childhood Experience and Vocational Choice: A Study of Lawyers, Dentists, and Social Workers.* Unpublished doctoral dissertation. Ann Arbor: University of Michigan.

Nachmansohn, M. (1951). "Concerning experimentally produced dreams." In Rapaport, D. (ed.), *Organization and Pathology of Thought.* New York: Columbia U.P.

Nauta, W. (1946). "Hypothalamic regulation of sleep in rats: An experimental study," *Journal of Neurophysiology,* **9,** 285-316.

Netter, F. (1953). *The Ciba Collection of Medical Illustrations, Vol I: Nervous System.* Summit, N.J.: Ciba Pharmaceutical.

Newton, N. and Newton, M. (1950). "Relationship of ability to breast feed and maternal attitudes toward breast feeding," *Pediatrics,* **5,** 869-875.

Noble, C. and Parker, G. (1960). "The Montana scale of meaningfulness (m)," *Psychological Reports,* **7,** 325-331.

——— and Taylor, A. (1959). "Influence of work distribution upon complex learning by the noncorrection and modified-correction methods," *Journal of Experimental Psychology,* **58,** 352-356.

Olds, J. (1955). "Physiological mechanisms of reward." In Jones, M. (ed.), *Nebraska Symposium on Motivation.* Lincoln: University of Nebraska Press.

——— (1956). "Pleasure centers in the brain," *Scientific American,* **195,** 108-118.

Osgood, C. (1953). *Method and Theory in Experimental Psychology.* New York: Oxford U.P.

Patel, A. and Gordon, J. (1960). "Some personal and situational determinants of yielding to influence," *Journal of Abnormal and Social Psychology,* **61,** 411-418.

Patrick, J. (1934). "Studies in rational behavior and emotional excitement: II. The effect of emotional excitement on rational behavior of human subjects," *Journal of Comparative Psychology,* **18,** 153-195.

Penfield, W. and Rasmussen, T. (1950). *The Cerebral Cortex of Man.* New York: Macmillan.

Piaget, J. (1926). *The Language and Thought of the Child.* New York: Harcourt.

Piquer y Jover, J. (1946). "El niño abandonada y delincuente," Madrid.

Postman, L., Bruner, J., and McGinnies, E. (1948). "Personal values as selective factors in perception," *Journal of Abnormal and Social Psychology,* **43,** 142-154.

Prokasy, W. (1956). "The acquisition of observing responses in the absence of differential external reinforcement," *Journal of Comparative and Physiological Psychology,* **49,** 131-134.

Proshansky, H. and Murphy, G. (1942). "The effects of reward and punishment on perception," *Journal of Psychology,* **13,** 295-305.

Radke, M. and Trager, H. (1950). "Children's perceptions of the social roles of Negroes and whites," *Journal of Psychology*, **29**, 3-33.

Rank, O. (1929). *The Trauma of Birth*. London: Routledge and Kegan Paul.

Rapaport, D. (1958). "The theory of ego autonomy: A generalization," *Bulletin of the Menninger Clinic*, **22**, 14-18.

Razran, G. (1955). "Conditioning and perception," *Psychological Review*, **62**, 83-95.

Rheingold, H., Gewirtz, J., and Ross, H. (1958). "Social conditioning of vocalizations in the infant," *Journal of Comparative and Physiological Psychology*, **52**, 68-73.

Ribble, M. (1944). "Infantile experience in relation to personality development." In Hunt, J. (ed.), *Personality and the Behavior Disorders*. New York: Ronald.

Riesman, D., Glazer, N., and Denney, R. (1953). *The Lonely Crowd*. New York: Doubleday.

Rogers, C. (1951). *Client-Centered Therapy*. Boston: Houghton.

———, (1961). *On Becoming A Person: A Therapist's View of Psychotherapy*. Boston: Houghton.

Rorschach, Hermann (1942). *Psychodiagnostik*. Berne: Huber.

Rosenzweig, S. (1944). "An outline of frustration theory." In Hunt, J. (ed.), *Personality and the Behavior Disorders*. New York: Ronald.

Rothschild, D. (1944). "The role of the premorbid personality in arteriosclerotic psychoses," *American Journal of Psychiatry*, **100**, 501-505.

Rotter, J. (1954). *Social Learning and Clinical Psychology*. Englewood Cliffs, N.J.: Prentice.

Samuels, I. (1959). "Reticular mechanisms and behavior," *Psychological Bulletin*, **56**, 1-25.

Sanford, R. (1936). "The effect of abstinence from food upon imaginal processes; a preliminary experiment," *Journal of Psychology*, **2**, 129-136.

——— (1937). "The effect of abstinence from food upon imaginal processes; a further experiment," *Journal of Psychology*, **3**, 145-149.

Sarnoff, I. (1960). "Reaction-formation and cynicism," *Journal of Personality*, **28**, 215-219.

Schachtel, E. (1959). *Metamorphosis*. New York: Basic Books.

Schachter, S. (1959). *Psychology of Affiliation*. Stanford: Stanford U.P.

Schlosberg, H. (1954). "Three dimensions of emotion," *Psychological Review*, **61**, 81-88.

Scodel, A. (1957). "Heterosexual somatic preference and fantasy dependency," *Journal of Consulting Psychology*, **21**, 371-374.

Scott, J. (1945). "Social behavior, organization, and leadership in a small flock of domestic sheep," *Comparative Psychology Monographs*, **18**, No. 4.

Scott, W. (1957). "Attitude change through reward of verbal behavior," *Journal of Abnormal and Social Psychology*, **55**, 72-75.

Sears, P. (1953). "Child-rearing factors as related to playing of sex-typed roles," *American Psychologist*, **8**, 431.

Sears, R. (1936). "Experimental studies of projection: I. Attribution of traits," *Journal of Social Psychology*, **7**, 151-163.

———, Hovland, C., and Miller, N. (1940). "Minor studies of aggression: I.

Sears, R., Hovland, C., and Miller, N. (1940), continued
Measurement of aggressive behavior," *Journal of Psychology,* **9,** 275-294.

———, Maccoby, E., and Levin, H. (1957). *Patterns of Child Rearing.* Evanston, Ill.: Row.

———, Pintler, M., and Sears, P. (1946). "Effect of father separation on pre-school children's doll play aggression," *Child Development,* **17,** 219-243.

———, Whiting, J., Nowlis, V., and Sears, P. (1953). "Some child-rearing antecedents of aggression and dependency in young children," *Genetic Psychology Monographs,* **47,** 135-234.

——— and Wise, G. (1950). "Relation of cup feeding in infancy to thumb-sucking and the oral drive." *American Journal of Orthopsychiatry.* **20,** 123-138.

Secord, P. and Jourard, S. (1956). "Mother-concepts and judgments of young women's faces," *Journal of Abnormal and Social Psychology,* **52,** 246-250.

Segal, S. (1953). *The Role of Personality in Vocational Choice: A Study of Accountants and Creative Writers.* Unpublished doctoral dissertation. Ann Arbor: University of Michigan.

Shaffer, L. (1947). "Fear and courage in aerial combat," *Journal of Consulting Psychology,* **11,** 137-143.

——— and Shoben, E. (1956). *The Psychology of Adjustment.* Boston: Houghton.

Sheffield, F., Wulff, J., and Backer, L. (1951). "Reward value of copulation without sex drive reduction," *Journal of Comparative and Physiological Psychology,* **44,** 3-8.

Shroder, H. and Rotter, J. (1952). "Rigidity as learned behavior," *Journal of Experimental Psychology,* **44,** 141-150.

Sidman, M. (1955). "On the persistence of avoidance behavior," *Journal of Abnormal and Social Psychology,* **50,** 217-220.

Siegel, P. and MacDonnell, M. (1954). "A repetition of the Calvin-Bicknell-Sperling study of conditioned drive," *Journal of Comparative and Physiological Psychology,* **47,** 250-252.

Siipola, E. (1935). "A study of some effects of preparatory set," *Psychological Monographs,* **46,** No. 210.

Skinner, B. (1938). *The Behavior of Organisms.* New York: Appleton.

Snygg, D. and Combs, A. (1949). *Individual Behavior.* New York: Harper.

Solomon, P. (ed.) (1961). *Sensory Deprivation.* Cambridge: Harvard U.P.

Spence, K. (1947). "The role of secondary reinforcement in delayed reward learning," *Psychological Review,* **54,** 1-8.

——— (1954). "Current interpretations of learning data and some recent developments in stimulus-response theory." In *Kentucky Symposium: Learning Theory, Personality Theory, and Clinical Research.* New York: Wiley.

Spitz, R. (1945). "Hospitalism: An inquiry into the genesis of psychiatric conditions in early childhood. In Freud, A. et al. (eds.), *The Psychoanalytic Study of the Child,* Vol. I. New York: International Universities Press.

——— (1946). "Hospitalism: A follow-up report on investigations described in Vol. I. 1945." In Freud, A. et al. (eds.), *The Psychoanalytic Study of the Child,* Vol. II. New York: International Universities Press.

Spock, B. (1946). *Pocket Book of Baby and Child Care.* New York: Pocket Books.

Stagner, R. and Krout, M. (1940). "Correlational study of personality develop-

Stagner, R. and Krout, M. (1940), continued
  ment and structure," *Journal of Abnormal and Social Psychology,* **35,** 339-355.
Stauffer, S. and Lumsdaine, A. (1947). *The American Soldier.* Princeton: Princeton U.P.
Stellar, E. (1954). "The physiology of motivation," *Psychological Review,* **61,** 5-22.
Szasz, T. (1960). "The myth of mental illness," *American Psychologist,* **15,** 113-118.
——— (1961). "The uses of naming and the origin of the myth of mental illness," *American Psychologist,* **16,** 59-65.
Tatz, S. (1956). "Symbolic mediation in 'learning without awareness.'" Paper read at Eastern Psychological Association, Atlantic City, March.
Taylor, J. (1958). "The duplication of chromosomes," *Scientific American,* **198,** 36-42.
Tepas, D. (1962). Personal communication.
Thigpen, C. and Cleckley, H. (1957). *The Three Faces of Eve.* New York: McGraw.
Thomas, A., Chess, S., Birch, H., and Hertzig, M. (1960). "A longitudinal study of primary reaction patterns in children," *Comprehensive Psychiatry,* **1,** 103-112.
Thorndike, E. and Lorge, I. (1944). *The Teacher's Word Book of 30,000 Words.* New York: Columbia U.P.
Toch, H. and Schulte, R. (in press). "Perception of violence as a result of police training," *British Journal of Psychology.*
Townsend, A. (1958). *The Relationship Between Parental Commitment and Certain Forms of Dependent Behavior.* Unpublished doctoral dissertation. Ann Arbor: University of Michigan.
Tsang, Y. (1938). "Hunger motivation in gastrectomized rats," *Journal of Comparative Psychology,* **26,** 1-17.
Tuddenham, R. (1959). "Correlates of yielding to a distorted group norm," *Journal of Personality,* **27,** 272-284.
Verplanck, W. (1956). "The operant conditioning of human motor behavior," *Psychological Bulletin,* **53,** 70-83.
Wagner, M. (1944). "Mental hazards in old age," *Family,* **25,** 132-137.
Walker, E. and Heyns, R. (1962). *An Anatomy for Conformity.* Englewood Cliffs, N.J.: Prentice.
Wallerstein, H. (1954). "An electromyographic study of attentive listening," *Canadian Journal of Psychology,* **8,** 228-238.
Walters, H. A. (1959). Unpublished research.
Wang, G. (1923). "The relation between 'spontaneous' activity and oestrous cycle in the white rat," *Comparative Psychology Monographs,* **2,** No. 6.
Wangensteen, O. and Carlson, A. (1931). "Hunger sensations in a patient after total gastrectomy," *Proceedings of the Society for Experimental Biology,* New York, **28,** 545-547.
Watson, J. and Raynor, R. (1920). "Conditioned emotional reactions," *Journal of Experimental Psychology,* **3,** 1-14.
Weber, M. (1958). *The Protestant Ethic and the Spirit of Capitalism.* New York: Scribner.
Weingarten, Linda L. (1962). *Correlates of Ambivalence Toward Parental Figures.*

Weingarten, Linda L. (1962), continued
    Unpublished doctoral dissertation. Ann Arbor: University of Michigan.
Welsh, G. and Dahlstrom, W. (eds.) (1956). *Basic Readings on the MMPI in Psychology and Medicine.* Minneapolis: University of Minnesota Press.
Wharton, E. (1922). *Ethan Frome.* New York: Scribner.
White, R. (1959). "Motivation reconsidered: The concept of competence," *Psychological Review,* **66,** 297-333.
Whiting, J. and Child, J. (1953). *Child Training and Personality.* New Haven: Yale U.P.
Whorf, B. (1956). *Language, Thought, and Reality;* ed. by J. Carroll. New York: Wiley.
Wilcoxon, H. (1952). "'Abnormal fixation' and learning," *Journal of Experimental Psychology,* **44,** 324-333.
Wilkins, L. and Richter, C. (1940). "A great craving for salt by a child with cortico-adrenal insufficiency," *Journal of the American Medical Association,* **114,** 866-868.
Williams, H. (1962). Personal communication.
Winch, R. (1950). "Some data bearing on the Oedipus complex," *Journal of Abnormal and Social Psychology,* **45,** 481-490.
Winterbottom, M. (1953). "The sources of achievement motivation in mothers' attitudes toward independence training." In McClelland, D. and others, *The Achievement Motive.* New York: Appleton.
Witkin, H. (1949). "The nature and importance of individual differences in perception," *Journal of Personality,* **18,** 145-170.
——— (1950). "Individual differences in ease of perception of embedded figures," *Journal of Personality,* **19,** 1-15.
——— (1959). "The perception of the upright," *Scientific American,* **200,** 50-56.
———, Lewis, H., Mackover, K., Meissner, P., and Wapner, S. (1954). *Personality Through Perception.* New York: Harper.
Wolberg, L. (1948). *Medical Hypnosis.* New York: Grune.
Wolf, S. and Wolff, H. (1946). "Psychosomatic aspects of peptic ulcer," *Scope,* **2,** 4-9.
Wolfe, J. (1936). "Effectiveness of token-rewards for chimpanzees," *Comparative Psychology Monographs,* **12,** No. 5.
Wolff, H. (1953). "Life stress and bodily disease." In Weider, A. (ed.), *Contributions Toward Medical Psychology,* Vol. I. New York: Ronald.
Wolff, W. (1933). "The experimental study of forms of expression." *Character and Personality,* **2,** 168-176.
——— (1935). "Involuntary self-expression in gait and other movements," *Character and Personality,* **3,** 327-344.
Zeigarnik, B. (1927). "Das Behalten von erledigten und unerledigten Handlungen," *Psychologische Forschung,* **9,** 1-85.
Zimmerman, D. (1957). "Durable secondary reinforcement; method and theory," *Psychological Review,* **64,** 373-383.

Index